Grade 7

Glencoe

Georgia Math

Volume 2

Bothell, WA • Chicago, IL • Columbus, OH • New York, NY

Cover: (tl) Red maple tree (Acer rubrum) on the shore of Lookout Lake in Dade County Georgia, (tr) The most recognizable of all the Georgia state symbols, the Georgia peach, (b) Hurricane Falls, Tallulah Gorge State Park in the town of Tallulah Falls, Georgia.

connectED.mcgraw-hill.com

STEM McGraw-Hill is committed to providing instructional materials in Science, Technology, Engineering, and Mathematics (STEM) that give all students a solid foundation, one that prepares them for college and careers in the 21st century.

Send all inquiries to:
McGraw-Hill Education
STEM Learning Solutions Center
8787 Orion Place
Columbus, OH 43240

ISBN: 978-0-07-665486-4 (*Volume 2*)
MHID: 0-07-665486-9

Printed in the United States of America.

11 12 13 QSX 20 19 18

Our mission is to provide educational resources that enable students to become the problem solvers of the 21st century and inspire them to explore careers within Science, Technology, Engineering, and Mathematics (STEM) related fields.

CONTENTS IN BRIEF

Units organized by the Georgia Grade 7 Curriculum Map

it's all at connectED.mcgraw-hill.com

Go to the Student Center for your eBook, Resources, Homework, and Messages.

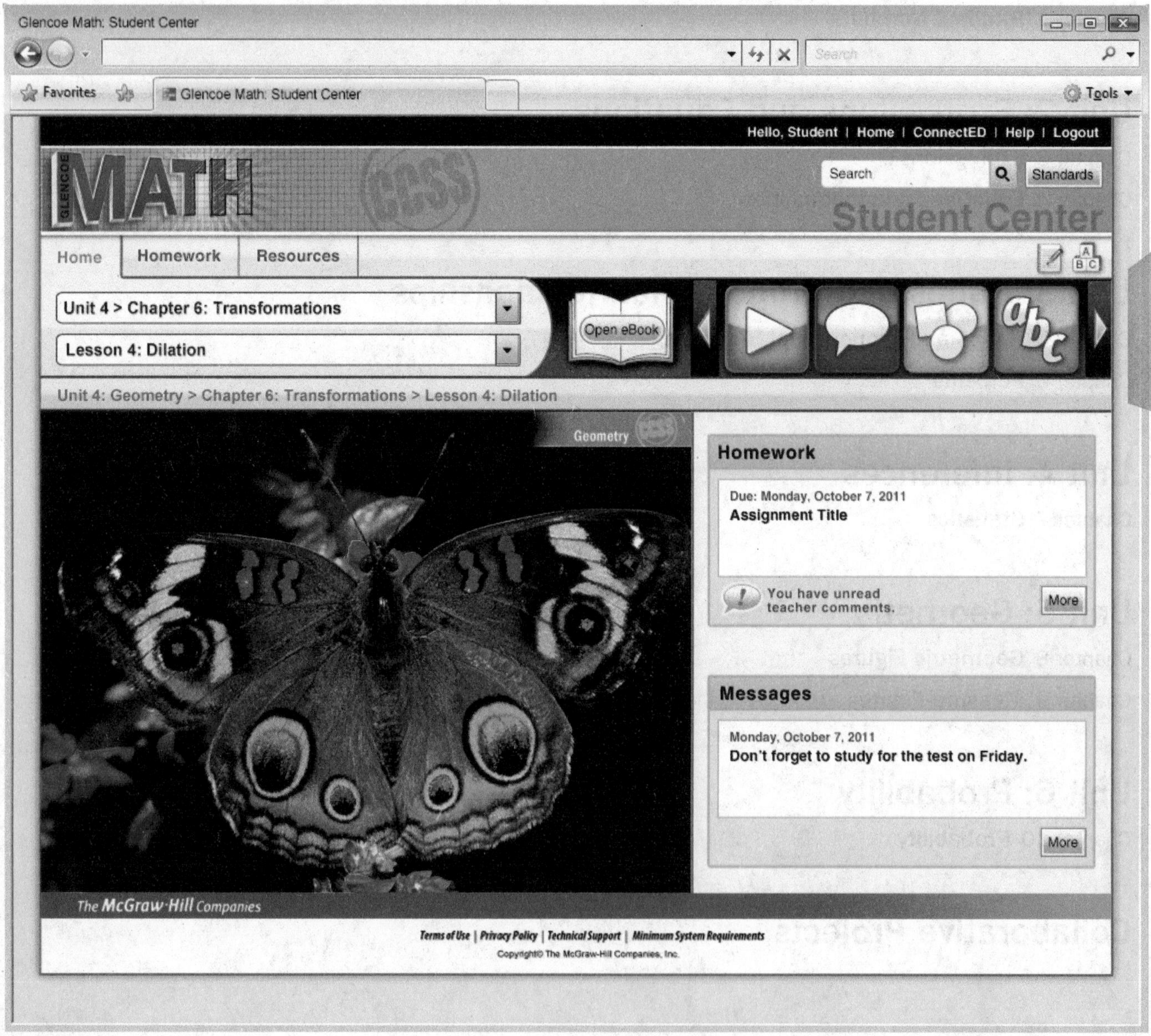

Glencoe Math: Student Center

Favorites | Glencoe Math: Student Center | Tools

Hello, Student | Home | ConnectED | Help | Logout

GLENCOE MATH CCSS

Search | Standards

Student Center

Home | Homework | Resources

Unit 4 > Chapter 6: Transformations

Lesson 4: Dilation

Open eBook

Unit 4: Geometry > Chapter 6: Transformations > Lesson 4: Dilation

Geometry

Homework

Due: Monday, October 7, 2011

Assignment Title

You have unread teacher comments.

More

Messages

Monday, October 7, 2011

Don't forget to study for the test on Friday.

More

The McGraw-Hill Companies

Terms of Use | Privacy Policy | Technical Support | Minimum System Requirements

Copyright© The McGraw-Hill Companies, Inc.

Write your Username ______ Password ______

Get your resources online to help you in class and at home.

Vocab

Find activities for building vocabulary.

Watch

Watch animations and videos.

Tutor

See a teacher illustrate examples and problems.

Tools

Explore concepts with virtual manipulatives.

Check

Self-assess your progress.

eHelp

Get targeted homework help.

Masters

Provides practice worksheets.

GO mobile

Scan this QR code with your smart phone* or visit mheonline.com/apps.

*May require quick response code reader app.

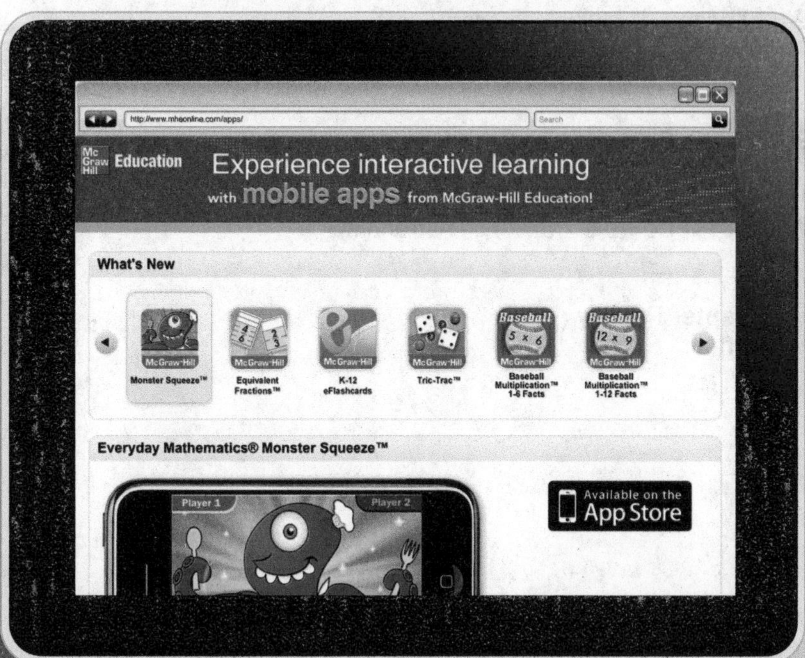

UNIT 1 Operations with Rational Numbers

Chapter 1 Integers

Online Transition Lessons

- Integers and Graphing
- Absolute Value
- Compare and Order Integers
- Graph on the Coordinate Plane
- Polygons on the Coordinate Plane

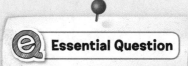

Essential Question

WHAT happens when you add, subtract, multiply, and divide integers?

Chapter 2 Rational Numbers

Essential Question

WHAT happens when you add, subtract, multiply, and divide fractions?

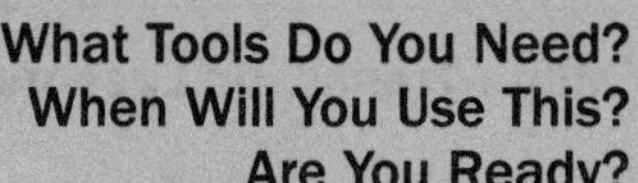

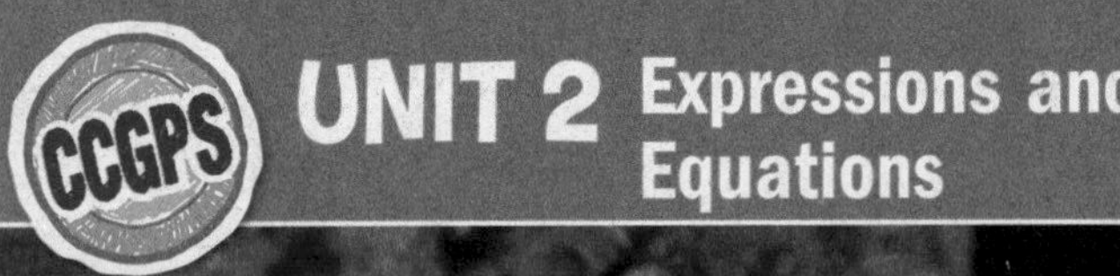

UNIT 2 Expressions and Equations

Chapter 3 Expressions

Online Transition Lessons

- **Inquiry Lab:** Equivalent Expressions
- Equivalent Expressions
- **Inquiry Lab:** Write Expressions
- Algebra: Write Expressions

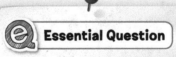

Essential Question

HOW can you use numbers and symbols to represent mathematical ideas?

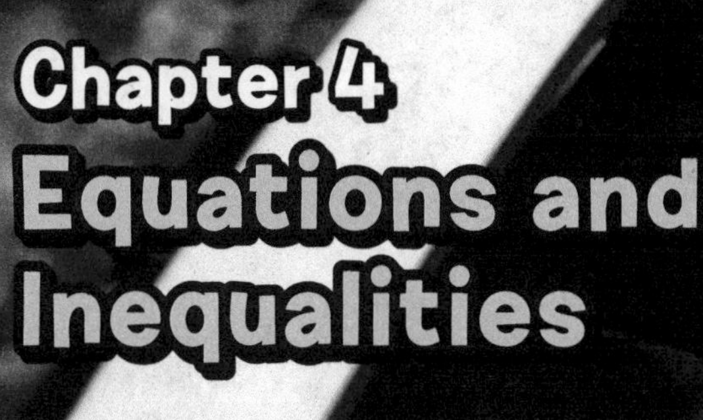

Chapter 4 Equations and Inequalities

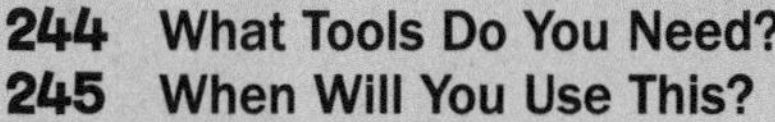

Online Transition Lessons

- **Inquiry Lab:** Inequalities
- Inequalities
- Write and Graph Inequalities
- **Inquiry Lab:** Solve One-Step Inequalities
- Solve One-Step Inequalities

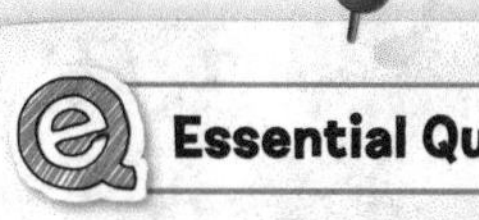

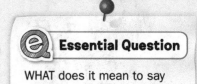

Essential Question

WHAT does it mean to say two quantities are equal?

UNIT 3 Ratios and Proportional Relationships

Chapter 5 Ratios and Proportional Reasoning

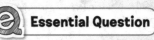

Essential Question

HOW can you show that two objects are proportional?

Chapter 6
Percents

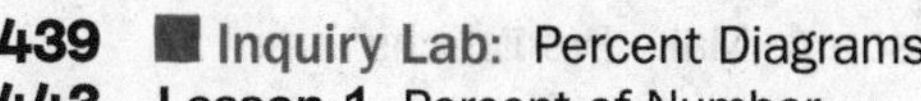

Essential Question

HOW can percent help you understand situations involving money?

UNIT 4 Inferences

Chapter 7 Statistics

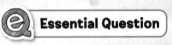

Essential Question

HOW do you know which type of graph to use when displaying data?

UNIT 5 Geometry

Chapter 8 Geometric Figures

Essential Question

HOW does geometry help us describe real-world objects?

Chapter 9
Measure Figures

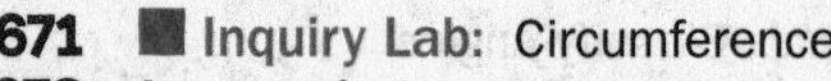

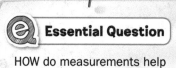

Essential Question

HOW do measurements help you describe real-world objects?

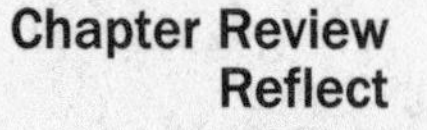

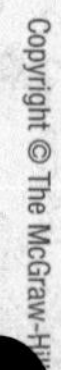

CCGPS **UNIT 6** Probability

Chapter 10 Probability

Essential Question

HOW can you predict the outcome of future events?

Georgia Grade 7 Curriculum Map

Georgia Math, Grade 7, focuses on teaching the CCGPS standards in the order of the Georgia Grade 7 Curriculum map.

Unit 1: Operations with Rational Numbers

MCCS addressed in Unit 1:

MCC7.NS 1 Apply and extend previous understandings of addition and subtraction to add and subtract rational numbers; represent addition and subtraction on a horizontal or vertical number line diagram.

MCC7.NS1.a Describe situations in which opposite quantities combine to make 0. For example, a hydrogen atom has 0 charge because its two constituents are oppositely charged.

MCC7.NS1.b Understand $p + q$ as the number located a distance $|q|$ from p, in the positive or negative direction depending on whether q is positive or negative. Show that a number and its opposite have a sum of 0 (are additive inverses). Interpret sums of rational numbers by describing real-world contexts.

MCC7.NS1.c Understand subtraction of rational numbers as adding the additive inverse, $p - q = p + (-q)$. Show that the distance between two rational numbers on the number line is the absolute value of their difference, and apply this principle in real-world context.

MCC7.NS1.d Apply properties of operations as strategies to add and subtract rational numbers.

MCC7.NS 2 Apply and extend previous understandings of multiplication and division and of fractions to multiply and divide rational numbers

MCC7.NS 2.a Understand that multiplication is extended from fractions to rational numbers by requiring that operations continue to satisfy the properties of operations, particularly the distributive property, leading to products such as $(-1)(-1) = 1$ and the rules for multiplying signed numbers. Interpret products of rational numbers by describing real-world contexts.

MCC7.NS 2.b Understand that integers can be divided, provided that the divisor is not zero, and every quotient of integers (with non-zero divisor) is a rational number. If p and q are integers, then $-(p/q) = (-p)/q = p/(-q)$. Interpret quotients of rational numbers by describing real-world contexts.

MCC7.NS 2.c Apply properties of operations as strategies to multiply and divide rational numbers.

MCC7.NS 2.d Convert a rational number to a decimal using long division; know that the decimal form of a rational number terminates in 0s or eventually repeats.

MCC7.NS 3 Solve real-world and mathematical problems involving the four operations with rational numbers.

Additional MCCS incorporated in Unit 1:

Real-world problem solving in these chapters also addresses:

MCC7.EE 3 *Solve multi-step real-life and mathematical problems posed with positive and negative rational numbers in any form (whole numbers, fractions, and decimals), using tools strategically. Apply properties of operations to calculate with numbers in any form; convert between forms as appropriate; and assess the reasonableness of answers using mental computation and estimation strategies.*

Transition Standard to be addressed:

MCC6.NS.5 *Understand that positive and negative numbers are used together to describe quantities having opposite directions or values (e.g. temperature above/below zero, elevation above/below sea level, debits/credits, positive/negative electric charge);*

Gerald Nowak/Westend61/Photolibrary

use positive and negative numbers to represent quantities in real-world contests, explaining the meaning of 0 in each situation.

MCC6.NS.6 *Understand a rational number as a point on the number line. Extend number line diagrams and coordinate axes familiar from previous grades to represent points on the line and in the plane with negative number coordinates.*

MCC6.NS.6a *Recognize opposite signs of numbers as indicating locations on opposite sides of 0 on the number line; recognize that the opposite of the opposite of a number is the number itself (e.g., $-(-3) = 3$, and that 0 is its own opposite.*

MCC6.NS.6b *Understand signs of numbers in ordered pairs as indicating locations in quadrants of the coordinate plane; recognize that when two ordered pairs differ only by signs, the locations of the points are related by reflections across one or both axes.*

MCC6.NS.6c *Find and position integers and other rational numbers on a horizontal or vertical number line diagram; find and position pairs of integers and other rational numbers on a coordinate plane.*

MCC6.NS.7 *Understand ordering and absolute value of rational numbers.*

MCC6.NS.7a *Interpret statements of inequality as statements about the relative position of two numbers on a number line diagram.*

MCC6.NS.7b *Write, interpret, and explain statements of order for rational numbers in real-world contexts.*

MCC6.NS.7c *Understand the absolute value of a rational number as its distance from 0 on the number line; interpret absolute value as magnitude for a positive or negative quantity in a real-world situation.*

MCC6.NS.7d *Distinguish comparisons of absolute value from statements about order.*

MCC6.NS.8 *Solve real-world and mathematical problems by graphing points in all four quadrants of the coordinate plane. Include use of coordinates and absolute value to find distances between points with the same first coordinates or the same second coordinates.*

MCC6.G.3 *Draw polygons in the coordinate plane given coordinates for the vertices; use coordinates to find the length of a side joining points with the same first coordinate or the same second coordinate. Apply these techniques in the context of solving real world and mathematical problems.*

Unit 2: Expressions and Equations

MCCS addressed in Unit 2:

MCC7.EE.1 Apply properties of operations as strategies to add, subtract, factor, and expand linear expressions with rational coefficients.

MCC7.EE.2 Understand that rewriting an expression in different forms in a problem context can shed light on the problem and how the quantities in it are related.

MCC7.EE.3 Solve multi step real life and mathematical problems posed with positive and negative rational numbers in any form (whole numbers, fractions, and decimals), using tools strategically. Apply properties of operations as strategies to calculate with numbers in any form; convert between forms as appropriate; and assess the reasonableness of answers using mental computation and estimation strategies.

MCC7.EE.4 Use variables to represent quantities in a real-world or mathematical problem, and construct simple equations and inequalities to solve problems by reasoning about the quantities.

7.EE.4a Solve word problems leading to equations of the form $px + q = r$ and $p(x + q) = r$, where p, q, and r are specific rational numbers. Solve equations of these forms fluently. Compare an algebraic solution to an arithmetic solution, identifying the sequence of the operations used in each approach.

7.EE.4b Solve word problems leading to inequalities of the form $px + q > r$ or $px + q < r$, where p, q, and r are specific rational numbers. Graph the solution set of the inequality and interpret it in the context of the problem.

Additional MCCS incorporated in Unit 2:

MCC7.NS 1 *Apply and extend previous understandings of addition and subtraction to add and subtract rational numbers; represent addition and subtraction on a horizontal or vertical number line diagram.*

MCC7.NS1.a *Describe situations in which opposite quantities combine to make 0. For example, a hydrogen atom has 0 charge because its two constituents are oppositely charged.*

MCC7.NS1.b *Understand $p + q$ as the number located a distance $|q|$ from p, in the positive or negative direction depending on whether q is positive or negative. Show that a number and its opposite have a sum of 0 (are additive inverses). Interpret sums of rational numbers by describing real-world contexts.*

MCC7.NS1.c *Understand subtraction of rational numbers as adding the additive inverse, $p - q = p + (-q)$. Show that the distance between two rational numbers on the number line is the absolute value of their difference, and apply this principle in real-world context.*

MCC7.NS1.d *Apply properties of operations as strategies to add and subtract rational numbers.*

MCC7.NS 2 *Apply and extend previous understandings of multiplication and division and of fractions to multiply and divide rational numbers*

MCC7.NS 2.a *Understand that multiplication is extended from fractions to rational numbers by requiring that operations continue to satisfy the properties of operations, particularly the distributive property, leading to products such as $(-1)(-1) = 1$ and the rules for multiplying signed numbers. Interpret products of rational numbers by describing real-world contexts.*

MCC7.NS 2.b *Understand that integers can be divided, provided that the divisor is not zero, and every quotient of integers (with non-zero divisor) is a rational number. If p and q are integers, then $-(p/q) = (-p)/q = p/(-q)$. Interpret quotients of rational numbers by describing real-world contexts.*

MCC7.NS 2.c *Apply properties of operations as strategies to multiply and divide rational numbers.*

MCC7.NS 2.d *Convert a rational number to a decimal using long division; know that the decimal form of a rational number terminates in 0s or eventually repeats.*

MCC7.NS 3 *Solve real-world and mathematical problems involving the four operations with rational numbers.*

Transition Standards to be addressed:

MCC6.EE.3 *Apply the properties of operations to generate equivalent expressions.*

MCC6.EE.4 *Identify when two expressions are equivalent (i.e., when the two expressions name the same number regardless of which value is substituted into them).*

MCC6.EE.6 *Use variables to represent numbers and write expressions when solving a real-world or mathematical problem; understand that a variable can represent an unknown number, or, depending on the purpose at hand, any number in a specified set.*

MCC6.EE.8 *Write an inequality of the form $x > c$ or $x < c$ to represent a constraint or condition in a real-world or mathematical problem. Recognize that inequalities of the form $x > c$ or $x < c$ have infinitely many solutions; represent solutions of such inequalities on number line diagrams.*

Unit 3: Ratios and Proportional Relationships

MCCS addressed in Unit 3:

MCC7.RP.1 Compute unit rates associated with ratios of fractions, including ratios of lengths, areas and other quantities measured in like or different units.

MCC7.RP.2 Recognize and represent proportional relationships between quantities.

MCC7.RP.2a Decide whether two quantities are in a proportional relationship, e.g., by testing for equivalent ratios in a table or graphing on a coordinate plane and observing whether the graph is a straight line through the origin.

MCC7.RP.2b Identify the constant of proportionality (unit rate) in tables, graphs, equations, diagrams, and verbal descriptions of proportional relationships.

MCC7.RP.2c Represent proportional relationships by equations.

MCC7.RP.2d Explain what a point (x, y) on the graph of a proportional relationship means in terms of the situation, with special attention to the points (0, 0) and $(1, r)$ where r is the unit rate.

MCC7.RP.3 Use proportional relationships to solve multistep ratio and percent problems. Examples: simple interest, tax, markups and markdowns, gratuities and commissions, fees, percent increase and decrease, percent error.

MCC7.G.1 Solve problems involving scale drawings of geometric figures, including computing actual lengths and areas from a scale drawing and reproducing a scale drawing at a different scale.

Additional MCCS incorporated in Unit 3:

MCC7.EE 3 *Solve multi-step real-life and mathematical problems posed with positive and negative rational numbers in any form (whole numbers, fractions, and decimals), using tools strategically. Apply properties of operations to calculate with numbers in any form; convert between forms as appropriate; and assess the reasonableness of answers using mental computation and estimation strategies.*

MCC7.NS 1 *Apply and extend previous understandings of addition and subtraction to add and subtract rational numbers; represent addition and subtraction on a horizontal or vertical number line diagram.*

MCC7.NS1.a *Describe situations in which opposite quantities combine to make 0. For example, a hydrogen atom has 0 charge because its two constituents are oppositely charged.*

MCC7.NS1.b *Understand $p + q$ as the number located a distance $|q|$ from p, in the positive or negative direction depending on whether q is positive or negative. Show that a number and its opposite have a sum of 0 (are additive inverses). Interpret sums of rational numbers by describing real-world contexts.*

MCC7.NS1.c *Understand subtraction of rational numbers as adding the additive inverse, $p - q = p + (-q)$. Show that the distance between two rational numbers on the number line is the absolute value of their difference, and apply this principle in real-world context.*

MCC7.NS1.d *Apply properties of operations as strategies to add and subtract rational numbers.*

MCC7.NS 2. *Apply and extend previous understandings of multiplication and division and of fractions to multiply and divide rational numbers*

MCC7.NS 2.a *Understand that multiplication is extended from fractions to rational numbers by requiring that operations continue to satisfy the properties of operations, particularly the distributive property, leading to products such as $(-1)(-1) = 1$ and the rules for multiplying signed numbers. Interpret products of rational numbers by describing real-world contexts.*

MCC7.NS 2.b *Understand that integers can be divided, provided that the divisor is not zero, and every quotient of integers (with non-zero divisor) is a rational number. If p and q are integers, then $-(p/q) = (-p)/q = p/(-q)$. Interpret quotients of rational numbers by describing real-world contexts.*

MCC7.NS 2.c *Apply properties of operations as strategies to multiply and divide rational numbers.*

MCC7.NS 2.d *Convert a rational number to a decimal using long division; know that the decimal form of a rational number terminates in 0s or eventually repeats.*

MCC7.NS 3 *Solve real-world and mathematical problems involving the four operations with rational numbers.*

Unit 4: Inferences

MCCS addressed in Unit 4:

MCC7.SP.1 Understand that statistics can be used to gain information about a population by examining a sample of the population; generalizations about a population from a sample are valid only if the sample is representative of that population. Understand that random sampling tends to produce representative samples and support valid inferences.

MCC7.SP.2 Use data from a random sample to draw inferences about a population with an unknown characteristic of interest. Generate multiple samples (or simulated samples) of the same size to gauge the variation in estimates or predictions.

MCC7.SP.3 Informally assess the degree of visual overlap of two numerical data distributions with similar variabilities, measuring the difference between the centers by expressing it as a multiple of a measure of variability.

MCC7.SP.4 Use measures of center and measures of variability for numerical data from random samples to draw informal comparative inferences about two populations.

Additional MCCS incorporated in Unit 4:

MCC7.EE 3 *Solve multi-step real-life and mathematical problems posed with positive and negative rational numbers in any form (whole numbers, fractions, and decimals), using tools strategically. Apply properties of operations to calculate with numbers in any form; convert between forms as appropriate; and assess the reasonableness of answers using mental computation and estimation strategies.*

MCC7.NS 1 *Apply and extend previous understandings of addition and subtraction to add and subtract rational numbers; represent addition and subtraction on a horizontal or vertical number line diagram.*

MCC7.NS1.a *Describe situations in which opposite quantities combine to make 0. For example, a hydrogen atom has 0 charge because its two constituents are oppositely charged.*

MCC7.NS1.b *Understand $p + q$ as the number located a distance $|q|$ from p, in the positive or negative direction depending on whether q is positive or negative. Show that a number and its opposite have a sum of 0 (are additive inverses). Interpret sums of rational numbers by describing real-world contexts.*

MCC7.NS1.c *Understand subtraction of rational numbers as adding the additive inverse, $p - q = p + (-q)$. Show that the distance between two rational numbers on the number line is the absolute value of their difference, and apply this principle in real-world context.*

MCC7.NS1.d *Apply properties of operations as strategies to add and subtract rational numbers.*

MCC7.NS 2 *Apply and extend previous understandings of multiplication and division and of fractions to multiply and divide rational numbers*

MCC7.NS 2.a *Understand that multiplication is extended from fractions to rational numbers by requiring that operations continue to satisfy the properties of operations, particularly the distributive property, leading to products such as $(-1)(-1) = 1$ and the rules for multiplying signed numbers. Interpret products of rational numbers by describing real-world contexts.*

MCC7.NS 2.b *Understand that integers can be divided, provided that the divisor is not zero, and every quotient of integers (with non-zero divisor) is a rational number. If p and q are integers, then $-(p/q) = (-p)/q = p/(-q)$. Interpret quotients of rational numbers by describing real-world contexts.*

MCC7.NS 2.c *Apply properties of operations as strategies to multiply and divide rational numbers.*

MCC7.NS 2.d *Convert a rational number to a decimal using long division; know that the decimal form of a rational number terminates in 0s or eventually repeats.*

MCC7.NS 3 *Solve real-world and mathematical problems involving the four operations with rational numbers.*

Unit 5: Geometry

MCCS addressed in Unit 5:

MCC7.G.2 Draw (freehand, with ruler and protractor, and with technology) geometric shapes with given condition. Focus on constructing triangles from three measures of angles or sides, noticing when the conditions determine a unique triangle, more than one triangle, or no triangle.

MCC7.G.3 Describe the two dimensional figures that result from slicing three dimensional figures, as in plane sections of right rectangular prisms and right rectangular pyramids.

MCC7.G.4 Know the formulas for the area and circumference of a circle and use them to solve problems; give an informal derivation of the relationship between the circumference and area of a circle.

MCC7.G.5 Use facts about supplementary, complementary, vertical, and adjacent angles in a multi step problem to write and solve simple equations for an unknown angle in a figure.

MCC7.G.6 Solve real world and mathematical problems involving area, volume and surface area of two and three dimensional objects composed of triangles, quadrilaterals, polygons, cubes, and right prisms.

Additional MCCS incorporated in Unit 5:

MCC7.G.1 *Solve problems involving scale drawings of geometric figures, including computing actual lengths and areas from a scale drawing and reproducing a scale drawing at a different scale.*

Unit 6: Probability

MCCS addressed in Unit 6:

MCC7.SP.5 Understand that the probability of a chance event is a number between 0 and 1 that expresses the likelihood of the event occurring. Larger numbers indicate greater likelihood. A probability near 0 indicates an unlikely event, a probability around 1/2 indicates an event that is neither unlikely nor likely, and a probability near 1 indicates a likely event.

MCC7.SP.6 Approximate the probability of a chance event by collecting data on the chance process that produces it and observing its long run relative frequency, and predict the approximate relative frequency given the probability.

MCC7.SP.7 Develop a probability model and use it to find probabilities of events. Compare probabilities from a model to observed frequencies; if the agreement is not good, explain possible sources of the discrepancy.

- **MCC7.SP.7a** Develop a uniform probability model by assigning equal probability to all outcomes, and use the model to determine probabilities of events.
- **MCC7.SP.7b** Develop a probability model (which may not be uniform) by observing frequencies in data generated from a chance process.

MCC7.SP.8 Find probabilities of compound events using organized lists, tables, tree diagrams, and simulation.

- **MCC7.SP.8a** Understand that, just as with simple events, the probability of a compound event is the fraction of outcomes in the sample space for which the compound event occurs.
- **MCC7.SP.8b** Represent sample spaces for compound events using methods such as organized lists, tables and tree diagrams. For an event described in everyday language (e.g., "rolling double sixes"), identify the outcomes in the sample space which compose the event.
- **MCC7.SP.8c** Design and use a simulation to generate frequencies for compound events.

Unit 7: Show What We Know

MCCS addressed in Unit 8:

ALL

UNIT 3

Ratios and Proportional Relationships

Essential Question

HOW can you use mathematics to describe change and model real-world situations?

Chapter 5
Ratios and Proportional Reasoning

Proportional relationships can be used to solve real-world problems. In this chapter, you will determine whether the relationship between two quantities is proportional. Then you will use proportions to solve multi-step problems.

Chapter 6
Percents

Proportional relationships can be used to solve percent problems. In this chapter, you will find percent of increase and decrease and use percents to solve problems involving sales tax, tips, markups and discounts, and simple interest.

Chapter 5

Ratios and Proportional Reasoning

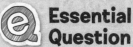

Essential Question

HOW can you show that two objects are proportional?

Common Core GPS

Content Standards
MCC7.RP.1, MCC7.RP.2, MCC7.RP.2a, MCC7.RP.2b, MCC7.RP.2c, MCC7.RP.2d, MCC7.RP.3, MCC7.NS.3

Mathematical Practices
1, 2, 3, 4, 5, 6

Math in the Real World

Airplanes used for commercial flights travel at a speed of about 550 miles per hour.

Suppose an airplane travels 265 miles in one-half hour. Draw an arrow on the speedometer below to represent the speed of the airplane in miles per hour.

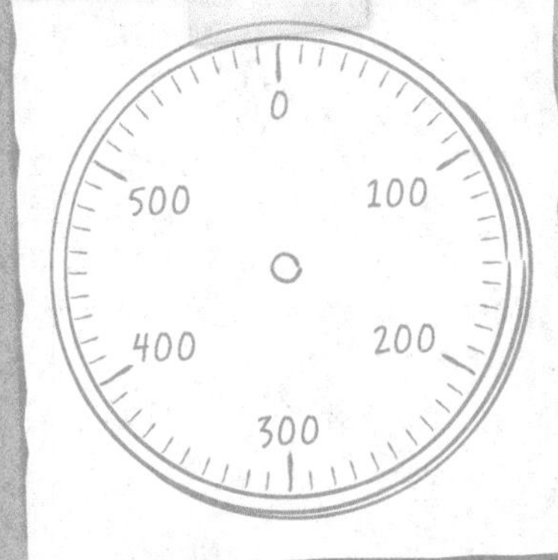

FOLDABLES®
Study Organizer

Cut out the correct Foldable from the FL pages in the back of this book.

Place your Foldable on the Key Concept page toward the end of this chapter.

Use the Foldable throughout this chapter as you learn about proportional reasoning.

What Tools Do You Need?

Vocabulary

complex fraction
constant of proportionality
constant rate of change
constant of variation
coordinate plane
cross products
dimensional analysis
direct variation
equivalent ratios
nonproportional
proportion
proportional
ordered pair
origin
quadrants
rate
rate of change
slope
unit rate
unit ratio
x-axis
x-coordinate
y-axis
y-coordinate

Review Vocabulary

Functions A function is a relationship that assigns exactly one output value for each input value. The function rule is the operation performed on the input. Perform each indicated operation on the input 10. Then write each output in the organizer.

Input	Rule	Output
10	Add 2.	
	Subtract 3.	
	Multiply by 4.	
	Divide by 5.	

When Will You Use This?

Your Turn! **You will solve this problem in the chapter.**

Try the Quick Check below.
Or, take the Online Readiness Quiz.

Quick Review

Common Core Review MCC6.RP.1, MCC6.RP.3

Example 1

Write the ratio of wins to losses as a fraction in simplest form.

Madison Mavericks	
Team Statistics	
Wins	10
Losses	12
Ties	8

wins → losses → $\frac{10}{12} = \frac{5}{6}$

The ratio of wins to losses is $\frac{5}{6}$.

Example 2

Determine whether the ratios 250 miles in 4 hours and 500 miles in 8 hours are equivalent.

Compare the ratios by writing them in simplest form.

250 miles : 4 hours = $\frac{250}{4}$ or $\frac{125}{2}$

500 miles : 8 hours = $\frac{500}{8}$ or $\frac{125}{2}$

The ratios are equivalent because they simplify to the same fraction.

Quick Check

Ratios **Write each ratio as a fraction in simplest form.**

Seventh-Grade Field Trip	
Students	180
Adults	24
Buses	4

1. adults : students ______
2. students : buses ______
3. buses : people ______

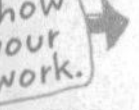

Equivalent Ratios **Determine whether the ratios are equivalent. Explain.**

4. 20 nails for every 5 shingles
   12 nails for every 3 shingles

5. 12 out of 20 doctors agree
   15 out of 30 doctors agree

Which problems did you answer correctly in the Quick Check? Shade those exercise numbers below.

1 2 3 4 5

HOW can you use a bar diagram to solve a real-world problem involving ratios?

Content Standards
Preparation for MCC7.RP.1, MCC7.RP.2, and MCC7.RP.2b

Mathematical Practices
1, 3, 4

Money When Jeremy gets his allowance, he agrees to save part of it. His savings and expenses are in the ratio 7:5. If his daily allowance is \$3, find how much he saves each day.

Investigation

Complete the bar diagram below by writing *savings, expenses,* and *\$3* in the correct boxes.

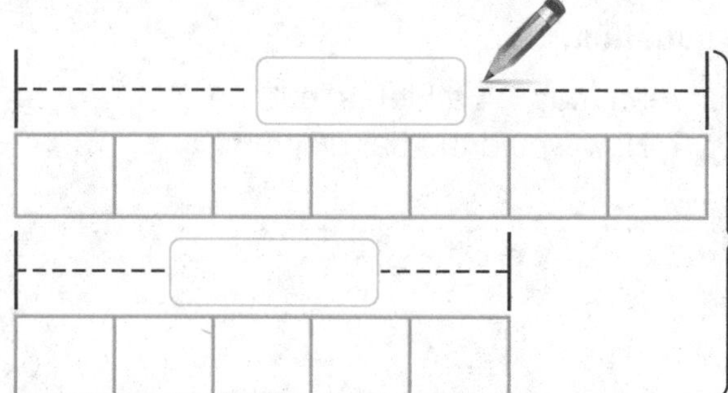

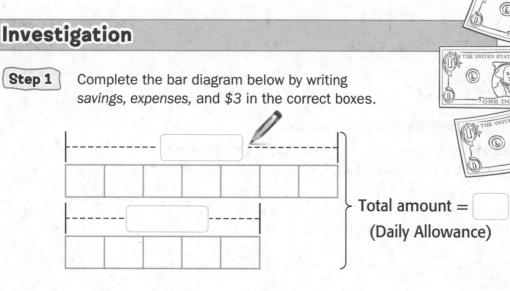

Total amount = ☐
(Daily Allowance)

Step 2 Let x represent each part of a bar. Write and solve an equation to find the amount of money each bar represents.

$7x + \square x = 3$	Write the equation.
$12x = 3$	There are 12 parts in all.
$\frac{12x}{12} = \frac{3}{12}$	Division Property of Equality
$x = \frac{\square}{\square}$ or 0.25	Simplify.

Determine the amount Jeremy saves each day. Since each part of the bar represents \$0.25, Jeremy's savings are represented by $7 \times \$\square$ or \$1.75.

So, Jeremy saves \$☐ each day.

Collaborate

Work with a partner to answer the following question.

1. The ratio of the number of boys to the number of girls on the swim team is 4:2. If there are 24 athletes on the swim team, how many more boys than girls are there? Use a bar diagram to solve. ______

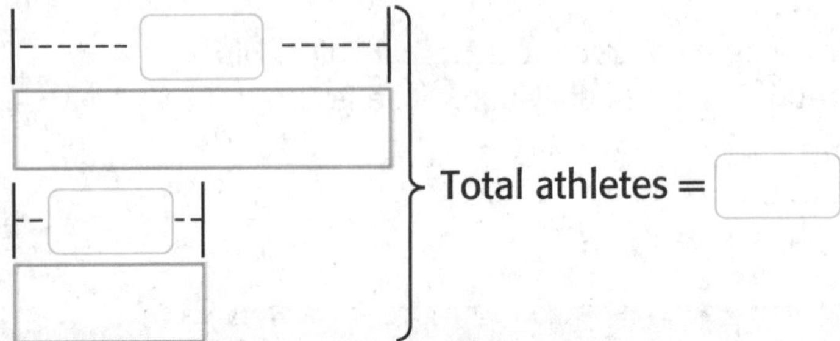

Work with a partner to answer the following question.

2. CCGPS **Reason Inductively** Suppose the swim team has 24 athletes, but the ratio of boys to girls on the swim team is 3 : 5. How would the bar diagram change? ______

3. CCGPS **Model with Mathematics** Write a real-world problem that could be represented by the bar diagram shown below. Then solve your problem.

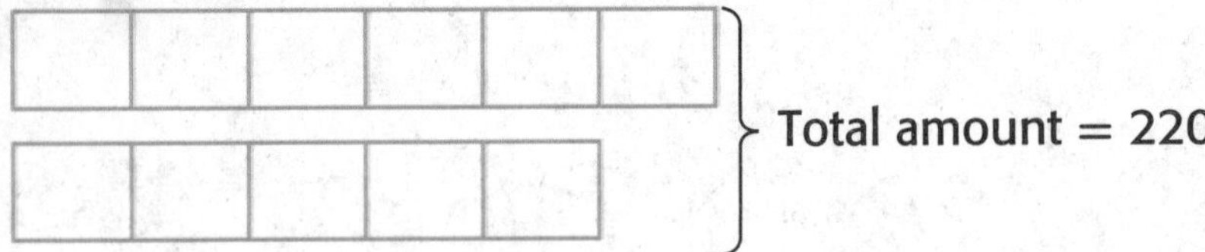

4. Inquiry HOW can you use a bar diagram to solve a real-world problem involving ratios?

Rates

What You'll Learn

Scan the lesson. Predict two things you will learn about rates.

- ______________________________
- ______________________________

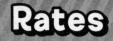

Essential Question

HOW can you show that two objects are proportional?

Vocabulary

rate
unit rate

Common Core GPS

Content Standards
MCC7.RP.2, MCC7.RP.2b

Mathematical Practices
1, 3, 4, 5

Real-World Link

Watch

Pulse Rate You can take a person's pulse by placing your middle and index finger on the underside of their wrist. Choose a partner and take their pulse for two minutes.

1. Record the results in the diagram below.

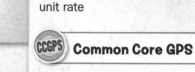

2. Use the results from Exercise 1 to complete the bar diagram and determine the number of beats per minute for your partner.

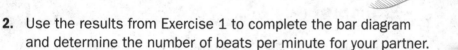

Beats in 2 minutes = ☐

Number of beats in 1 minute.	Number of beats in 1 minute.
☐ beats	☐ beats

So, your partner's heart beats ☐ times per minute.

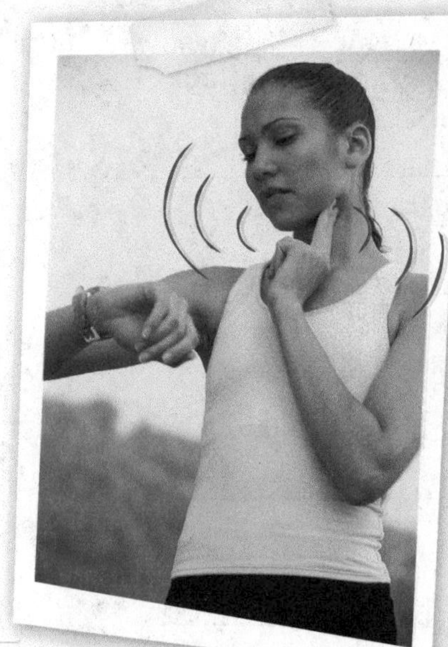

3. Use the results from Exercise 1 to determine the number of beats for $\frac{1}{2}$ minute for your partner.

____

Work Zone

Find a Unit Rate

A ratio that compares two quantities with different kinds of units is called a **rate**. When you found each other's pulse, you were actually finding the heart *rate*.

$$\frac{\text{160 beats}}{\text{2 minutes}}$$

The units *beats* and *minutes* are different.

When a rate is simplified so that it has a denominator of 1 unit, it is called a **unit rate**.

$$\frac{\text{80 beats}}{\text{1 minute}}$$

The denominator is 1 unit.

The table below shows some common unit rates.

Rate	Unit Rate	Abbreviation	Name
$\frac{\text{number of miles}}{\text{1 hour}}$	miles per hour	mi/h or mph	average speed
$\frac{\text{number of miles}}{\text{1 gallon}}$	miles per gallon	mi/gal or mpg	gas mileage
$\frac{\text{number of dollars}}{\text{1 pound}}$	price per pound	dollars/lb	unit price

Example

1. Adrienne biked 24 miles in 4 hours. If she biked at a constant speed, how many miles did she ride in one hour?

24 miles in 4 hours $= \frac{24 \text{ mi}}{4 \text{ h}}$ Write the rate as a fraction.

$= \frac{24 \text{ mi} \div 4}{4 \text{ h} \div 4}$ Divide the numerator and the denominator by 4.

$= \frac{6 \text{ mi}}{1 \text{ h}}$ Simplify.

Adrienne biked 6 miles in one hour.

STOP and Reflect

Circle the unit rate below that represents 18 cans for $6.

$\frac{\text{9 cans}}{\$3}$ $\frac{\text{3 cans}}{\$1}$ $\frac{\text{4 cans}}{\$1}$

Got It? Do these problems to find out.

Find each unit rate. Round to the nearest hundredth if necessary.

a. $300 for 6 hours

b. 220 miles on 8 gallons

Show your work.

a. ____________

b. ____________

Example

2. Find the unit price if it costs \$2 for eight juice boxes.

$\$2 \text{ for eight boxes} = \frac{\$2}{8 \text{ boxes}}$ — Write the rate as a fraction.

$= \frac{\$2 \div 8}{8 \text{ boxes} \div 8}$ — Divide the numerator and the denominator by 8.

$= \frac{\$0.25}{1 \text{ box}}$ — Simplify.

The unit price is \$0.25 per juice box.

Got It? **Do this problem to find out.**

c. Find the unit price if a 4-pack of mixed fruit sells for \$2.12.

c. ________

Example

3. The prices of 3 different bags of dog food are given in the table. Which size bag has the lowest price per pound rounded to the nearest cent?

Dog Food Prices	
Bag Size (lb)	**Price (\$)**
40	49.00
20	23.44
8	9.88

- 40-pound bag
  \$49.00 ÷ 40 pounds ≈ \$1.23 per pound
- 20-pound bag
  \$23.44 ÷ 20 pounds ≈ \$1.17 per pound
- 8-pound bag
  \$9.88 ÷ 8 pounds ≈ \$1.24 per pound

The 20-pound bag sells for the lowest price per pound.

Alternative Method

One 40-lb bag is equivalent to two 20-lb bags or five 8-lb bags. The cost for one 40-lb bag is \$49, the cost for two 20-lb bags is about 2 x \$23 or \$46, and the cost for five 8-lb bags is about 5 x \$10 or \$50. So, the 20-lb bag has the lowest price per pound.

Got It? **Do this problem to find out.**

d. Tito wants to buy some peanut butter to donate to the local food pantry. Tito wants to buy as much peanut butter as possible. Which brand should he buy?

Peanut Butter Sales	
Brand	**Sale Price**
Nutty	12 ounces for \$2.19
Grandma's	18 ounces for \$2.79
Bee's	28 ounces for \$4.69
Save-A-Lot	40 ounces for \$6.60

d. ________

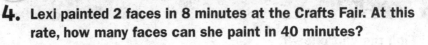

Example

4. Lexi painted 2 faces in 8 minutes at the Crafts Fair. At this rate, how many faces can she paint in 40 minutes?

Method 1 **Draw a Bar Diagram**

time to paint one face	time to paint one face

8 min (total); 4 min | 4 min

It takes 4 minutes to paint one face. In 40 minutes, Lexi can paint 40 ÷ 4 or 10 faces.

Method 2 **Find a Unit Rate**

2 faces in 8 minutes $= \frac{2 \text{ faces} \div 8}{8 \text{ min} \div 8} = \frac{0.25 \text{ face}}{1 \text{ min}}$ Find the unit rate.

Multiply the unit rate by 40 minutes.

$\frac{0.25 \text{ face}}{1 \cancel{\text{min}}} \cdot 40 \cancel{\text{min}} = 10 \text{ faces}$ Divide out the common units.

Using either method, Lexi can paint 10 faces in 40 minutes.

Guided Practice

1. CD Express offers 4 CDs for \$60. Music Place offers 6 CDs for \$75. Which store offers the better buy? (Examples 1–3)

2. After 3.5 hours, Pasha had traveled 217 miles. If she travels at a constant speed, how far will she have traveled after 4 hours? (Example 4)

3. Write 5 pounds for \$2.49 as a unit rate. Round to the nearest hundredth. (Example 2)

4. **Building on the Essential Question** Use an example to describe how a *rate* is a measure of one quantity per unit of another quantity.

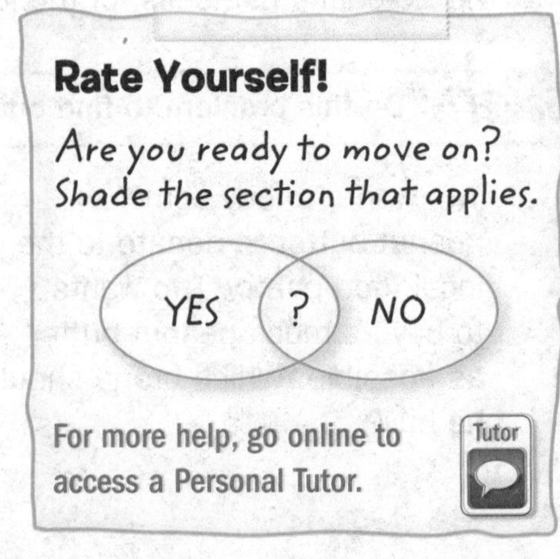

Rate Yourself!
Are you ready to move on? Shade the section that applies.
YES
?
NO
For more help, go online to access a Personal Tutor.
Tutor

Independent Practice

Go online for Step-by-Step Solutions eHelp

Find each unit rate. Round to the nearest hundredth if necessary. (Examples 1 and 2)

1. 360 miles in 6 hours ______

2. 6,840 customers in 45 days ______

3. 45.5 meters in 13 seconds ______

4. $7.40 for 5 pounds ______

5. Estimate the unit rate if 12 pairs of socks sell for $5.79. (Examples 1 and 2)

______

6. CCGPS **Justify Conclusions** The results of a swim meet are shown. Who swam the fastest? Explain your reasoning. (Example 3)

______

Name	Event	Time (s)
Tawni	50-m Freestyle	40.8
Pepita	100-m Butterfly	60.2
Susana	200-m Medley	112.4

7. Ben can type 153 words in 3 minutes. At this rate, how many words can he type in 10 minutes? (Example 4)

______

8. Kenji buys 3 yards of fabric for $7.47. Then he realizes that he needs 2 more yards. How much will the extra fabric cost? (Example 4)

______

9. The record for the Boston Marathon's wheelchair division is 1 hour, 18 minutes, and 27 seconds.

   a. The Boston Marathon is 26.2 miles long. What was the average speed of the record winner of the wheelchair division?

   Round to the nearest hundredth. ______

   b. At this rate, about how long would it take this competitor to complete a 30-mile race? ______

10. At Tire Depot, a pair of new tires sells for $216. The manager's special advertises the same tires selling at a rate of $380 for 4 tires. How much do you save per tire if you purchase the manager's special? ______

H.O.T. Problems Higher Order Thinking

11. CCGPS **Use Math Tools** Find examples of grocery item prices in a newspaper, on television, or on the Internet. Compare unit prices of two different brands of the same item. Explain which item is the better buy.

12. CCGPS **Find the Error** Seth is trying to find the unit price for a package of blank compact discs on sale at 10 for $5.49. Find his mistake and correct it.

CCGPS **Persevere with Problems Determine whether each statement is *sometimes, always,* or *never* true. Give an example or a counterexample.**

13. A ratio is a rate.

14. A rate is a ratio.

Georgia Test Practice

15. The table shows the total distance traveled by a car driving at a constant rate of speed. How far will the car have traveled after 10 hours?

Time (h)	Distance (mi)
2	130
3.5	227.5
4	260
7	455

Ⓐ 520 miles

Ⓑ 585 miles

Ⓒ 650 miles

Ⓓ 715 miles

Name ______________________ My Homework

Extra Practice

Find each unit rate. Round to the nearest hundredth if necessary.

16. 150 people for 5 classes

30 people per class

$\frac{150 \text{ people} \div 5}{5 \text{ classes} \div 5} = \frac{30 \text{ people}}{1 \text{ class}}$

Homework Help

30 people per class

17. 815 Calories in 4 servings

203.75 Calories per serving

$\frac{815 \text{ Calories} \div 4}{4 \text{ servings} \div 4} = \frac{203.75 \text{ Calories}}{1 \text{ serving}}$

203.75 Calories per serving

18. $1.12 for 8.2 ounces

19. 144 miles on 4.5 gallons

20. CCGPS **Justify Conclusions** A grocery store sells a 6-pack of bottled water for $3.79, a 9-pack for $4.50, and a 12-pack for $6.89. Which package costs the least per bottle? Explain your reasoning.

21. CCGPS **Justify Conclusions** Dalila earns $108.75 for working 15 hours as a holiday helper wrapping gifts. At this rate, how much money will she earn if she works 18 hours the next week? Explain.

22. CCGPS **Use Math Tools** Use the graph that shows the average number of heartbeats for an active adult brown bear and a hibernating brown bear.

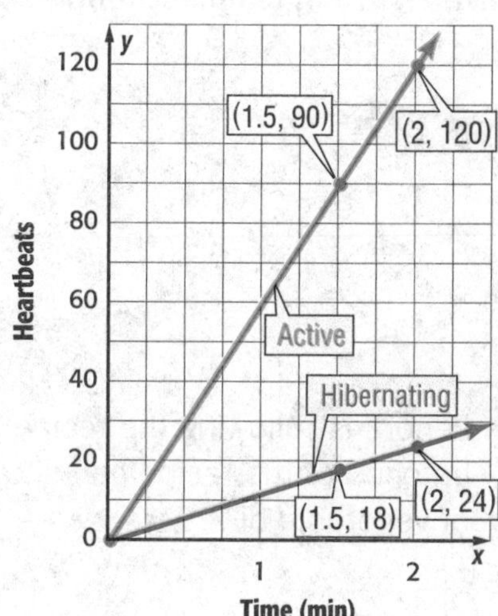

a. What does the point (2, 120) represent on the graph?

b. What does the ratio of the y-coordinate to the x-coordinate for each pair of points on the graph represent?

c. Use the graph to find the bear's average heart rate when it is active and when it is hibernating.

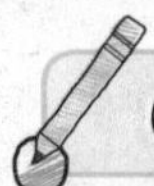

Georgia Test Practice

23. Mrs. Ross needs to buy dish soap. There are four different sized containers.

Dish Soap Prices	
Brand	**Price**
Lots of Suds	$0.98 for 8 ounces
Bright Wash	$1.29 for 12 ounces
Spotless Soap	$3.14 for 30 ounces
Lemon Bright	$3.45 for 32 ounces

Which brand costs the least per ounce?

Ⓐ Lots of Suds
Ⓑ Bright Wash
Ⓒ Spotless Soap
Ⓓ Lemon Bright

24. **Short Response** Bonita spent $2.00 for 20 pencils, Jamal spent $1.50 for 10 pencils, and Hasina spent $2.10 for 15 pencils. List the students from least to greatest according to unit price paid.

25. The Jimenez family took a four-day road trip. They traveled 300 miles in 5 hours on Sunday, 200 miles in 3 hours on Monday, 150 miles in 2.5 hours on Tuesday, and 250 miles in 6 hours on Wednesday. On which day did they average the greatest miles per hour?

Ⓕ Sunday
Ⓖ Monday
Ⓗ Tuesday
Ⓘ Wednesday

26. **Short Response** Suppose that 1 euro is worth $1.25. In Europe, a book costs 19 euros. In Los Angeles, the same book costs $22.50. In which location is the book less expensive?

Common Core Review

Solve. Write in simplest form. MCC5.NF.4

27. $\frac{1}{2} \times \frac{4}{7} = \frac{\square}{\square}$

28. $\frac{2}{3} \times \frac{1}{6} = \frac{\square}{\square}$

29. $\frac{1}{4} \div \frac{3}{8} = \frac{\square}{\square}$

30. Lenora is following the recipe at the right. How many batches of the recipe can she make if she has 5 cups of vegetable oil? MCC5.NF.4

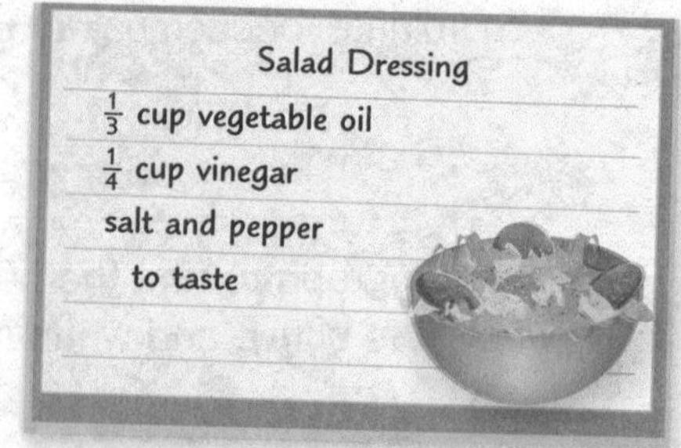

Complex Fractions and Unit Rates

What You'll Learn

List two headings you would use to make an outline of the lesson.

-

-

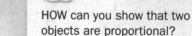

Essential Question

HOW can you show that two objects are proportional?

Vocabulary

complex fraction

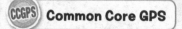

Common Core GPS

Content Standards
MCC7.RP.1, MCC7.NS.3

Mathematical Practices
1, 3, 4, 6

Real-World Link

Speed Skating Dana is skating laps to train for a speed skating competition. She can skate 1 lap in 40 seconds.

1. Write a ratio in simplest form comparing Dana's time to her number of laps.

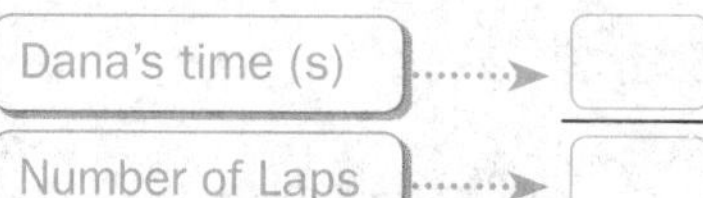

2. Suppose Dana skates for 20 seconds. How many laps will she skate?

3. Write the ratio of Dana's time from Exercise 2 to her number of laps.

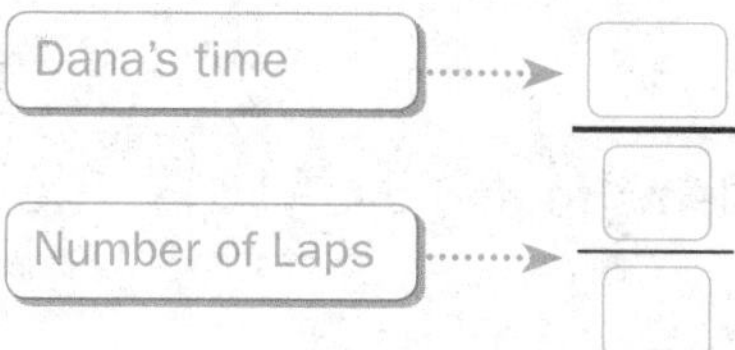

4. How could you simplify the ratio you wrote in Exercise 3?

Work Zone

Simplify a Complex Fraction

Fractions like $\frac{20}{\frac{1}{2}}$ are called complex fractions. **Complex fractions** are fractions with a numerator, denominator, or both that are also fractions. Complex fractions are simplified when both the numerator and denominator are integers.

Examples

Divide Fractions

To divide by a whole number, first write it as a fraction with a denominator of 1. Then multiply by the reciprocal.

So, $\frac{\frac{1}{4}}{2}$ can be written as $\frac{1}{4} \div \frac{2}{1}$.

1. Simplify $\frac{\frac{1}{4}}{2}$.

Recall that a fraction can also be written as a division problem.

$\frac{\frac{1}{4}}{2} = \frac{1}{4} \div 2$ Write the complex fraction as a division problem.

$= \frac{1}{4} \times \frac{1}{2}$ Multiply by the reciprocal of 2, which is $\frac{1}{2}$.

$= \frac{1}{8}$ Simplify.

So, $\frac{\frac{1}{4}}{2}$ is equal to $\frac{1}{8}$.

2. Simplify $\frac{1}{\frac{1}{2}}$.

Write the fraction as a division problem.

$\frac{1}{\frac{1}{2}} = 1 \div \frac{1}{2}$ Write the complex fraction as a division problem.

$= \frac{1}{1} \times \frac{2}{1}$ Multiply by the reciprocal of $\frac{1}{2}$, which is $\frac{2}{1}$.

$= \frac{2}{1}$ or 2 Simplify.

So, $\frac{1}{\frac{1}{2}}$ is equal to 2.

Got It? Do these problems to find out.

a. $\frac{2}{\frac{2}{3}}$

b. $\frac{6}{\frac{1}{3}}$

c. $\frac{\frac{2}{3}}{7}$

d. $\frac{\frac{2}{4}}{2}$

a. ____

b. ____

c. ____

d. ____

Find Unit Rates

When the fractions of a complex fractions represent different units, you can find the unit rate.

Examples

3. Josiah can jog $1\frac{1}{3}$ miles in $\frac{1}{4}$ hour. Find his average speed in miles per hour.

Write a rate that compares the number of miles to hours.

$$\frac{1\frac{1}{3}\text{ mi}}{\frac{1}{4}\text{ h}} = 1\frac{1}{3} \div \frac{1}{4}$$ Write the complex fraction as a division problem.

$$= \frac{4}{3} \div \frac{1}{4}$$ Write the mixed number as an improper fraction.

$$= \frac{4}{3} \times \frac{4}{1}$$ Multiply by the reciprocal of $\frac{1}{4}$, which is $\frac{4}{1}$.

$$= \frac{16}{3} \text{ or } 5\frac{1}{3}$$ Simplify.

So, Josiah jogs at an average speed of $5\frac{1}{3}$ miles per hour.

4. Tia is painting her house. She paints $34\frac{1}{2}$ square feet in $\frac{3}{4}$ hour. At this rate, how many square feet can she paint each hour?

Write a ratio that compares the amount of square feet to hours.

$$\frac{34\frac{1}{2}\text{ ft}^2}{\frac{3}{4}\text{ h}} = 34\frac{1}{2} \div \frac{3}{4}$$ Write the complex fraction as a division problem.

$$= \frac{69}{2} \div \frac{3}{4}$$ Write the mixed number as an improper fraction.

$$= \frac{69}{2} \times \frac{4}{3}$$ Multiply by the reciprocal of $\frac{3}{4}$, which is $\frac{4}{3}$.

$$= \frac{276}{6} \text{ or } 46$$ Simplify.

So, Tia can paint 46 square feet per hour.

Got It? **Do these problems to find out.**

e. Mr. Ito is spreading mulch in his yard. He spreads $4\frac{2}{3}$ square yards in 2 hours. How many square yards can he mulch per hour?

f. Aubrey can walk $4\frac{1}{2}$ miles in $1\frac{1}{2}$ hours. Find her average speed in miles per hour.

e. ________

f. ________

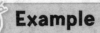

Example

5. On Javier's soccer team, about $33\frac{1}{3}\%$ of the players have scored a goal. Write $33\frac{1}{3}\%$ as a fraction in simplest form.

$$33\frac{1}{3}\% = \frac{33\frac{1}{3}}{100}$$ Definition of percent

$$= 33\frac{1}{3} \div 100$$ Write the complex fraction as a division problem.

$$= \frac{100}{3} \div 100$$ Write $33\frac{1}{3}$ as an improper fraction.

$$= \frac{\overset{1}{\cancel{100}}}{3} \times \frac{1}{\underset{1}{\cancel{100}}}$$ Multiply by the reciprocal of 100, which is $\frac{1}{100}$.

$$= \frac{1}{3}$$ Simplify.

So, about $\frac{1}{3}$ of Javier's team has scored a goal.

Guided Practice

Simplify. (Examples 1 and 2)

1. $\frac{18}{\frac{3}{4}} =$ ______

2. $\frac{\frac{3}{6}}{4} =$ ______

3. $\frac{\frac{1}{3}}{\frac{1}{4}} =$ ______

4. Pep Club members are making spirit buttons. They make 490 spirit buttons in $3\frac{1}{2}$ hours. Find the number of buttons the Pep Club makes per hour. (Examples 3 and 4) ______

5. A county sales tax is $6\frac{2}{3}\%$. Write the percent as a fraction in simplest form. (Example 5) ______

6. **Building on the Essential Question** What is a complex fraction? ______

Rate Yourself!

How confident are you about simplifying complex fractions? Check the box that applies.

For more help, go online to access a Personal Tutor.

Name ________________ My Homework ________________

Independent Practice

Go online for Step-by-Step Solutions

Simplify. (Examples 1 and 2)

1. $\frac{\frac{1}{2}}{3} =$ ______

2. $\frac{2}{\frac{3}{11}} =$ ______

3. $\frac{\frac{8}{9}}{6} =$ ______

4. $\frac{\frac{2}{5}}{9} =$ ______

5. $\frac{\frac{4}{5}}{10} =$ ______

6. $\frac{\frac{1}{4}}{\frac{7}{10}} =$ ______

7. Mary is making pillows for her Life Skills class. She bought $2\frac{1}{2}$ yards of fabric. Her total cost was \$15. What was the cost per yard? (Examples 3 and 4)

______

8. Doug entered a canoe race. He rowed $3\frac{1}{2}$ miles in $\frac{1}{2}$ hour. What is his average speed in miles per hour? (Examples 3 and 4)

______

9. Monica reads $7\frac{1}{2}$ pages of a mystery book in 9 minutes. What is her average reading rate in pages per minute? (Examples 3 and 4) ______

Write each percent as a fraction in simplest form. (Example 5)

10. $56\frac{1}{4}\% =$ ______

11. $15\frac{3}{5}\% =$ ______

12. $13\frac{1}{3}\% =$ ______

13. A bank is offering home loans at an interest rate of $5\frac{1}{2}\%$. Write the percent as a fraction in simplest form. (Example 5) ______

14. **Be Precise** Karl measured the wingspan of the butterfly and the moth shown below. How many times larger is the moth than the butterfly?

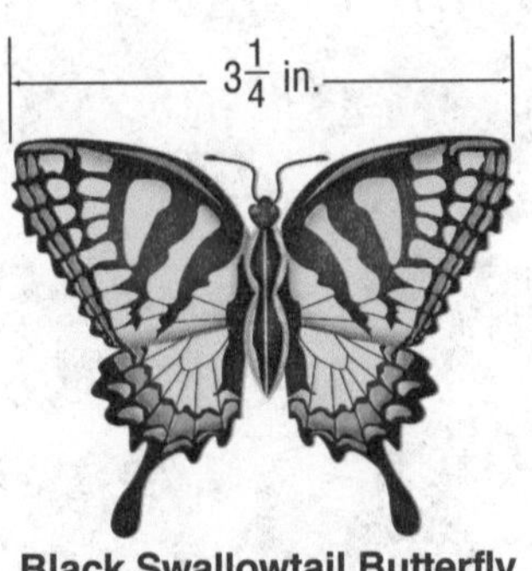

Black Swallowtail Butterfly

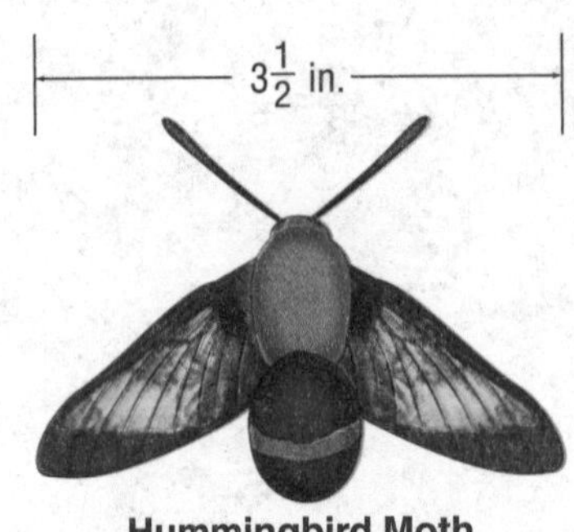

Hummingbird Moth

H.O.T. Problems Higher Order Thinking

15. **Construct an Argument** Explain how complex fractions can be used to solve problems involving ratios.

16. **Reason Inductively** Write three different complex fractions that simplify to $\frac{1}{4}$.

17. **Persevere with Problems** Use mental math to find the value of $\frac{15}{124} \cdot \frac{230}{30} \div \frac{230}{124}$.

Georgia Test Practice

18. Which statement explains how to use the model to simplify the complex fraction?

$$\frac{\frac{2}{3}}{\frac{1}{12}}$$

$\frac{1}{12}$	$\frac{1}{12}$	$\frac{1}{12}$	$\frac{1}{12}$	$\frac{1}{12}$	$\frac{1}{12}$	$\frac{1}{12}$	$\frac{1}{12}$	$\frac{1}{12}$	$\frac{1}{12}$	$\frac{1}{12}$	$\frac{1}{12}$

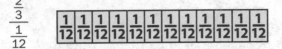

Ⓐ Count the twelfths that fit within $\frac{2}{3}$ of the figure.
Ⓑ Remove $\frac{2}{3}$ of the twelfths, and count those remaining.
Ⓒ Count the number of thirds in the figure. Multiply this number by 12.
Ⓓ Count the number of rectangles in the figure. Divide this number by 3.

Extra Practice

Simplify.

19. $\frac{1}{\frac{1}{4}} = 4$

$\frac{1}{\frac{1}{4}} = 1 \div \frac{1}{4}$

$= \frac{1}{1} \times \frac{4}{1}$

$= \frac{4}{1}$ or 4

Homework Help

20. $\frac{12}{\frac{3}{5}} =$ ______

21. $\frac{\frac{9}{10}}{9} =$ ______

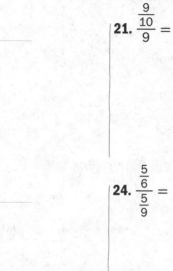

22. $\frac{\frac{1}{2}}{\frac{1}{4}} =$ ______

23. $\frac{\frac{1}{12}}{\frac{5}{6}} =$ ______

24. $\frac{\frac{5}{6}}{\frac{5}{9}} =$ ______

25. Mrs. Frasier is making costumes for the school play. Each costume requires 0.75 yard of fabric. She bought 6 yards of fabric. How many costumes can Mrs. Frasier make?

______

26. A lawn company advertises that they can spread 7,500 square feet of grass seed in $2\frac{1}{2}$ hours. Find the number of square feet of grass seed that can be spread per hour.

______

Write each percent as a fraction in simplest form.

27. $2\frac{2}{5}\% =$ ______

28. $7\frac{3}{4}\% =$ ______

29. $8\frac{1}{3}\% =$ ______

30. CCGPS **Justify Conclusions** The value of a certain stock increased by $1\frac{1}{4}\%$. Explain how to write $1\frac{1}{4}\%$ as a fraction in simplest form. ______

______

______

Georgia Test Practice

31. Debra can run $20\frac{1}{2}$ miles in $2\frac{1}{4}$ hours. How many miles per hour can she run?

Ⓐ $46\frac{1}{8}$ miles per hour

Ⓑ $22\frac{3}{4}$ miles per hour

Ⓒ $18\frac{1}{4}$ miles per hour

Ⓓ $9\frac{1}{9}$ miles per hour

32. Which of the following is equivalent to $\frac{1}{2}$?

Ⓕ $\frac{\frac{1}{4}}{\frac{1}{2}}$

Ⓗ $\frac{\frac{1}{4}}{\frac{1}{4}}$

Ⓖ $\frac{\frac{1}{2}}{\frac{1}{2}}$

Ⓘ $\frac{\frac{1}{8}}{\frac{1}{2}}$

33. Tina wants to give away 6 bundles of thyme from her herb garden. If she has $\frac{1}{2}$ pound of thyme, how much will each bundle weigh?

Ⓐ $\frac{1}{2}$ lb

Ⓑ 3 lb

Ⓒ $\frac{1}{12}$ lb

Ⓓ 12 lb

34. **Short Response** Write $32\frac{1}{8}\%$ as a fraction in simplest form.

____

Common Core Review

Fill in each box with the equivalent customary measurement. MCC5.MD.1

35. 2 feet = ☐ inches

36. 5 tons = ☐ pounds

37. 8 gallons = ☐ quarts

Fill in each box with the equivalent metric measurement. MCC5.MD.1

38. 1 meter = ☐ centimeters

39. 1 liter = ☐ milliliters

40. 1 kilogram = ☐ grams

Convert Unit Rates

What You'll Learn

Scan the lesson. Write the definitions of unit ratio and dimensional analysis.

- ______________________________
- ______________________________

Essential Question

HOW can you show that two objects are proportional?

Vocabulary

unit ratio
dimensional analysis

Common Core GPS

Content Standards
MCC7.RP.2, MCC7.RP.3

Mathematical Practices
1, 3, 4, 5

Real-World Link

Animals Squirrels, chipmunks, and rabbits are capable of running at fast speeds. The table shows the top running speeds of these animals.

Animal	Speed (mph)
Squirrel	10
Chipmunk	15
Cottontail Rabbit	30

1. How many feet are in 1 mile? 10 miles?

   1 mile = ______ feet

   10 miles = ______ feet

2. How many seconds are in 1 minute? 1 hour?

   1 minute = ______ seconds

   1 hour = ______ seconds

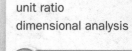

3. How could you determine the number of feet per second a squirrel can run?

   ____

   ____

4. Complete the following statement. Round to the nearest tenth.

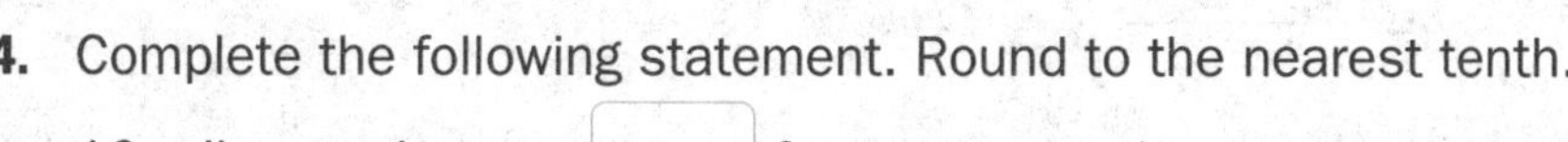

   10 miles per hour ≈ ☐ feet per second

Work Zone

Convert Rates

The relationships among some commonly used customary and metric units of measure are shown in the tables below.

Customary Units of Measure	
Smaller	**Larger**
12 inches	1 foot
16 ounces	1 pound
8 pints	1 gallon
3 feet	1 yard
5,280 feet	1 mile

Metric Units of Measure	
Smaller	**Larger**
100 centimeters	1 meter
1,000 grams	1 kilogram
1,000 milliliters	1 liter
10 millimeters	1 centimeter
1,000 milligrams	1 gram

Each of the relationships in the tables can be written as a **unit ratio**. Like a unit rate, a unit ratio is one in which the denominator is 1 unit. Below are three examples of unit ratios.

$$\frac{\text{12 inches}}{\text{1 foot}} \qquad \frac{\text{16 ounces}}{\text{1 pound}} \qquad \frac{\text{100 centimeters}}{\text{1 meter}}$$

The numerator and denominator of each of the unit ratios shown are equal. So, the value of each ratio is 1.

You can convert one rate to an equivalent rate by multiplying by a unit ratio or its reciprocal. When you convert rates, you include the units in your computation.

The process of including units of measure as factors when you compute is called **dimensional analysis**.

$$\frac{10 \text{ ft}}{1 \text{ s}} = \frac{10 \not{\text{ft}}}{1 \text{ s}} \cdot \frac{12 \text{ in.}}{1 \not{\text{ft}}} = \frac{10 \cdot 12 \text{ in.}}{1 \text{ s} \cdot 1} = \frac{120 \text{ in.}}{1 \text{ s}}$$

Example

1. A remote control car travels at a rate of 10 feet per second. How many inches per second is this?

$$\frac{10 \text{ ft}}{1 \text{ s}} = \frac{10 \text{ ft}}{1 \text{ s}} \cdot \frac{12 \text{ in.}}{1 \text{ ft}}$$ Use 1 foot = 12 inches. Multiply by $\frac{12 \text{ in.}}{1 \text{ ft}}$.

$$= \frac{10 \text{ ft}}{1 \text{ s}} \cdot \frac{12 \text{ in.}}{1 \text{ ft}}$$ Divide out common units.

$$= \frac{10 \cdot 12 \text{ in.}}{1 \text{ s} \cdot 1}$$ Simplify.

$$= \frac{120 \text{ in.}}{1 \text{ s}}$$ Simplify.

So, 10 feet per second equals 120 inches per second.

Examples

2. A swordfish can swim at a rate of 60 miles per hour. How many feet per hour is this?

You can use 1 mile = 5,280 feet to convert the rates.

$\frac{60 \text{ mi}}{1 \text{ h}} = \frac{60 \text{ mi}}{1 \text{ h}} \cdot \frac{5{,}280 \text{ ft}}{1 \text{ mi}}$ Multiply by $\frac{5{,}280 \text{ ft}}{1 \text{ mi}}$.

$= \frac{60 \cancel{\text{mi}}}{1 \text{ h}} \cdot \frac{5{,}280 \text{ ft}}{1 \cancel{\text{mi}}}$ Divide out common units.

$= \frac{60 \cdot 5{,}280 \text{ ft}}{1 \cdot 1 \text{ h}}$ Simplify.

$= \frac{316{,}800 \text{ ft}}{1 \text{ h}}$ Simplify.

A swordfish can swim at a rate of 316,800 feet per hour.

3. Marvin walks at a speed of 7 feet per second. How many feet per hour is this?

You can use 60 seconds = 1 minute and you can use 60 minutes = 1 hour to convert the rates.

$\frac{7 \text{ ft}}{1 \text{ s}} = \frac{7 \text{ ft}}{1 \text{ s}} \cdot \frac{60 \text{ s}}{1 \text{ min}} \cdot \frac{60 \text{ min}}{1 \text{ h}}$ Multiply by $\frac{60 \text{ s}}{1 \text{ min}}$ and $\frac{60 \text{ min}}{1 \text{ h}}$.

$= \frac{7 \text{ ft}}{1 \cancel{\text{s}}} \cdot \frac{60 \cancel{\text{s}}}{1 \cancel{\text{min}}} \cdot \frac{60 \cancel{\text{min}}}{1 \text{ h}}$ Divide out common units.

$= \frac{7 \cdot 60 \cdot 60 \text{ ft}}{1 \cdot 1 \cdot 1 \text{ h}}$ Simplify.

$= \frac{25{,}200 \text{ ft}}{1 \text{ h}}$ Simplify.

Marvin walks 25,200 feet in 1 hour.

and Reflect

To convert meters per hour to kilometers per hour, circle the relationship you need to know.

100 cm = 1 m

60 s = 1 min

1,000 m = 1 km

Got It? **Do these problems to find out.**

a. A gull can fly at a speed of 22 miles per hour. About how many feet per hour can the gull fly?

b. An AMTRAK train travels at 125 miles per hour. Convert the speed to miles per minute. Round to the nearest tenth.

a. ______________

b. ______________

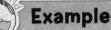

Example

4. The average speed of one team in a relay race is about 10 miles per hour. What is this speed in feet per second?

We can use 1 mile = 5,280 feet, 1 hour = 60 minutes, and 1 minute = 60 seconds to convert the rates.

$$\frac{10 \text{ mi}}{1 \text{ h}} = \frac{10 \text{ mi}}{1 \text{ h}} \cdot \frac{5{,}280 \text{ ft}}{1 \text{ mi}} \cdot \frac{1 \text{ h}}{60 \text{ min}} \cdot \frac{1 \text{ min}}{60 \text{ s}}$$ Multiply by distance and time unit ratios.

$$= \frac{10 \not{\text{mi}}}{1 \not{\text{h}}} \cdot \frac{5{,}280 \text{ ft}}{1 \not{\text{mi}}} \cdot \frac{1 \not{\text{h}}}{60 \not{\text{min}}} \cdot \frac{1 \not{\text{min}}}{60 \text{ s}}$$ Divide out common units.

$$= \frac{10 \cdot 5{,}280 \cdot 1 \cdot 1 \text{ ft}}{1 \cdot 1 \cdot 60 \cdot 60 \text{ s}}$$ Simplify.

$$= \frac{52{,}800 \text{ ft}}{3{,}600 \text{ s}}$$ Simplify.

$$\approx \frac{14.7 \text{ ft}}{1 \text{ s}}$$ Simplify.

The relay team runs at an average speed of 14.7 feet per second.

Guided Practice

1. Water weighs about 8.34 pounds per gallon. About how many ounces per gallon is the weight of the water? (Examples 1 and 2) ______

2. A skydiver is falling at about 176 feet per second. How many feet per minute is he falling? (Example 3) ______

3. Lorenzo rides his bike at a rate of 5 yards per second. About how many miles per hour can Lorenzo ride his bike? (***Hint***: 1 mile = 1,760 yards) (Example 4)

4. **Building on the Essential Question** Explain why the ratio $\frac{3 \text{ feet}}{1 \text{ yard}}$ has a value of one.

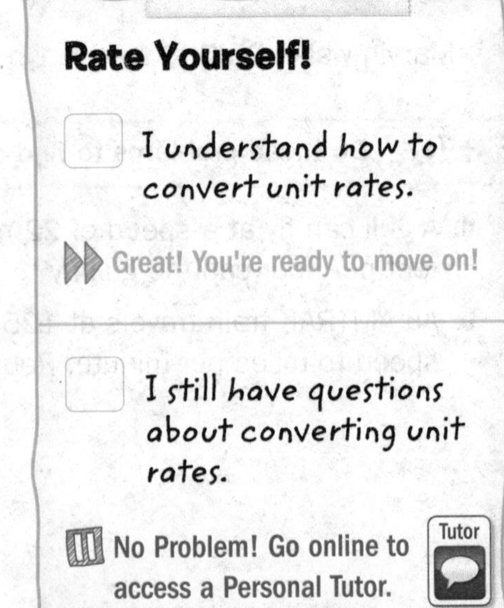

Rate Yourself!
I understand how to convert unit rates.
Great! You're ready to move on!
I still have questions about converting unit rates.
No Problem! Go online to access a Personal Tutor.
Tutor

Name ______ My Homework ______

Independent Practice

Go online for Step-by-Step Solutions

1. A go-kart's top speed is 607,200 feet per hour. What is the speed in miles per hour? (Examples 1 and 2)

2. The fastest a human has ever run is 27 miles per hour. How many miles per minute did the human run? (Example 3)

3. A peregrine falcon can fly 322 kilometers per hour. How many meters per hour can the falcon fly? (Example 3)

4. A pipe is leaking at 1.5 cups per day. About how many gallons per week is the pipe leaking? (***Hint***: 1 gallon = 16 cups) (Example 4)

5. Charlie runs at a speed of 3 yards per second. About how many miles per hour does Charlie run? (Example 4)

6. CCGPS **Model with Mathematics** Refer to the graphic novel frame below. Seth traveled 1 mile in 57.1 seconds. About how fast does Seth travel in miles per hour?

Watch
Replay it online!
SKREEECH!
3
I can't believe how fast I was going.

7. The speed at which a certain computer can access the Internet is 2 megabytes per second. How fast is this in megabytes per hour?

8. CCGPS **Use Math Tools** The approximate metric measurement of length is given for a U.S. customary unit of length. Use your estimation skills to complete the graphic organizer below. Fill in each blank with *foot, yard, inch,* or *mile*.

Metric		Customary
2.54 centimeters	→	1
0.30 meter	→	1
0.91 meter	→	1
1.61 kilometers	→	1

H.O.T. Problems Higher Order Thinking

9. CCGPS **Model with Mathematics** Give an example of a unit rate used in a real-world situation.

10. CCGPS **Reason Inductively** When you convert 100 feet per second to inches per second, will there be more or less than 100 inches. Explain.

11. CCGPS **Persevere with Problems** Use the information in Exercise 8 to convert 7 meters per minute to yards per hour. Round to the nearest tenth.

Georgia Test Practice

12. A salt truck drops 39 kilograms of salt per minute. How many grams of salt does the truck drop per second?

Ⓐ 600 Ⓒ 650

Ⓑ 625 Ⓓ 6,000

Name ______ My Homework ______

Extra Practice

13. 20 mi/h = 1,760 ft/min

$\frac{20 \text{ mi}}{1 \text{ h}} \cdot \frac{5{,}280 \text{ ft}}{1 \text{ mi}} \cdot \frac{1 \text{ h}}{60 \text{ min}} =$

$\frac{105{,}600 \text{ ft}}{60 \text{ min}} = 1{,}760 \text{ ft/min}$

14. 16 cm/min = 9.6 m/h

$\frac{16 \text{ cm}}{1 \text{ min}} \cdot \frac{1 \text{ m}}{100 \text{ cm}} \cdot \frac{60 \text{ min}}{1 \text{ h}} =$

$\frac{960 \text{ m}}{100 \text{ h}} = 9.6 \text{ m/h}$

15. 45 mi/h = ______ ft/s

16. 26 cm/s = ______ m/min

17. 24 mi/h = ______ ft/s

18. 105.6 L/h = ______ L/min

19. The table shows the speed and number of wing beats per second for various flying insects.

Flying Insects		
Insect	**Speed (miles per hour)**	**Wing Beats per Second**
Housefly	4.4	190
Honeybee	5.7	250
Dragonfly	15.6	38
Hornet	12.8	100
Bumblebee	6.4	130

a. What is the speed of a housefly in feet per second? Round to the nearest hundredth.

______

b. How many times does a dragonfly's wing beat per minute?

______

c. About how many miles can a bumblebee travel in one minute?

______

d. How many times can a honeybee beat its wings in one hour?

______

Georgia Test Practice

20. Thirty-five miles per hour is the same rate as which of the following?

    Ⓐ 150 feet per minute

    Ⓑ 1,500 feet per minute

    Ⓒ 2,200 feet per minute

    Ⓓ 3,080 feet per minute

21. A boat is traveling at an average speed of 15 meters per second. How many kilometers per second is the boat traveling?

    Ⓕ 1.5

    Ⓖ 0.15

    Ⓗ 0.015

    Ⓘ 1,500

22. **Short Response** An oil tanker empties at 3.5 gallons per minute. Convert this rate to cups per second. Round to the nearest tenth. Show the steps you used.

Common Core Review

Determine if each pair of rates are equivalent. Explain your reasoning.

MCC6.RP.3b

23. $36 for 4 baseball hats; $56 for 7 baseball hats

24. 12 posters for 36 students; 21 posters for 63 students

25. An employer pays $22 for 2 hours. Use the ratio table to determine how much she charges for 5 hours. MCC6.RP.3a

Payment	$22		
Hours	2		5

Proportional and Nonproportional Relationships

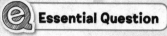

What You'll Learn

Scan the lesson. Write the definitions of proportional and nonproportional.

- proportional

- nonporportional

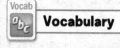

Essential Question

HOW can you show that two objects are proportional?

Vocabulary

proportional
nonproportional
equivalent ratios

Common Core GPS

Content Standards
MCC7.RP.2, MCC7.RP.2a, MCC7.RP.2b

Mathematical Practices
1, 3, 4

Real-World Link

Pizza Party Ms. Cochran is planning a year-end pizza party for her students. Ace Pizza offers free delivery and charges $8 per medium pizza.

1. Complete the table to determine the cost for different numbers of pizzas ordered.

Cost ($)	8				
Pizza	1	2	3	4	5

2. For each number of pizzas, fill in the boxes to write the relationship of the cost and number of pizzas as a ratio in simplest form.

$\frac{16}{2} = \frac{\square}{1}$ $\frac{24}{3} = \frac{\square}{\square}$

$\frac{32}{\square} = \frac{\square}{\square}$ $\frac{\square}{5} = \frac{\square}{\square}$

3. What do you notice about the simplified ratios?

Work Zone

Identify Proportional Relationships

Two quantities are **proportional** if they have a constant ratio or unit rate. For relationships in which this ratio is not constant, the two quantities are **nonproportional**.

In the pizza example on the previous page, the cost of an order is *proportional* to the number of pizzas ordered.

$$\frac{\text{cost of order}}{\text{pizzas ordered}} = \frac{8}{1} = \frac{16}{2} = \frac{24}{3} = \frac{32}{4} = \frac{40}{5} \text{ or \$8 per pizza}$$

All of the ratios above are **equivalent ratios** because they all have the same value.

Example

1. Andrew earns $18 per hour for mowing lawns. Is the amount of money he earns proportional to the number of hours he spends mowing? Explain.

Find the amount of money he earns for working a different number of hours. Make a table to show these amounts.

Earnings ($)	18	36	54	72
Time (h)	1	2	3	4

For each number of hours worked, write the relationship of the amount he earned and hour as a ratio in simplest form.

$$\frac{\text{amount earned}}{\text{number of hours}} \rightarrow \frac{18}{1} \text{ or } 18 \quad \frac{36}{2} \text{ or } 18 \quad \frac{54}{3} \text{ or } 18 \quad \frac{72}{4} \text{ or } 18$$

All of the ratios between the two quantities can be simplified to 18.

The amount of money he earns is proportional to the number of hours he spends mowing.

Got It? **Do this problem to find out.**

a. At Lakeview Middle School, there are 2 homeroom teachers assigned to every 48 students. Is the number of students at this school proportional to the number of teachers? Explain your reasoning.

a. ____________

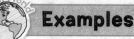

Examples

2. Uptown Tickets charges $7 per baseball game ticket plus a $3 processing fee per order. Is the cost of an order proportional to the number of tickets ordered? Explain.

Cost ($)	10	17	24	31
Tickets Ordered	1	2	3	4

For each number of tickets, write the relationship of the cost and number of tickets as a ratio in simplest form.

$\frac{\text{cost of order}}{\text{tickets ordered}} \rightarrow \frac{10}{1}$ or 10 $\quad \frac{17}{2}$ or 8.5 $\quad \frac{24}{3}$ or 8 $\quad \frac{31}{4}$ or 7.75

Since the ratios of the two quantities are not the same, the cost of an order is *not* proportional to the number of tickets ordered.

3. You can use the recipe shown to make a fruit punch. Is the amount of sugar used proportional to the amount of mix used? Explain.

Find the amount of sugar and mix needed for different numbers of batches. Make a table to help you solve.

Cups of Sugar	$\frac{1}{2}$	1	$1\frac{1}{2}$	2
Envelopes of Mix	1	2	3	4

For each number of cups of sugar, write the relationship of the cups and number of envelopes of mix as a ratio in simplest form.

$\frac{\text{cups of sugar}}{\text{envelopes of mix}} \rightarrow \frac{\frac{1}{2}}{1}$ or 0.5 $\quad \frac{1}{2}$ or 0.5 $\quad \frac{1\frac{1}{2}}{3}$ or 0.5 $\quad \frac{2}{4}$ or 0.5

All of the ratios between the two quantities can be simplified to 0.5. The amount of mix used is proportional to the amount of sugar used.

Got It? **Do this problem to find out.**

b. At the beginning of the year, Isabel had $120 in the bank. Each week, she deposits another $20. Is her account balance proportional to the number of weeks of deposits? Use the table below. Explain your reasoning.

Time (wk)	1	2	3
Balance ($)			

b. ____________

Example

4. The tables shown represent the number of pages Martin and Gabriel read over time. Which situation represents a proportional relationship between the time spent reading and the number of pages read? Explain.

Pages Martin Read	2	4	6
Time (min)	5	10	15

Pages Gabriel Read	3	4	7
Time (min)	5	10	15

Write the ratios for each time period in simplest form.

$\frac{\text{pages}}{\text{minutes}} \rightarrow \frac{2}{5}, \frac{4}{10} \text{ or } \frac{2}{5}, \frac{6}{15} \text{ or } \frac{2}{5}$ $\quad \frac{3}{5}, \frac{4}{10} \text{ or } \frac{2}{5}, \frac{7}{15}$

All of the ratios between Martin's quantities are $\frac{2}{5}$. So, Martin's reading rate represents a proportional relationship.

Guided Practice

For Exercises 1 and 2, use a table to solve. Then explain your reasoning.

1. The Vista Marina rents boats for $25 per hour. In addition to the rental fee, there is a $12 charge for fuel. Is the number of hours you can rent the boat proportional to the total cost? Explain. (Examples 1–3)

Rental Time (h)			
Cost ($)			

2. Which situation represents a proportional relationship between the hours worked and amount earned for Matt and Jane? Explain. (Example 4)

Matt's Earnings ($)	12	20	31
Time (h)	1	2	3

Jane's Earnings ($)	12	24	36
Time (h)	1	2	3

3. **Building on the Essential Question** Explain what makes two quantities proportional.

Rate Yourself!

How confident are you about determining proportional relationships? Shade the ring on the target.

For more help, go online to access a Personal Tutor.

FOLDABLES *Time to update your Foldable!*

Independent Practice

Go online for Step-by-Step Solutions 

For Exercises 1 and 2, use a table to solve. Then explain your reasoning.
(Examples 1 and 2)

1. An adult elephant drinks about 225 liters of water each day. Is the number of days the water supply lasts proportional to the number of liters of water the elephant drinks?

Time (days)	1	2	3	4
Water (L)				

2. An elevator *ascends*, or goes up, at a rate of 750 feet per minute. Is the height to which the elevator ascends proportional to the number of minutes it takes to get there? (Examples 1–3)

Time (min)	1	2	3	4
Height (ft)				

3. Which situation represents a proportional relationship between the number of laps run by each student and their time? (Example 4)

Desmond's Time (s)	146	292	584
Laps	2	4	8

Maria's Time (s)	150	320	580
Laps	2	4	6

Copy and Solve **Use a table to help you solve. Then explain your reasoning. Show your work on a separate piece of paper.**

4. Plant A is 18 inches tall after one week, 36 inches tall after two weeks, 56 inches tall after three weeks. Plant B is 18 inches tall after one week, 36 inches tall after two weeks, 54 inches tall after three weeks. Which situation represents a proportional relationship between the plants' height and number of weeks? (Example 4)

5. Determine whether the measures for the figure shown are proportional.
   a. the length of a side and the perimeter
   b. the length of a side and the area

6. **Justify Conclusions** MegaMart collects a sales tax equal to $\frac{1}{16}$ of the retail price of each purchase. The tax is sent to the state government.

a. Is the amount of tax collected proportional to the cost of an item before tax is added? Explain.

Retail Price ($)	16	32	48	64
Tax Collected ($)				

b. Is the amount of tax collected proportional to the cost of an item after tax has been added? Explain.

Retail Price ($)	16	32	48	
Tax Collected ($)				
Cost Including Tax ($)				

H.O.T. Problems Higher Order Thinking

7. **Find the Error** Blake ran laps around the gym. His times are shown in the table. Blake is trying to decide whether the number of laps is proportional to the time. Find his mistake and correct it.

Time (min)	1	2	3	4
Laps	4	6	8	10

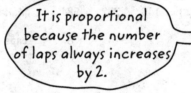

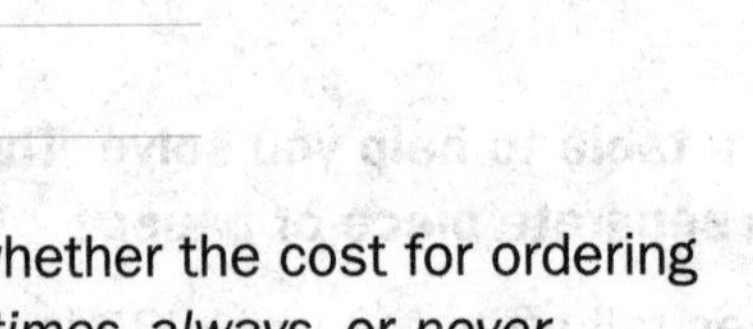

It is proportional because the number of laps always increases by 2.

8. **Persevere with Problems** Determine whether the cost for ordering multiple items that will be delivered is *sometimes*, *always*, or *never* proportional. Explain your reasoning.

Georgia Test Practice

9. Which relationship has a unit rate of 60 miles per hour?

Ⓐ 300 miles in 6 hours
Ⓑ 300 miles in 5 hours
Ⓒ 240 miles in 6 hours
Ⓓ 240 miles in 5 hours

Name ____________________ My Homework ____________________

Extra Practice

For Exercises 10-12, use a table to solve. Then explain your reasoning.

10. A vine grows 7.5 feet every 5 days. Is the length of the vine on the last day proportional to the number of days of growth?

Homework Help

Yes; the length to time ratios are all equal to 1.5 ft per day.

Time (days)	5	10	15	20
Length (ft)	7.5	15	22.5	30

11. STEM To convert a temperature in degrees Celsius to degrees Fahrenheit, multiply the Celsius temperature by $\frac{9}{5}$ and then add 32°. Is a temperature in degrees Celsius proportional to its equivalent temperature in degrees Fahrenheit?

Degrees Celsius	0	10	20	30
Degrees Fahrenheit				

12. On Saturday, Querida gave away 416 coupons for a free appetizer at a local restaurant. The next day, she gave away about 52 coupons an hour.

a. Is the number of coupons Querida gave away on Sunday proportional to the number of hours she worked that day?

Hours Worked on Sunday	1	2	3	4
Coupons Given Away on Sunday				

b. Is the total number of coupons Querida gave away on Saturday and Sunday proportional to the number of hours she worked on Sunday?

Hours Worked on Sunday	1	2	3	4
Coupons Given Away on Weekend				

13. CCGPS **Justify Conclusions** The fee for ride tickets at a carnival is shown in the table at the right.

Tickets	5	10	15	20
Fee ($)	5	9.50	13.50	16

a. Is the fee for ride tickets proportional to the number of tickets? Explain your reasoning.

b. Can you determine the fee for 30 ride tickets? Explain.

Georgia Test Practice

14. Mr. Martinez is comparing the price of oranges from several different markets. Which market's pricing guide is based on a constant unit price?

Ⓐ

Number of Oranges	5	10	15	20
Total Cost ($)	3.50	6.00	8.50	11.00

Ⓑ

Number of Oranges	5	10	15	20
Total Cost ($)	3.50	6.50	9.50	12.50

Ⓒ

Number of Oranges	5	10	15	20
Total Cost ($)	3.00	5.00	7.00	9.00

Ⓓ

Number of Oranges	5	10	15	20
Total Cost ($)	3.00	6.00	9.00	12.00

15. Short Response The middle school is planning a family movie night where popcorn will be served. The constant relationship between the number of people n and the number of cups of popcorn p is shown in the table. How many people can be served with 519 cups of popcorn?

n	30	60	120	
p	90	180	360	519

Common Core Review

Find the value of each expression if $x = 12$. MCC6.EE.2

16. $3x$ ______

17. $2x - 4$ ______

18. $5x + 30$ ______

19. $3x - 2x$ ______

20. $x - 12$ ______

21. $\frac{x}{4}$ ______

Make a table to solve the situation. MCC6.RP.3a

22. Brianna downloads 9 songs each month onto her MP3 player. Show the total number of songs downloaded after 1, 2, 3, and 4 months.

Month				
Number of Songs				

The Four-Step Plan

Content Standards
MCC7.RP.2
Mathematical Practices
1, 3, 4

Case #1 'Round and 'Round

The Forte family visited the Mall of America in Minneapolis. The Ferris wheel in the mall's amusement park is about 22.5 meters tall.

What is the approximate height of the Mall of America Ferris wheel in feet if 1 foot is about 0.3 meter?

In mathematics, there is a *four-step problem-solving plan* you can use to help you solve any problem. The four steps are *Understand, Plan, Solve,* and *Check*.

Understand *What are the facts?*

- The Mall of America Ferris wheel is about 22.5 meters tall.
- You need to find the height of the Ferris wheel in feet.

Plan *What is your strategy to solve this problem?*

To solve the problem, write an expression that converts meters to feet. Then divide out common units.

Solve *How can you apply the strategy?*

One foot is about 0.3 meter. Convert 22.5 meters to feet.

$22.5 \text{ meters} \cdot \frac{1 \text{ foot}}{0.3 \text{ meter}} \approx \frac{22.5}{0.3}$ or ☐ feet

So, the Ferris wheel is about 75 feet tall.

Check *Does the answer make sense?*

There is a little more than 3 feet in a meter.

Since 3 • 22.5 is 67.5 and 75 feet is a little more than 67.5 feet, the answer is reasonable.

Analyze the Strategy

Tutor

Reason Inductively Explain in your own words how the four-step plan helps you solve real-world problems.

Case #2 Cool Treats

Mr. Martino's class learned the average American consumes about 23 quarts of ice cream every year. The class also learned the average American in the north-central United States consumes about 19 quarts more.

How much ice cream in gallons is consumed every year by the average American in the north-central United States?

Understand

Read the problem. What are you being asked to find?

I need to find ____

____.

Fill in each box with the information you know.

The average American consumes about ☐ quarts of ice cream.

The average American in the north-central United States consumes about ☐ quarts more.

Plan

Choose two operations to solve the problem.

I will ____.

Solve

How will you use the operations?

I will ____.

Find total quarts. Convert to gallons.

☐ + ☐ = ☐ ☐ $\cancel{\text{quarts}} \cdot \dfrac{1 \text{ gallon}}{\square \ \cancel{\text{quarts}}}$ = ______ gallons

The average American in the north-central United States consumes about ☐ gallons of ice cream each year.

Check

Use information from the problem to check your solution.

____.

Collaborate Work with a small group to solve the following cases. Show your work on a separate piece of paper.

Case #3 Financial Literacy

Terry opened a savings account in December with $150 and deposited $30 each month beginning in January.

What is the value of Terry's account at the end of July?

Case #4 STEM

About how many centimeters longer is the average femur than the average tibia? (Hint: 1 inch ≈ 2.54 centimeters)

Bones in a Human Leg	
Bone	**Length (in.)**
Femur (upper leg)	19.88
Tibia (inner lower leg)	16.94
Fibula (outer lower leg)	15.94

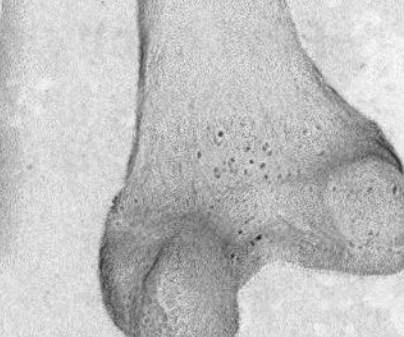

Case #5 Patterns

Numbers that can be represented by a triangular arrangement of dots are called *triangular numbers*. The first four triangular numbers are shown.

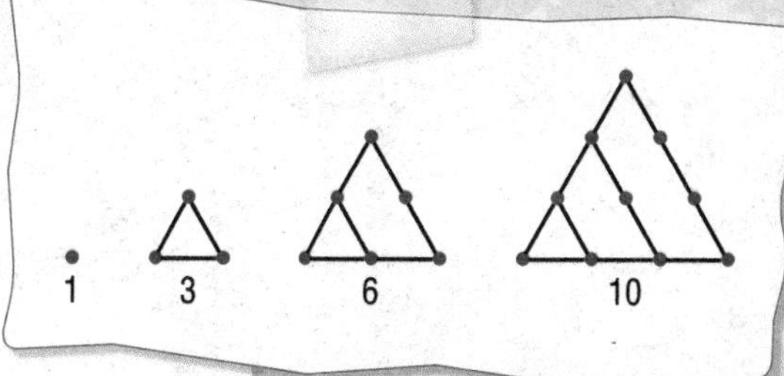

Describe the pattern in the first four numbers. Then list the next three triangular numbers.

Circle a strategy below to solve the problem.

- Draw a diagram.
- Solve a simpler problem.
- Guess, check, and revise.
- Make a table.

Case #6 School

The Boosters expect 500 people at the annual awards banquet.

If each table seats 8 people, how many tables are needed?

Mid-Chapter Check

Vocabulary Check

1. CCGPS **Be Precise** Define *complex fraction*. Give two examples of a complex fraction. (Lesson 2)

2. Fill in the blank in the sentence below with the correct term. (Lesson 1)

   When a rate is simplified so that it has a denominator of 1 unit, it is called a(n) ________________ rate.

Skills Check and Problem Solving

Find each unit rate. Round to the nearest hundredth if necessary. (Lesson 1)

3. 750 yards in 25 minutes ________________

4. $420 for 15 tickets ________________

Simplify. (Lesson 2)

5. $\dfrac{9}{\frac{1}{3}} =$ ________________

6. $\dfrac{\frac{1}{2}}{4} =$ ________________

7. $\dfrac{\frac{1}{6}}{1\frac{3}{8}} =$ ________________

8. A tourist information center charges $10 per hour to rent a bicycle. Is the rental charge proportional to the number of hours you rent the bicycle? Justify your response. (Lesson 4)

9. **Georgia Test Practice** Which of the following is the same as 2,088 feet per minute? (Lesson 3)

   Ⓐ 696 meters per minute
   Ⓑ 696 yards per minute
   Ⓒ 696 feet per minute
   Ⓓ 696 yards per second

Graph Proportional Relationships

What You'll Learn

Scan the lesson. Predict two things you will learn about graphing proportional relationships.

-
-

Essential Question

HOW can you show that two objects are proportional?

Vocabulary

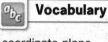

coordinate plane
quadrants
ordered pair
x-coordinate
y-coordinate
y-axis
origin
x-axis

Common CoreGPS

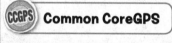

Content Standards
MCC7.RP.2, MCC7.RP.2a

Mathematical Practices
1, 2, 3, 4

Vocabulary Start-Up

Maps have grids to locate cities. The **coordinate plane** is a type of grid that is formed when two number lines intersect at their zero points. The number lines separate the coordinate plane into four regions called **quadrants**.

An **ordered pair** is a pair of numbers, such as (1, 2), used to locate or graph points on the coordinate plane.

The ***x*-coordinate** corresponds to a number on the *x*-axis. → (1, 2) ← The ***y*-coordinate** corresponds to a number on the *y*-axis.

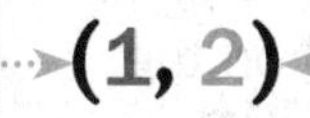

Label the coordinate plane with the terms *ordered pair*, *x-coordinate*, and *y-coordinate*.

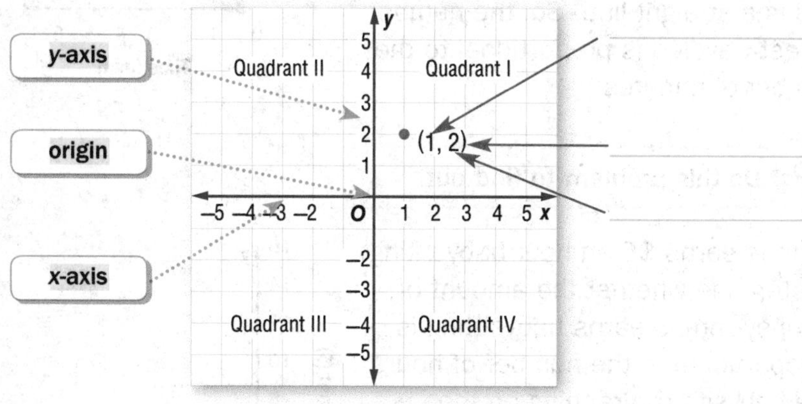

Graph points (2, 3) and (−3, −2) above. Connect the three points on the coordinate plane. Describe the graph.

Work Zone

Identify Proportional Relationships

Another way to determine whether two quantities are proportional is to graph the quantities on the coordinate plane. If the graph of the two quantities is a straight line through the origin, then the two quantities are proportional.

Real World

Example

Linear Relationships
Relationships that have straight-line graphs are called linear relationships.

1. The slowest mammal on Earth is the tree sloth. It moves at a speed of 6 feet per minute. Determine whether the number of feet the sloth moves is proportional to the number of minutes it moves by graphing on the coordinate plane. Explain your reasoning.

Step 1 Make a table to find the number of feet walked for 0, 1, 2, 3, and 4 minutes.

Time (min)	0	1	2	3	4
Distance (ft)	0	6	12	18	24

Step 2 Graph the ordered pairs (time, distance) on the coordinate plane. Then connect the ordered pairs.

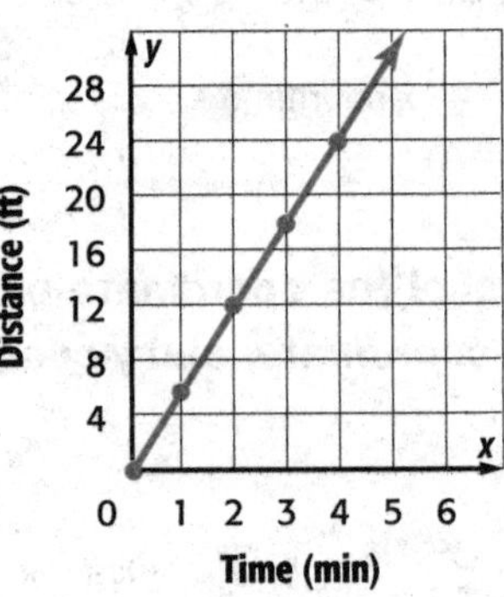

The line passes through the origin and is a straight line. So, the number of feet traveled is proportional to the number of minutes.

Got It? Do this problem to find out.

a. ______________

a. James earns $5 an hour babysitting. Determine whether the amount of money James earns babysitting is proportional to the number of hours he babysits by graphing on the coordinate plane. Explain your reasoning in the work zone.

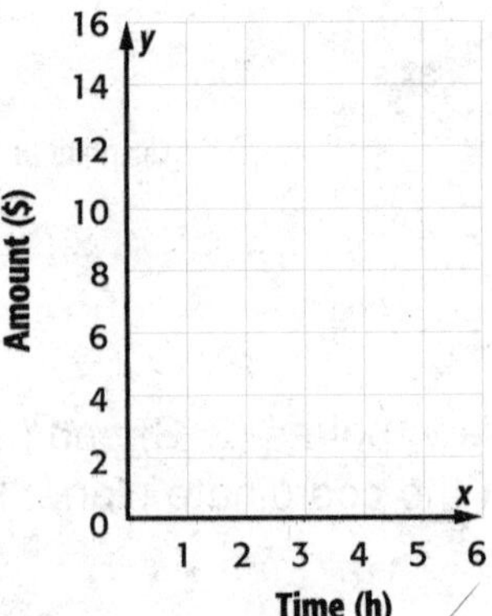

Example

Tutor

2. The cost of renting video games from Games Inc. is shown in the table. Determine whether the cost is proportional to the number of games rented by graphing on the coordinate plane. Explain your reasoning.

Video Game Rental Rates	
Number of Games	Cost ($)
1	3
2	5
3	7
4	9

Step 1 Write the two quantities as ordered pairs (number of games, cost).

The ordered pairs are (1, 3), (2, 5), (3, 7), and (4, 9).

Step 2 Graph the ordered pairs on the coordinate plane. Then connect the ordered pairs and extend the line to the *y*-axis.

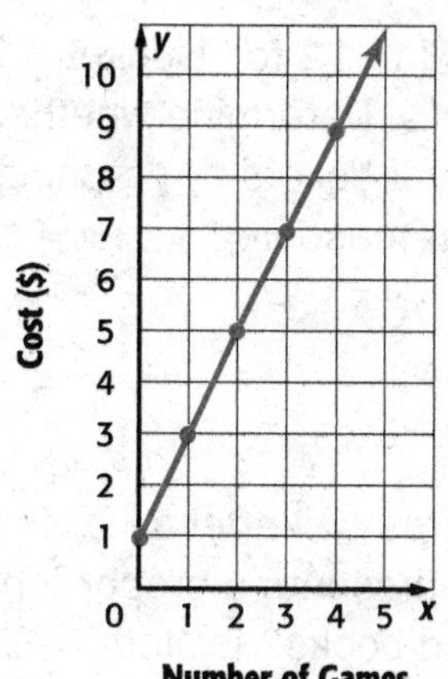

The line does not pass through the origin. So, the cost of the video games is not proportional to the number of games rented.

Check The ratios are not constant. $\frac{1}{3} \neq \frac{2}{5}$ ✓

Quick Review

When drawing a graph, include a title and labels for the horizontal and vertical axes.

Got It? Do this problem to find out.

b. The table shows the number of Calories an athlete burned per minute of exercise. Determine whether the number of Calories burned is proportional to the number of minutes by graphing on the coordinate plane. Explain your reasoning in the Work Zone.

Calories Burned	
Number of Minutes	Number of Calories
0	0
1	4
2	8
3	13

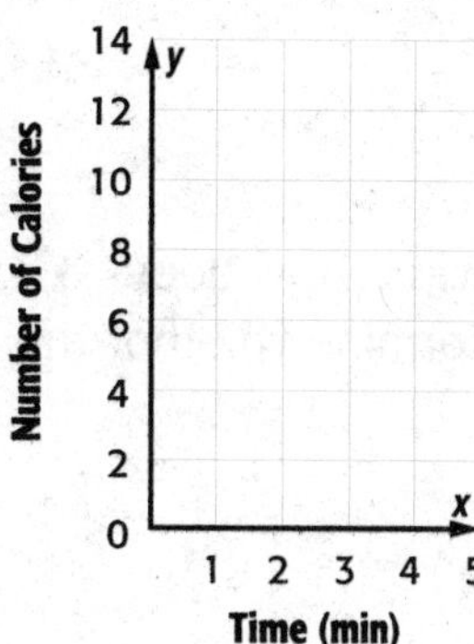

b. __________

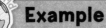

Real-World Example

Tutor

3. Which batting cage represents a proportional relationship between the number of pitches thrown and the cost? Explain.

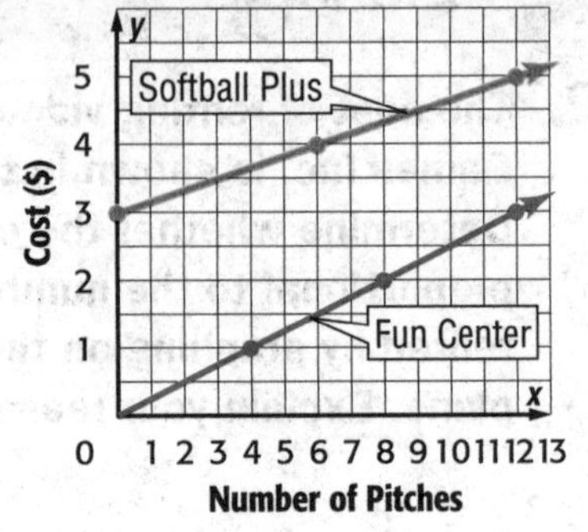

The graph for Softball Plus is a straight line, but it does not pass through the origin. So, the relationship is not proportional.

The graph for the Fun Center is a straight line through the origin. So, the relationship between the number of the pitches thrown and the cost is proportional.

Guided Practice

Check

1. The cost of 3-D movie tickets is $12 for 1 ticket, $24 for 2 tickets, and $36 for 3 tickets. Determine whether the cost is proportional to the number of tickets by graphing on the coordinate plane. Explain your reasoning. (Examples 1 and 2)

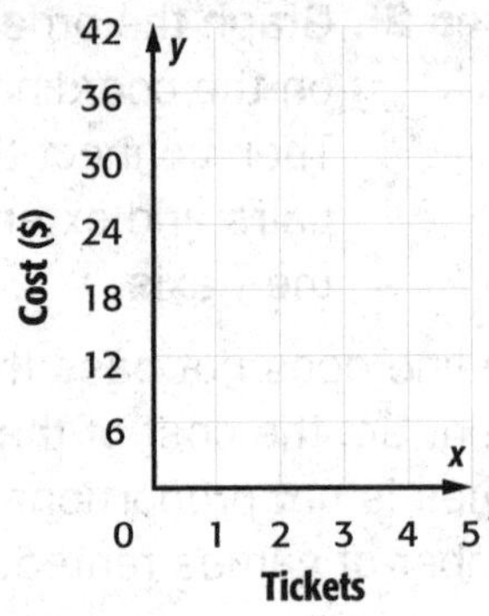

2. The number of books two stores sell after 1, 2, and 3 days is shown. Which book sale represents a proportional relationship between time and books? Explain. (Example 3)

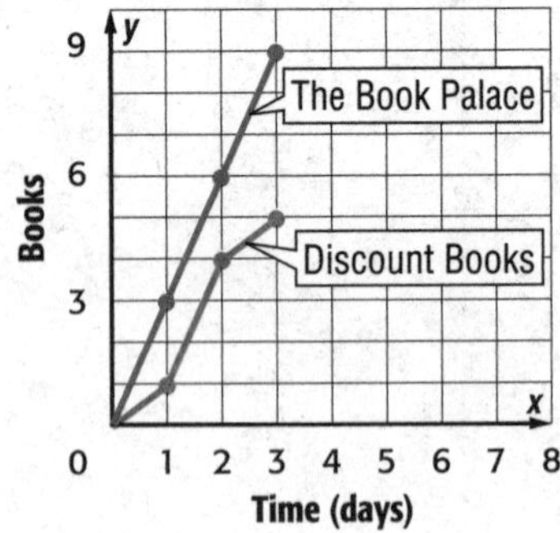

3. **Building on the Essential Question** How does graphing relationships help you determine whether the relationship is proportional or not?

Rate Yourself!

How confident are you about identifying proportional relationships by graphing? Check the box that applies.

For more help, go online to access a Personal Tutor.

FOLDABLES *Time to update your Foldable!*

Independent Practice

Go online for Step-by-Step Solutions

CCGPS Model with Mathematics Determine whether the relationship between the two quantities shown in each table are proportional by graphing on the coordinate plane. Explain your reasoning. (Examples 1 and 2)

1.

Savings Account	
Week	**Account Balance ($)**
1	125
2	150
3	175

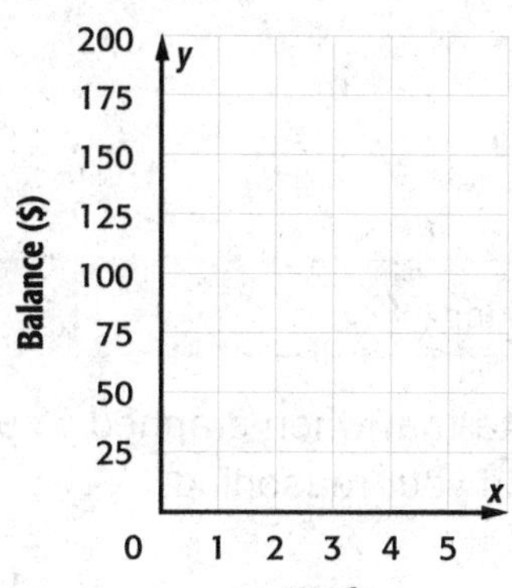

____

____

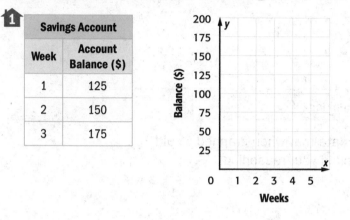

2.

Calories in Fruit Cups	
Servings	**Calories**
1	70
3	210
5	350

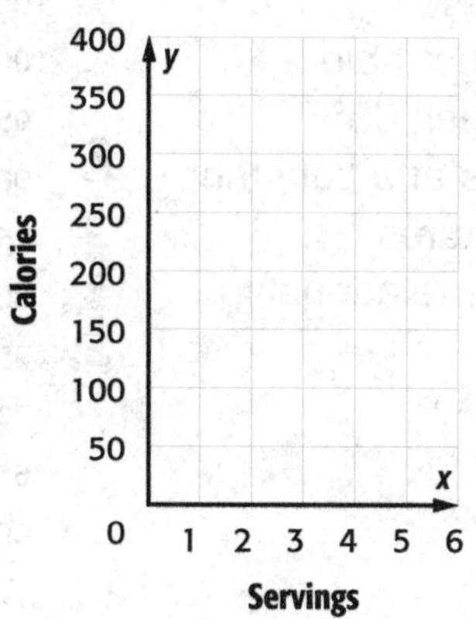

____

____

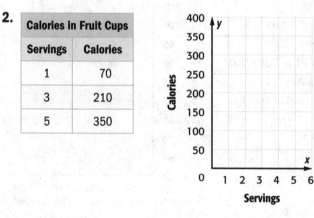

3. The height of two plants is recorded after 1, 2, and 3 weeks as shown in the graph at the right. Which plants' growth represents a proportional relationship between time and height? Explain. (Example 3)

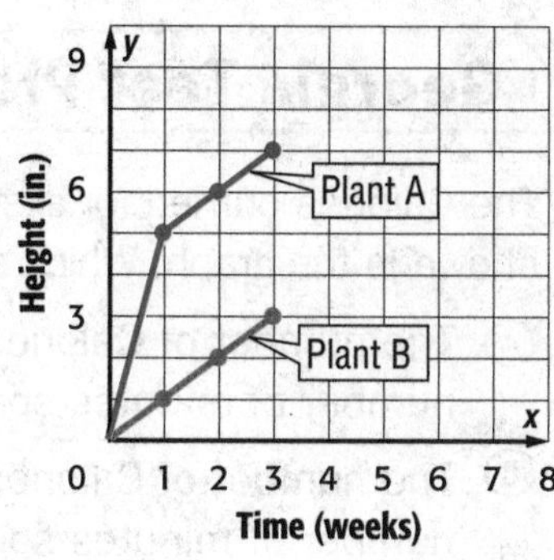

____

____

4. The perimeter of a square is 4 times as great as the length of any of its sides. Determine if the perimeter of a square is proportional to its side length. Explain.

5. A health club charges $35 a month for membership fees. Determine whether the cost of membership is proportional to the number of months. Explain your reasoning.

H.O.T. Problems Higher Order Thinking

6. CCGPS **Reason Abstractly** Describe some data that when graphed would represent a proportional relationship. Explain your reasoning.

7. CCGPS **Persevere with Problems** The greenhouse temperatures at certain times are shown in the table. The greenhouse maintains temperatures between 65°F and 85°F. Suppose the temperature increases at a constant rate. Create a graph of the time and temperatures at each hour from 1:00 P.M. to 8:00 P.M. Is the relationship proportional? Explain.

Time	Temperature (°F)
1:00 P.M.	66
6:00 P.M.	78.5
8:00 P.M.	83.5

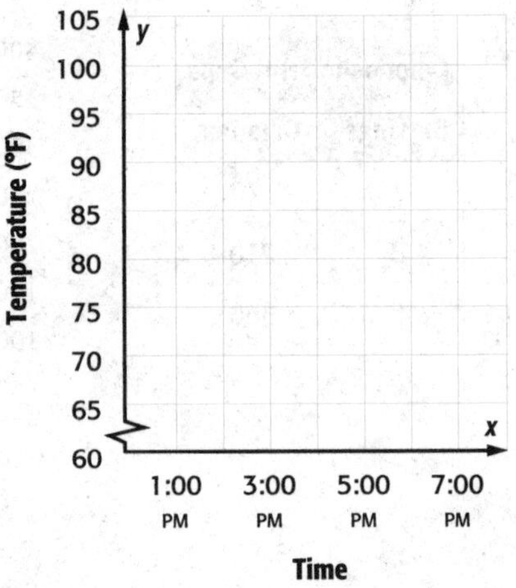

Georgia Test Practice

8. The Calories burned for exercising various number of minutes are shown in the graph. Which statement about the graph is *not* true?

Ⓐ The number of Calories burned is proportional to the number of minutes spent exercising.

Ⓑ The number of Calories burned is *not* proportional to the number of minutes spent exercising.

Ⓒ If the line were extended, it would pass through the origin.

Ⓓ The line is straight.

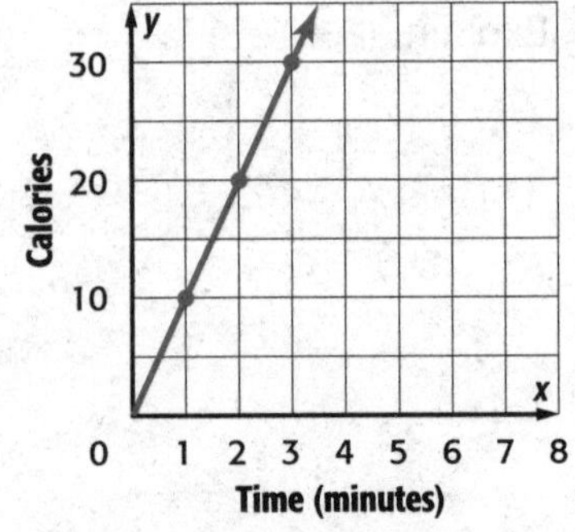

Name ______________________ My Homework ______________________

Extra Practice

Determine whether the relationship between the two quantities shown in each table are proportional by graphing on the coordinate plane. Explain your reasoning.

9.

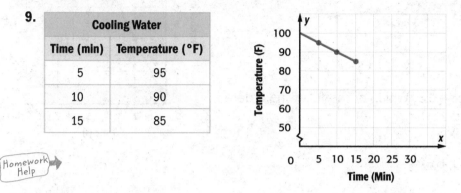

Cooling Water	
Time (min)	**Temperature (°F)**
5	95
10	90
15	85

Temperature (F): 100, 90, 80, 70, 60, 50; y; x
Time (Min): 0, 5, 10, 15, 20, 25, 30

Homework Help

Not proportional; The graph does not pass through the origin.

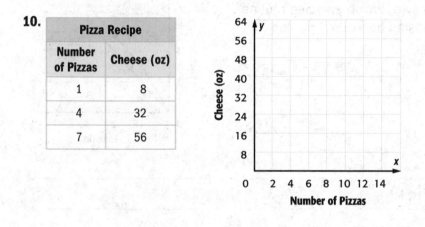

10.

Pizza Recipe	
Number of Pizzas	**Cheese (oz)**
1	8
4	32
7	56

Cheese (oz): 64, 56, 48, 40, 32, 24, 16, 8; y; x
Number of Pizzas: 0, 2, 4, 6, 8, 10, 12, 14

____

Copy and Solve **Determine if each situation represents a proportional relationship. Graph on a separate piece of paper. Write an explanation for each situation.**

11. CCGPS **Justify Conclusions** An airplane is flying at an altitude of 4,000 feet and descends at a rate of 200 feet per minute. Determine whether the altitude is proportional to number of minutes. Explain your reasoning.

12. Frank and Allie purchased cell phone plans through different providers. Their costs for several minutes are shown. Graph each plan to determine whose plan is proportional to the number of minutes the phone is used. Explain your reasoning.

Cell Phone Plans		
Time (min)	**Frank's Cost ($)**	**Allie's Cost ($)**
0	0	4.00
3	1.50	4.50
6	3.00	5.00

Georgia Test Practice

13. **Short Response** Determine whether the relationship between the number of heartbeats and the time shown in the graph is proportional. Explain your reasoning.

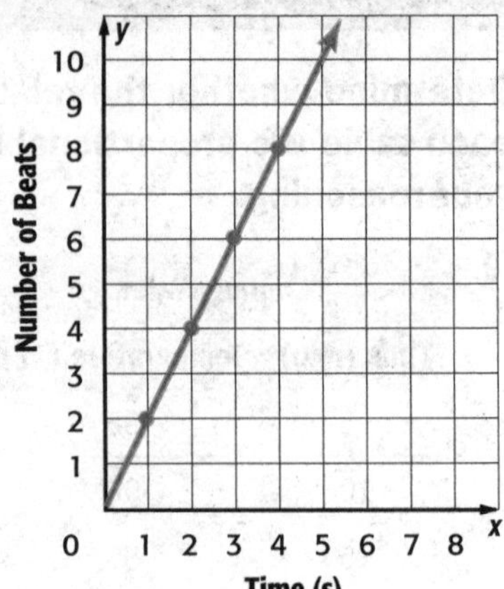

14. Refer to the graph in Exercise 13. Which of the following ordered pairs represent the unit rate?

Ⓐ (0, 0)
Ⓑ (1, 2)
Ⓒ (2, 4)
Ⓓ (3, 6)

15. **Short Response** The distance Charlie and Samora travel after 1, 2, and 3 hours of jogging is shown. Which exercise routine represents a proportional relationship between time and distance? Explain.

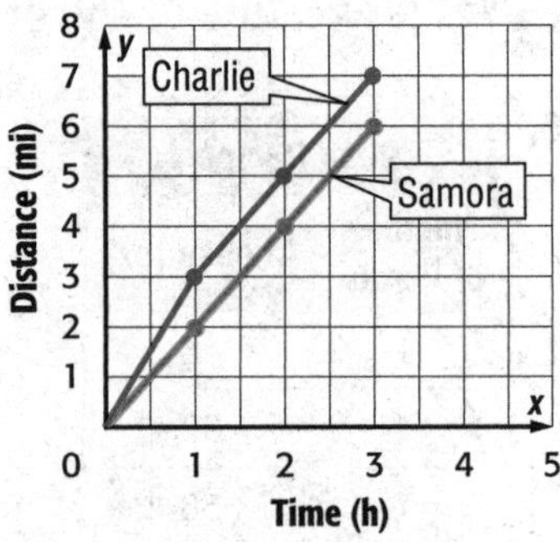

Common Core Review

Write each ratio as a fraction in simplest form. MCC6.RP.1

16. A class has 10 boys and 15 girls. What is the ratio of boys to girls? ______

17. A car dealership has 55 cars and 11 vans. What is the ratio of cars to vans? ______

18. A drawer has 4 red shirts and 8 green shirts. What is the ratio of red shirts to the total number of shirts? ______

19. A store sells 13 coffees and 65 hot chocolates. What is the ratio of coffees to hot chocolates? ______

Inquiry Lab

Proportional and Nonproportional Relationships

HOW are proportional and nonproportional linear relationships alike? HOW are they different?

Content Standards
MCC7.RP.2, MCC7.RP.2a

Mathematical Practices
1, 3, 4

Albert and Bianca joined an online discussion group. Each student posted four comments. The number of replies to each of their comments is shown in the table. Determine if each data set represents a proportional relationship.

Investigation

Step 1 Arrange centimeter cubes to model the number of replies per comment as shown in the diagram below.

Student	Albert				Bianca			
Comment Number	1	2	3	4	1	2	3	4
Number of Replies								

Step 2 Complete each table. Then graph the data on the coordinate plane. You may wish to use a different color pencil for each data set.

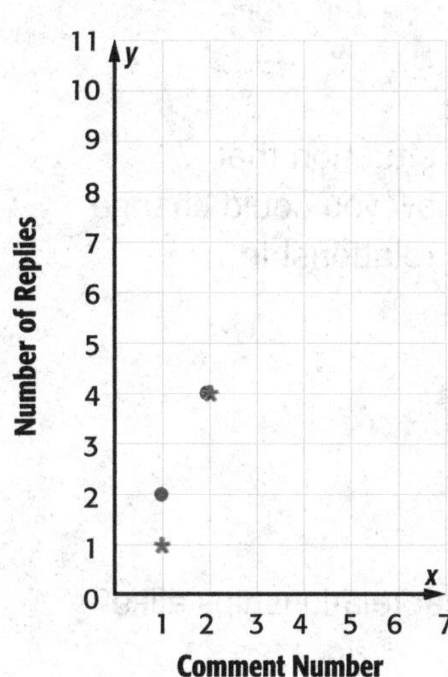

Albert's Comments	
Comment Number (x)	Number of Replies (y)
1	2
2	4
3	
4	

Bianca's Comments	
Comment Number (x)	Number of Replies (y)
1	1
2	4
3	
4	

Collaborate

Work with a partner to answer the following questions.

1. **CCGPS Justify Conclusions** Does Albert's graph represent a proportional relationship? Does Bianca's? Explain.

2. How can you use constant ratios to determine if a relationship is proportional?

Analyze

Work with a partner to complete the table. Describe the type of relationship shown by each set of ordered pairs. The first one is already done for you.

	Ordered Pairs	Type of Relationship
	(0, 5), (1, 7), (2, 9), (3, 11), (4, 13)	linear and nonproportional
3.	(0, 0), (1, 3), (2, 6), (3, 9), (4, 12)	
4.	(0, 0), (1, 1), (2, 4), (3, 9), (4, 16)	

Reflect

5. **CCGPS Model with Mathematics** Describe a real-world situation that represents a proportional relationship. Then explain how you could change your situation so that it represents a nonproportional relationship.

6. **Inquiry** HOW are proportional and nonproportional linear relationships alike? HOW are they different?

Solve Proportional Relationships

What You'll Learn

Scan the lesson. Write the definitions of equivalent ratios and proportion.

- equivalent ratios ______________________________
- proportion ______________________________

Essential Question

HOW can you show that two objects are proportional?

Vocabulary

proportion
cross product

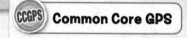

Common Core GPS

Content Standards
MCC7.RP.2, MCC7.RP.2b, MCC7.RP.2c, MCC7.RP.3

Mathematical Practices
1, 2, 3, 4

Real-World Link

Fruit Smoothies Katie and some friends want to buy fruit smoothies. They go to a health food store that advertises a sale of 2 fruit smoothies for $5.

1. Fill in the boxes to write a ratio that compares the cost to the number of fruit smoothies.

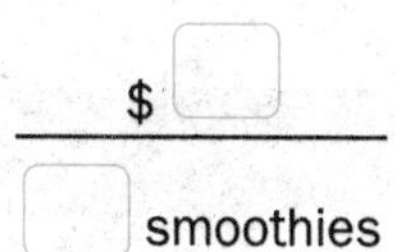

2. Suppose Katie and her friends buy 6 fruit smoothies. Complete the ratio that compares the cost to the number of fruit smoothies.

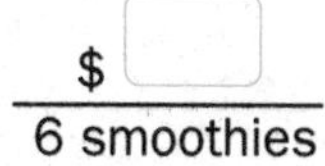

3. Is the cost proportional to the number of fruit smoothies for two and six smoothies? Explain.

____

____

____

Key Concept Write and Solve Proportions

Words A **proportion** is an equation stating that two ratios or rates are equivalent.

Numbers	Algebra
$\frac{6}{8} = \frac{3}{4}$	$\frac{a}{b} = \frac{c}{d}, b \neq 0, d \neq 0$

Work Zone

Consider the following proportion.

$$\frac{a}{b} = \frac{c}{d}$$

$$\frac{a}{\cancel{b}_1} \cdot \overset{1}{\cancel{b}}d = \frac{c}{\cancel{d}_1} \cdot b\overset{1}{\cancel{d}}$$ Multiply each side by *bd* and divide out common factors.

$$ad = bc$$ Simplify.

The products *ad* and *bc* are called the **cross products** of this proportion. The cross products of any proportion are equal.

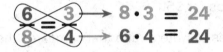

$$\frac{6}{8} = \frac{3}{4} \rightarrow 8 \cdot 3 = 24$$
$$\rightarrow 6 \cdot 4 = 24$$

Real World

Example

Tutor

1. After 2 hours, the air temperature had risen 7°F. Write and solve a proportion to find the amount of time it will take at this rate for the temperature to rise an additional 13°F.

Write a proportion. Let *t* represent the time in hours.

temperature → $\frac{7}{2} = \frac{13}{t}$ ← temperature
time → ← time

$7 \cdot t = 2 \cdot 13$ Find the cross products.

$7t = 26$ Multiply

$\frac{7t}{7} = \frac{26}{7}$ Divide each side by 7.

$t \approx 3.7$ Simplify.

It will take about 3.7 hours to rise an additional 13°F.

Show your work.

a. ________

b. ________

c. ________

Got It? Do these problems to find out.

Solve each proportion.

a. $\frac{x}{4} = \frac{9}{10}$ b. $\frac{2}{34} = \frac{5}{y}$ c. $\frac{7}{3} = \frac{n}{21}$

Example

2. If the ratio of Type O to non-Type O donors at a blood drive was 37:43, how many donors would be Type O, out of 300 donors?

Type O donors → total donors → $\frac{37}{37 + 43}$ or $\frac{37}{80}$

Write a proportion. Let t represent the number of Type O donors.

Type O donors → total donors → $\frac{37}{80} = \frac{t}{300}$ ← Type O donors ← total donors

$37 \cdot 300 = 80t$ Find the cross products.

$11{,}100 = 80t$ Multiply.

$\frac{11{,}100}{80} = \frac{80t}{80}$ Divide each side by 80.

$138.75 = t$ Simplify.

There would be about 139 Type O donors.

Got It? Do this problem to find out.

d. The ratio of 7th grade students to 8th grade students in a soccer league is 17:23. If there are 200 students in all, how many are in the 7th grade?

d. ______

Use Unit Rate

You can also use the unit rate to write an equation expressing the relationship between two proportional quantities.

Examples

3. Olivia bought 6 containers of yogurt for \$7.68. Write an equation relating the cost c to the number of yogurts y. How much would Olivia pay for 10 yogurts at this same rate?

Find the unit rate between cost and containers of yogurt.

$\frac{\text{cost in dollars}}{\text{containers of yogurt}} = \frac{7.68}{6}$ or \$1.28 per container

The cost is \$1.28 times the number of containers of yogurt.

$c = 1.28y$ Let c represent the cost. Let y represent the number of yogurts.

$= 1.28(10)$ Replace y with 10.

$= 12.80$ Multiply.

The cost for 10 containers of yogurt is \$12.80.

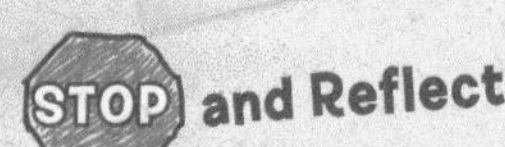

Consider the proportion $\frac{6}{b} = \frac{c}{7}$. What is true about bc?

4. Jaycee bought 8 gallons of gas for $31.12. Write an equation relating the cost c to the number of gallons g of gas. How much would Jaycee pay for 11 gallons at this same rate?

Find the unit rate between cost and gallons.

$$\frac{\text{cost in dollars}}{\text{gasoline in gallons}} = \frac{31.12}{8} \text{ or \$3.89 per gallon}$$

The cost is $3.89 times the number of gallons.

$c = 3.89g$ — Let c represent the cost. Let g represent the number of gallons.

$= 3.89(11)$ — Replace g with 11.

$= 42.79$ — Multiply.

The cost for 11 gallons of gas is $42.79.

Got It? Do this problem to find out.

e. Olivia typed 2 pages in 15 minutes. Write an equation relating the number of minutes *m* to the number of pages *p* typed. How long will it take her to type 10 pages at this rate?

e. ____________

Guided Practice

Solve each proportion. (Examples 1 and 2)

1. $\frac{k}{7} = \frac{32}{56}$ $k =$ ____________

2. $\frac{3.2}{9} = \frac{n}{36}$ $n =$ ____________

3. $\frac{41}{x} = \frac{5}{2}$ $x =$ ____________

4. Trina earns $28.50 tutoring for 3 hours. Write an equation relating her earnings *m* to the number of hours *h* she tutors. Assuming the situation is proportional, how much would Trina earn tutoring for 2 hours? for 4.5 hours? (Examples 3 and 4)

____

5. **Building on the Essential Question** How do you solve a proportion?

____

____

Rate Yourself!

How confident are you about solving proportions? Check the box that applies.

For more help, go online to access a Personal Tutor.

FOLDABLES Time to update your Foldable!

Name _______________ My Homework _______________

Independent Practice

Go online for Step-by-Step Solutions

Solve each proportion. (Examples 1 and 2)

1. $\frac{1.5}{6} = \frac{10}{p}$ $p =$ ______

2. $\frac{44}{p} = \frac{11}{5}$ $p =$ ______

3. $\frac{2}{w} = \frac{0.4}{0.7}$ $w =$ ______

Assume the situations are proportional. Write and solve by using a proportion. (Examples 1 and 2)

4. Evarado paid $1.12 for a dozen eggs at his local grocery store. Determine the cost of 3 eggs.

5. Sheila mixed 3 ounces of blue paint with 2 ounces of yellow paint. She decided to create 20 ounces of the same mixture. How many ounces of yellow paint does Sheila need for the new mixture?

Assume the situations are proportional. Use the unit rate to write an equation, then solve. (Examples 3 and 4)

6. A car can travel 476 miles on 14 gallons of gas. Write an equation relating the distance *d* to the number of gallons *g*. How many gallons of gas does this car need to travel 578 miles.

7. Mrs. Baker paid $2.50 for 5 pounds of bananas. Write an equation relating the cost *c* to the number of pounds *p* of bananas. How much would Mrs. Baker pay for 8 pounds of bananas?

8. A woman who is 64 inches tall has a shoulder width of 16 inches. Write an equation relating the height *h* to the width *w*. Find the height of a woman who has a shoulder width of 18.5 inches.

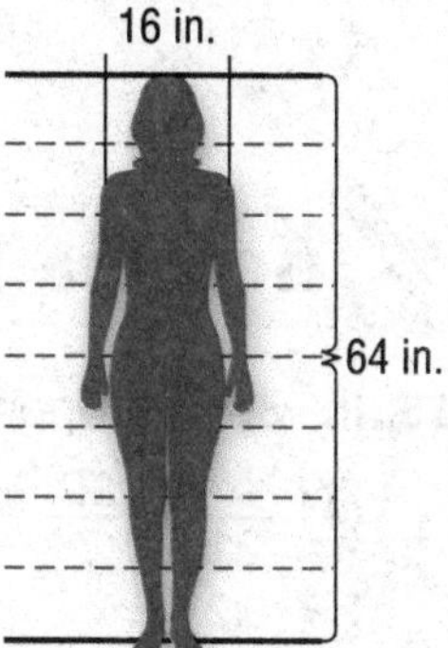

9. At an amusement park, 360 visitors rode the roller coaster in 3 hours. Write and solve a proportion to find the number of visitors at this rate who will ride the roller coaster in 7 hours. (Examples 3 and 4)

10. **Reason Abstractly** Use the table to write a proportion relating the weights on two planets. Then find the missing weight. Round to the nearest tenth.

Weights on Different Planets Earth Weight = 120 pounds	
Mercury	45.6 pounds
Venus	109.2 pounds
Uranus	96 pounds
Jupiter	304.8 pounds

a. Earth: 90 pounds; Venus: ☐ pounds

b. Mercury: 55 pounds; Earth: ☐ pounds

c. Jupiter: 350 pounds; Uranus: ☐ pounds

d. Venus: 115 pounds; Mercury: ☐ pounds

H.O.T. Problems Higher Order Thinking

11.  **Justify Conclusions** A powdered drink mix calls for a ratio of powder to water of 1 : 8. If there are 32 cups of powder, how many total cups of water are needed? Explain your reasoning.

Persevere with Problems **Solve each equation.**

12. $\frac{2}{3} = \frac{18}{x+5}$

13. $\frac{x-4}{10} = \frac{7}{5}$

14. $\frac{4.5}{17-x} = \frac{3}{8}$

Georgia Test Practice

15. In which proportion does x have a value of 4?

Ⓐ $\frac{x}{21} = \frac{12}{7}$

Ⓑ $\frac{12}{21} = \frac{x}{7}$

Ⓒ $\frac{5}{2} = \frac{1}{x}$

Ⓓ $\frac{1}{x} = \frac{5}{200}$

Name ______________________ My Homework ______________

Extra Practice

Solve each proposition.

16. $\frac{x}{13} = \frac{18}{39}$ $x =$ 6

$x \cdot 39 = 13 \cdot 18$

$39x = 234$

$\frac{39x}{39} = \frac{234}{39}$

$x = 6$

17. $\frac{6}{25} = \frac{d}{30}$ $d =$ ______

18. $\frac{2.5}{6} = \frac{h}{9}$ $h =$ ______

Assume the situations are proportional. Write and solve by using a proportion.

19. For every person who has the flu, there are 6 people who have only flu-like symptoms. If a doctor sees 40 patients, determine approximately how many patients you would expect to have only flu-like symptoms.

____

20. For every left-handed person, there are about 4 right-handed people. If there are 30 students in a class, predict the number of students who are right-handed.

____

21. Jeremiah is saving money from a tutoring job. After the first three weeks, he saved $135. Assume the situation is proportional. Use the unit rate to write an equation relating the amount saved *s* to the number of weeks *w* worked. At this rate, how much will Jeremiah save after eight weeks?

____

22. CCGPS **Make a Prediction** A speed limit of 100 kilometers per hour (kph) is approximately equal to 62 miles per hour (mph). Write an equation relating kilometers per hour *k* to miles per hour *m*. Then predict the following measures. Round to the nearest tenth.

a. a speed limit in mph for a speed limit of 75 kph

____

b. a speed limit in kph for a speed limit of 20 mph

____

Georgia Test Practice

23. A recipe for making 3 dozen muffins requires 1.5 cups of flour. At this rate, how many cups of flour are required to make 5 dozen muffins?

Ⓐ 2 cups
Ⓑ 2.5 cups
Ⓒ 3 cups
Ⓓ 3.5 cups

24. An amusement park line is moving about 4 feet every 15 minutes. At this rate, approximately how long will it take for a person at the back of the 50-foot line to reach the front of the line?

Ⓕ 1 hour
Ⓖ 3 hours
Ⓗ 5 hours
Ⓘ 13 hours

25. **Short Response** Crystal's mother kept a record of Crystal's height at different ages. She recorded the information in a table.

Age (yr)	Height (in.)
0 (birth)	19
1	25
2	30
5	42
10	55
12	60

Is the relationship between Crystal's age and her height proportional? Explain.

Common Core Review

26. The table shows the cost to have various numbers of pizzas delivered from Papa's Slice of Italy pizzeria. Is the relationship between the cost and the number of pizzas proportional? Explain. MCC7.RP.2a

Number of Pizzas	Cost ($)
1	12.50
2	20
3	27.50
4	35

27. Brenna charges $15, $30, $45, and $60 for babysitting 1, 2, 3, and 4 hours, respectively. Is the relationship between the amount charged and the number of hours proportional? If so, find the unit rate. If not, explain why not. MCC7.RP.2a

Find each unit rate. MCC6.RP.3b

28. 50 miles on 2.5 gallons

29. 2,500 kilobytes in 5 minutes

HOW is unit rate related to rate of change?

Content Standards
MCC7.RP.2, MCC7.RP.2b

Mathematical Practices
1, 3

Pets Happy Hound is a doggie daycare where people drop off their dogs while they are at work. It costs \$3 for 1 hour, \$6 for 2 hours, and \$9 for 3 hours of doggie daycare. Farah takes her dog to Happy Hound several days a week. Farah wants to determine if the number of hours of daycare is related to the cost.

Investigation

Step 1 Assume the pattern in the table continues. Complete the table shown.

Happy Hound Doggie Daycare	
Number of Hours	Cost (\$)
1	3
2	6
3	9
4	
5	

Step 2 The cost depends on the number of hours. So, the cost is the output y, and the number of hours is the ________. Graph the data on the coordinate plane below.

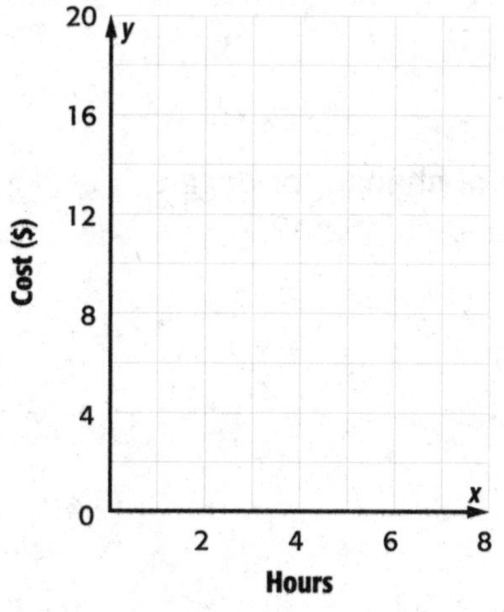

Collaborate

Refer to the Investigation. Work with a partner.

1. CCGPS **Justify Conclusions** Is the graph linear? Explain.

2. What is the cost per hour, or unit rate, charged by Happy Hound?

3. CCGPS **Justify Conclusions** Is the relationship proportional? Explain.

4. Use the graph to examine any two consecutive points. By how much does y change? By how much does x change?

5. The first two ordered pairs on the graph are (1, 3) and (2, 6). You can find the *rate of change* by writing the ratio of the change in y to the change in x.

   Find the rate of change shown in the graph. ______

Analyze

Work with a partner to answer the following question.

6. Pampered Pooch charges $5 for 1 hour of doggie daycare, $10 for 2 hours, and $15 for 3 hours.

   a. What is the unit rate? ______

   b. What is the rate of change? ______

   c. CCGPS **Reason Inductively** How do the rates of change for doggie daycare at Pampered Pooch and Happy Hound compare?

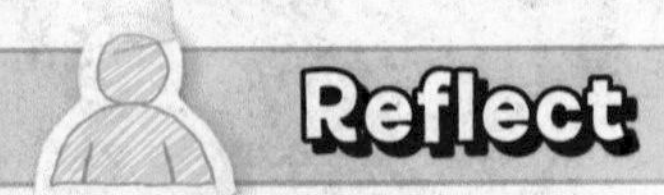

Reflect

7. Inquiry HOW is unit rate related to rate of change?

Lesson 7

Constant Rate of Change

What You'll Learn

Scan the text on the following two pages. Write two facts you learned about constant rate of change.

- ______________________________
- ______________________________

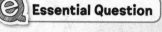

Essential Question

HOW can you show that two objects are proportional?

Vocabulary

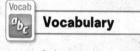

rate of change
constant rate of change

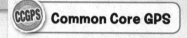

Common Core GPS

Content Standards
MCC7.RP.2, MCC7.RP.2b, MCC7.RP.2d

Mathematical Practices
1, 3, 4

Vocabulary Start-Up

A **rate of change** is a rate that describes how one quantity changes in relation to another. In a linear relationship, the rate of change between any two quantities is the same. A linear relationship has a **constant rate of change**.

Real-World Link

A computer programmer charges customers per line of code written. Fill in the blanks with the amount of change between consecutive numbers.

Lines of Code	50	100	150	200
Cost ($)	1,000	2,000	3,000	4,000

Label the diagram below with the terms *change in lines*, *change in dollars*, and *constant rate of change*.

$$\frac{\square}{\square} = \frac{\$1,000}{50 \text{ lines}}$$

$$= \frac{\$20}{1 \text{ line}} \quad \text{unit rate}$$

The ______________________ is $20 per line of programming code.

Work Zone

Use a Table

You can use a table to find a constant rate of change.

Example

1. The table shows the amount of money a booster club makes washing cars for a fundraiser. Use the information to find the constant rate of change in dollars per car.

Cars Washed	
Number	**Money ($)**
5	40
10	80
15	120
20	160

+5, +5, +5 (Number); +40, +40, +40 (Money)

Find the unit rate to determine the constant rate of change.

$$\frac{\text{change in money}}{\text{change in cars}} = \frac{40 \text{ dollars}}{5 \text{ cars}}$$ The money earned increases by $40 for every 5 cars.

$$= \frac{8 \text{ dollars}}{1 \text{ car}}$$ Write as a unit rate.

So, the number of dollars earned increases by $8 for every car washed.

Unit Rate
A rate of change is usually expressed as a unit rate.

Got It? **Do these problems to find out.**

a. The table shows the number of miles a plane traveled while in flight. Use the information to find the approximate constant rate of change in miles per minute.

Time (min)	30	60	90	120
Distance (mi)	290	580	870	1,160

b. The table shows the number of students that buses can transport. Use the table to find the constant rate of change in students per school bus.

Number of Buses	2	3	4	5
Number of Students	144	216	288	360

a. ____________

b. ____________

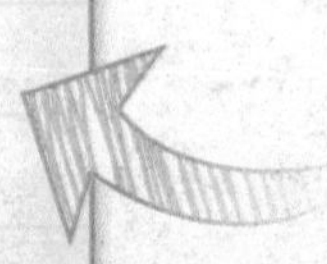

Use a Graph

You can also use a graph to find a constant rate of change and to analyze points on the graph.

Examples

2. The graph represents the distance traveled while driving on a highway. Find the constant rate of change.

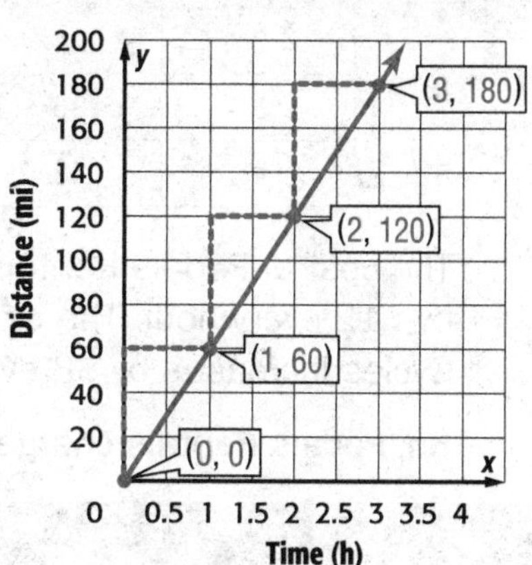

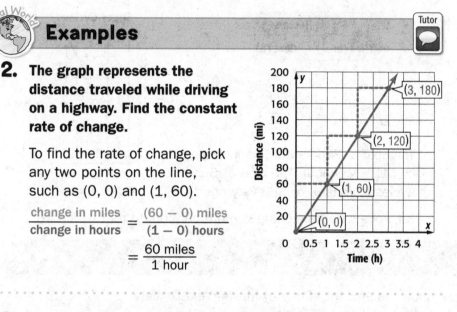

To find the rate of change, pick any two points on the line, such as (0, 0) and (1, 60).

$$\frac{\text{change in miles}}{\text{change in hours}} = \frac{(60 - 0)\text{ miles}}{(1 - 0)\text{ hours}}$$

$$= \frac{60\text{ miles}}{1\text{ hour}}$$

3. Explain what the points (0, 0) and (1, 60) represent.

The point (0, 0) represents traveling zero miles in zero hours. The point (1, 60) represents traveling 60 miles in 1 hour. Notice that this is the constant rate of change.

Got It? Do these problems to find out.

c. Use the graph to find the constant rate of change in miles per hour while driving in the city.

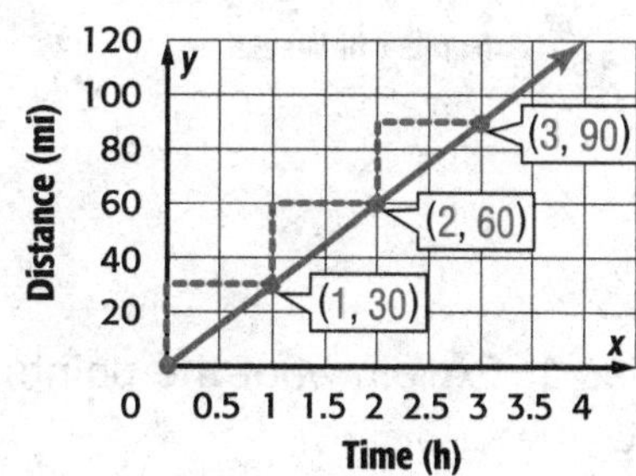

d. On the lines below, explain what the points (0, 0) and (1, 30) represent.

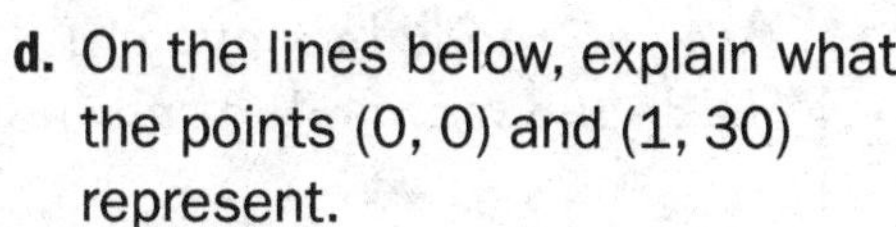

Ordered Pairs
The ordered pair (2, 120) represents traveling 120 miles in 2 hours.

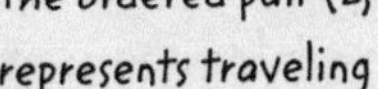

c. ______

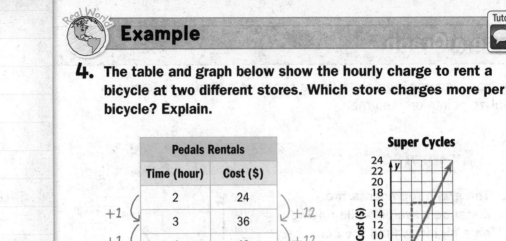

Example

4. The table and graph below show the hourly charge to rent a bicycle at two different stores. Which store charges more per bicycle? Explain.

Pedals Rentals	
Time (hour)	Cost ($)
2	24
3	36
4	48

+1 +1 +12 +12

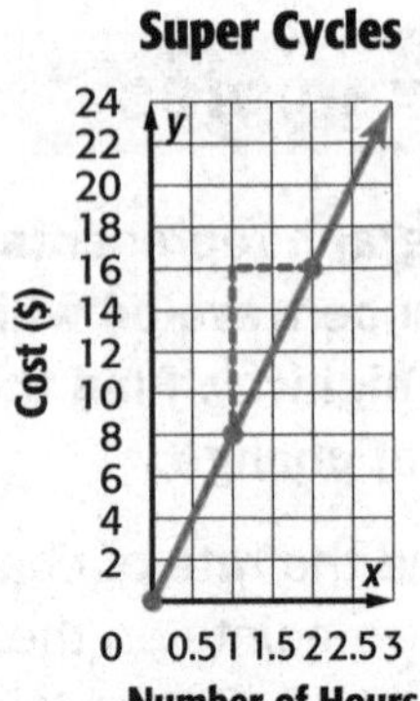

The cost at Pedals Rentals increases by $12 every hour. The cost at Super Cycles increases by $8 every hour.

So, Pedals Rentals charges more per hour to rent a bicycle.

Guided Practice

1. The table and graph below show the amount of money Mi-Ling and Daniel save each week. Who saves more each week? Explain. (Examples 1, 2, and 4)

Mi-Ling's Savings	
Time (weeks)	Savings ($)
2	$30
3	$45
4	$60

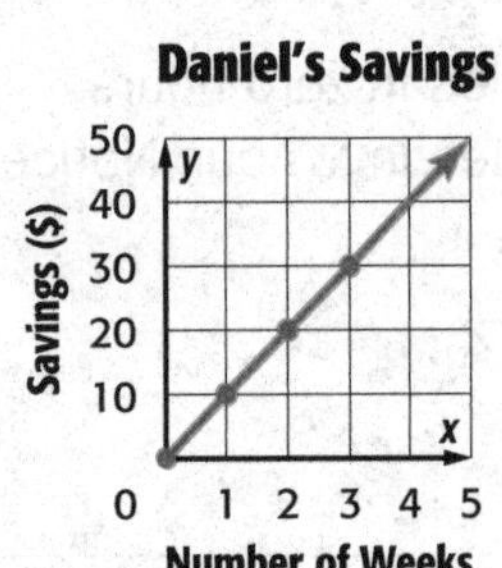

2. Refer to the graph in Exercise 1. Explain what the points (0, 0) and (1, 10) represent. (Example 3)

3. **Building on the Essential Question** How can you find the unit rate on a graph that goes through the origin?

Rate Yourself!

Are you ready to move on? Shade the section that applies.

For more help, go online to access a Personal Tutor.

Name ______________________ My Homework ______________________

Independent Practice

Go online for Step-by-Step Solutions

Find the constant rate of change for the table. (Example 1)

1.

Time (s)	Distance (m)
1	6
2	12
3	18
4	24

2.

Items	Cost ($)
2	18
4	36
6	54
8	72

3. The graph shows the cost of purchasing T-shirts. Find the constant rate of change for the graph. Then explain what points (0, 0) and (1, 9) represent. (Examples 2 and 3)

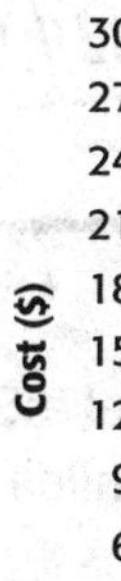

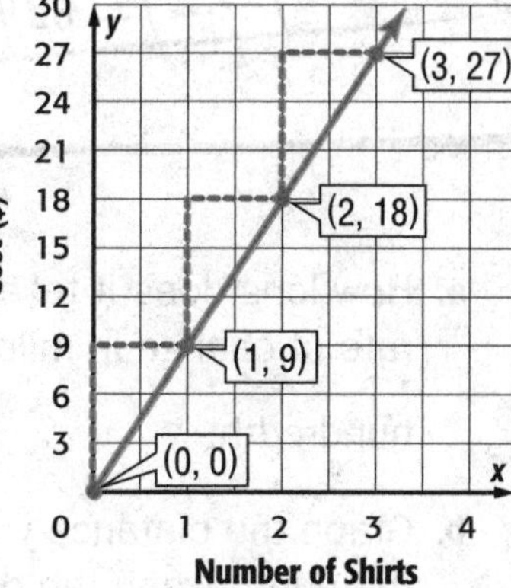

4. The Guzman and Hashimoto families each took a 4-hour road trip. The distances traveled by each family are shown in the table and graph below. Which family averaged fewer miles per hour? Explain. (Example 4)

Guzman's Road Trip	
Time (hours)	**Distance (miles)**
2	90
3	135
4	180

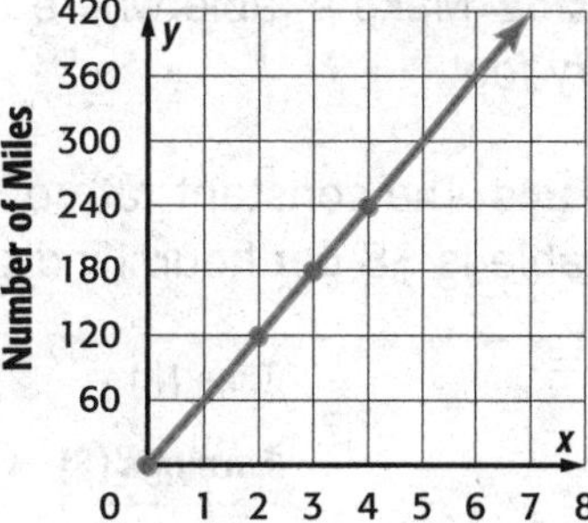

5. At 1:00 P.M., the water level in a pool is 13 inches. At 1:30 P.M., the water level is 18 inches. At 2:30 P.M., the water level is 28 inches. What is the constant rate of change?

 **Model with Mathematics** Refer to the lap times for Exercises **a** and **b**.

Watch Replay it online!

The race is 20 laps, which is 5 miles. Assuming your speed is constant...
Let's calculate Seth's times.
Lap 4 8 12 16 20
Distance(mi) 1 2 3 4 5
Time(s) 57.1 114.2 171.3

a. How long does it take Seth to race 1 mile? Write the constant rate of change in miles per second. Round to the nearest hundredth. ____________

b. Graph the distance y and time x on the coordinate plane at the right. Graph the distance on the y-axis and the time on the x-axis.

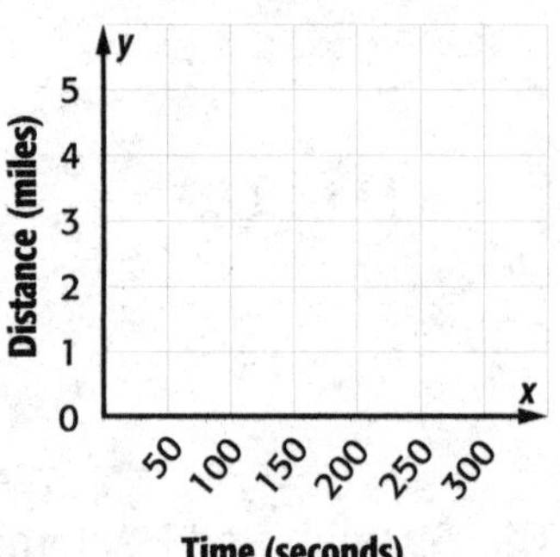

H.O.T. Problems

7. **Model with Mathematics** Make a table where the constant rate of change is 6 inches for every foot.

Feet	Inches

8. **Persevere with Problems** The constant rate of change for the relationship shown in the table is \$8 per hour. Find the missing values.

$x =$ ______ $y =$ ______ $z =$ ______

Time (h)	1	2	3
Earnings (\$)	x	y	z

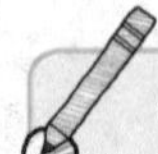

Georgia Test Practice

9. The information in the table represents a constant rate of change. Find the missing value.

Ⓐ 30
Ⓑ 90
Ⓒ 105
Ⓓ 120

Number of Packages	2	4	7
Number of Raisins	30	60	x

Extra Practice

Find the constant rate of change for each table.

10.

Time (h)	0	1	2	3
Wage ($)	0	9	18	27

$9 per hour

$$\frac{\text{change in wages}}{\text{change in hours}} = \frac{\$9}{1 \text{ hour}}$$

11.

Minutes	1,000	1,500	2,000	2,500
Cost ($)	38	53	68	83

____

12. Use the graph to find the constant rate of change. Then, explain what the points (0, 0) and (6, 72) represent.

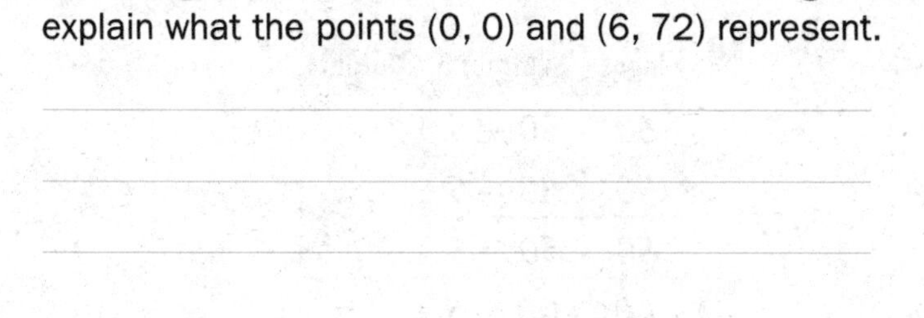

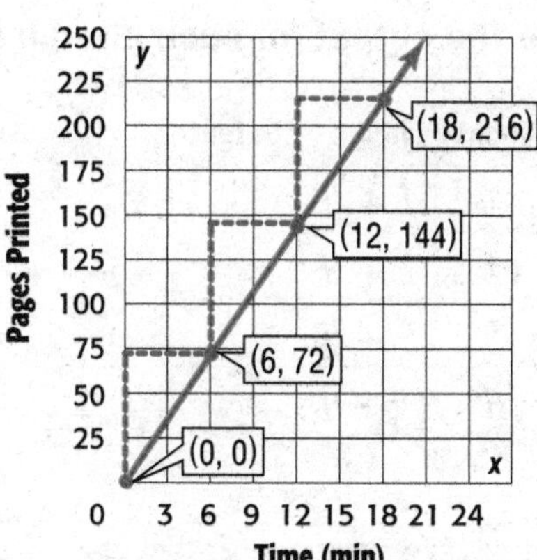

13. CCGPS **Justify Conclusions** Ramona and Josh earn money by babysitting. The amounts earned for one evening are shown in the table and graph. Who charged more per hour? Explain.

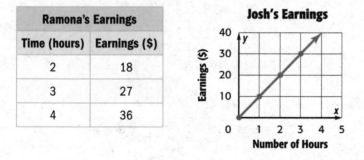

Ramona's Earnings	
Time (hours)	**Earnings ($)**
2	18
3	27
4	36

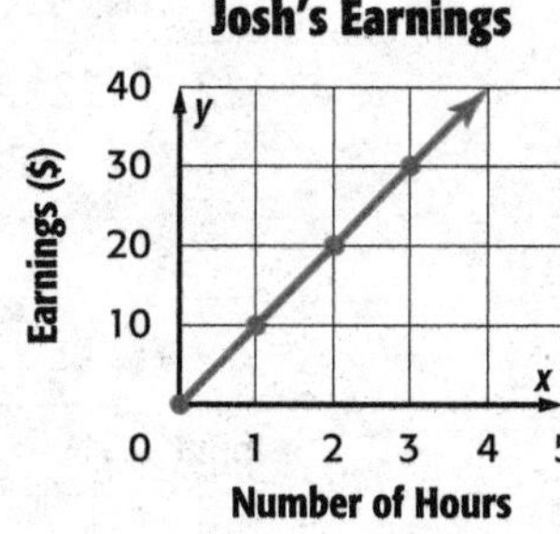

____

____

14. The cost of 1 movie ticket is $7.50. The cost of 2 movie tickets is $15. Based on this constant rate of change, what is the cost of 4 movie tickets? ________

Georgia Test Practice

15. Use the information in the table to find the constant rate of change.

Number of Apples	3	7	11
Number of Seeds	30	70	110

Ⓐ $\frac{10}{1}$

Ⓑ $\frac{1}{10}$

Ⓒ $\frac{40}{4}$

Ⓓ $\frac{4}{40}$

16. **Short Response** Reggie started a running program to prepare for track season. Every day for 60 days, he ran a half hour in the morning and a half hour in the evening. He averaged 6.5 miles per hour. At this rate, what is the total number of miles Reggie ran over the 60-day period? ____________

Common Core Review

Write the output for each given input in the tables below. MCC5.OA.3

17.

Input	Add 4	Output
1	1 + 4	
2	2 + 4	
3	3 + 4	
4	4 + 4	

18.

Input	Subtract 5	Output
30	30 − 5	
40	40 − 5	
50	50 − 5	
60	60 − 5	

19.

Input	Multiply by 2	Output
1	1 × 2	
2	2 × 2	
3	3 × 2	
4	4 × 2	

20.

Input	Divide by 3	Output
3	3 ÷ 3	
6	6 ÷ 3	
9	9 ÷ 3	
12	12 ÷ 3	

Write the rule shown in each table. MCC5.OA.3

21.

Input		Output
4	?	10
5	?	11
6	?	12
7	?	13

22.

Input		Output
2	?	10
4	?	20
6	?	30
8	?	40

Slope

What You'll Learn

Scan the lesson. Predict two things you will learn about slope.

- ______________________________
- ______________________________

Essential Question

HOW can you show that two objects are proportional?

Vocabulary

slope

Common Core GPS

Content Standards
MCC7.RP.2, MCC7.RP.2b

Mathematical Practices
1, 3, 4

Real-World Link

Recycling Hero Comics prints on recycled paper. The table shows the total number of pounds of recycled paper that has been used each day during the month.

Day of Month	Total Recycled (lbs)
3	36
5	60
6	72
7	84
12	144

1. Graph the ordered pairs on the coordinate plane.

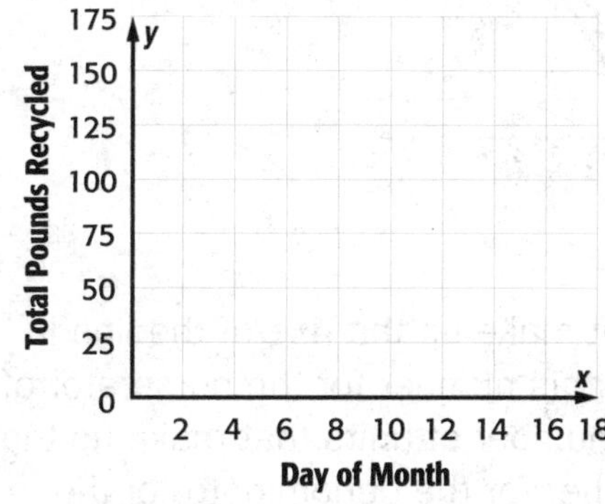

2. Explain why the graph is linear. ______________________________

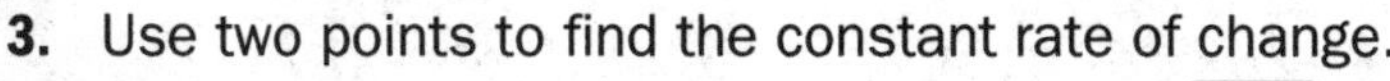

3. Use two points to find the constant rate of change.

Point 1: ________ $\frac{\text{change in pounds}}{\text{change in days}}$ → $\frac{\square \text{ pounds}}{\square \text{ days}}$

Point 2: ________

So, the constant rate of change is $\frac{24}{2}$ or $\square$ pounds per day.

Key Concept Slope

Slope is the rate of change between any two points on a line.

Work Zone

$$\text{slope} = \frac{\text{change in } y}{\text{change in } x} \begin{array}{l} \leftarrow \text{vertical change} \\ \leftarrow \text{horizontal change} \end{array}$$

$$= \frac{2}{1} \text{ or } 2$$

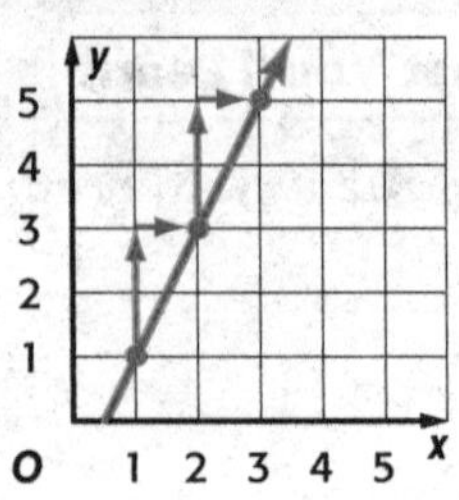

In a linear relationship, the vertical change (change in *y*-value) per unit of horizontal change (change in *x*-value) is always the same. This ratio is called the **slope** of the function. The constant rate of change, or unit rate, is the same as the slope of the related linear relationship.

The slope tells how steep the line is. The vertical change is sometimes called "rise" while the horizontal change is called "run." You can say that slope $= \frac{\text{rise}}{\text{run}}$.

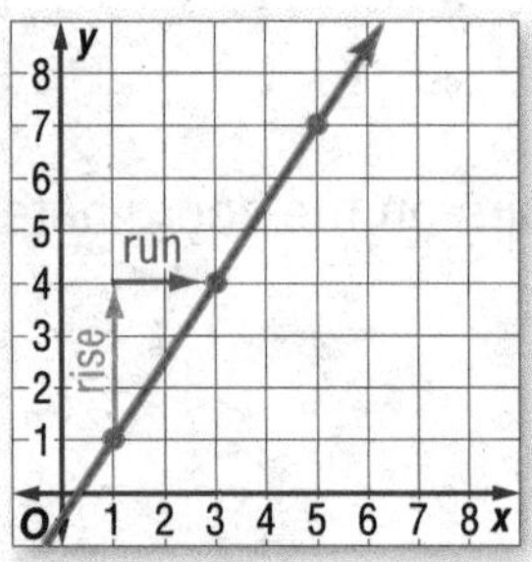

Count the number of units that make up the rise of the line in the graph shown above. Write this number for the numerator of the fraction below. Count the number of units that make up the run of the line. Write this number for the denominator of the fraction below.

$$\frac{\text{rise}}{\text{run}} = \frac{\square}{\square}$$

So, the slope of the line is $\frac{3}{2}$.

Example

1. The table below shows the relationship between the number of seconds y it takes to hear thunder after a lightning strike and the miles x you are from the lightning. Graph the data and find the slope. Explain what the slope represents.

Miles (x)	0	1	2	3	4	5
Seconds (y)	0	5	10	15	20	25

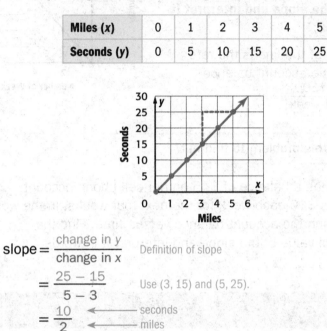

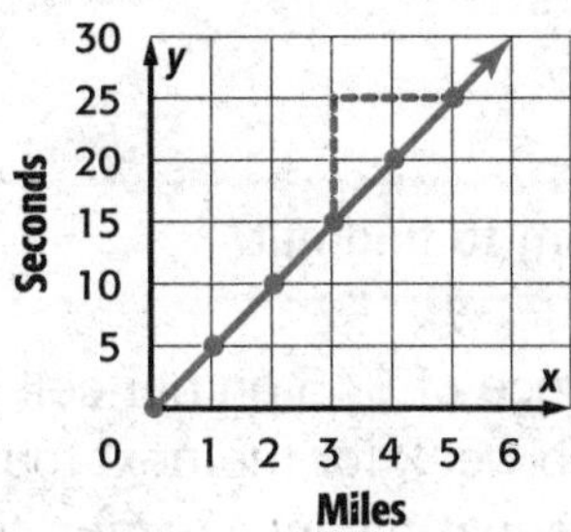

$$\text{slope} = \frac{\text{change in } y}{\text{change in } x}$$ Definition of slope

$$= \frac{25 - 15}{5 - 3}$$ Use (3, 15) and (5, 25).

$$= \frac{10}{2}$$ ← seconds, ← miles

$$= \frac{5}{1}$$ Simplify.

So, for every 5 seconds between a lightning flash and the sound of thunder, there is 1 mile between you and the lightning strike.

Slope In everyday language, slope means inclination or slant.

In math language, slope means the ratio of vertical change per unit of horizontal change; the steepness of a line.

Got It? Do this problem to find out.

a. Graph the data about plant height for a science fair project. Then find the slope of the line. Explain what the slope represents in the work zone.

Week	Plant Height (cm)
1	1.5
2	3
3	4.5
4	6

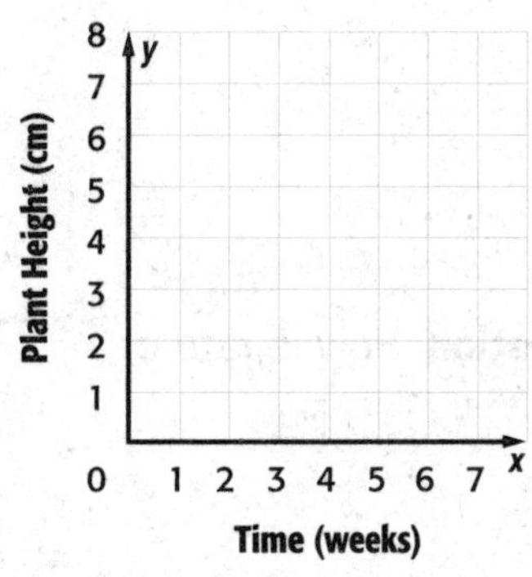

a. ______________

Example

2. Renaldo opened a savings account. Each week he deposits $300. Draw a graph of the the account balance versus time. Find the numerical value of the slope and interpret it in words.

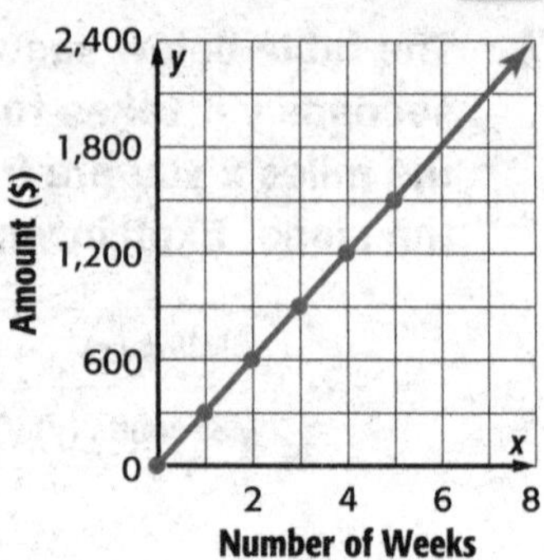

The slope of the line is the rate at which the account balance rises, or $\frac{\$300}{1 \text{ week}}$.

Account Balance ($)
80
60
40
20
0
1 2 3 4
Number of Weeks

Got It? Do this problem to find out.

b. ____________

b. Jessica has a balance of $45 on her cell phone account. She adds $10 each week for the next four weeks. In the work zone, graph the account balance versus time. Find the numerical value of the slope and interpret it in words.

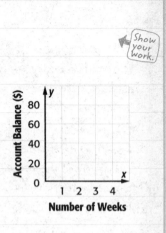

Guided Practice

1. The table at the right shows the number of small packs of fruit snacks y per box x. Graph the data. Then find the slope of the line. Explain what the slope represents. (Examples 1 and 2)

Boxes, x	3	5	7
Fruit Snacks, y	12	20	28

____

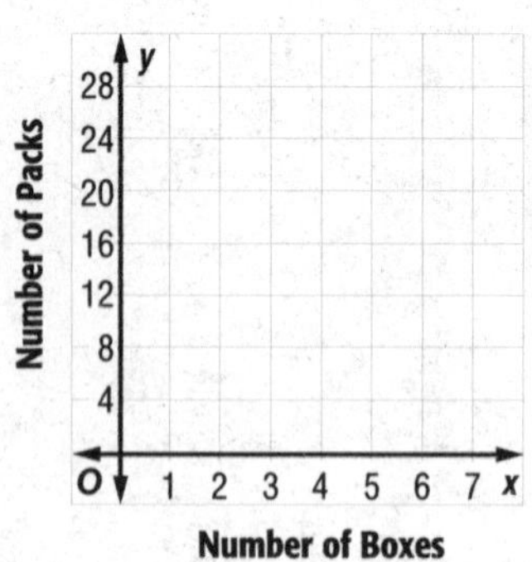

2. **Building on the Essential Question** How is rate of change related to slope? ____________

____

____

____

Rate Yourself!

How well do you understand slope? Circle the image.

Clear

Somewhat Clear

Not So Clear

For more help, go online to access a Personal Tutor.

Independent Practice

Go online for Step-by-Step Solutions 

1 The table shows the number of pages Adriano read in *x* hours. Graph the data. Then find the slope of the line. Explain what the slope represents. (Example 1)

Time (h)	1	2	3	4
Number of pages	50	100	150	200

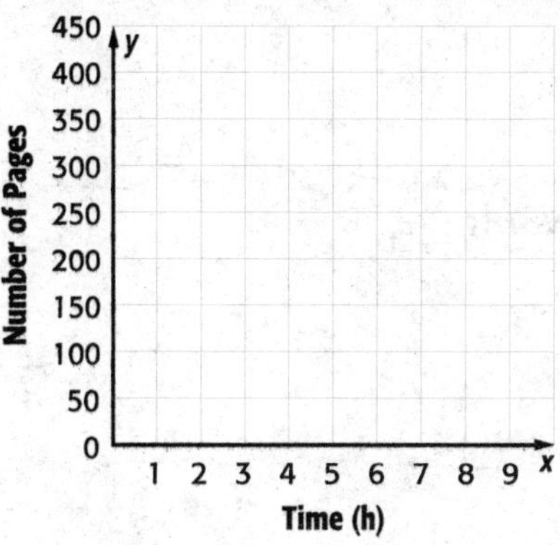

2. Graph the data. Find the numerical value of the slope and interpret it in words. (Example 2)

Number of Yards	1	2	3
Number of Feet	3	6	9

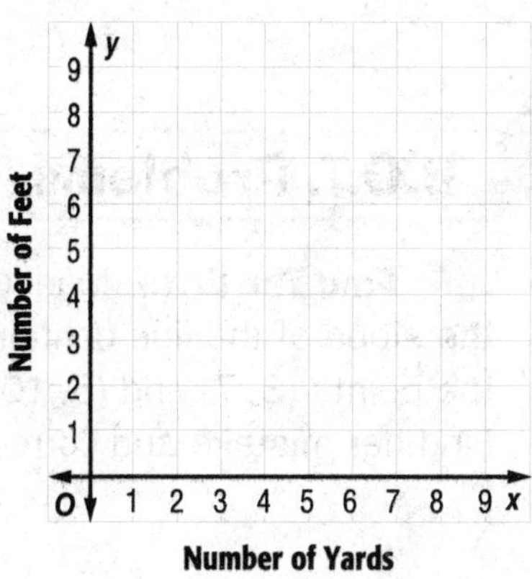

3 The graph shows the average speed of two cars on the highway.

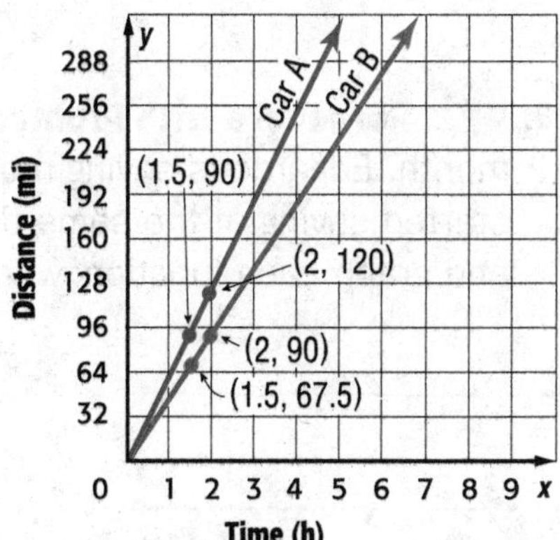

a. What does (2, 120) represent? ______

b. What does (1.5, 67.5) represent? ______

c. What does the ratio of the *y*-coordinate to the *x*-coordinate for each pair of points on the graph represent?

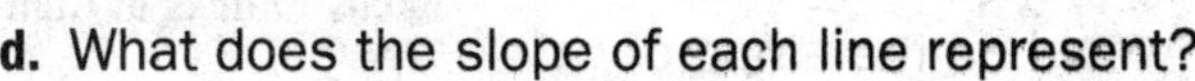

d. What does the slope of each line represent?

e. Which car is traveling faster? How can you tell from the graph?

4. **Multiple Representations** Complete the graphic organizer on slope.

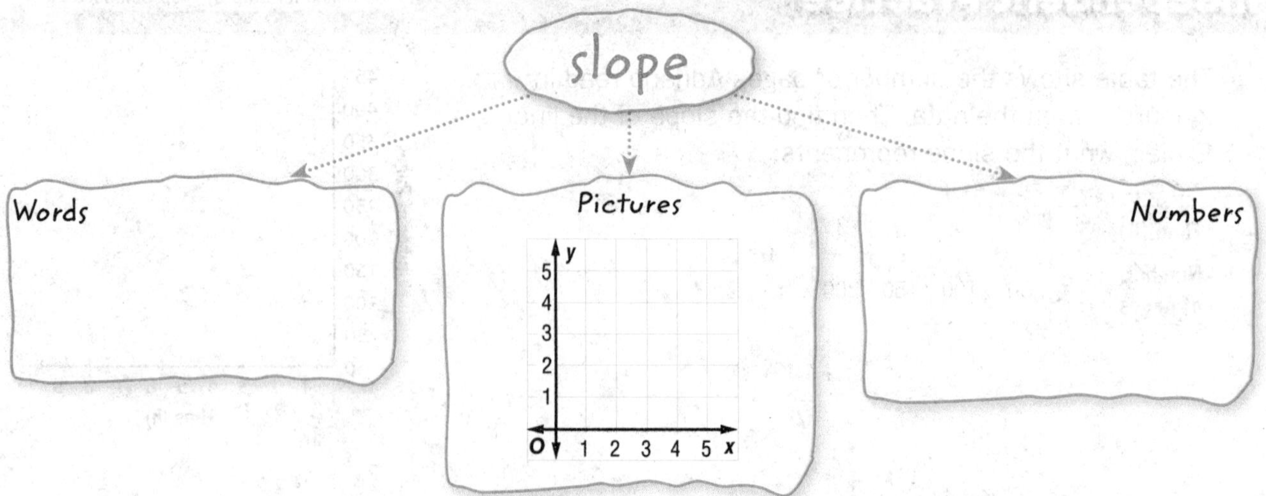

H.O.T. Problems Higher Order Thinking

5. **Find The Error** Marisol is finding the slope of the line containing the points (3, 7) and (5, 10). Find her mistake and correct it.

The slope between the two points (3, 7) and (5, 10) is found like this:
$\text{slope} = \frac{\text{rise}}{\text{run}} = \frac{5-3}{10-7}$
$= \frac{2}{3}$

6. **Persevere with Problems** Kaya is saving money at a rate of $30 per month. Edgardo is saving money at a rate of $35 per month. They both started saving at the same time. If you were to create a table of values and graph each function, what would be the slope of each graph?

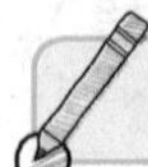

Georgia Test Practice

7. The table shows the number of packs and the number of sticks of chewing gum. If the data were graphed, what would be the slope of the line?

Packs	Sticks of Gum
1	5
2	10
3	15
4	20

Ⓐ (1, 5)

Ⓑ (5, 1)

Ⓒ $\frac{1}{5}$

Ⓓ $\frac{5}{1}$

Extra Practice

8. CCGPS **Justify Conclusions** The table to the right shows the number of markers per box. Graph the data. Then find the slope of the line. Explain what the slope represents.

Boxes	1	2	3	4
Markers	8	16	24	32

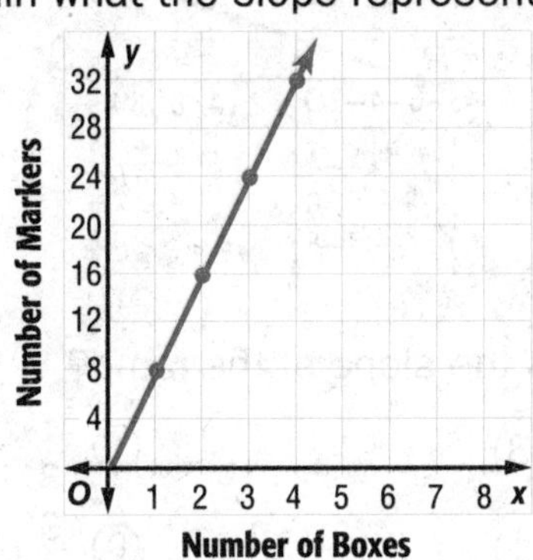

Use (1, 8) and (2, 16).

$$\text{slope} = \frac{\text{change in } y}{\text{change in } x}$$

$$= \frac{16 - 8}{2 - 1}$$

$$= \frac{8}{1}$$

So, there are 8 markers in every 1 box.

9. The table shows the cost to rent a paddle boat from two businesses.

Paddle Boat Rentals		
Number of Hours	Water Wheels Cost ($)	Fun in the Sun Cost ($)
1	20	25
2	40	50
3	60	75
4	80	100

a. What does (1, 20) represent?

____

b. What does (2, 50) represent?

____

Copy and Solve **For Exercises 10–13, draw a graph on a separate sheet of grid paper to find each slope. Then record each slope and interpret its meaning.**

10. The table shows the amount Maggie earns for various numbers of hours she babysits. Graph the data. Then find the slope of the line. Explain what the slope represents.

Number of Hours	Earnings ($)
1	8
2	16
3	24
4	32

11. Joshua swims 25 meters in 1 minute. Draw a graph of meters swam versus time. Find the value of the slope and interpret it in words.

12. The Jackson family rents 6 movies each month. Draw a graph of movies rented versus time. Find the value of the slope and interpret it in words.

13. Zack completes 20 homework problems in 1 hour. Draw a graph of homework problems versus time. Find the value of the slope and interpret it in words.

Georgia Test Practice

14. **Short Response** Find the slope of the line below that shows the distance Jairo traveled while jogging.

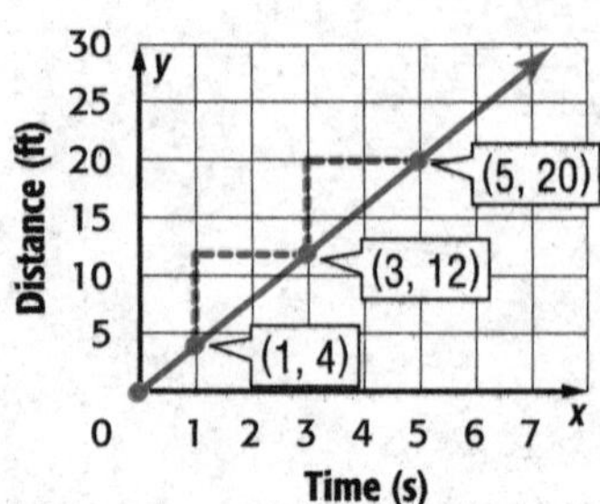

15. Line *RS* represents a bike ramp.

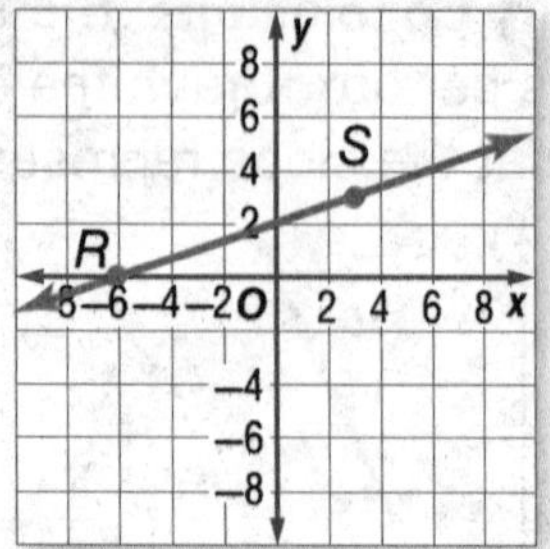

What is the slope of the ramp?

Ⓐ (1, 3)

Ⓑ (3, 1)

Ⓒ $\frac{1}{3}$

Ⓓ $\frac{3}{1}$

16. **Short Response** Two weeks ago, Audrey earned $84 for 7 hours of work. This week, she earned $132 for 11 hours of work. Find the numerical value of the slope of the line that would represent Audrey's earnings.

Common Core Review

Determine if each situation is proportional. Explain your reasoning. MCC7.RP.2

17. Taxi cab passengers are charged $2.50 upon entering a cab. They are then charged $1.00 for every mile traveled.

18. A restaurant charges $5 for one sandwich, $9.90 for two sandwiches, and $14.25 for three sandwiches.

19.

Tickets Purchased	1	2	3	4
Cost ($)	7.50	15	22.50	30

20.

Cups of Flour	3	6	9	12
Cups of Sugar	2	4	6	8

Direct Variation

What You'll Learn

Scan the text on the following two pages. Write the definitions of direct variation and constant of proportionality.

- direct variation ______________________
- constant of proportionality ______________________

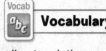

Essential Question

HOW can you show that two objects are proportional?

Vocabulary

direct variation
constant of variation
constant of proportionality

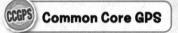

Common Core GPS

Content Standards
MCC7.RP.2, MCC7.RP.2a, MCC7.RP.2b

Mathematical Practices
1, 2, 3, 4

Real-World Link

Speed The distance d a car travels after t hours can be represented by $d = 65t$. The table and graph also represent the situation.

Time (hours)	Distance (miles)
2	130
3	195
4	260

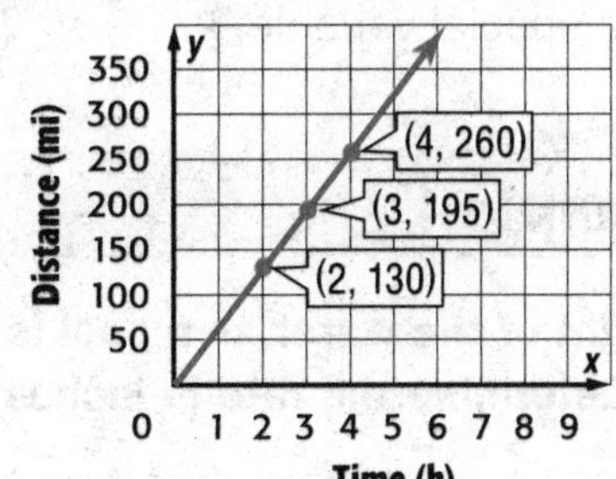

1. Fill in the blanks to find the constant ratio.

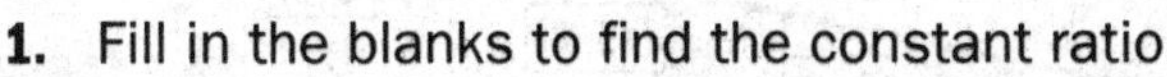

$$\frac{\text{distance traveled}}{\text{driving time}} = \frac{130}{2} = \frac{195}{\square} = \frac{\square}{4}$$

The constant ratio is ☐ miles per hour.

2. The constant rate of change, or slope, of the line is $\frac{\text{change in miles}}{\text{change in time}}$, which is equal to $\frac{195 - 130}{3 - 2}$ or ☐ miles per hour.

3. Write a sentence that compares the constant rate of change and the constant ratio.

____

Work Zone

Key Concept Direct Variation

Words A linear relationship is a direct variation when the ratio of y to x is a constant, k. We say y varies directly with x.

Symbols $\frac{y}{x} = k$ or $y = kx$, where $k \neq 0$

Example $y = 3x$

Model

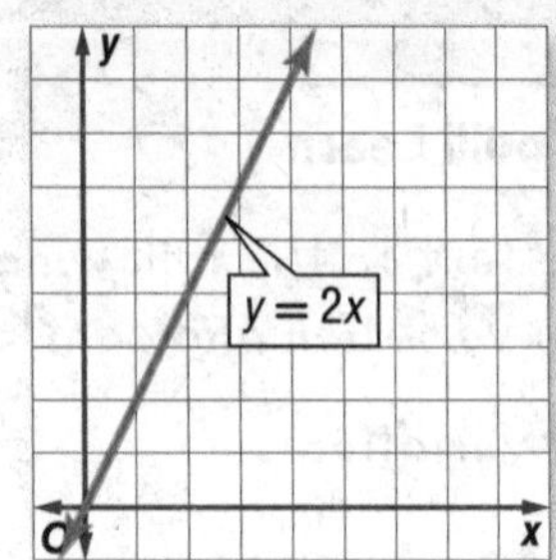

When two variable quantities have a constant ratio, their relationship is called a **direct variation**. The constant ratio is called the **constant of variation**. The constant of variation is also known as the **constant of proportionality**.

In a direct variation equation, the constant rate of change, or slope, is assigned a special variable, k.

Real World Example

Tutor

1. The height of the water as a pool is being filled is shown in the graph. Determine the rate in inches per minute.

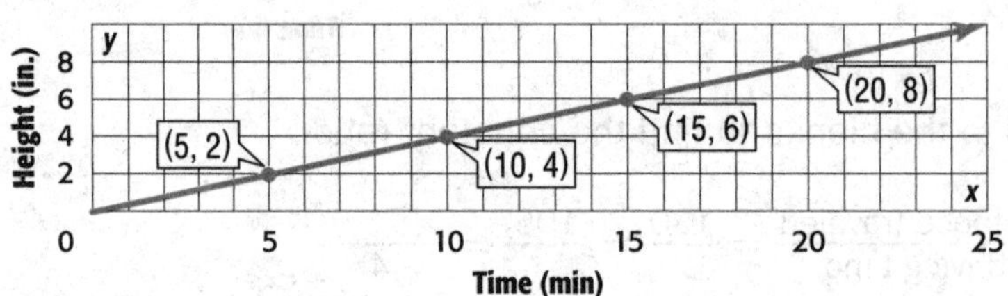

Since the graph of the data forms a line, the rate of change is constant. Use the graph to find the constant of proportionality.

$\frac{\text{height}}{\text{time}} \rightarrow \frac{2}{5}$ or $\frac{0.4}{1}$ $\quad \frac{4}{10}$ or $\frac{0.4}{1}$ $\quad \frac{6}{15}$ or $\frac{0.4}{1}$ $\quad \frac{8}{20}$ or $\frac{0.4}{1}$

The pool fills at a rate of 0.4 inch every minute.

Direct Variation
When a relationship varies directly, the graph of the function will always go through the origin, (0, 0). Also, the unit rate r is located at $(1, r)$.

Got It? Do this problem to find out.

a. Two minutes after a diver enters the water, he has descended 52 feet. After 5 minutes, he has descended 130 feet. At what rate is the scuba diver descending?

Show your work.

a. ______________

Example

2. The equation $y = 10x$ represents the amount of money y Julio earns for x hours of work. Identify the constant of proportionality. Explain what it represents in this situation.

$$y = kx$$
$$y = 10x$$

Compare the equation to $y = kx$, where k is the constant of proportionality.

The constant of proportionality is 10. So, Julio earns $10 for every hour that he works.

Got It? **Do this problem to find out.**

b. The distance y traveled in miles by the Chang family in x hours is represented by the equation $y = 55x$. Identify the constant of proportionality. Then explain what it represents.

b. ______

Determine Direct Variation

Not all situations with a constant rate of change are proportional relationships. Likewise, not all linear functions are direct variations.

Example

3. Pizzas cost $8 each plus a $3 delivery charge. Show the cost of 1, 2, 3, and 4 pizzas. Is there a direct variation?

Number of Pizzas	1	2	3	4
Cost ($)	$11	$19	$27	$35

$\frac{\text{cost}}{\text{number of pizzas}} \rightarrow \frac{11}{1}, \frac{19}{2}$ or 9.5, $\frac{27}{3}$ or 9, $\frac{35}{4}$ or 8.75

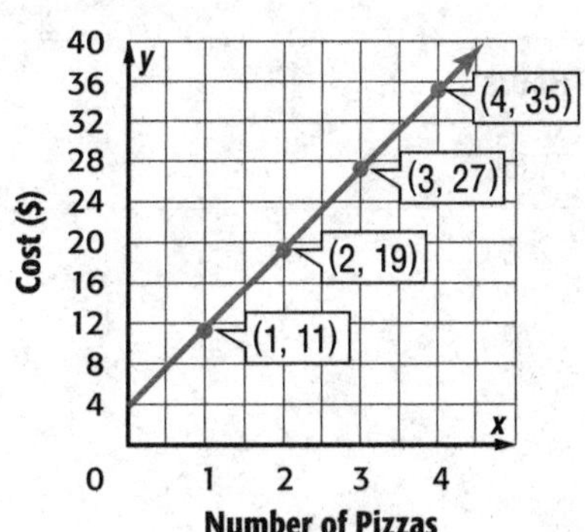

There is no constant ratio and the line does not go through the origin. So, there is no direct variation.

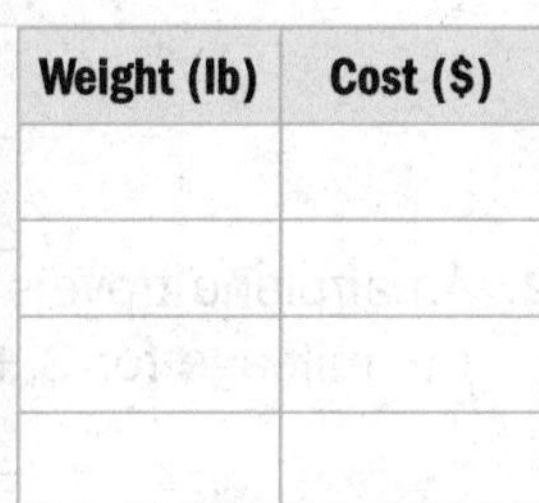

Weight (lb)	Cost ($)

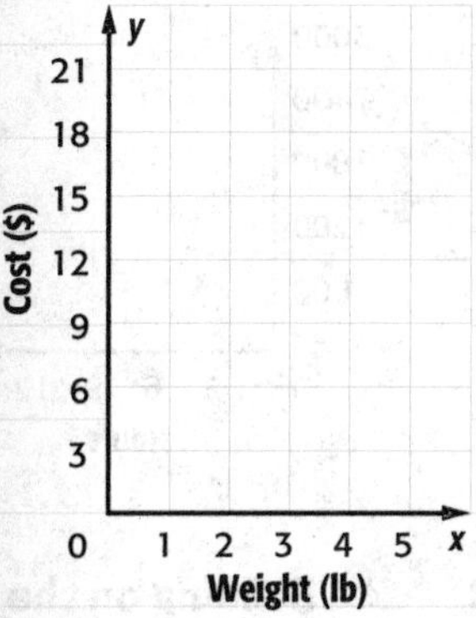

Got It? **Do this problem to find out.**

c. Two pounds of cheese cost $8.40. Show the cost of 1, 2, 3, and 4 pounds of cheese. Is there a direct variation? Explain.

c. ______

Example

4. Determine whether the linear relationship is a direct variation. If so, state the constant of proportionality.

Time, x	1	2	3	4
Wages ($), y	12	24	36	48

Compare the ratios to check for a common ratio.

$\frac{\text{wages}}{\text{time}} \rightarrow \frac{12}{1} \quad \frac{24}{2} \text{ or } \frac{12}{1} \quad \frac{36}{3} \text{ or } \frac{12}{1} \quad \frac{48}{4} \text{ or } \frac{12}{1}$

Since the ratios are the same, the relationship is a direct variation. The constant of proportionality is $\frac{12}{1}$.

Guided Practice

1. The number of cakes baked varies directly with the number of hours the caterers work. What is the ratio of cakes baked to hours worked? (Examples 1 and 2) ______

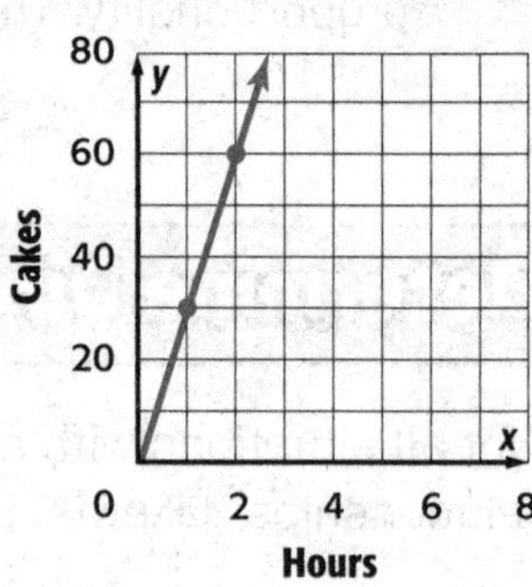

2. An airplane travels 780 miles in 4 hours. Make a table and graph to show the mileage for 2, 8, and 12 hours. Is there a direct variation? Explain.

(Examples 3 and 4) ______

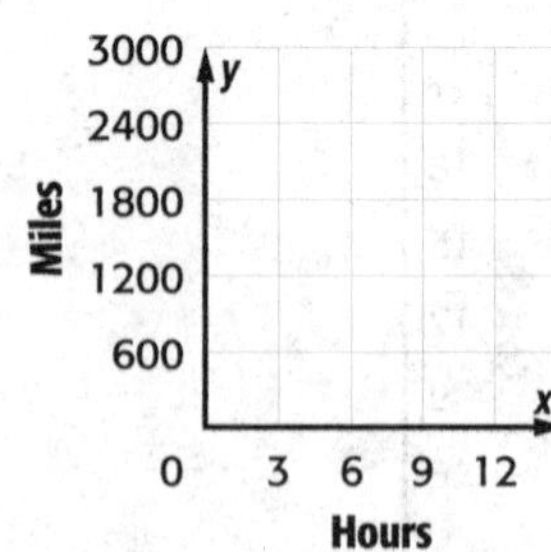

Hours			
Miles			

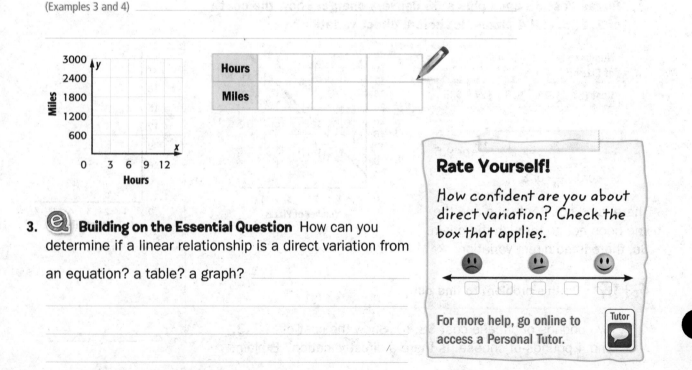

3. **Building on the Essential Question** How can you determine if a linear relationship is a direct variation from an equation? a table? a graph? ______

Rate Yourself!

How confident are you about direct variation? Check the box that applies.

For more help, go online to access a Personal Tutor.

Independent Practice

Go online for Step-by-Step Solutions 

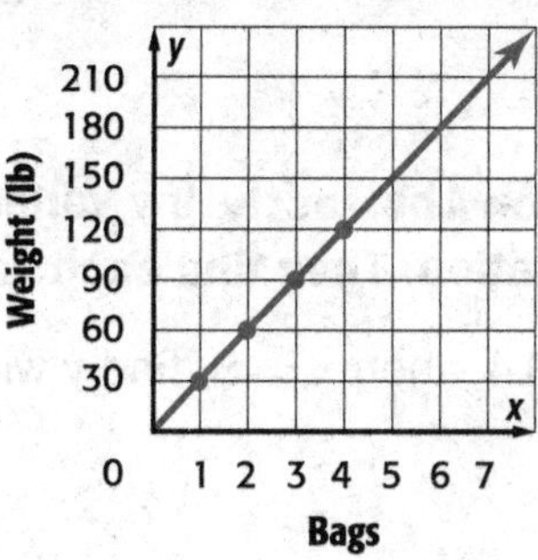

1. Veronica is mulching her front yard. The total weight of mulch varies directly with the number of bags of mulch.

   What is the rate of change? (Example 1) ______________

2. The Spanish club held a car wash to raise money. The equation $y = 5x$ represents the amount of money y club members made for washing x cars. Identify the constant of proportionality. Then explain what it represents in this situation. (Example 2) ______________

3. A technician charges $25 per hour plus $50 for a house call to repair home computers. Make a table and a graph to show the cost for 1, 2, 3, and 4 hours of home computer repair service. Is there a direct variation? (Example 3)

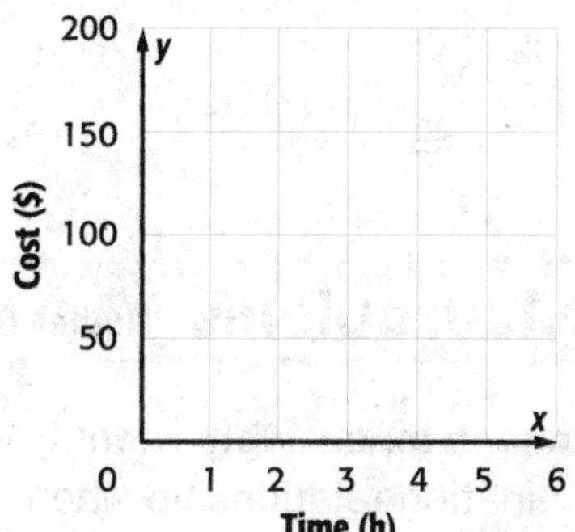

Time (h)				
Charge ($)				

Determine whether each linear relationship is a direct variation. If so, state the constant of proportionality. (Example 4)

4.

Pictures, x	3	4	5	6
Profit, y	24	32	40	48

5.

Minutes, x	185	235	275	325
Cost, y	60	115	140	180

6.

Year, x	5	10	15	20
Height, y	12.5	25	37.5	50

7.

Game, x	2	3	4	5
Points, y	4	5	7	11

8. At a 33-foot depth underwater, the pressure is 29.55 pounds per square inch (psi). At a depth of 66 feet, the pressure reaches 44.4 psi. At what rate is the pressure increasing? ____________

Reason Abstractly **If y varies directly with x, write an equation for the direct variation. Then find each value.**

9. If $y = 14$ when $x = 8$, find y when $x = 12$.

____

10. Find y when $x = 15$ if $y = 6$ when $x = 30$.

____

11. If $y = 6$ when $x = 24$, what is the value of x when $y = 7$?

____

12. Find x when $y = 14$, if $y = 7$ when $x = 8$.

____

H.O.T. Problems Higher Order Thinking

13. **Reason Inductively** Identify two additional values for x and y in a direct variation relationship where $y = 11$ when $x = 18$.

$x =$ ______ $y =$ ______ and $x =$ ______ $y =$ ______

14. **Persevere with Problems** Find y when $x = 14$ if y varies directly with x^2, and $y = 72$ when $x = 6$. ____________

Georgia Test Practice

15. Which of the following relationships represent a direct variation?

Ⓐ

Hours, x	1	2	3	4
Wages ($), y	10	22	36	50

Ⓑ

Hours, x	1	2	3	4
Wages ($), y	10	25	30	50

Ⓒ

Hours, x	1	2	3	4
Wages ($), y	10	20	30	40

Ⓓ

Hours, x	1	2	3	4
Wages ($), y	6	16	30	48

Extra Practice

16. The money Shelley earns varies directly with the number of dogs she walks. How much does Shelley earn for each dog she walks?

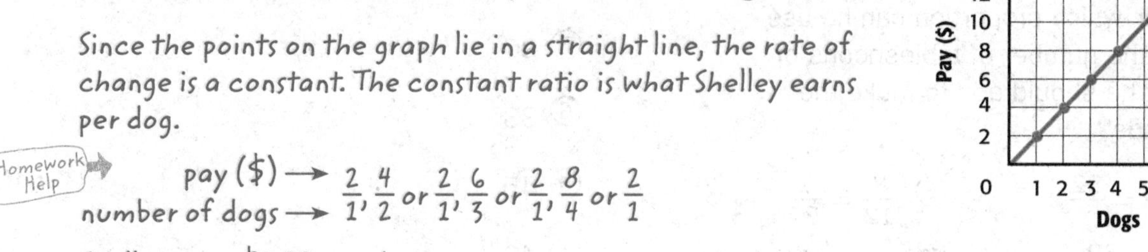

Since the points on the graph lie in a straight line, the rate of change is a constant. The constant ratio is what Shelley earns per dog.
Homework Help
pay ($) → $\frac{2}{1}, \frac{4}{2}$ or $\frac{2}{1}, \frac{6}{3}$ or $\frac{2}{1}, \frac{8}{4}$ or $\frac{2}{1}$
number of dogs →
Shelley earn $2.00 per dog.

17. A cake recipe requires $3\frac{1}{4}$ cups of flour for 13 servings and $4\frac{1}{2}$ cups of flour for 18 servings. How much flour is required to make a cake that serves 28? ______

Determine whether each linear relationship is a direct variation. If so, state the constant of variation.

18.

Age, x	11	13	15	19
Grade, y	5	7	9	11

______

19.

Price, x	20	25	30	35
Tax, y	4	5	6	7

______

20. CCGPS **Multiple Representations** Robert is in charge of the community swimming pool. Each spring he drains it in order to clean it. Then he refills the pool, which holds 120,000 gallons of water. Robert fills the pool at a rate of 10 gallons each minute.

a. Words What is the rate at which Robert will fill the pool? Is it constant? ______

b. Graph Graph the relationship on the grid shown.

c. Algebra Write an equation for the direct variation.

______

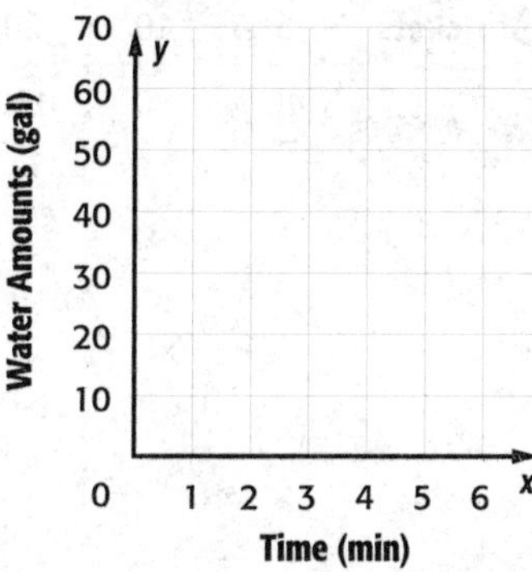

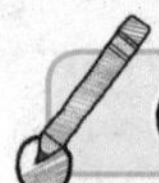

Georgia Test Practice

21. To make lemonade, Andy adds 8 tablespoons of sugar for every 12 ounces of water. If he uses 32 ounces of water, which proportion can he use to find the number of tablespoons of sugar x he should add to make the lemonade?

Ⓐ $\frac{8}{12} = \frac{32}{x}$

Ⓑ $\frac{8}{x} = \frac{32}{12}$

Ⓒ $\frac{8}{12} = \frac{x}{32}$

Ⓓ $\frac{x}{12} = \frac{8}{32}$

22. Anjuli read 22 pages during a 30-minute study hall. At this rate, how many pages would she read in 45 minutes?

Ⓕ 30

Ⓖ 33

Ⓗ 45

Ⓘ 48

23. Short Response Determine whether the linear function is a direct variation. If so, state the constant of proportionality. ______________

Hours, x	3	5	7	9
Miles, y	108	180	252	324

Common Core Review

24. The table below shows the number of sheets of paper in various numbers of packages. Graph the data. MCC6.RP.3b

Number of Packages	1	2	3	4
Number of Sheets	50	100	150	200

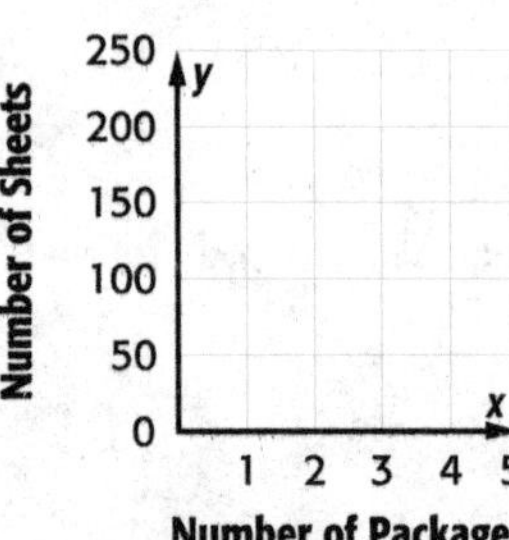

25. The cost of various numbers of tickets to a festival is shown in the table. Graph the data. Then find the slope of the line. Explain what the slope represents. MCC6.RP.3b

Number of Tickets	5	10	20	25
Cost ($)	40	80	160	200

____

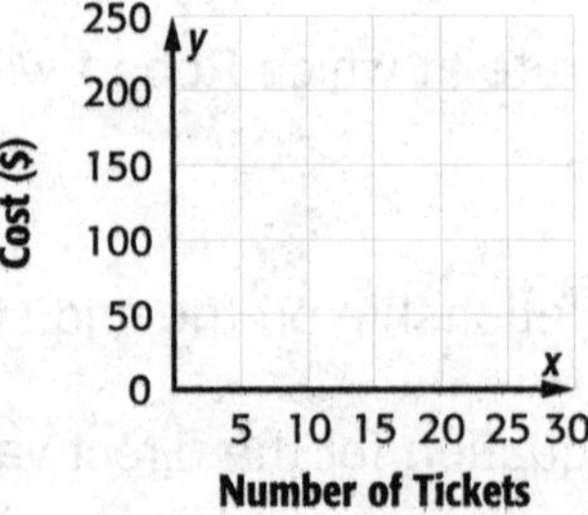

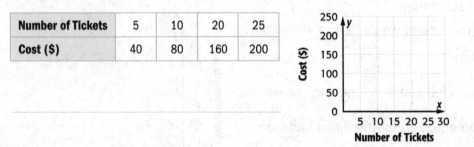

21ST CENTURY CAREER in Engineering

Biomechanical Engineering

Did you know that more than 700 pounds of force are exerted on a 140-pound long-jumper during the landing? Biomechanical engineers understand how forces travel through the shoe to an athlete's foot and how the shoes can help reduce the impact of those forces on the legs. If you are curious about how engineering can be applied to the human body, a career in biomechanical engineering might be a great fit for you.

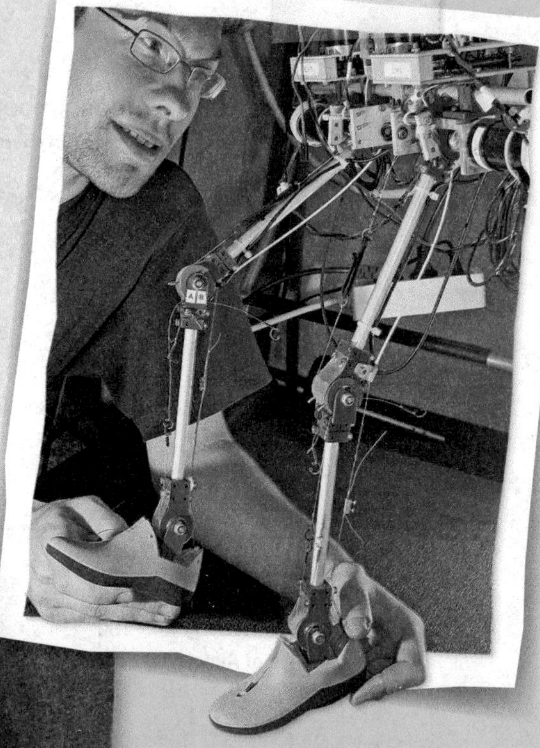

Explore college and careers at ccr.mcgraw-hill.com

Is This the Career for You?

Are you interested in a career as a biomechanical engineer? Take some of the following courses in high school.

- Biology
- Calculus
- Physics
- Trigonometry

Find out how math relates to a career in Biomechanical Engineering.

Start Off on the Right Foot

Use the information in the graph to solve each problem.

1. Find the constant rate of change for the data shown in the graph below Exercise 2. Interpret its meaning.

2. Is there a proportional relationship between the weight of an athlete and the forces that are generated from running? Explain your reasoning.

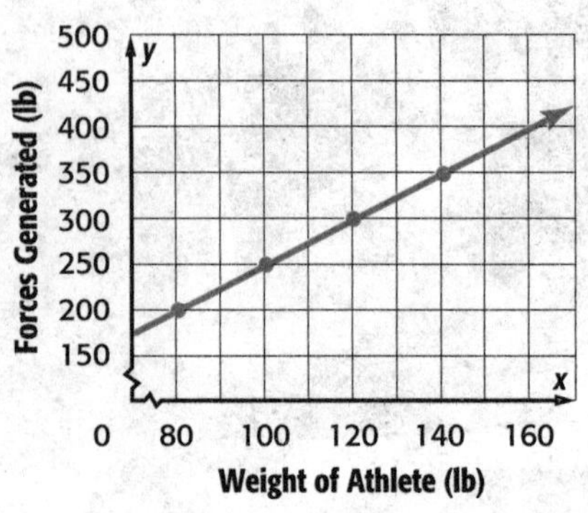

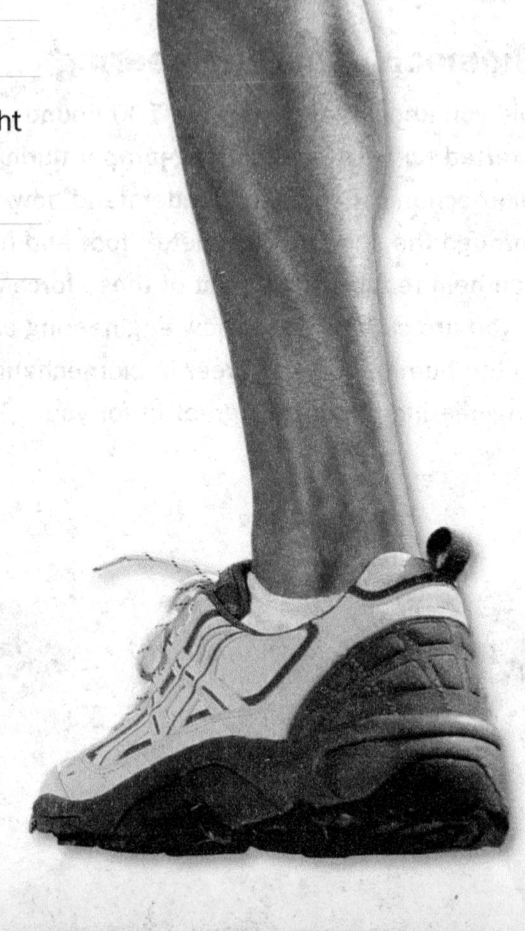

Career Project

It's time to update your career portfolio! Use the Internet or another source to research the fields of biomechanical engineering, biomedical engineering, and mechanical engineering. Write a brief summary comparing and contrasting the fields. Describe how they are all related.

What subject in school is the most important to you? How would you use that subject in this career?

Chapter Review

Vocabulary Check

Complete each sentence using the vocabulary list at the beginning of the chapter. Then circle the word that completes the sentence in the word search.

1. A ____________ is a ratio that compares two quantities with different kinds of units.

2. A rate that has a denominator of 1 unit is called a ____________ rate.

3. A pair of numbers used to locate a point in the coordinate plane is an ____________ pair.

4. (0, 0) represents the ____________.

5. A ____________ fraction has a fraction in the numerator, denominator, or both.

6. A ____________ variation is the relationship between two variable quantities with a constant ratio.

7. The ____________ is the rate of change between any two points on a line.

8. One of the four regions into which a coordinate plane is separated is called a ____________.

9. A ____________ is an equation stating that two ratios or rates are equal.

10. The rate of ____________ describes how one quantity changes in relation to another.

11. ____________ analysis is the process of including units of measurement when you compute.

Key Concept Check

Use Your FOLDABLES®

Use your Foldable to help review the chapter.

Tab 1

Table

Graph

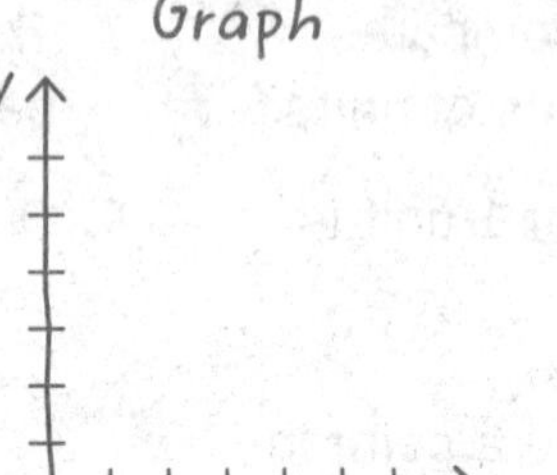

Equation

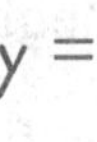

Table

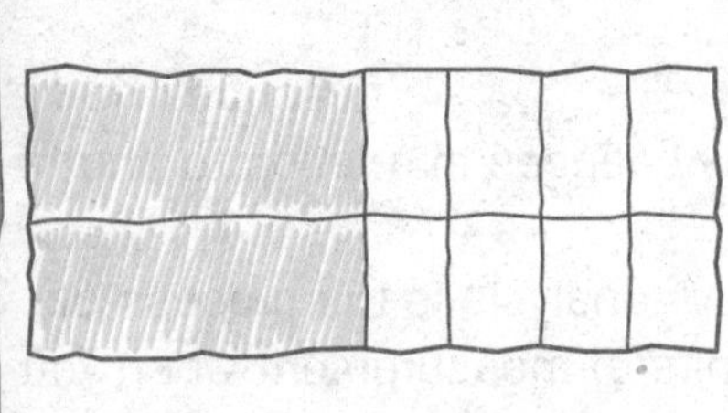

Graph

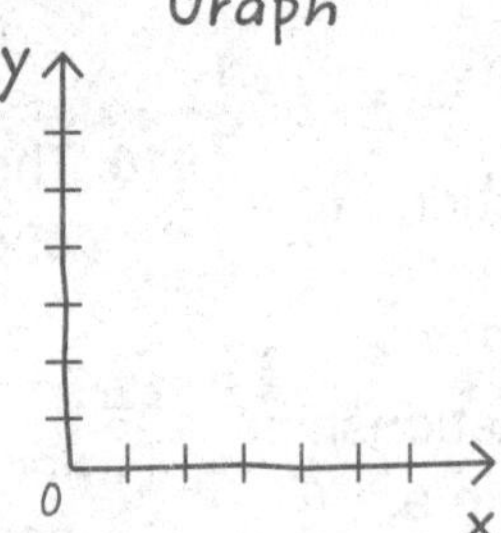

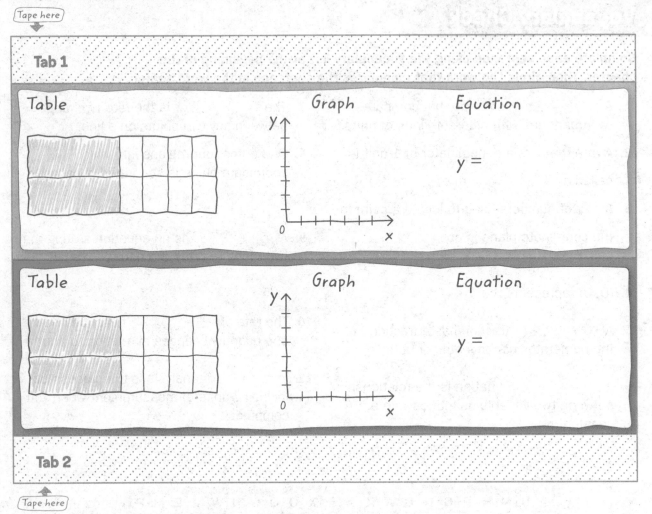

Equation

y =

Tab 2

Got it?

Identify the Correct Choice Write the correct term or number to complete each sentence.

1. When a rate is simplified so that it has a (numerator, denominator) of 1 unit, it is called a unit rate.

2. If Dinah can skate $\frac{1}{2}$ lap in 15 seconds, she can skate 1 lap in (7.5, 30) seconds.

3. Slope is the ratio of (horizontal change to vertical change, vertical change to horizontal change).

4. When two quantities have a constant ratio, their relationship is called a (direct, linear) variation.

Problem Solving

1. Which bottle of shampoo shown at the right costs less per ounce? (Lesson 1)

Bottle	Price
12 oz	$2.59
16 oz	$3.19

2. An airplane is traveling at an average speed of 245 meters per second. How many kilometers per second is the plane traveling? (Lesson 3)

3. An Internet company charges $30 a month. There is also a $30 installation fee. Is the number of months you can have Internet proportional to the total cost? Explain. (Lesson 4)

4. Damon runs 8 meters in 1 second, 16 meters in 2 seconds, 24 meters in 3 seconds, and 32 meters in 4 seconds. Determine whether Damon's distance is proportional to the number of seconds he runs by graphing on the coordinate grid at the right. Explain your reasoning. (Lesson 5)

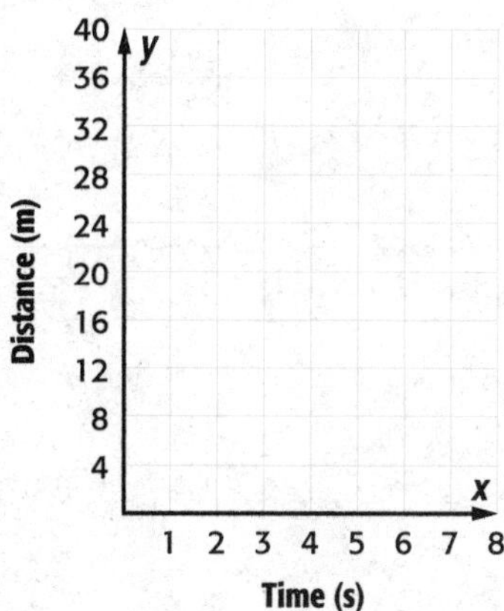

5. Suppose 3 televisions weigh 240.6 pounds. How much do 9 of the same televisions weigh? (Lesson 6)

6. The table and the graph show the amount of rainfall for 2 different days. Which day had a greater rate of change? Explain. (Lesson 8)

Saturday	
Time (h)	Rainfall (in.)
1	1.5
2	3
3	4.5
4	6

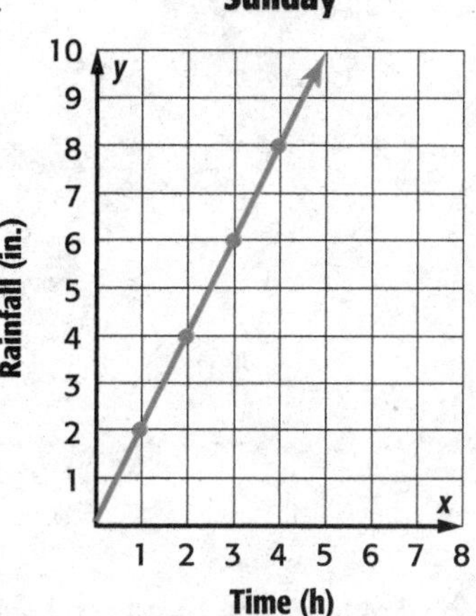

Reflect

Answering the Essential Question

Use what you learned about ratios and proportional reasoning to complete the graphic organizer.

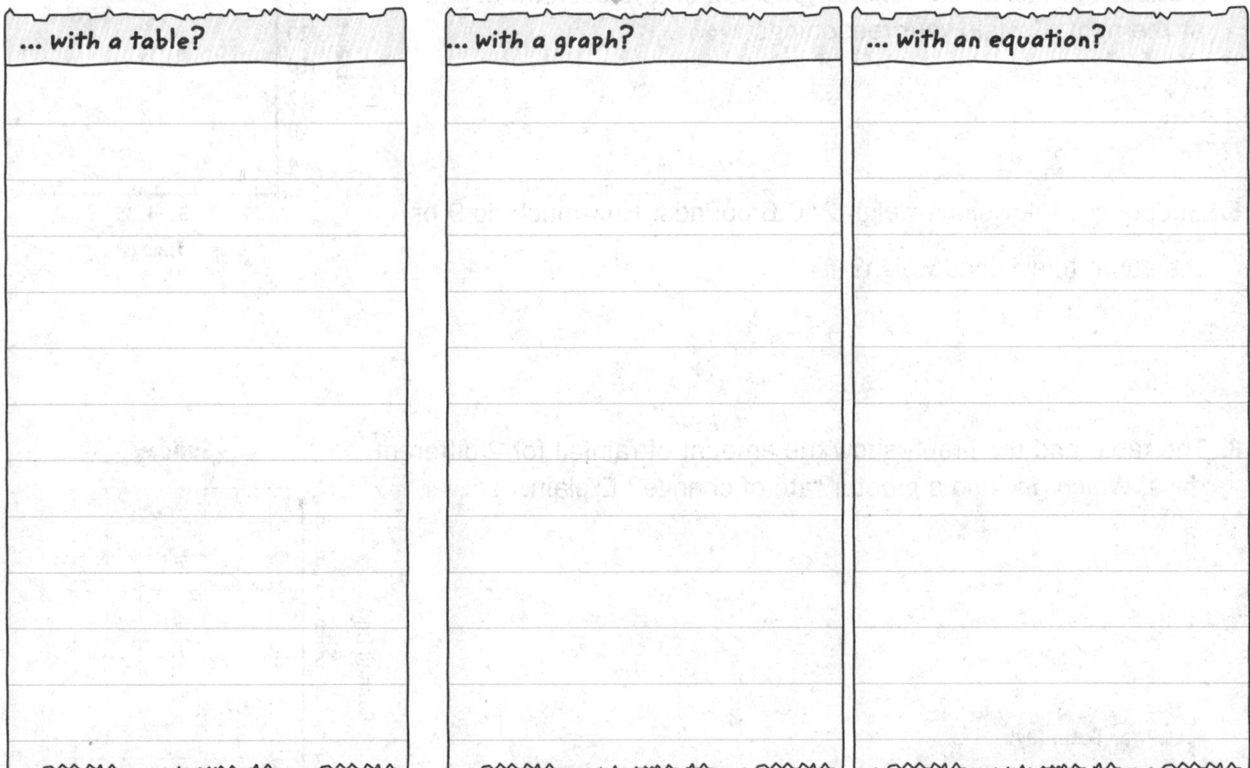
Essential Question
HOW can you show that two objects are proportional...
... with a table?
... with a graph?
... with an equation?

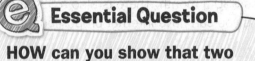

Answer the Essential Question. HOW can you show that two objects are proportional?

Chapter 6

Percents

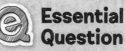

Essential Question

HOW can percent help you understand situations involving money?

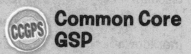

Common Core GSP

Content Standards
MCC7.RP.2, MCC7.RP.2c, MCC7.RP.3, MCC7.EE.2, MCC7.EE.3

Mathematical Practices
1, 2, 3, 4, 5, 6

Math in the Real World

Biking The class goal for a biking fundraiser was to make $300 by the end of the pledge week. Halfway through the week, the students had made $210. Fill in the graph below to show the percent of the goal achieved.

FOLDABLES® Study Organizer

Cut out the correct Foldable from the FL pages in the back of this book.

Place your Foldable on the Key Concept page toward the end of this chapter.

Use the Foldable throughout this chapter to help you learn about percents.

What Tools Do You Need?

Vocabulary

discount	percent error	principal	selling price
gratuity	percent of change	sales tax	simple interest
markdown	percent of decrease	scale drawing	tip
markup	percent of increase	scale model	
percent equation	percent proportion	scale	

Study Skill: Studying Math

Draw a Picture Drawing a picture can help you better understand numbers. For example, a *number map* shows how numbers are related to each other.

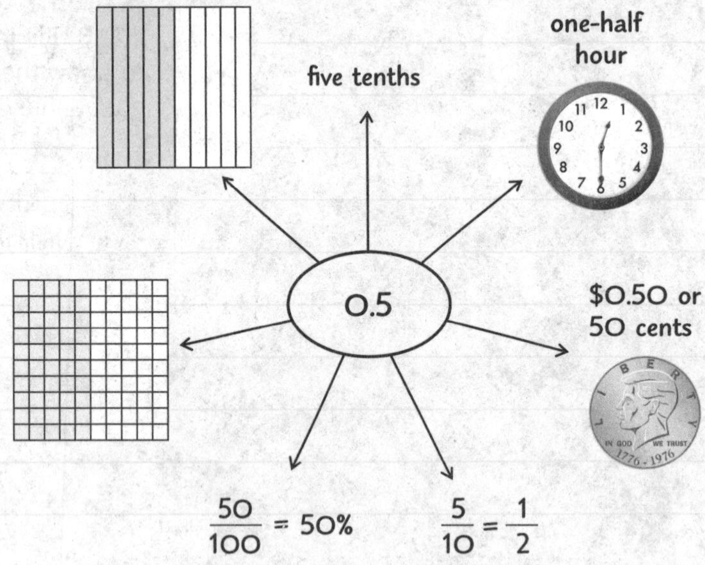

In the space below, make a number map for 0.75.

When Will You Use This?

Your Turn! **You will solve this problem in the chapter.**

Try the Quick Check below.
Or, take the Online Readiness Quiz.

Quick Review

Common Core Review MCC6.NS.3, MCC6.RP.3c

Example 1

Evaluate 240 × 0.03 × 5.

240 × 0.03 × 5
= 7.2 × 5 Multiply 240 by 0.03.
= 36 Simplify.

Example 2

Write 0.35 as a percent.

0.35 = 35% Move the decimal point two places to the right and add the percent symbol.

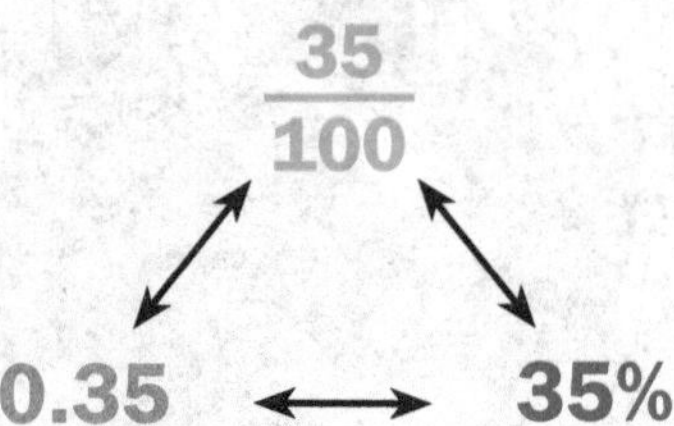

Quick Check

Multiply Decimals Find each product.

1. 300 × 0.02 × 8 = ______

2. 85 × 0.25 × 3 = ______

3. Suppose Nicole saves $2.50 every day. How much money will she have in 4 weeks? ______

Decimals and Percents Write each decimal as a percent.

4. 0.675 = ______

5. 0.725 = ______

6. 0.95 = ______

7. Approximately 0.92 of a watermelon is water. What percent represents this decimal? ______

Which problems did you answer correctly in the Quick Check? Shade those exercise numbers below.

1 2 3 4  5  6 7

Inquiry Lab
Percent Diagrams

Inquiry HOW are percent diagrams used to solve real-world problems?

Content Standards
MCC7.RP.3, MCC7.EE.3

Mathematical Practices
1, 3, 4

Musical Instruments One fourth of the students in Mrs. Singh's music class chose a guitar as their favorite musical instrument. There are 24 students in Mrs. Singh's music class. How many students chose a guitar as their favorite musical instrument?

What do you know? ______________________________

____

____

What do you need to find? ______________________________

____

Investigation 1

Bar diagrams can be used to represent a part of a whole as a fraction and as a percent.

Step 1 The bar diagram represents 100% of the class. Shade the bar diagram to show that $\frac{1}{4}$ or ☐% of the class chose guitar as their favorite instrument.

				100%

|--- ☐% ---|

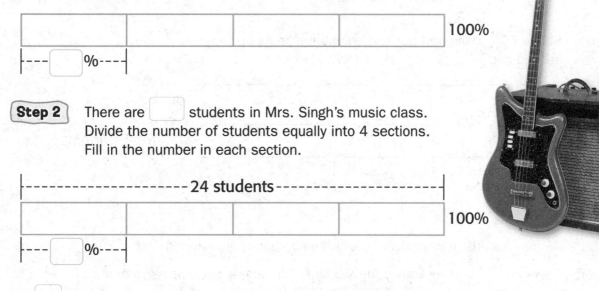

Step 2 There are ☐ students in Mrs. Singh's music class. Divide the number of students equally into 4 sections. Fill in the number in each section.

|----------------------24 students----------------------|

				100%

|--- ☐% ---|

So, ☐ students chose a guitar as their favorite musical instrument.

Investigation 2

Music There are 500 seventh-grade students at Heritage Middle School. Sixty percent of them play a musical instrument. How many seventh-grade students play a musical instrument?

Step 1 Supply the missing information for the second bar.

percent | | 100%

students | | ☐ total students

Step 2 Divide each bar into ten equal parts. Write 10% in each section of the first bar.

percent | **10%** | | 100%

students | | | ☐ total students

Step 3 Determine what number to write in each section of the second bar. Fill in that number.

percent | **10%** | | 100%

students | | | ☐ total students

Step 4 Shade 60% of the first bar and an equal amount on the second bar.

percent | **10%** | | 100%

students | | | ☐ total students

|---------- ☐ ----------|

Since ☐ % corresponds to 6 sections, count the number of students in 6 sections. There are ☐ seventh-grade students who play a musical instrument.

Work with a partner. Use bar diagrams to solve each problem.

1. The seventh-grade class at Fort Couch Middle School has a goal of selling 300 tickets to the annual student versus teacher basketball game. The eighth-grade class has a goal of selling 400 tickets.

   a. By the end of the first week, the eighth-grade students sold 30% of their goal. How many tickets has the eighth grade sold? ______

   percent [   ] 100%

   tickets [   ] [ ]

   b. The seventh grade sold 60% of their goal. How many tickets do the students still need to sell? Explain. ______

   ______ [   ] 100%

   ______ [   ] [ ]

2. **Justify Conclusions** The graph shows the results of a survey asking 500 teens about their allowances. How many teens did *not* receive between \$10 and \$20? Explain.

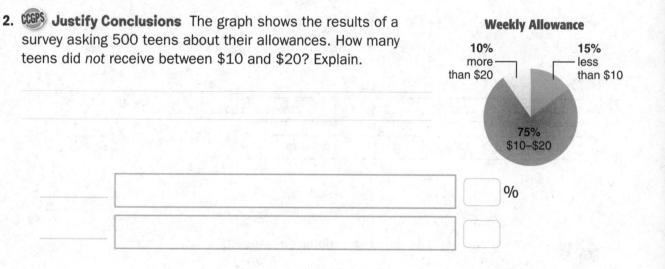

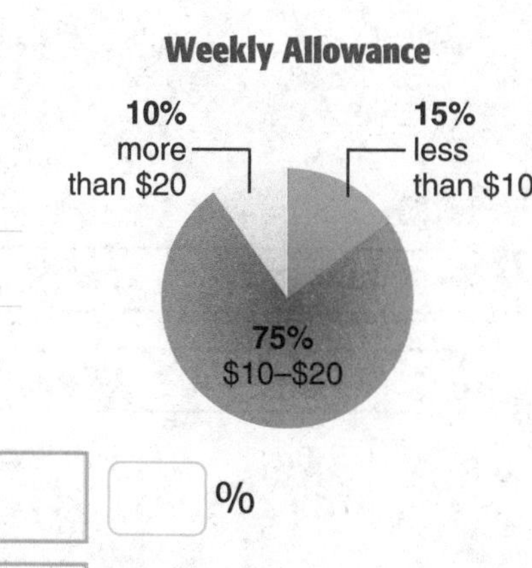

______ [   ] [ ] %

______ [   ] [ ]

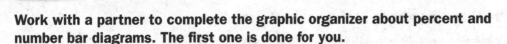

Work with a partner to complete the graphic organizer about percent and number bar diagrams. The first one is done for you.

	Percent	Rate per 100	Whole	Part
	30%	$\frac{30}{100}$	150	45
3.	40%	$\frac{40}{100}$	150	
4.	50%	$\frac{50}{100}$	150	

5. Analyze the table above. Do you see any patterns?

CCGPS **Model with Mathematics** Write a real-world problem for the bar diagrams shown. Then solve your problem.

6.

10%	10%	10%	10%	10%	10%	10%	10%	10%	10%	100%
25	25	25	25	25	25	25	25	25	25	250

7.

25%	25%	25%	25%	100%
15	15	15	15	60

8. Inquiry HOW are percent diagrams used to solve real-world problems?

Lesson 1

Percent of a Number

What You'll Learn

Scan the rest of the lesson. List two headings you would use to make an outline of the lesson.

-
-

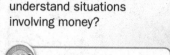

Essential Question

HOW can percent help you understand situations involving money?

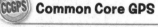

Common Core GPS

Content Standards
MCC7.RP.3, MCC7.EE.3

Mathematical Practices
1, 3, 4

Real-World Link

Pets Some students are collecting money for a local pet shelter. The model shows that they have raised 60% of their $2,000 goal or $1,200.

	Percent	Decimal	Fractions
$2,000	100%	1	$\frac{5}{5}$ or 1
$1,600	80%		
$1,200	60%		
$800	40%		
$400	20%		$\frac{1}{5}$
$0	0%	0	0

1. Fill in the decimal and fractional equivalents for each of the percents shown in the model.

2. Use the model to write two multiplication sentences that are equivalent to 60% of 2,000 = 1,200.

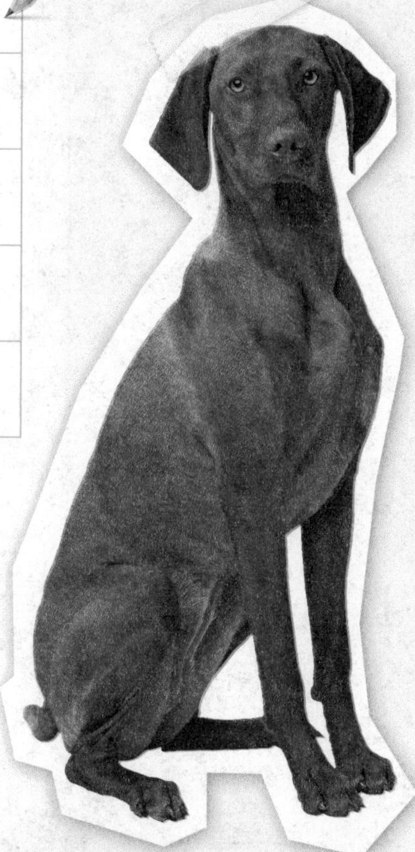

Work Zone

Find the Percent of a Number

To find the percent of a number such as 60% of 2,000, you can use either of the following methods.

- Write the percent as a fraction and then multiply.
- Write the percent as a decimal and then multiply.

Examples

Percent as a Rate
Find a percent of a quantity as a rate per 100.
For example, 5% of a quantity means $\frac{5}{100}$ times the quantity.

1. Find 5% of 300 by writing the percent as a fraction.

Write 5% as $\frac{5}{100}$ or $\frac{1}{20}$. Then find $\frac{1}{20}$ of 300.

$\frac{1}{20}$ of $300 = \frac{1}{20} \times 300$ Write a multiplication expression.

$= \frac{1}{\cancel{20}_1} \times \frac{\cancel{300}^{15}}{1}$ Write 300 as $\frac{300}{1}$. Divide out common factors.

$= \frac{1 \times 15}{1 \times 1}$ Multiply numerators and denominators.

$= \frac{15}{1}$ or 15 Simplify.

So, 5% of 300 is 15.

2. Find 25% of 180 by writing the percent as a decimal.

Write 25% as 0.25. Then multiply 0.25 and 180.

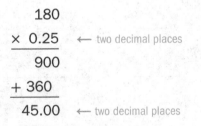

$$\begin{array}{r} 180 \\ \times\ 0.25 \\ \hline 900 \\ +\ 360 \\ \hline 45.00 \end{array}$$

× 0.25 ← two decimal places

45.00 ← two decimal places

So, 25% of 180 is 45.

Show your work.

Got It? Do these problems to find out.

Find the percent of each number.

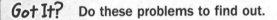

a. 40% of 70 **b.** 15% of 100

c. 55% of 160 **d.** 75% of 280

a. ______

b. ______

c. ______

d. ______

Use Percents Greater Than 100%

Percents that are greater than 100% can be written as improper fractions, mixed numbers, or decimals greater than 1.

$$150\% = \frac{150}{100} = \frac{3}{2} = 1\frac{1}{2} = 1.5$$

Examples

3. Find 120% of 75 by writing the percent as a fraction.

Write 120% as $\frac{120}{100}$ or $\frac{6}{5}$. Then find $\frac{6}{5}$ of 75.

$\frac{6}{5}$ of $75 = \frac{6}{5} \times 75$ — Write a multiplication expression.

$= \frac{6}{\cancel{5}_1} \times \frac{\cancel{75}^{15}}{1}$ — Write 75 as $\frac{75}{1}$. Divide out common factors.

$= \frac{6 \times 15}{1 \times 1}$ — Multiply numerators and denominators.

$= \frac{90}{1}$ or 90 — Simplify.

So, 120% of 75 is 90.

Alternate Method
You can solve Example 3 using a decimal, and you can solve Example 4 using a fraction.

4. Find 150% of 28 by writing the percent as a decimal.

Write 150% as 1.5. Then find 1.5 of 28.

```
   28
 × 1.5   ← one decimal place
  140
 + 28
 42.0    ← one decimal place
```

So, 150% of 28 is 42.

Got It? Do these problems to find out.

Show your work.

Find each number.

e. 150% of 20 **f.** 160% of 35

e. ______

f. ______

Example

5. Refer to the graph. If 275 students took the survey, how many can be expected to have 3 televisions each in their houses?

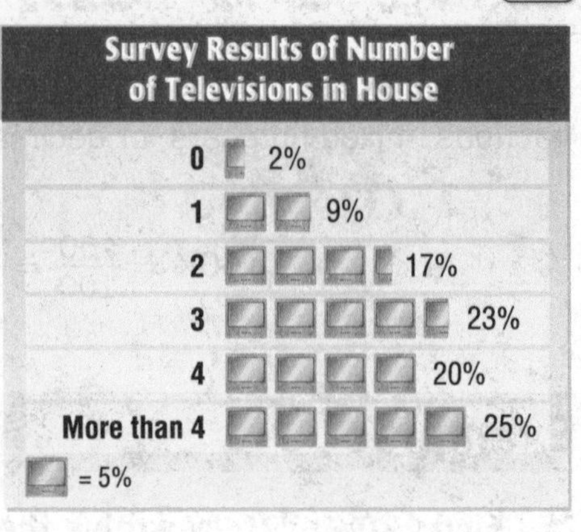

Write the percent as a decimal. Then multiply.

$$23\% \text{ of } 275 = 23\% \times 275$$
$$= 0.23 \times 275$$
$$= 63.25$$

So, about 63 students can be expected to have 3 televisions each.

Commission
Refer to Exercise g. It is common for people who work in the sales industry to earn a commission on the products they sell.

Got It? **Do this problem to find out.**

Show your work.

g. Mr. Sudimack earned a 4% commission on the sale of a hot tub that cost $3,755. How much did he earn?

g. ________

Guided Practice

Find each number. Round to the nearest tenth if necessary. (Examples 1–4)

1. 8% of 50 = ________

2. 95% of 40 = ________

3. 110% of 70 = ________

4. Mackenzie wants to buy a backpack that costs $50. If the tax rate is 6.5%, how much tax will she pay? (Example 5)

____

5. **Building on the Essential Question** Give an example of a real-world situation in which you would find the percent of a number. ________

Rate Yourself!

Are you ready to move on? Shade the section that applies.

I have a few questions. | I'm ready to move on. | I have a lot of questions.

For more help, go online to access a Personal Tutor.

Name ______________________ My Homework ______________________

Independent Practice

Go online for Step-by-Step Solutions 

Find each number. Round to the nearest tenth if necessary. (Examples 1–4)

1. 65% of 186 = ______

Show your work.

2. 45% of \$432 = ______

3. 23% of \$640 = ______

4. 130% of 20 = ______

5. 175% of 10 = ______

6. 150% of 128 = ______

7. 32% of 4 = ______

8. 5.4% of 65 = ______

9. 23.5% of 128 = ______

10. Suppose there are 20 questions on a multiple-choice test. If 25% of the answers are choice B, how many of the answers are *not* choice B?

(Example 5) ______________________

11. CCGPS **Model with Mathematics** Refer to the graphic novel frame below. Find the dollar amount of the group discount each student would receive at each park.

____

12. In addition to her salary, Ms. Lopez earns a 3% *commission,* or fee paid based on a percent of her sales, on every vacation package that she sells. One day, she sold the three vacation packages shown. Fill in the table for each packages' commission. What was her total commission?

Package	Sale Price	Commission
#1	$2,375	
#2	$3,950	
#3	$1,725	

Copy and Solve For Exercises 13–21, find each number. Round to the nearest hundredth. Show your work on a separate piece of paper.

13. $\frac{4}{5}$% of 500

14. $5\frac{1}{2}$% of 60

15. $20\frac{1}{4}$% of 3

16. 1,000% of 99

17. 520% of 100

18. 0.15% of 250

19. 200% of 79

20. 0.3% of 80

21. 0.28% of 50

H.O.T. Problems Higher Order Thinking

22. CCGPS **Persevere with Problems** Suppose you add 10% of a number to the number, and then you subtract 10% of the total. Is the result *greater than, less than,* or *equal to* the original number? Explain your reasoning.

23. CCGPS **Reason Inductively** When is it easiest to find the percent of a number using a fraction? using a decimal?

Georgia Test Practice

24. Marcos earned $300 mowing lawns this month. Of his earnings, he plans to spend 18% repairing lawn equipment, put 20% in his savings, and use 35% for camp fees. He will spend the rest. How much will Marcos have left to spend?

Ⓐ $27.00

Ⓑ $55.00

Ⓒ $81.00

Ⓓ $100.00

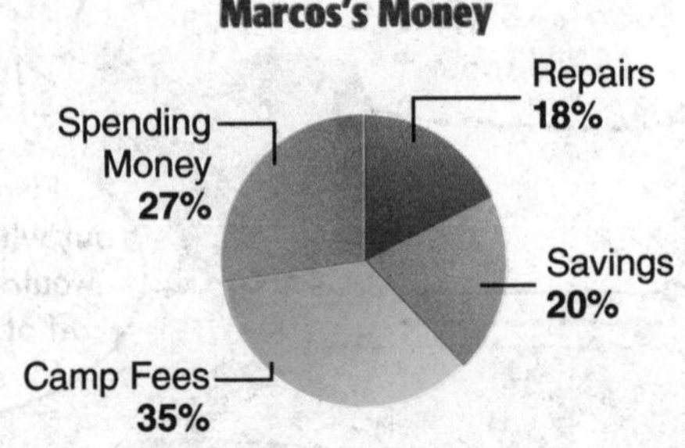

Name ______________________ My Homework ______________________

Extra Practice

Find each number. Round to the nearest tenth if necessary.

25. 54% of 85 = 45.9

Homework Help

$0.54 \times 85 = 45.9$

26. 12% of \$230 = \$27.60

$\frac{12}{100} \times 230 = \frac{3}{25} \times 230$

$= \frac{3}{5} \times 46$

$= \frac{138}{5}$ or 27.6

27. 98% of 15 = ______

28. 250% of 25 = ______

29. 108% of \$50 = ______

30. 75.2% of 130 = ______

31. 0.5% of 60 = ______

32. 2.4% of 20 = ______

33. 7.5% of 30 = ______

34. In a recent year, 17.7% of households watched the finals of a popular reality series. There are 110.2 million households in the United States. How many households watched the finals?

______

35. A family pays \$19 each month for Internet access. Next month, the cost will increase by 5% because of an equipment fee. After this increase, what will be the cost for the Internet access?

______

36. CCGPS **Persevere with Problems** 250 people were asked to name their favorite fruit.

a. Of those surveyed, how many people prefer peaches?

______

Favorite Fruit	
Berries	44%
Peaches	32%
Cherries	24%

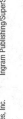

b. Which type of fruit did more than 100 people prefer?

______

Georgia Test Practice

37. **Short Response** Tanner has 200 baseball cards. Of those, 42% are in mint condition. How many of the cards are in mint condition? ____________

____

38. The table shows the results of a survey of 200 movie rental customers.

Favorite Type of Movie	Percent of Customers
Comedy	15
Mystery	10
Horror	46
Science Fiction	29

How many customers prefer horror movies?

Ⓐ 20
Ⓑ 30
Ⓒ 46
Ⓓ 92

39. The graph shows the Ramirez family budget. Their budget is based on a monthly income of $3,000.

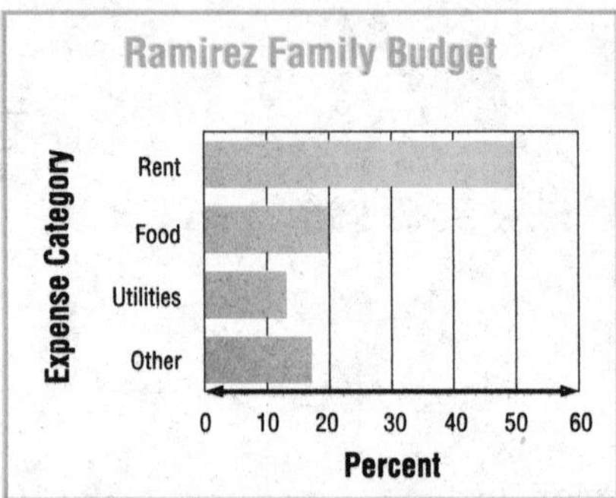

Which of the following is *true*?

Ⓕ The family budgeted $1,000 for rent.
Ⓖ The family budgeted $600 for food.
Ⓗ The family budgeted $100 more for utilities than for other expenses.
Ⓘ The family budgeted $900 more for food than for rent.

Common Core Review

Multiply. MCC6.NS.3

40. $1.7 \times 54 =$ ________

41. $1.5 \times 3.65 =$ ________

42. $49.6 \times 2.7 =$ ________

43. Trent spent 50 minutes at the neighbor's house. He spent $\frac{2}{5}$ of the time swimming. How many minutes did Trent spend swimming? MCC5.NF.4 ____________

50 min

____

44. There are 240 seventh-graders at Yorktown Middle School. Two-thirds of the students participate in after-school activities. How many students participate in after-school activities? MCC5.NF.4

____

Percent and Estimation

What You'll Learn

Scan the rest of the lesson. List two headings you would use to make an outline of the lesson.

- __________
- __________

Essential Question

HOW can percent help you understand situations involving money?

Common Core GPS

Content Standards
MCC7.RP.3, MCC7.EE.3

Mathematical Practices
1, 3, 4, 5

Real-World Link

Music Suppose 200 people are surveyed to find out how they learned to play an instrument. The results are shown in the table below.

Type of Teaching	Actual Percent	Estimated Percent	Fraction
Private Lessons	42%	40%	$\frac{2}{5}$
Lessons at School	32%		
Self-Taught	26%		

1. Estimate each percent. Choose an estimate that can be represented by a fraction that is easy to use. Then, write each estimated percent as a fraction in simplest form.

2. About how many people took lessons at school?

3. Sarah estimates the percent of people who taught themselves to play an instrument as 25%, and then she found $\frac{1}{4}$ of 200. Would her answer be less than or greater than the actual number of people who were self taught? Explain.

Work Zone

Estimate the Percent of a Number

Sometimes an exact answer is not needed when using percents. One way to estimate the percent of a number is to use a fraction.

Another method for estimating the percent of a number is first to find 10% of the number and then multiply.

$$70\% = 7 \cdot 10\%$$

So, 70% equals 7 times 10% of a number.

Examples

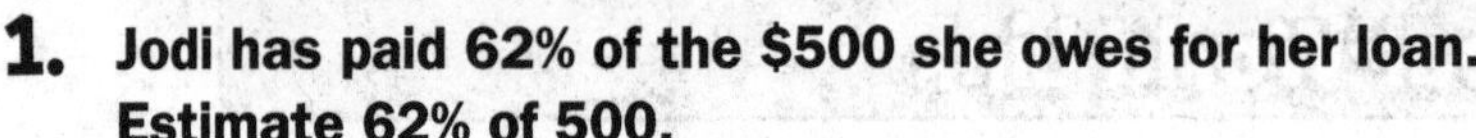

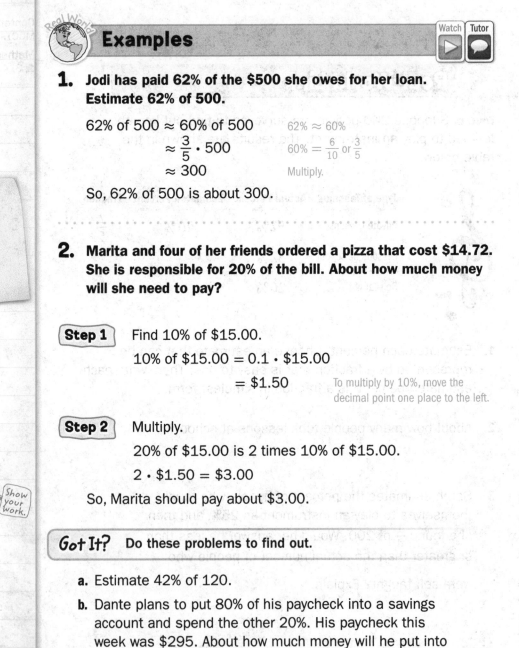

1. Jodi has paid 62% of the $500 she owes for her loan. Estimate 62% of 500.

$62\% \text{ of } 500 \approx 60\% \text{ of } 500$	$62\% \approx 60\%$
$\approx \frac{3}{5} \cdot 500$	$60\% = \frac{6}{10} \text{ or } \frac{3}{5}$
≈ 300	Multiply.

So, 62% of 500 is about 300.

What are two ways to estimate 22% of 130? Explain below.

2. Marita and four of her friends ordered a pizza that cost $14.72. She is responsible for 20% of the bill. About how much money will she need to pay?

Step 1 Find 10% of $15.00.

$10\% \text{ of } \$15.00 = 0.1 \cdot \$15.00$

$= \$1.50$ — To multiply by 10%, move the decimal point one place to the left.

Step 2 Multiply.

20% of $15.00 is 2 times 10% of $15.00.

$2 \cdot \$1.50 = \$3.00$

So, Marita should pay about $3.00.

Got It? Do these problems to find out.

a. Estimate 42% of 120.

b. Dante plans to put 80% of his paycheck into a savings account and spend the other 20%. His paycheck this week was $295. About how much money will he put into his savings account?

a. __________

b. __________

Percents Greater Than 100 or Less Than 1

You can also estimate percents of numbers when the percent is greater than 100 or less than 1.

Check for Reasonableness
When the percent is greater than 100, the estimate will always be greater than the number.

Example

3. Estimate 122% of 50.

122% is about 120%.

$$120\% \text{ of } 50 = 100\% \text{ of } 50 + 20\% \text{ of } 50 \quad 120\% = 100\% + 20\%$$
$$= (1 \cdot 50) + \left(\frac{1}{5} \cdot 50\right) \quad 100\% = 1 \text{ and } 20\% = \frac{1}{5}$$
$$= 50 + 10 \text{ or } 60 \quad \text{Simplify.}$$

So, 122% of 50 is about 60.

Got It? Do these problems to find out.

c. 174% of 200 **d.** 298% of 45 **e.** 347% of 80

c. ______

d. ______

e. ______

Example

4. There are 789 seventh grade students at Washington Middle School. About $\frac{1}{4}$% of the seventh grade students have traveled overseas. What is the approximate number of seventh grade students that have traveled overseas? Explain.

$\frac{1}{4}$% is one fourth of 1%. 789 is about 800.

$$1\% \text{ of } 800 = 0.01 \cdot 800 \quad \text{Write 1\% as 0.01.}$$
$$= 8 \quad \text{To multiply by 1\%, move the decimal point two places to the left.}$$

One fourth of 8 is $\frac{1}{4} \cdot 8$ or 2.

So, about 2 seventh grade students have traveled overseas.

Got It? Do this problem to find out.

f. A county receives $\frac{3}{4}$% of a state sales tax. About how much money would the county receive from the sale of a computer that costs $1,020?

f. ______

Example

5. Last year, 639 students attended a summer camp. Of those who attended this year, 0.5% also attended summer camp last year. About how many students attended the summer camp two years in a row?

0.5% is half of 1%.

$1\% \text{ of } 639 = 0.01 \cdot 639$

≈ 6

So, 0.5% of 639 is about $\frac{1}{2}$ of 6 or 3.

About 3 students attended summer camp 2 years in a row.

Guided Practice

Estimate. (Examples 1–4)

1. 52% of 10 ≈ ______

2. 79% of 489 ≈ ______

3. 151% of 70 ≈ ______

4. $\frac{1}{2}$% of 82 ≈ ______

5. Of the 78 teenagers at a youth camp, 63% have birthdays in the spring. About how many teenagers have birthdays in the spring? (Example 2)

______

6. About 0.8% of the land in Maine is federally owned. If Maine has 19,847,680 acres, about how many acres are federally owned? (Example 5) ______

7. **Building on the Essential Question** How can you estimate the percent of a number? ______

Rate Yourself!
How confident are you about estimating percents? Shade the ring on the target.
I'm on target.
I need help.
For more help, go online to access a Personal Tutor.
Tutor

Name ______ My Homework ______

Independent Practice

Go online for Step-by-Step Solutions

Estimate. (Examples 1–4)

1. 47% of 70 ≈ ______

2. 39% of 120 ≈ ______

3. 21% of 90 ≈ ______

4. 65% of 152 ≈ ______

5. 72% of 238 ≈ ______

6. 132% of 54 ≈ ______

7. 224% of 320 ≈ ______

8. $\frac{3}{4}$% of 168 ≈ ______

9. 0.4% of 510 ≈ ______

10. **Financial Literacy** Carlie spent $42 at the salon. Her mother loaned her the money. Carlie will pay her mother 15% of $42 each week until the loan is repaid. About how much will Carlie pay each week? (Example 2)

______

11. The United States has 12,383 miles of coastline. If 0.8% of the coastline is located in Georgia, about how many miles of coastline are in Georgia? (Example 5)

______

12. CCGPS **Persevere with Problems** Use the graph shown.

a. About how many more hours does Avery spend sleeping than doing the activities in the "other" category? Justify your answer.

______

b. What is the approximate number of minutes Avery spends each day on extracurricular activities?

______

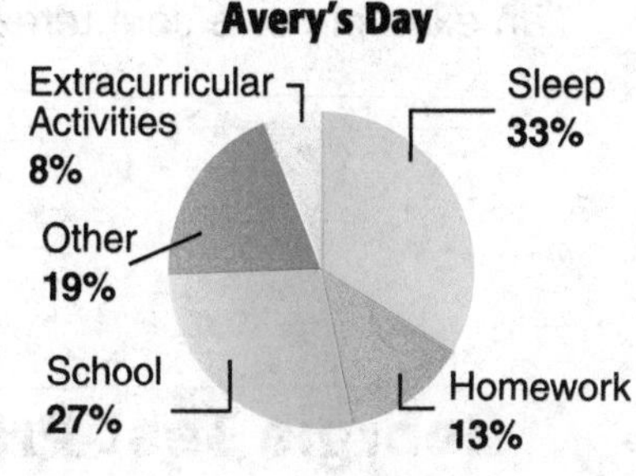

Estimate.

13. 67% of 8.7 ≈ ______

14. 54% of 76.8 ≈ ______

15. 10.5% of 238 ≈ ______

16. The average white rhinoceros gives birth to a single calf that weighs about 3.8% as much as its mother. If the mother rhinoceros weighs 3.75 tons, about how many pounds does its calf weigh? ______

17. The students at Monroe Junior High sponsored a canned food drive. The seventh-grade class collected 129% of its canned food goal.

a. About how many canned foods did the seventh-graders collect if their goal was 200 cans? ______

b. About how many canned foods did the seventh-graders collect if their goal was 595 cans? ______

H.O.T. Problems Higher Order Thinking

18. CCGPS **Persevere with Problems** Explain how you could find $\frac{3}{8}$% of $800.

19. CCGPS **Use MathTools** Is an estimate for the percent of a number *always*, *sometimes*, or *never* greater than the actual percent of the number? Give an example or a counterexample to support your answer.

Georgia Test Practice

20. Mallory is buying bedroom furniture for $1,789.43. The dresser is 39.7% of the total cost. Which is the best estimate for the cost of the dresser?

Ⓐ $540 Ⓑ $630 Ⓒ $720 Ⓓ $810

Extra Practice

Estimate.

21. 76% of 180 ≈ 135

$\frac{3}{4} \cdot 180 = 135$ or

Homework Help

$0.1 \cdot 180 = 18$

$7.5 \cdot 18 = 135$

22. 57% of 29 ≈ 18

$\frac{3}{5} \cdot 30 = 18$ or

$0.1 \cdot 30 = 3$

$6 \cdot 3 = 18$

23. 92% of 104 ≈ ______

24. $\frac{1}{2}$% of 412 ≈ ______

25. 0.9% of 74 ≈ ______

26. 32% of 89.9 ≈ ______

27. You use 43 muscles to frown. When you smile, you use 32% of these same muscles. About how many muscles do you use when you smile?

28. CCGPS **Justify Conclusions** The coastline of the Atlantic Coast is 2,069 miles long. Approximately $\frac{6}{10}$% of the coastline lies in New Hampshire. About how many miles of the coastline lie in New Hampshire? Explain how you estimated.

29. The table shows the number of passes attempted and the percent completed by the top quarterbacks in the NFL for a recent season.

a. Estimate the number of passes that Tom Brady completed.

b. Is your estimate greater or less than the actual number of passes he completed? Explain.

c. Without calculating, determine whether Tony Romo or David Garrard completed more passes. Justify your reasoning.

NFL Quarterbacks		
Player	Passes Attempted	Percent Completed
T. Brady	578	69
P. Manning	515	65
T. Romo	520	64
D. Garrard	325	64

Georgia Test Practice

30. The graph shows the results of a survey of 510 students.

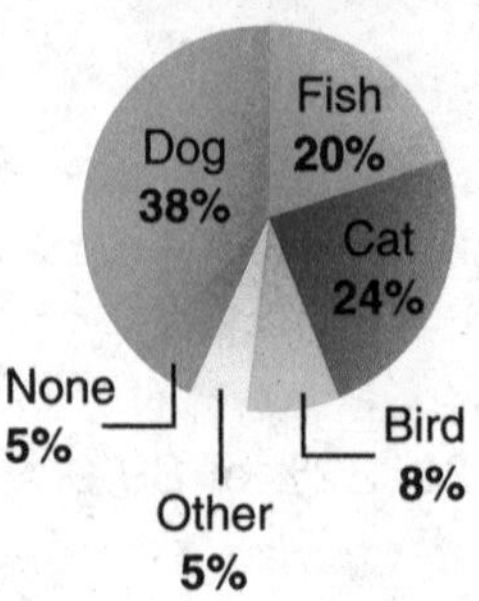

Which is the best estimate for the percent of students who prefer cats?

Ⓐ 75 Ⓒ 225

Ⓑ 125 Ⓓ 450

31. Abbey asked 50 students to vote for the school issue that was most important to them. The results are shown below.

Issue	Votes
Library use	10%
Time to change classes	12%
Use of electronics	18%
Lunch room rules	20%
Dress code	40%

About how many students chose "Time to change classes" as the most important issue?

Ⓕ 3 Ⓗ 9

Ⓖ 5 Ⓘ 12

Common Core Review

Solve each equation. Show your work. MCC6.EE.7

32. $5n = 120$

33. $1{,}200 = 4a$

34. $6x = 39$

35. Marquita created the design at the right. She created the design from 8 equal-size rectangles. Write a fraction in simplest form that represents the yellow portion of the design. MCC5.NF.1

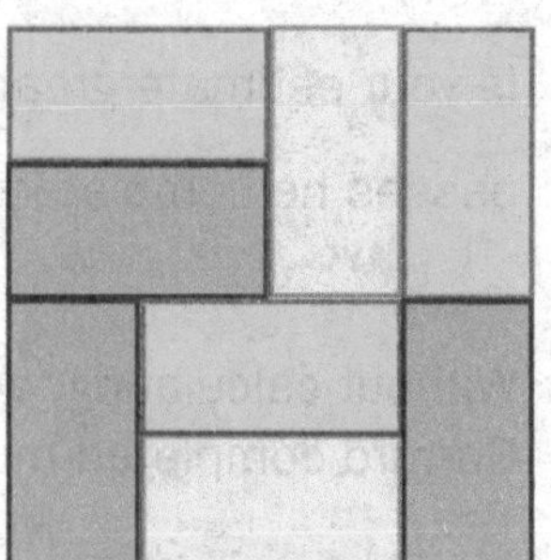

36. Write three fractions equivalent to $\frac{3}{5}$. MCC5.NF.1

HOW is percent used to solve real-world problems?

Content Standards
MCC7.RP.3, MCC7.EE.3

Mathematical Practices
1, 3, 4

Drama The eighth grade had 300 tickets to sell to the school play and the seventh grade had 250 tickets to sell. One hour before the show, the eighth grade had sold 225 tickets and the seventh grade had sold 200 tickets. Complete the investigation below to find which grade sold the greater percent of tickets.

Investigation

Step 1 The bar diagrams below show 100% for each grade. Label the total tickets to be sold above each bar. Divide each bar into 10 equal sections. So, each section will represent 10%.

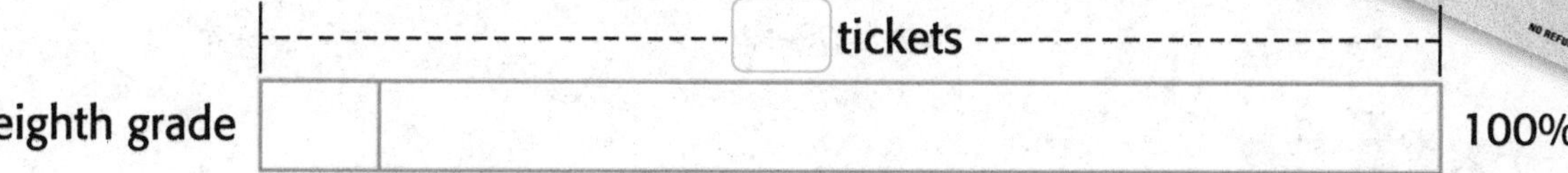

tickets

seventh grade | 100%

Step 2 Find the number that belongs in each section for both of the bars. Then write that number in the sections.

Eighth grade:

$300 \div 10 =$ ☐

Seventh grade:

$250 \div 10 =$ ☐

Step 3 Find the number of sections to shade for each bar. Then shade the sections.

Eighth grade:

$225 \div 30 =$ ☐

Seventh grade:

$200 \div 25 =$ ☐

The eighth grade sold ☐ % of their tickets. The seventh grade sold ☐ % of their tickets.

The ________ grade sold the greater percent of their tickets.

Collaborate

Work with a partner. Show your work using bar diagrams.

1. **Model with Mathematics** Vanlue Middle School has 600 students and Memorial Middle School has 450 students. Vanlue has 270 girls and Memorial has 225 girls. Which school has the greater percent of girls? Explain. ____________________

____

____

____

students

Vanlue 100%

students

Memorial 100%

Analyze

Work with a partner to answer the following question.

2. **Model with Mathematics** Seventy-five students were in the audience for a 3-D screening of a movie. Fifty students were in the audience for a 2-D screening of the same movie. Describe a situation in which the percent of students who went to the 2-D screening is greater than the percent of students who went to the 3-D screening. ____________________

____

____

____

Reflect

3. **Inquiry** HOW is percent used to solve real-world problems? ____________________

____

____

____

Lesson 3

The Percent Proportion

What You'll Learn

Scan the lesson. Predict two things you will learn about the percent proportion.

- ______________________________

- ______________________________

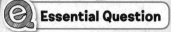

Essential Question

HOW can percent help you understand situations involving money?

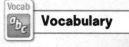

Vocabulary

percent proportion

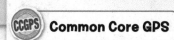

Common Core GPS

Content Standards
MCC7.RP.3

Mathematical Practices
1, 3, 4

Real-World Link

Monster Trucks The tires on a monster truck weigh approximately 2 tons. The entire truck weighs about 6 tons.

1. Write the ratio of tire weight to total weight as a fraction.

$\frac{\text{Part}}{\text{Whole}} = \frac{\square}{\square}$

2. Represent the fraction above by shading in the model.

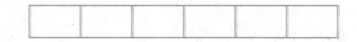

3. Write the fraction as a decimal to the nearest hundredth.

____

4. About what percent of the monster truck's weight is the tires?

____

Key Concept Use the Percent Proportion

Type	Example	Proportion
Find the Percent	What percent of 5 is 4?	$\frac{4}{5} = \frac{n}{100}$
Find the Part	What number is 80% of 5?	$\frac{p}{5} = \frac{80}{100}$
Find the Whole	4 is 80% of what number?	$\frac{4}{w} = \frac{80}{100}$

Work Zone

In a **percent proportion**, one ratio or fraction compares part of a quantity to the whole quantity. The other ratio is the equivalent percent written as a fraction with a denominator of 100.

4 out of 5 is 80%

$$\frac{\text{part}}{\text{whole}} \rightarrow \frac{4}{5} = \frac{80}{100} \} \text{ percent}$$

Example

1. What percent of $15 is $9?

The Percent Proportion
The word *of* is usually followed by the whole.

Words	What percent of $15 is $9?
Variable	Let n represent the percent.
Proportion	$\frac{\text{part}}{\text{whole}} \rightarrow \frac{9}{15} = \frac{n}{100}$ } percent

$\frac{9}{15} = \frac{n}{100}$ Write the proportion.

$9 \cdot 100 = 15 \cdot n$ Find the cross products.

$900 = 15n$ Simplify.

$\frac{900}{15} = \frac{15n}{15}$ Divide each side by 15.

$60 = n$

So, $9 is 60% of $15.

a. ________

b. ________

Got It? **Do these problems to find out.**

a. What percent of 25 is 20? **b.** $12.75 is what percent of $50?

Example

2. What number is 40% of 120?

Words	What number is 40% of 120?
Variable	Let p represent the part.
Proportion	part → whole → $\frac{p}{120} = \frac{40}{100}$ } percent

$\frac{p}{120} = \frac{40}{100}$ Write the proportion.

$p \cdot 100 = 120 \cdot 40$ Find the cross products.

$100p = 4{,}800$ Simplify.

$\frac{100p}{100} = \frac{4{,}800}{100}$ Divide each side by 100.

$p = 48$ So, 48 is 40% of 120.

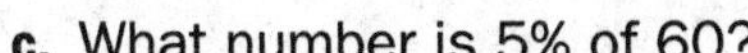

Got It? Do these problems to find out.

c. What number is 5% of 60? **d.** 12% of 85 is what number?

Show your work.

c. ________

d. ________

Example

3. 18 is 25% of what number?

Words	18 is 25% of what number?
Variable	Let w represent the whole.
Proportion	part → whole → $\frac{18}{w} = \frac{25}{100}$ } percent

$\frac{18}{w} = \frac{25}{100}$ Write the proportion.

$18 \cdot 100 = w \cdot 25$ Find the cross products.

$1{,}800 = 25w$ Simplify.

$\frac{1{,}800}{25} = \frac{25w}{25}$ Divide each side by 25.

$72 = w$ So, 18 is 25% of 72.

In the proportion $\frac{3}{20} = \frac{15}{100}$, identify the part, whole, and percent.

part = ______

whole = ______

percent = ______

Got It? Do these problems to find out.

e. 40% of what number is 26? **f.** 84 is 75% of what number?

e. ________

f. ________

Example

4. The average adult male Western Lowland gorilla eats about 33.5 pounds of fruit each day. How much food does the average adult male gorilla eat each day?

Western Lowland Gorilla's Diet	
Food	**Percent**
Fruit	67%
Seeds, leaves, stems, and pith	17%
Insects/ insect larvae	16%

You know that 33.5 pounds is the part. You need to find the whole.

$\frac{33.5}{w} = \frac{67}{100}$ Write the proportion.

$33.5 \cdot 100 = w \cdot 67$ Find the cross products.

$3{,}350 = 67w$ Simplify.

$\frac{3{,}350}{67} = \frac{67w}{67}$ Divide each side by 67.

$50 = w$

The average adult male gorilla eats 50 pounds of food each day.

Guided Practice

Find each number. Round to the nearest tenth if necessary. (Examples 1–3)

1. What percent of \$90 is \$9? ________

2. What number is 2% of 35? ________

3. 62 is 90.5% of what number? ________

4. Brand A cereal contains 10 cups of cereal. How many more cups of cereal are in Brand B cereal? (Example 4)

____

5. **Building on the Essential Question** How can you use the percent proportion to solve real-world problems?

____

____

____

____

Rate Yourself!

How confident are you about using the percent proportion? Shade the ring on the target.

For more help, go online to access a Personal Tutor.

FOLDABLES *Time to update your Foldable!*

Independent Practice

Go online for Step-by-Step Solutions 

Find each number. Round to the nearest tenth if necessary. (Examples 1–3)

1. What percent of 60 is 15? ______

2. What number is 15% of 60? ______

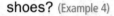

3. 9 is 12% of which number? ______

4. 12% of 72 is what number? ______

5. What percent of 50 is 18? ______

6. 12 is 90% of what number? ______

7. A pair of sneakers is on sale as shown. This is 75% of the original price. What was the original price of the shoes? (Example 4) ______

8. Of the 60 books on a bookshelf, 24 are nonfiction. What percent of the books are nonfiction? (Example 4) ______

Find each number. Round to the nearest hundredth if necessary.

9. 40 is 50% of what number? ______

10. 12.5% of what number is 24? ______

11. What percent of 300 is 0.6? ______

12. What number is 0.5% of 8? ______

Find each number. Round to the nearest hundredth if necessary.

13. **STEM** Use the table shown.

Planet	Radius (km)
Mercury	2,440
Mars	3,397
Jupiter	71,492

a. Mercury's radius is what percent of Jupiter's radius?

b. If the radius of Mars is about 13.7% of Neptune's radius, what is the radius of Neptune?

c. Earth's radius is about 261.4% of Mercury's radius. What is the radius of Earth?

H.O.T. Problems Higher Order Thinking

14. **CCGPS Reason Inductively** Seventy percent of the 100 students in a middle school cafeteria bought their lunch. Some of the students that bought their lunch leave the cafeteria to attend an assembly. Now only 60% of the remaining students bought their lunch. How many students are remaining in the cafeteria? Explain.

15. **CCGPS Persevere with Problems** Without calculating, arrange the following from greatest to least value. Justify your reasoning.

20% of 100, 20% of 500, 5% of 100

Georgia Test Practice

16. One hundred ninety-two students were surveyed about their favorite kind of TV programs. The results are shown in the table. Which kind of program did 25% of the students report as their favorite?

Ⓐ Music
Ⓑ Reality
Ⓒ Comedy
Ⓓ Sports

Favorite TV Programs	
Kind	**Number**
Music	48
Reality	44
Comedy	41
Sports	36
Drama	23

Extra Practice

Find each number. Round to the nearest tenth if necessary.

17. What number is 25% of 180? 45

$\frac{n}{180} = \frac{25}{100}$

$\frac{n}{180} = \frac{1}{4}$

$4n = 180$

$n = 45$

18. $3 is what percent of $40? 7.5%

$\frac{3}{40} = \frac{p}{100}$

$40p = 300$

$p = 7.5\%$

19. 9 is 45% of what number? ______

20. 75 is 20% of what number? ______

21. What percent of 60 is 12? ______

22. What number is 5% of 46? ______

23. CCGPS **Justify Conclusions** Roman has 2 red pencils in his backpack. If this is 25% of the total number of pencils, how many pencils are in his backpack? Explain.

______

24. CCGPS **Justify Conclusions** Eileen and Michelle scored 48% of their team's points. If their team had a total of 50 points, how many points did they score? Explain.

______

Find each number. Round to the nearest hundredth if necessary.

25. What percent of 25 is 30? ______

26. What number is 8.2% of 50? ______

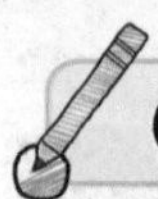

Georgia Test Practice

27. Of the 273 students in a school, 95 volunteered to work the book sale. About what percent of the students volunteered?

Ⓐ 35%

Ⓑ 65%

Ⓒ 70%

Ⓓ 75%

28. Brian ate 3 granola bars. This is 25% of the total number of granola bars in a box. How many granola bars are in a box?

Ⓕ 10

Ⓖ 11

Ⓗ 12

Ⓘ 13

29. **Short Response** The types of flowers shown in the table make up an arrangement. What percent of the flowers in the arrangement are roses?

Flower Arrangement	
Lilies	4
Roses	15
Snapdragons	6

CCGPS Common Core Review

Multiply. MCC5.NF.4

30. $\frac{1}{2} \times \frac{2}{3} =$ ______

31. $\frac{3}{5} \times \frac{1}{4} =$ ______

32. $\frac{2}{7} \times \frac{1}{6} =$ ______

Divide. MCC6.NS.1

33. $\frac{2}{5} \div \frac{3}{4} =$ ______

34. $\frac{1}{3} \div \frac{5}{6} =$ ______

35. $\frac{1}{5} \div \frac{5}{7} =$ ______

36. A store had a sale as shown at the right. A pair of shoes cost $80. What is $\frac{3}{4}$ of $80? MCC5.NF.4

The Percent Equation

What You'll Learn

Scan the lesson. Predict two things you will learn about using the percent equation.

-
-

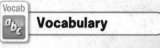

Essential Question

HOW can percent help you understand situations involving money?

Vocabulary

percent equation

Common Core GPS

Content Standards
MCC7.RP.2, MCC7.RP.2c, MCC7.RP.3, MCC7.EE.3

Mathematical Practices
1, 2, 3, 4

Vocabulary Start-Up

You have used a percent proportion to find the missing part (p), percent (n), or whole (w). You can also use a **percent equation**. The percent equation is part = percent • whole.

Label the diagram that shows the relationship between the percent proportion and the percent equation with the terms *part, whole,* and *percent.* Use each term once.

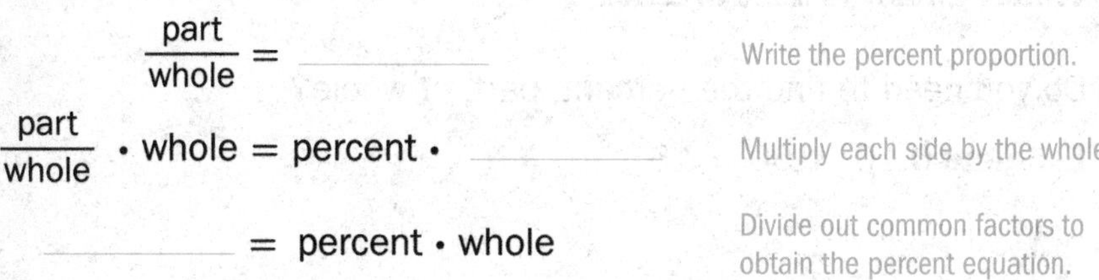

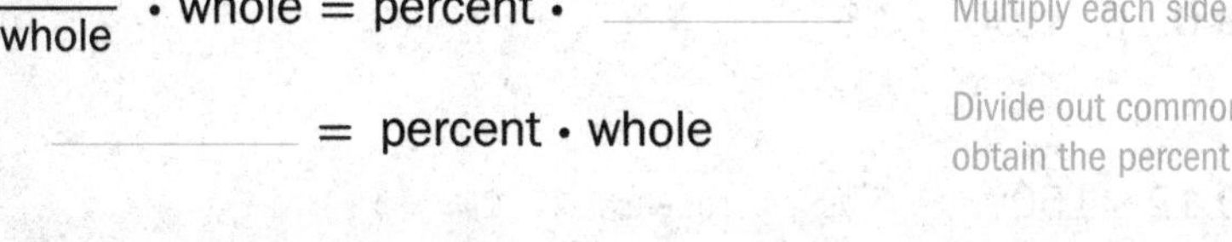

$\frac{\text{part}}{\text{whole}} =$ ______ Write the percent proportion.

$\frac{\text{part}}{\text{whole}} \cdot \text{whole} = \text{percent} \cdot$ ______ Multiply each side by the whole.

______ $= \text{percent} \cdot \text{whole}$ Divide out common factors to obtain the percent equation.

Real-World Link

A survey found that 16% of all seventh-graders at Lincoln Middle school think that tarantulas are the scariest creatures. There are 150 seventh-graders at the school. How would you write a percent equation to find how many seventh-graders said that tarantulas are the scariest creatures?

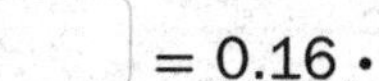

☐ $= 0.16 \cdot$ ☐

Key Concept — Use the Percent Equation

Type	Example	Equation
Find the Percent	3 is what percent of 6?	$3 = n \cdot 6$
Find the Part	What number is 50% of 6?	$p = 0.5 \cdot 6$
Find the Whole	3 is 50% of what number?	$3 = 0.5 \cdot w$

Work Zone

You can use the percent equation to solve problems that involve percent.

3 is 50% of 6

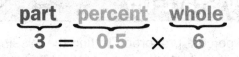

$$\underbrace{3}_{\text{part}} = \underbrace{0.5}_{\text{percent}} \times \underbrace{6}_{\text{whole}}$$

Note that the percent is written as a decimal.

Example

Percent Equation
A percent must always be converted to a decimal or a fraction when it is used in an equation.

1. What number is 12% of 150?

Do you need to find the percent, part, or whole? ______

Estimate $0.10 \cdot 150 = 15$

part = percent · whole

$p = 0.12 \cdot 150$ — Write the percent equation. $12\% = 0.12$

$p = 18$ — Multiply.

So, 18 is 12% of 150.

18 is close to the estimate of 15. So, the answer is reasonable. You can also check your answer using the percent proportion.

Check $\frac{18}{150} \stackrel{?}{=} \frac{12}{100}$

$18 \cdot 100 \stackrel{?}{=} 150 \cdot 12$

$1{,}800 = 1{,}800$ ✓

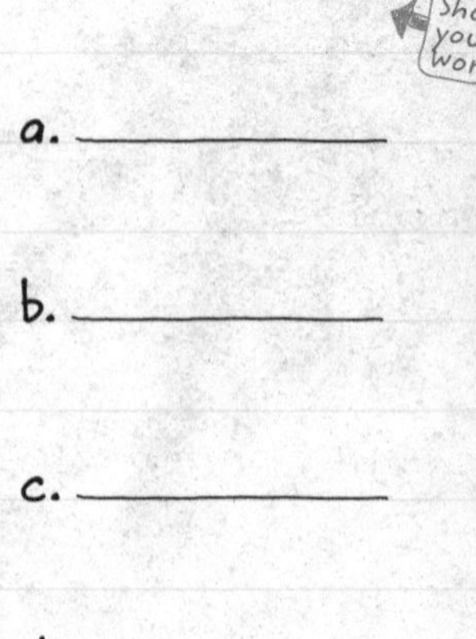

Got It? Do these problems to find out.

Write an equation for each problem. Then solve.

a. What is 6% of 200?

b. Find 72% of 50.

c. What is 14% of 150?

d. Find 50% of 70.

Example

2. 21 is what percent of 40?

Do you need to find the percent, part, or whole? ________

Estimate $\frac{21}{40} \approx \frac{1}{2}$ or 50%

part = percent · whole

$21 = n \cdot 40$ Write the percent equation.

$\frac{21}{40} = \frac{40n}{40}$ Divide each side by 40.

$0.525 = n$ Simplify.

So, 21 is 52.5% of 40.

Check 52.5% ≈ 50% ✓

Percent
Remember to write the decimal as a percent in your final answer.

Got It? Do these problems to find out.

Write an equation for each problem. Then solve. Round to the nearest tenth if necessary.

e. What percent of 40 is 9?

f. 27 is what percent of 150?

e. ________

f. ________

Example

3. 13 is 26% of what number?

Do you need to find the percent, part, or whole? ________

Estimate $\frac{1}{4}$ of 48 = 12

part = percent · whole

$13 = 0.26 \cdot w$ Write the percent equation. 26% = 0.26

$\frac{13}{0.26} = \frac{0.26w}{0.26}$ Divide each side by 0.26.

$50 = w$ Simplify.

So, 13 is 26% of 50.

Check 50 ≈ 48. ✓

Got It? Do these problems to find out.

Write an equation for each problem. Then solve. Round to the nearest tenth if necessary.

g. 39 is 84% of what number?

h. 26% of what number is 45?

g. ________

h. ________

Example

4. A survey found that 25% of people aged 18–24 gave up their home phone and only use a cell phone. If 3,264 people only use a cell phone, how many people were surveyed?

Words	3,264 people is 25% of what number of people?
Variable	Let w represent the number of people.
Equation	$3{,}264 \quad = \quad 0.25 \quad \cdot \quad w$

$3{,}264 = 0.25 \cdot w$ Write the percent equation. 25% = 0.25

$\frac{3{,}264}{0.25} = \frac{0.25w}{0.25}$ Divide each side by 0.25. Use a calculator.

$13{,}056 = w$ Simplify.

About 13,056 people were surveyed.

Guided Practice

Write an equation for each problem. Then solve. Round to the nearest tenth if necessary. (Examples 1–3)

1. What number is 88% of 300? ______

2. 24 is what percent of 120? ______

3. 3 is 12% of what number? ______

4. A local bakery sold 60 loaves of bread in one day. If 65% of these were sold in the afternoon, how many loaves were sold in the afternoon? (Example 4) ______

5. **Building on the Essential Question** When might it be easier to use the percent equation rather than the percent proportion? ______

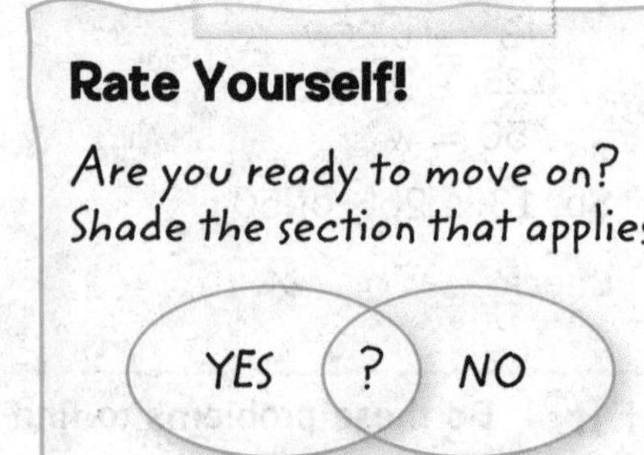

Rate Yourself!
Are you ready to move on?
Shade the section that applies.
YES
?
NO

For more help, go online to access a Personal Tutor.

FOLDABLES Time to update your Foldable!

Independent Practice

Go online for Step-by-Step Solutions

Write an equation for each problem. Then solve. Round to the nearest tenth if necessary. (Examples 1–3)

1. 75 is what percent of 150? ________

2. 84 is 60% of what number? ________

3. What number is 65% of 98? ________

4. Find 39% of 65. ________

5. Find 24% of 25. ________

6. What number is 53% of 470? ________

7. Ruben bought 6 new books for his collection. This increased his collection by 12%. How many books did he have before his purchases? (Example 4)

8. A store sold 550 video games during the month of December. If this made up 12.5% of its yearly video game sales, about how many video games did the store sell all year? (Example 4)

9. CCGPS **Persevere with Problems** About 142 million people in the United States watch online videos. Use the graph that shows what type of videos they watch.

   a. About what percent of viewers watch comedy, jokes, and bloopers? ________

   b. About what percent watch news stories? ________

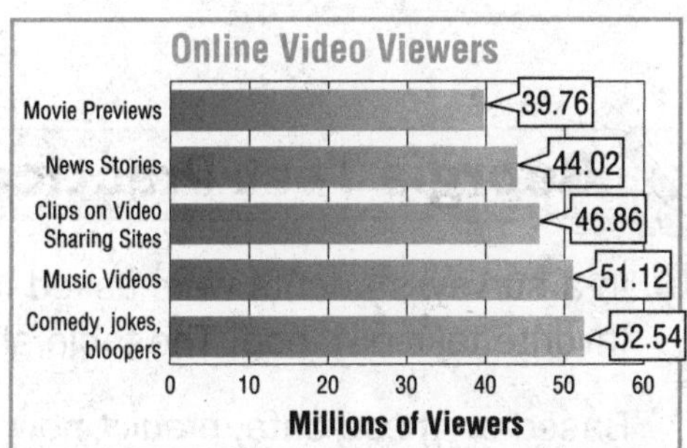

Write an equation for each problem. Then solve. Round to the nearest tenth if necessary.

10. Find 135% of 64. ________

11. What number is 0.4% of 82.1? ________

12. 450 is 75.2% of what number? ________

13. What percent of 200 is 230? ________

H.O.T. Problems Higher Order Thinking

14. CCGPS **Model with Mathematics** Write a percent problem for which the percent is greater than 100 and the part is known. Use the percent equation to solve your problem to find the whole.

15. CCGPS **Persevere with Problems** If you need to find the percent of a number, explain how you can predict whether the part will be *less than*, *greater than*, or *equal* to the number.

Georgia Test Practice

16. In a survey, students were asked to choose their favorite take-out food. The table shows the results.

Based on these data, predict how many out of 1,800 students would choose sandwiches.

Ⓐ 504 Ⓒ 680

Ⓑ 576 Ⓓ 720

Favorite Take-Out Food	
Type of Food	**Percent**
Pizza	40
Sandwiches	32
Chicken	28

Extra Practice

Write an equation for each problem. Then solve. Round to the nearest tenth if necessary.

17. 9 is what percent of 45? 20%

$9 = n \times 45$

$\frac{9}{45} = \frac{45n}{45}$

0.2 or $20\% = n$

18. What percent of 96 is 26? 27.1%

$26 = n \times 96$

$\frac{26}{96} = \frac{96n}{96}$

0.271 or $27.1\% = n$

19. What percent of 392 is 98? ______

20. 30 is what percent of 64? ______

21. 33% of what number is 1.45? ______

22. 84 is 75% of what number? ______

23. 17 is 40% of what number? ______

24. 80% of what number is 64? ______

25. The length of Giselle's arm is 27 inches. The length of her lower arm is 17 inches. About what percent of Giselle's arm is her lower arm?

______

26. Approximately 0.02% of North Atlantic lobsters are born bright blue in color. Out of 5,000 North Atlantic lobsters, how many would you expect to be blue in color?

______

27. **Financial Literacy** Suppose you earn $6 per hour at your part-time job. What will your new hourly rate be after a 2.5% raise? Explain.

______

______

Georgia Test Practice

28. If 60% of a number is 18, what is 90% of the number?

Ⓐ 3
Ⓑ 16
Ⓒ 27
Ⓓ 30

29. Which equation represents the statement below?

80% of what number is 64?

Ⓕ $64 = 0.8 \times w$
Ⓖ $80 = 64 \times w$
Ⓗ $64 = 80 \times w$
Ⓘ $64 = 8.0 \times w$

30. Taryn's grandmother took her family out to dinner. If the dinner was $74 and Taryn's dinner was 20% of the bill, how much was Taryn's dinner?

Ⓐ $6.80
Ⓑ $7.20
Ⓒ $9.50
Ⓓ $14.80

CCGPS Common Core Review

Fill in each ◯ with <, >, or = to make a true statement. MCC5.NBT.3b

31. 5.56 ◯ $5\frac{5}{7}$

32. 4.027 ◯ 4.0092

33. 88% ◯ 0.9

34. Last week, a jacket cost $39.50. This week, the price of the jacket decreased by $4.50. What is the price of the jacket after the decrease? How much would it cost to purchase 2 jackets this week? MCC5.NBT.5

Use the graph to solve.

35. What number represents 100% of the fall student athletes?

Explain. MCC6.SP.5a

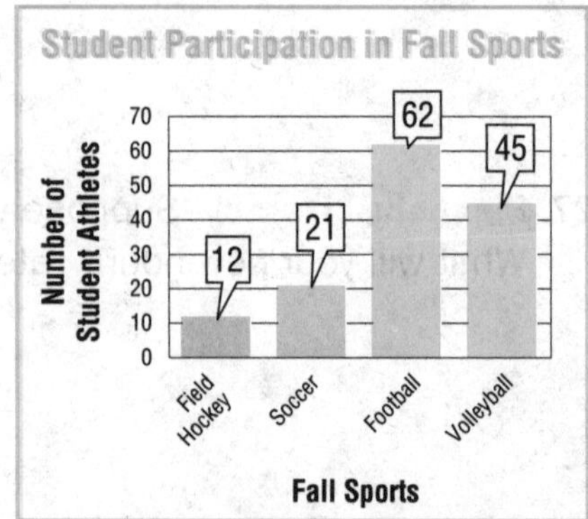

Determine Reasonable Answers

Content Standards
MCC7.RP.3, MCC7.EE.3
Mathematical Practices
1, 3, 4

Case #1 Vacations

Wesley's family spent $1,400 on a trip to the Grand Canyon. They spent 30% of the total on a sightseeing helicopter flight. Wesley estimates that his family spent about $450 on the flight.

Determine whether Wesley's estimate is reasonable.

Understand *What are the facts?*

- Wesley's family spent $1,400 on vacation.
- Thirty percent of the total was spent on a helicopter flight.
- Wesley estimates that 30% is about $450.

Plan *What is your strategy to solve this problem?*

Make a bar diagram that represents 100%.

Solve *How can you apply the strategy?*

Fill in each section of the diagram with 10% of $1,400.

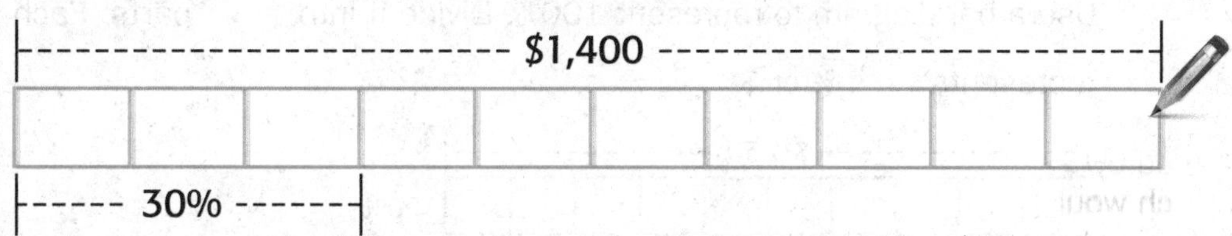

Add three sections to get a total of ______.
So, the helicopter flight cost $420.

Check *Does the answer make sense?*

Wesley estimated the cost of the helicopter flight to be $450. Since $450 is close to $420, his estimate was reasonable.

Analyze the Strategy

Make a Conjecture How can you use $\frac{1}{3}$ to determine if Wesley's estimate is reasonable? Explain.

Case #2 Don't forget the tip!

At a local Italian restaurant, Brett's bill was $17.50. He decides to leave a 20% tip for the server.

Is $4 a reasonable tip?

Understand

Read the problem. What are you being asked to find?

I need to ______________________________.

Is there any information that you do *not* need to know?

I do not need to know ______________________________.

Plan

Choose a problem-solving strategy.

I will use the ______________________________ *strategy.*

Solve

Use your problem-solving strategy to solve the problem.

Use a bar diagram to represent 100%. Divide it into ☐ parts. Each part represents ☐% or $☐.

$17.50									

100%

|-- tip --|

Two parts, or ☐%, equal $☐ + $☐ = $☐.

Is $4 a reasonable tip? ______________________________

Check

Use information from the problem to check your answer.

____

____

Collaborate Work with a small group to solve the following cases. Show your work on a separate piece of paper.

Case #3 Travel

A travel agency surveyed 140 families about their favorite vacation spots.

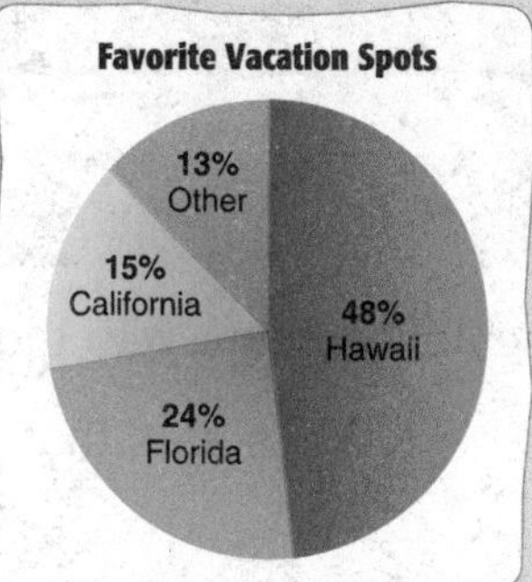

Is 60, 70, or 80 families a reasonable estimate for the number of families that did not choose Hawaii?

Case #4 Exercise

A survey showed that 61% of middle school students do some kind of physical activity every day.

Suppose there are 828 middle school students in your school. Would the number of students who exercise be about 300, 400, or 500?

Case #5 School

Of 423 students, 57.6% live within 5 miles of the school.

What is a reasonable estimate for the number of students living within 5 miles of the school?

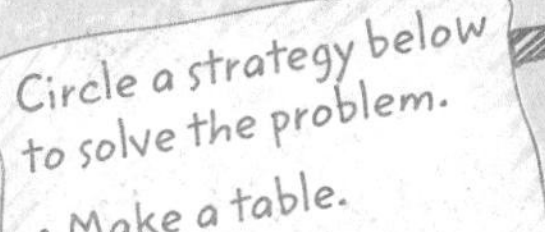

Circle a strategy below to solve the problem.
• Make a table.
• Draw a diagram
• Act it out.

Case #6 Bowling

In bowling, you get a spare when you knock down the ten pins in two throws.

How many possible ways are there to get a spare?

Mid-Chapter Check

Vocabulary Check

1. Fill in the blank in the sentence below with the correct term. (Lesson 4)

   The ______________________ states that the part equals the percent multiplied by the whole.

Skills Check and Problem Solving

Find each number. Round to the nearest tenth if necessary. (Lessons 1 and 3)

2. What percent of 84 is 12? ________

3. 15 is 25% of what number? ________

Estimate. (Lesson 2)

4. 20% of 392 ________

5. 78% of 112 ________

Write an equation for each problem. Then solve. Round to the nearest tenth if necessary. (Lesson 4)

6. CCGPS **Use Math Tools** A computer costs $849.75 and the hard drive is 61.3% of the total cost. What is a reasonable estimate for the cost of the hard drive? (Lesson 2)

   ____

7. What number is 35% of 72? ________

8. 16.1 is what percent of 70? ________

9. **Georgia Test Practice** Ayana has 220 coins in her piggy bank. Of those, 45% are pennies. How many coins are *not* pennies? (Lesson 1)

   Ⓐ 121　　Ⓒ 99
   Ⓑ 116　　Ⓓ 85

HOW can you use a bar diagram to show a percent of change?

Content Standards
MCC7.RP.3, MCC7.EE.3
Mathematical Practices
1, 3, 4

Admission The admission price for the state fair has increased by 50% in the last five years. The admission price was \$6 five years ago. What is the current admission price? Do the Investigation below to find out.

Investigation

Use a bar diagram to solve.

Step 1 The bar diagram represents 100%.

price 5 years ago = \$6	100%

Since $50\% = \frac{1}{2}$, divide the bar diagram in half. Fill in the missing information.

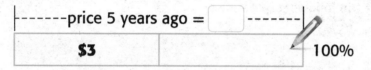

price 5 years ago = ☐

\$3		100%

Step 2 The admission price increased by 50%. Complete the bar diagram that represents 150% of the price 5 years ago.

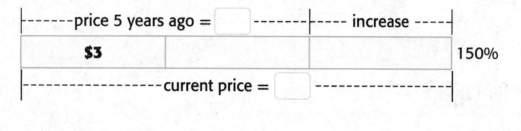

price 5 years ago = ☐ | increase

\$3			150%

current price = ☐

So, the current admission price is ☐ + ☐ or ☐.

Collaborate

Work with a partner to solve the following problems.

1. The height of a tree was 8 feet. After a year, the tree's height increased by 25%. Use a bar diagram to find the new height of the tree? ________

2. CCGPS **Model with Mathematics** The model below describes the following scenario: Ryan put $160 in a bank account. After 2 months, the total in his account decreased by 25%. Fill in the amount in Ryan's account after 2 months.

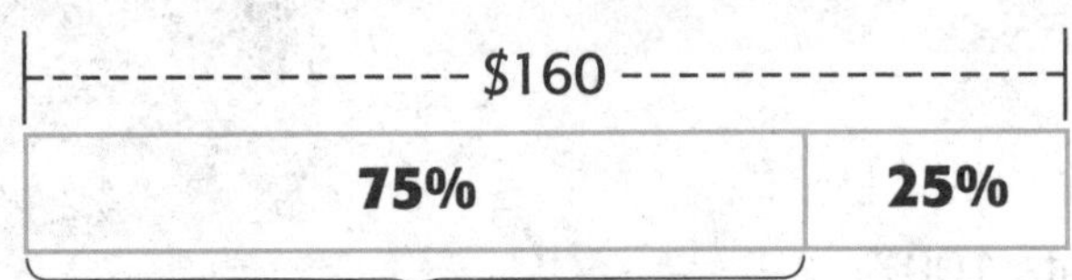

The amount in Ryan's account after 2 months is ☐.

Work with a partner to answer the following questions.

3. Find 125% of 8 two different ways.

____

____

4. CCGPS **Reason Inductively** Refer to Exercises 1 and 3. How can you find the new amount of a quantity that has increased over a period of time?

____

____

____

Reflect

5. Inquiry HOW can you use a bar diagram to show a percent of change?

____

____

____

Percent of Change

What You'll Learn

Scan the lesson. Predict two things you will learn about percent of change.

- ____
- ____

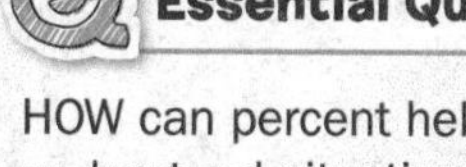

Essential Question

HOW can percent help you understand situations involving money?

Vocabulary

percent of change
percent of increase
percent of decrease
percent error

Common Core GPS

Content Standards
MCC7.RP.3, MCC7.EE.3

Mathematical Practices
1, 3, 4, 5, 6

Real-World Link

Watch

Speed Racer The Indy 500 is one of the world's great motor races. The table shows the average speed of the winning race cars for various years.

Year	Speed (mph)
1922	94
1955	128
2010	162

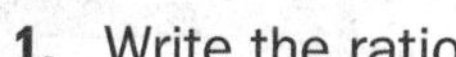

1. Write the ratio $\frac{\text{speed increase from 1922 to 1955}}{\text{speed in 1922}}$.

Then write the ratio as a percent.

Round to the nearest whole percent.

$\frac{\square}{94} = \square\%$

2. Write the ratio $\frac{\text{speed increase from 1955 to 2010}}{\text{speed in 1955}}$.

Then write the ratio as a percent.

Round to the nearest whole percent.

$\frac{\square}{128} = \square\%$

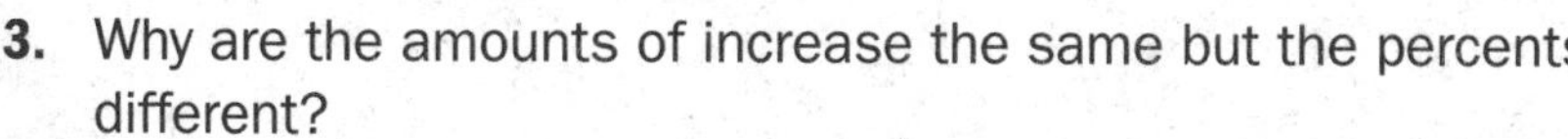

3. Why are the amounts of increase the same but the percents different?

____

____

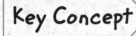

Key Concept

Percent of Change

Work Zone

Words A **percent of change** is a ratio that compares the change in quantity to the original amount.

Equation $\text{percent of change} = \frac{\text{amount of change}}{\text{original amount}}$

When you compare the amount of change to the original amount in a ratio, you are finding the percent of change. The percent of change is based on the original amount.

If the original quantity is increased, then it is called a **percent of increase**. If the original quantity is decreased, then it is called a **percent of decrease**.

$\text{percent of increase} = \frac{\text{amount of increase}}{\text{original amount}}$

$\text{percent of decrease} = \frac{\text{amount of decrease}}{\text{original amount}}$

Examples

1. Find the percent of change in the cost of gasoline from 1970 to 2010. Round to the nearest whole percent if necessary.

Since the 2010 price is greater than the 1970 price, this is a percent of increase.

Step 1 Find the amount of increase.
$2.95 − $1.30 = $1.65

Step 2 Find the percent of increase.

$$\text{percent of increase} = \frac{\text{amount of increase}}{\text{original amount}}$$

$$= \frac{\$1.65}{\$1.30} \quad \text{Substitution}$$

$$\approx 1.27 \quad \text{Simplify.}$$

$$\approx 127\% \quad \text{Write 1.27 as a percent.}$$

The cost of gasoline increased by about 127% from 1970 to 2010.

Percents
In the percent of change formula, the decimal repesenting the percent of change must be written as a percent.

2. Yusuf bought a DVD recorder for $280. Now, it is on sale for $220. Find the percent of change in the price. Round to the nearest whole percent if necessary.

Since the new price is less than the original price, this is a percent of decrease.

Step 1 Find the amount of decrease.
$\$280 - \$220 = \$60$

Step 2 Find the percent of decrease.

$$\text{percent of decrease} = \frac{\text{amount of decrease}}{\text{original amount}}$$

$$= \frac{\$60}{\$280} \quad \text{Substitution}$$

$$\approx 0.21 \quad \text{Simplify.}$$

$$\approx 21\% \quad \text{Write 0.21 as a percent.}$$

The price of the DVD recorder decreased by about 21%.

Percent of Change
Always use the original amount as the whole when finding percent of change.

Got It? **Do these problems to find out.**

a. Find the percent of change from 10 yards to 13 yards.

b. The price of a radio was $20. It is on sale for $15. What is the percent of change in the price of a radio?

a. ______________

b. ______________

Percent Error

Key Concept

Words The **percent error** is a ratio that compares the inaccuracy of an estimate, or amount of error, to the actual amount.

Equation $\text{percent error} = \frac{\text{amount of error}}{\text{actual amount}}$

Finding the percent error is similar to finding the percent of change. Instead of finding the amount of increase or decrease, you will find the amount an estimate is greater or less than the actual amount.

Suppose you guess there are 300 gum balls in a jar, but there are actually 400.

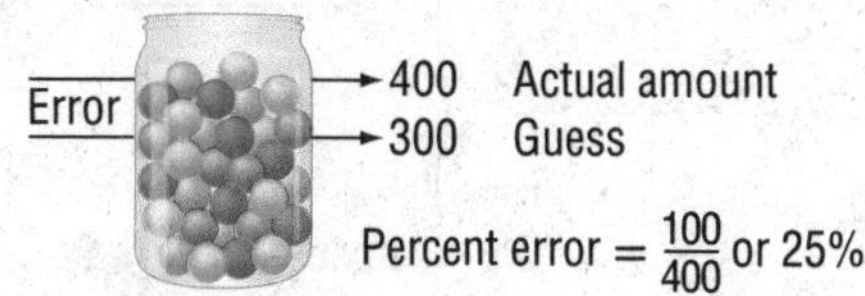

Example

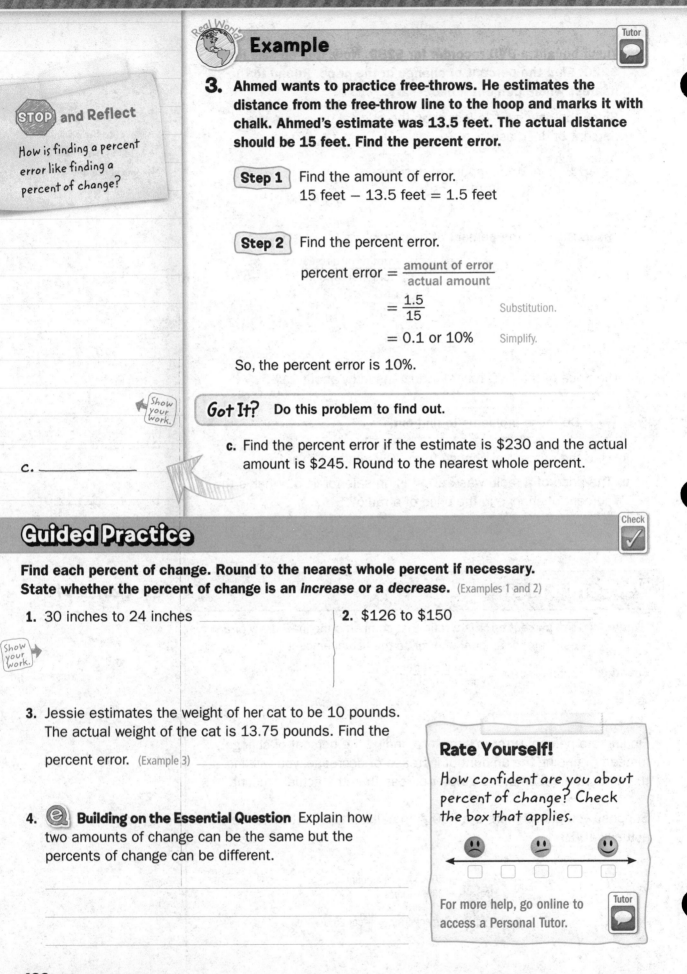

3. Ahmed wants to practice free-throws. He estimates the distance from the free-throw line to the hoop and marks it with chalk. Ahmed's estimate was 13.5 feet. The actual distance should be 15 feet. Find the percent error.

STOP and Reflect

How is finding a percent error like finding a percent of change?

Step 1 Find the amount of error.
15 feet − 13.5 feet = 1.5 feet

Step 2 Find the percent error.

$$\text{percent error} = \frac{\text{amount of error}}{\text{actual amount}}$$

$$= \frac{1.5}{15} \quad \text{Substitution.}$$

$$= 0.1 \text{ or } 10\% \quad \text{Simplify.}$$

So, the percent error is 10%.

Got It? **Do this problem to find out.**

c. Find the percent error if the estimate is $230 and the actual amount is $245. Round to the nearest whole percent.

c. ______

Guided Practice

Find each percent of change. Round to the nearest whole percent if necessary. State whether the percent of change is an *increase* or a *decrease*. (Examples 1 and 2)

1. 30 inches to 24 inches ______

2. $126 to $150 ______

3. Jessie estimates the weight of her cat to be 10 pounds. The actual weight of the cat is 13.75 pounds. Find the percent error. (Example 3) ______

4. **Building on the Essential Question** Explain how two amounts of change can be the same but the percents of change can be different.

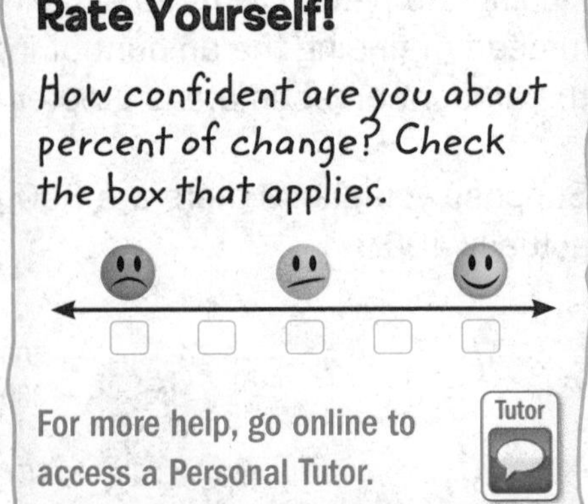

Rate Yourself!
How confident are you about percent of change? Check the box that applies.
For more help, go online to access a Personal Tutor.
Tutor

Name ____________________ My Homework ____________________

Independent Practice

Go online for Step-by-Step Solutions

Find each percent of change. Round to the nearest whole percent if necessary. State whether the percent of change is an *increase* or a *decrease*. (Examples 1 and 2)

1. 15 yards to 18 yards

2. 100 acres to 140 acres

3. $15.60 to $11.70

4. 125 centimeters to 87.5 centimeters

5. 1.6 hours to 0.95 hour

6. 132 days to 125.4 days

CCGPS **Be Precise** **Find the percent error.** (Example 3)

7. Each week, Mr. Jones goes to the grocery store. Mr. Jones estimates that he will spend $120 when he goes to the grocery store this week. He actually spends $94.

8. Marcus estimates that 230 people will attend choir concert. There was an actual total of 300 people who attended the choir concert.

For each situation, find each percent of change. Round to the nearest whole percent if necessary. State whether the percent of change is an *increase* or a *decrease*. (Examples 1 and 2)

9. Three months ago, Santos could walk 2 miles in 40 minutes. Today he can walk 2 miles in 25 minutes.

10. Last school year the enrollment of Genoa Middle School was 465 students. This year the enrollment is 525.

11. Refer to the rectangle at the right. Suppose the side lengths are doubled.

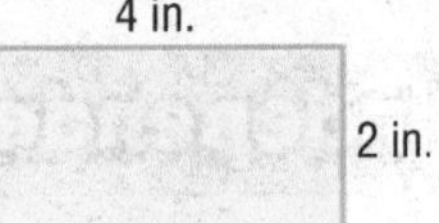

a. Find the percent of change in the perimeter. ______

b. Find the percent of change in the area. ______

12. CCGPS **Use Math Tools** Find examples of data reflecting change over a period of time in a newspaper or magazine, on television, or on the Internet. Determine the percent of change. Explain whether the data show a percent of increase or decrease.

13. Use the graph shown to find the percent of change in CD sales from 2011 to 2012. ______

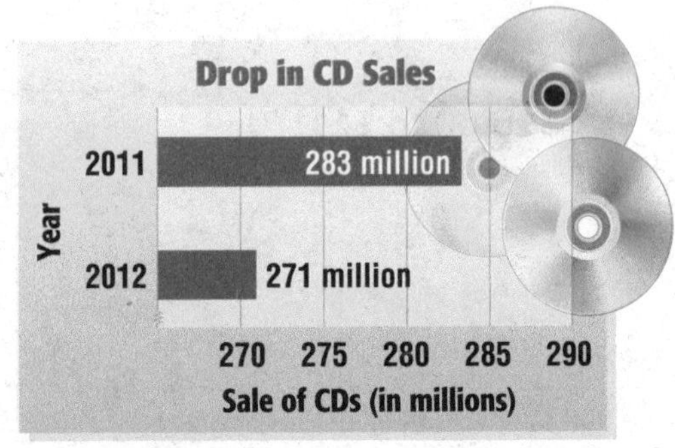

H.O.T. Problems Higher Order Thinking

14. CCGPS **Persevere with Problems** The costs of two sound systems were decreased by $10. The original costs of the systems were $90 and $60. Without calculating, which had a greater percent of decrease? Explain.

15. CCGPS **Find the Error** Dario is finding the percent of change from $52 to $125. Find his mistake and correct it.

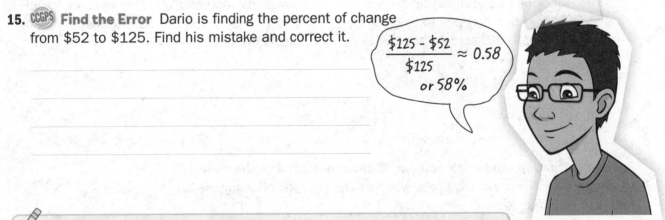

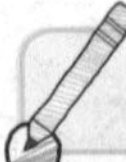

Georgia Test Practice

16. Which of the following represents the least percent of change?

Ⓐ A coat that was originally priced at $90 is now $72.

Ⓑ A puppy who weighed 6 ounces at birth now weighs 96 ounces.

Ⓒ A child grew from 54 inches to 60 inches in 1 year.

Ⓓ A savings account increased from $500 to $550 in 6 months.

Extra Practice

Find each percent of change. Round to the nearest whole percent. State whether the percent of the change is an *increase* or *decrease*.

17. \$12 to \$6

50%; decrease

$12 - 6 = 6$

$\frac{6}{12} = 0.5$ or 50%

18. 48 notebooks to 14 notebooks

19. \$240 to \$320

20. 624 feet to 702 feet

21. The table shows the number of youth 7 years and older who played soccer from 2004 to 2012.

a. Find the percent of change from 2008 to 2012. Round to the nearest tenth of a percent. Is it an increase or decrease?

b. Find the percent of change from 2006 to 2008. Round to the nearest tenth of a percent. Is it an increase or decrease?

Playing Soccer	
Year	**Number (millions)**
2004	12.9
2006	13.7
2008	13.3
2010	14.0
2012	13.8

22. Shoe sales for a certain company were \$25.9 billion. Sales are expected to increase by about 20% in the next year. Find the projected amount of shoe sales next year. ______

23. CCGPS **Be Precise** Eva estimates that 475 songs will fit on her MP3 player. The actual amount of songs that fit is 380. Find the percent error. ______

24. The table shows Catalina's babysitting hours. She charges \$6.50 per hour. Write a sentence that compares the percent of change in the amount of money earned from April to May to the percent of change in the amount of money earned from May to June. Round to the nearest percent if needed.

Month	Hours Worked
April	30
May	35
June	45

Georgia Test Practice

25. Short Response A music video Web site received 5,000 comments on a new song they released. After the artist performed the song on television, the number of comments increased by 30% the next day. How many new comments were on the Web site at the end of the next day?

______

26. Students in a reading program gradually increased the amount of time they read. The first week, they read 20 minutes per day. Each week thereafter, they increased their reading time by 50% until they read an hour per day. In what week of the program did the students begin reading an hour per day?

Ⓐ Week 2 Ⓒ Week 4

Ⓑ Week 3 Ⓓ Week 5

27. Short Response Find the percent of change in the perimeter of the square below if its side length is tripled. ______

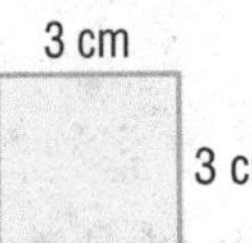

Common Core Review

Find each sum. MCC6.NS.3

28. 1.5 + 2.25 = ______

29. 32.5 + 13.43 = ______

30. \$66.99 + \$8.15 = ______

31. The distances around Earth at the equator and through the North and South Poles are shown at the right. How many miles would you travel if you circled Earth along both routes? MCC6.NS.3

______

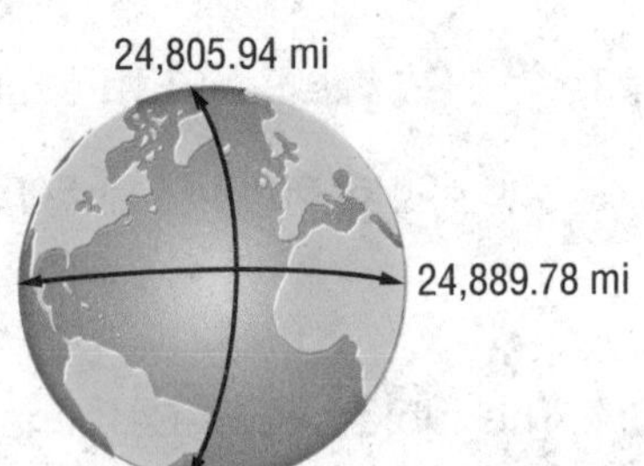

32. The table shows the prices of various grocery items. What is the cost of 3 cans of chicken broth and 2 cans of vegetable soup? MCC6.NS.3

______

Item	Price ($)
chicken broth	0.99
chili	2.49
vegetable soup	1.49

Sales Tax, Tips, and Markup

What You'll Learn

Scan the rest of the lesson. List two headings you would use to make an outline of the lesson.

-
-

Essential Question

HOW can percent help you understand situations involving money.

Vocabulary

sales tax
tip
gratuity
markup
selling price

Common Core GPS

Content Standards
MCC7.RP.3, MCC7.EE.2, MCC7.EE.3

Mathematical Practices
1, 3, 4

Real-World Link

Kayaks Alonso plans to buy a new kayak that costs $2,100. But when he buys the kayak, it actually costs more because he lives in a county where there is a 7% sales tax.

You can find the amount of tax on an item by multiplying the price by the tax percentage.

1. Circle the amount below that shows the amount of tax Alonso will pay for the kayak.

$350 $235 $147

2. Use the amount of tax from Exercise 1 to fill in the receipt at the right. Then find the total cost Alonso will pay for the kayak.

Jimmie's Kayaks

Kayak ______
Sales Tax + ______
Total ______

3. Multiply 1.07 and $2,100. How does the result compare to your answer in Exercise 2?

4. On Alonso's kayaking trip, hiring a guide costs $50. Alonso wants to give the guide a 10% tip. Explain how to find the amount of the tip.

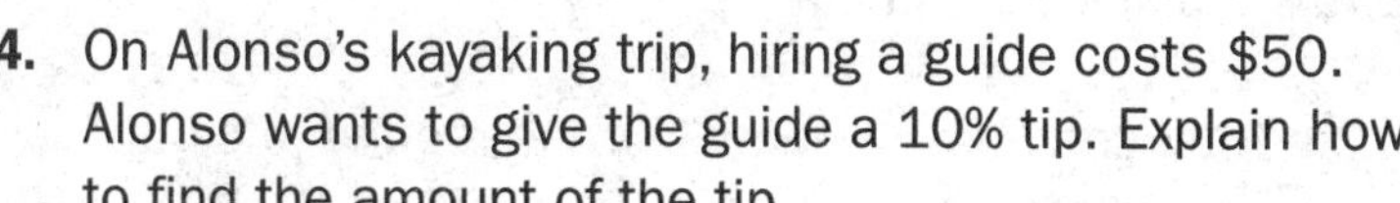

Work Zone

Sales Tax and Total Cost

Sales tax is an additional amount of money charged on items that people buy. The total cost of an item is the regular price plus the sales tax.

Example

1. Drew wants to buy exercise equipment that costs \$140 and the sales tax is 5.75%. What is the total cost of the equipment?

Method 1 **Add sales tax to the regular price.**

First, find the sales tax.

Let t represent the sales tax.

part = percent × whole	Write the percent equation.
$t = 0.0575 \times 140$	$5.75\% = 0.0575$
$t = 8.05$	Multiply.

Next, add the sales tax to the regular price.

\$8.05 + \$140 = \$148.05

Method 2 **Add the percent of tax to 100%.**

$100\% + 5.75\% = 105.75\%$	Add the percent of tax to 100%.

Let t represent the total.

part = percent × whole	Write the percent equation.
$t = 1.0575 \times 140$	$105.75\% = 1.0575$
$t = \$148.05$	Multiply.

The total cost of the exercise equipment is \$148.05.

Got It? **Do this problem to find out.**

a. What is the total cost of a sweatshirt if the regular price is \$42 and the sales tax is $5\frac{1}{2}\%$?

a. ________

Tips and Markups

A **tip** or **gratuity** is a small amount of money in return for a service. The total price is the regular price of the service plus the tip.

A store sells items for more than it pays for those items. The amount of increase is called the **markup**. The **selling price** is the amount the customer pays for an item.

Examples

2. A customer wants to tip 15% on a restaurant bill that is $35. What will be the total bill with tip?

Method 1 **Add the tip to the regular price.**

First, find the tip. Let t represent the tip.

part = percent × whole

$t = 0.15 \times 35$ — 15% = 0.15

$t = 5.25$ — Multiply.

Next, add the tip to the bill.

$5.25 + $35 = $40.25 — Add.

Method 2 **Add the percent of tip to 100%.**

100% + 15% = 115% — Add the percent of tip to 100%.

The total cost is 115% of the bill. Let t represent the total.

part = percent × whole

$t = 1.15 \times 35$ — 115% = 1.15

$t = 40.25$ — Multiply.

Using either method, the total cost of the bill with tip is $40.25.

3. A haircut costs $20. Sales tax is 4.75%. Is $25 sufficient to cover the haircut with tax and a 15% tip?

Sales tax is 4.75% and the tip is 15%, so together they will be 19.75%.

Let t represent the tax and tip.

part = percent × whole

$t = 0.1975 \times 20$ — $0.15 + 0.0475 = 0.1975$

$t = 3.95$ — Multiply.

$20 + $3.95 = $23.95 — Add.

Since $23.95 < $25, $25 is sufficient to cover the total cost.

Mental Math

10% of a number can be found by moving the decimal one place to the left. 10% of $20 is $2. So, 20% of $20 is $4.

Got It? **Do these problems to find out.**

b. Scott wants to tip his taxicab driver 20%. If his commute costs $15, what is the total cost?

c. Find the total cost of a spa treatment of $42 including 6% tax and 20% tip.

b. ____________

c. ____________

Example

4. A store pays $56 for a GPS navigation system. The markup is 25%. Find the selling price.

Markup
In Example 4, you could find the selling price by finding 125% of the amount the store pays.

First, find the markup. Let m represent the markup.

part = percent × whole	Write the percent equation.
$m = 0.25 \times 56$	25% = 0.25
$m = 14$	Mulitply.

Next, add the markup to the amount the store pays.

$14 + $56 = $70   Add.

The selling price of the GPS navigation system is $70.

Got It? **Do this problem to find out.**

d. A store pays $150 for a portable basketball backboard and the markup is 40%. What is the selling price?

d. ________

Guided Practice

Find the total cost to the nearest cent. (Examples 1 and 2)

1. $2.95 notebook; 5% tax ________

2. $28 lunch; 15% tip ________

3. Jaimi went to have a manicure that cost $30. She wanted to tip the technician 20% and tax is 5.75%. How much did she spend total for the manicure? (Example 3)

____

4. Find the selling price of a $62.25 karaoke machine with a 60.5% markup. (Example 4) ________

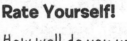

5. **Building on the Essential Question** Describe two methods for finding the total price of a bill that includes a 20% tip. Which method do you prefer? ________

____

____

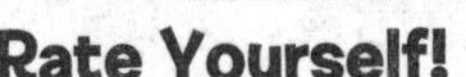

Rate Yourself!

How well do you understand finding sales tax, tips, and markups? Circle the image that applies.

Clear   Somewhat Clear   Not So Clear

For more help, go online to access a Personal Tutor.

Name ______________________ My Homework ______________________

Independent Practice

Go online for Step-by-Step Solutions

Find the total cost to the nearest cent. (Examples 1 and 2)

1. $58 bill; 20% tip ______

2. $43 dinner; 18% gratuity ______

3. $1,500 computer; 7% tax ______

4. $46 shoes; 2.9% tax ______

5. **Financial Literacy** A restaurant bill comes to $28.35. Find the total cost if the tax is 6.25% and a 20% tip is left on the amount before tax. (Example 3) ______

6. Toru takes his dog to be groomed. The fee to groom the dog is $75 plus 6.75% tax. Is $80 enough to pay for the service? Explain. (Example 3) ______

7. Find the selling price of a $270 bicycle with a 24% markup. (Example 4) ______

8. Find the selling price of a $450 painting with a 45% markup. (Example 4) ______

9. What is the sales tax on the chair shown if the tax rate is 5.75%? ______

10. A store pays $10 for a bracelet, and the markup is 115%. A customer will also pay a $5\frac{1}{2}$% sales tax. What will be the total cost of the bracelet to the nearest cent? ______

H.O.T. Problems Higher Order Thinking

11. **Persevere with Problems** The Leather Depot buys a coat from a supplier for $90 wholesale and marks up the price by 40%. If the retail price is $134.82, what is the sales tax? ______

12. **Model with Mathematics** Give an example of the regular price of an item and the total cost including sales tax if the tax rate is 5.75%.

13. **Which One Doesn't Belong?** In each pair, the first value is the regular price of an item and the second value is the price with gratuity. Identify the pair that does not belong with the other three. Explain your reasoning to a classmate.

$30, $34.50	$54, $64.80	$16, $18.40	$90, $103.50

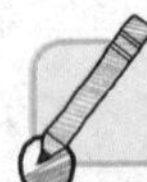

Georgia Test Practice

14. Prices for several cell phones are listed in the table below. The table shows the regular price p and the price with tax t.

Phone	Regular Price (p)	Price with Tax (t)
Flip phone	$80	$86.40
Slide phone	$110	$118.80
Video phone	$120	$129.60

Which formula can be used to calculate the price with tax?

Ⓐ $t = p \times 0.8$
Ⓑ $t = p - 0.8$
Ⓒ $t = p \times 0.08$
Ⓓ $t = p \times 1.08$

Extra Practice

Find the total cost to the nearest cent.

15. \$99 CD player; 5% tax \$103.95

$0.05 \times 99 = 4.95$

\$99.00
+ 4.95
\$103.95

16. \$13 haircut; 15% tip \$14.95

$0.15 \times 13 = 1.95$

\$13.00
+ 1.95
\$14.95

17. \$7.50 meal; 6.5% tax ________

18. \$39 pizza order; 15% tip ________

19. \$89.75 scooter; $7\frac{1}{4}$% tax ________

20. \$8.50 yoga mat; 75% markup ________

21. CCGPS **Reason Inductively** Diana and Sujit clean homes for a summer job. They charge \$70 for the job plus 5% for supplies. A homeowner gave them a 15% tip. Did they receive more than \$82 for their job? Explain.

22. CCGPS **Find the Error** Jamar is finding the selling price of a pair of \$40 skates with a 30% markup. Find his mistake and correct it.

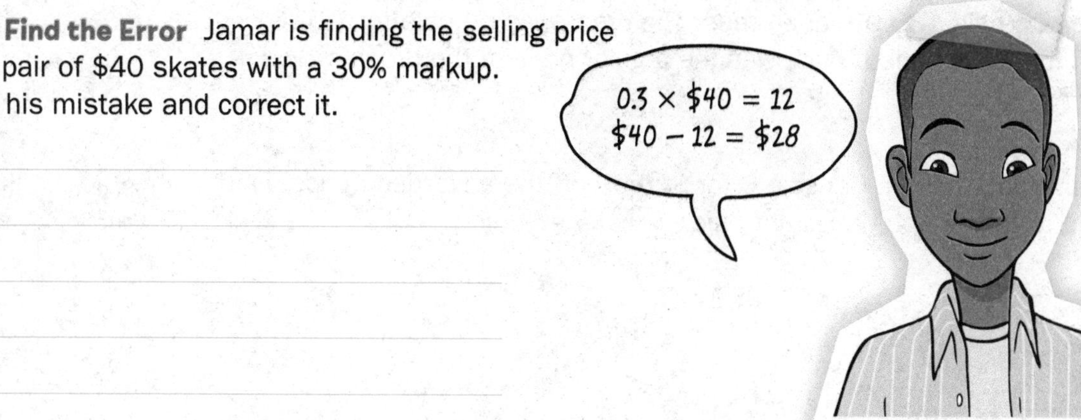

Georgia Test Practice

23. Ms. Taylor bought a water tube to pull behind her boat. The tube cost $87.00 and 9% sales tax was added at the register. Ms. Taylor gave the cashier five $20 bills. How much change should she have received?

Ⓐ $4.83
Ⓑ $5.17
Ⓒ $94.83
Ⓓ $117.00

24. A trampoline costs $220 and the sales tax is 6.25%. What is the total cost of the trampoline?

Ⓕ $13.75
Ⓖ $15.75
Ⓗ $233.75
Ⓘ $240

25. **Short Response** The same pair of boots are at different stores. The cost and sales tax on the boots at each store are shown in the table. In which store would you pay less for the boots? Explain.

Store	Price	Tax
A	$54.90	6%
B	$53.25	7%

Common Core Review

Solve. MCC6.NS.3

26. 45 – 4.5 = ______

27. 89 – 31.15 = ______

28. $102 – $25.75 = ______

29. Renata paid $35.99 for a dress. The dress was on sale for $14.01 off its regular price. What was the regular price of the dress? MCC6.NS.3

30. Mr. Durant bought Console B for $20.99 off the advertised price. Find the total amount Mr. Durant paid. MCC6.NS.3

Game Console	Advertised Price ($)
A	128.99
B	138.99
C	148.99

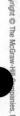

Discount

Essential Question

HOW can percent help you understand situations involving money?

Vocabulary

discount
markdown

Common Core GPS

Content Standards
MCC7.RP.3, MCC7.EE.3

Mathematical Practices
1, 3, 4, 5

What You'll Learn

Scan the lesson. List two real-world scenarios in which you would use discounts.

- ______________________________
- ______________________________

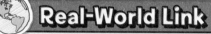

Real-World Link

Water Parks A pass at a water park is $58 dollars at the beginning of the season. The cost of the pass decreases each month.

1. Each month 10% is taken off the price of a season pass. Find the discounted price for August by completing the fill-ins below.

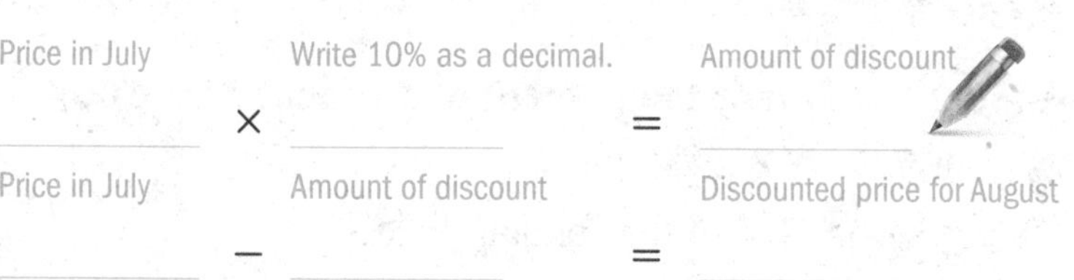

Price in July × Write 10% as a decimal. = Amount of discount
Price in July − Amount of discount = Discounted price for August

2. Multiply 0.9 and $52.20. How does the result compare to your answer in Exercise 1?

3. Write the definition of *discount* in your own words.

Work Zone

Find Sale Price and Original Price

Discount or **markdown** is the amount by which the regular price of an item is reduced. The sale price is the regular price minus the discount.

Example

1. **A DVD normally costs \$22. This week it is on sale for 25% off the original price. What is the sale price of the DVD?**

Original Price
\$22

Sale Price | 25%

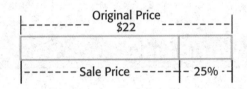

Method 1 **Subtract the discount from the regular price.**

First, find the amount of the discount.

Let d represent the discount.

part = percent × whole	Write the percent equation.
$d = 0.25 \times 22$	25% = 0.25.
$d = 5.50$	Multiply.

Next, subtract the discount from the regular price.

$\$22 - \$5.50 = \$16.50$

Method 2 **Subtract the percent of discount from 100%.**

100% − 25% = 75% — Subtract the discount from 100%.

The sale price is 75% of the regular price.

Let s represent the sale price.

part = percent × whole	Write the percent equation.
$s = 0.75 \times 22$	75% = 0.75
$s = 16.50$	Multiply.

The sale price of the DVD is \$16.50.

Got It? **Do this problem to find out.**

a. ______

a. A shirt is regularly priced at \$42. It is on sale for 15% off of the regular price. What is the sale price of the shirt?

Example

2. A boogie board that has a regular price of \$69 is on sale at a 35% discount. What is the sale price with 7% tax?

Step 1 Find the amount of the discount.

Let d represent the discount.

part = percent × whole	Write the percent equation.
$d = 0.35 \times 69$	35% = 0.35
$d = 24.15$	Multiply.

Step 2 Subtract the discount from the regular price.

\$69 − \$24.15 = \$44.85

Step 3 The percent of tax is applied after the discount is taken.

7% of \$44.85 = 0.07 • 44.85	Write 7% as a decimal.
= 3.14	The tax is \$3.14.
\$44.85 + \$3.14 = \$47.99	Add the tax to the sale price.

The sale price of the boogie board including tax is \$47.99.

Got It? Do this problem to find out.

b. A CD that has a regular price of \$15.50 is on sale at a 25% discount. What is the sale price with 6.5% tax?

b. ________

Example

3. A cell phone is on sale for 30% off. If the sale price is \$239.89, what is the original price?

The sale price is 100% − 30% or 70% of the original price.

Let p represent the original price.

part = percent × whole	
$239.89 = 0.7 \times p$	
$\frac{239.89}{0.7} = \frac{0.7p}{0.7}$	Divide each side by 0.7.
$342.70 = p$	Simplify.

The original price is \$342.70.

Percent Equation

Remember that in the percent equation, the percent must be written as a decimal. Since the sale price is 70% of the original price, use 0.7 to represent 70% in the percent equation.

Got It? Do this problem to find out.

c. Find the original price if the sale price of the cell phone is \$205.50.

c. ________

Example

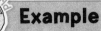

4. Clothes Are Us and Ratcliffe's are having sales. At Clothes Are Us, a pair of sneakers is on sale for 40% off the regular price of $50. At Ratcliffe's, the same brand of sneakers is discounted by 30% off of the regular price of $40. Which store has the better sale price? Explain.

Find the sale price of the sneakers at each store.

Clothes Are Us	**Ratcliffe's**
60% of \$50 = 0.6 × \$50	70% of \$40 = 0.7 × \$40
= \$30	= \$28
The sale price is \$30.	The sale price is \$28.

Since \$28 < \$30, the sale price at Ratcliffe's is the better buy.

Got It? **Do this problem to find out.**

d. If the sale at Clothes Are Us was 50% off, which store would have the better buy? Explain.

d. __________

Guided Practice

1. Mary and Roberto bought identical backpacks at different stores. Mary's backpack originally cost \$65 and was discounted 25%. Roberto's backpack originally cost \$75 and was on sale for 30% off of the original price. Which backpack was the better buy? Explain. (Examples 1, 2, and 4)

2. A pair of in-line skates is on sale for \$90. If this price represents a 9% discount from the original price, what is the original price to the nearest cent? (Example 3)

3. **Building on the Essential Question** Describe two methods for finding the sale price of an item that is discounted 30%.

Rate Yourself!
Are you ready to move on? Shade the section that applies.
I have a few questions.
I'm ready to move on.
I have a lot of questions.
For more help, go online to access a Personal Tutor.
Tutor

Name ______ My Homework ______

Independent Practice

Go online for Step-by-Step Solutions

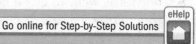

Find the sale price to the nearest cent. (Examples 1 and 2)

1. $64 jacket; 20% discount ______

2. $1,200 TV; 10% discount ______

3. $7.50 admission; 20% off; 5.75% tax ______

4. $4.30 makeup; 40% discount; 6% tax ______

5. A bottle of hand lotion is on sale for $2.25. If this price represents a 50% discount from the original price, what is the original price to the nearest cent? (Example 3)

______

6. A tennis racket at Sport City costs $180 and is discounted 15%. The same model racket costs $200 at Tennis World and is on sale for 20% off. Which store is offering the better deal? Explain. (Example 4)

______

______

7. **Model with Mathematics** Refer to the graphic novel frame below.

a. Find the price that a student would pay including the group discount for each amusement park. ______

______

b. Which is the best deal? ______

8. The Wares want to buy a new computer. The regular price is $1,049. The store is offering a 20% discount and a sales tax of 5.25% is added after the discount. What is the total cost? ________

Find the original price to the nearest cent.

9. calendar: discount, 75%; sale price, $2.25 ________

10. telescope: discount, 30%; sale price, $126 ________

11. CCGPS **Use Math Tools** Compare and contrast tax and discount.

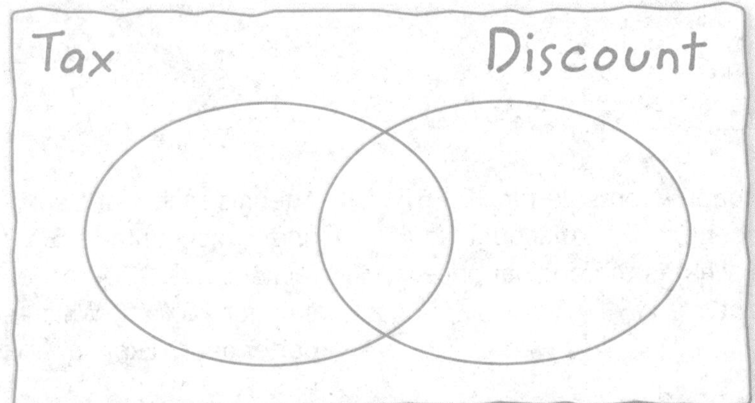

H.O.T. Problems Higher Order Thinking

12. CCGPS **Model with Mathematics** Give an example of the sale price of an item and the total cost including sales tax if the tax rate is 5.75% and the item is 25% off. ________

13. CCGPS **Persevere with Problems** A store is having a sale in which all items are discounted 20%. Including tax, Colin paid $21 for a picture. If the sales tax rate is 5%, what was the original price of the picture? ________

Georgia Test Practice

14. A computer software store is having a sale. The table shows the regular price r and the sale price s of various items. Which formula can be used to calculate the sale price?

Ⓐ $s = r \times 0.2$
Ⓑ $s = r - 0.2$
Ⓒ $s = r \times 0.8$
Ⓓ $s = r - 0.8$

Item	Regular Price (r)	Sale Price (s)
A	$5.00	$4.00
B	$8.00	$6.40
C	$10.00	$8.00
D	$15.00	$12.00

Name _______________ My Homework _______________

Extra Practice

Find the sale price to the nearest cent.

15. $119.50 skateboard; 20% off; 7% tax $102.29

0.20 × $119.50 = $23.90
$119.50 – $23.90 = $95.60
0.07 × $95.60 = $6.69
$95.60 + $6.69 = $102.29

16. $40 sweater; 33% discount ________

17. $199 MP3 player; 15% discount ________

18. $12.25 pen set; 60% discount ________

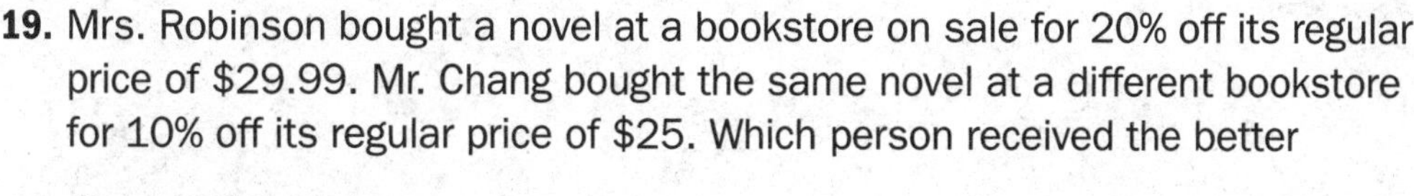

19. Mrs. Robinson bought a novel at a bookstore on sale for 20% off its regular price of $29.99. Mr. Chang bought the same novel at a different bookstore for 10% off its regular price of $25. Which person received the better discount? Explain. ________

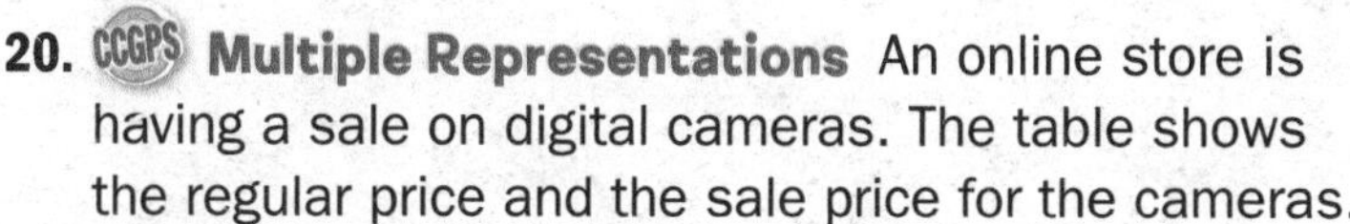

20. CCGPS **Multiple Representations** An online store is having a sale on digital cameras. The table shows the regular price and the sale price for the cameras.

Camera Model	Regular Price	Sale Price	Discount
A	$97.99	$83.30	
B	$102.50	$82.00	
C	$75.99	$65.35	
D	$150.50	$135.45	

a. Words Write a rule that can be used to find the percent of decrease for any of the cameras.

____

b. Table Complete the table for the discount.

c. Numbers Which model has the greatest percent discount?

____

Georgia Test Practice

21. A chair that costs $210 was reduced by 40% for a one-day sale. After the sale, the sale price was increased by 40%. What is the price of the chair?

Ⓐ $176.40
Ⓑ $185.30
Ⓒ $205.50
Ⓓ $210.00

22. Carmen paid $10.50 for a T-shirt at the mall. It was on sale for 30% off. What was the original price before the discount?

Ⓕ $3.15
Ⓖ $7.35
Ⓗ $15.00
Ⓘ $35.00

Common Core Review

Find the percent of change. Round to the nearest whole percent if necessary. State whether the percent of change is an *increase* or *decrease*.

MCC7.RP.3

23. 35 birds to 45 birds

24. 60 inches to 38 inches

25. $2.75 to $1.80

26. Complete the table to express each number of months in years. Write in simplest form. The first one is done for you. MCC6.RP.3a

Number of Months	1	2	3	4	6
Time in Years	$\frac{1}{12}$				

27. Carlos, Karen, and Beng saved money for an overseas trip. Carlos saved for $1\frac{1}{2}$ years. Karen saved for $1\frac{1}{3}$ years. Beng saved for $1\frac{1}{6}$ years. For how many months did each person save? MCC5.MD.1

Financial Literacy: Simple Interest

What You'll Learn

Scan the lesson. Predict two things you will learn about financial literacy.

-
-

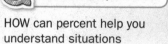

Essential Question

HOW can percent help you understand situations involving money?

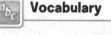

Vocabulary

principal
simple interest

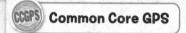

Common Core GPS

Content Standards
MCC7.RP.3, MCC7.EE.3

Mathematical Practices
1, 3, 4

Vocabulary Start-Up

Principal is the amount of money deposited or borrowed. **Simple interest** is the amount paid or earned for the use of money.

The simple interest formula is shown below. Fill in the diagram using the correct words from the word bank.

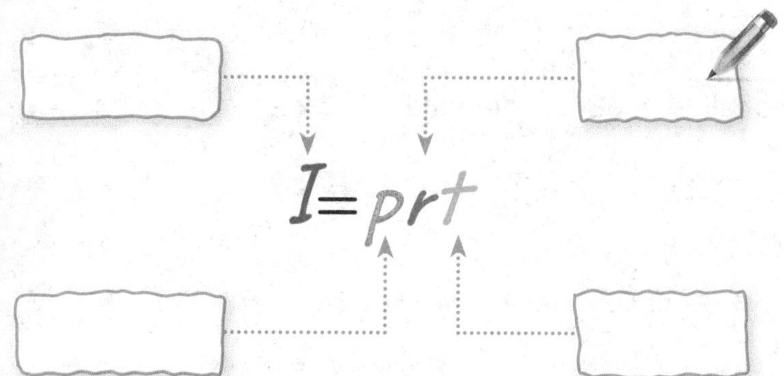

Word Bank
interest
principal
rate
time

Real-World Link

Mrs. Ramirez is investing $400 in a savings account at a simple interest rate of 2% to purchase a laptop computer. She plans on investing the money for 18 months.

Based on this real-world situation, fill in the blanks with the correct numbers. Write the rate as a decimal. Time is expressed in years.

principal = ______ rate = ______ time = ______ years

Key Concept Simple Interest Formula

Words Simple interest I is the product of the principal p, the annual interest rate r, and the time t, expressed in years.

Symbols $I = prt$

Work Zone

If you have a savings account, the bank pays you interest for the use of your money. Use the formula $I = prt$ to find the amount of interest that will be earned.

Examples

Arnold puts \$580 into a savings account. The account pays 3% simple interest. How much interest will he earn in each amount of time?

1. 5 years

$I = prt$	Formula for simple interest
$I = 580 \cdot 0.03 \cdot 5$	Replace p with \$580, r with 0.03, and t with 5.
$I = 87$	Simplify.

So, Arnold will earn \$87 in interest in 5 years.

2. 6 months

6 months $= \frac{6}{12}$ or 0.5 year	Write the time as years.
$I = prt$	Formula for simple interest
$I = 580 \cdot 0.03 \cdot 0.5$	$p = \$580, r = 0.03, t = 0.5$
$I = 8.7$	Simplify.

So, Arnold will earn \$8.70 in interest in 6 months.

Got It? **Do these problems to find out.**

a. Jenny puts \$1,560 into a savings account. The account pays 2.5% simple interest. How much interest will she earn in 3 years?

b. Marcos invests \$760 into a savings account. The account pays 4% simple interest. How much interest will he earn after 5 years?

a. ____________

b. ____________

Interest on Loans and Credit Cards

If you borrow money from a bank, you pay the bank interest for the use of their money. You also pay interest to a credit card company if you have an unpaid balance. Use the formula $I = prt$ to find the amount of interest owed.

Examples

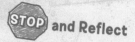

3. Rondell's parents borrow $6,300 from the bank for a new car. The interest rate is 6% per year. How much simple interest will they pay if they take 2 years to repay the loan?

$I = prt$ Formula for simple interest

$I = 6{,}300 \cdot 0.06 \cdot 2$ Replace p with $6,300, r with 0.06, and t with 2.

$I = 756$ Simplify.

Rondell's parents will pay $756 in interest in 2 years.

4. Derrick's dad bought new tires for $900 using a credit card. His card has an interest rate of 19%. If he has no other charges on his card and does not make a payment, how much money will he owe after one month?

$I = prt$ Formula for simple interest

$I = 900 \cdot 0.19 \cdot \frac{1}{12}$ Replace p with $900, r with 0.19, and t with $\frac{1}{12}$.

$I = 14.25$ Simplify.

The interest owed after one month is $14.25.

So, the total amount owed would be $900 + $14.25 or $914.25.

and Reflect

Explain in the space below how you would find the simple interest on a $500 loan at a 6% interest rate for 18 months.

Got It? Do these problems to find out.

c. Mrs. Hanover borrows $1,400 at a rate of 5.5% per year. How much simple interest will she pay if it takes 8 months to repay the loan?

d. An office manager charged $425 worth of office supplies on a credit card. The credit card has an interest rate of 9.9%. How much money will he owe at the end of one month if he makes no other charges on the card and does not make a payment?

c. ________

d. ________

Example

5. Luis is taking out a car loan for $5,000. He plans on paying off the car loan in 2 years. At the end of 2 years, Luis will have paid $300 in interest. What is the simple interest rate on the car loan?

$I = prt$	Formula for simple interest
$300 = 5{,}000 \cdot r \cdot 2$	Replace I with 300, p with 5,000, and t with 2.
$300 = 10{,}000r$	Simplify.
$\frac{300}{10{,}000} = \frac{10{,}000r}{10{,}000}$	Divide each side by 10,000.
$0.03 = r$	

The simple interest rate is 0.03 or 3%.

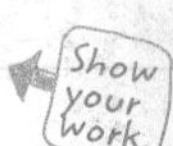

Got It? **Do this problem to find out.**

e. __________

e. Maggie is taking out a student loan for $2,600. She plans on paying off the loan in 3 years. At the end of 3 years, Maggie will have paid $390 in interest. What is the simple interest rate on the student loan?

Guided Practice

1. The Masters family financed a computer that cost $1,200. If the interest rate is 19%, how much will the family owe for the computer after one month if no payments are made? (Examples 1–4) __________

2. Samantha received a loan from the bank for $4,500. She plans on paying off the loan in 4 years. At the end of 4 years, Samantha will have paid $900 in interest. What is the simple interest rate on the bank loan? (Example 5)

____

3. **Building on the Essential Question** How can you use a formula to find simple interest?

____

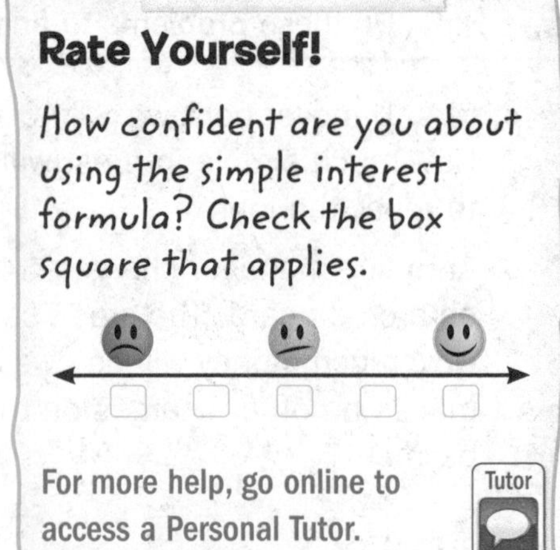

Rate Yourself!
How confident are you about using the simple interest formula? Check the box square that applies.
For more help, go online to access a Personal Tutor.
Tutor

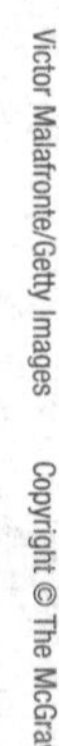

Independent Practice

Go online for Step-by-Step Solutions 

Find the simple interest earned to the nearest cent for each principal, interest rate, and time. (Examples 1 and 2)

1. $640, 3%, 2 years ________

2. $1,500, 4.25%, 4 years ________

3. $580, 2%, 6 months ________

4. $1,200, 3.9%, 8 months ________

Find the simple interest paid to the nearest cent for each loan amount, interest rate, and time. (Example 3)

5. $4,500, 9%, 3.5 years ________

6. $290, 12.5%, 6 months ________

7. Leon charged $75 at an interest rate of 12.5%. How much will Leon have to pay after one month if he makes no payments? (Example 4)

____

8. Jamerra received a $3,000 car loan. She plans on paying off the loan in 2 years. At the end of 2 years, Jamerra will have paid $450 in interest. What is the simple interest rate on the car loan? (Example 5)

____

9. CCGPS **Justify Conclusions** Pablo has $4,200 to invest for college.

   a. If Pablo invests $4,200 for 3 years and earns $630, what is the simple interest rate? ________

   b. Pablo's goal is to have $5,000 after 4 years. Is this possible if he invests with a rate of return of 6%? Explain. ________

____

10. **Financial Literacy** The table shows interest owed for a home improvement loan based on how long it takes to pay off the loan.

a. What is the simple interest owed on $900 for 9 months? ______

b. Find the simple interest owed on $2,500 for 18 months. ______

c. Find the simple interest owed on $5,600 for 6 months. ______

Time	Rate
6 months	2.4%
9 months	2.9%
12 months	3.0%
18 months	3.1%

H.O.T. Problems Higher Order Thinking

11. CCGPS **Justify Conclusions** Suppose you earn 3% on a $1,200 deposit for 5 years. Explain how the simple interest is affected if the rate is increased by 1%. What happens if the time is increased by 1 year?

______

______

______

12. CCGPS **Persevere with Problems** Dustin bought a $2,000 computer with a credit card. The minimum payment each month is $35. Each month 1% of the unpaid balance is added to the amount he owes.

a. If Dustin pays only $35 the first month, what will he owe the second month? ______

b. If Dustin makes the minimum payment, what will he owe the third month? ______

Georgia Test Practice

13. Jada invests $590 in a money market account. Her account pays 7.2% simple interest. If she does not add or withdraw any money, how much interest will Jada's account earn after 4 years of simple interest?

Ⓐ $75.80
Ⓑ $158.67
Ⓒ $169.92
Ⓓ $220.67

Extra Practice

Find the simple interest earned to the nearest cent for each principal, interest rate, and time.

14. \$1,050, 4.6%, 2 years $96.60

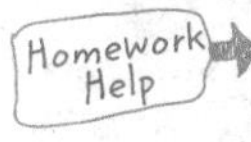

$I = prt$

$I = \$1,050 \cdot 0.046 \cdot 2$

$I = 96.60$

15. \$500, 3.75%, 4 months ______

16. \$250, 2.85%, 3 years ______

17. \$3,000, 5.5%, 9 months ______

Find the simple interest paid to the nearest cent for each loan amount, interest rate, and time.

18. \$1,000, 7%, 2 years ______

19. \$725, 6.25%, 1 year ______

20. \$2,700, 8.2%, 3 months ______

21. \$175.80, 12%, 8 months ______

22. Jake received a student loan for \$12,000. He plans on paying off the loan in 5 years. At the end of 5 years, Jake will have paid \$3,600 in interest. What is the simple interest rate on the student loan?

______

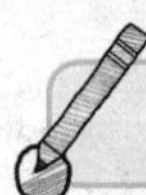

Georgia Test Practice

23. Mei-Ling invested $2,000 in a simple interest account for 3 years. At the end of 3 years, she had earned $150 in interest. What was the simple interest rate of the account?

Ⓐ 0.025%
Ⓑ 0.25%
Ⓒ 2.5%
Ⓓ 25%

24. Mr. Sprockett borrows $3,500 from his bank to buy a used car. The loan has a 7.4% annual simple interest rate. If it takes Mr. Sprockett two years to pay back the loan, what is the total amount he will be paying?

Ⓕ $3,012
Ⓖ $3,598
Ⓗ $4,018
Ⓘ $4,550

Common Core Review

Label the number line below from 0 to 10. Then graph each number. MCC6.NS.6

25. 2.5

26. $8\frac{1}{4}$

27. 5.9

28. $\frac{1}{1}$

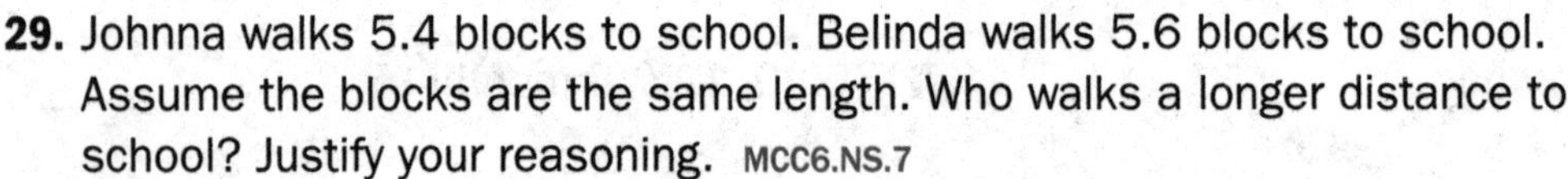

29. Johnna walks 5.4 blocks to school. Belinda walks 5.6 blocks to school. Assume the blocks are the same length. Who walks a longer distance to school? Justify your reasoning. MCC6.NS.7

30. Use the Commutative and Associative Properties of Addition to mentally find (11 + 64) + 9. Then justify each step. MCC6.EE.3

Inquiry Lab

Spreadsheet: Compound Interest

HOW is compound interest different from simple interest?

Content Standards
MCC7.RP.3
Mathematical Practices
1, 3, 5

College Jin Li's parents deposit $2,000 in a college savings account. The account pays an interest rate of 4% compounded annually. Complete the Investigation to find how much money will be in the account after 9 years.

Investigation

Compound interest is interest earned on the original principal and on interest earned in the past. At the end of each time period, the interest earned is added to the principal, which becomes the new principal for the next time period.

A computer spreadsheet is a useful tool for quickly performing calculations involving compound interest. To perform a calculation in a spreadsheet cell, first enter the equals sign. For example, enter =A4+B4 to find the sum of Cells A4 and B4.

Create a spreadsheet like the one shown.

Compound Interest

◇	A	B	C	D
1	Rate	0.04		
2				
3	Principal	Interest	New Principal	Time (YR)
4	$2000.00	$80.00	$2080.00	1
5	$2080.00	$83.20	$2163.20	2
6	$2163.20	$86.53	$2249.73	3
7	$2249.73	$89.99	$2339.72	4
8	$2339.72	$93.59	$2433.31	5
9	$2433.31	$97.33	$2530.64	6
10	$2530.64	$101.23	$2631.86	7
11	$2631.86	$105.27	$2737.14	8
12				

Sheet 1 Sheet 2 Sheet 3

The interest rate is entered as a decimal.

The spreadsheet evaluates the formula A4×B1.

The interest is added to the principal every year. The spreadsheet evaluates the formula A4+B4.

What formula would the spreadsheet use to find the new principal at the end of Year 9? ________________

So, the account will have a balance of __________ after 9 years.

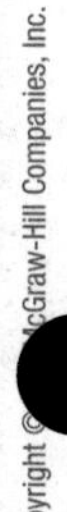

Collaborate

Work with a partner. Create spreadsheets for the situations below. Then answer the questions.

1. Lakeesha deposits $1,500 into a Young Savers account. The account receives 4% interest compounded annually. What is the balance in Lakeesha's account after 2 years? after 3 years?

   2 Years: ________ 3 Years: ________

2. Michael deposits $2,650 into an account. The interest rate on the account is 6% compounded annually. What is the balance in Michael's account after 2 years? after 3 years?

   2 Years: ________ 3 Years: ________

Analyze

Work with a partner to answer the following question.

3. CCGPS **Reason Inductively** Suppose you deposit $1,000 into a bank account paying 4.75% interest compounded annually. At the same time, a friend deposits $1,000 in a separate account that pays 5% simple interest. You and your friend withdraw your money from the accounts after 6 years. Predict which account made more money. Explain.

Reflect

4. Inquiry HOW is compound interest different from simple interest?

Investigate Online Maps and Scale Drawings

HOW is the zoom feature of an online map like the scale of a drawing?

Content Standards
MCC7.G.1

Mathematical Practices
1, 3, 5

Online Maps Maps and blueprints are *scale drawings* of the locations and buildings they represent. Unlike maps printed on paper, online map services allow users the opportunity to view a location from different distances.

Maps | Directions | Info

Start Here — Country

Business or Name: Name of your School

Address or location

City: Your Town — State — Zip Code

Investigation 1

Step 1 Use the online map service provided to you by your teacher. Locate your school on a map.

Step 2 Measure the length of the scale bar in centimeters on the online map. Find the scale distance of the map. Write these values in the Original View table in Step 4.

Step 3 Click on the satellite or aerial view. Use the zoom feature to zoom in until your school shows up on the map.

Step 4 Measure the length of the scale bar in centimeters. Find the new scale distance for the map. Write these values in the Zoom View table.

Original View	
Scale Bar	
Scale Distance	

Zoom View	
Scale Bar	
Scale Distance	

What happens when you use the zoom feature?

Describe the appearance of the map as you zoomed in.

CCGPS **Use Math Tools** **Work with a partner to answer the following questions about using an online map service.**

1. Locate the local public library on the map. Write the scale bar and scale distance values in the Original View table below Exercise 2.

2. Click on the satellite or aerial view. Use the zoom feature to zoom in until the building shows up on the map. Write the scale bar and scale distance values in the Zoom View table.

Original View	
Scale Bar	
Scale Distance	

Zoom View	
Scale Bar	
Scale Distance	

Work with a partner to answer the following questions about using an online map.

3. Refer to Investigation 1. Write a ratio $\frac{\text{scale bar}}{\text{scale distance}}$ for the original view and the zoom view.

   Original View: ______ Zoom View: ______

4. How many times bigger is the zoom view?

5. Refer to the table in Exercise 2. Write a ratio $\frac{\text{scale bar}}{\text{scale distance}}$ for the original view and the zoom view.

   Original View: ______ Zoom View: ______

6. How many times bigger is the zoom view?

Investigation 2

The diagram shown represents a garden. The scale is 1 centimeter = 30 meters.

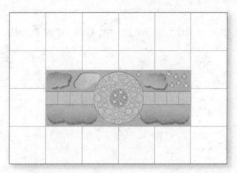

Step 1 Write the length and width of the drawing of the garden.

Length: ________ centimeters Width: ________ centimeters

Step 2 Use the scale to find the dimensions of the garden.

Length: ________ meters Width: ________ meters

Step 3 On the grid below, draw the garden so that the scale is 1 centimeter = 10 meters. Write the dimensions of your drawing.

Length: ________ centimeters Width: ________ centimeters

Step 4 Use the scale on your drawing to compute the dimensions of the garden. How do the dimensions compare to the dimensions in Step 2?

Length: ________ meters Width: ________ meters

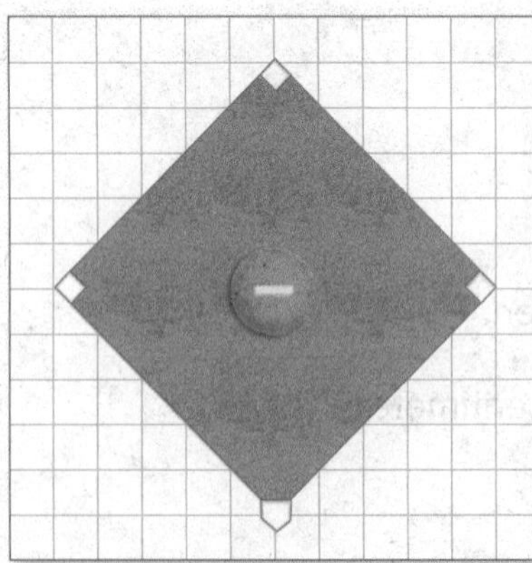

Collaborate

Work with a partner to answer the following questions about reproducing a scale drawing.

7. Recreate the drawing of the baseball diamond below using the new scale.

current scale: 1 unit = 15 ft
new scale: 1 unit = 30 ft

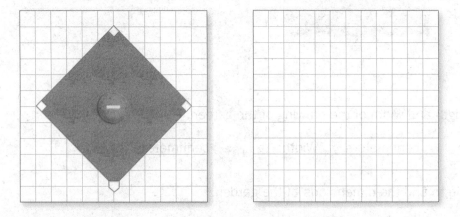

8. A drawing of the Statue of Liberty is 3 inches tall. The scale is 1 inch = 50 feet. How tall would the drawing be if the scale were 0.5 inch = 100 feet? ______

Analyze

9. CCGPS **Reason Inductively** The triangle shown in the drawing has an area of 40 square feet. What is the scale of the drawing? ______

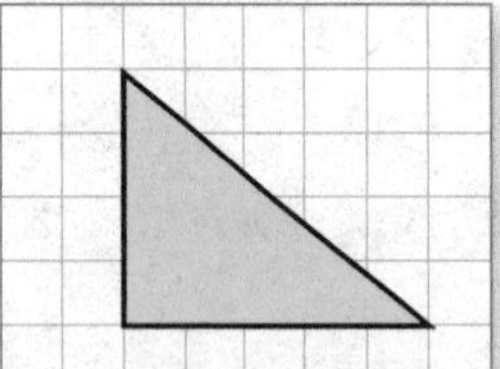

Reflect

10. Inquiry HOW is the zoom feature of an online map like the scale of a drawing?

______

______

______

Scale Drawings

What You'll Learn

Scan the lesson. Predict two things you will learn about scale drawings.

- ______________________________
- ______________________________

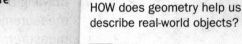

Essential Question

HOW does geometry help us describe real-world objects?

Vocabulary

scale drawing
scale model
scale
scale factor

Common CoreGPS

Content Standards
MCC7.G.1

Mathematical Practices
1, 2, 3, 4, 5

Real-World Link

Room Model Architects make detailed drawings of rooms and buildings. Conner made a drawing of a bedroom. Follow the steps below to make a model of a room of your choosing.

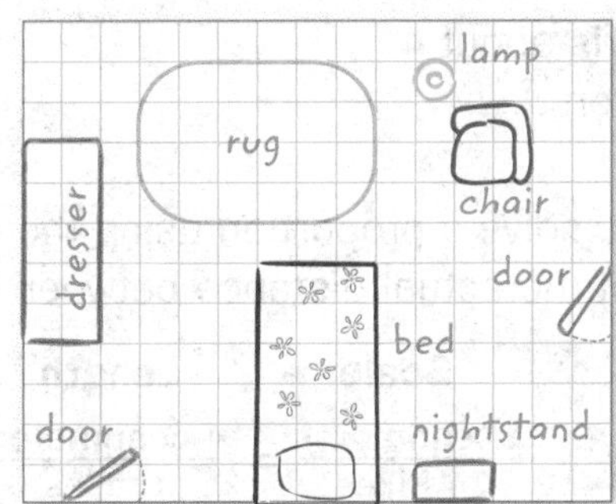

Step 1 Measure the length of three objects in the room. Record each length to the nearest $\frac{1}{2}$ foot in the table below.

Object	Length (ft)	Length (units)

Step 2 Let 1 unit represent 2 feet. So, 4 units = 8 feet. Convert all your measurements to units. Record these values.

Step 3 On grid paper, make a drawing of your room like the one shown.

Work Zone

Use a Scale Drawing or a Scale Model

Scale drawings and **scale models** are used to represent objects that are too large or too small to be drawn or built at actual size. The **scale** gives the ratio that compares the measurements of the drawing or model to the measurements of the real object. The measurements on a drawing or model are proportional to the measurements on the actual object.

Example

1. What is the actual distance between Hagerstown and Annapolis?

Step 1 Use a centimeter ruler to find the map distance between the two cities. The map distance is about 4 centimeters.

Step 2 Write and solve a proportion using the scale. Let d represent the actual distance between the cities.

	Scale		Length	
map → actual →	$\frac{1 \text{ centimeter}}{24 \text{ miles}}$	=	$\frac{4 \text{ centimeter}}{d \text{ miles}}$	← map ← actual

$1 \times d = 24 \times 4$ Cross products

$d = 96$ Simplify.

The distance between the cities is about 96 miles.

Scale

A map scale can be written in different ways, including the following:

1 cm = 20 mi

1 cm : 20 mi

$\frac{1 \text{ cm}}{20 \text{ mi}}$

Got It? Do this problem to find out.

a. ________

a. On the map of Arkansas shown, find the actual distance between Clarksville and Little Rock. Use a ruler to measure.

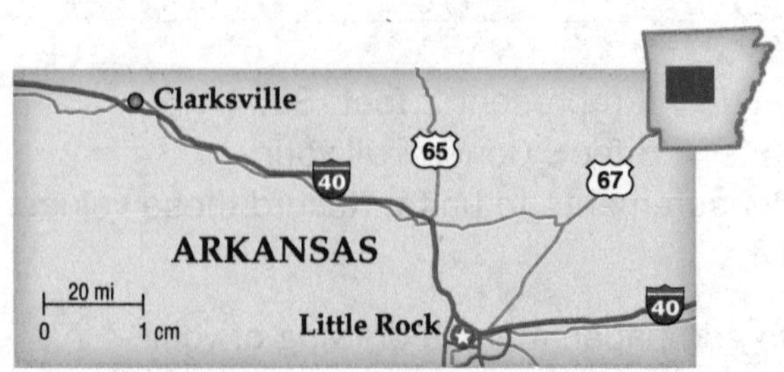

Example

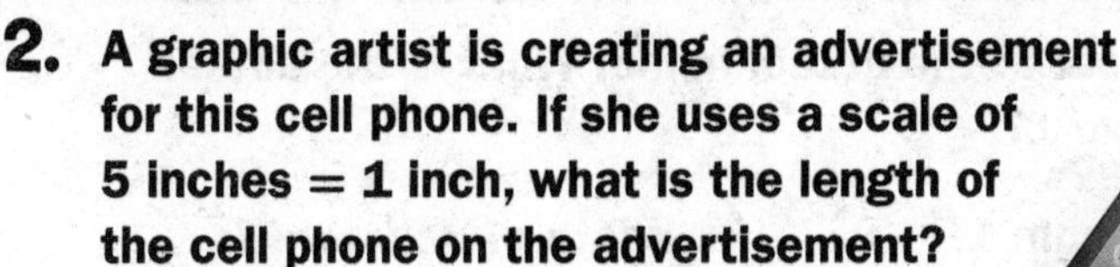

2. A graphic artist is creating an advertisement for this cell phone. If she uses a scale of 5 inches = 1 inch, what is the length of the cell phone on the advertisement?

Write a proportion using the scale. Let *a* represent the length of the advertisement cell phone.

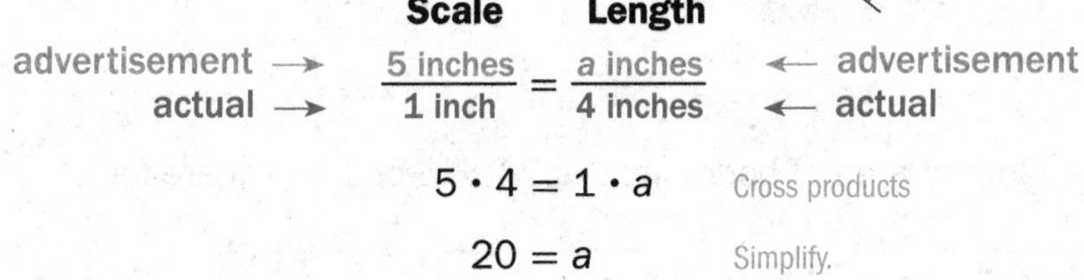

	Scale		Length	
advertisement →	5 inches	=	*a* inches	← advertisement
actual →	1 inch		4 inches	← actual

$$5 \cdot 4 = 1 \cdot a \quad \text{Cross products}$$

$$20 = a \quad \text{Simplify.}$$

The length of the cell phone on the advertisement is 20 inches long.

Scale
The scale is the ratio of the drawing/model measure to the actual measure. It is not always the ratio of a smaller measure to a larger measure.

Got It? Do this problem to find out.

b. A scooter is $3\frac{1}{2}$ feet long. Find the length of a scale model of the scooter if the scale is 1 inch = $\frac{3}{4}$ feet.

b. ________

Find a Scale Factor

A scale written as a ratio without units in simplest form is called the **scale factor.**

Example

3. Find the scale factor of a model sailboat if the scale is 1 inch = 6 feet.

$$\frac{1 \text{ inch}}{6 \text{ feet}} = \frac{1 \text{ inch}}{72 \text{ inches}} \quad \text{Convert 6 feet to inches.}$$

$$= \frac{1}{72} \quad \text{Divide out the common units.}$$

The scale factor is $\frac{1}{72}$.

Got It? Do this problem to find out.

c. What is the scale factor of a model car if the scale is 1 inch = 2 feet?

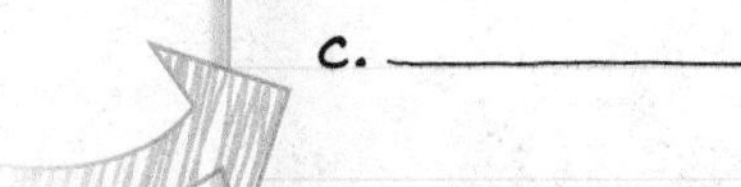

c. ________

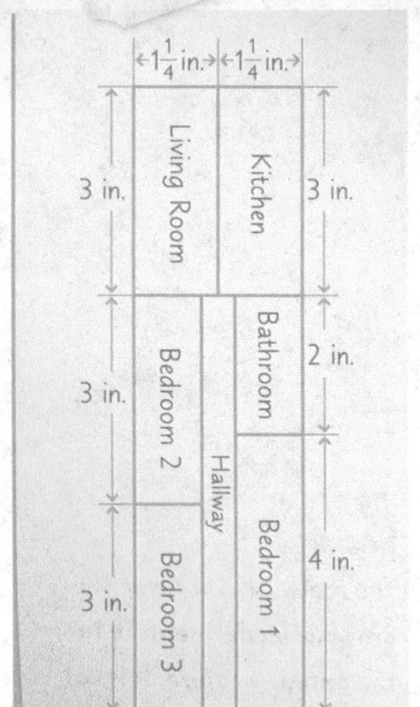

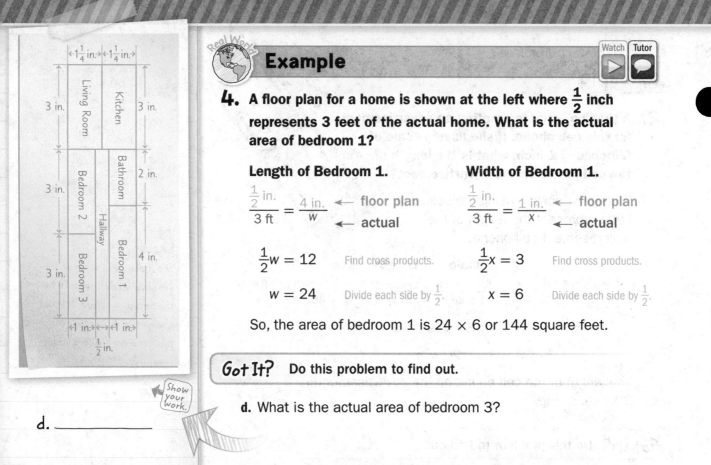

Example

4. A floor plan for a home is shown at the left where $\frac{1}{2}$ inch represents 3 feet of the actual home. What is the actual area of bedroom 1?

Length of Bedroom 1.

$\frac{\frac{1}{2}\text{ in.}}{3\text{ ft}} = \frac{4\text{ in.}}{w}$ ← floor plan ← actual

$\frac{1}{2}w = 12$ Find cross products.

$w = 24$ Divide each side by $\frac{1}{2}$.

Width of Bedroom 1.

$\frac{\frac{1}{2}\text{ in.}}{3\text{ ft}} = \frac{1\text{ in.}}{x}$ ← floor plan ← actual

$\frac{1}{2}x = 3$ Find cross products.

$x = 6$ Divide each side by $\frac{1}{2}$.

So, the area of bedroom 1 is 24×6 or 144 square feet.

Got It? **Do this problem to find out.**

Show your work.

d. What is the actual area of bedroom 3?

d. ____________

Guided Practice

1. On a map, the distance from Akron to Cleveland measures 2 centimeters. What is the actual distance if the scale of the map shows that 1 centimeter is equal to 30 kilometers? (Example 1)

2. An engineer makes a model of a bridge using a scale of 1 inch = 3 yards. The length of the actual bridge is 50 yards. What is the length of the model? (Example 2)

3. Julie is constructing a scale model of her room. The rectangular room is $10\frac{1}{4}$ inches by 8 inches. If 1 inch represents 2 feet of the actual room, what is the scale factor and the actual area of the room? (Examples 3 and 4)

4. **Building on the Essential Question** Explain how you could use a map to estimate the actual distance between Miami, Florida, and Atlanta, Georgia.

Rate Yourself!

How well do you understand scale drawings? Circle the image that applies.

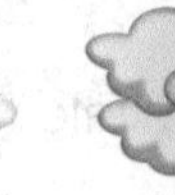

Clear | Somewhat Clear | Not So Clear

For more help, go online to access a Personal Tutor.

Name ________________ My Homework ________________

Independent Practice

Go online for Step-by-Step Solutions 

CCGPS Use Math Tools Find the actual distance between each pair of locations in South Carolina. Use a ruler to measure. (Example 1)

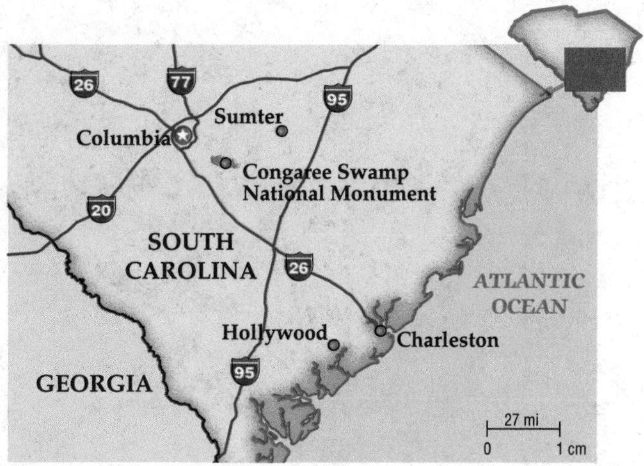

1. Columbia and Charleston ________

2. Hollywood and Sumter ________

Find the length of each model. Then find the scale factor. (Examples 2 and 3)

3. 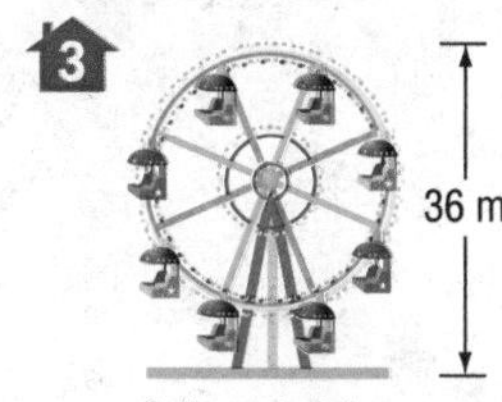

4. 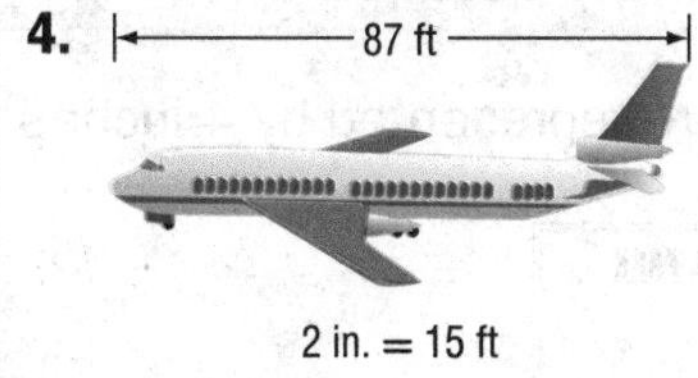

5. A model of an apartment is shown where $\frac{1}{4}$ inch represents 3 feet in the actual apartment. Find the actual area of the master bedroom. (Example 4)

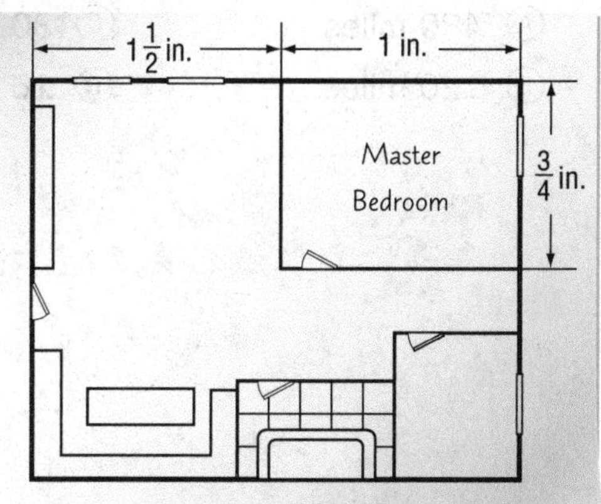

H.O.T. Problems Higher Order Thinking

6. CCGPS **Model with Mathematics** On the grid paper, create a scale drawing of a room in your home. Include the scale that you used.

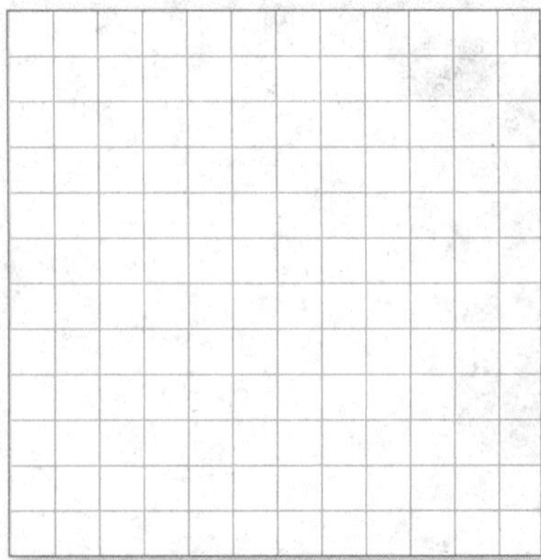

7. CCGPS **Reason Abstractly** A statue of Thomas Jefferson was made using a scale of 3 feet = 1 foot. Write an expression to represent the height of the statue if Thomas Jefferson is x feet in height. Then find his actual height if the height of the statue is 19 feet.

Georgia Test Practice

8. How many miles are represented by 4 inches on this map?

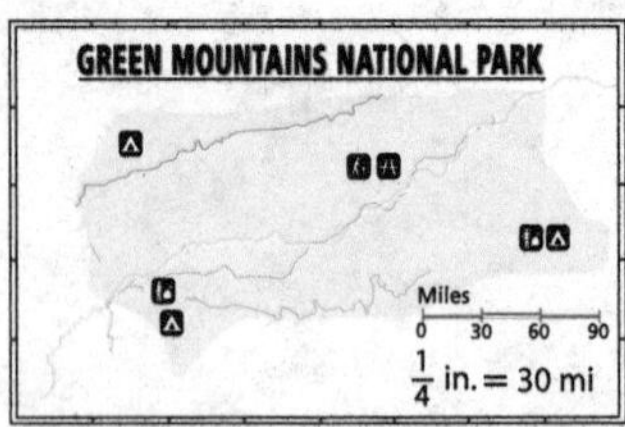

Ⓐ 480 miles

Ⓑ 120 miles

Ⓒ 30 miles

Ⓓ 16 miles

Extra Practice

CCGPS Use Math Tools Find the actual distance between each pair of cities in New Mexico. Use a ruler to measure.

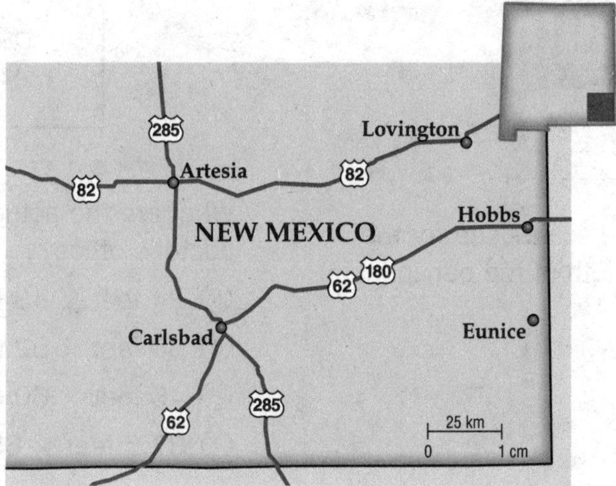

9. Carlsbad and Artesia 50 km

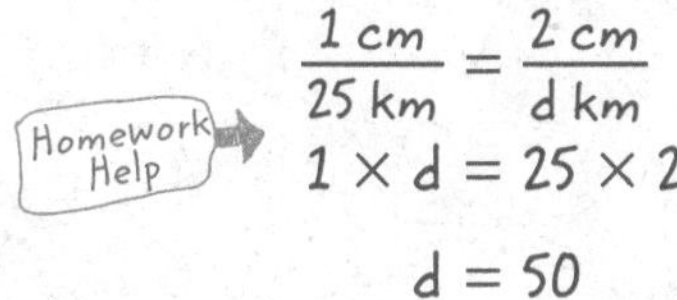

Homework Help
$\frac{1 \text{ cm}}{25 \text{ km}} = \frac{2 \text{ cm}}{d \text{ km}}$
$1 \times d = 25 \times 2$
$d = 50$

10. Artesia and Eunice ______

11. Lovington and Carlsbad ______

12. Find the length of the model. Then find the scale factor. The length of an actual bird is shown at the right.

______

1 in. = 0.5 in.

Copy and Solve Show your work on a separate piece of paper.

13. A model of a tree is made using a scale of 1 inch = 25 feet. What is the height of the actual tree if the height of the model is $4\frac{3}{8}$ inches?

14. A map of Bakersfield has a scale of 1 inch = 5 miles. If the city is $5\frac{1}{5}$ inches across on the map, what is the actual distance across the city?

15. Tyson is creating a scale drawing of the area of his school. The rectangular drawing shows the length as 20 inches and the width as 19 inches. The drawing uses a scale of 1 inch = 3 feet. What is the actual area of the school in square feet?

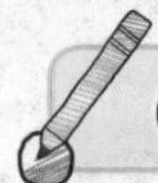

Georgia Test Practice

16. A landscape designer created the scale drawing below showing the bench that will be in the garden area.

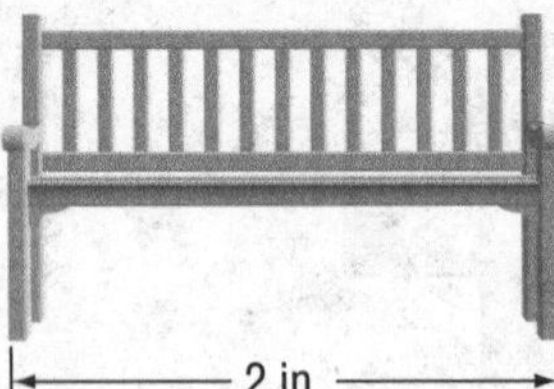

Which of these was the scale used for the drawing if the actual width of the bench is 6 feet?

Ⓐ $\frac{1}{4}$ inch = 1 foot

Ⓑ 3 inches = 1 foot

Ⓒ $\frac{2}{3}$ inch = 1 foot

Ⓓ 1 inch = 3 feet

17. A scale drawing of a doctor's office is shown.

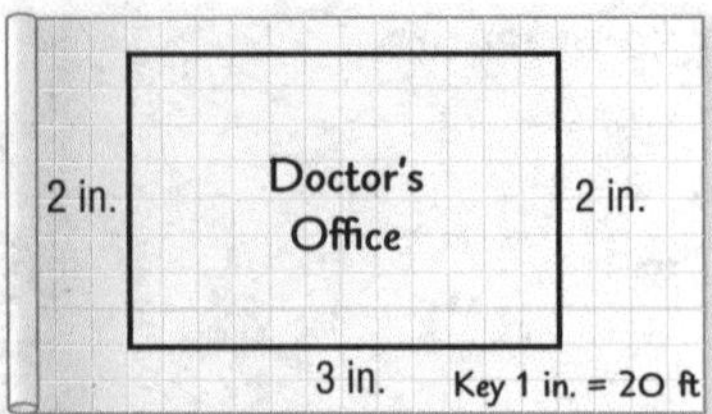

What are the actual dimensions of the doctor's office?

Ⓕ 24 feet × 48 feet

Ⓖ 30 feet × 52 feet

Ⓗ 40 feet × 60 feet

Ⓘ 37.5 feet × 65 feet

18. **Short Response** Ernesto drew a map of his school. He used a scale of 1 inch : 50 feet. What distance in inches on Ernesto's map should represent the 625 feet between the cafeteria and the science lab?

Common Core Review

19. A carpenter sawed a piece of wood into 3 pieces. The ratio of wood pieces is 1 : 3 : 6. The longest piece is 2.5 feet longer than the shortest piece. Use the *draw a diagram* strategy to find the length of the original piece. MCC6.RP.1

Solve each proportion. MCC7.RP.2C

20. $\frac{2}{5} = \frac{b}{25}$

21. $\frac{3}{7} = \frac{a}{49}$

22. $\frac{2}{9} = \frac{x}{99}$

Content Standards
MCC7.G.1

Mathematical Practices
1, 3, 5

WHAT happens to the size of a scale drawing when it is reproduced using a different scale?

Miniature Golf The owner of the miniature golf course wants to create a sign with an image of the 18th hole on it. Use the dimensions shown to create a scale drawing using the Geometer's Sketchpad®. Use the scale 1 centimeter = 3 meters.

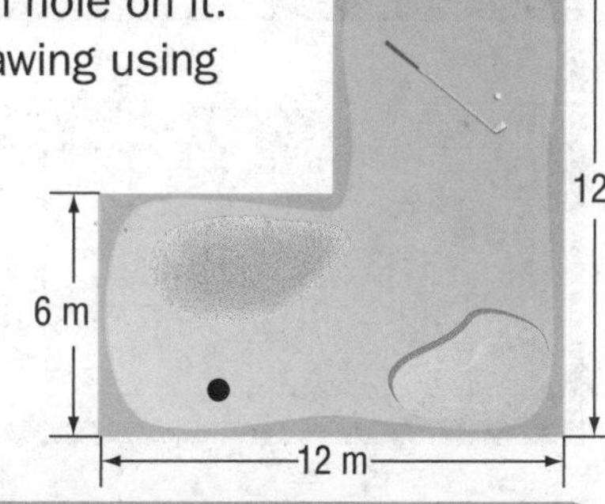

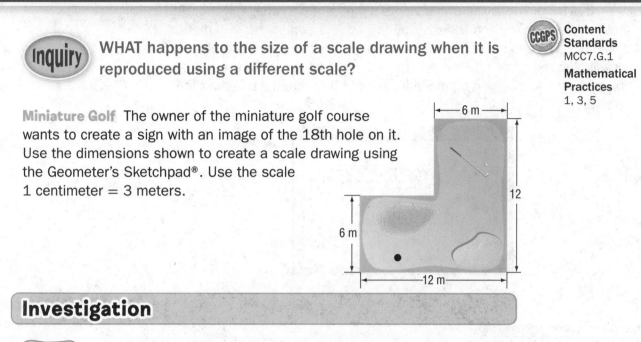

Investigation

Step 1 Determine the length the 6 meter side and the 12 meter side will be in the drawing.

Scale	Length	Scale	Length
$\frac{1 \text{ cm}}{3 \text{ m}} =$	$\frac{x \text{ cm}}{6 \text{ cm}}$	$\frac{1 \text{ cm}}{3 \text{ m}} =$	$\frac{x \text{ cm}}{12 \text{ m}}$

$1 \cdot 6 = 3 \cdot x$ $\qquad$ $1 \cdot 12 = 3 \cdot x$

$x =$ ☐ $\qquad$ $x =$ ☐

So, the 6 meter side will be ☐ centimeters and the 12 meter side will be ☐ centimeters in the drawing.

Step 2 Create the drawing using a dynamic geometry software. Then fill in the correct length for each line segment.

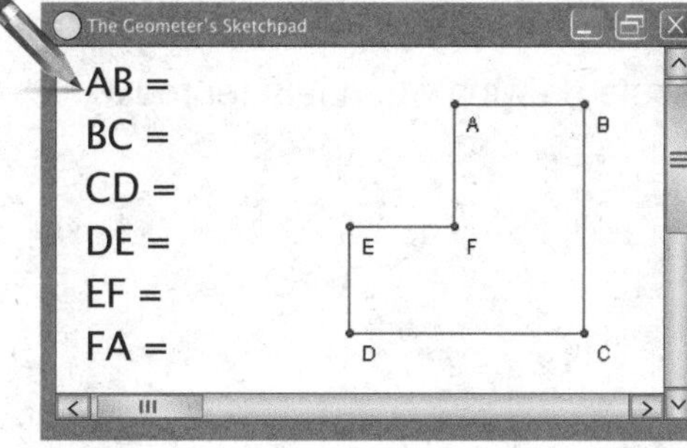

Collaborate

Work with a partner. Use a dynamic geometry software.

1. **Use Math Tools** The owner wants a different size image of the 18th hole to place on the scorecards. Use the scale 1 centimeter = 6 meters. Fill in the new lengths of the line segments and draw the new scale drawing on the screen below. (*Hint:* You don't have to redraw the figure. Try clicking and dragging on the sides of your first drawing to adjust the side lengths.)

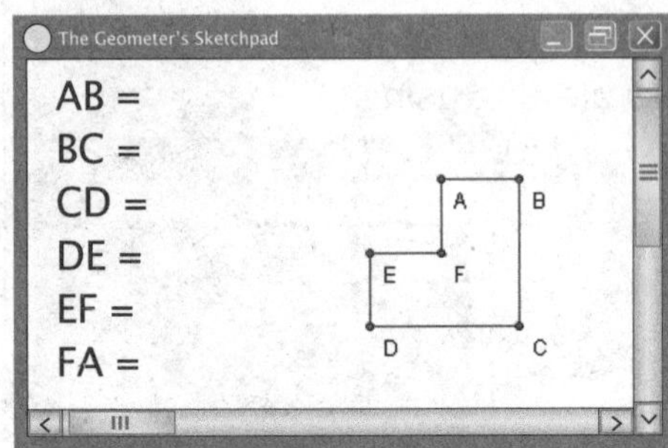

Analyze

2. What happened to the size of the scale drawing when the scale changed from 1 centimeter = 3 meters to 1 centimeter = 6 meters?

3. **Reason Inductively** Suppose you drew the miniature golf hole again at the scale 1 centimeter = 2 meters. Would the size of your drawing be larger or smaller than the drawing in the Investigation? Explain.

Reflect

4. **Inquiry** WHAT happens to the size of a scale drawing when it is reproduced using a different scale?

21ST CENTURY CAREER
in Video Game Design

Video Game Designer

Are you passionate about computer gaming? You might want to explore a career in video game design. A video game designer is responsible for a game's concept, layout, character development, and game-play. Game designers use math and logic to compute how different parts of a game will work.

College & Career READINESS

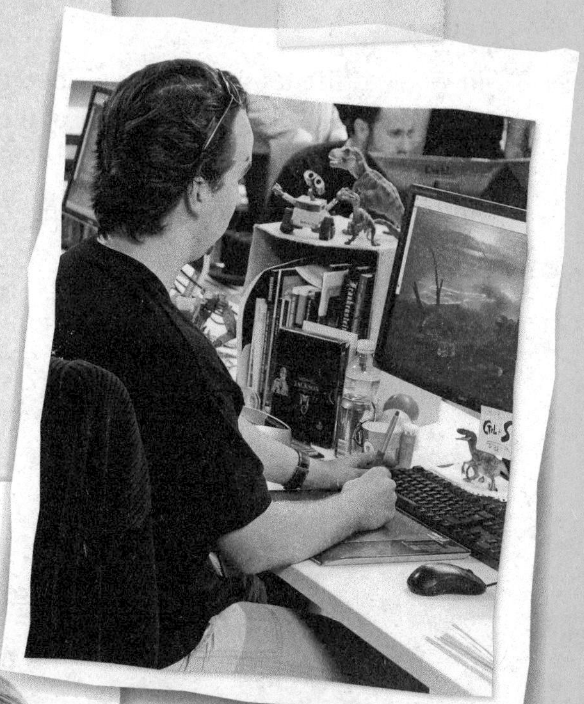

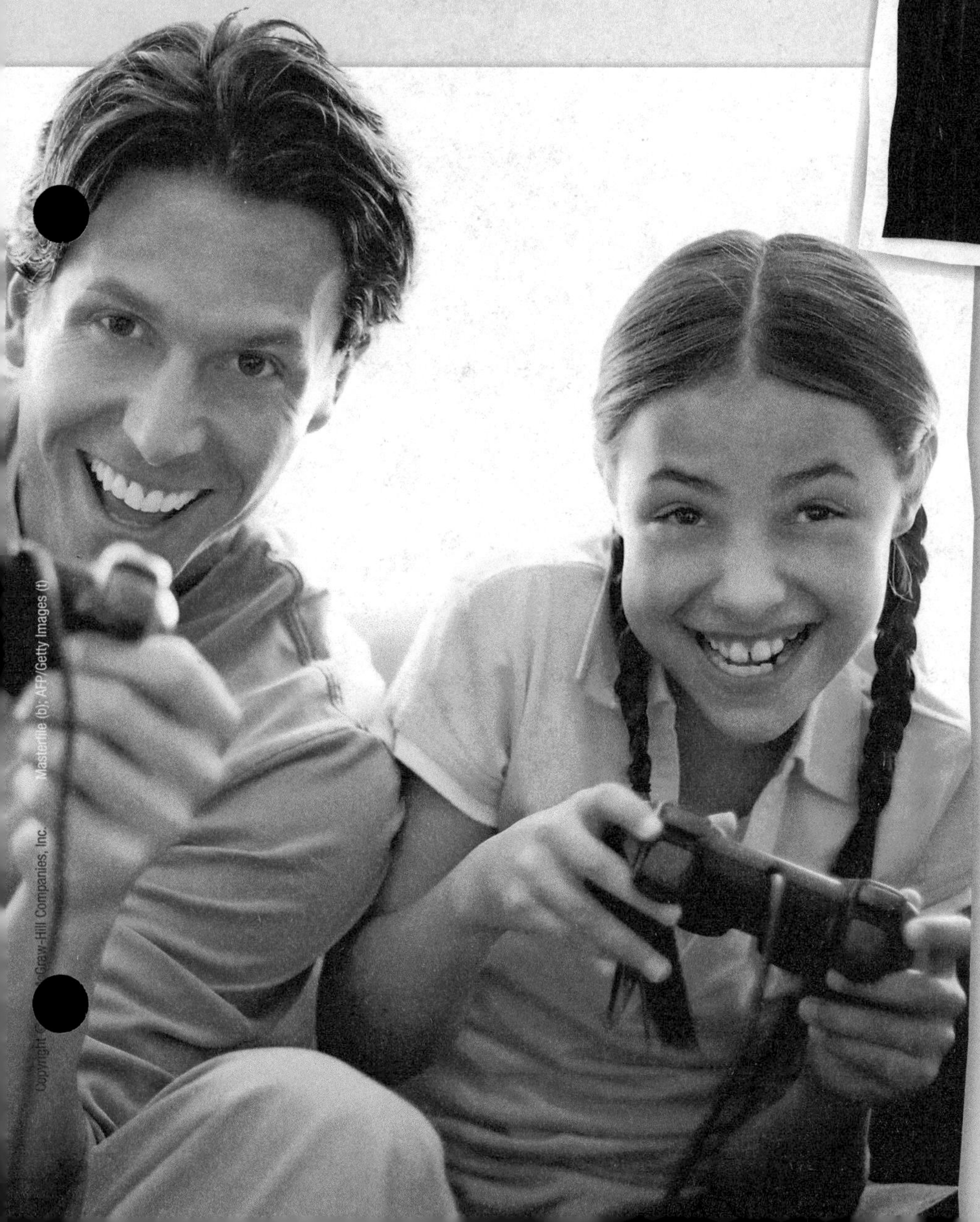

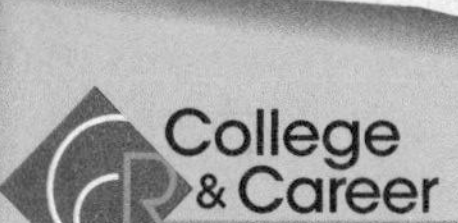

Explore college and careers at ccr.mcgraw-hill.com

Is This the Career for You?

Are you interested in a career as a video game designer? Take some of the following courses in high school.

- 3-D Digital Animation
- Introduction to Computer Literacy
- Introduction to Game Development

Find out how math relates to a career in Video Game Design.

All Fun and Games

Use the information in the circle graph and the table to solve the problems below.

1. How many of the top 20 video games sold were sports games? ______
2. Out of the top 20 video games sold, how many more music games were there than racer games? ______
3. In Week 1, the total sales for a video game were $2,374,136. What percent of the total sales was from the United States? Round to the nearest whole percent. ______
4. Find the percent of change in sales of the video game from Week 1 to Week 3 in Japan. Round to the nearest whole percent. ______
5. Which country had a greater percent decrease in sales from Week 1 to Week 2: Japan or the United States? Explain.

______

______

______

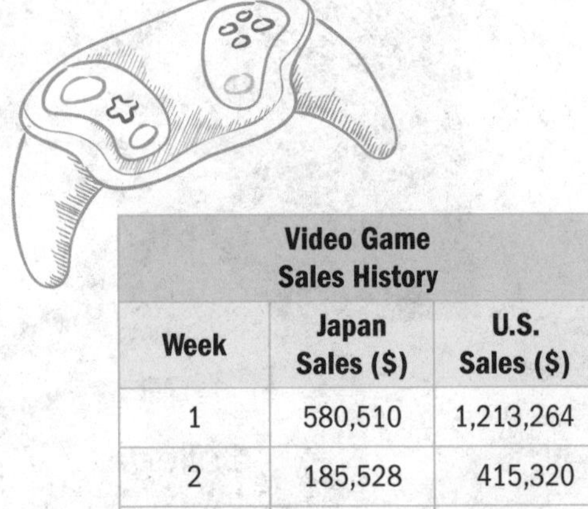

Video Game Sales History		
Week	**Japan Sales ($)**	**U.S. Sales ($)**
1	580,510	1,213,264
2	185,528	415,320
3	149,045	263,825

Top 20 Video Games in United States

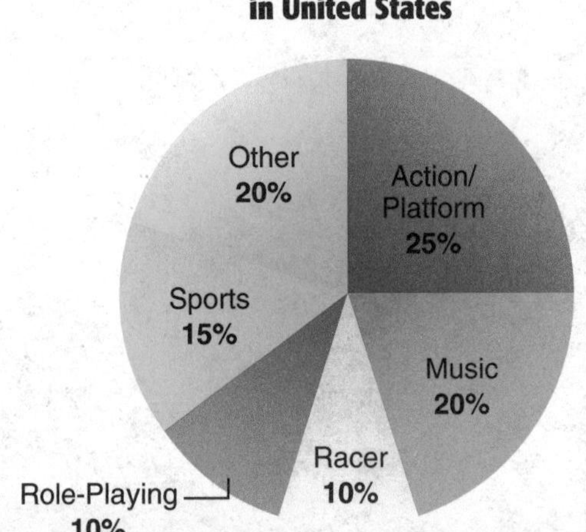

Career Project

It's time to update your career portfolio! Choose one of your favorite video games. Make a list of what you think are the best features of the game. Then describe any changes that you, as a video game designer, would make to the game.

______

______

______

______

______

List the strengths you have that would help you succeed in this career.

- ______
- ______
- ______
- ______
- ______

Vocabulary Check

Complete the crossword puzzle using the vocabulary list at the beginning of the chapter.

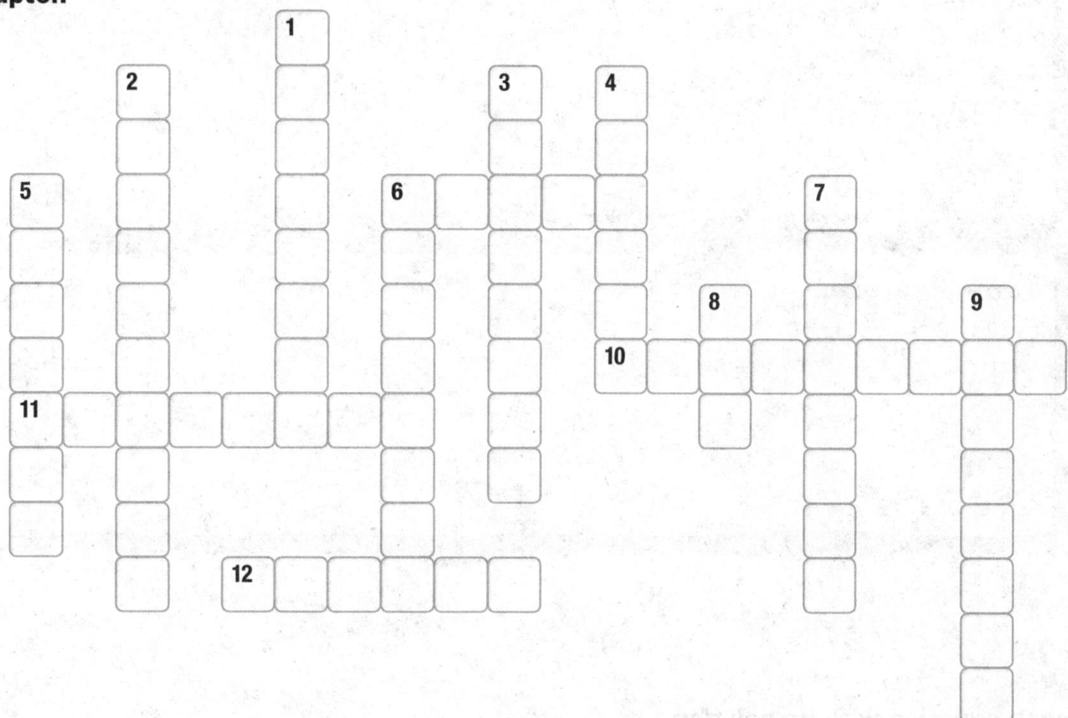

Down

1. type of percent when the final amount is greater than the original amount
2. statement that two ratios are equal
3. amount that the regular price is reduced
4. difference between what a store pays for an item and what a customer pays
5. price that a customer pays for an item
6. mathematical sentence stating that two expressions are equal
7. another term for the term in 3 down
8. gratuity
9. additional amount of money charged to items that people buy

Across

6. type of percent that compares the inaccuracy of an estimate to the actual amount
10. amount of money deposited or borrowed
11. amount paid or earned for the use of money
12. type of percent that compares the final and original amounts

Key Concept Check

Use Your FOLDABLES

Use your Foldable to help review the chapter.

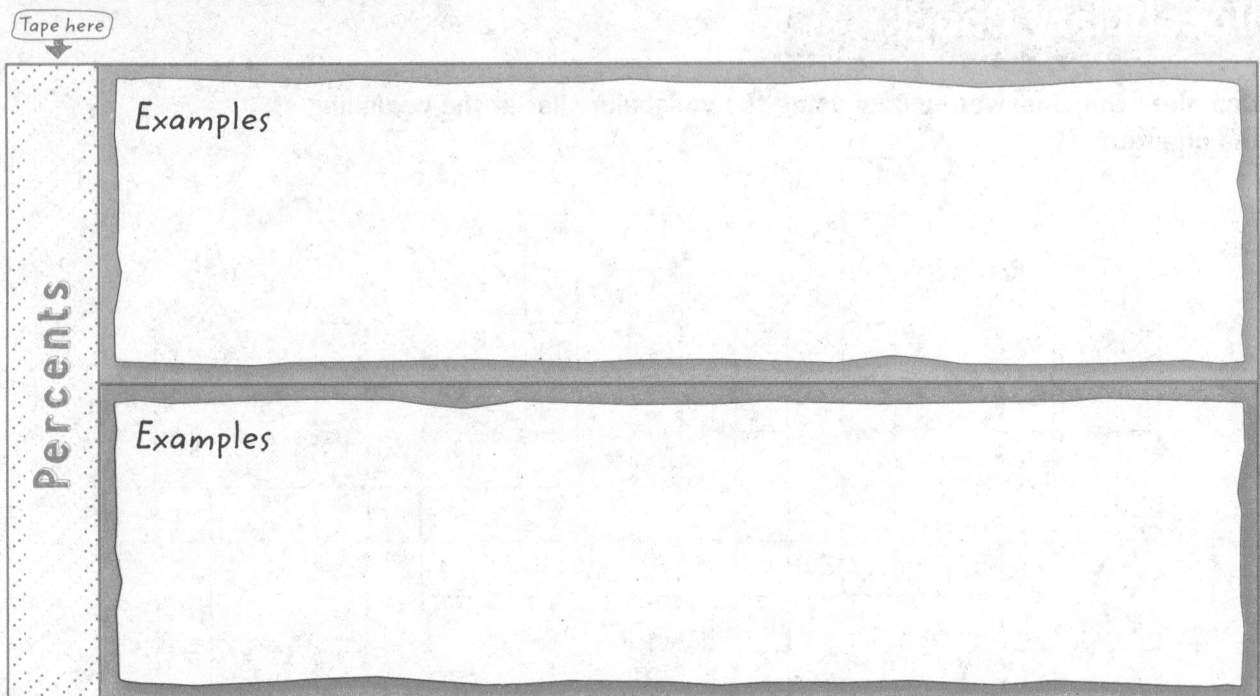

Got it?

Match each equation with its solution.

1. $0.15w = 45$

2. $15 = 20n$

3. $0.3(60) = p$

4. $600n = 750$

5. $0.15(80) = x$

6. $20 = 0.8w$

a. 125%

b. 12

c. 300

d. 18

e. 75%

f. 25

Problem Solving

1. CCGPS **Justify Conclusions** The table shows the results of a survey in which 175 students were asked what type of food they wanted for a class party. How many students chose Italian food? Explain. (Lesson 1)

Type of Food	Percent
Subs	32%
Tex-Mex	56%
Italian	12%

2. A soccer team lost 30% of its games. Suppose the team won 14 games. How many games did the team play? (Lesson 3) ____________

3. Tyree bought a collectible comic book for $49.62 last year. This year, he sold it for $52.10. Find the percent of change of the price of the comic book. Round to the nearest percent. (Lesson 5) ____________

4. CCGPS **Justify Conclusions** A restaurant bill comes to $42.75. Suppose the sales tax is 6% and a 15% tip is left on the amount after the tax is added. How much in all did the customer pay? Explain. (Lesson 6)

5. A new radio is priced at $30. An electronics store has an end-of-the-year sale. All of the items in the store are discounted by 40%. What is the sale price of the radio? (Lesson 7) ____________

6. **Financial Literacy** Aleta deposited $450 into a savings account earning 3.75% simple interest. How much interest will she earn in 6 years? Explain. (Lesson 8)

Reflect

Answering the Essential Question

Use what you learned about percent to complete the graphic organizer. For each situation, circle an arrow to show if the final amount would be greater or less than the original amount. Then write a real-world percent problem and an equation that models it.

Essential Question

HOW can percent help you understand situations involving money?

Sales Tax	Simple Interest	Discount
⇧ ⇩	⇧ ⇩	⇧ ⇩
Equation:	Equation:	Equation:

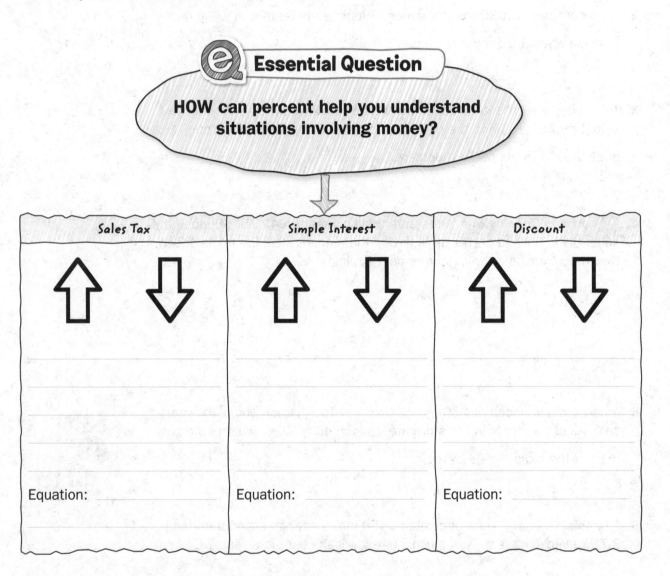

Answer the Essential Question. HOW can percent help you understand situations involving money?

UNIT 4

Inferences

Essential Question

WHY is learning mathematics important?

Chapter 7
Statistics

Statistics can be used to draw conclusions about a population. In this chapter, you will use random samples to make predictions and compare populations.

Chapter 7
Statistics

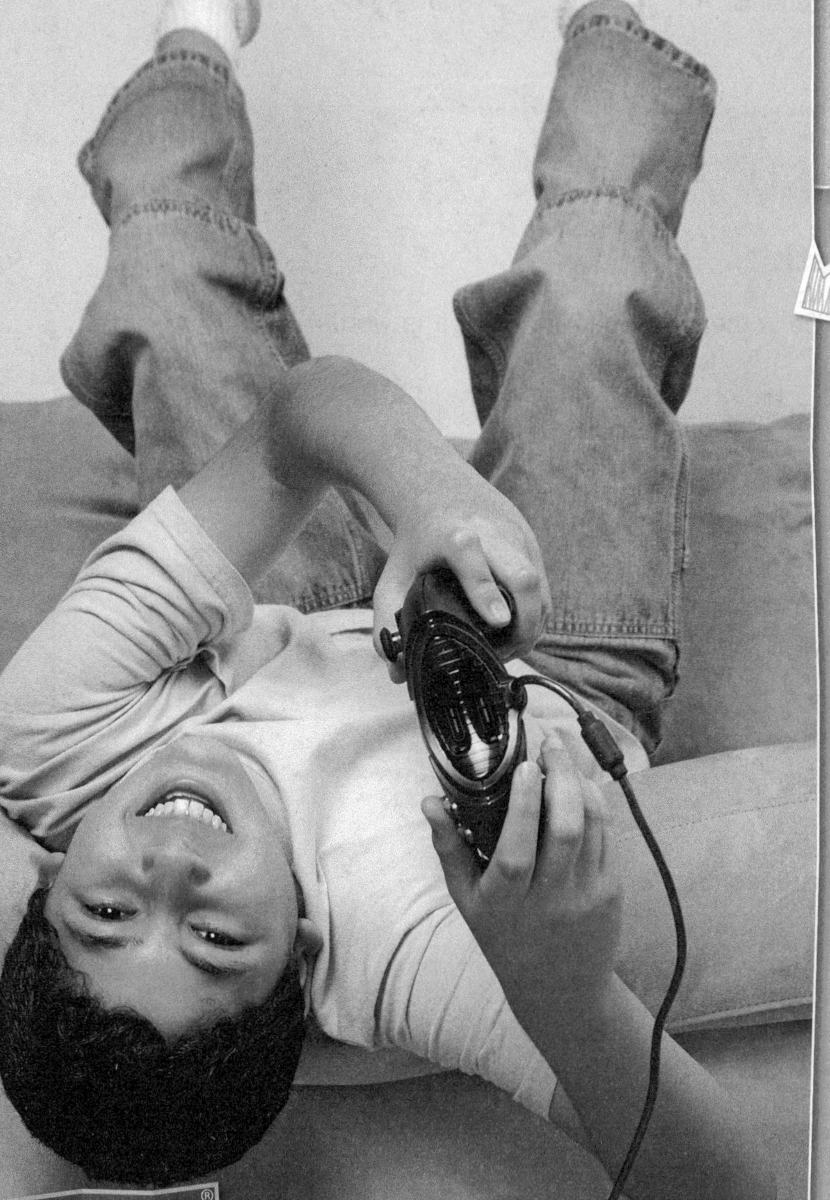

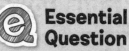

Essential Question

HOW do you know which type of graph to use when displaying data?

Common Core GPS

Content Standards
MCC7.SP.1, MCC7.SP.2, MCC7.SP.3, MCC7.SP.4

Mathematical Practices
1, 3, 4, 5, 6

Math in the Real World

Surveys are used to collect information. Survey results can be shown in graphs.

The results of a survey of 50 middle school students are shown in the table. On the circle graph, write the percent of students who preferred each activity.

Activity	Number of Students
Gaming	22
Social Networking	18
Viewing Movies	6
Other	4

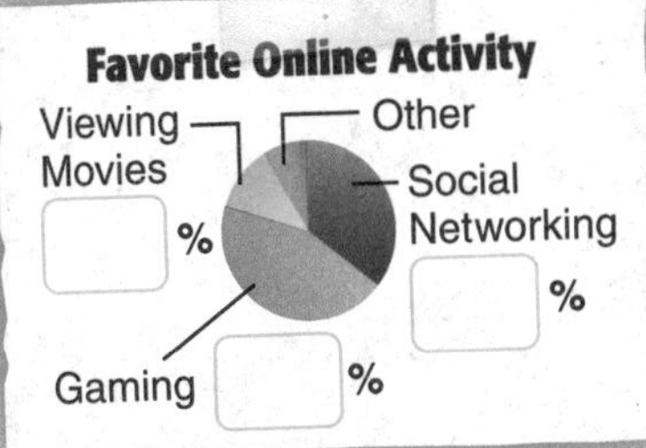

FOLDABLES® Study Organizer

1. Cut out the correct Foldable from the FL pages in the back of this book.
2. Place your Foldable on the Key Concept page toward the end of this chapter.
3. Use the Foldable throughout this chapter to help you learn about statistics.

What Tools Do You Need?

Vocabulary

biased sample	population	survey
convenience sample	sample	systematic random sample
double box plot	simple random sample	unbiased sample
double dot plot	statistics	voluntary response sample

Study Skill: Writing Math

Describe Data When you *describe* something, you represent it in words.

The table shows the prices for takeout orders at Lombardo's Restaurant.

Takeout	Price ($)
Main Dish	8.00
Side Dish	2.50
Dessert	4.00

Use the table to complete the following statements.

1. The price of a dessert is ________________.
2. The price of a main dish is twice the price of ________________.
3. A ________________ is the least expensive item.

Write two other statements that describe the data.

4. ________________

5. ________________

When Will You Use This?

Your Turn! You will solve this problem in the chapter.

Are You Ready?

Try the Quick Check below.
Or, take the Online Readiness Quiz.

Quick Review

Common Core Review MCC6.SP.5c, MCC6.NS.4

Example 1

Which players average more than 10 points per game?

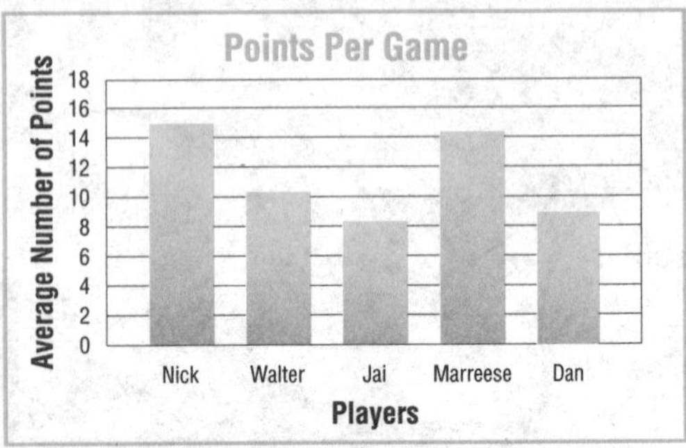

Nick, Walter, and Marreese averaged more than 10 points per game.

Example 2

Use the circle graph. Suppose 300 people were surveyed. How many people have two accounts?

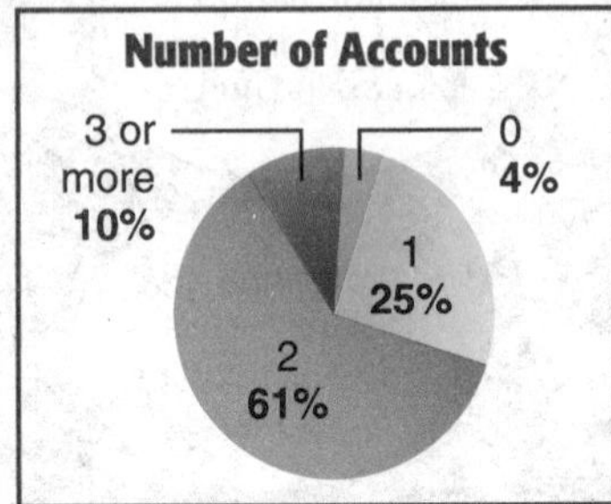

Find 61% of 300.

$$\begin{aligned} 61\% \text{ of } 300 &= 61\% \times 300 \\ &= 0.61 \times 300 \text{ or } 183 \end{aligned}$$

So, 183 people have two accounts.

Quick Check

Graphs **The bar graph at the right shows the number of items each student obtained during a scavenger hunt.**

Scavenger Hunt

Number of Items Obtained: 0, 2, 4, 6, 8, 10, 12, 14, 16

Student: Ty, Jill, Gui, Rihanna, Karl

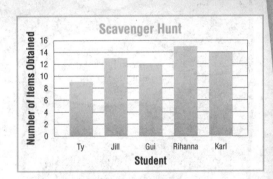

1. Who obtained the most items?

2. Who obtained the least items?

3. Refer to the circle graph in Example 2. Suppose 300 people were surveyed. How many people have 1 account?

Which problems did you answer correctly in the Quick Check? Shade those exercise numbers below.

1 2 3

Make Predictions

What You'll Learn

Scan the lesson. List two headings you will use to make an outline of the lesson.

•

•

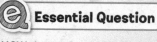

Essential Question

HOW do you know which type of graph to use when displaying data?

Vocabulary

statistics
survey
population
sample

Common Core GPS

Content Standards
MCC7.SP.1, MCC7.SP.2

Mathematical Practices
1, 3, 4

Vocabulary Start-Up

Statistics deal with collecting, organizing, and interpreting data. A **survey** is a method of collecting information. The group being studied is the **population**. Sometimes the population is very large. To save time and money, part of the group, called a **sample**, is surveyed.

For each survey topic, determine which set represents the population and which represents a sample of the population. Write *population* or *sample*.

	Survey Topic	Set A	Set B
1.	dress code changes	the students in a middle school	the seventh graders in the middle school
2.	favorite flavors of ice cream	the customers at an ice cream shop in the town	the residents of a town

Real-World Link

Logan wants to survey students in his school about their favorite and least favorite ice cream flavors. Describe a possible sample Logan could survey instead of surveying the entire school.

Work Zone

Make Predictions Using Ratios

You can use the results of a survey or past actions to predict the actions of a larger group. Since the ratios of the responses of a good sample are often the same as the ratios of the responses of the population.

Examples

The students in Mr. Blackwell's class brought photos from their summer break. The table shows how many students brought each type of photo.

Summer Break Photos	
Location	**Students**
beach	6
campground	4
home	7
theme park	11

1. What is the probability that a student brought a photo taken at a theme park?

$$P(\text{theme park}) = \frac{\text{number of theme park photos}}{\text{number of students with a photo}} = \frac{11}{28}$$

So, the probability of a theme park photo is $\frac{11}{28}$.

2. There are 560 students at the school where Mr. Blackwell teaches. Predict how many students would bring in a photo taken at a theme park.

Let s represent the number of theme park photos.

$\frac{11}{28} = \frac{s}{560}$ Write an equivalent ratio.

$\frac{11}{28} \underset{\times 20}{\overset{\times 20}{=}} \frac{s}{560}$ Since $28 \times 20 = 560$, multiply 11 by 20 to find s.

$\frac{11}{28} = \frac{220}{560}$ $s = 220$

Of the 560 students, you can expect about 220 to bring a photo from a theme park.

Got It? Do these problems to find out.

A survey found that 6 out of every 10 students have a blog.

a. ____________

b. ____________

a. What is the probability that a student at the school has a blog?

b. Suppose there are about 250 students at the school. About how many have a blog?

Make Predictions Using Equations

You can also use the percent equation to make predictions.

Examples

3. **A survey found that 85% of people use emoticons on their instant messengers. Predict how many of the 2,450 students at Washington Middle School use emoticons.**

Words	What number of students is 85% of 2,450 students?			
Variable	Let n represent the number of students.			
Equation	n	$=$	0.85	$\cdot$ $2{,}450$

$n = 0.85 \cdot 2{,}450$ Write the percent equation.

$n = 2{,}082.5$ Multiply.

About 2,083 of the students use emoticons.

4. **The circle graph shows the results of a survey in which children ages 8 to 12 were asked whether they have a television in their bedroom. Predict how many out of 1,725 students would not have a television in their bedroom.**

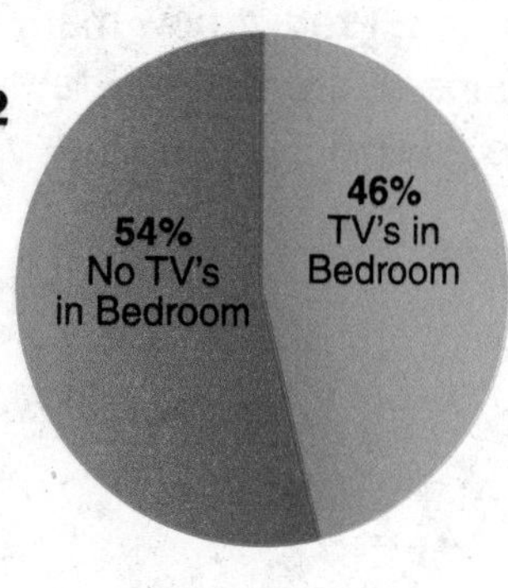

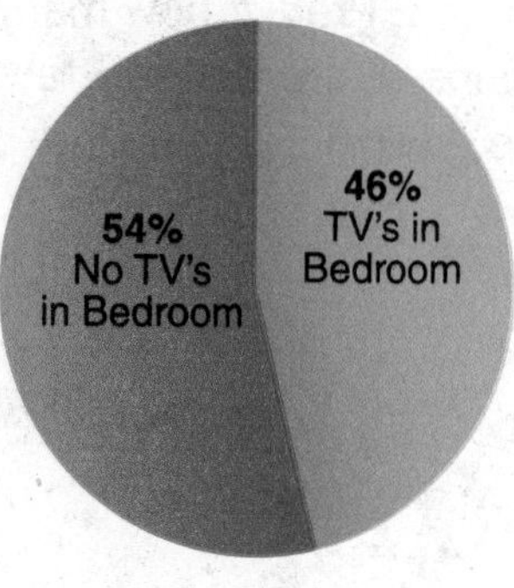

You can use the percent equation and the survey results to predict what part p of the 1,725 students have no TV in their bedroom.

part = percent · whole

$p = 0.54 \cdot 1{,}725$ Survey results: 54%

$p = 931.5$ Multiply.

About 932 students do not have a television in their bedroom.

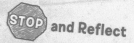

STOP and Reflect

What proportion could you use to solve Example 4? Write your answer below.

Got It? **Do this problem to find out.**

c. Refer to Example 4. Predict how many out of 1,370 students have a television in their bedroom.

c. ________

Guided Practice

The table shows the results of a survey of Hamilton Middle School seventh graders. Use the table to find the following probabilities. (Examples 1 and 2)

Career Field	Students
Entertainment	17
Education	14
Medicine	11
Public service	6
Sports	2

1. the probability of choosing a career in public service

2. the probability of choosing a career in education

3. the probability of choosing a career in sports

4. Predict how many students out of 400 will enter the education field.

5. Predict how many students out of 500 will enter the medical field.

6. Use the circle graph that shows the results of a poll to which 60,000 teens responded. Predict how many of the approximately 28 million teens in the United States would buy a music CD if they were given $20. (Examples 3 and 4)

How Would You Spend a Gift of $20?

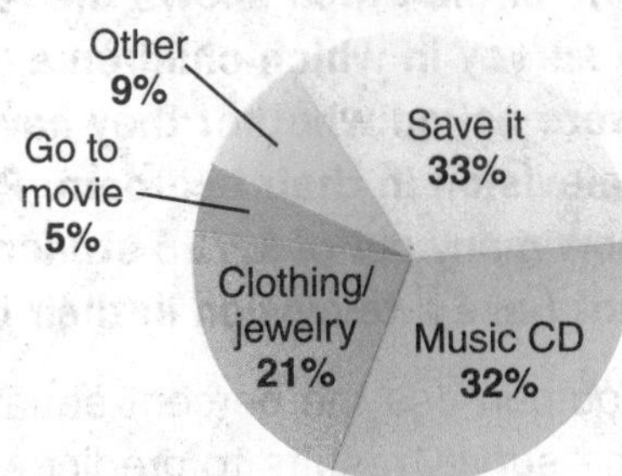

7. **Building on the Essential Question** When can statistics be used to gain information about a population from a sample?

Rate Yourself!

How confident are you about making predictions? Check the box that applies.

For more help, go online to access a Personal Tutor.

Independent Practice

Go online for Step-by-Step Solutions

The table shows the results of a survey of 150 students. Use the table to find the probability of a student participating in each sport. (Example 1)

Sport	Students
Baseball/softball	36
Basketball	30
Football	45
Gymnastics	12
Tennis	18
Volleyball	9

Show your work.

1. football

2. tennis

3. gymnastics

4. volleyball

5. Three out of every 10 students ages 6–14 have a magazine subscription. Suppose there are 30 students in Annabelle's class. About how many will have a magazine subscription? (Example 2)

6. Use the graph that shows the percent of cat owners who train their cats in each category. (Examples 3 and 4)

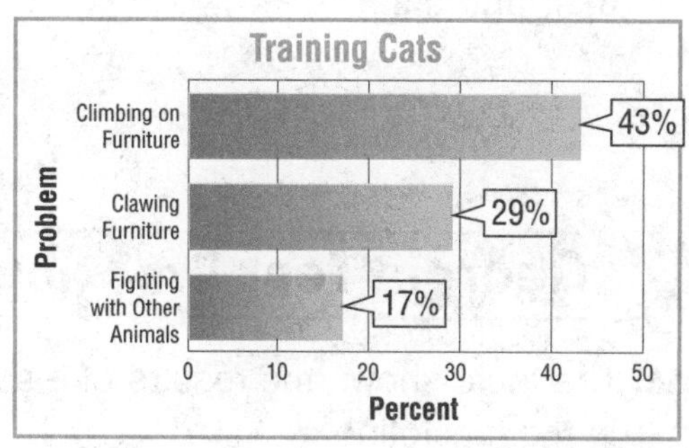

   a. Out of 255 cat owners, predict how many owners trained their cat not to climb on furniture.

   b. Out of 316 cat owners, predict how many cat owners trained their cat not to claw on furniture.

7. CCGPS **Make a Prediction** The school librarian recorded the types of books students checked out on a typical day. Suppose there are 605 students enrolled at the school. Predict the number of students that prefer humor books. Compare this to the number of students at the school who prefer nonfiction.

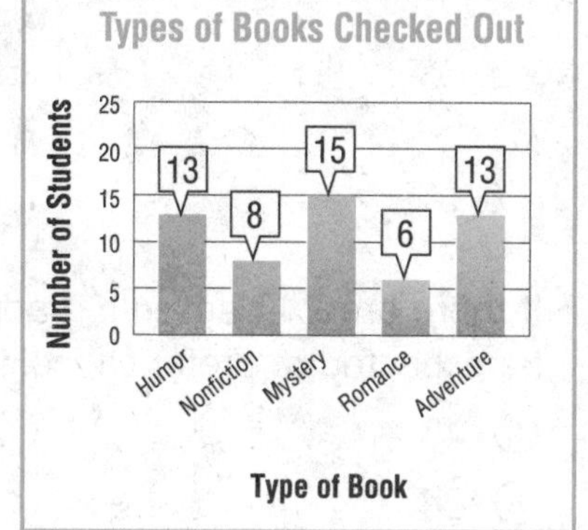

H.O.T. Problems Higher Order Thinking

8. **CCGPS Find the Error** A survey of a seventh-grade class showed that 4 out of every 10 students are taking a trip during spring break. There are 150 students in the seventh grade. Caitlyn is trying to determine how many of the seventh-grade students can be expected to take a trip during spring break. Find her mistake and correct it.

9. **CCGPS Persevere with Problems** One letter tile is drawn from the bag and replaced 300 times. Predict how many times a consonant will *not* be picked.

10. **CCGPS Persevere with Problems** A survey found that 80% of teens enjoy going to the movies in their free time. Out of 5,200 teens, predict how many said that they do not enjoy going to the movies in their free time.

Georgia Test Practice

11. The table shows the results of a survey of seventh-grade students in the lunch line.

Favorite Drink	
Drink	**Students**
Chocolate Milk	15
Soda	12
Milk	6
Water	2

If there are 245 seventh graders in the school, how many can be expected to prefer chocolate milk?

Ⓐ 45 Ⓒ 90

Ⓑ 84 Ⓓ 105

Extra Practice

Solve.

12. Luther won 12 of the last 20 video games he played. Find the probability of Luther winning the next game he plays. $\frac{3}{5}$, 0.6, or 60%

$$P(\text{winning}) = \frac{\text{number of games won}}{\text{number of games played}}$$
$$= \frac{12}{20} \text{ or } \frac{3}{5}$$

13. Refer to Exercise 12. Suppose Luther plays a total of 60 games with his friends over the next month. Predict how many of these games Luther will win. _______________

14. Use the graph that shows the number of times teens volunteer.

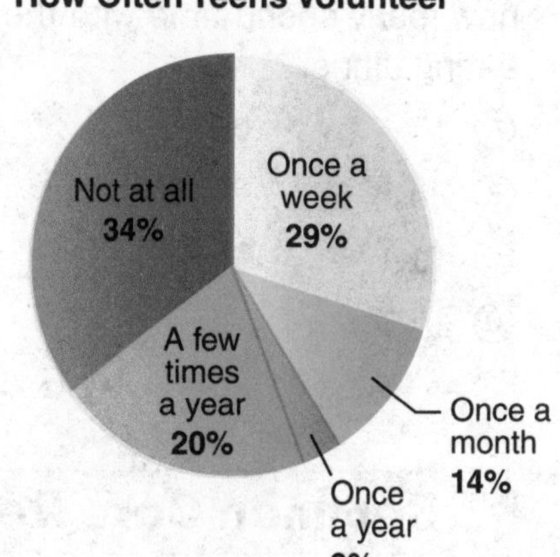

a. About 300,000 teens ages 12–14 live in Virginia. Predict the number of teens in this age group who volunteer a few times a year.

____

b. Tennessee has about 250,000 teens ages 12–14. Predict the number of teens in this age group who volunteer once a week.

____

c. About 240,000 teens ages 12–14 live in Missouri. Predict the number of teens in this age group who volunteer once a year.

____

15. CCGPS **Make a Prediction** The probability of Jaden making a free throw is 15%. Predict the number of free throws that he can expect to make if he attempts 40 free throws.

____

Draw a line to match each situation with the appropriate equation or proportion.

16. 27 MP3s is what percent of 238 MP3s? — **a.** $n = 27 \cdot 2.38$

17. 238% of 27 is what number? — **b.** $\frac{27}{100} = \frac{p}{238}$

18. 27% of MP3 owners download music weekly. Predict how many MP3 owners out of 238 owners download music weekly. — **c.** $\frac{27}{238} = \frac{n}{100}$

Georgia Test Practice

19. The table shows how students spend time with their family.

How Students Spend Time with Family	
Eating Dinner	34%
Watching TV	20%
Talking	14%
Playing Sports	14%
Taking Walks	4%
Other	14%

Of the 515 students surveyed, about how many spend time with their family eating dinner?

Ⓐ 17

Ⓑ 34

Ⓒ 119

Ⓓ 175

20. Yesterday, a bakery baked 54 loaves of bread in 20 minutes. Today, the bakery needs to bake 375 loaves of bread. At this rate, predict how long it will take to bake the bread.

Ⓕ 1.5 hours

Ⓖ 2.3 hours

Ⓗ 3.0 hours

Ⓘ 3.75 hours

21. Short Response Suppose 7 out of 30 students are going on a ski trip. Predict the number of students out of 150 that are going on the ski trip.

Common Core Review

Solve each proportion. MCC6.RP.1, MCC6.RP.3

22. $\frac{1}{4} = \frac{x}{72}$ $x =$ ______

23. $\frac{8}{n} = \frac{0.5}{0.9}$ $n =$ ______

24. $\frac{1}{3} = \frac{m}{153}$ $m =$ ______

25. $\frac{0.2}{a} = \frac{1.8}{18}$ $a =$ ______

26. A school librarian surveyed students about their favorite type of novel. The results are shown in the table at the right. What percent of students chose science fiction as their favorite type of novel? Round to the nearest whole percent. MCC6.RP.3c

Type of Novel	Number of Students
mystery	18
romance	10
science fiction	26
other	4

Lesson 2

Unbiased and Biased Samples

What You'll Learn

Scan the lesson. Define unbiased sample and biased sample.

- unbiased sample ______________________

- biased sample ______________________

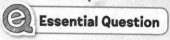

Essential Question

HOW do you know which type of graph to use when displaying data?

Vocabulary

unbiased sample
simple random sample
systematic random sample
biased sample
convenience sample
voluntary response sample

Common Core GPS

Content Standards
MCC7.SP.1, MCC7.SP.2

Mathematical Practices
1, 3, 4, 5

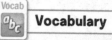

Real-World Link

Entertainment A T.V. programming manager wants to conduct a survey to determine which reality television show is the favorite of viewers in a certain viewing area. He is considering the three samples shown. Draw an X through the two samples that would not fairly represent all of the people in the viewing area.

Sample 1
100 people that are trying out for a reality show

Sample 2
100 students at your middle school

Sample 3
Every 100th person at a shopping mall

Explain why the two samples that you crossed out do *not* fairly represent all of the people in the viewing area? Explain.

____

____

____

____

Work Zone

Biased and Unbiased Samples

To get valid results, a sample must be chosen very carefully. An **unbiased sample** is selected so that it accurately represents the entire population. Two ways to pick an unbiased sample are listed below.

Unbiased Samples		
Type	**Description**	**Example**
Simple Random Sample	Each item or person in the population is as likely to be chosen as any other.	Each student's name is written on a piece of paper. The names are placed in a bowl, and names are picked without looking.
Systematic Random Sample	The items or people are selected according to a specific time or item interval.	Every 20th person is chosen from an alphabetical list of all students attending a school.

In a **biased sample**, one or more parts of the population are favored over others. Two ways to pick a biased sample are listed below.

Biased Samples		
Type	**Description**	**Example**
Convenience Sample	A convenience sample consists of members of a population that are easily accessed.	To represent all the students attending a school, the principal surveys the students in one math class.
Voluntary Response Sample	A voluntary response sample involves only those who want to participate in the sampling.	Students at a school who wish to express their opinions complete an online survey.

Everyday Use
Bias is a tendency or prejudice

Math Use
Bias is an error introduced by selecting or encouraging a specific outcome

Examples

Determine whether the conclusion is valid. Justify your answer.

1. A random sample of students at a middle school shows that 10 students prefer listening to rock, 15 students prefer listening to hip hop, and 25 students prefer no music while they exercise. It can be concluded that half the students prefer no music while they exercise.

This is a simple random sample. So, the sample is unbiased and the conclusion is valid.

Determine whether each conclusion is valid. Justify your answer.

2. **Every tenth person who walks into a department store is surveyed to determine his or her music preference. Out of 150 customers, 70 stated that they prefer rock music. The manager concludes that about half of all customers prefer rock music.**

Since the population is every tenth customer of a department store, the sample is an unbiased, systematic random sample. The conclusion is valid.

3. **The customers of a music store are surveyed to determine their favorite leisure time activity. The results are shown in the graph. The store manager concludes that most people prefer to listen to music in their leisure time.**

Leisure Time Activities

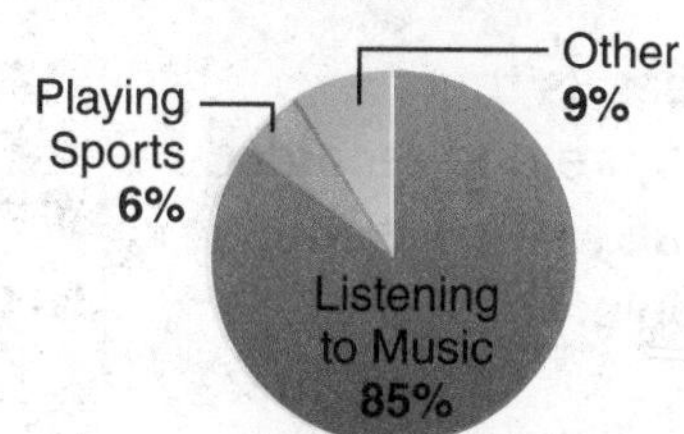

The customers of a music store probably like to listen to music in their leisure time. The sample is a biased, convenience sample since all of the people surveyed are in one specific location. The conclusion is not valid.

Got It? **Do this problem to find out.**

Show your work.

a. A radio station asks its listeners to indicate their preference for one of two candidates in an upcoming election. Seventy-two percent of the listeners who responded preferred candidate A, so the radio station announced that candidate A would win the election. Is the conclusion valid? Justify your answer.

a. ____________

Use Sampling to Predict

A valid sampling method uses unbiased samples. If a sampling method is valid, you can make generalizations about the population.

Example

4. A store sells 3 types of pants: jeans, capris, and cargos. The store workers survey 50 customers at random about their favorite type of pants. The survey responses are indicated at the right. If 450 pairs of pants are ordered, how many should be jeans?

Type	Number
Jeans	25
Capris	15
Cargos	10

First, determine whether the sample method is valid. The sample is a simple random sample since customers were randomly selected. Thus, the sample method is valid.

$\frac{25}{50}$ or 50% of the customers prefer jeans. So, find 50% of 450.

$0.5 \times 450 = 225$, so about 225 pairs of jeans should be ordered.

Guided Practice

1. Zach is trying to decide which of three golf courses is the best. He randomly surveyed people at a sports store and recorded the results in the table. Is the sample method valid? If so, suppose Zach surveyed 150 more people. How many people would be expected to vote for Rolling Meadows? (Example 4)

Course	Number
Whispering Trail	10
Tall Pines	8
Rolling Meadows	7

2. To find how much money the average American family spends to cool their home, 100 Alaskan families are surveyed at random. Of the families, 85 said that they spend less than $75 per month on cooling. The researcher concluded that the average American family spends less than $75 on cooling per month. Is the conclusion valid? Explain. (Examples 1–3)

3. **Building on the Essential Question** How is using a survey one way to determine experimental probability?

Rate Yourself!
Are you ready to move on?
Shade the section that applies.
YES
?
NO
For more help, go online to access a Personal Tutor.
Tutor
FOLDABLES Time to update your Foldable!

Name ______________________ My Homework ______________

Independent Practice

Go online for Step-by-Step Solutions 

Determine whether each conclusion is valid. Justify your answer.
(Examples 1–3)

1. To evaluate the quality of their product, a manufacturer of cell phones checks every 50th phone off the assembly line. Out of 200 phones tested, 4 are defective. The manager concludes that about 2% of the cell phones produced will be defective.

2. To determine whether the students will attend an arts festival at the school, Oliver surveys his friends in the art club. All of Oliver's friends plan to attend. So, Oliver assumes that all the students at his school will also attend.

3. A random sample of people at a mall shows that 22 prefer to take a family trip by car, 18 prefer to travel by plane, and 4 prefer to travel by bus. Is the sample method valid? If so, how many people out of 500 would you expect to say they prefer to travel by plane? (Example 4)

Preferred Ways to Travel

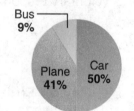

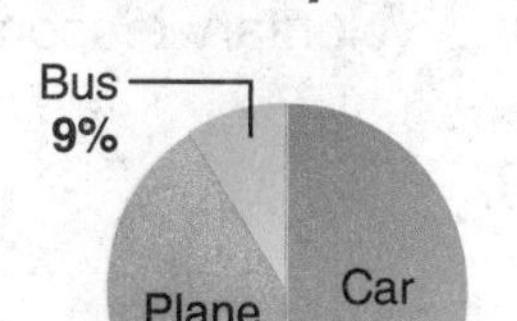

4. **Use Math Tools** Use the organizer to determine whether the conclusion is valid.

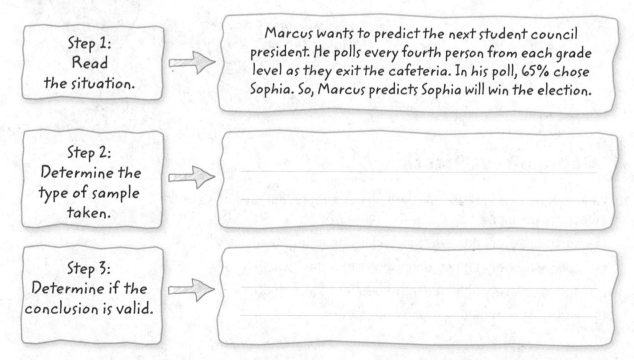

Step 1: Read the situation.	Marcus wants to predict the next student council president. He polls every fourth person from each grade level as they exit the cafeteria. In his poll, 65% chose Sophia. So, Marcus predicts Sophia will win the election.
Step 2: Determine the type of sample taken.	
Step 3: Determine if the conclusion is valid.	

H.O.T. Problems Higher Order Thinking

5. **Persevere with Problems** How could the wording of a question or the tone of voice of the interviewer affect a survey? Provide an example.

Justify Conculsions Determine whether each statement is *sometimes*, *always*, or *never* true. Explain your reasoning to a classmate.

6. A biased sample is valid.

7. A simple random sample is valid.

8. A voluntary response sample is valid.

9. **Find the Error** Marisol wants to determine how many students plan to attend the girls' varsity basketball game. Find her mistake and correct it.

I will survey students at the boys' varsity basketball game.

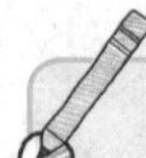

Georgia Test Practice

10. Which of the following samples will be most representative of an entire student population?

Ⓐ surveying every fifth seventh-grader who enters the library

Ⓑ surveying every fifth student who enters the library

Ⓒ surveying every fifth student who enters the school

Ⓓ surveying every fifth girl who enters the school

Extra Practice

Determine whether each conclusion is valid. Justify your answer.

11. To determine what people in California think about a proposed law, 5,000 people from the state are randomly surveyed. Of the people surveyed, 58% are against the law. The legislature concludes that the law should not be passed.

Homework Help

This is an unbiased, simple random sample because randomly selected Californians were surveyed. So, the conclusion is valid.

12. A magazine asks its readers to complete and return a questionnaire about popular television actors. The majority of those who replied liked one actor the most, so the magazine decides to write more articles about that actor.

13. The Student Council advisor asked every tenth student in the lunch line how they preferred to be contacted with school news. The results are shown in the table. Is this a random sample? If yes, suppose there are 684 students at the school. How many can be expected to prefer E-mail?

Method	Number
E-mail	16
Newsletter	12
Announcement	5
Telephone	3

CCGPS **Justify Conclusions** **Each of the following surveys results in a biased sample. For each situation, explain why the survey is biased. Then explain how you would change the survey to obtain an unbiased sample.**

14. A store manager sends an E-mail survey to customers who have registered at the store's Web site.

15. A school district surveys the family of every tenth student to determine if they would vote in favor of the construction of a new school building.

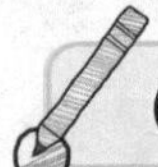

Georgia Test Practice

16. Maci surveyed all the members of her softball team about their favorite sport.

Sport	Number of Members
Softball	12
Basketball	5
Soccer	3
Volleyball	8

From these results, Maci concluded that softball was the favorite sport among all her classmates. Which is the best explanation for why her conclusion might *not* be valid?

Ⓐ The softball team meets only on weekdays.

Ⓑ She should have asked only people who do not play sports.

Ⓒ The survey should have been done daily for a week.

Ⓓ The sample was not representative of all of her classmates.

17. Ms. Hernandez determined that 60% of the students in her classes brought an umbrella to school when the weather forecast predicted rain. If she has a total of 150 students, which statement does *not* represent Ms. Hernandez's data?

Ⓕ On days when rain is forecasted, less than $\frac{2}{5}$ of her students bring an umbrella to school.

Ⓖ On days when rain is forecasted, 90 of her students bring an umbrella to school.

Ⓗ On days when rain is forecasted, more than $\frac{1}{2}$ of her students bring an umbrella to school.

Ⓘ On days when rain is forecasted, 60 of her students do not bring an umbrella to school.

Common Core Review

For Exercises 18 and 19, use the table that shows Alana's first six math test scores. MCC6.SP.3

Test	1	2	3	4	5	6
Score	88%	92%	70%	96%	84%	96%

18. Find the mean, median, and mode of Alana's test scores. Round to the nearest tenth if necessary.

mean: ________ median: ________ mode: ________

19. Determine which measure of center best represents Alana's performance. Justify your reasoning.

WHY is it important to analyze multiple samples of data before making predictions?

Content Standards
MCC7.SP.2
Mathematical Practices
1, 3, 4, 5

Crayons A hostess at a restaurant randomly hands out crayons to young children. There are three different color crayons: green (G), red (R), and blue (B). The server gives out the green crayon 40% of the time, the red crayon 40% of the time, and the blue crayon 20% of the time.

Investigation 1

When you draw a conclusion about a population from a sample of data, you are drawing an *inference* about that population. Sometimes, drawing inferences about a population from only one sample is not as accurate as using multiple samples of data.

Use a spinner to simulate the situation above.

Step 1 Create a spinner with five equal sections. Label two sections G. Label another two sections R and label one section B.

Step 2 Each spin of the spinner represents a young child receiving a crayon. Spin the spinner 20 times. Record the number of times each color of crayon was received in the column labeled Sample 1 in the table below. Repeat two more times. Record the results in the columns labeled Sample 2 and Sample 3 in the table.

Color	Sample 1 Frequency	Sample 2 Frequency	Sample 3 Frequency
Green			
Red			
Blue			

Compare the results of the 3 samples. Do you notice any differences?

Computer Keyboards The most commonly used keyboard is the QWERTY keyboard. However, there is another type of keyboard called the Dvorak keyboard that is based on letter frequency. Complete the Investigation below about letter frequencies.

Investigation 2

The table at the right contains fifteen randomly selected words from the English language dictionary.

Sample 1		
airport	juggle	sewer
blueberry	lemon	standard
costume	mileage	thread
doorstop	percentage	vacuum
instrument	print	whale

Step 1 Find the frequency of each letter. Record the frequencies in the Sample 1 rows of the tables below.

Letter	a	b	c	d	e	f	g	h	i	j	k	l	m
Sample 1 Frequency													
Sample 2 Frequency													
Sample 3 Frequency													

Letter	n	o	p	q	r	s	t	u	v	w	x	y	z
Sample 1 Frequency													
Sample 2 Frequency													
Sample 3 Frequency													

Step 2 Randomly select another 15 words from a dictionary. Record the frequency of the letters in the rows labeled Sample 2 in the tables above.

Step 3 Repeat Step 2. Record the frequency of the letters in the rows labeled Sample 3.

Work with a partner to collect multiple samples based on the following situation.

Janet and Masao are making centerpieces for their school's fall dance. They randomly select a ribbon to use in each centerpiece. There are four different colors of ribbon to choose from: brown (B), green (G), orange (O), and yellow (Y).

1. CCGPS **Model with Mathematics** Design a method to simulate how many times each ribbon will be selected. Describe your simulation.

2. Use the method you described in Exercise 1 to simulate the ribbon selection 20 times. Record the frequency of each color selection in the Sample 1 Frequency column of the table below.

Color	Sample 1 Frequency	Sample 2 Frequency	Sample 3 Frequency
Brown			
Green			
Orange			
Yellow			

3. Repeat the process described in Exercise 2 two more times. Record the frequencies of each color selection in the Sample 2 and Sample 3 columns.

4. Which color was selected the most often in each sample?

5. The *relative frequency* of a color being selected is the ratio of the number of times the color was selected to the total number of selections. Find the relative frequency of an orange ribbon being selected for each sample.

Sample 1: ______ Sample 2: ______ Sample 3: ______

6. Masao predicts that 5 out of 10 centerpieces will have an orange ribbon. How far off is Masao's prediction? Explain.

Analyze

Work with a partner to answer the following questions. Refer to Investigation 2.

7. What is the relative frequency for the letter e for each sample? Round to the nearest hundredth.

   Sample 1: ________ Sample 2: ________ Sample 3: ________

8. What is the mean relative frequency of the letter e for the three samples? the median relative frequency? Round to the nearest tenth if necessary.

   mean relative frequency: ________ median relative frequency: ________

9. CCGPS **Use Math Tools** Research on the Internet to find the actual relative frequency of the letter e for words in the English language. How do your sample results compare to the actual relative frequency?

10. CCGPS **Reason Inductively** Write a few sentences describing the inferences you can make about the frequency of letters in the words in the English language using your three samples.

11. CCGPS **Justify Conclusions** Research on the Internet to find the relative frequency of other letters in words in the English language. How do your sample results compare to the actual frequencies? Note any differences.

Reflect

12. Inquiry WHY is it important to analyze multiple samples of data before making predictions?

Misleading Graphs and Statistics

What You'll Learn

Scan the lesson. List two scenarios that might involve misleading graphs or statistics.

•

•

Essential Question

HOW do you know which type of graph to use when displaying data?

Common Core GPS

Content Standards
Extension of MCC7.SP.1

Mathematical Practices
1, 3, 4

Real-World Link

Hockey The Stanley Cup is awarded annually to the champion team in the National Hockey League. The graph shows the total number of points scored in Stanley Cup playoff games by three players during their careers.

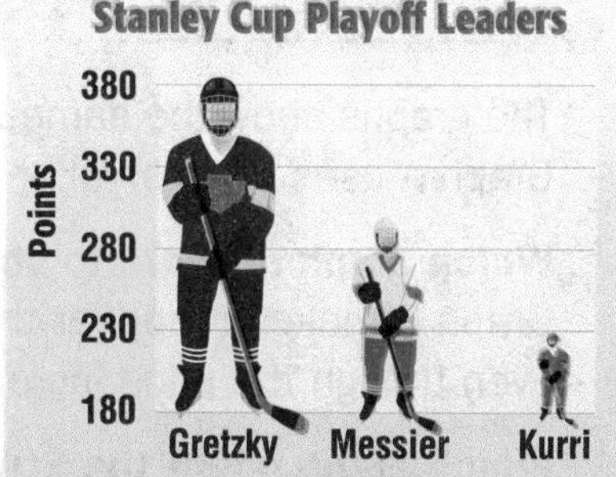

1. According to the size of the players, how many times more points does Messier appear to have than Kurri?

2. Do you think this is representative of the players' number of points? Explain.

3. What reason could someone have for intentionally creating a misleading Stanley Cup graph?

Work Zone

Identify a Misleading Graph

Graphs let readers analyze data easily, but are sometimes made to influence conclusions by misrepresenting the data.

Example

Changing Scales
To emphasize a change over time, reduce the scale interval on the vertical axis.

1. Explain how the graphs differ.

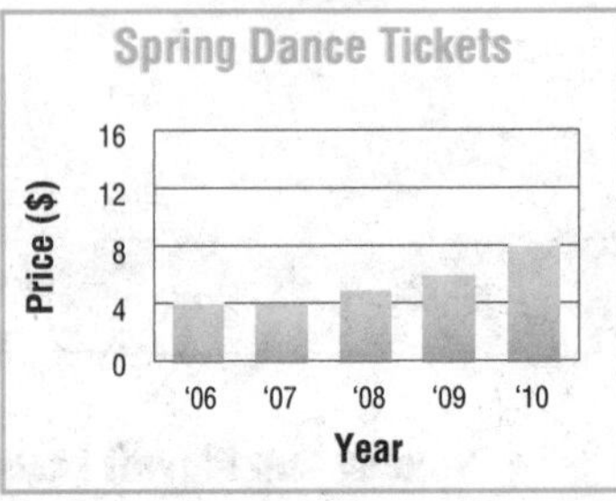

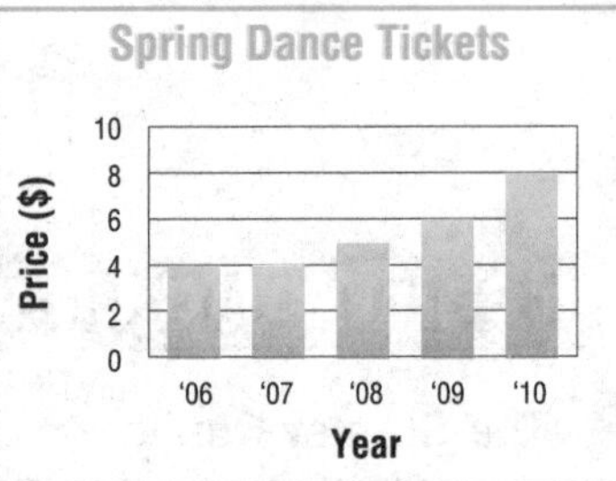

The graphs show the same data. However, the graphs differ in that Graph A uses an interval of 4, and Graph B uses an interval of 2.

Which graph appears to show a sharper increase in price?
Graph B makes it appear that the prices increased more rapidly even though the price increase is the same.

Which graph might the Student Council use to show that while ticket prices have risen, the increase is not significant? Why?
They might use Graph A. The scale used on the vertical axis of this graph makes the increase appear less significant.

Got It? **Do this problem to find out.**

a. The line graphs show monthly profits of a company from October to March. Which graph suggests that the business is extremely profitable? Is this a valid conclusion? Explain.

a. ______________

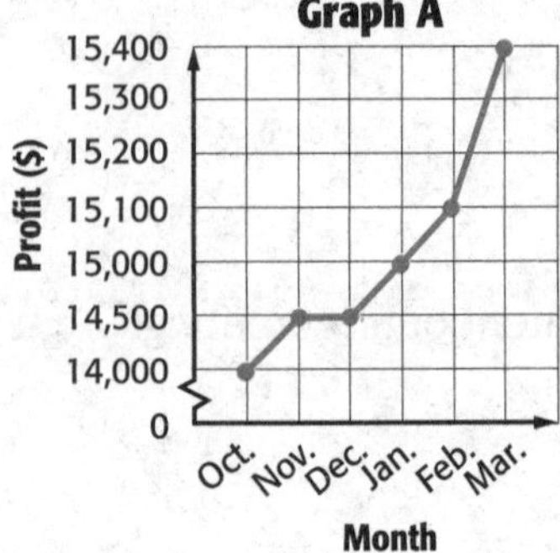

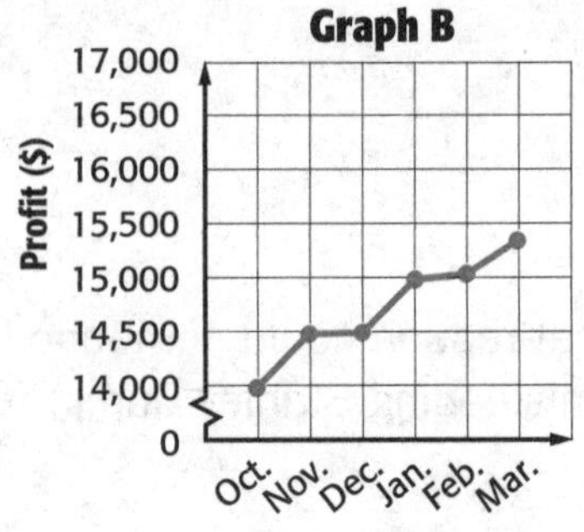

Misleading Statistics

Statistics can also be used to influence conclusions.

Example

2. **An amusement park boasts that the average height of their roller coasters is 170 feet. Explain how this might be misleading.**

Park Roller Coaster Heights	
Coaster	**Height (ft)**
Viper	109
Monster	135
Red Zip	115
Tornado	365
Riptide	126

Mean $\frac{109 + 135 + 115 + 365 + 126}{5} = \frac{850}{5}$

$= 170$

Median 109, 115, 126, 135, 365

Mode none

The average used by the park was the mean. This measure is much greater than most of the heights listed because of the coaster that is 365 feet. So, it is misleading to use this measure to attract visitors.

A more appropriate measure to describe the data is the median, 126 feet, which is closer to the height of most of the coasters.

Mode
The mode is the number or numbers that appear most often in a set of data.

Got It? Do this problem to find out.

b. Find the mean, median, and mode of the sofa prices shown in the table. Which measurement might be misleading in describing the average cost of a sofa? Explain.

Sofa Prices	
Sofa Style	**Cost**
leather	$1,700
reclining	$1,400
DIY assembly	$350
sectional	$1,600
micro-fiber	$1,400

b. ______________

Guided Practice

1. The graph suggests that Cy Young had three times as many wins as Jim Galvin. Is this a valid conclusion? Explain. (Example 1)

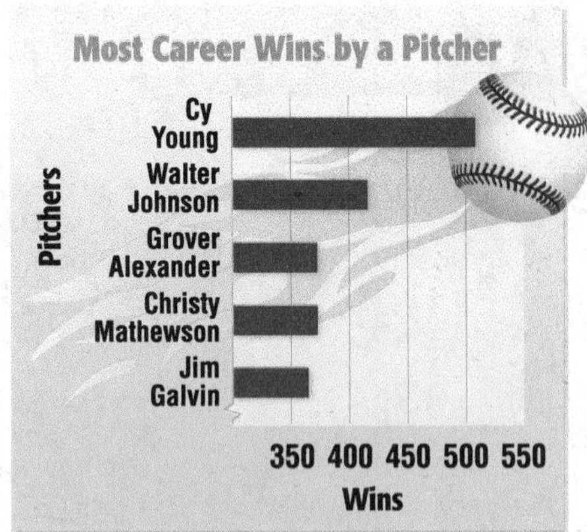

2. The graph at the right shows the results of a survey to determine students' favorite pets. Why is the graph misleading? (Example 1)

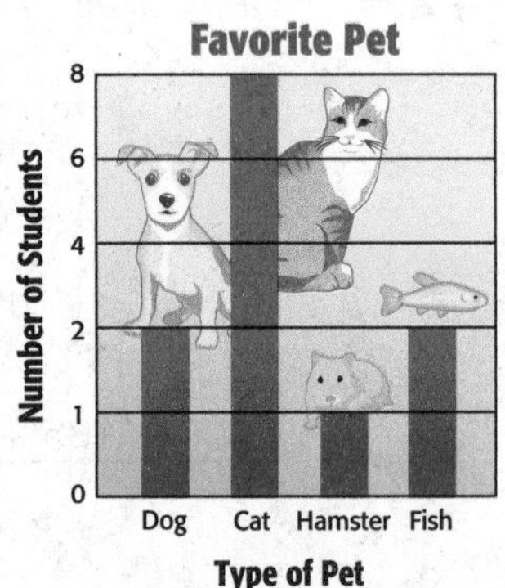

3. The table lists the five largest land vehicle tunnels in the United States. Write a convincing argument for which measure of center you would use to emphasize the average length length of the tunnels. (Example 2)

U.S. Vehicle Tunnels	Length (ft)
Anton Anderson Memorial	13,300
E. Johnson Memorial	8,959
Eisenhower Memorial	8,941
Allegheny	6,072
Liberty Tubes	5,920

4. **Building on the Essential Question** Describe at least two ways in which the display of data can influence the conclusions reached.

Rate Yourself!

How well do you understand misleading graphs and statistics? Circle the image that applies.

Clear Somewhat Clear Not So Clear

For more help, go online to access a Personal Tutor.

Name ______________________ My Homework ______________________

Independent Practice

Go online for Step-by-Step Solutions

1. Which graph could be used to indicate a greater increase in monthly gas prices? Explain. (Example 1)

Graph A

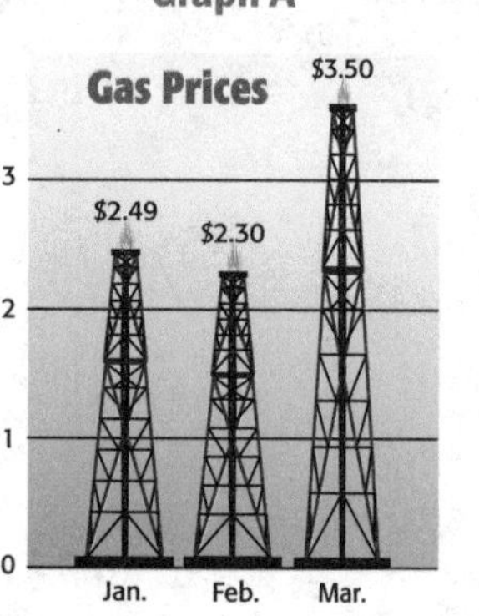

Graph B

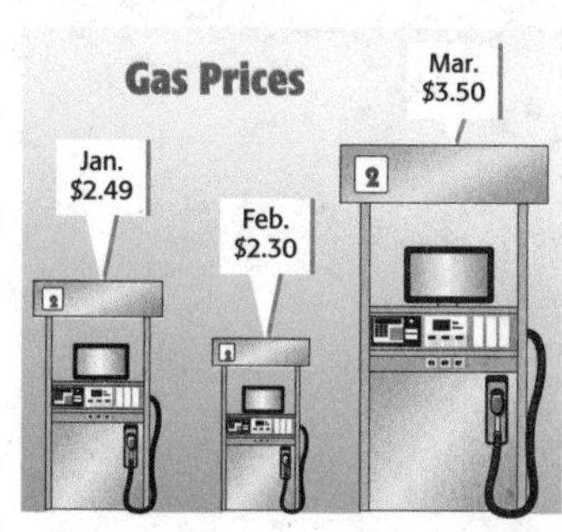

For Exercises 2 and 3, use the table. (Example 2)

2. Find the mean, median, and mode of the data. Which measure might be misleading in describing the average annual number of visitors who visit these sights? Explain.

Annual Sight-Seeing Visitors

Sight	Visitors
Cape Cod	4,600,000
Grand Canyon	4,500,000
Lincoln Memorial	4,000,000
Castle Clinton	4,600,000
Smoky Mountains	10,200,000

3. Which measure would be best if you wanted a value close to the most number of visitors? Explain.

4. CCGPS **Model with Mathematics** Refer to the graphic novel frame below.

Which measure of center should the students use? ______________________

For Exercises 5 and 6, create a display that would support each argument. The monthly costs to rent an apartment for the last five years are $500, $525, $560, $585, and $605.

5. Rent has remained fairly stable.

6. Rent has increased dramatically.

H.O.T. Problems Higher Order Thinking

7. CCGPS **Reason Inductively** How could the graph you created in Exercise 5 help influence someone's decision to rent the apartment?

8. CCGPS **Persevere with Problems** Does adding values that are much greater or much less than the other values in a set of data affect the median of the set? Give an example to support your answer.

Georgia Test Practice

9. A restaurant claims its average menu price is $3.50. Which statement below helps explain how this might be misleading.

Ⓐ The mean price of the items listed is actually $4.00.

Ⓑ The mean price of the items listed is actually $3.90.

Ⓒ The restaurant is calculating the average price by including coffee, a low priced item.

Ⓓ The median of the data is $3.90.

Menu	
Hamburger	$4.00
Fish Sandwich	$4.45
Chicken Sandwich	$4.35
Garden Salad	$3.90
Coffee	$0.80

Extra Practice

10. To determine how often his students are tardy, Mr. Kessler considered the attendance record for his first period class. Why is this graph misleading?

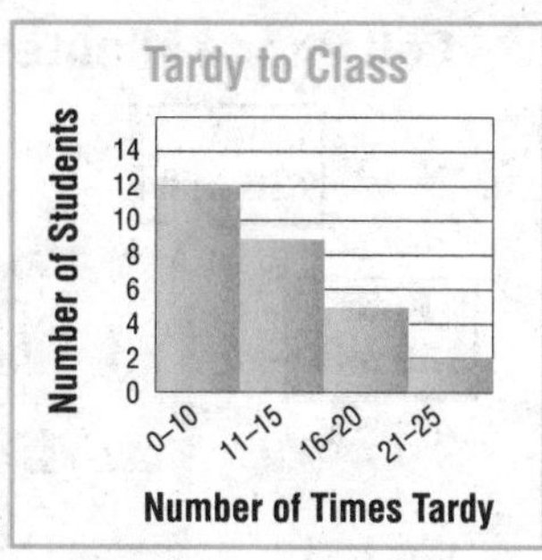

There are not equal intervals on the horizontal axis. So, the height of the bars is not representative of the sample.

11. The graph shows the height of a plant after 9 weeks of growth. Why is the graph misleading?

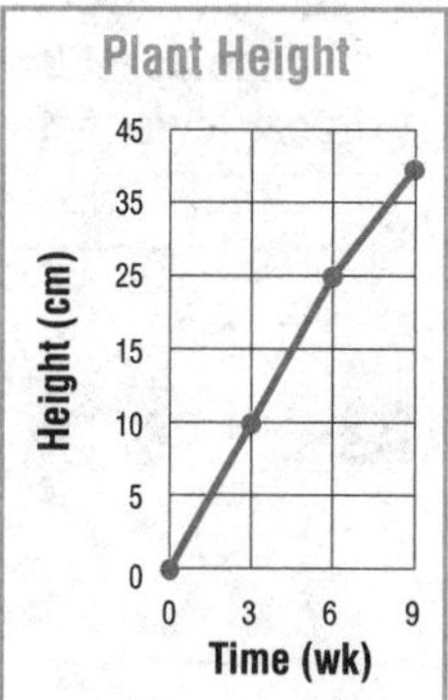

12. CCGPS **Justify Conclusions** Each of the graphs below show the distance Romerio travels on his bike. Romerio wants to impress his friends with the distance he travels. Which graph should he show his friends? Explain.

Graph A

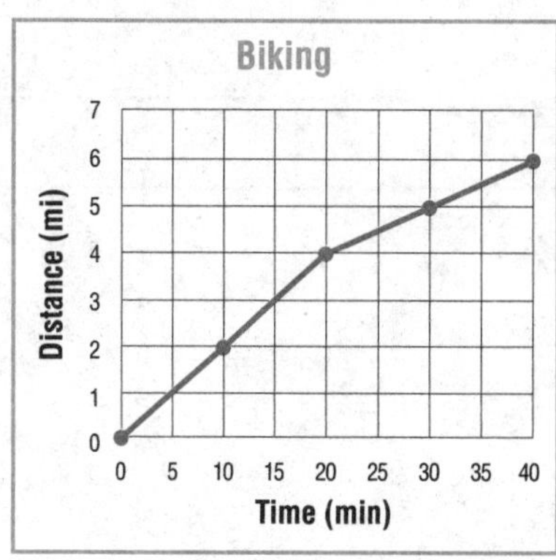

Graph B

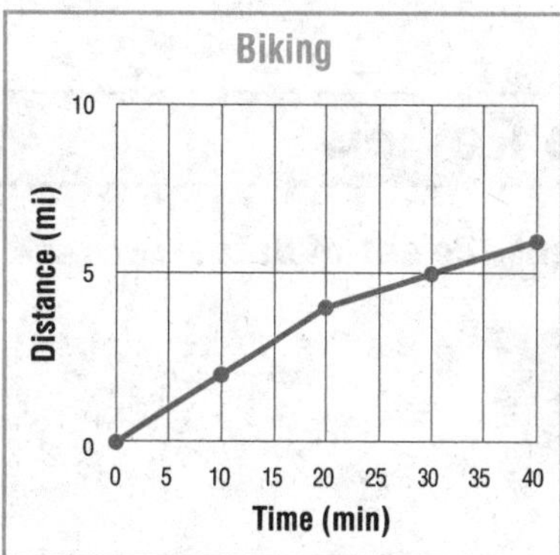

13. The scores Emily received on her math tests were 80, 90, 85, 100, 100, and 84. Why might it be misleading for Emily to say that most of the time she receives a score of 100?

Georgia Test Practice

14. The bar graph shows the average number of hours each week that a group of students attend an extracurricular activity after school.

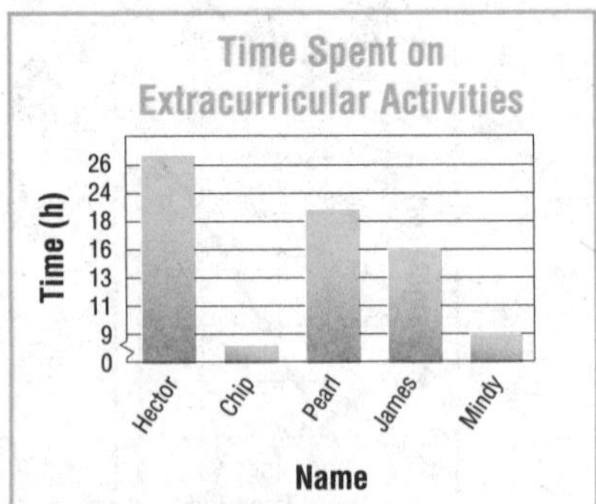

Which statement best tells why the graph may be misleading?

Ⓐ The vertical scale should show days instead of hours.

Ⓑ The graph does not show the number of hours each person attended.

Ⓒ The intervals on the vertical scale are inconsistent.

Ⓓ The graph's title is misleading.

15. **Short Response** Janet kept track of the minutes she used on her cell phone for 2 months. How many more minutes did Janet use in July than June? Explain why the graph could be misleading.

Cell Phone Minutes

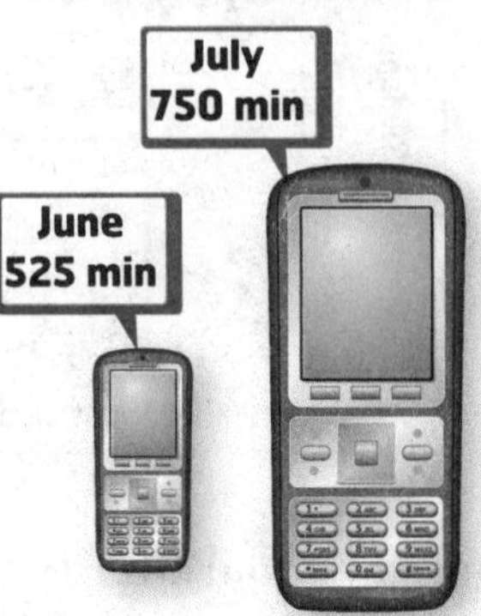

Common Core Review

Draw a histogram to represent the set of data. MCC6.SP.4

16.

Test Scores		
Percent	**Tally**	**Frequency**
50-59	|	1
60-69	||	2
70-79	||||	4
80-89	~~||||~~ ~~||||~~ |	11
90-99	~~||||~~ |||	8

Use a Graph

Content Standards
MCC7.SP.1
Mathematical Practices
1, 3, 4

Case #1 Fishy Waters

Tess recently purchased a saltwater aquarium. She needs to add 1 tablespoon of sea salt for every 5 gallons of water.

Sea Salt Requirements						
Tablespoons of Sea Salt	1	2	3	4	5	6
Capacity of Tank (gallons)	5	10	15	20	25	30

How can she use a graph to show the number of tablespoons of salt required for a 50-gallon saltwater fish tank?

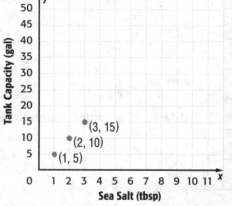

Understand *What are the facts?*

You know the number of gallons of the tank. You need to show the number of tablespoons of sea salt.

Plan *What is your strategy to solve this problem?*

Organize the rest of the data in a graph so you can easily see any trends.

Solve *How can you apply the strategy?*

Tank Capacity (gal) (y-axis: 0, 5, 10, 15, 20, 25, 30, 35, 40, 45, 50)
Sea Salt (tbsp) (x-axis: 0, 1, 2, 3, 4, 5, 6, 7, 8, 9, 10, 11)
Points: (1, 5), (2, 10), (3, 15)

Continue the graph until you align horizontally with 50 gallons. Graph a point. What value of sea salt corresponds with the point?

4 Check *Does the answer make sense?*

Find the unit rate of tablespoons of sea salt per gallon of water. Multiply the unit rate by the number of gallons to find the number of tablespoons of sea salt.

$$\frac{0.2 \text{ tbsp salt}}{1 \text{ gal water}} \times \frac{50 \text{ gal water}}{1} = \square \text{ tbsp salt} \checkmark$$

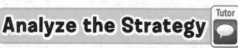

Analyze the Strategy

Make a Prediction Suppose the tank holds 32 gallons. Predict how much sea salt is required.

Case #2 Calories

The table shows the average number of Calories burned while sleeping for various numbers of hours. Assume the trend continues.

Calories Burned While Sleeping	
Hours	Calories
6	386
7	450
8	514
9	579

Make a graph to determine the approximate number of Calories that are burned by sleeping for 10 hours.

Understand

Read the problem. What are you being asked to find?

I need to find ______________________.

What information do you know?

There is an average of ________ Calories burned while sleeping for 6 hours and 514 Calories burned while sleeping for ________ hours.

Plan

Choose a problem-solving strategy.

I will use the ______________________ strategy.

Solve

Use your problem-solving strategy to solve the problem.

Continue the graph until it is aligned vertically with 10 hours. Graph a point. Find what value of Calories corresponds with the point. So, about ________ Calories are burned while sleeping for 10 hours.

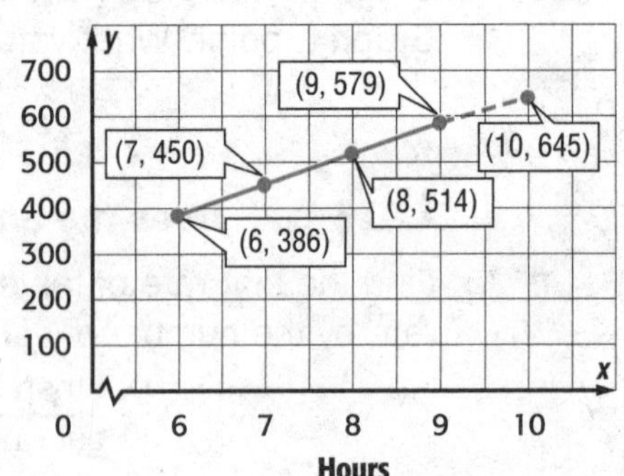

Check

Review the data in the table.

$450 - 386 = 64$; $514 - 450 = 64$; $579 - 514 = 65$. $645 - 579 = 66$.

So, the answer seems reasonable.

Collaborate Work with a small group to solve the following cases. Show your work on a separate piece of paper.

Case #3 Postage

The table shows the postage stamp rate from 1999 to 2009.

Make a graph of the data. Predict the year the postage rate will reach $0.52.

Postage Stamp Rates

Year	Cost ($)
1999	0.33
2001	0.34
2002	0.37
2006	0.39
2007	0.41
2008	0.42
2009	0.44

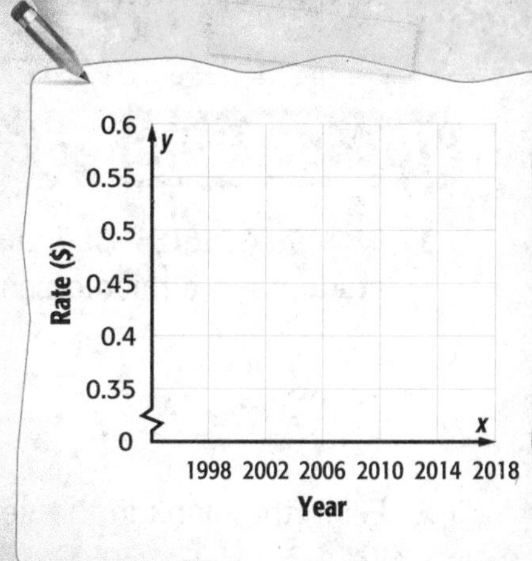

Case #4 Trains

The lengths of various train rides are 4, 1, 2, 3, 6, 2, 3, 2, 5, 8, and 4 hours.

Draw a box plot for the data set. Then write a sentence that can be supported by the graph.

Case #5 Advertising

A local newspaper charges $14.50 for every three lines of a classified ad.

Predict the cost of a 7-line ad.

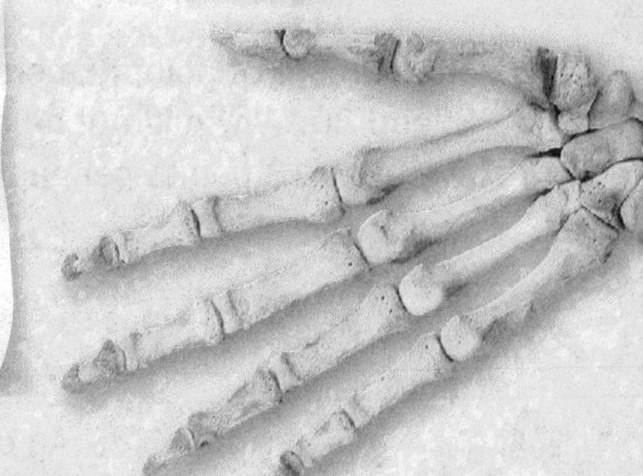

Circle a strategy below to solve the problem.

- Determine reasonable answers.
- Work backward.
- Draw a diagram.

Case #6 Anatomy

Each human hand has 27 bones. There are 6 more bones in the fingers than in the wrist. There are 3 fewer bones in the palm than in the wrist.

How many bones are in each part of the hand?

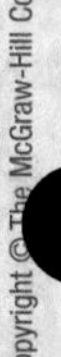

Mid-Chapter Check

Vocabulary Check

1. **CCGPS Be Precise** Define *sample*. Give an example of a sample of the students in a middle school. (Lesson 1)

2. Fill in the blank in the sentence below with the correct terms. (Lesson 2)

_______________ and _______________ are two types of unbiased samples.

Skills Check and Problem-Solving

3. A travel agent surveyed her customers to determine their favorite vacation locations. Use the table to find the probability of choosing a beach vacation. (Lesson 1)

4. Refer to the table. Suppose 120 customers are planning vacations. Predict how many will plan a national park vacation. (Lesson 1)

Vacation Locations	
Location	**Customers**
amusement park	2
beach	11
campground	8
national park	4

5. The number of points Emerson scored in 5 basketball games is 10, 8, 9, 8, and 30. Why might it be misleading for Emerson to say that she averages 13 points per game? (Lesson 3)

6. **Georgia Test Practice** An owner of a restaurant wants to conduct a survey about possible menu changes. Which of the following sampling methods would produce a valid sample? (Lesson 2)

Ⓐ survey every fifth person entering the mall

Ⓑ survey five of his friends

Ⓒ survey every fifth person eating at the owner's restaurant

Ⓓ survey every fifth person registered at the restaurant's Web site

HOW can you use the measures of center and the range to compare two populations?

Content Standards
MCC7.SP.3, MCC7.SP.4

Mathematical Practices
1, 3, 4

Sleep Studies show that teens need around 9 hours of sleep each night to stay healthy.

Investigation

Step 1 The results of a survey that asked 24 teens how many hours they slept last night are shown below. The teens were split into two populations, male and female.

Males	7	7	6	8	6	8	7	6	7	6	8	6
Females	8	8	7	6	8	7	6	6	7	8	9	7

Step 2 Graph the data for each population on a single line plot.

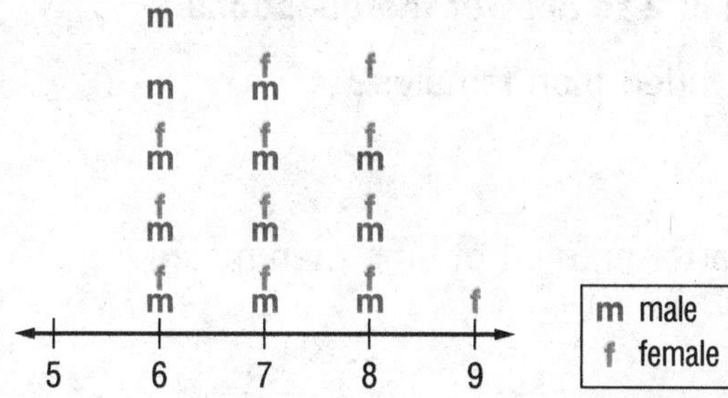

Step 3 Find the measures of center and range for each population.

	Mean	Median	Mode	Range
Males	6.8$\overline{3}$			
Females				

Are the data for males more or less varied than females?

____

Which measure most accurately represents the data of the whole class?

Explain. ______________________________

____

____

Collaborate

Work with a partner.

1. **Model with Mathematics** Collect data about the number of hours of sleep your classmates got last night from 5 males and 5 females. Then graph the data for each population on the single line plot below.

Males					
Females					

2. Find the measures of center and range for each population.

	Mean	Median	Mode	Range
Males				
Females				

Analyze

Work with a partner. Use Exercises 1 and 2 to answer the questions.

3. Are the data for males more or less varied than females?

4. Did females sleep for a longer or shorter amount of time than males?

5. **Justify Conclusions** Which measure most accurately represents the data of the whole class? Explain.

Reflect

6. **Inquiry** HOW can you use the measures of center and the range to compare two populations?

Compare Populations

What You'll Learn

Scan the lesson. List two-real world scenarios in which you would compare two populations.

- ______________________________
- ______________________________

Essential Question

HOW do you know which type of graph to use when displaying data?

Vocabulary

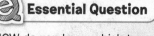

double box plot
double dot plot

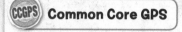

Common Core GPS

Content Standards
MCC7.SP.4

Mathematical Practices
1, 3, 4, 6

Real-World Link

Exercise Mr. Singh surveyed the students in his first period gym class to find out how many times they exercised this month. The box plot below shows the results.

How Many Times Have You Exercised This Month?

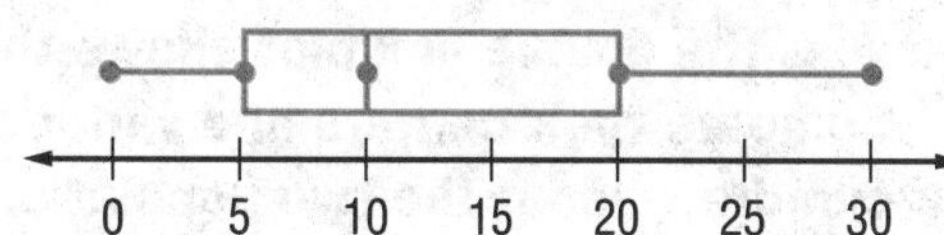

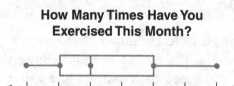

1. Find the following values.

Minimum: ☐ First Quartile: ☐

Maximum: ☐ Third Quartile: ☐

Range: ☐ Interquartile Range: ☐

2. What is the median? What does the median represent?

____

3. Write a conclusion that you can make from the box plot.

____

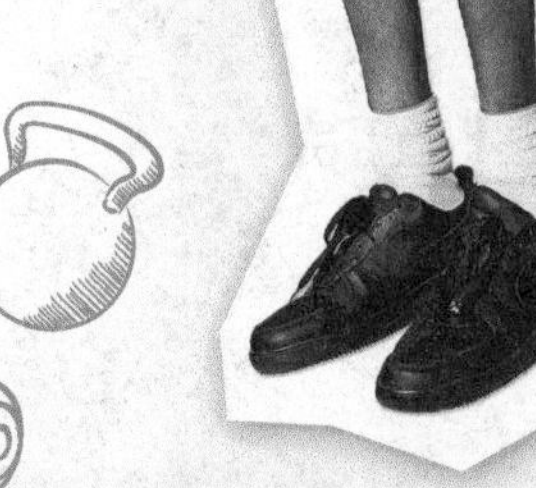

Work Zone

Compare Two Populations

A **double box plot** consists of two box plots graphed on the same number line. A **double dot plot** consists of two dot plots that are drawn on the same number line. You can draw inferences about two populations in a double box plot or double dot plot by comparing their centers and variations. The centers and variations to use are shown.

Box-plots
A box plot is symmetric if the data are balanced at the center.

Symmetric

Not Symmetric

Most Appropriate Measures			
	Both sets of data are symmetric.	**Neither set of data is symmetric.**	**Only one set of data is symmetric.**
Measure of Center	mean	median	median
Measure of Variation	mean absolute deviation	interquartile range	interquartile range

Example

1. Kacey surveyed a different group of students in her science and math classes. The double box plot shows the results for both classes. Compare their centers and variations. Write an inference you can draw about the two populations.

How Many Times Have You Posted A Blog This Month?

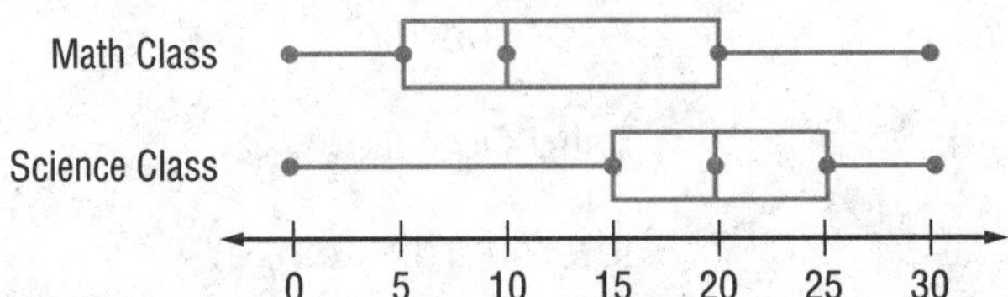

Neither box plot is symmetric. Use the median to compare the centers and the interquartile range to compare the variations.

	Math Class	**Science Class**
Median	10	20
Interquartile Range	20 – 5, or 15	25 – 15, or 10

Overall, the science students posted more blogs than the math students. The median for the science class is twice the median for the math class. There is a greater spread of data around the median for the math class than the science class.

Got It? Do this problem to find out.

Show your work.

a. The double box plot shows the costs of MP3 players at two different stores. Compare the centers and variations of the two populations. Write an inference you can draw about the two populations.

a. ______________

Cost of MP3 Players ($)

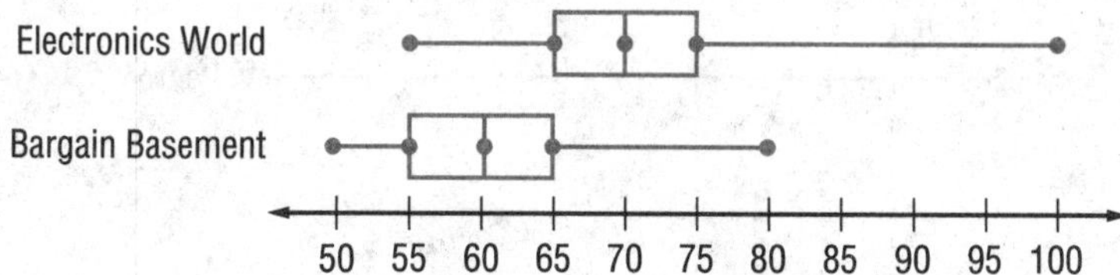

Example

2. The double dot plot below shows the daily high temperatures for two cities for thirteen days. Compare the centers and variations of the two populations. Write an inference you can draw about the two populations.

Daily High Temperatures (°F)

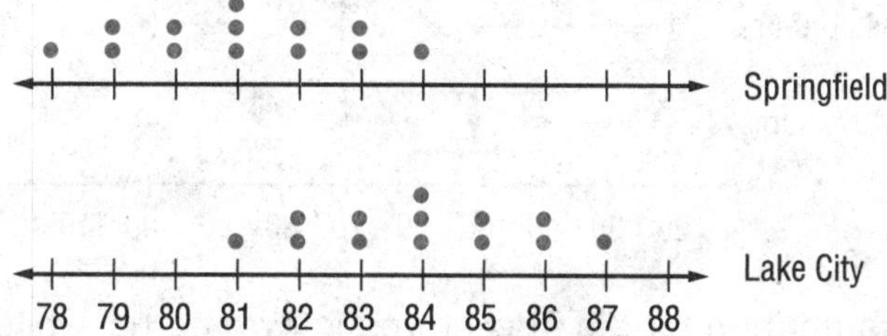

Both dot plots are symmetric. Use the mean to compare the centers and use the mean absolute deviation, rounded to the nearest tenth, to compare the variations.

	Springfield	Lake City
Mean	81	84
Mean Absolute Deviation	1.4	1.4

While both cities have the same variation, or spread of data about each of their means, Lake City has a greater mean temperature than Springfield.

Mean Absolute Deviation

To find the mean absolute deviation, find the absolute values of the differences between each value and the mean. Then find the average of those differences.

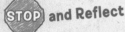

Show your work.

b. ____________

Got It? Do this problem to find out.

b. The double dot plot shows the number of new E-mails in each of Pedro's and Annika's inboxes for sixteen days. Compare the centers and variations of the two populations. Write an inference you can draw about the two populations.

Number of E-mails in Inbox

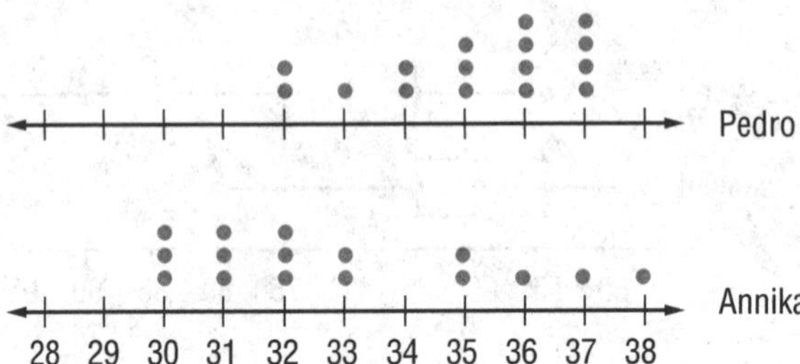

Examples

3. The double box plot shows the daily participants for two zip line companies for one month. Compare the centers and variations of the two populations. Which company has the greater number of daily participants?

Number of Daily Participants

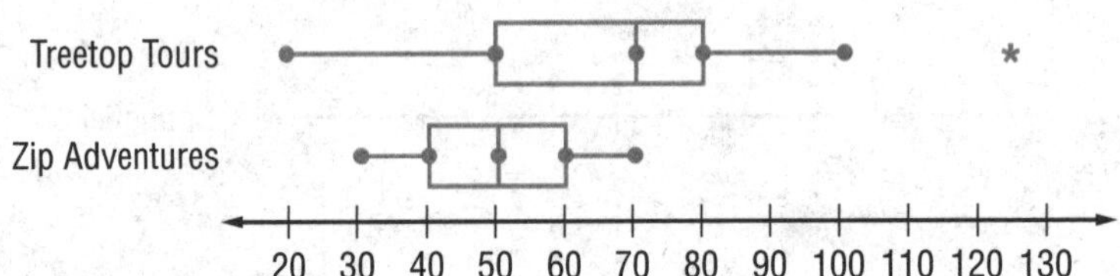

The distribution for Zip Adventures is symmetric, while the distribution for Treetop Tours is not symmetric. Use the median and the interquartile range to compare the populations.

	Treetop Tours	Zip Adventures
Median	70	50
Interquartile Range	30	20

Overall, Treetop Tours has a greater number of daily participants. However, Treetop Tours also has a greater variation, so it is more difficult to predict how many participants they may have each day. Zip Adventures has a greater consistency in their distribution.

STOP and Reflect

What can you tell about the set of data for Zip Adventures by looking at its box plot? Write your answer in the space below.

4. **The double dot plot shows Jada's and Angel's number of hours worked in a week at their part-time jobs. Compare the centers and variations of the two populations. Who typically works the greater number of hours in a week?**

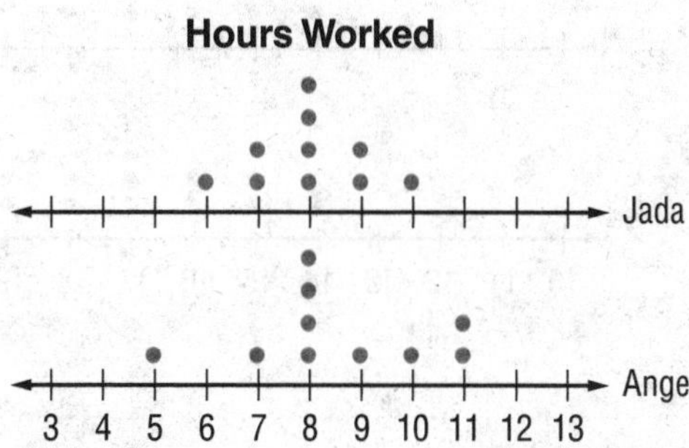

The distribution for Jada's number of hours is symmetric, while the distribution for Angel's number of hours is not symmetric. Use the median and interquartile range to compare the populations.

	Jada	Angel
Median	8	8
Interquartile Range	2	2

The median and interquartile range for both sets of data are the same. However, the interquartile range for Angel's number of hours worked is the difference of 10 and 8, while the interquartile range for Jada's number of hours is the difference of 9 and 7. So, Angel typically works more per week.

Got It? **Do this problem to find out.**

c. The double dot plot shows Kareem's and Martin's race times for a three-mile race. Compare the centers and variations of the two populations. Which runner is more likely to run a faster race?

c. ______________

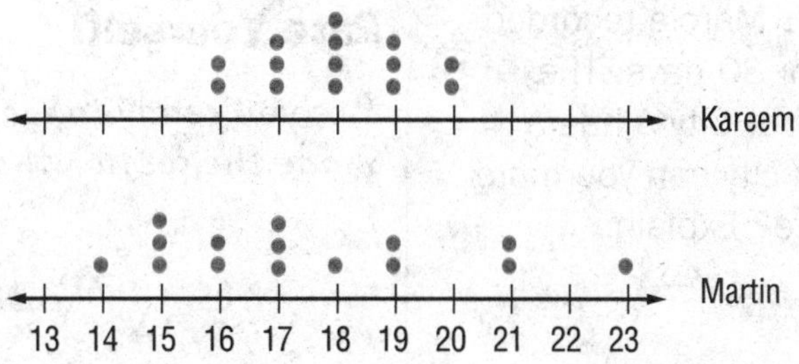

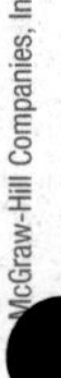

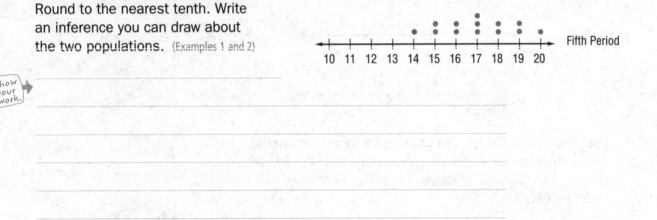

Guided Practice

1. The double dot plot below shows the quiz scores out of 20 points for two different class periods. Compare the centers and variations of the two populations. Round to the nearest tenth. Write an inference you can draw about the two populations. (Examples 1 and 2)

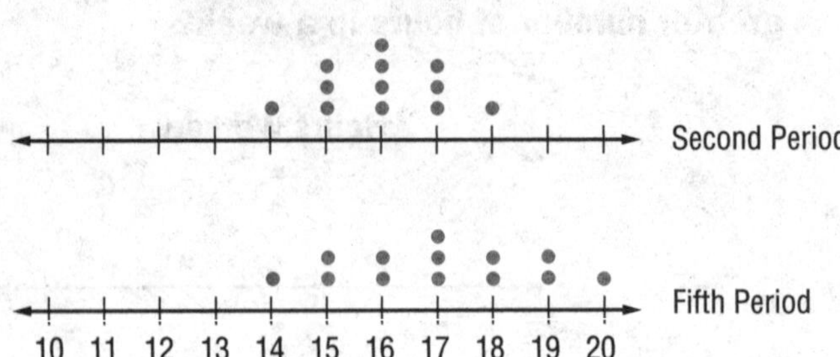

Show your work.

2. The double box plot shows the speeds of cars recorded on two different roads in Hamilton County. Compare the centers and variations of the two populations. On which road are the speeds greater? (Examples 3 and 4)

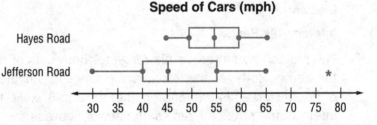

Speed of Cars (mph)

Hayes Road

Jefferson Road

30 35 40 45 50 55 60 65 70 75 80

3. **Building on the Essential Question** Marcia recorded the daily temperatures for two cities for 30 days. The two populations have similar centers, but City A has a greater variation than City B. For which city can you more accurately predict the daily temperature? Explain.

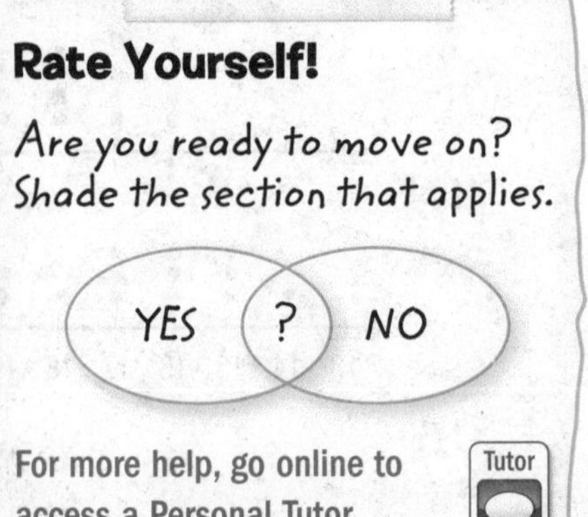

Rate Yourself!
Are you ready to move on?
Shade the section that applies.
YES
?
NO
For more help, go online to access a Personal Tutor.
Tutor

Name ________________ My Homework ________________

Independent Practice

Go online for Step-by-Step Solutions

1. Jordan randomly asked customers at two different restaurants how long they waited for a table before they were seated. The double box plot shows the results. Compare their centers and variations. Write an inference you can draw about the two populations. (Examples 1 and 2)

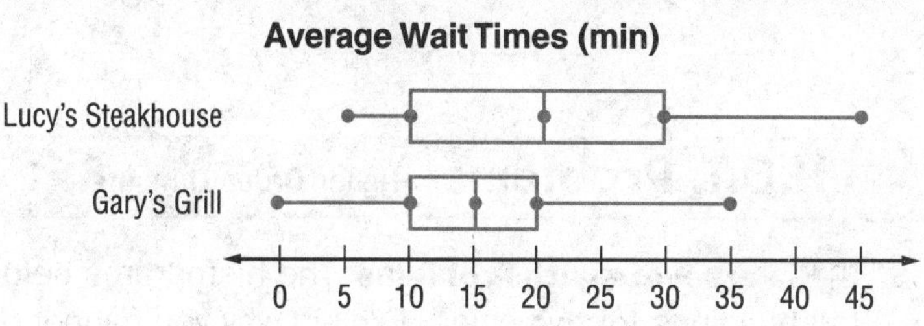

Show your work.

2. The double dot plot shows the times, in hours, for flights of two different airlines flying out of the same airport. Compare the centers and variations of the two populations. Which airline's flights had shorter flight times? (Examples 3 and 4)

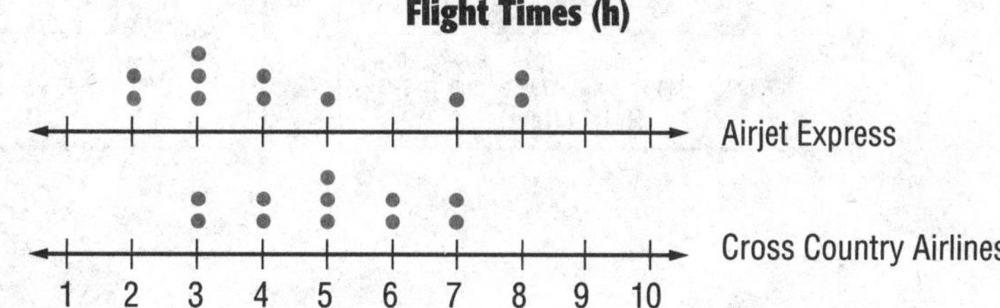

Copy and Solve **Write your answers for Exercise 3 on a separate piece of paper.**

3. CCGPS **Multiple Representations** For a science project, Mackenzie is measuring the growth of two plants.

Weekly Plant Growth (cm)								
	Week 1	**Week 2**	**Week 3**	**Week 4**	**Week 5**	**Week 6**	**Week 7**	**Week 8**
Plant A	2	3	2	2.5	3.4	3	2.5	3
Plant B	3	2.5	3	3.4	3.2	3.8	3.5	2.5

a. **Numbers** Find the median and interquartile range for both plants.

b. **Graphs** Graph the data using a double box plot.

c. **Words** Write an inference you can draw about the two populations.

4. The median and interquartile range of a set of data is shown. Write a set of data consisting of seven values for the pair of measures.

Median: 6 Interquartile Range: 5

H.O.T. Problems Higher Order Thinking

5. **CCGPS Persevere with Problems** The histograms below show the number of tall buildings for two cities. Explain why you cannot describe the specific location of the centers and spreads of the histograms.

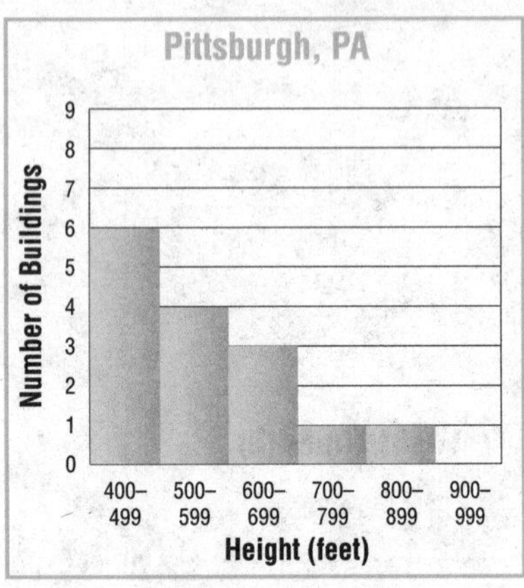

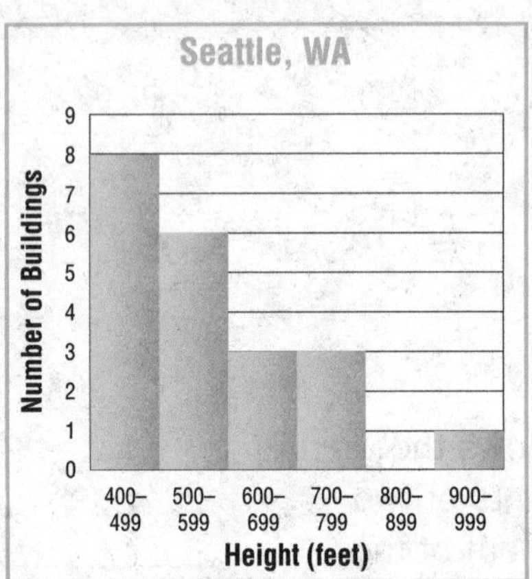

6. **CCGPS Model with Mathematics** Refer to Exercise 1. What is a specific question you could ask about the two populations?

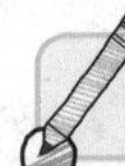

Georgia Test Practice

7. Which of the following is *not* true about the double box plot?

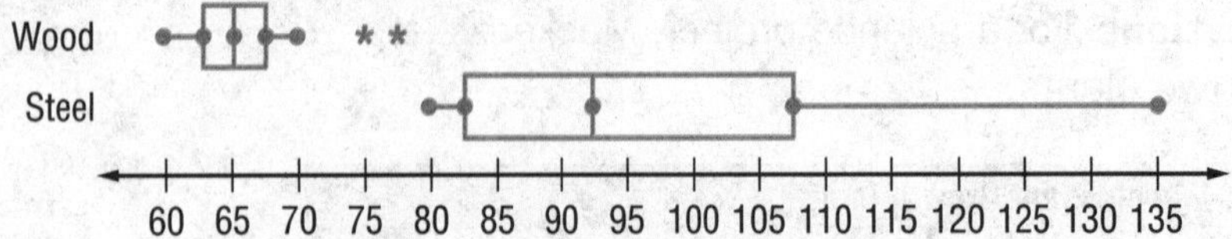

Ⓐ The data for the steel coaster is symmetric.

Ⓑ The data for the steel coaster is *not* symmetric.

Ⓒ The fastest steel coaster travels 135 miles per hour.

Ⓓ The slowest wooden coaster travels 60 miles per hour.

Name ______________________________ My Homework ____________________

Extra Practice

8. The double dot plot shows the heights in inches for the girls and boys in Franklin's math class. Compare the centers and variations of the two populations. Round to the nearest tenth. Write an inference you can draw about the two populations.

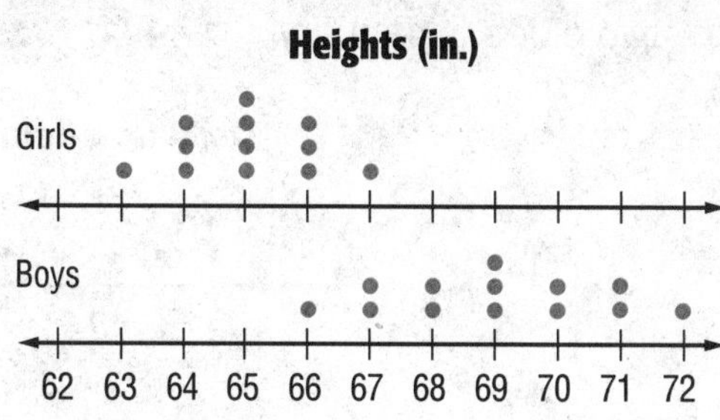

Homework Help Both plots are symmetric. The girls' heights have a mean of 65 inches with a mean absolute deviation of about 0.8 inch. The boys' heights have a mean of 69 inches with a mean absolute deviation of about 1.4 inches. Overall, the girls' heights are lower than the boys' heights and are also more consistently grouped together.

9. The double box plot shows the number of points scored by the football team for two seasons. Compare the centers and variations of the two populations. During which season was the team's performance more consistent?

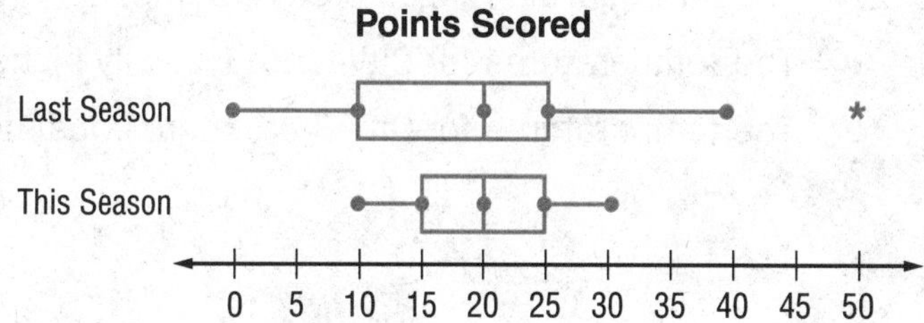

10. The double box plot shows the number of daily visitors to two different parks. Compare the centers and variations of the two populations. In general, which park has more daily visitors?

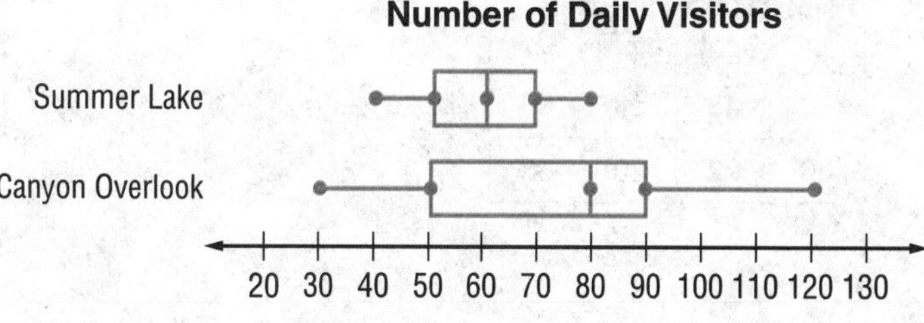

11. CCGPS **Be Precise** The median and interquartile range of a set of data is shown. Write a set of data consisting of seven values for the pair of measures.

Median: 5 Interquartile Range: 5

Georgia Test Practice

12. The double dot plot below shows the daily low temperatures of two cities in January.

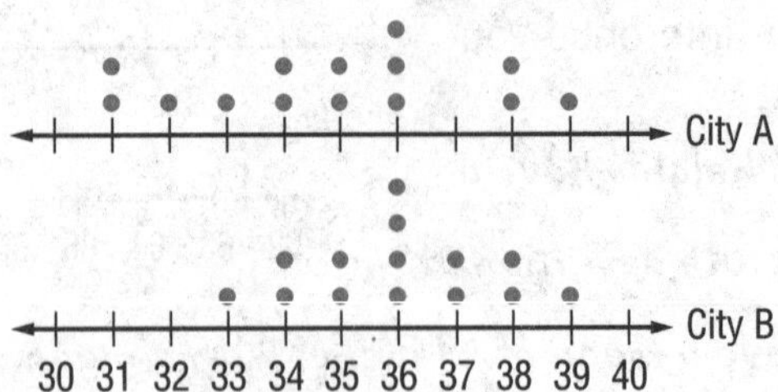

Which of the following statements about the two populations is true?

Ⓐ The medians are the same.

Ⓑ The interquartile ranges are the same.

Ⓒ The temperatures for City A are typically higher.

Ⓓ The temperatures for City B are more consistent.

Common Core Review

Find the mean absolute deviation of each set of data. Round to the nearest hundredth if necessary. MCC6.SP.5c

13. ________

Maximum Speeds of Boats (mph)			
40	48	58	60
66	72	80	88

14. ________

Populations of Largest U.S. Cities (millions)			
1.3	3.8	1.5	8.4
0.9	1.4	2.3	1.3

15. Refer to the graph in Exercise 2. Describe the shape of the distribution of the data for Airjet Express. MCC6.SP.5d

16. Refer to the graph in Exercise 10. Describe the shape of the distribution of the data for Canyon Overlook. MCC6.SP.5d

Inquiry Lab

Visual Overlap of Data Distributions

WHAT does the ratio $\frac{\text{difference in means}}{\text{mean absolute deviation}}$ tell you about how much visual overlap there is between two distributions with similar variation?

Content Standards
MCC7.SP.3

Mathematical Practices
1, 3

Texting A survey was done. The tables below show the number of text messages sent and received daily for two different age groups.

Text Messages Ages 12–15			
70	90	80	90
85	75	85	80
90	80	75	95
100	85	95	85

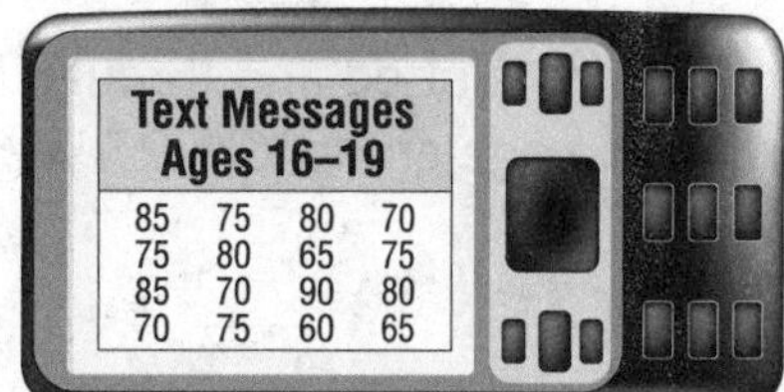

Text Messages Ages 16–19			
85	75	80	70
75	80	65	75
85	70	90	80
70	75	60	65

Investigation

You can compare two numerical data sets by comparing the shape of their distributions. The **visual overlap** of two distributions with similar variation is a visual demonstration that compares their centers to their variation, or spread.

Step 1 Use a double dot plot to display the data in each table.

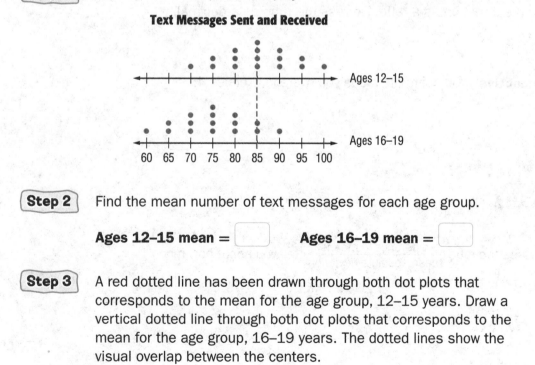

Text Messages Sent and Received

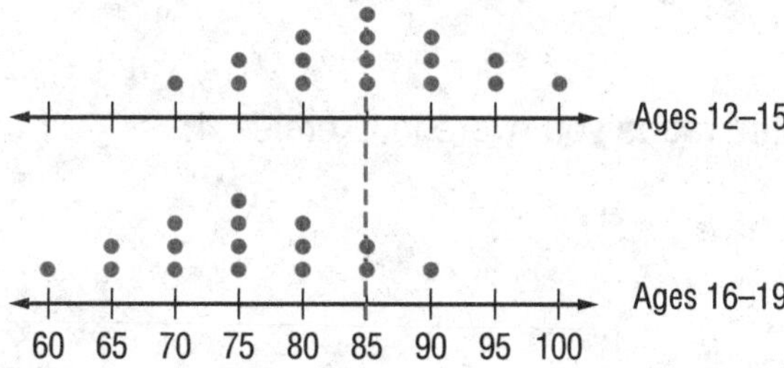

Step 2 Find the mean number of text messages for each age group.

Ages 12–15 mean = ☐ **Ages 16–19 mean =** ☐

Step 3 A red dotted line has been drawn through both dot plots that corresponds to the mean for the age group, 12–15 years. Draw a vertical dotted line through both dot plots that corresponds to the mean for the age group, 16–19 years. The dotted lines show the visual overlap between the centers.

Collaborate

Work with a partner. The double dot plot compares the number of text messages sent and received by a third age group to the age group, 12–15 years.

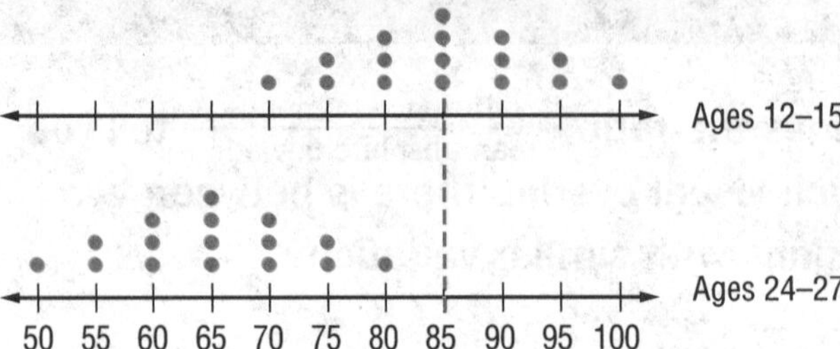

1. What is the mean number of texts for the age group, 24–27 years?

2. In the graph above, draw a vertical dotted line through both dot plots that corresponds to the mean for the age group, 24–27 years.

Work with a partner.

3. What is the difference between the means of the distributions for the Investigation? for Exercise 1?

4. The mean absolute deviation of each distribution is 6.25 texts. For the Investigation and Exercise 1, write the difference between the means and the mean absolute deviation as a ratio. Express the ratio as a decimal.

5. CCGPS **Reason Inductively** Compare the ratios you wrote in Exercise 4.

Reflect

6. Inquiry What does the ratio $\frac{\text{difference in means}}{\text{mean absolute deviation}}$ tell you about how much visual overlap there is between two distributions with similar variation?

Lesson 5

Select an Appropriate Display

What You'll Learn

Scan the lesson. Predict two things you will learn about selecting an appropriate display.

•

•

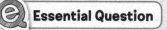

Essential Question

HOW do you know which type of graph to use when displaying data?

Common Core GPS

Content Standards
Extension of MCC7.SP.1

Mathematical Practices
1, 3, 4

Real-World Link

There are many different types of graphs that are used to display all kinds of statistical data. List all of the types of graphs you can think of below.

The graphs below display the total number of pounds of plastic recycled each week during a ten-week period in different ways.

Weekly Recycling

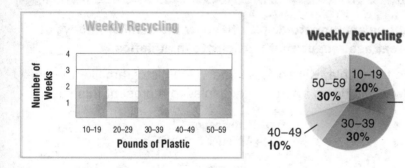

10–19 **20%**
20–29 **10%**
30–39 **30%**
40–49 **10%**
50–59 **30%**

1. On the line below each graph, write the type of graph used.

2. Which display more easily shows the number of weeks the class collected between 30 and 39 pounds of plastic? ________

3. Which display more easily shows the percent of time that 40 to 49 pounds of plastic was recycled? ________

Key Concept — Select an Appropriate Display

Type of Display	Best Used to...
Bar Graph	show the number of items in specific categories
Box Plot	show measures of variation for a set of data; also useful for very large sets of data
Circle Graph	compare parts of the data to the whole
Double Bar Graph	compare two sets of categorical data
Histogram	show frequency of data divided into equal intervals
Line Graph	show change over a period of time
Line Plot	show frequency of data with a number line

Work Zone

Data Displays
Many situations have more than one appropriate display.

When deciding what type of display to use, ask these questions.

- What type of information is given?
- What do you want the display to show?
- How will the display be analyzed?

Example

1. Select an appropriate display to show the number of boys of different age ranges that participate in athletics.

Since the display will show an interval, a histogram like the one below would be an appropriate display to represent this data.

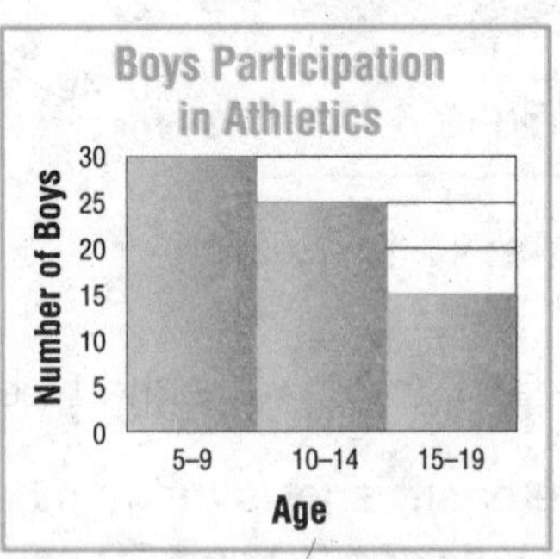

Got It? Do this problem to find out.

Show your work.

a. Select an appropriate display for the percent of students in each grade at a middle school.

a. ________

Example

2. Select an appropriate type of display to compare the percent of ethanol production by state. Justify your reasoning. Then construct the display. What can you conclude from your display?

Ethanol Production by State Per Year						
State	Iowa	Nebraska	Illinois	Minnesota	Indiana	Other
Gallons (millions)	3,534	1,665	1,135	1,102	1,074	5,098

You are asked to compare parts to a whole. A circle graph would be an appropriate display.

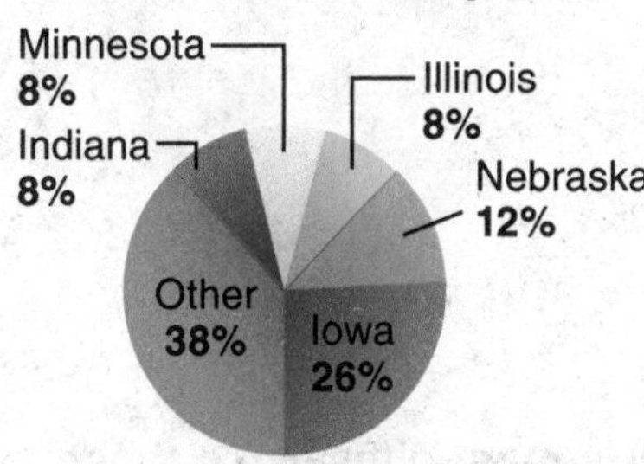

Indiana, Minnesota, and Illinois produce about the same amount of ethanol.

Got It? **Do this problem to find out.**

b. The table lists the ticket prices for school musicals during recent years. Select an appropriate display to predict the price of a ticket in 2013. Justify your reasoning. Then construct the display. What can you conclude from your display?

Ticket Prices	
Year	**Price ($)**
2009	5.00
2010	5.50
2011	6.50
2012	7.00

Guided Practice

Select an appropriate display for each situation. Justify your reasoning. (Example 1)

1. the number of people who have different kinds of pets

2. the percent of different ways electricity is generated

3. The prices of sandwiches at a restaurant are $4.50, $5.59, $3.99, $2.50, $4.99, $3.75, $2.99, $3.29, and $4.19. Select an appropriate display to determine how many sandwiches range from $3.00 to $3.99. Justify your reasoning. Then construct the display. What can you conclude from your display? (Example 2)

4. A survey asked teens which subject they felt was most difficult. Of those who responded, 25 said English, 39 said social studies, 17 said English and social studies equally, and 19 said neither subject. Construct an appropriate display of the data. Justify your reasoning. Then name one thing you can conclude from the display. (Example 2)

5. **Building on the Essential Question** What are some of the factors to consider when selecting an appropriate display for a set of data?

Rate Yourself!

How confident are you about selecting an appropriate display? Shade the ring on the target.

For more help, go online to access a Personal Tutor.

Independent Practice

Go online for Step-by-Step Solutions

Select an appropriate display for each situation. Justify your reasoning. (Example 1)

1. the median age of members in a community band

2. the number of students that favor chocolate or vanilla as a frosting

3. Select an appropriate display for the data. Justify your reasoning. Then construct the display. What can you conclude from your display? (Example 2)

Number of Push-ups			
45	35	42	37
44	40	36	42
45	40	42	39
44	43	36	39

4. CCGPS **Model with Mathematics** Refer to the graphic novel frame below. What is the best type of display to use for this data? Explain.

5. Refer to the situations described below.

Situation A	Situation B
the number of customers ages 12–19 compared to all age groups	the number of customers ages 12, 13, 14, 15, and 16 who made a purchase

a. Which situation involves data that is best displayed in a bar graph? Explain your reasoning.

b. Refer to the situation you selected in part **a.** Could you display the data using another type of display? If so, which display? Explain.

H.O.T. Problems **H**igher **O**rder **T**hinking

6. CCGPS **Model with Mathematics** Give an example of a data set that would be best represented in a line graph.

7. CCGPS **Reason Inductively** Determine if the following statement is *always*, *sometimes*, or *never* true. Justify your response.

A circle graph can be used to display data from a bar graph.

8. CCGPS **Persevere with Problems** Determine if the following statement is *true* or *false*. Explain your reasoning.

A line plot can be used to display data from a histogram.

Georgia Test Practice

9. Select an appropriate display for showing the temperature change for the last three hours.

Ⓐ bar graph
Ⓑ circle graph
Ⓒ line graph
Ⓓ box plot

Name ______________________ My Homework ______________

Extra Practice

Justify Conclusions **Select an appropriate display for each situation. Justify your reasoning.**

10. the resale value of a person's car over time

line graph; A line graph compares change over time.

11. the percent of people that drink 0, 1, 2, 3, or more than 3 glasses of water a day

12. the number of different colored cars at a car dealership

13. The circle graph shows the approximate percent of the total volume of each Great Lake.

a. Display the data using another type of display.

Volume of the Great Lakes

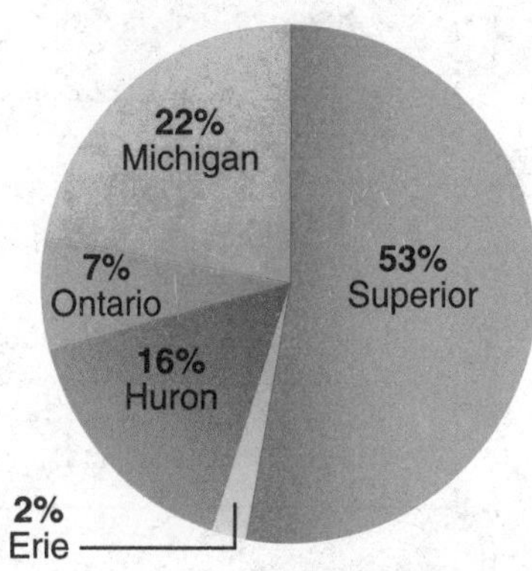

b. Write a convincing argument telling which display is more appropriate.

Copy and Solve **Select an appropriate display for each situation. Then justify your reasoning and construct the display on a separate sheet of paper. What can you conclude from your display?**

14.

Favorite Movies	
Type of Movie	**Number of People**
Comedy	48
Action	17
Drama	5
Horror	2

15.

Age Group	Number of Texts per Day
11–15	25
16–20	23
21–25	17
26–30	10

Georgia Test Practice

16. Moira surveyed 25 of her classmates to find out how many E-mails they received. Which of the following displays gives the most detail about the data?

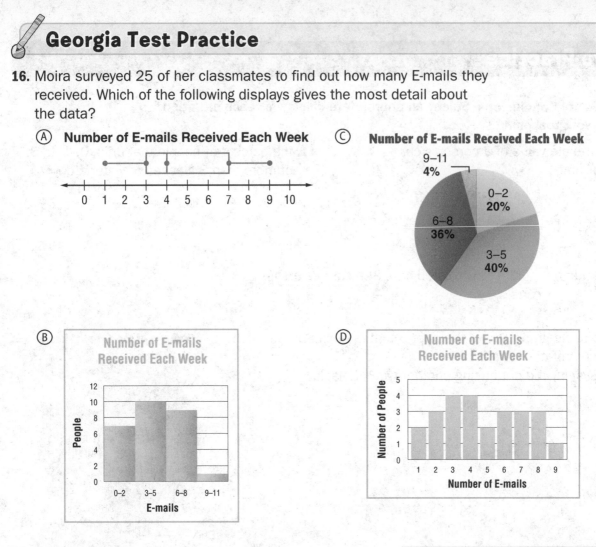

Ⓐ **Number of E-mails Received Each Week**

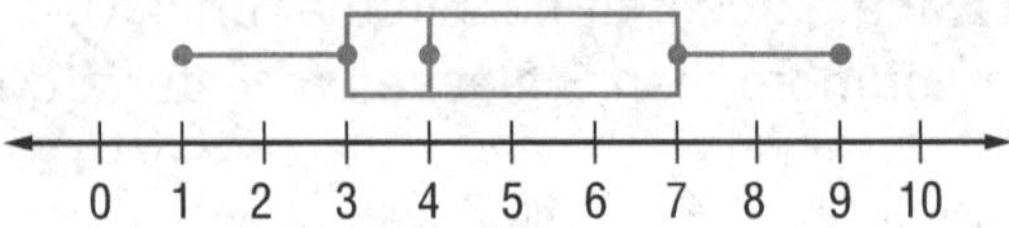

Ⓒ **Number of E-mails Received Each Week**

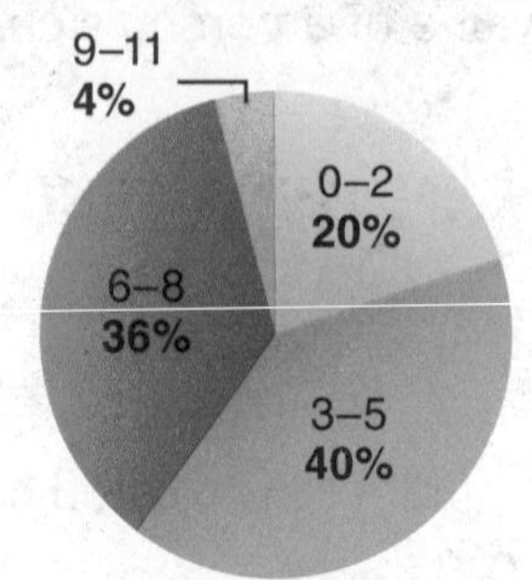

Ⓑ

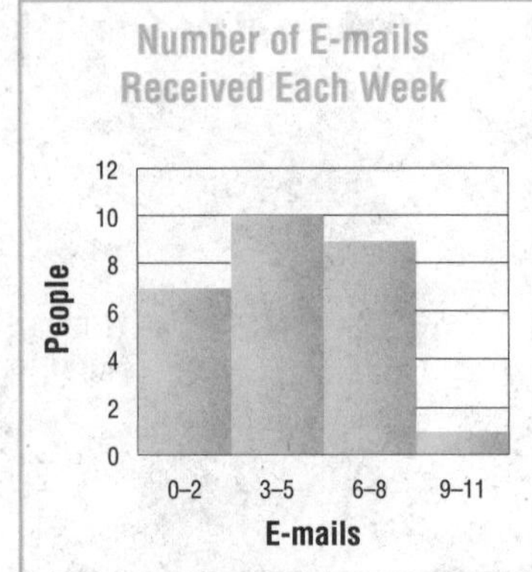

Ⓓ

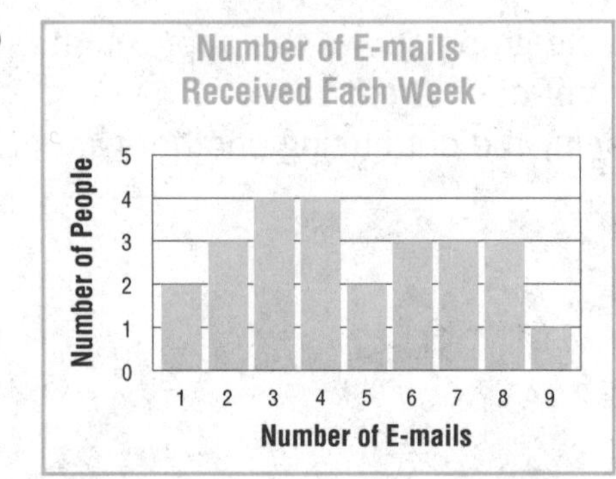

17. The number of home runs hit by each player of a high school baseball team is shown in the table. What type of display would be most appropriate to show the frequency of data?

Ⓕ line graph　　Ⓗ bar graph

Ⓖ circle graph　　Ⓘ line plot

Home Runs					
10	15	5	10	12	5
12	12	4	5	10	7

Common Core Review

Use the graph to answer Exercises 18–20. The graph shows the number of male and the number of female students that chose certain occupations to research. MCC6.SP.5

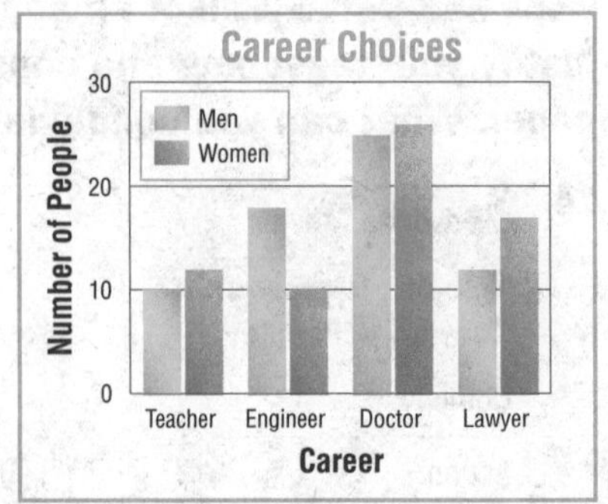

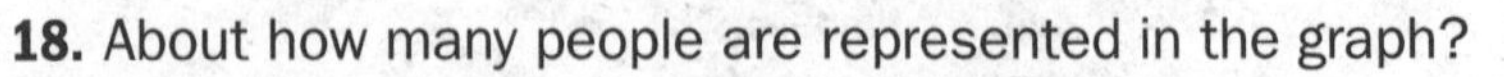

18. About how many people are represented in the graph? ________

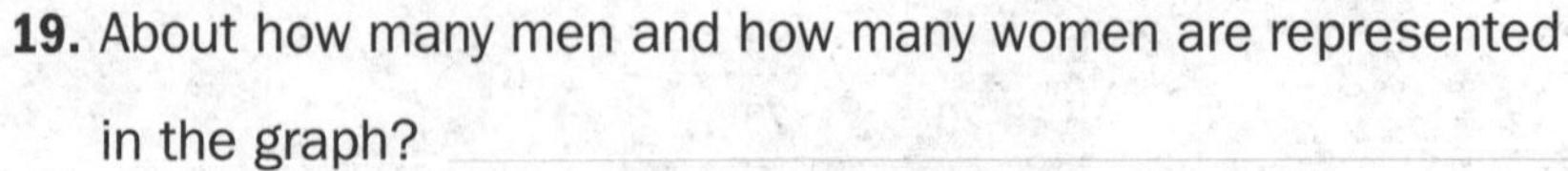

19. About how many men and how many women are represented in the graph? ________

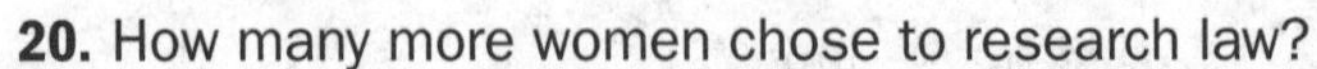

20. How many more women chose to research law? ________

21ST CENTURY CAREER in Market Research

Market Research Analyst

Do you think that gathering and analyzing information about people's opinions, tastes, likes, and dislikes sounds interesting? If so, then you should consider a career in market research. Market research analysts help companies understand what types of products and services consumers want. They design Internet, telephone, or mail response surveys and then analyze the data, identify trends, and present their conclusions and recommendations. Market research analysts must be analytical, creative problem-solvers, have strong backgrounds in mathematics, and have good written and verbal communication skills.

Explore college and careers at ccr.mcgraw-hill.com

Is This the Career for You?

Are you interested in a career as a market research analyst? Take some of the following courses in high school.

- Algebra
- Calculus
- Computer Science
- English
- Statistics

Find out how math relates to a career in Market Research.

Keeping Your Eye on the Target Market!

Use the results of the survey in the table below to solve each problem.

1. At Hastings Middle School, 560 of the students use social networking sites. Predict how many of them use the sites to make plans with friends. ________

2. Suppose 17.9 million teens use online social networks. Predict how many will be using the sites to make new friends.

____

3. According to the survey, what percent of a teen's networking site friends are people they regularly see? ________

4. Landon randomly selects a friend from his social networking site. What is the probability that it is someone he never sees in person? Write as a percent. ________

5. Paris wants to leave a message on 8 of her friends' social networking sites. In how many ways can she leave a message on her friends' sites? ________

Survey Results: Teens and Social Networking	
Reason to Use Social Networks	**Percent of Respondents**
Stay in touch with friends	91%
Make plans with friends	72%
Make new friends	49%
Friends on Social Networking Sites	**Average Number**
People who are regularly seen	43
People who are occasionally seen	23
People who are never seen in person	33
Total	99

Career Project

It's time to update your career portfolio! Use the Internet or another source to research a career as a market research analyst. Write a paragraph that summarizes your findings.

What skills would you need to improve to succeed in this career?

-
-
-
-
-

Chapter Review 

Vocabulary Check 

Complete the crossword puzzle using the vocabulary list at the beginning of the chapter.

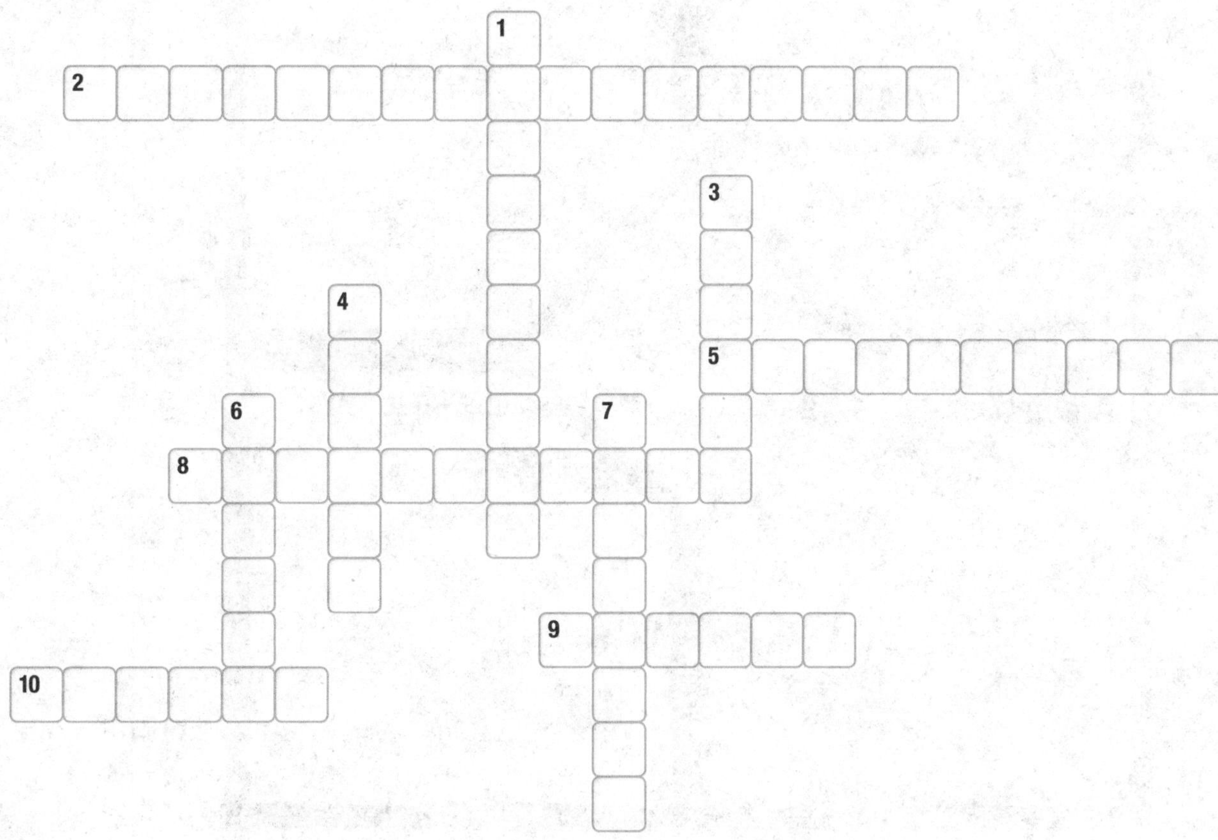

Across

2. sample involving only those who want to participate (two words)

5. the group being studied

8. sample in which members of a population are easily accessed

9. part of a group

10. sample in which one or more parts of the population are favored over other parts

Down

1. random sample in which items are selected according to a specific time or interval

3. random sample in which each item is as likely to be chosen as any other item

4. a method of collecting information

6. two box plots on the same number line

7. sample that represents the entire population

Key Concept Check

Use Your FOLDABLES

Use your Foldable to help review the chapter.

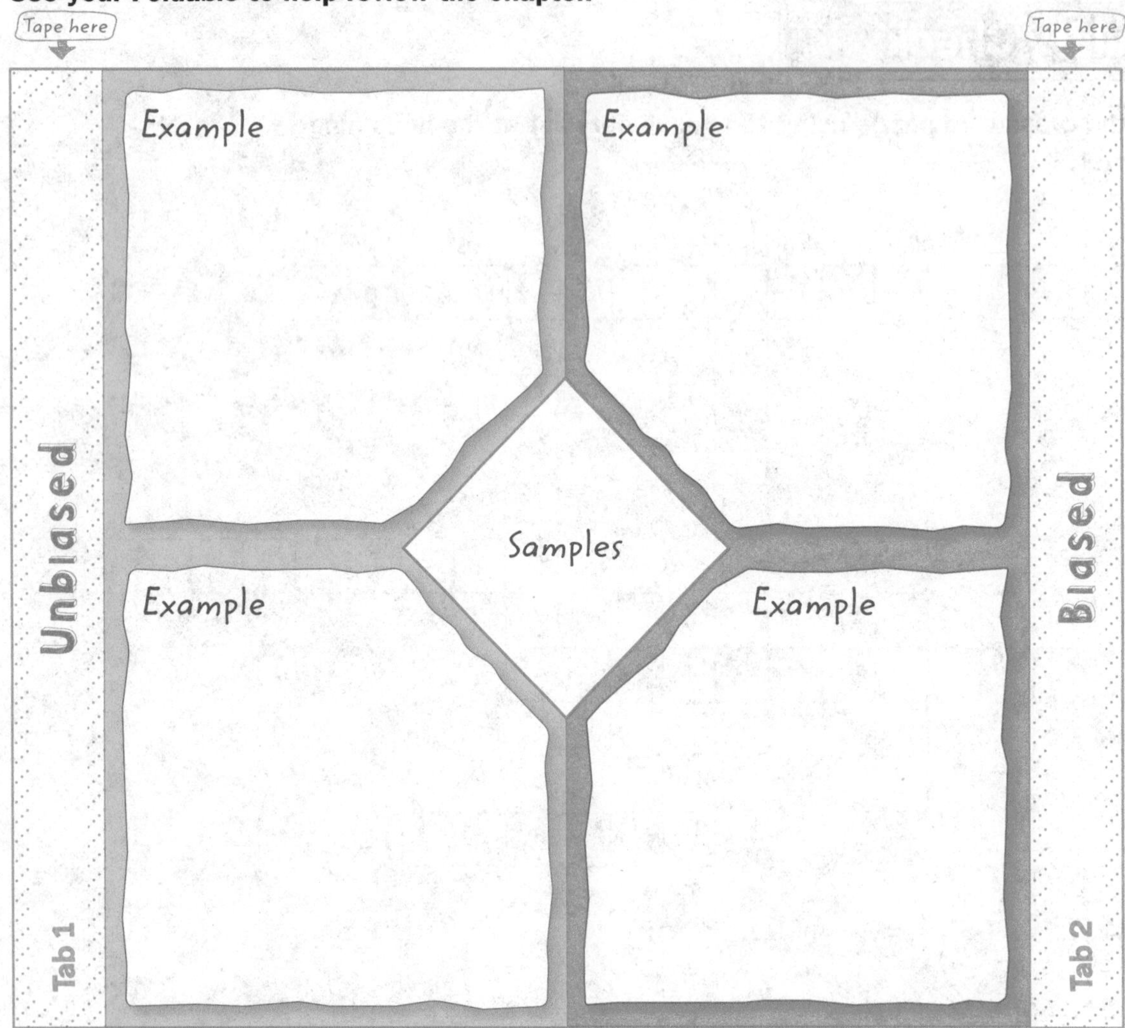

Got it?

Match each phrase with the correct term.

1. a method of collecting information

2. the group being studied

3. when one or more parts of the population is favored

4. a sample that involves only those who want to participate

a. voluntary response sample

b. biased sample

c. survey

d. population

e. convenience sample

Problem Solving

A survey at a college found that 3 out of every 10 students wanted to earn a degree in medicine.

1. Based on this survey, what is the probability that a student at the school wants to earn a degree in medicine? (Lesson 1)

2. **Make a Prediction** Suppose there are about 350 students at the school. About how many students want to earn a degree in medicine? (Lesson 1)

3. Mrs. Jenkins is taking a survey to find how many seventh-grade students would attend a school dance. Describe the sample if Mrs. Jenkins asks every tenth student in seventh grade. (Lesson 2)

4. The bar graph shows the monthly electric bill for the condominium that Toshiko is interested in renting. Why is the graph misleading? (Lesson 3)

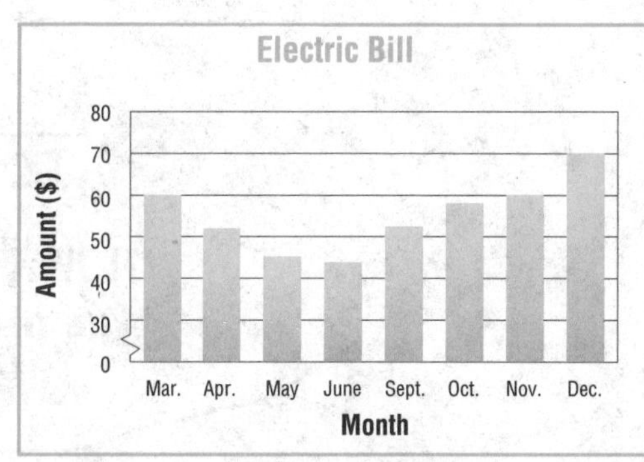

5. The double box plot shows the scores of two different classes on a biology test. How does the median score for Class A compare with the median score for Class B? (Lesson 4)

Scores on a Biology Test

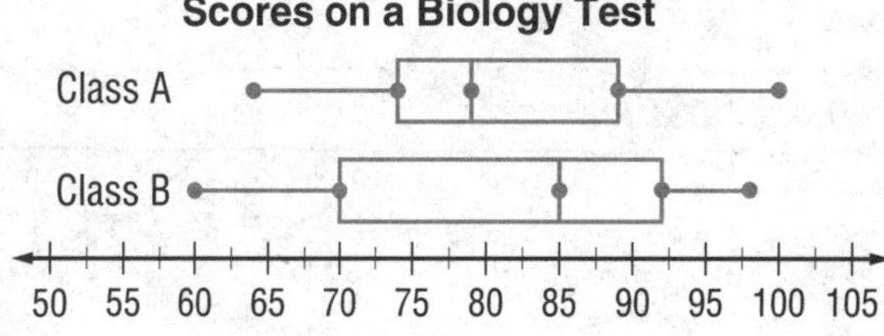

6. What is an appropriate display to show the variation in daily high temperatures of a city in March? (Lesson 5)

7. Is a circle graph an appropriate display to represent the number of calls made each day? (Lesson 5)

Reflect

Answering the Essential Question

Use what you learned about statistics to complete the graphic organizer.

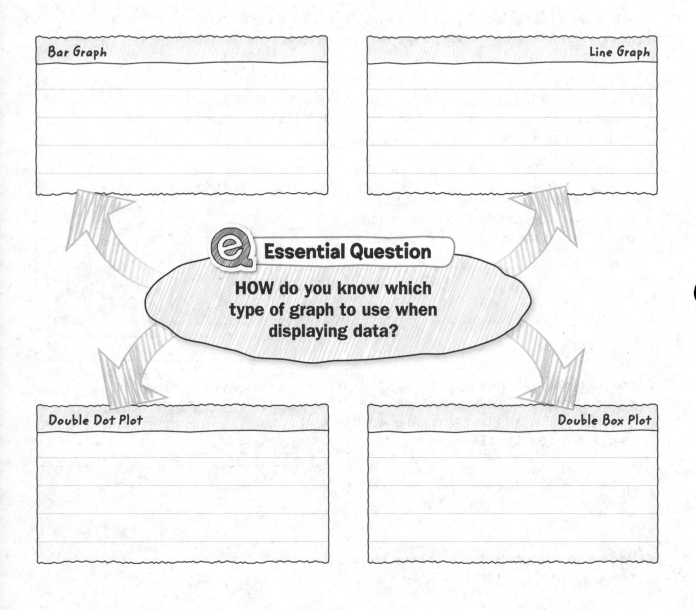

Bar Graph

Line Graph

Essential Question

HOW do you know which type of graph to use when displaying data?

Double Dot Plot

Double Box Plot

Answer the Essential Question. HOW do you know which type of graph to use when displaying data?

UNIT 5

CCGPS Geometry

Essential Question

HOW can you use different measurements to solve real-life problems?

Chapter 8

Geometric Figures

Geometric shapes can be drawn freehand, with a ruler and protractor, or using technology. In this chapter, you will draw two- and three-dimensional figures. You will also solve problems involving scale drawings of geometric figures.

Chapter 9

Measure Figures

Real-life problems involving area, surface area, and volume can be solved by using formulas. In this chapter, you will use formulas to find the area and circumference of a circle and to find the surface area and volume of prisms and pyramids.

Chapter 8

Geometric Figures

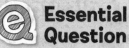

Essential Question

HOW does geometry help us describe real-world objects?

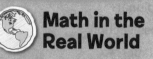

Common Core GPS

Content Standards
MCC7.G.1, MCC7.G.2, MCC7.G.3, MCC7.G.5

Mathematical Practices
1, 2, 3, 4, 5, 6, 7, 8

Math in the Real World

Robots that could be programmed and digitally operated were invented by George Devol in 1954.

The actual length of the robot's arm is 15 inches. A drawing of the robot is $\frac{1}{5}$ the size of the actual robot. Fill in the blank below with the correct measurement for the robot's arm.

FOLDABLES® Study Organizer

1. Cut out the correct Foldable from the FL pages in the back of this book.
2. Place your Foldable on the Key Concept page toward the end of this chapter.
3. Use the Foldable throughout this chapter to help you learn about geometric figures.

What Tools Do You Need?

Vocabulary

acute angle
acute triangle
adjacent angles
base
complementary angles
cone
congruent
congruent segments
coplanar
cross section
cylinder
diagonal
edge
equilateral triangle
face
isosceles triangle
obtuse angle
obtuse triangle
plane
polyhedron
prism
pyramid
right angle
right triangle
scale model
scalene triangle
straight angle
supplementary angles
triangle
vertex
vertical angles

Study Skill: Reading Math

The Language of Mathematics Many of the words you use in math and science are also used in everyday language, such as the leg of a person and the leg of a right triangle.

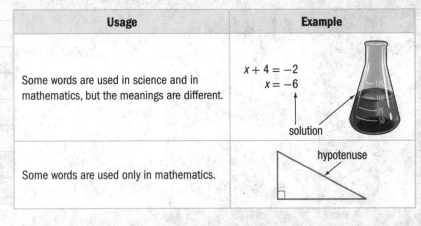

Usage	Example
Some words are used in science and in mathematics, but the meanings are different.	$x + 4 = -2$ $x = -6$ solution
Some words are used only in mathematics.	hypotenuse

Explain how the everyday meaning of *face* is different than its mathematical meaning.

Everyday meaning: ____________________

Mathematical meaning: ____________________

When Will You Use This?

Your Turn! You will solve this problem in the chapter.

Are You Ready?

Try the Quick Check below.
Or, take the Online Readiness Quiz. 

Quick Review

Common Core Review MCC4.MD.6, MCC6.G.1

Example 1

Use a protractor to measure angle *ABC*.

Align the center of the protractor with the vertex of the angle.

Make sure one ray of the angle passes through zero on the protractor.

Read the measure on the protractor where the other ray crosses the protractor.

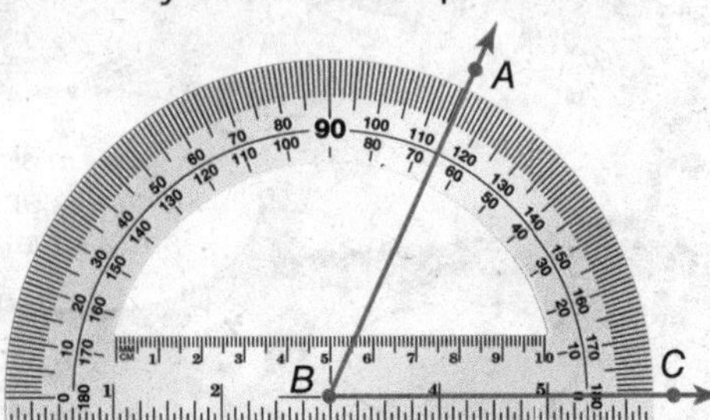

The angle measures 65°.

Example 2

Find the area of the triangle.

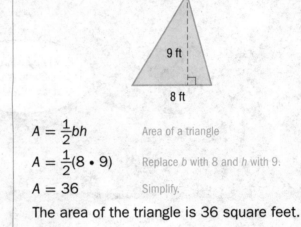

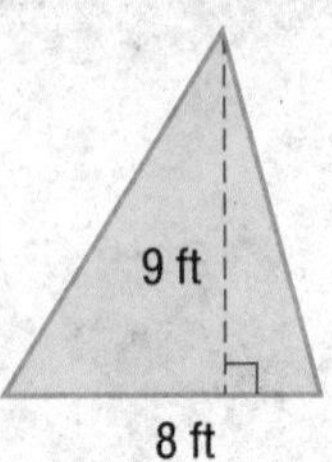

$A = \frac{1}{2}bh$ Area of a triangle

$A = \frac{1}{2}(8 \cdot 9)$ Replace b with 8 and h with 9.

$A = 36$ Simplify.

The area of the triangle is 36 square feet.

Quick Check

Angle Measures **Use a protractor to measure each angle.**

Show your work.

1. 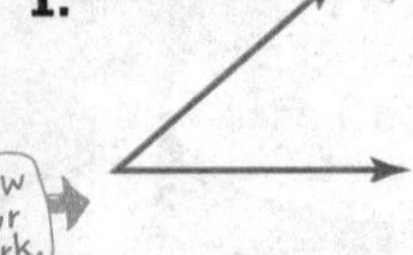

2. 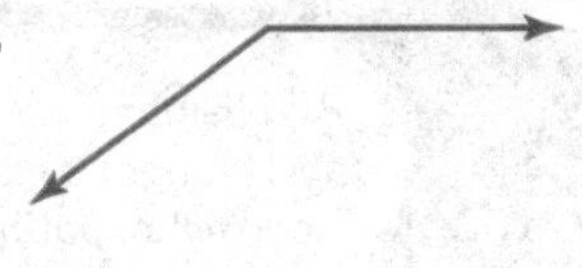

3. 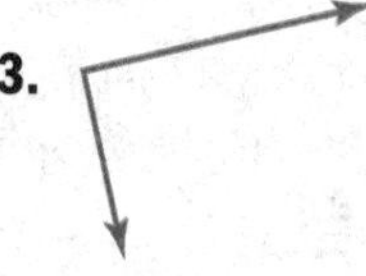

Area **Find the area of each triangle.**

4. 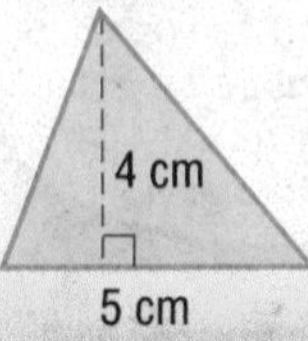

5. base: 3.2 yd
height: 4.2 yd

How Did You Do?

Which problems did you answer correctly in the Quick Check? Shade those exercise numbers below.

① ② ③ ④ ⑤

Classify Angles

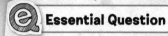

What You'll Learn

Scan the lesson. Write the definitions of a right angle and a straight angle.

- right angle ______
- straight angle ______

 **Essential Question**

HOW does geometry help us describe real-world objects?

 **Vocabulary**

vertex
right angle
acute angle
obtuse angle
straight angle
vertical angles
congruent
adjacent angles

Math Symbols

∠
≅

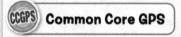

 **Common Core GPS**

Content Standards
MCC7.G.5

Mathematical Practices
1, 3, 4, 7

Vocabulary Start-Up

An angle is formed by two rays that share a common endpoint. The **vertex** is the point where the two rays meet.

Complete the table by drawing the hands of a clock to represent each angle.

Type of Angle			
Right	Acute	Obtuse	Straight
exactly 90°	less than 90°	greater than 90°	exactly 180°
(clock)	(clock)	(clock)	(clock)

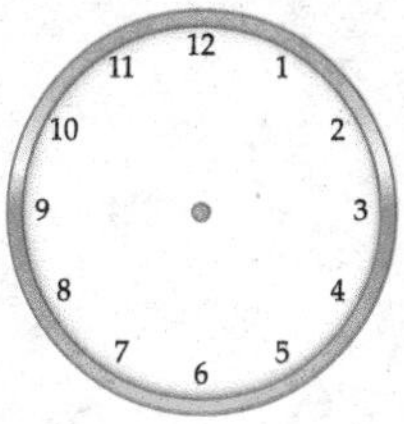

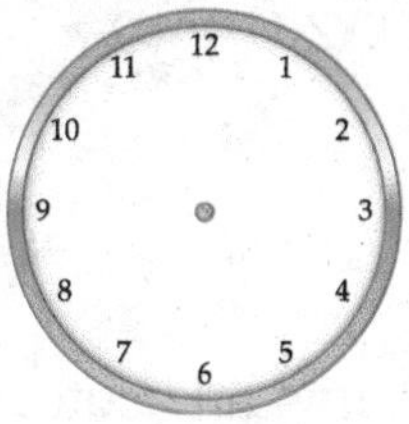

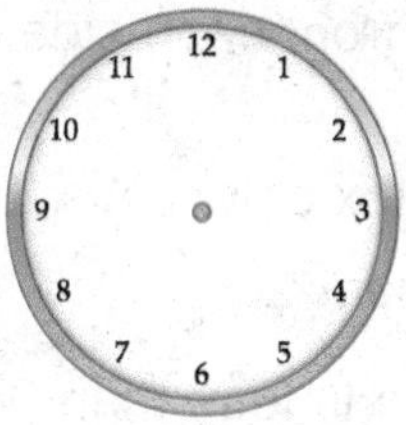

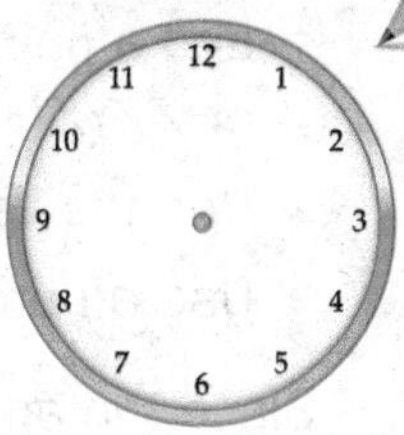

Real-World Link

The angle formed by a bike ramp is shown.

1. What type of angle is formed?

______

2. Estimate the measure of the angle.

______

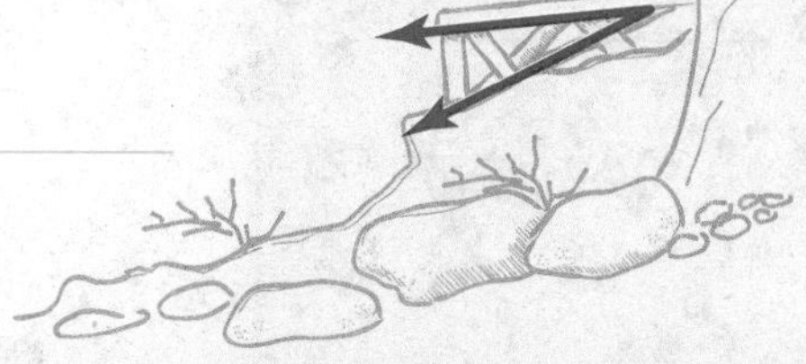

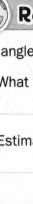

Key Concept Name and Identify Angles

Words	Models	Symbols
Two angles are **vertical** if they are opposite angles formed by the intersection of two lines. Vertical angles are **congruent** or have the same measure.	∠1 and ∠3, ∠2 and ∠4	∠1 ≅ ∠3 ∠2 ≅ ∠4
Two angles are **adjacent** if they share a common vertex, a common side, and do not overlap.	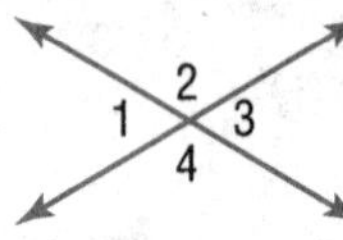	Adjacent angle pairs are ∠1 and ∠2, ∠2 and ∠3, ∠3 and ∠4, and ∠4 and ∠1.

Work Zone

You can name an angle by its vertex and by its points.

Example

1. Name the angle shown at the right. Then classify it as *acute, right, obtuse,* or *straight*.

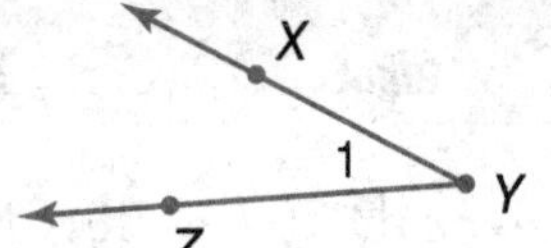

- Use the vertex as the middle letter and a point from each side, ∠*XYZ* or ∠*ZYX*.
- Use the vertex only, ∠*Y*.
- Use a number, ∠1.

Since the angle is less than 90°, it is an acute angle.

Symbols
The symbol for angle is ∠.
The symbol ≅ means is congruent to.

Got It? Do these problems to find out.

Name each angle in four ways. Then classify each angle as *acute, right, obtuse,* or *straight*.

a.
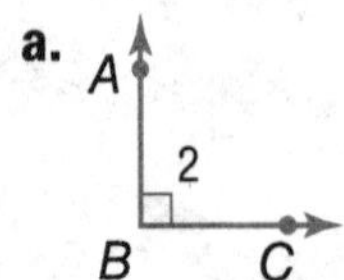

b.
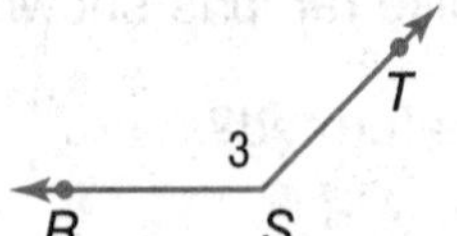

c.
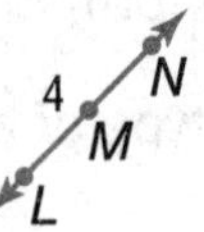

a. ____________

b. ____________

c. ____________

Example

2. Identify a pair of vertical angles and adjacent angles in the diagram at the right. Justify your response.

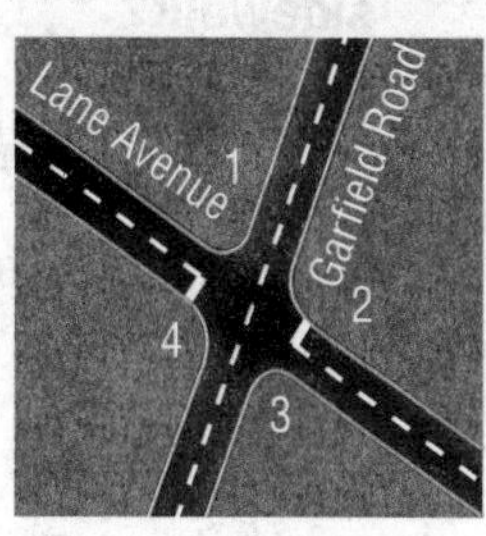

Since ∠2 and ∠4 are opposite angles formed by the intersection of two lines, they are vertical angles.

Since ∠1 and ∠2 share a common side and vertex, and they do not overlap, they are adjacent angles.

Got It? **Do this problem to find out.**

d. Refer to the diagram in Example 2. Identify different pairs of vertical and adjacent angles. Justify your response.

d. ___________

Find a Missing Measure

You can use what you learned about vertical and adjacent angles to find the value of a missing measure.

Example

3. What is the value of x in the figure?

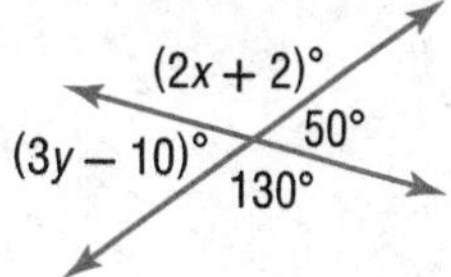

The angle labeled $(2x + 2)°$ and the angle labeled 130° are vertical angles.

Since vertical angles are congruent, $(2x + 2)°$ equals 130°.

$2x + 2 = 130$ Write the equation.

$-2 = -2$ Subtract 2 from each side.

$\frac{2x}{2} = \frac{128}{2}$ Divide each side by 2.

$x = 64$

So, the value of x is 64.

Got It? **Do this problem to find out.**

e. What is the value of y in the figure in Example 2?

e. ___________

Example

Tutor

4. What is the value of x shown in the sidewalk?

The angle labeled 115° and the angle labeled 5x are adjacent angles. Together they form a straight angle or 180°.

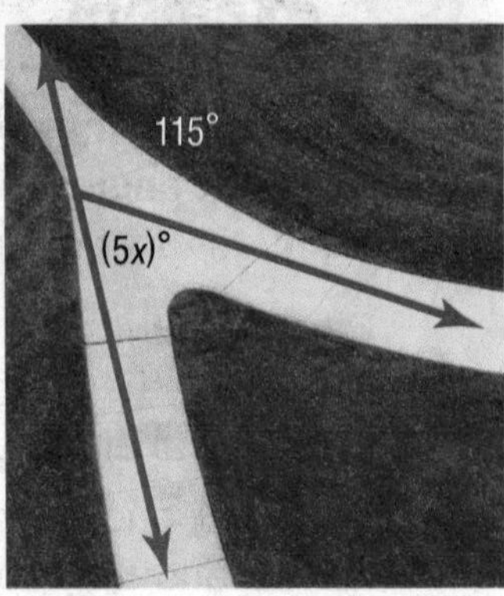

$$115 + 5x = 180 \quad \text{Write the equation.}$$
$$-115 \quad = -115 \quad \text{Subtract 115 from each side.}$$
$$\frac{5x}{5} = \frac{65}{5} \quad \text{Divide each side by 5.}$$
$$x = 13$$

So, the value of x is 13.

Guided Practice

1. Name the angle below in four ways. Then classify it as *acute, right, obtuse,* or *straight.* (Example 1)

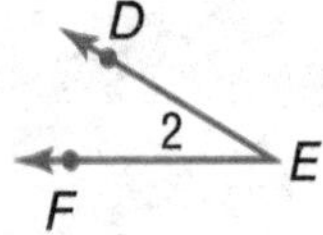

2. Find the value of x in each figure. (Examples 3–4)

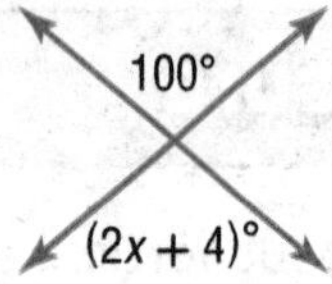

3. Identify a pair of vertical angles and adjacent angles on the railroad crossing sign. Justify your response. (Example 2)

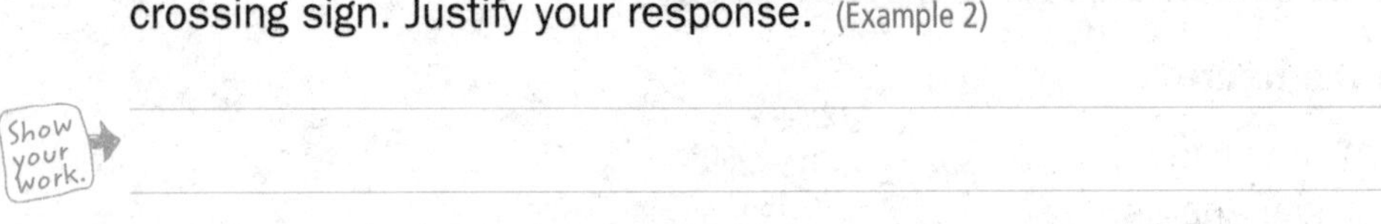

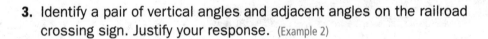

4. **Building on the Essential Question** Describe the differences between vertical and adjacent angles.

Rate Yourself!
How confident are you about classifying angles? Check the box that applies.
For more help, go online to access a Personal Tutor.
Tutor
FOLDABLES Time to update your Foldable!

Name ______________________ My Homework ______________

Independent Practice

Go online for Step-by-Step Solutions

Name each angle in four ways. Then classify the angle as *acute, right, obtuse,* or *straight*. (Example 1)

1. 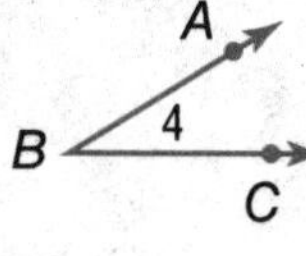

Show your work.

2. 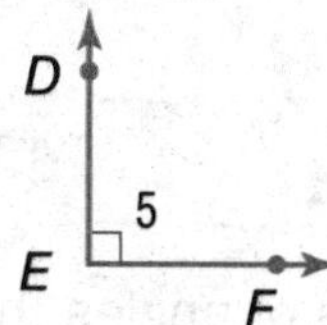

3. 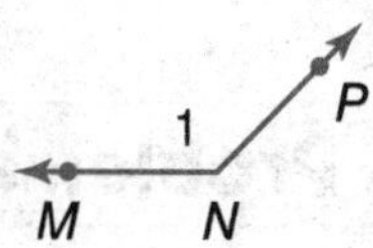

Identify Structure Refer to the diagram at the right. Identify each angle pair as *adjacent, vertical,* or *neither*. (Example 2)

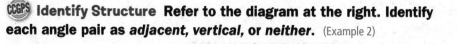

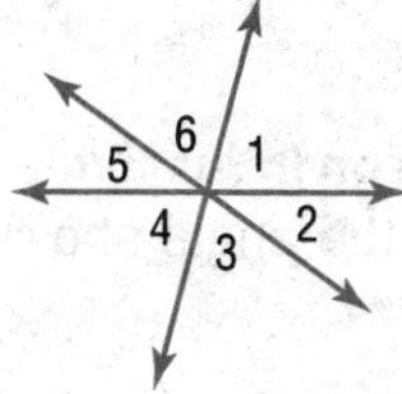

4. $\angle 2$ and $\angle 5$ ______

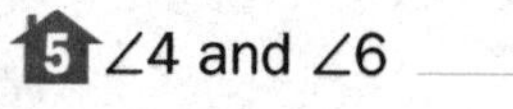

5. $\angle 4$ and $\angle 6$ ______

6. $\angle 3$ and $\angle 4$ ______

7. $\angle 5$ and $\angle 6$ ______

8. $\angle 1$ and $\angle 3$ ______

9. $\angle 1$ and $\angle 4$ ______

10. What is the value of x in the figure at the right? (Examples 3 and 4) ______

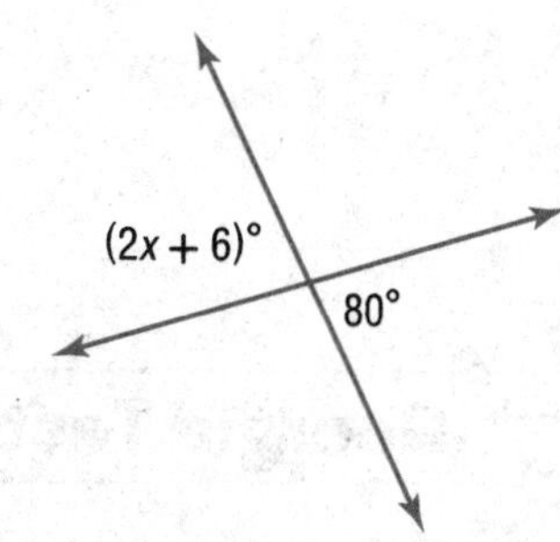

11. What is the value of x in the figure at the right? (Examples 3 and 4) ______

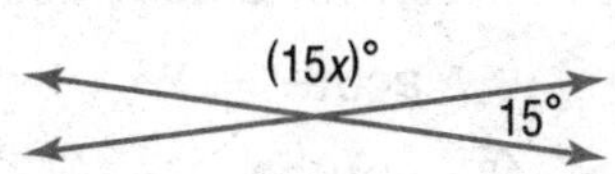

12. Angles *ABC* and *DBE* are vertical angles. If the measure of ∠*ABC* is 40°, what is the measure of ∠*ABD*?

H.O.T. Problems Higher Order Thinking

13. CCGPS **Model with Mathematics** Draw examples of angles that represent real-world objects. Be sure to include at least three of the following angles: acute, right, obtuse, straight, vertical, and adjacent. Verify by measuring the angles.

14. CCGPS **Reason Inductively** Explain how you can use a protractor to measure the angle shown. Find the measure of the angle.

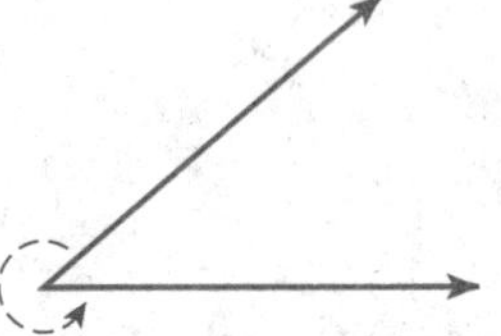

CCGPS **Persevere with Problems Determine whether each statement is *true* or *false*. If the statement is true, provide a diagram to support it. If the statement is false, explain why.**

15. A pair of obtuse angles can also be vertical angles.

16. A pair of straight angles can also be adjacent angles.

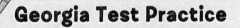

Georgia Test Practice

17. Which word best describes the angle marked in the figure?

Ⓐ acute

Ⓑ obtuse

Ⓒ right

Ⓓ straight

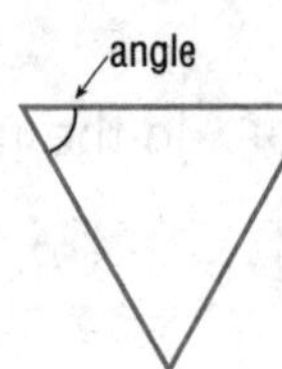

Name ______________________ My Homework ______________________

Extra Practice

Name each angle in four ways. Then classify the angle as *acute, right, obtuse,* or *straight.*

18. M 7 P N

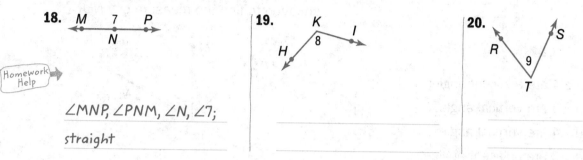

Homework Help

∠MNP, ∠PNM, ∠N, ∠7;

straight

19.

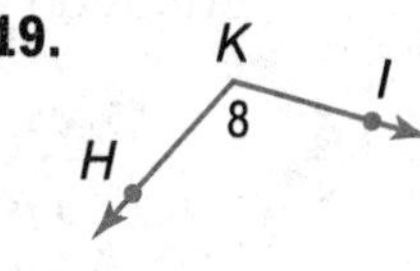

20. R S 9 T

21. The corner where the states of Utah, Arizona, New Mexico, and Colorado meet is called the Four Corners.

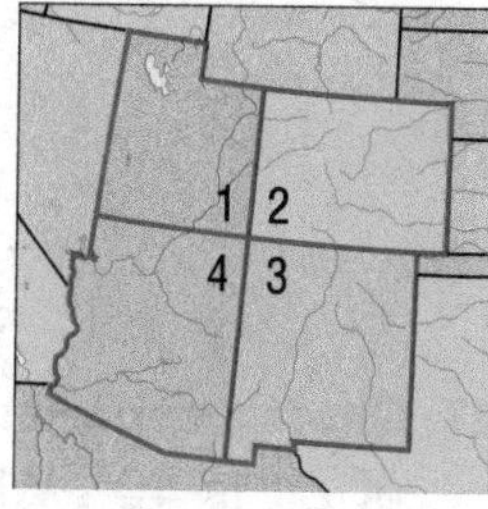

a. Identify a pair of vertical angles. Justify your response.

b. Identify a pair of adjacent angles. Justify your response.

22. What is the value of x in the figure at the right?

23. What is the value of x in the figure at the right?

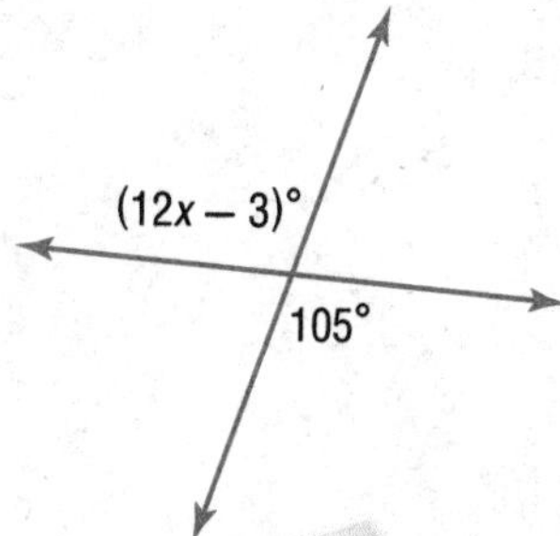

24. CCSS **Identify Structure** The John Hancock Center in Chicago is shown at the right. Classify each pair of angles.

a. ∠1 and ∠2 ____________

b. ∠2 and ∠4 ____________

c. ∠3 and ∠4 ____________

d. ∠1 and ∠3 ____________

e. If the measure of ∠2 is 66°, what are the measures of the other angles? ____________

Georgia Test Practice

25. Which statement is true?

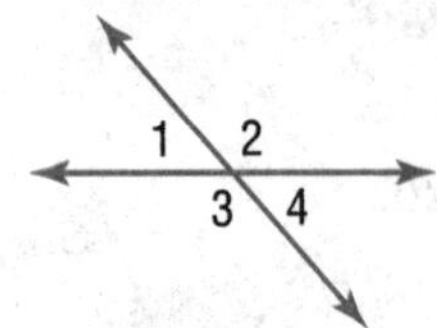

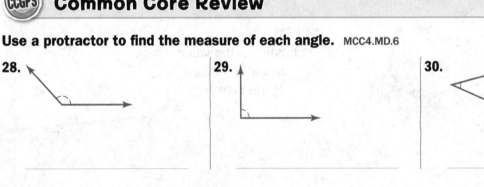

Ⓐ ∠1 and ∠4 are adjacent angles.
Ⓑ ∠2 and ∠3 are vertical angles.
Ⓒ ∠3 and ∠4 are vertical angles.
Ⓓ ∠2 and ∠3 are adjacent angles.

26. **Short Response** In the figure below, the measure of ∠*NLM* is 60° and the measure of ∠*PLR* is 102°. Write and solve an equation to find the measure of ∠*NLR*.

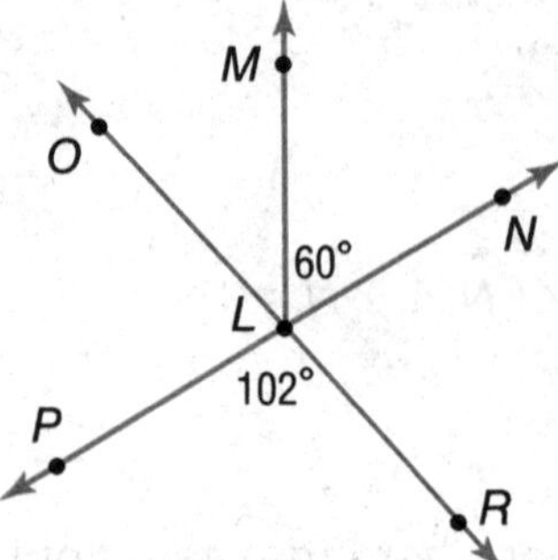

27. **Short Response** Refer to the figure in Exercise 25. Suppose the measure of ∠1 is 40°. What is the measure of ∠4?

Common Core Review

Use a protractor to find the measure of each angle. MCC4.MD.6

28.

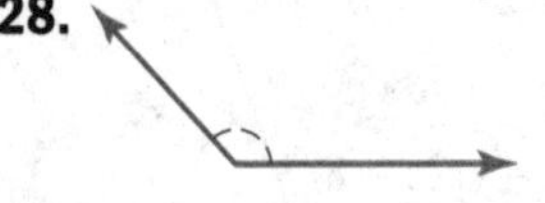

29.

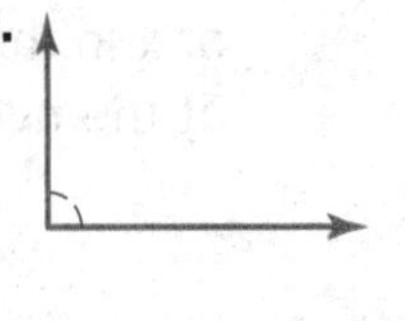

30.

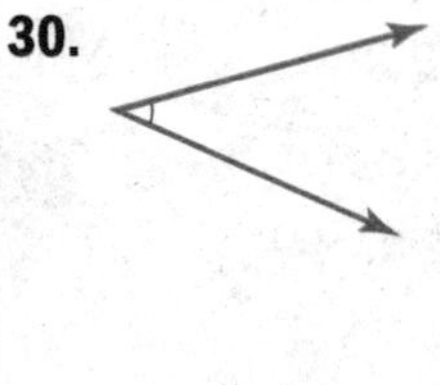

31. Name the line segment at the right in two ways. MCC5.G.4 A B

32. What is the name for a quadrilateral with all right angles and opposite sides that are parallel and congruent? MCC5.G.3

Complementary and Supplementary Angles

What You'll Learn

Scan the lesson. List two headings you would use to make an outline of the lesson.

-
-

Essential Question

HOW does geometry help us describe real-world objects?

Vocabulary

complementary angles
supplementary angles

Math Symbols

$m\angle 1$

Common Core GPS

Content Standards
MCC7.G.5

Mathematical Practices
1, 3, 4, 7

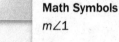

Real-World Link

Watch

Bridges Engineers use angles to construct bridges. The Golden Gate Bridge is created by combining angles as shown.

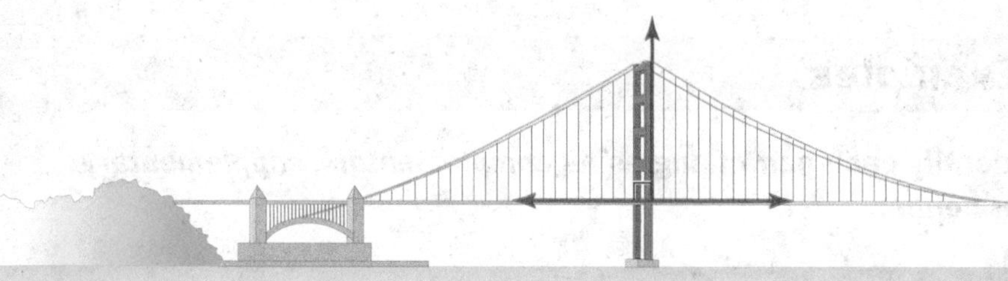

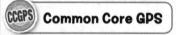

1. What types of angles make up the two angles marked in the drawing of the bridge? ____________

2. What is the sum of the two angles marked in the drawing of the bridge? ________

3. In the space below, draw a figure that contains two angles that have a sum of 90°.

Key Concept Pairs of Angles

Work Zone

Words	Models	Symbols
Two angles are **complementary** if the sum of their measures is 90°.	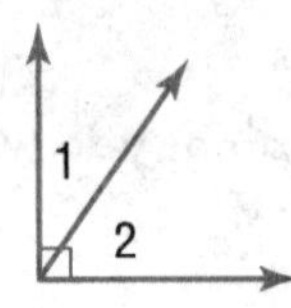	$m\angle 1 + m\angle 2 = 90°$
Two angles are **supplementary** if the sum of their measures is 180°.	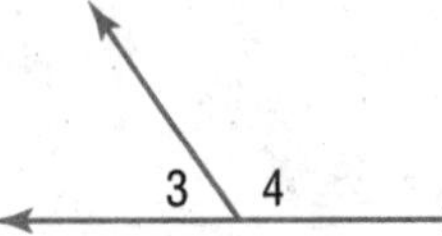	$m\angle 3 + m\angle 4 = 180°$

A special relationship exists between two angles with a sum of 90°. A special relationship also exists between two angles with a sum of 180°. The symbol $m\angle 1$ means *the measure of angle 1*.

Examples

Identify each pair of angles as *complementary, supplementary,* or *neither*.

1.

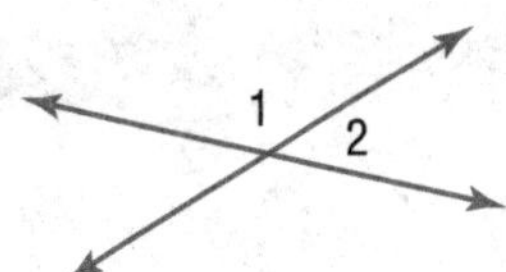

$\angle 1$ and $\angle 2$ form a straight angle. So, the angles are supplementary.

2.

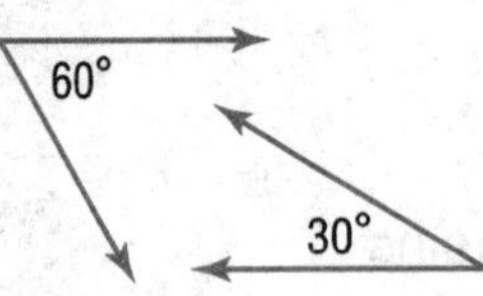

$60° + 30° = 90°$ The angles are complementary.

Adjacent
As shown in Example 2, angles do not need to be adjacent to be complementary or supplementary angles.

Got It? Do these problems to find out.

Show your work.

a.

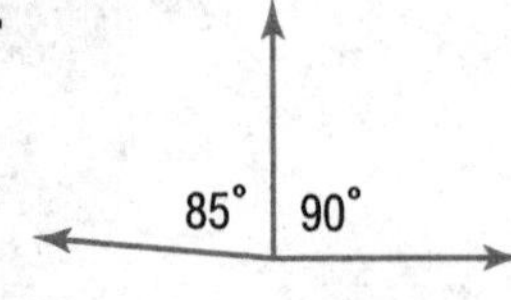

b.

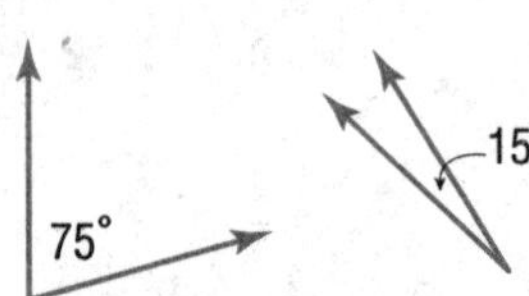

a. ____________

b. ____________

Find a Missing Measure

You can use angle relationships to find missing measures.

Examples

3. Find the value of x.

Since the two angles form a right angle, they are complementary.

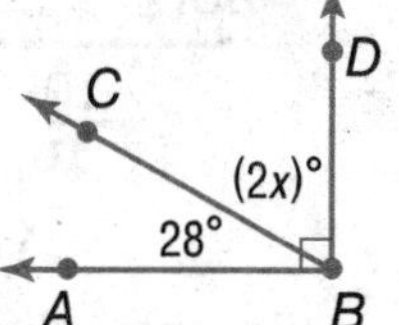

Words	The sum of the measures of ∠ABC and ∠CBD	is	90°.
Variable	Let $2x$ represent the measure of ∠CBD.		
Equation	$28 + 2x$	=	90

$28 + 2x = 90$ Write the equation.

$-28 \quad = -28$ Subtract 28 from each side.

$\frac{2x}{2} = \frac{62}{2}$ Divide each side by 2.

$x = 31$

So, the value of x is 31.

4. The angles shown are supplementary. Find the value of x.

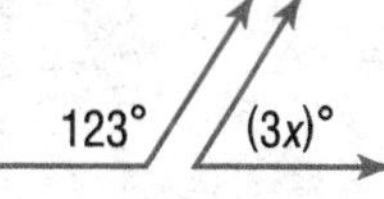

$123 + 3x = 180$ Write the equation.

$-123 \quad = -123$ Subtract 123 from each side.

$\frac{3x}{3} = \frac{57}{3}$ Divide each side by 3.

$x = 19$

So, the value of x is 19.

STOP and Reflect

Circle true or false. The sum of two angles that are supplementary is 180°.

True False

Got It? Do this problem to find out.

c. Find the value of x.

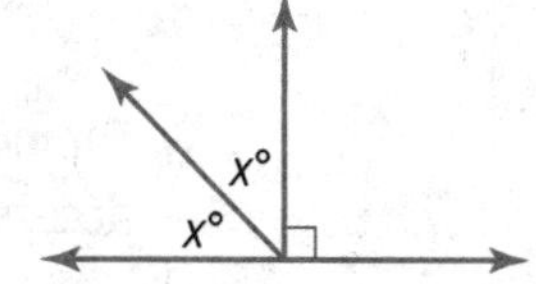

c. ______

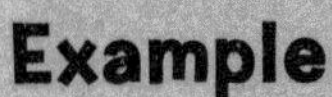

Example

5. The picture shows a support brace for a gate. Find the value of x.

The angle labeled 80° and the angle labeled 10x are supplementary angles.

$$80 + 10x = 180 \quad \text{Write the equation.}$$
$$-80 \quad = -80 \quad \text{Subtract 80 from each side.}$$
$$\frac{10x}{10} = \frac{100}{10} \quad \text{Divide each side by 10.}$$
$$x = 10$$

So, the value of x is 10.

Got It? Do this problem to find out.

Show your work.

d. ______

d. A pair of scissors forms the angle shown. What is the value of x?

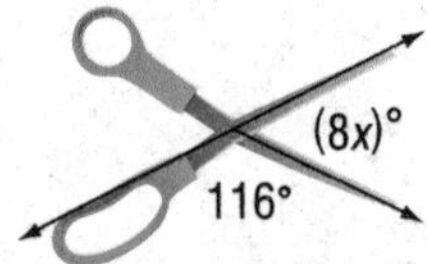

Guided Practice

Check

Identify each pair of angles as *complementary, supplementary,* or *neither*.
(Examples 1 and 2)

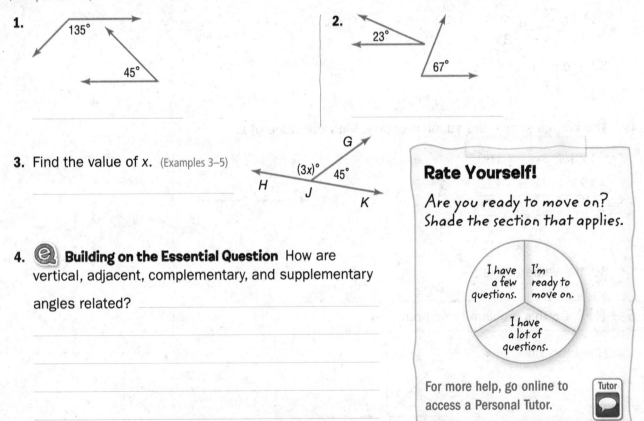

1.

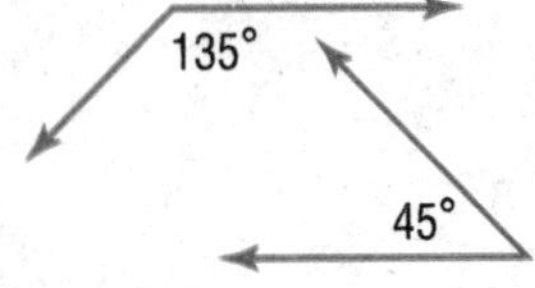

______

2.

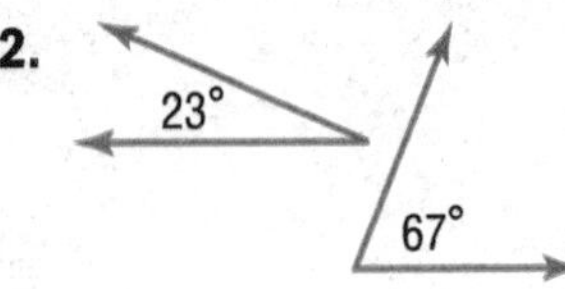

______

3. Find the value of x. (Examples 3–5)

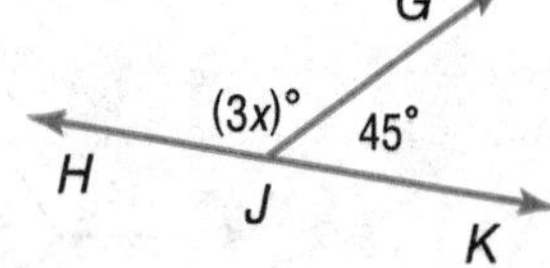

______

4. **Building on the Essential Question** How are vertical, adjacent, complementary, and supplementary angles related? ______

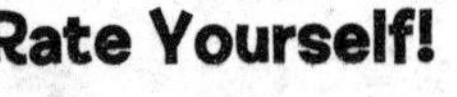

Rate Yourself!

Are you ready to move on? Shade the section that applies.

For more help, go online to access a Personal Tutor.

Independent Practice

Go online for Step-by-Step Solutions

Identify each pair of angles as *complementary, supplementary,* or *neither.*
(Examples 1 and 2)

1. 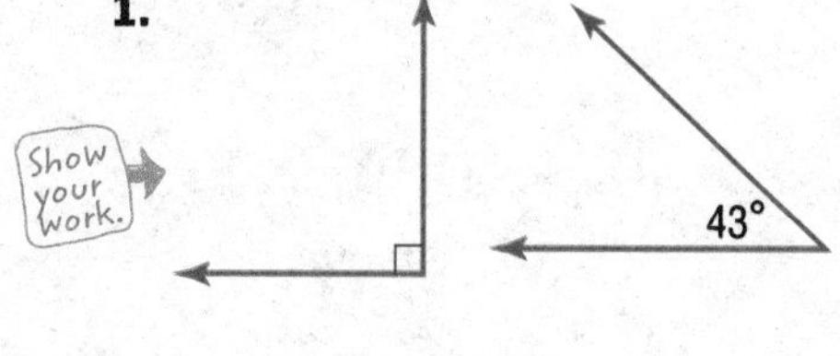

2. 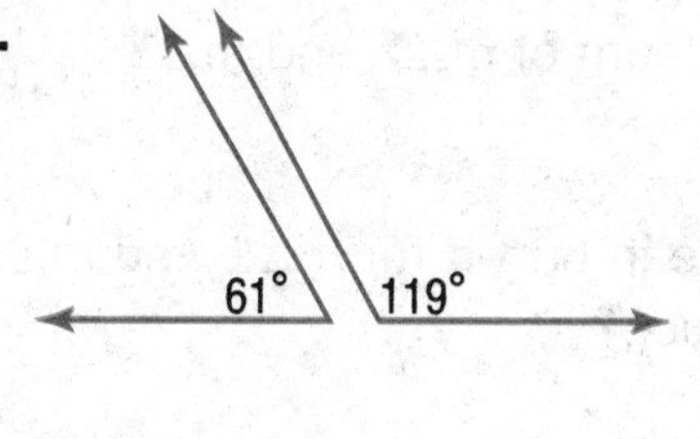

3 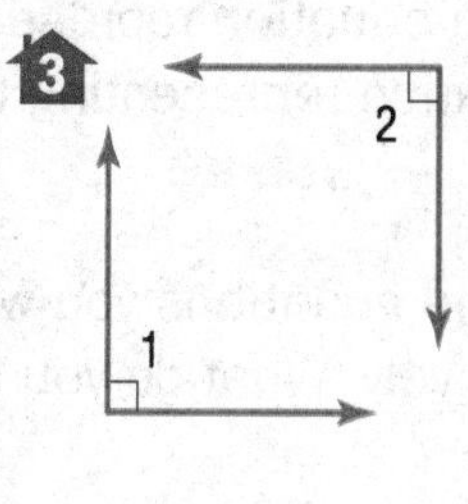

Show your work.

Find the measure of *x* in each figure. (Examples 3 and 4)

4. 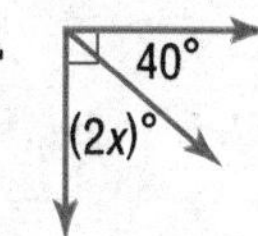

5. 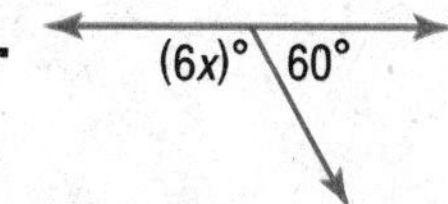

6. ∠A and ∠B are complementary angles. The measure of ∠B is $(4x)°$, and the measure of ∠A is 50°. What is the value of *x*? (Example 5)

7 A skateboard ramp forms a 42° angle as shown.

Find the value of *x*. (Example 5)

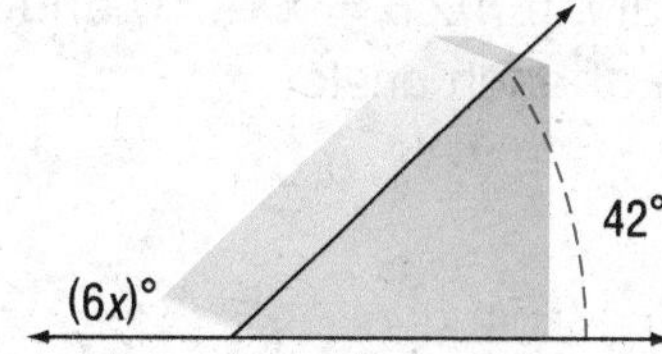

Use the figure at the right to name the following.

8. a pair of supplementary angles

9. a pair of complementary angles

10. a pair of vertical angles

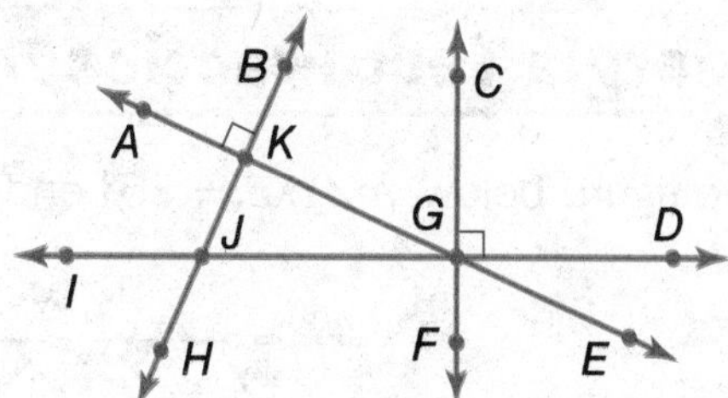

11. Use the figure at the right.

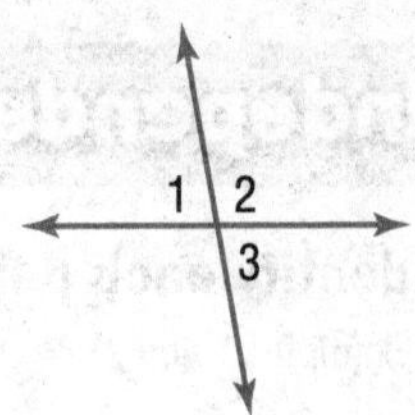

a. Are $\angle 1$ and $\angle 2$ vertical angles, adjacent angles, or neither? $\angle 2$ and $\angle 3$? $\angle 1$ and $\angle 3$?

b. Write an equation representing the sum of $m\angle 1$ and $m\angle 2$. Then write an equation representing the sum of $m\angle 2$ and $m\angle 3$.

c. Solve the equations you wrote in part **b** for $m\angle 1$ and $m\angle 3$, respectively. What do you notice?

d. CCGPS **Make a Conjecture** Use your answer from part **c** to make a conjecture as to the relationship between vertical angles.

H.O.T. Problems Higher Order Thinking

12. CCGPS **Reason Inductively** When a basketball hits a hard, level surface, it bounces off at the same angle at which it hits. Use the figure to find the angle at which the ball hit the floor.

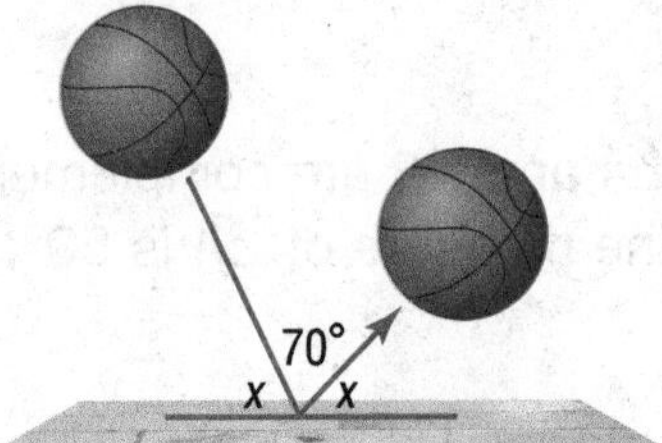

13. CCGPS **Persevere with Problems** Angles E and F are complementary. If $m\angle E = x - 10$ and $m\angle F = x + 2$, find the measure of each angle.

Georgia Test Practice

14. In the figure below, $m\angle YXZ = 35°$ and $m\angle WXV = 40°$. What is $m\angle ZXW$?

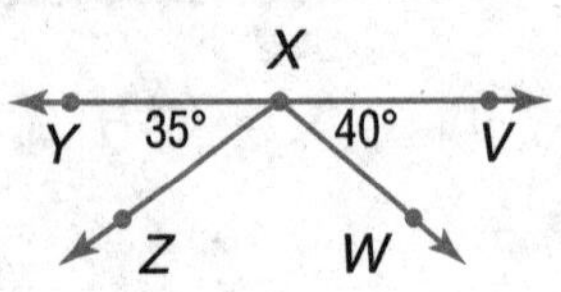

Ⓐ 180° Ⓒ 75°

Ⓑ 105° Ⓓ 15°

Extra Practice

Identify each pair of angles as *complementary, supplementary,* or *neither.*

15. 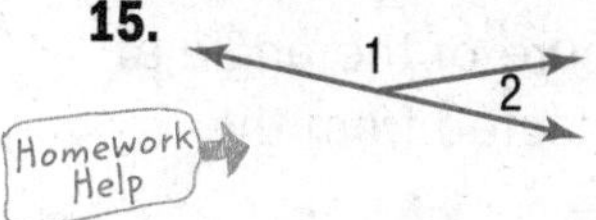

Homework Help

∠1 and ∠2 form a straight angle. So, the angles are supplementary.

16. 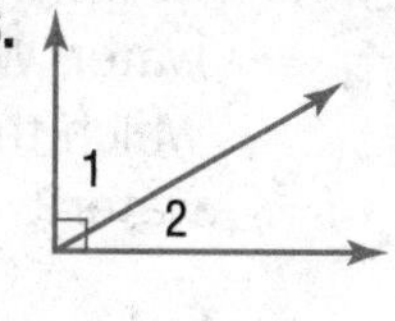

17. 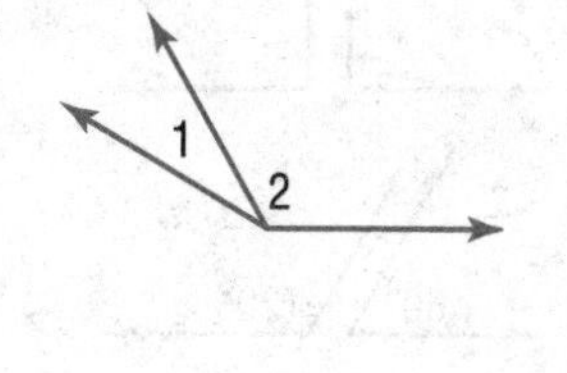

18. ∠*J* and ∠*K* are supplementary. The measure of ∠*J* is $(9x)°$ and the measure of ∠*K* is 45°. What is the value of *x*?

19. ∠*C* and ∠*D* are complementary. The measure of ∠*C* is $(4x)°$ and the measure of ∠*D* is 26°. What is the value of *x*?

CCGPS **Identify Structure Determine whether each statement is *always, sometimes,* or *never* true. Explain your reasoning.**

20. Two obtuse angles are supplementary.

21. Two vertical angles are complementary.

22. CCGPS **Multiple Representations** Line *a* passes through (1, 4) and (−4, −1). Line *b* passes through (−3, 4) and (2, −1).

a. Graphs Graph each line on the same coordinate plane.

b. Words Describe the lines.

c. Numbers What is the slope of each line?

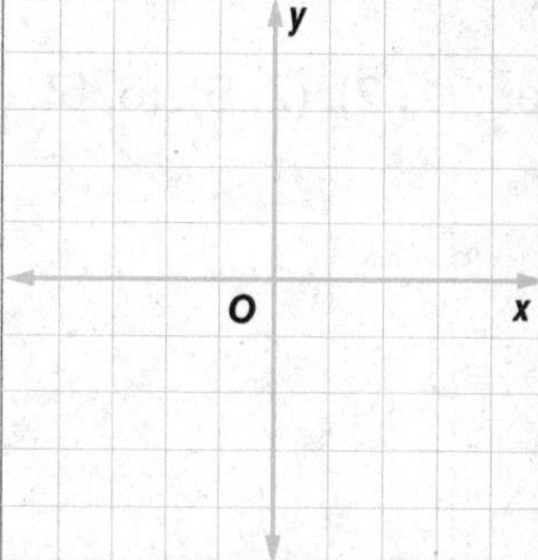

Georgia Test Practice

23. Which angle pairs are *not* supplementary?

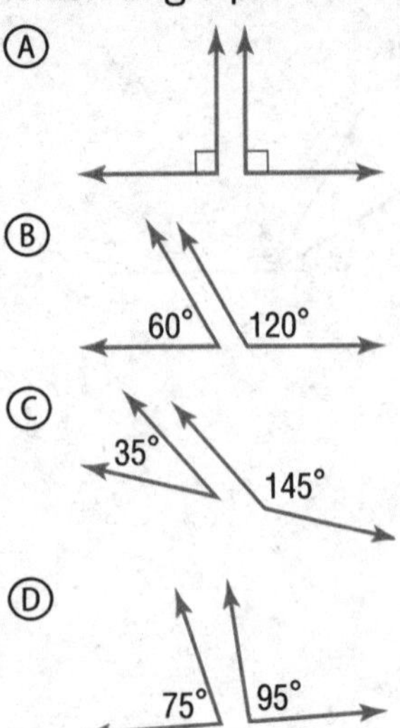

24. **Short Response** The angle at which the light ray hits the water is equal to the angle at which the light ray is reflected from the water. What is the measure of the angle at which the light ray is reflected from the water?

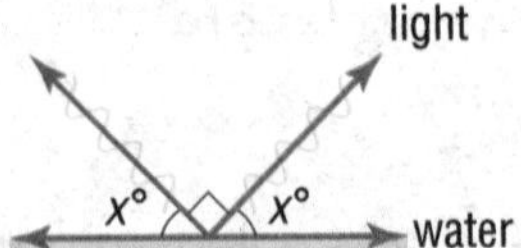

Common Core Review

Graph each figure with the given vertices on the coordinate plane. Then classify each figure. MCC6.G.3

25. Vertices: (1, 2), (5, 2), (5, 6), and (1, 6)

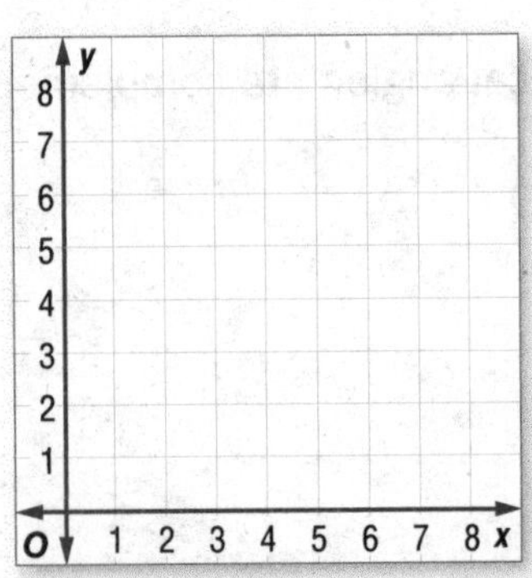

26. Vertices: (1, 3), (1, 6), (5, 5), and (5, 3)

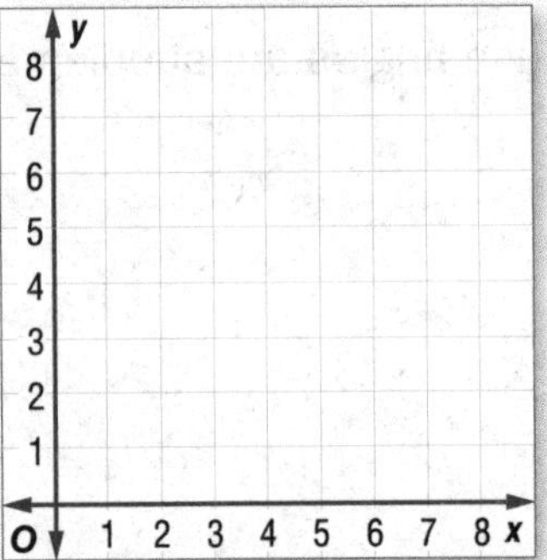

27. Vertices: (1, 2), (2, 5), (6, 5), and (5, 2)

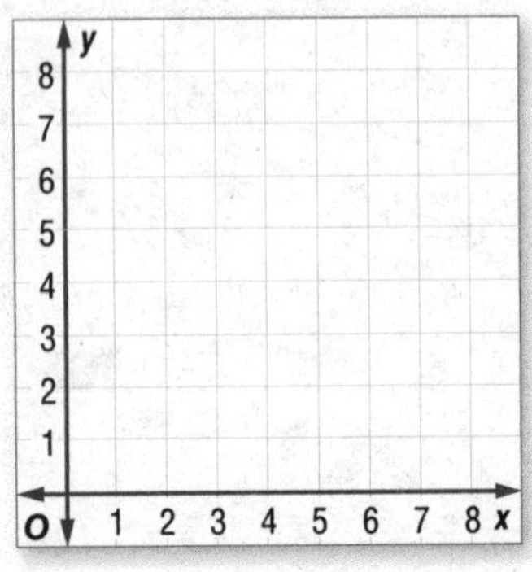

28. Vertices: (3, 2), (3, 6), (5, 6), and (5, 2)

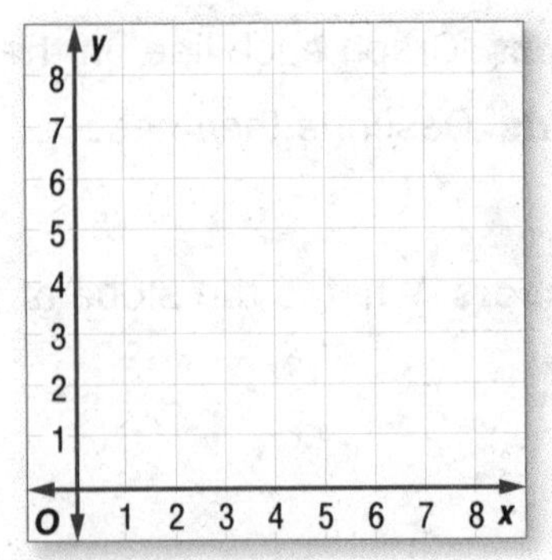

Inquiry Lab

Create Triangles

Inquiry **WHAT do you notice about the measures of the sides or the measures of the angles that form triangles?**

CCGPS **Content Standards**
MCC7.G.2
Mathematical Practices
1, 3, 5, 8

Sailing Dennis has a sailboat. The sail on his boat is in the shape of a triangle with side lengths of 6 feet, 8 feet, and 10 feet. These dimensions work to form a triangle, but not just any three lengths form a triangle. Complete the Investigation below to determine which side lengths form triangles.

Investigation 1

Step 1 Measure and cut several plastic straws into lengths that equal 3, 4, 4, 5, 8, 8, 8, 13, 15, 15, 15, and 15 centimeters.

Step 2 Arrange three of the pieces that each measure 15 centimeters to see if you can form a triangle.

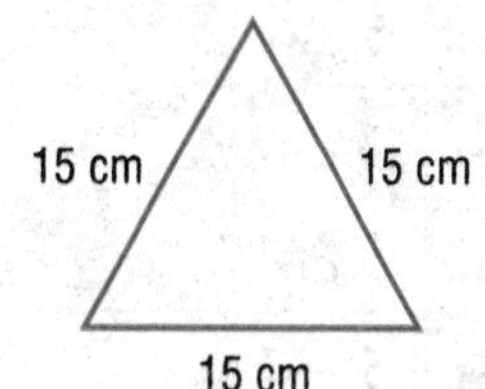

So, you can form a triangle with side lengths of 15 centimeters, 15 centimeters, and 15 centimeters.

Step 3 Continue using pieces of straw to try to form triangles using the different combinations of side lengths given. Determine whether or not the lengths form a triangle. Complete the table.

Side 1	Side 2	Side 3	Do the sides form a triangle?
15 cm	15 cm	15 cm	yes
3 cm	4 cm	5 cm	
8 cm	8 cm	13 cm	
3 cm	4 cm	8 cm	
4 cm	4 cm	5 cm	
8 cm	3 cm	15 cm	
4 cm	8 cm	15 cm	

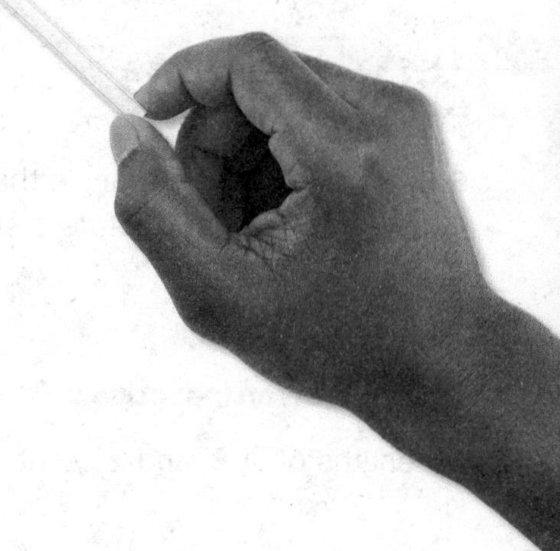

Collaborate

Work with a partner. Try to create triangles using the given side lengths. Circle *yes* if you can make a triangle or *no* if you cannot.

1. 5 cm, 8 cm, 15 cm

Yes or No

2. 13 cm, 8 cm, 15 cm

Yes or No

3. 13 cm, 4 cm, 4 cm

Yes or No

Work with a partner.

4. The table below contains the dimensions you used in Step 3 of the Investigation. Transfer your results from the Investigation into the fourth column and then complete the fifth column.

Side 1	Side 2	Side 3	Do the sides form a triangle?	Is Side 1 + Side 2 greater than or less than Side 3?
15 cm	15 cm	15 cm	yes	greater than
3 cm	4 cm	5 cm		
8 cm	8 cm	13 cm		
3 cm	4 cm	8 cm		
4 cm	4 cm	5 cm		
8 cm	3 cm	15 cm		
4 cm	8 cm	15 cm		

5. What do you notice about the figures with a Side 1 and Side 2 sum that is less than the length of Side 3? ______________________________

6. Can you create a triangle that has the same shape as the triangle in the Investigation, but different side lengths? Explain.

____

7. CCGPS **Reason Inductively** Could you form a triangle using the side lengths of 7, 8, and 25 centimeters? Explain. ______________________________

Investigation 2

Use angles of different sizes to determine which ones form a triangle.

Step 1 Draw two sets of angles measuring 30°, 45°, 60°, and 90° on different pieces of patty paper. Extend the rays of each angle to the edges of the patty paper.

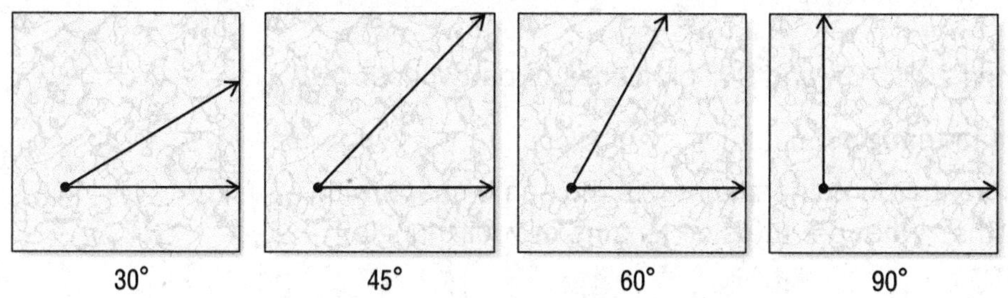

Step 2 Try to form a triangle with one 90° angle and two 45° angles.

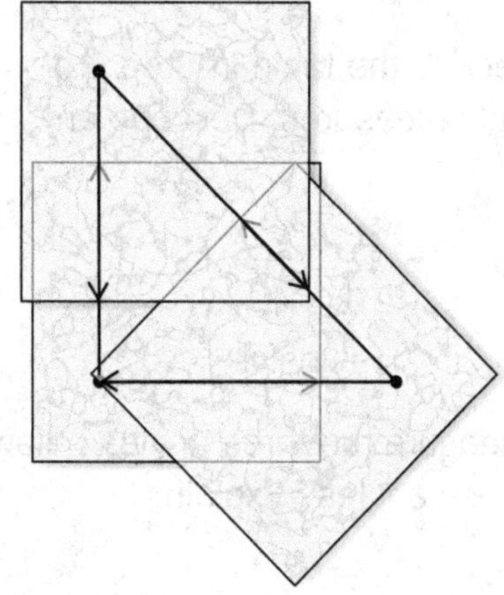

So, a 90° angle and two 45° angles form a triangle.

Step 3 Try to form triangles using the angle measures that are given in the table. Fill in *yes* or *no* in the fourth column of the table.

Angle 1	Angle 2	Angle 3	Do the angles form a triangle?
90°	45°	45°	yes
30°	60°	90°	
30°	45°	60°	
30°	30°	60°	

Collaborate

Work with a partner.

8. Draw another 60° angle on a piece of patty paper. Describe the angles and side lengths of the figure you form using three 60° angles.

Show your work.

9. Draw angles measuring 20°, 70°, and 90° on pieces of patty paper.

a. Do the angles form a triangle? ______

b. Can you create more than one triangle that is the same shape with different side lengths? What are the side lengths of your triangle?

Analyze

10. CCGPS **Identify Repeated Reasoning** Refer back to the table in Step 3 of Investigation 2. Compare the sum of the angle measures. Describe any patterns that are found.

11. CCGPS **Use Math Tools** Use a protractor to measure the three angles below. Would you be able to form a triangle from these angles? Explain.

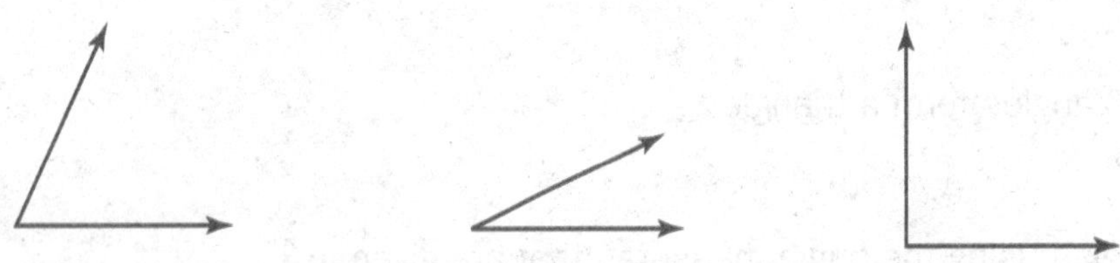

Reflect

12. Inquiry WHAT do you notice about the measures of the sides or the measures of the angles that form triangles?

Triangles

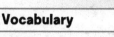

What You'll Learn

Scan the lesson. List two headings you would use to make an outline of the lesson.

-
-

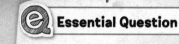

Essential Question

HOW does geometry help us describe real-world objects?

Vocabulary

acute triangle
right triangle
obtuse triangle
scalene triangle
isosceles triangle
equilateral triangle
triangle
congruent segments

Math Symbols

△

Content Standards
MCC7.G.2

Mathematical Practices
1, 2, 3, 4

Real-World Link

Ramps Julia practices jumping on a ski ramp. The front of the ramp is a triangle like the one shown below.

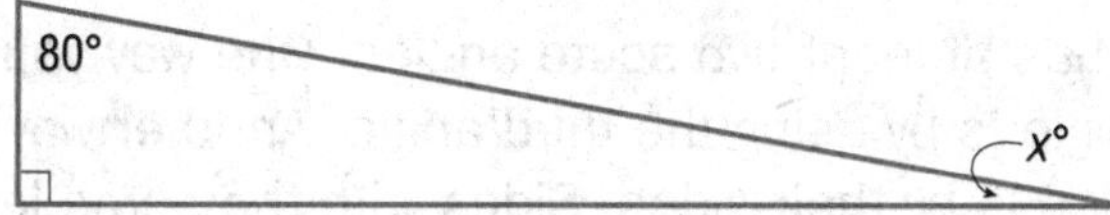

1. Draw an X through the type of angle that is not shown in the triangle.

   right   acute   obtuse

2. Measure the unkown angle. Describe the relationship between the 80° angle and the unknown angle.

3. Draw a triangle with one obtuse angle.

4. Is it possible to draw a triangle with two obtuse angles? Explain.

Key Concept: Classify Triangles

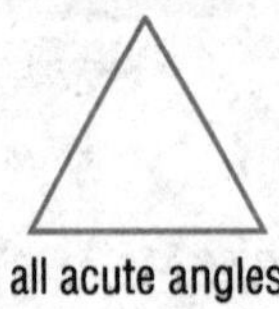

all acute angles

acute triangle

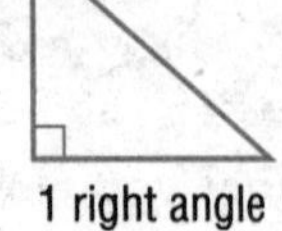

1 right angle

right triangle

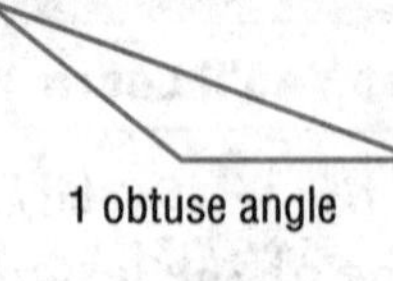

1 obtuse angle

obtuse triangle

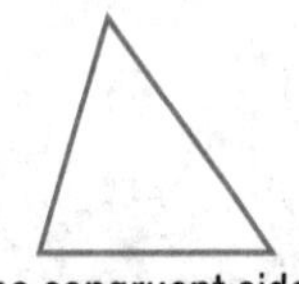

no congruent sides

scalene triangle

at least 2 congruent sides

isosceles triangle

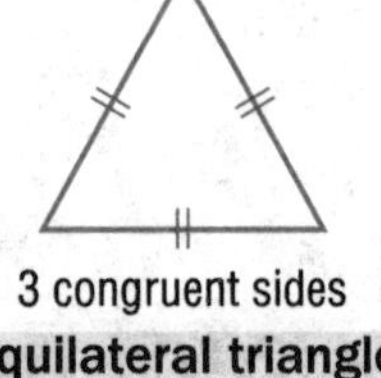

3 congruent sides

equilateral triangle

Work Zone

Congruent Segments
The tick marks on the sides of the triangle indicate that those sides are congruent.

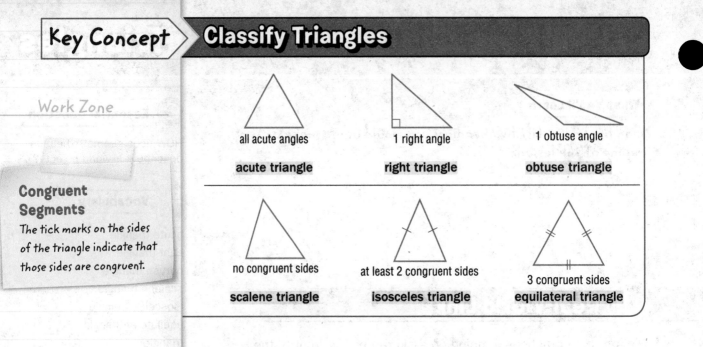

A **triangle** is a figure with three sides and three angles. The symbol for triangle is △.

Every triangle has at least two acute angles. One way you can classify a triangle is by using the third angle. Another way to classify triangles is by their sides. Sides with the same length are **congruent segments**.

Example

1. Draw a triangle with one obtuse angle and no congruent sides. Then classify the triangle.

Draw an obtuse angle.
The two segments of the angle should have different lengths.

Connect the two segments to form a triangle.

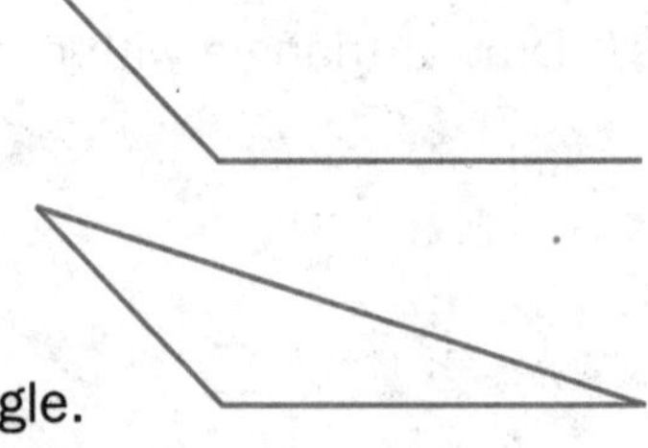

The triangle is an obtuse scalene triangle.

Got It? Do these problems to find out.

Draw a triangle that satisfies the set of conditions below. Then classify the triangle.

a. a triangle with one right angle and two congruent sides

a. ________

Example

2. Classify the triangle on the house by its angles and by its sides.

The triangle has one obtuse angle and two congruent sides. So, it is an obtuse isosceles triangle.

STOP and Reflect

How would you classify a triangle with a right angle and two congruent sides?

Got It? Do this problem to find out.

b. Classify the triangle shown by its angles and by its sides.

b. ____________

Angles of a Triangle

Key Concept

Words The sum of the measures of the angles of a triangle is 180°.

Algebra $x + y + z = 180$

Model

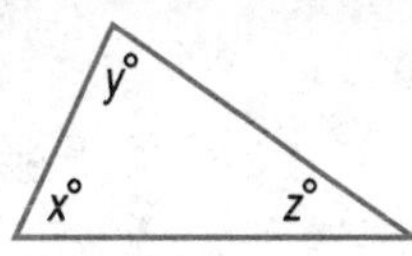

You can write and solve an equation to find the missing angle measure of a triangle.

Example

3. Find $m\angle Z$.

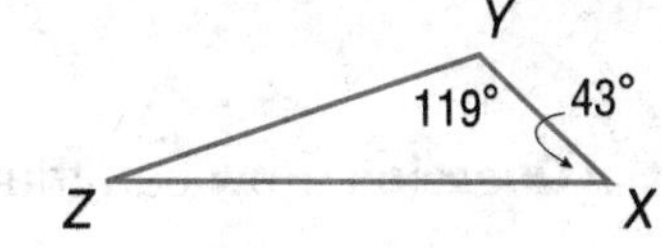

The sum of the angle measures in a triangle is 180°.

$$m\angle Z + 43° + 119° = 180°$$ Write the equation.

$$m\angle Z + 162° = 180°$$ Simplify.

$$-162° = -162°$$ Subtract 162° from each side.

$$m\angle Z = 18°$$

So, $m\angle Z$ is 18°.

Got It? Do this problem to find out.

c. In $\triangle ABC$, if $m\angle A = 25°$ and $m\angle B = 108°$, what is $m\angle C$?

c. ____________

Example 

4. The Alabama state flag is shown. What is the missing measure in the triangle?

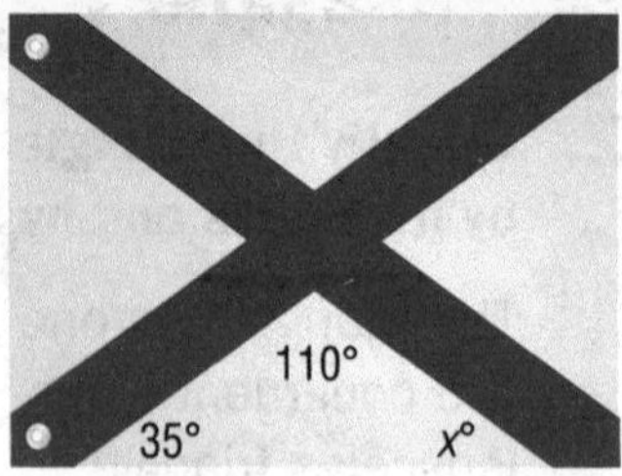

To find the missing measure, write and solve an equation.

$x + 110 + 35 = 180$	The sum of the measures is 180.
$x + 145 = 180$	Simplify.
$-145 = -145$	Subtract 145 from each side.
$x = 35$	

The missing measure is 35°.

Guided Practice 

1. Draw a triangle with three acute angles and two congruent sides. Classify the triangle. (Examples 1 and 2) ______

2. Find $m\angle T$ in $\triangle RST$ if $m\angle R = 37°$ and $m\angle S = 55°$. (Example 3) ______

3. A triangle is used in the game of pool to rack the pool balls. Find the missing measure of the triangle. (Example 4)

______

4. **Building on the Essential Question** How can triangles be classified?

______

Rate Yourself!

Are you ready to move on? Shade the section that applies.

YES ? NO

For more help, go online to access a Personal Tutor. 

FOLDABLES Time to update your Foldable!

Name ______________________ My Homework ______________________

Independent Practice

Go online for Step-by-Step Solutions 

Draw a triangle that satisfies each set of conditions. Then classify the triangle. (Example 1)

1. a triangle with three acute angles and three congruent sides ______________

2. a triangle with one right angle and no congruent sides ______________

Classify the marked triangle by its angles and by its sides. (Example 2)

3. 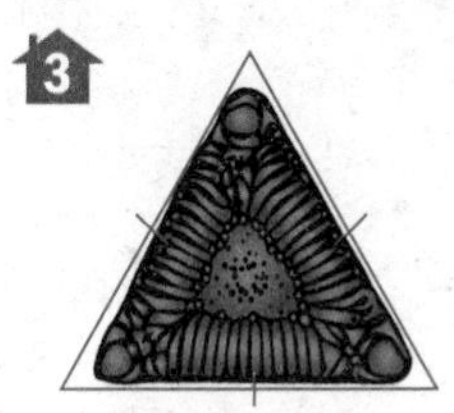

____

4. ______________

5. 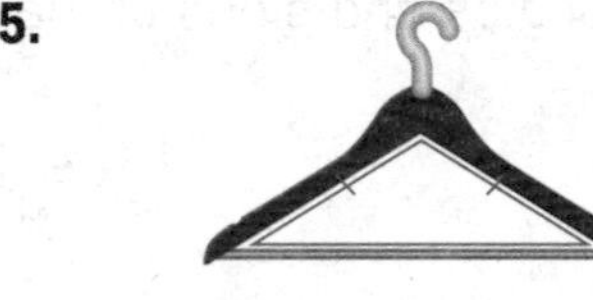

____

Find the value of *x*. (Examples 3 and 4)

6. 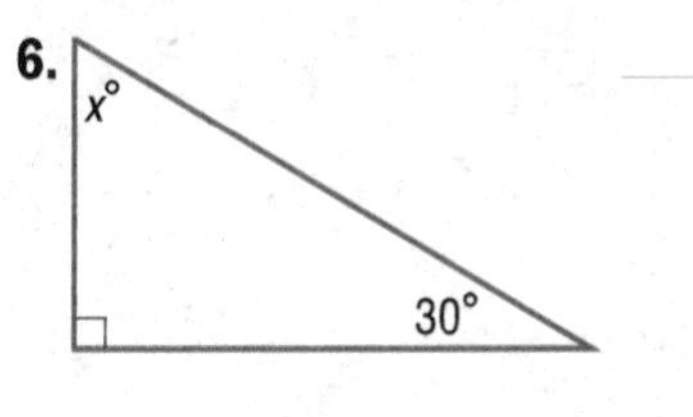

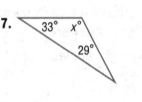

____

7. 33°, x°, 29° ______________

8. 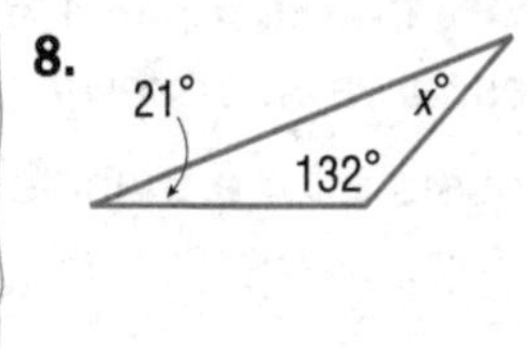

____

9. CCGPS **Model with Mathematics** Refer to the graphic novel below. Classify the triangle formed by the cabin, ropes course, and mess hall by its angles and sides.

____

10. Triangle *ABC* is formed by two parallel lines and two other intersecting lines. Find the measure of each angle *A*, *B*, and *C* of the triangle.

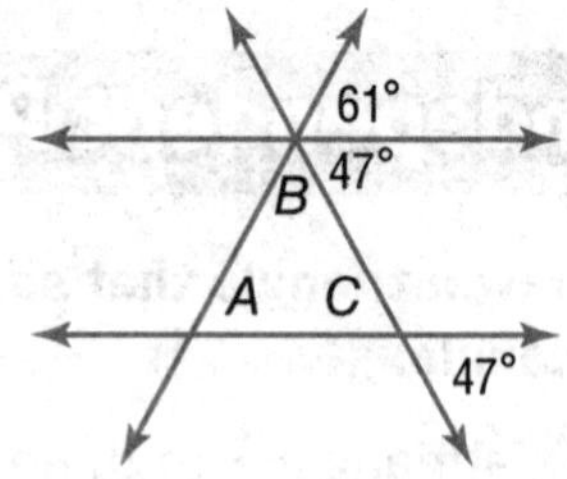

H.O.T. Problems Higher Order Thinking

11. CCGPS **Persevere with Problems** Apply what you know about triangles to find the missing angle measures in the figure.

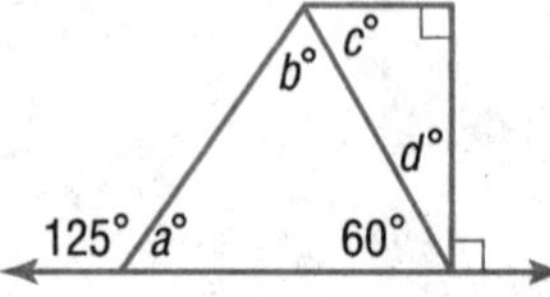

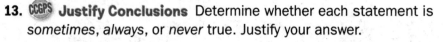

12. CCGPS **Model with Mathematics** Draw an acute scalene triangle. Describe the angles and sides of the triangle.

13. CCGPS **Justify Conclusions** Determine whether each statement is *sometimes*, *always*, or *never* true. Justify your answer.

a. It is possible for a triangle to have two right angles.

b. It is possible for a triangle to have two obtuse angles.

Georgia Test Practice

14. Which of the following is an acute triangle?

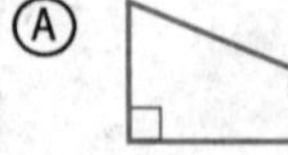
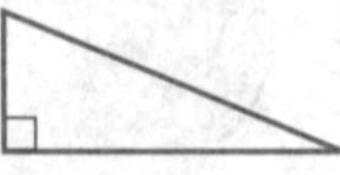

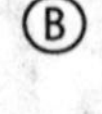
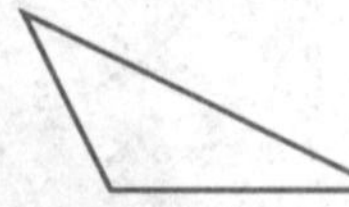

Ⓐ Ⓑ Ⓒ Ⓓ

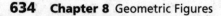

Extra Practice

Classify the marked triangle in each object by its angles and by its sides.

15.

The triangle has all acute angles and two congruent sides. It is an acute isosceles triangle.

16.

____

17.

____

Draw a triangle that satisfies each set of conditions. Then classify the triangle.

18. a triangle with three acute angles and no congruent sides ______________________

19. a triangle with one obtuse angle and two congruent sides ______________________

Find the value of x.

20.

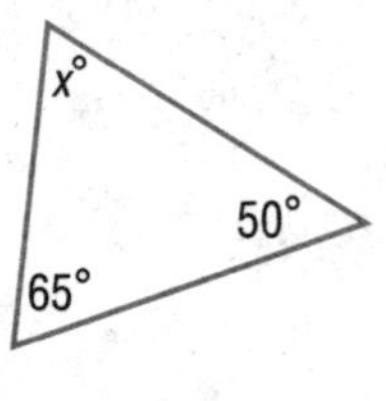

____

21.

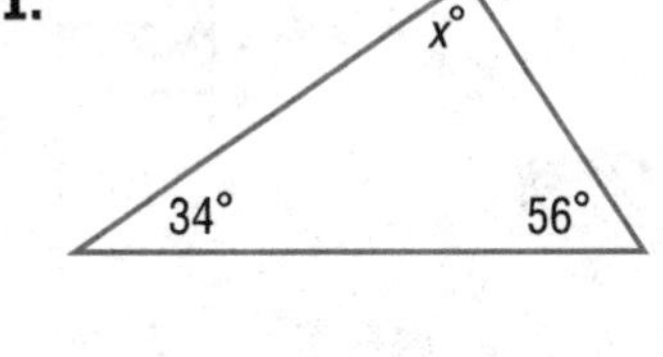

____

22.

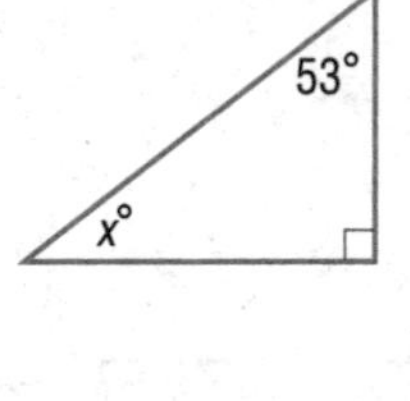

____

23. Find $m\angle Q$ in $\triangle QRS$ if $m\angle R = 25°$ and $m\angle S = 102°$. ______________________

Reason Abstractly **Find the value of x in each triangle.**

24.

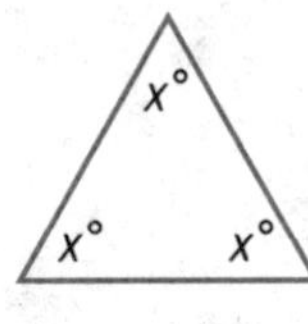

____

25.

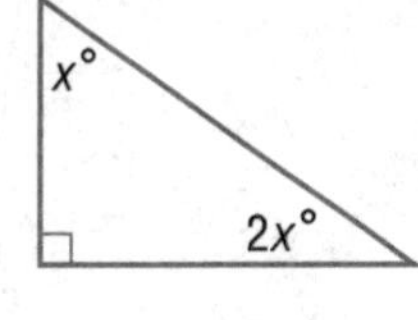

____

26.

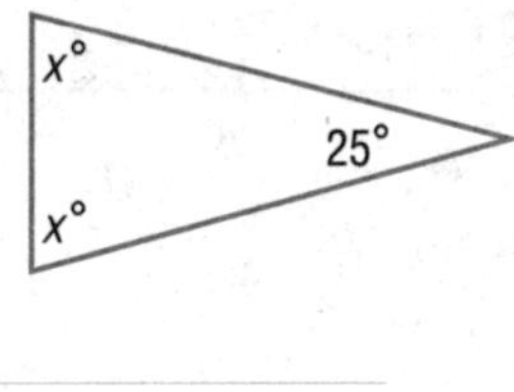

____

Georgia Test Practice

27. How would you find $m\angle R$?

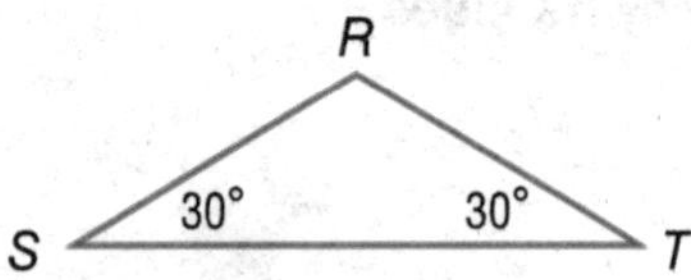

Ⓐ Add 30° to 180°.

Ⓑ Subtract 60° from 180°.

Ⓒ Subtract 30° from 90°.

Ⓓ Subtract 180° from 60°.

28. Which statement is true about the relationship between the measures of $\angle A$ and $\angle B$, two acute angles of an obtuse triangle?

Ⓕ $m\angle A + m\angle B = 90°$

Ⓖ $m\angle A + m\angle B = 180°$

Ⓗ $m\angle A + m\angle B > 90°$

Ⓘ $m\angle A + m\angle B < 90°$

29. **Short Response** What is the value of b in the triangle below? ______

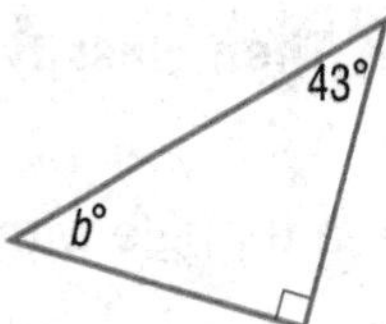

Common Core Review

Find the area of each figure. MCC6.G.1

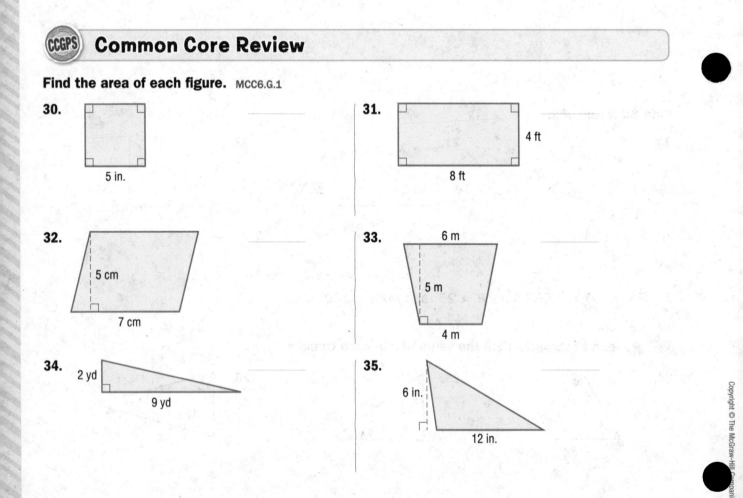

30. ______

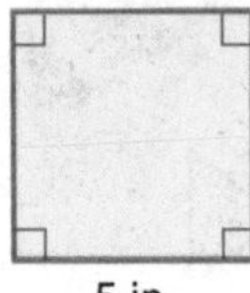

31. ______

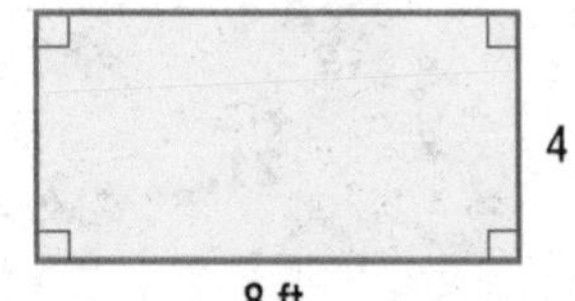

32. ______

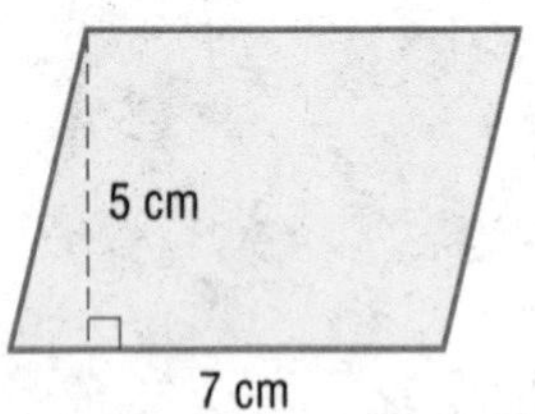

33. ______

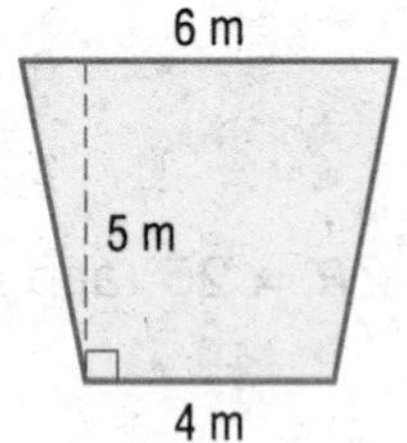

34. ______

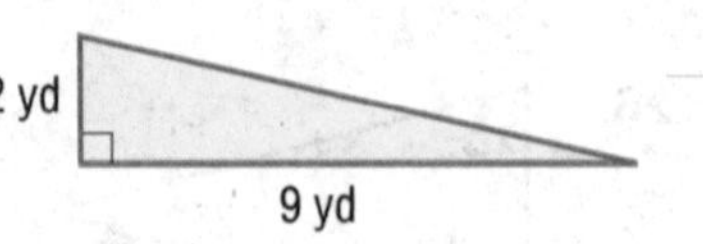

35. ______

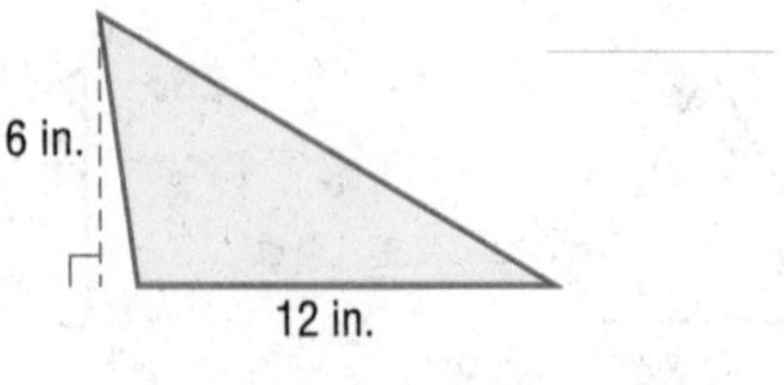

Inquiry Lab

Draw Triangles

Inquiry HOW can you use technology to draw geometric shapes?

Content Standards
MCC7.G.2

Mathematical Practices
1, 3, 5

The Spirit Club is selling triangular-shaped pennants for Homecoming. Teresa is making a poster to advertise the pennants. She wants to use a computer program to draw a model of the pennant.

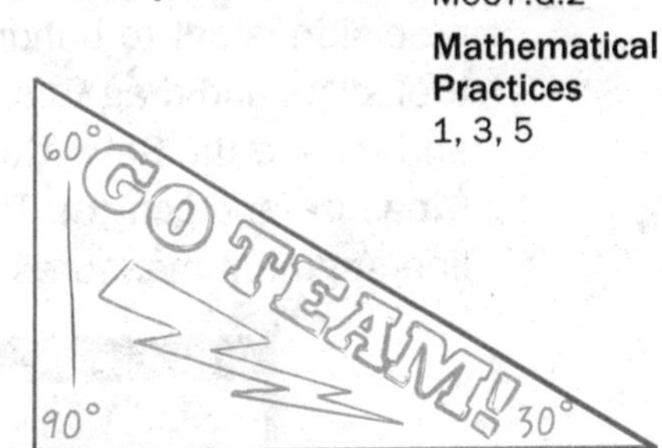

Investigation 1

You can use dynamic geometry software such as The Geometer's Sketchpad® to draw triangles given three angle measures. In this investigation, you will draw a triangle with angle measures of 30°, 60°, and 90°.

Step 1 First, click on **Edit**. Go to **Preferences**. Change the angle precision from *hundredths* to *units*. Next, use the **Straightedge (segment)** tool. Click and drag three times to create a triangle like the one shown.

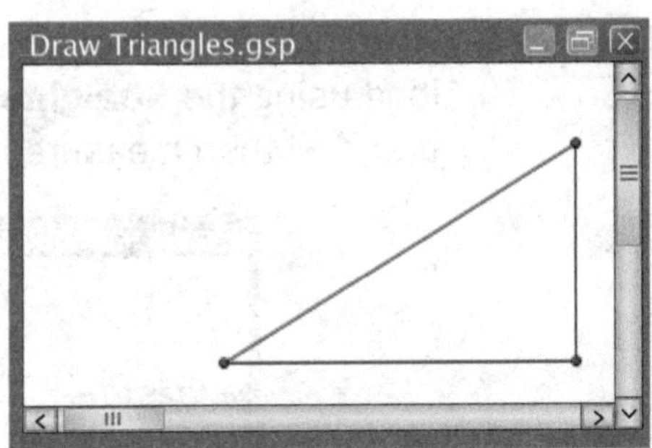

Step 2 Using the **Selection Arrow**, click on each of the vertex points *A*, *B*, and *C*. Then select **Measure** and **Angle**. Labels will automatically be assigned to the vertices. You found that the measure of $\angle ABC$ is ______.

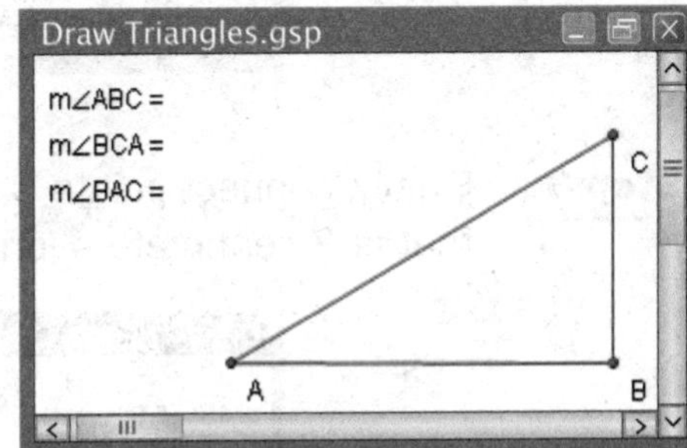

Step 3 Click on points *B*, *C*, and *A*. Click **Measure** and **Angle** again. Repeat for points *B*, *A*, and *C*. The angle measures should be displayed on your screen.

Step 4 If the angles do not measure 30°, 60°, and 90°, use the **Selection Arrow** to move the vertices. Click and drag one or more points so that the angles move.

Investigation 2

You can also use The Geometer's Sketchpad® to draw triangles given three side measures. In this investigation, you will draw a triangle with side measures of 3 centimeters, 4 centimeters, and 5 centimeters.

Step 1 First, click on **Edit**. Go to **Preferences**. Check that the distance precision is set to hundredths. Using the **Straightedge (segment)** tool, click and drag to create a line segment with endpoints *A* and *B*. Use the **Selection Arrow** to select the segment. Click on **Measure** and **Length**. Then drag one of the endpoints so that the line segment measures 5 centimeters.

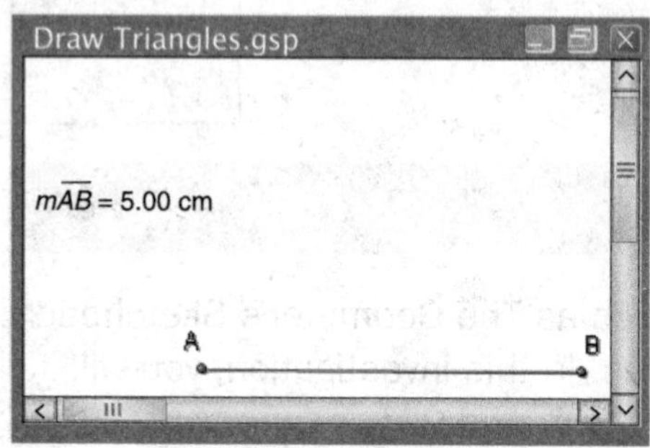

Step 2 Next, create a line segment from point *A* that is 4 centimeters long using the **Straightedge (segment)** tool. Draw the segment first and then measure it to make sure it is 4 centimeters.

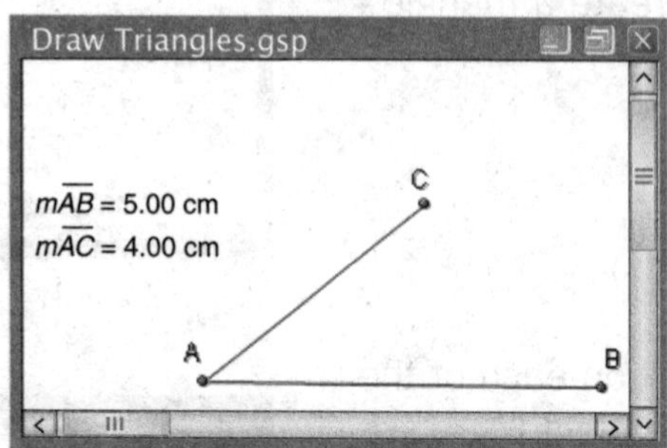

Step 3 Finally, connect points *C* and *B* with a line segment that is 3 centimeters long.

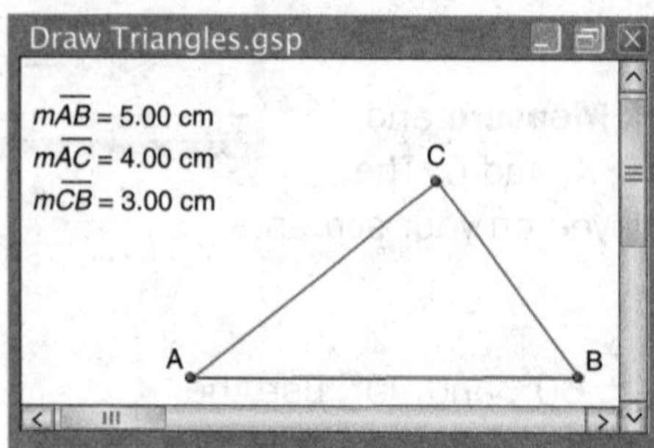

You have created a triangle with side lengths of 3 centimeters, 4 centimeters, and 5 centimeters.

Use Math Tools **Work with a partner to construct each triangle. Once you have constructed a triangle, draw the text and image that appears on your display.**

1. $\angle ABC = 90°$

$\angle BCA = 70°$

$\angle BAC = 20°$

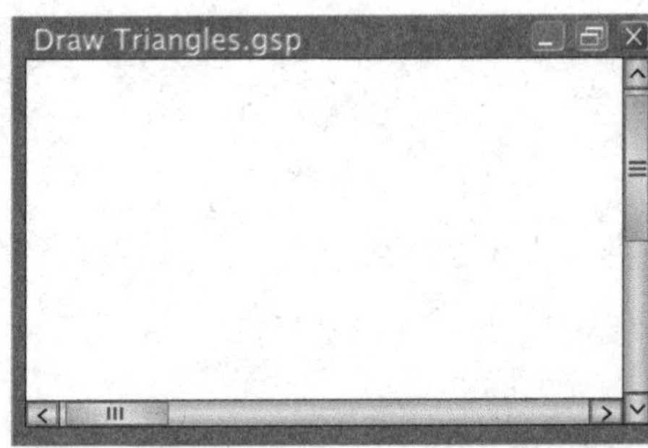

2. $\angle ABC = 90°$

$\angle BCA = 45°$

$\angle BAC = 45°$

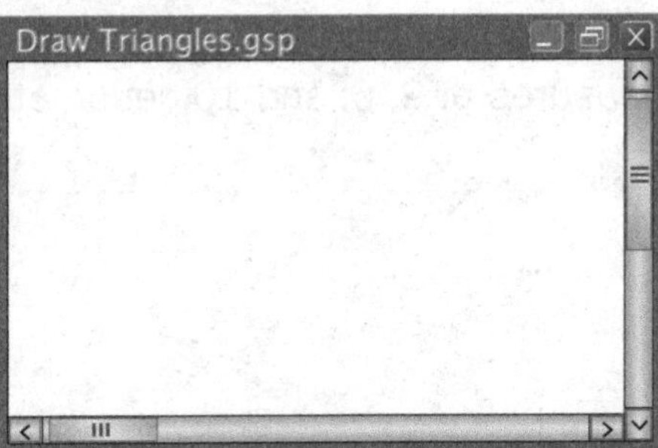

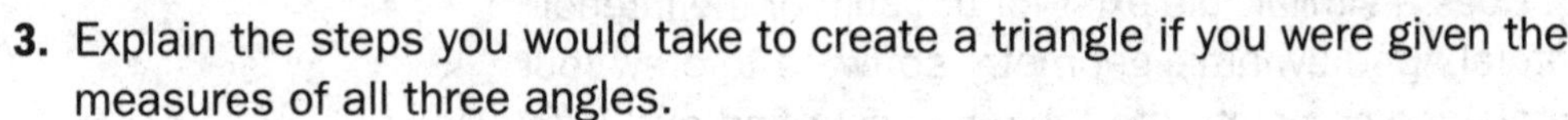

3. Explain the steps you would take to create a triangle if you were given the measures of all three angles.

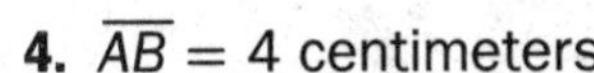

4. $\overline{AB} = 4$ centimeters

$\overline{AC} = 6$ centimeters

$\overline{CB} = 9$ centimeters

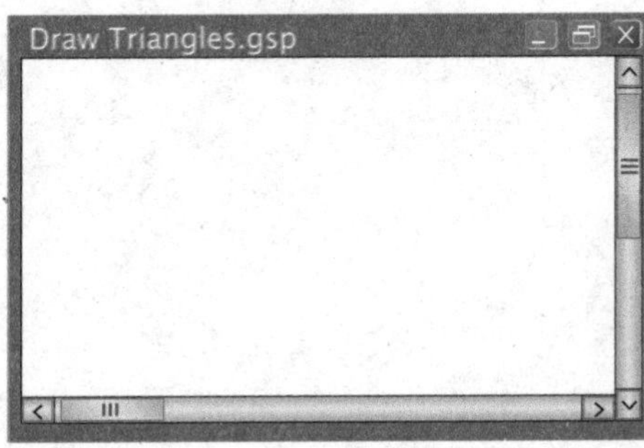

5. $\overline{AB} = 2$ centimeters

$\overline{AC} = 5$ centimeters

$\overline{CB} = 4$ centimeters

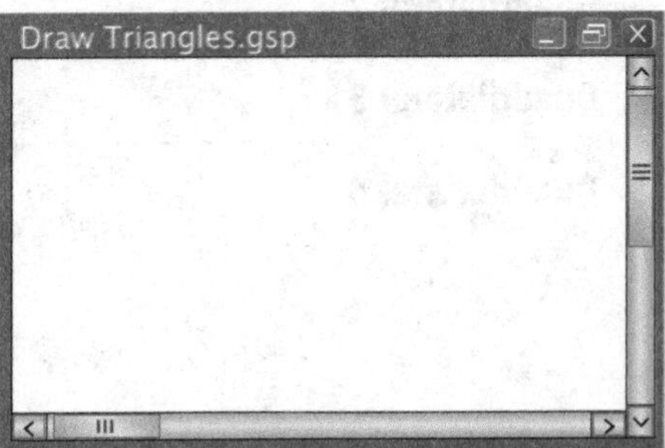

6. **Justify Conclusions** Explain the steps you would take to create a triangle if you were given the lengths of all three sides.

Analyze

Work with a partner to answer each of the following questions.

7. Is it possible to use dynamic geometry software to draw a triangle with angles of 50°, 65°, and 70°? Explain.

8. Is it possible to use dynamic geometry software to draw a triangle with side measures of 3, 6, and 10 centimeters? Explain.

9. CCGPS **Reason Inductively** You know the rule to find the sum of the interior angles of a triangle. Does a similar rule exist for the sum of the interior angles of a quadrilateral? Use dynamic geometry software to draw four different quadrilaterals and complete the table below to find out. (*Hint:* Do not draw more than one square or rectangle.)

	$m\angle 1$	$m\angle 2$	$m\angle 3$	$m\angle 4$	Sum of Angles
Quadrilateral 1					
Quadrilateral 2					
Quadrilateral 3					
Quadrilateral 4					

Reflect

10. Inquiry HOW can you use technology to draw geometric shapes?

Make a Model

Content Standards
MCC7.G.1
Mathematical Practices
1, 4, 6

Case #1 Science Project

Jordan is making a model of Mount Saint Helens for a science project. The height of the actual volcano is about 2,500 meters. She uses a scale of 250 meters equals 1 centimeter.

What is the height of the volcano in Jordan's model?

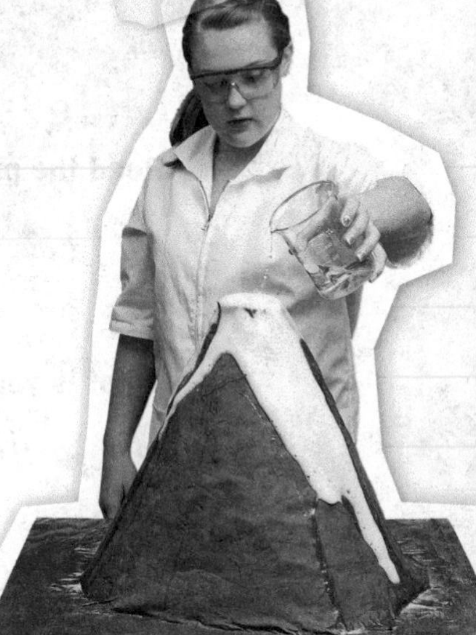

Understand What are the facts?

- The height of the actual volcano is about 2,500 meters.
- The scale for her model is 250 meters = 1 centimeter.

Plan What is your strategy to solve this problem?

Draw a model that represents the actual volcano and Jordan's volcano to help you visualize the problem.

Solve How can you apply the strategy?

The scale is 250 meters = 1 centimeter.
Write and solve a proportion using the scale.

$$\frac{250 \text{ m}}{1 \text{ cm}} = \frac{\square \text{ m}}{x \text{ cm}}$$

$$250 \cdot x = 1 \cdot \square$$

$$x = \square \text{ cm}$$

x

2,500 m

So, Jordan's model has a height of ______.

Check Does the answer make sense?

Multiply the height of the model by 250 to see if it matches the actual height.

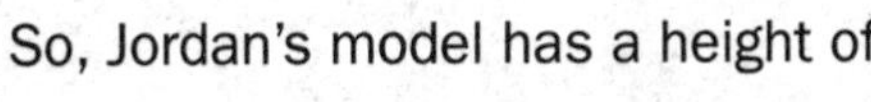

Analyze the Strategy

Be Precise The height of Mount Saint Helens is about 8,500 feet. What scale could Jordan use to represent the model in the U.S. Customary System?

______

Case #2 Portraits

Alicia created a portrait that is 10 inches wide by 13 inches long. She wants to put it in a frame that is $2\frac{1}{4}$ inches wide on each side.

What is the area of the framed portrait?

Understand

Read the problem. What are you being asked to find?

I need to find ______________________.

Plan

What is your strategy to solve this problem?

I will use the ______________________ strategy.

Solve

How can you apply the strategy?

I will ______________________.

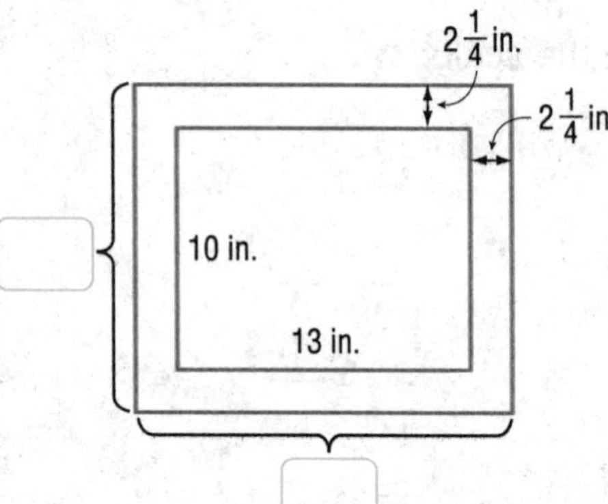

The inner rectangle is the portrait and the outer rectangle is the frame.

Label the combined length and width of the portrait and the frame.

The area of the framed portrait is ______________________

______________________.

Check

Estimate the product of the length and width of the framed portrait to determine if your answer is reasonable.

____

____

Collaborate Work with a small group to solve the following cases. Show your work on a separate piece of paper.

Case #3 Tables

Members of Student Council are setting up tables end-to-end for an awards banquet.

How many square tables will they need to put together for 32 people? Each table will seat one person on each side.

Case #4 Tile

The diagram shows the design of a tile border around a rectangular swimming pool that measures 7 meters by 4 meters. Each tile is a square measuring 1 meter on each side.

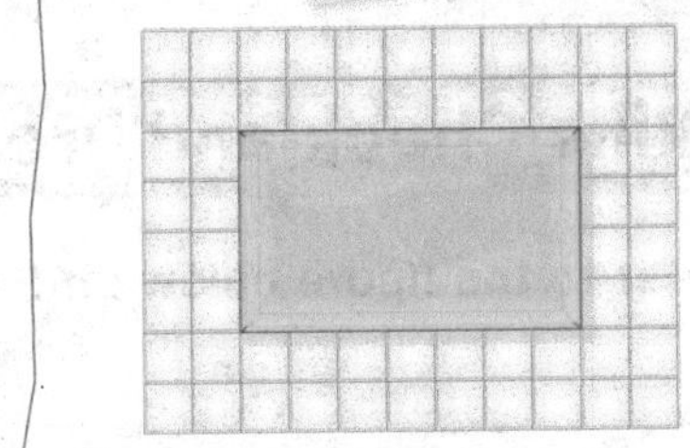

a. What is the area of the pool? ______

b. What is the area of both the pool and the tiles? ______

c. Explain a method you could use to find the area of just the tiles.

Case #5 Patterns

Mrs. Padilla is making a quilt using the following pattern.

How many squares would be in the 20th figure in this pattern?

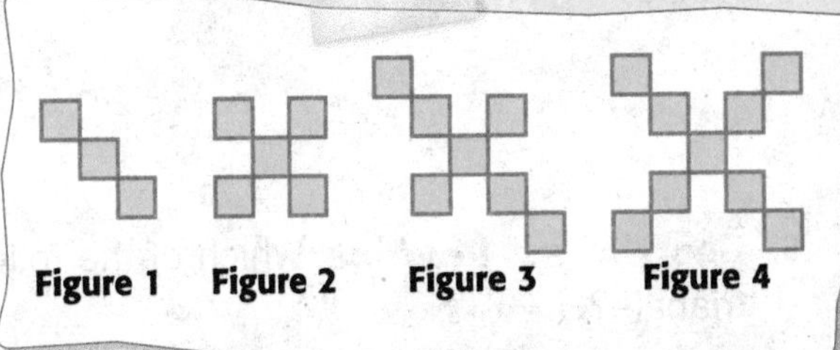

Circle a strategy below to solve the problem.

- Draw a diagram.
- Guess, check, and revise.
- Make a table.

Case #6 Money

Ken borrowed $250 from his parents for a camping trip. He has already repaid them $82.

If he plans to pay them $14 each week, how many weeks will it take Ken to repay his parents?

Mid-Chapter Check

Vocabulary Check

1. CCGPS **Be Precise** Define *complementary angles*. Give an example of two angles that would be complementary. (Lesson 2)

____

____

2. Fill in the blank in the sentence below with the correct term. (Lesson 3)

A ______________________ triangle is made up of one right angle and no congruent sides.

Skills Check and Problem Solving

Refer to the figure below for Exercises 3 and 4. (Lessons 1 and 2)

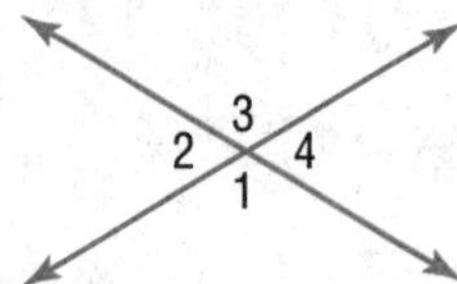

3. Identify a pair of vertical angles.

____

4. Identify a pair of supplementary angles.

____

5. **Georgia Test Practice** Which of the following is *not* a scalene triangle? (Lesson 3)

Ⓐ 

Ⓒ  

Ⓑ 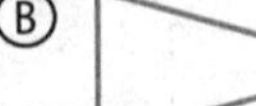 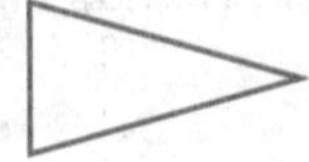

Ⓓ  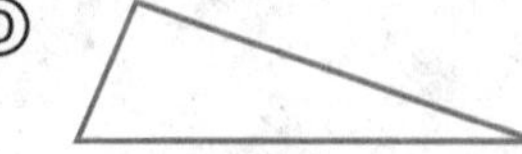

Lesson 4

Draw Three-Dimensional Figures

What You'll Learn

Scan the lesson. Predict two things you will learn about three-dimensional figures.

-
-

Essential Question

HOW does geometry help us describe real-world objects?

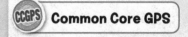

Common Core GPS

Content Standards
Preparation for MCC7.G.3

Mathematical Practices
1, 3, 4

Real-World Link

New York City In art class, Rasheed studied buildings known for their unusual architecture. He studied the Flatiron Building shown.

Three-dimensional figures, such as the Flatiron Building, have length, width, and height. They can be viewed from different perspectives, including the *side* view and the *top* view.

1. What is the two-dimensional figure that makes up the side view?

2. What is the two-dimensional figure that makes up the top view?

3. Sketch the side view of the Flatiron Building.

4. Sketch the top view of the Flatiron Building.

5. The top view, side view, and front view of a three-dimensional figure are shown below. Sketch the figure.

top 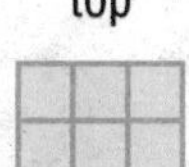 side 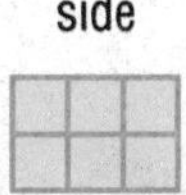 front 

Work Zone

Draw a Three-Dimensional Figure

You can draw different views of three-dimensional figures. The most common views drawn are the top, side, and front views.

The top, side, and front views of a three-dimensional figure can be used to draw a corner view of the figure.

Examples

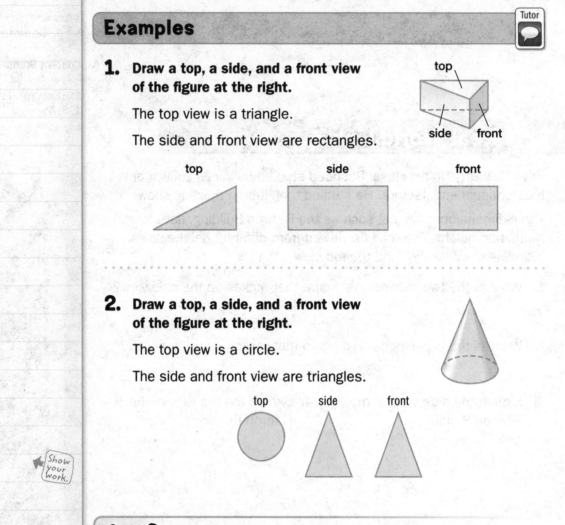

1. Draw a top, a side, and a front view of the figure at the right.

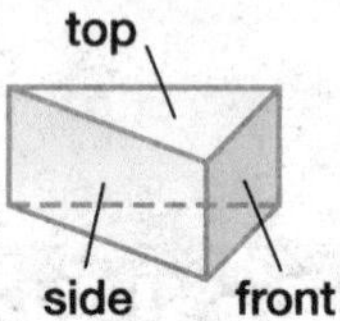

The top view is a triangle.

The side and front view are rectangles.

top 

side 

front 

2. Draw a top, a side, and a front view of the figure at the right.

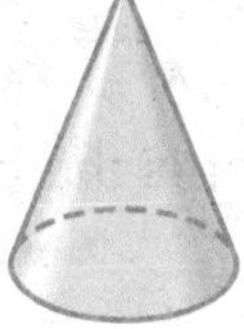

The top view is a circle.

The side and front view are triangles.

top 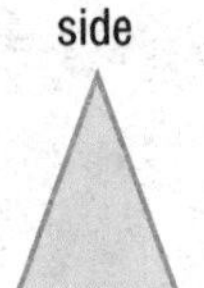

side 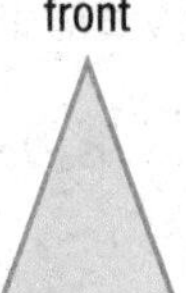

front

Got It? Do this problem to find out.

a. Draw a top, a side, and a front view of the figure at the right.

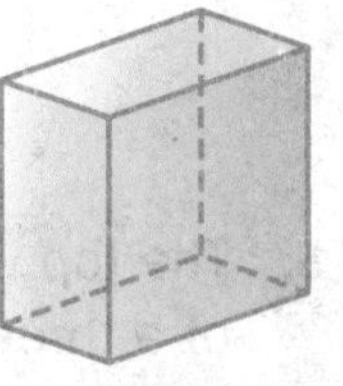

a. ____________

Example

3. Draw a top, a side, and a front view of the video console shown.

The top view is a rectangle.

The side and front views are also rectangles.

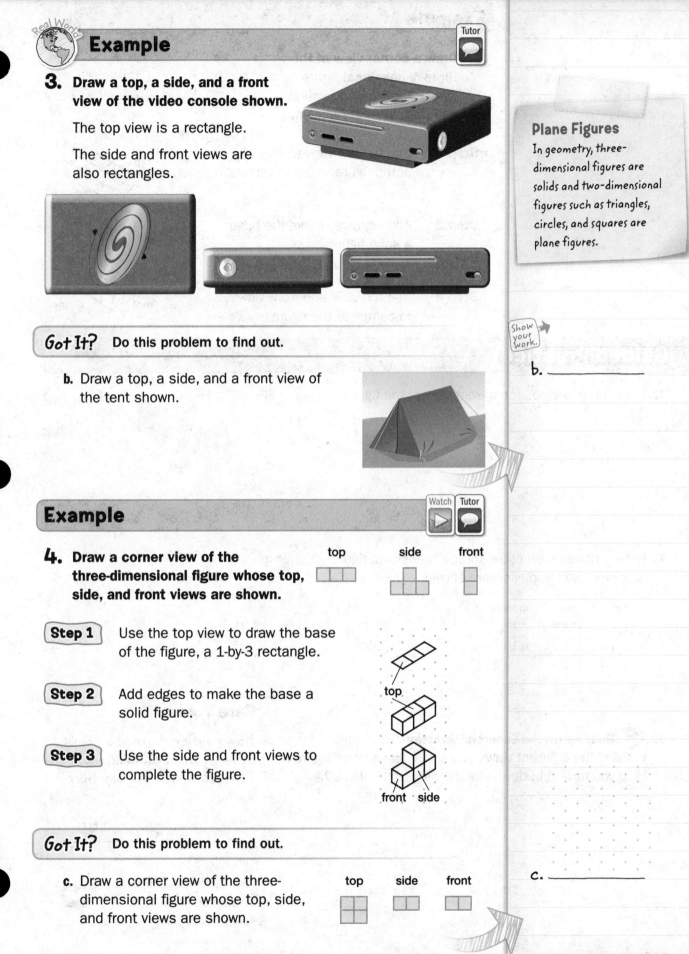

Plane Figures
In geometry, three-dimensional figures are solids and two-dimensional figures such as triangles, circles, and squares are plane figures.

Got It? **Do this problem to find out.**

b. Draw a top, a side, and a front view of the tent shown.

Show your work.

b. ________

Example

Watch Tutor

4. Draw a corner view of the three-dimensional figure whose top, side, and front views are shown.

top side front

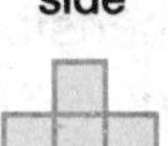

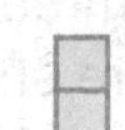

Step 1 Use the top view to draw the base of the figure, a 1-by-3 rectangle.

Step 2 Add edges to make the base a solid figure.

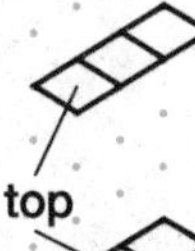

Step 3 Use the side and front views to complete the figure.

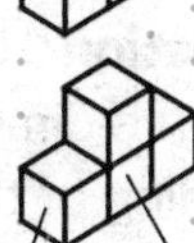

Got It? **Do this problem to find out.**

c. Draw a corner view of the three-dimensional figure whose top, side, and front views are shown.

top side front

c. ________

Example

5. Draw a corner view of the three-dimensional figure whose top view, side view, and front view are shown.

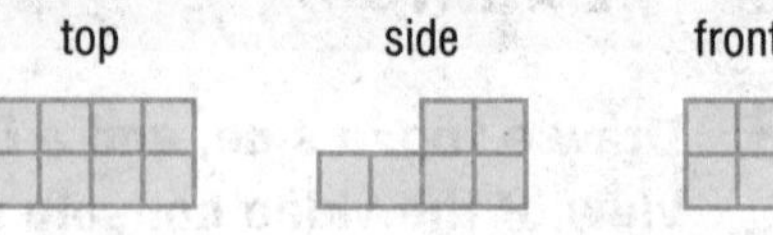

Step 1 Use the top view to draw the base of the figure, a 2-by-4 rectangle.

Step 2 Add edges to make the base a solid figure.

Step 3 Use the side and front views to complete the figure.

Guided Practice

1. Draw a top, a side, and a front view of the figure. (Examples 1–3)

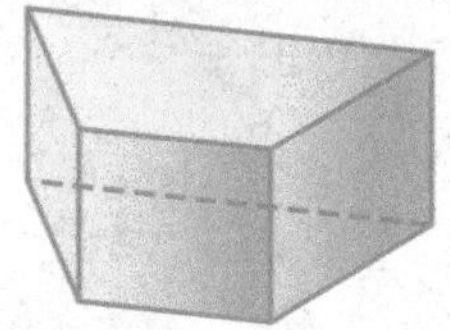

2. Draw a corner view of the three-dimensional figure whose top view, side view, and front view are shown. (Examples 4–5)

top side front

3. **Building on the Essential Question** How does drawing the different views of a three-dimensional figure help you have a better understanding of the figure?

Rate Yourself!

How confident are you about drawing three-dimensional figures? Check the box that applies.

For more help, go online to access a Personal Tutor.

Independent Practice

Go online for Step-by-Step Solutions

Draw a top, a side, and a front view of each figure. (Examples 1–2)

1

2.

3 Draw a top, a side, and a front view of the eraser shown. (Example 3)

Draw a corner view of each three-dimensional figure whose top view, side view, and front view are shown. (Examples 4–5)

4. **top** **side** **front**

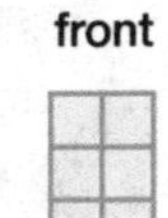

5. **top** **side** **front**

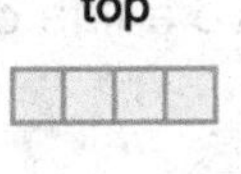

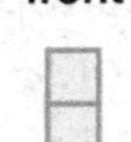

6. Name a real-world object that has a top view of a triangle, and a side and front view that are each rectangles. ______________________

7. **Model with Mathematics** The Quetzalcoatl pyramid in Mexico is shown. Use the photo to sketch views from the top, side, and front of the pyramid.

Show your work.

H.O.T. Problems Higher Order Thinking

8. **Model with Mathematics** Choose an object in your classroom or in your home. Sketch any view of the object. Choose among a top, a side, or a front view.

9. **Which One Doesn't Belong?** Identify the figure that does not have the same characteristic as the other three. Explain your reasoning.

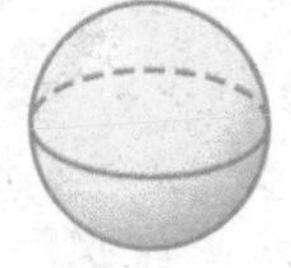
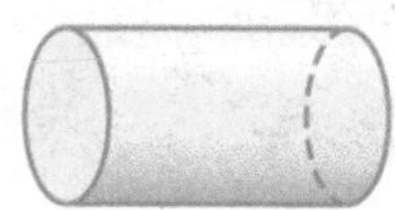
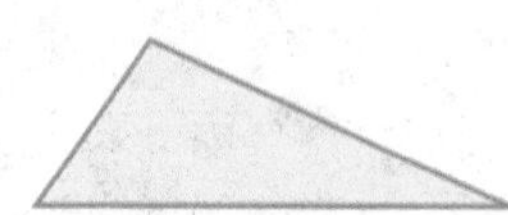
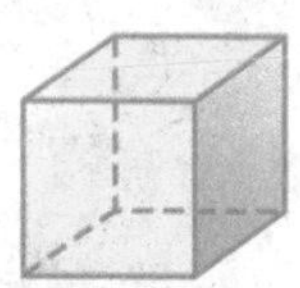

10. **Persevere with Problems** Draw a three-dimensional figure in which the front and top views each have a line of symmetry but the side view does not.

Georgia Test Practice

11. Which three-dimensional figure is represented by the two-dimensional views?

Ⓐ Triangular Prism   Ⓒ Cube
Ⓑ Square Pyramid   Ⓓ Cone

top
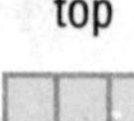
side
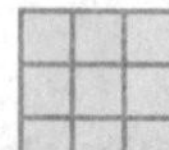
front
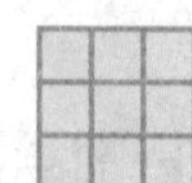

Extra Practice

Draw a top, a side, and a front view of each figure.

12.

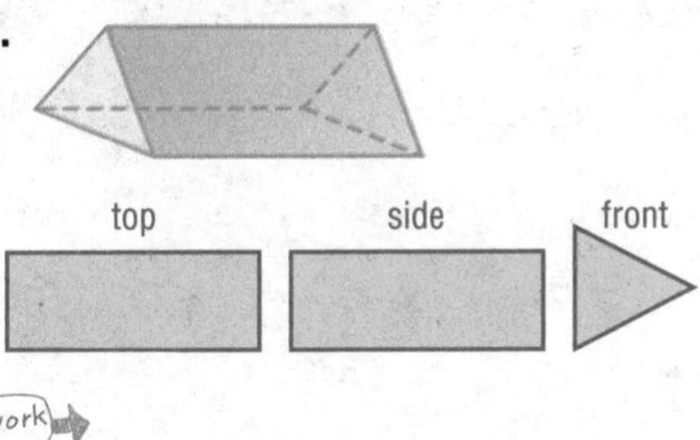

Homework Help

13.

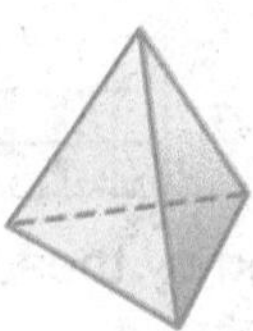

Draw a corner view of each three-dimensional figure whose top view, side view, and and front view are shown.

14. top side front

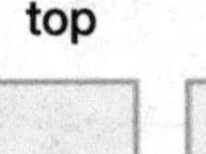

15. top side front

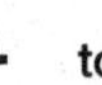

Draw a top, a side, and a front view of each figure.

16.

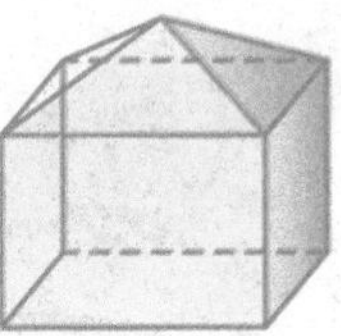

17.

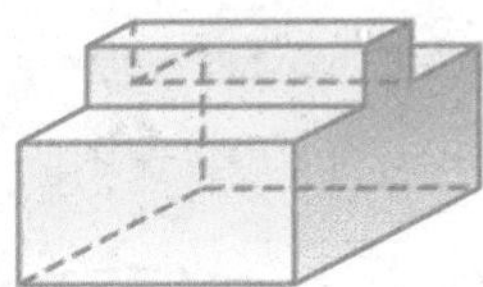

18. CCGPS **Find the Error** Raul drew the side, top, and front view of the figure shown at the right. Find his mistake and correct it.

side top front

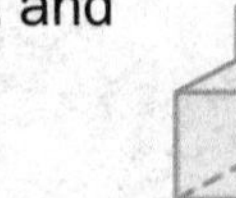

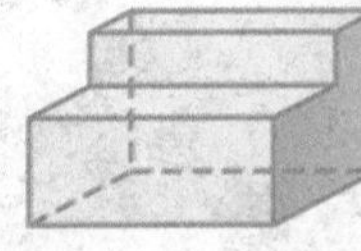

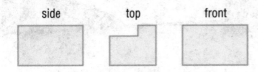

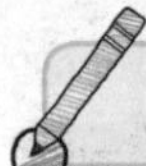

Georgia Test Practice

19. The top, side, and front view of a figure made of cubes are shown.

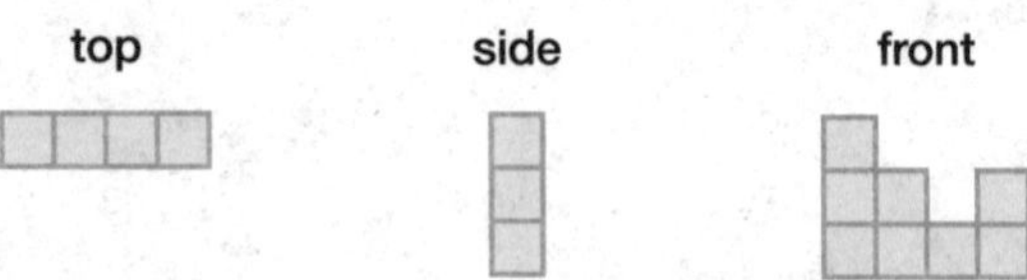

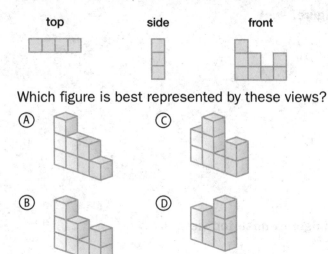

Which figure is best represented by these views?

Ⓐ 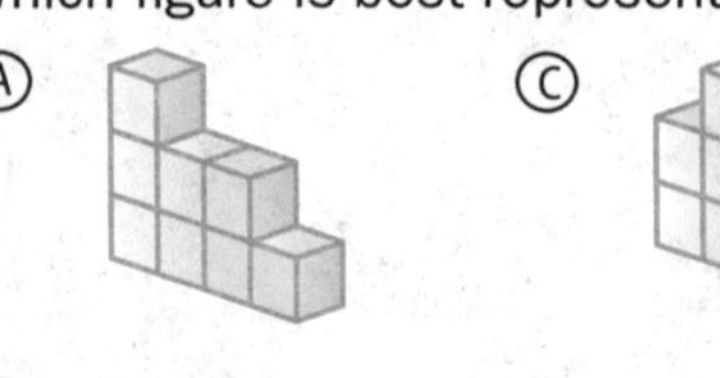

Ⓑ 

Ⓒ

Ⓓ 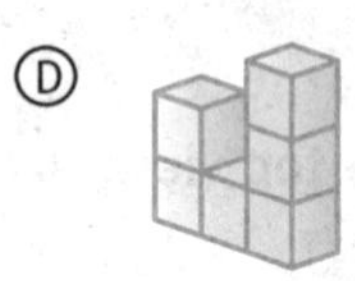

CCGPS Common Core Review

20. CCGPS **Model with Mathematics** Refer to the graphic novel frame at the beginning of the chapter. The scale on the map shows that 1 centimeter is equal to 75 yards. If the red line represents the path they took, how far have Raul, Caitlyn, and Jamar traveled since they left the lake? The red line is 17 centimeters long. MCC7.G.1

Watch
Replay it online!
Wow! We are finally here. How far do you think we traveled since we left the lake?
Our map has shown to be very handy. Review the map at the start of the chapter one more time.

Lesson 5

Cross Sections

What You'll Learn

Scan the lesson. Write the definitions of polyhedron and face.

- polyhedron ______________________________
- face ______________________________

Essential Question

HOW does geometry help us describe real-world objects?

Vocabulary

prism
bases
pyramid
plane
coplanar
parallel
polyhedron
edge
face
vertex
diagonal
cylinder
cone
cross section

Common Core State Standards

Content Standards
7.G.3

Mathematical Practices
1, 3, 4

Vocabulary Start-Up

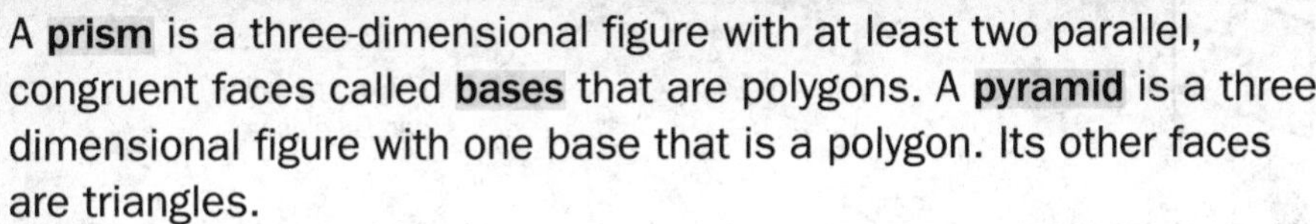

A **prism** is a three-dimensional figure with at least two parallel, congruent faces called **bases** that are polygons. A **pyramid** is a three-dimensional figure with one base that is a polygon. Its other faces are triangles.

Write *prism* or *pyramid* on the line below each figure.

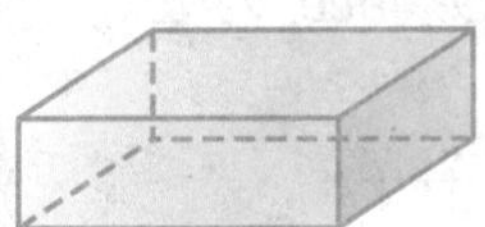

____

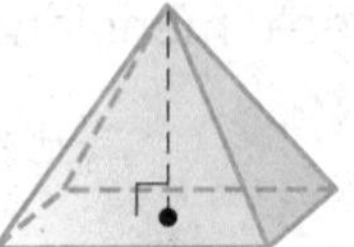

____

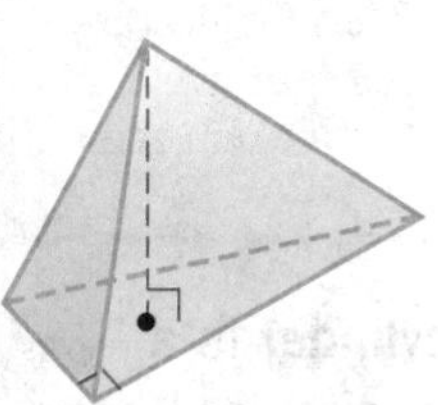

____

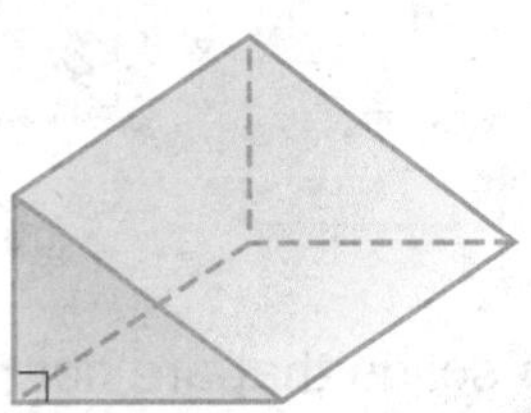

____

Real-World Link

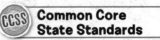

The Rock and Roll Hall of Fame is shown at the right. Is the shape of the building a *prism* or *pyramid*? Explain.

____

____

Work Zone

Identify Three-Dimensional Figures

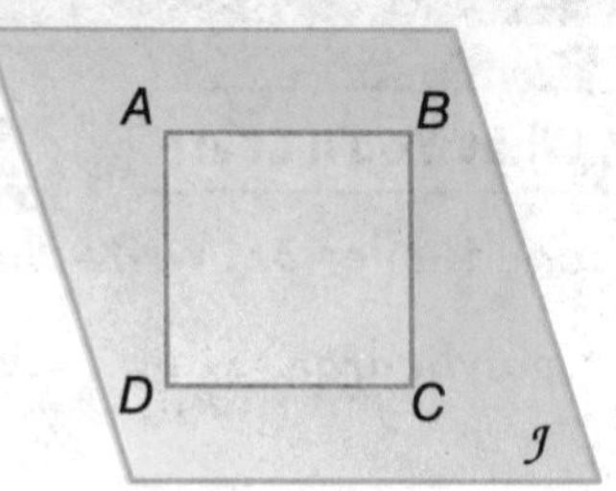
A
B
D
C
J

A **plane** is a flat surface that goes on forever in all directions. The figure at the right shows rectangle *ABCD*. Line segments *AB* and *DC* are **coplanar** because they lie in the same plane. They are also **parallel** because they will never intersect, no matter how far they are extended.

Just as two lines in a plane can intersect or be parallel, there are different ways that planes may be related in space.

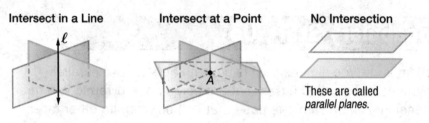

Intersect in a Line | **Intersect at a Point** | **No Intersection**

ℓ

A

These are called *parallel planes*.

Intersecting planes can form three-dimensional figures. A **polyhedron** is a three-dimensional figure with flat surfaces that are polygons. Prisms and pyramids are both polyhedrons. Some terms associated with three-dimensional figures are *edge, face, vertex*, and *diagonal*.

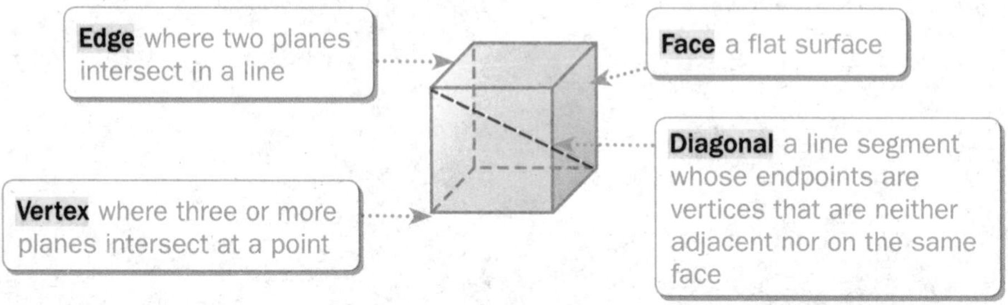
Edge where two planes intersect in a line
Face a flat surface
Diagonal a line segment whose endpoints are vertices that are neither adjacent nor on the same face
Vertex where three or more planes intersect at a point

There are also solids that are not polyhedrons. A **cylinder** is a three-dimensional figure with two parallel congruent circular bases connected by a curved surface. A **cone** has one circular base connected by a curved side to a single vertex.

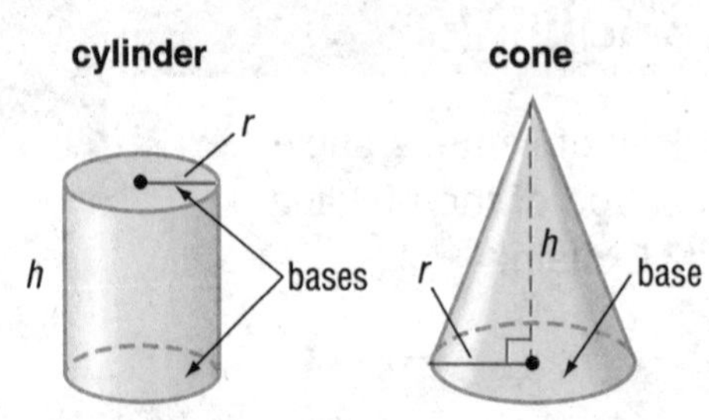
cylinder
cone
r
h
bases
r
h
base

Polygons

The table below lists some common names of polygons.

Sides	Name
5	pentagon
6	hexagon
7	heptagon
8	octagon
9	nonagon
10	decagon

Examples

Identify the figure. Name the bases, faces, edges, and vertices.

1.

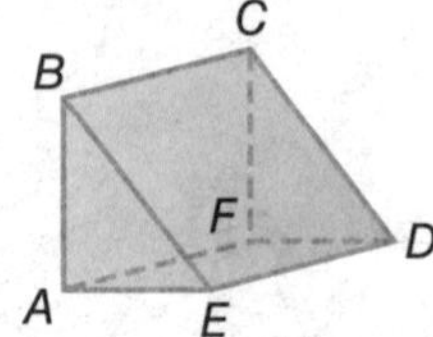

The figure has two parallel congruent bases that are triangles, so it is a triangular prism.

bases: *ABE, FCD*

faces: *ABE, FCD, BCDE, FAED, ABCF*

edges: $\overline{AB}$, $\overline{BE}$, $\overline{EA}$, $\overline{FC}$, $\overline{CD}$, $\overline{DF}$, $\overline{BC}$, $\overline{ED}$, $\overline{AF}$

vertices: *A, B, C, D, E, F*

2.

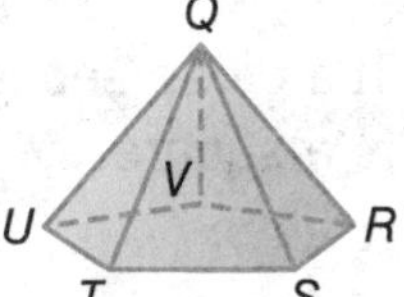

The figure has one base that is a pentagon, so it is a pentagonal pyramid.

base: *RSTUV*

faces: *RSTUV, QVR, QRS, QST, QTU, QUV*

edges: $\overline{QR}$, $\overline{QS}$, $\overline{QT}$, $\overline{QU}$, $\overline{QV}$, $\overline{VR}$, $\overline{RS}$, $\overline{ST}$, $\overline{TU}$, $\overline{UV}$

vertices: *Q, R, S, T, U, V*

3.

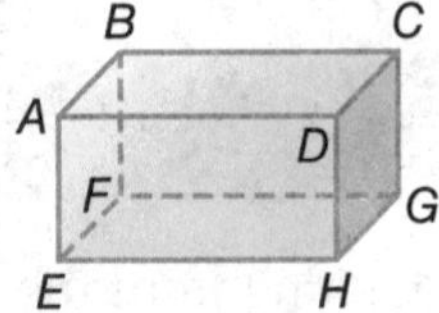

The figure has rectangular bases that are parallel and congruent, so it is a rectangular prism.

bases: *ABCD* and *EFGH*, *ABFE* and *DCGH*, *ADHE* and *BCGF*

faces: *ABCD, EFGH, ABFE, DCGH, ADHE, BCGF*

edges: $\overline{AB}$, $\overline{BC}$, $\overline{CD}$, $\overline{AD}$, $\overline{EF}$, $\overline{FG}$, $\overline{GH}$, $\overline{EH}$, $\overline{AE}$, $\overline{BF}$, $\overline{CG}$, $\overline{DH}$

vertices: *A, B, C, D, E, F, G, H*

Common Error

In the drawing of a rectangular prism, the bases do not have to be on the top and bottom. Any two parallel rectangles are bases. In a triangular pyramid, any face is a base.

Got It? Do this problem to find out.

a.

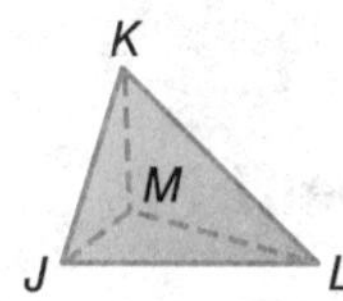

Figure name: ______________

base: ______________

faces: ______________

edges: ______________

vertices: ______________

Identify Cross Sections

The intersection of a solid and a plane is called a **cross section** of the solid.

Example

4. **Describe the shape resulting from a vertical, angled, and horizontal cross section of a square pyramid.**

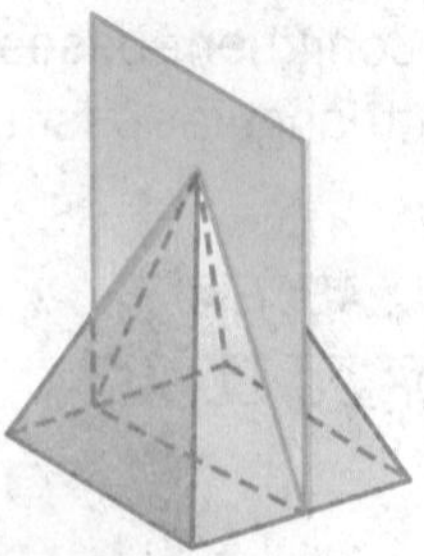

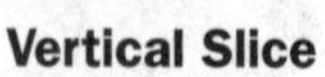

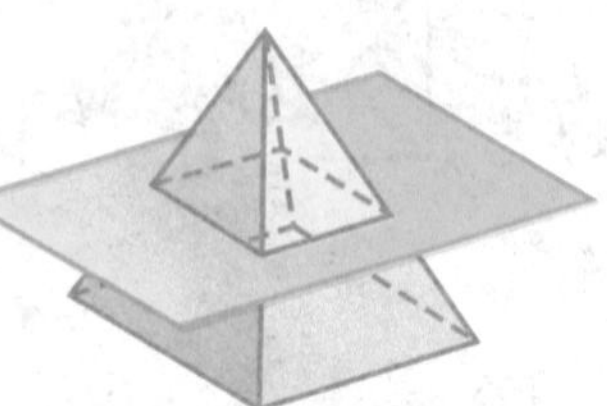

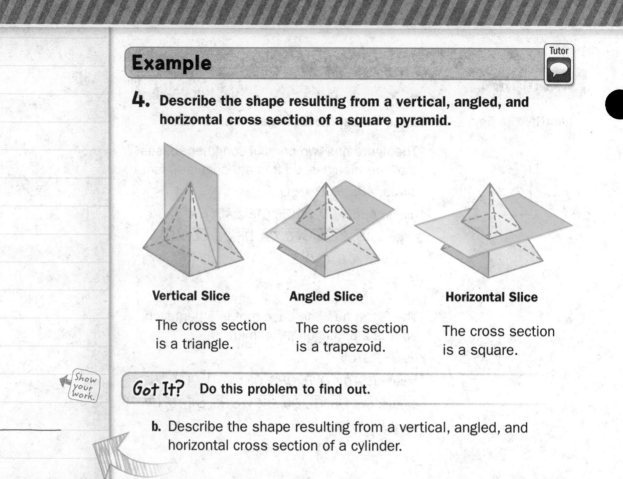

Vertical Slice

The cross section is a triangle.

Angled Slice

The cross section is a trapezoid.

Horizontal Slice

The cross section is a square.

Got It? **Do this problem to find out.**

b. ____________

b. Describe the shape resulting from a vertical, angled, and horizontal cross section of a cylinder.

Guided Practice

1. Identify the figure. Then name the bases, faces, edges, and vertices. (Examples 1–3)

Q R T U S V

Figure name: ____________

bases: ____________

faces: ____________

edges: ____________

vertices: ____________

2. Describe the shape resulting from the cross section shown. (Example 4) ____________

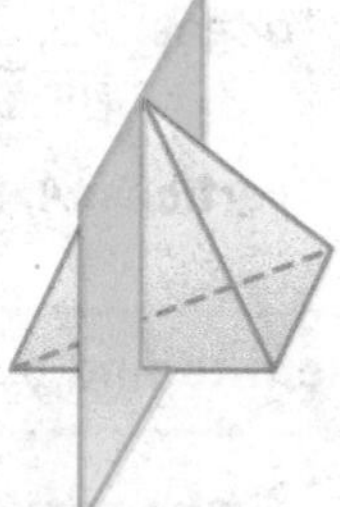

3. **Building on the Essential Question** How can knowing the shape of the base of a three-dimensional figure help you name the figure?

____

____

____

Rate Yourself!

Are you ready to move on? Shade the section that applies.

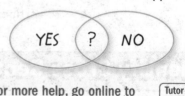

YES ? NO

For more help, go online to access a Personal Tutor.

Independent Practice

Go online for Step-by-Step Solutions

Identify each figure. Then name the bases, faces, edges, and vertices. (Examples 1–3)

1. 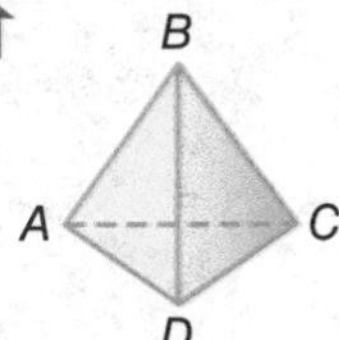

Figure name: ______

bases: ______

faces: ______

edges: ______

vertices: ______

2. 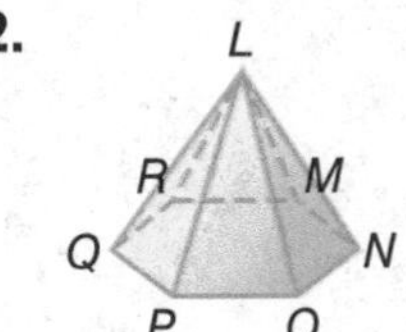

Figure name: ______

bases: ______

faces: ______

edges: ______

vertices: ______

Describe the shape resulting from each cross section. (Example 4)

3. 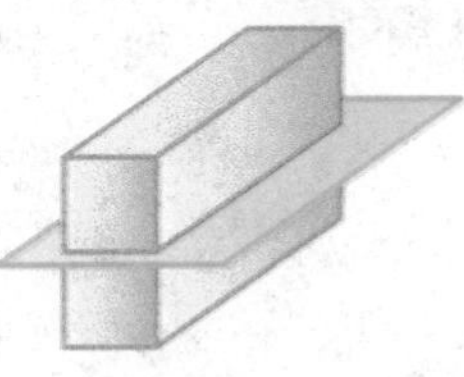

______

4. 

______

5. 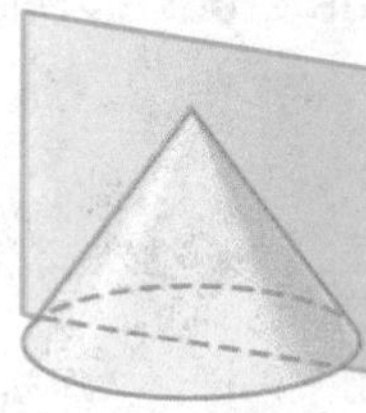

______

6. A basketball is shaped like a *sphere*.

   a. Draw a basketball with a vertical, angled, and horizontal slice.

   b. Describe the cross section made by each slice.

   ______

   c. Is the basketball a polyhedron? Explain.

   ______

7. **Use a Counterexample** State whether the following conjecture is *true* or *false*. If *false*, provide a counterexample.

Two planes in three-dimensional space can intersect at one point.

H.O.T. Problems Higher Order Thinking

8. **Model with Mathematics** Draw the cross sections of a polyhedron, cylinder, or cone. Exchange papers with another student. Identify the three-dimensional figures represented by the cross sections.

Persevere with Problems Determine whether each statement is *always*, *sometimes*, or *never* true. Explain your reasoning.

9. A prism has 2 bases and 4 faces.

10. A pyramid has parallel faces.

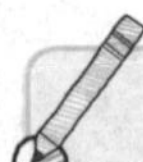

Georgia Test Practice

11. Benita received the gift box shown.

Which of the following is *not* a possible cross section of the triangular prism?

Ⓐ 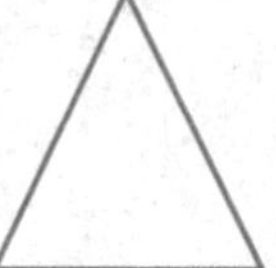

Ⓒ 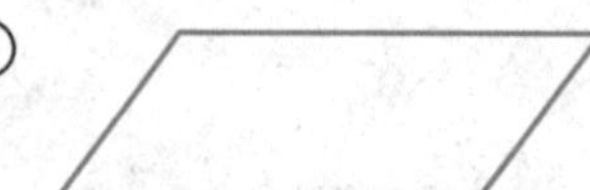

Ⓑ 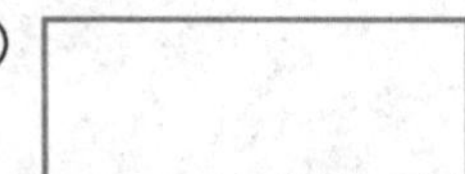

Ⓓ 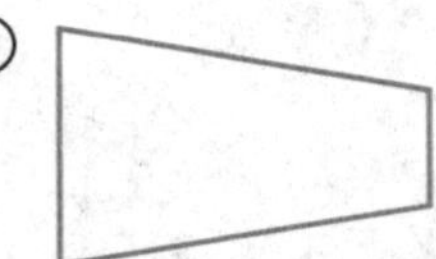

Extra Practice

Identify each figure. Then name the bases, faces, edges, and vertices.

12.

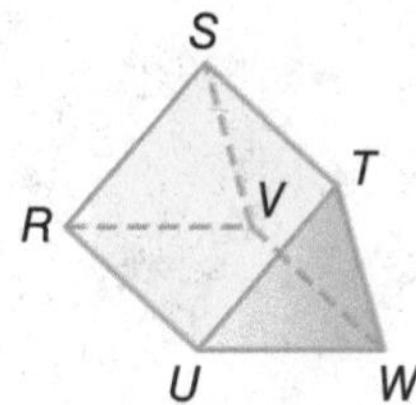

Figure name: triangular prism

Homework Help

bases: RSV and UTW

faces: RSV, UTW, RSTU, SVWT, VRUW

edges: $\overline{RS}$, $\overline{SV}$, $\overline{RV}$, $\overline{UT}$, $\overline{TW}$, $\overline{UW}$, $\overline{RU}$, $\overline{VW}$, $\overline{ST}$

vertices: R, S, T, U, V, W

13.

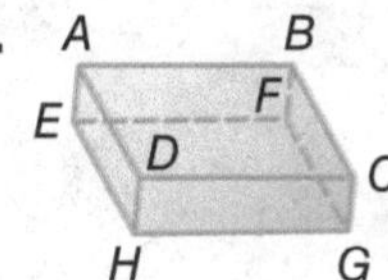

Figure name: ______

bases: ______

faces: ______

edges: ______

vertices: ______

Describe the shape resulting from each cross section. (Example 4)

14.

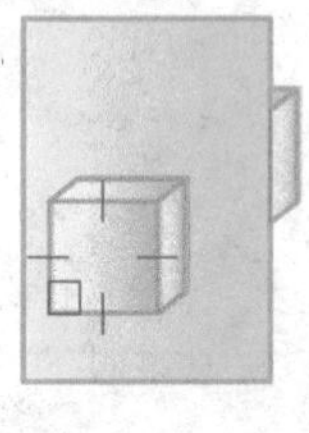

______

15.

______

16.

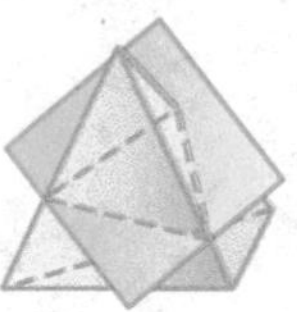

______

17. CCGPS **Find the Error** Hannah is identifying the figure below. Find her mistake and correct it.

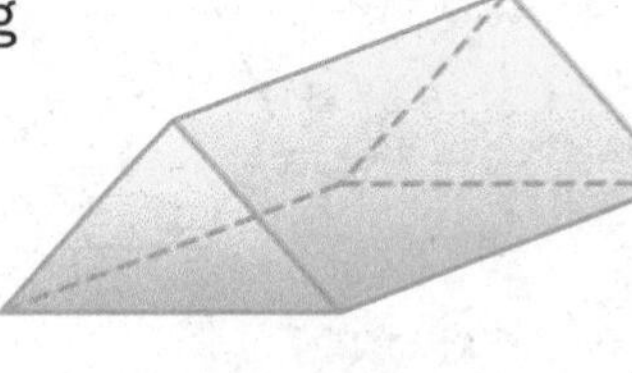

The figure has a triangular base. It is a triangular pyramid.

Georgia Test Practice

18. Which of the following describes the shape resulting from the cross section shown?

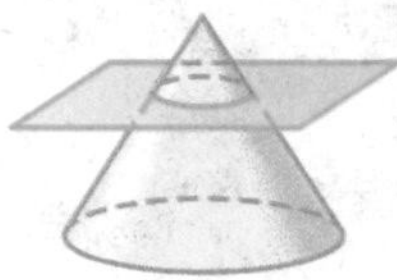

Ⓐ triangle
Ⓑ oval
Ⓒ circle
Ⓓ rectangle

19. Which of the following is *not* an example of a polyhedron?

Ⓕ cylinder
Ⓖ rectangular prism
Ⓗ octagonal pyramid
Ⓘ triangular prism

20. The figure below is a square pyramid.

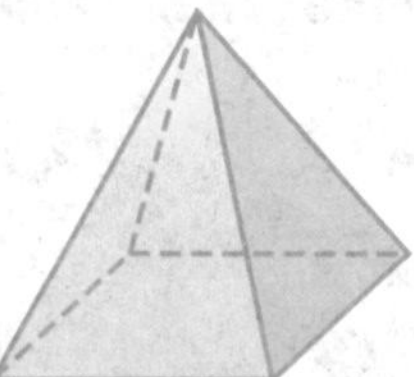

Which of the following is *not* a cross section from the square pyramid?

Ⓐ 

Ⓑ 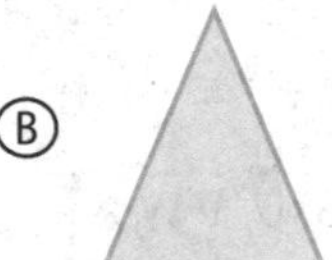

Ⓒ 

Ⓓ 

Common Core Review

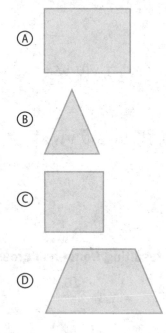

Name each polygon. MCC5.G.3

21. 

22. 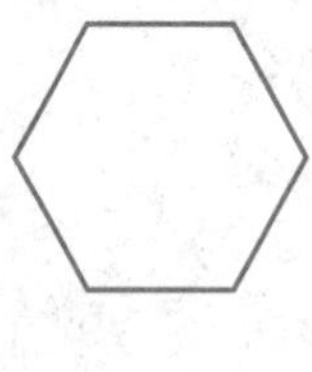

23. 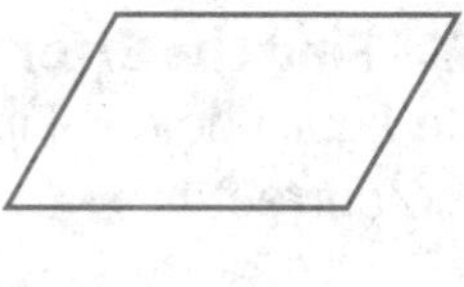

24. Find the measure of the missing angle of the polygon. MCC5.G.3

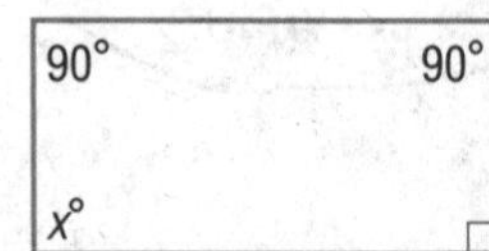

21ST CENTURY CAREER in Design Engineering

Roller Coaster Designer

If you have a passion for amusement parks, a great imagination, and enjoy building things, you might want to consider a career in roller coaster design. Roller coaster designers combine creativity, engineering, mathematics, and physics to develop rides that are both exciting and safe. In order to analyze data and make precise calculations, a roller coaster designer must have a solid background in high school math and science.

Explore college and careers at ccr.mcgraw-hill.com

Is This the Career for You?

Are you interested in a career as a roller coaster designer? Take some of the following course in high school to get you started in the right direction.

- Algebra
- Calculus
- Geometry
- Physics
- Trigonometry

Turn the page to find out how math relates to a career in Design Engineering.

A Thrilling Ride

Use the information in the table to solve each problem.

1. In a scale drawing of SheiKra, a designer uses a scale of 1 inch = 16 feet. What is the height of the roller coaster in the drawing? ______

2. On a model of Montu, the height of the loop is 13 inches. What is the scale? ______

3. In a scale drawing of Montu, the height of the roller coaster is 10 inches. What is the scale factor? ______

4. SheiKra has a hill that goes through a tunnel. On a model of the roller coaster, the hill is 23 inches tall and the scale is 1 inch = 6 feet. What is the actual height of the tunnel hill? ______

5. An engineer is building a model of SheiKra. She wants the model to be about 32 inches high. Choose an appropriate scale for the model. Then use it to find the loop height of the model. ______

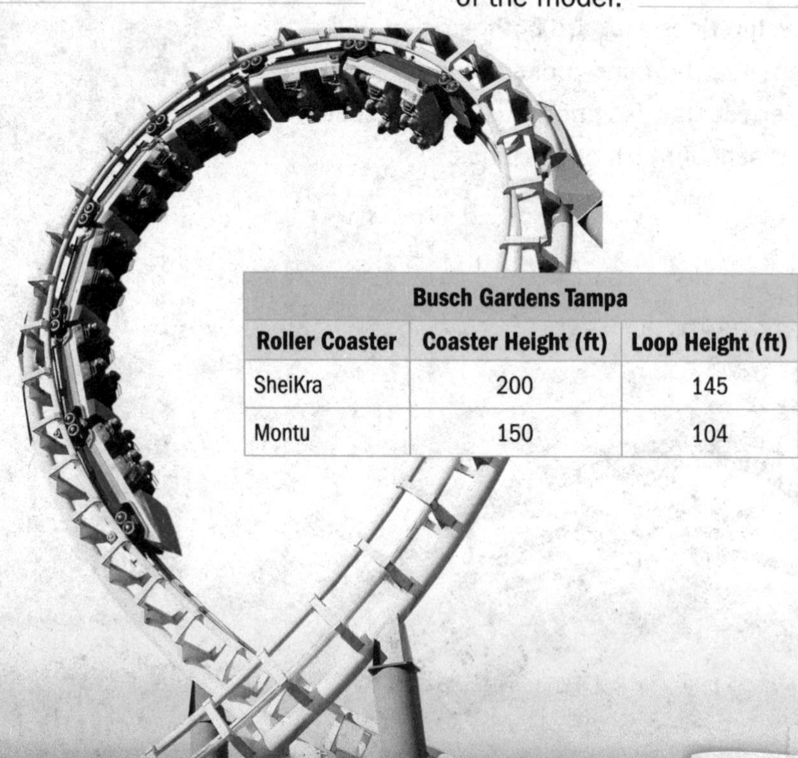

Busch Gardens Tampa		
Roller Coaster	**Coaster Height (ft)**	**Loop Height (ft)**
SheiKra	200	145
Montu	150	104

Career Project

It's time to update your career portfolio! Describe a roller coaster that you, as a roller coaster designer, would create. Include the height and angle of the tallest drop, the total length, maximum speed, number of loops and tunnels, and color scheme. Be sure to include the name of your roller coaster.

What problem-solving skills might you use as a roller coaster designer?

-
-
-
-
-

Chapter Review

Vocabulary Check

Complete the crossword puzzle using the vocabulary list at the beginning of the chapter.

Across

2. a three-dimensional figure with two parallel, congruent bases that are polygons
4. a triangle with an angle greater than 90 and less than 180 degrees
7. a three-dimensional figure with two parallel congruent circular bases connected by a curved surface
10. a triangle with three congruent sides
11. segments with the same length
13. two angles with a sum of 90 degrees

Down

1. angles that share a common vertex, a common side, and do not overlap
3. two angles with a sum of 180 degrees
5. a figure with three sides and three angles
6. opposite angles that are formed by the intersection of two lines
7. a three-dimensional figure with one circular base connected by a curved side to a single vertex
8. an angle less than 90 degrees
9. where two rays meet to form an angle
12. a 90 degree angle

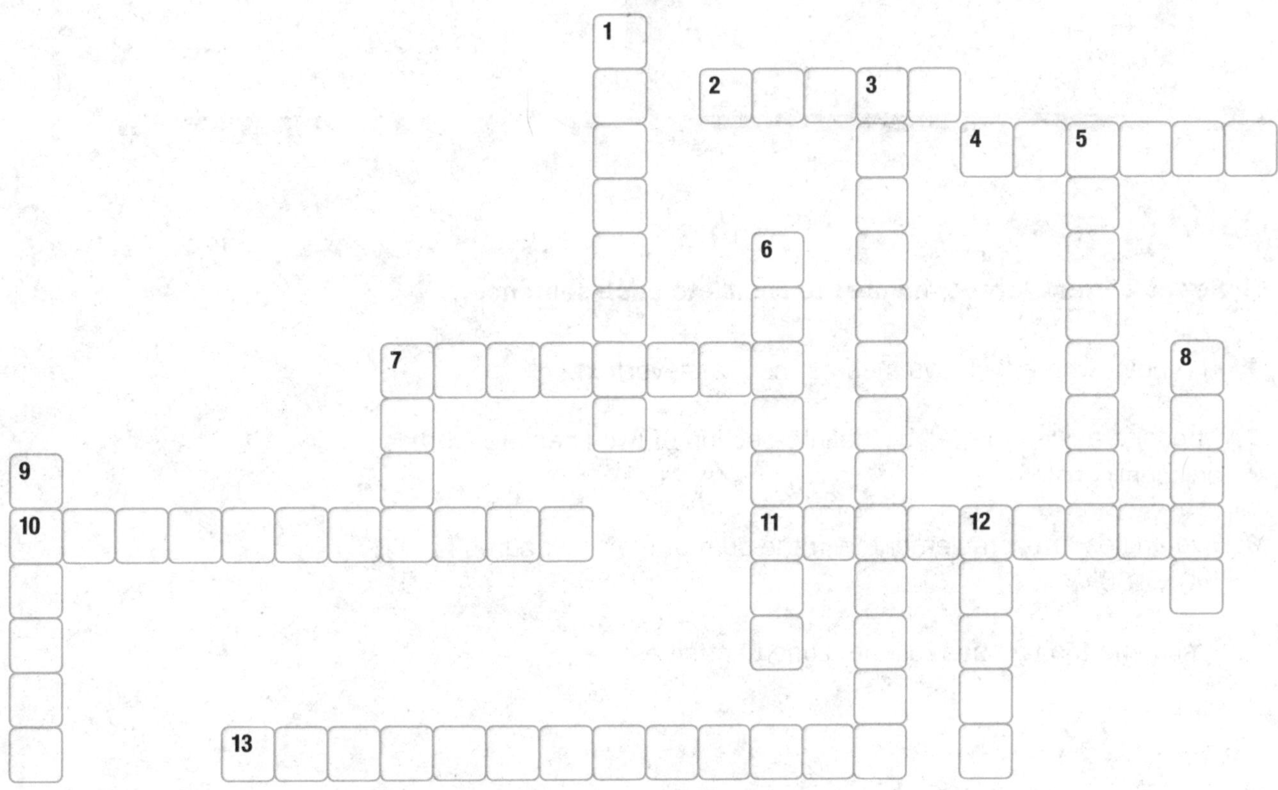

Key Concept Check

Use Your FOLDABLES

Use your Foldable to help review the chapter.

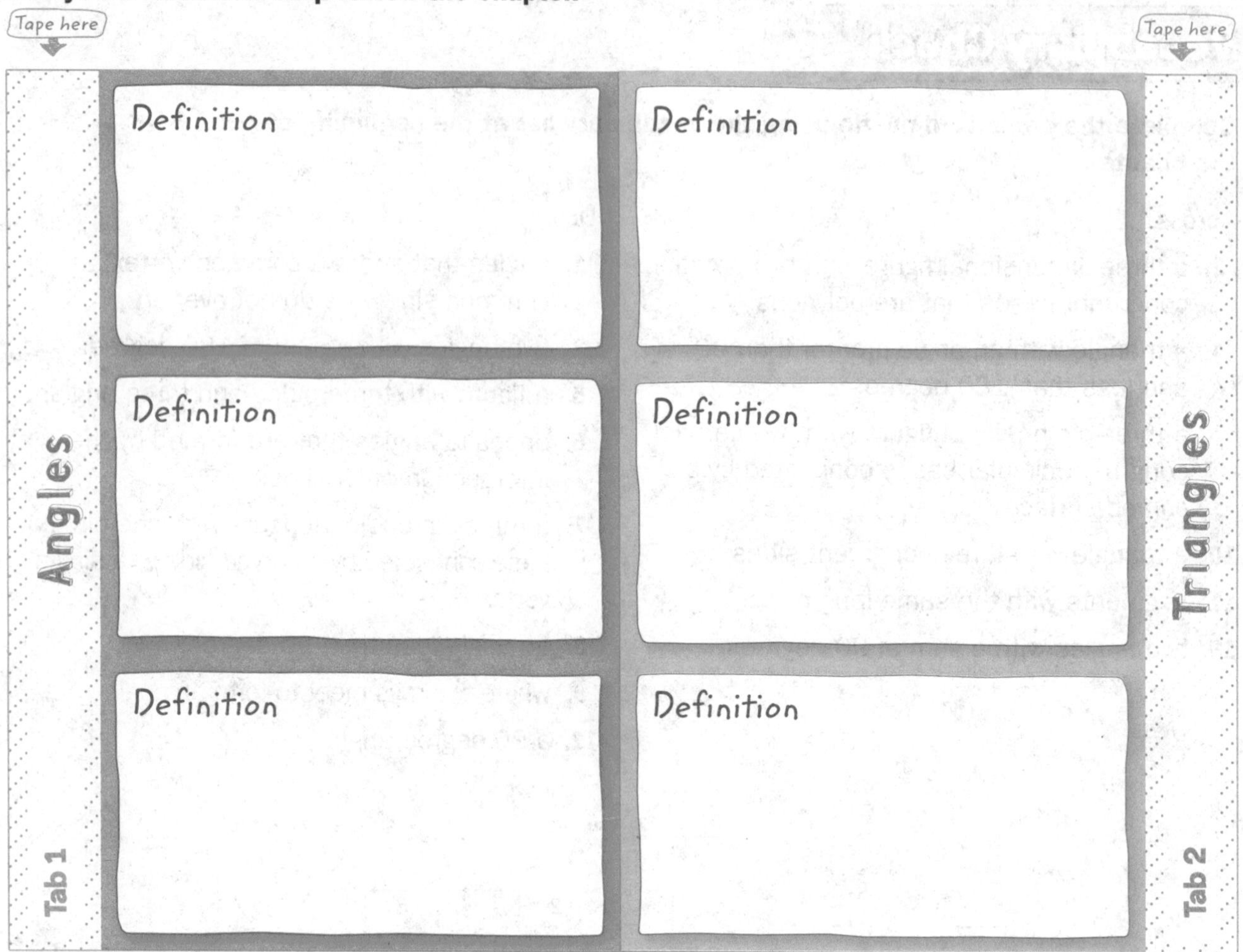

Got it?

Circle the correct term or number to complete each sentence.

1. The point where two rays meet is the (base, vertex).
2. Opposite angles formed by the intersection of two lines are (vertical, adjacent) angles.
3. Two angles are complementary if the sum of their measures is (90°, 180°).
4. A scalene triangle has (all, no) congruent sides.

Problem Solving

1. On a trip, Juan bought the kite shown at the right. Identify a pair of vertical angles and adjacent angles. (Lesson 1) ______

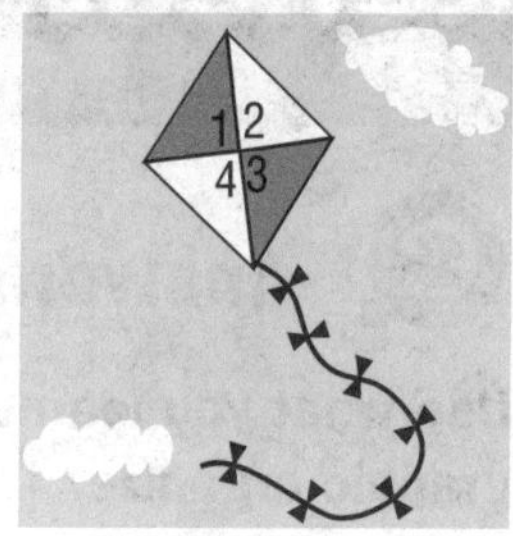

2. Angle Y and $\angle Z$ are complementary, and the measure of $\angle Z$ is 35°. What is the measure of $\angle Y$? (Lesson 2) ______

3. Maddie entered her design for an environmental club flag in the school contest. What is the value of x in her flag? (Lesson 3) ______

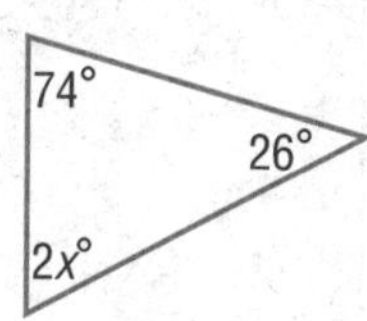

4. Lena is decorating the figure at the right. She is covering the faces with fabric and attaching ribbon to its edges. Identify the figure. Then name the faces and edges. (Lesson 5)

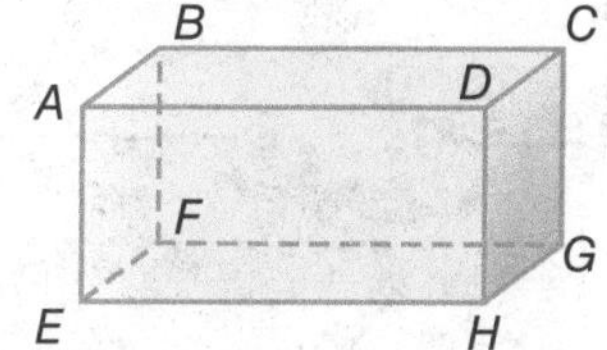

figure name: ______

faces: ______

edges: ______

5. CCGPS Model with Mathematics Draw a top, a side, and a front view of a rectangular table. (Lesson 4)

Reflect

Answering the Essential Question

Use what you learned about geometric figures to complete the graphic organizer.

How do polygons help us describe real-world objects?

Essential Question

HOW does geometry help us describe real-world objects?

How do polyhedrons help us describe real-world objects?

Answer the Essential Question. HOW does geometry help us describe real-world objects?

Chapter 9

Measure Figures

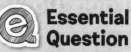

Essential Question

How do measurements help you describe real-world objects?

Common Core GPS

Content Standards
MCC7.G.4, MCC7.G.6

Mathematical Practices
1, 2, 3, 4, 5, 6, 8

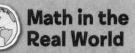

Math in the Real World

Soccer is a sport that is played on a rectangular field. The dimensions of a regulation size soccer field are 100 yards long and 60 yards wide.

What is the area of the soccer field shown?

$A =$ ______ square yards

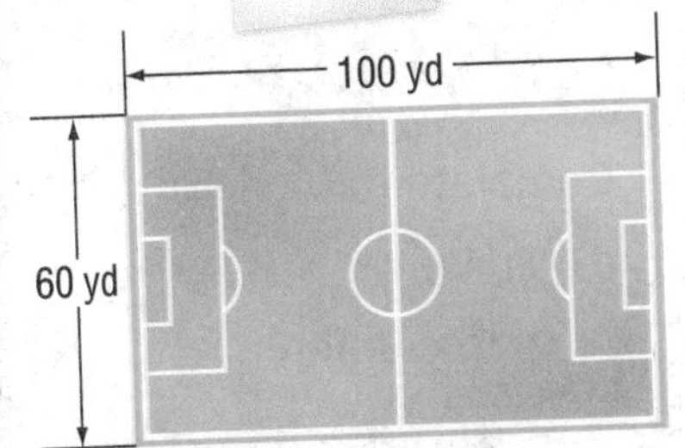

Cut out the correct Foldable from the FL pages in the back of this book.

Place your Foldable on the Key Concept page toward the end of this chapter.

Use the Foldable throughout this chapter to help you learn about measuring figures.

What Tools Do You Need?

Vocabulary

center	lateral face	semicircle
circle	lateral surface area	slant height
circumference	pi	surface area
composite figure	radius	volume
diameter	regular pyramid	

Study Skill: Studying Math

Power Notes *Power notes* are similar to lesson outlines, but they are simpler to organize. Power notes use the numbers 1, 2, 3, and so on. You can have more than one detail under each power. You can even add drawings or examples to your power notes.

Power 1: This is the main idea.
Power 2: This provides details about the main idea.
Power 3: This provides details about Power 2.
and so on...

Complete the following sample of power notes for this chapter.

1: Circles
2: Circumference
3: ______
3: ______
2: Area
3: ______

When Will You Use This?

Your Turn! **You will solve this problem in the chapter.**

Are You Ready?

Try the Quick Check below.
Or, take the Online Readiness Quiz.

Quick Review

Common Core Review MCC6.G.1

Example 1

Find the area of the rectangle.

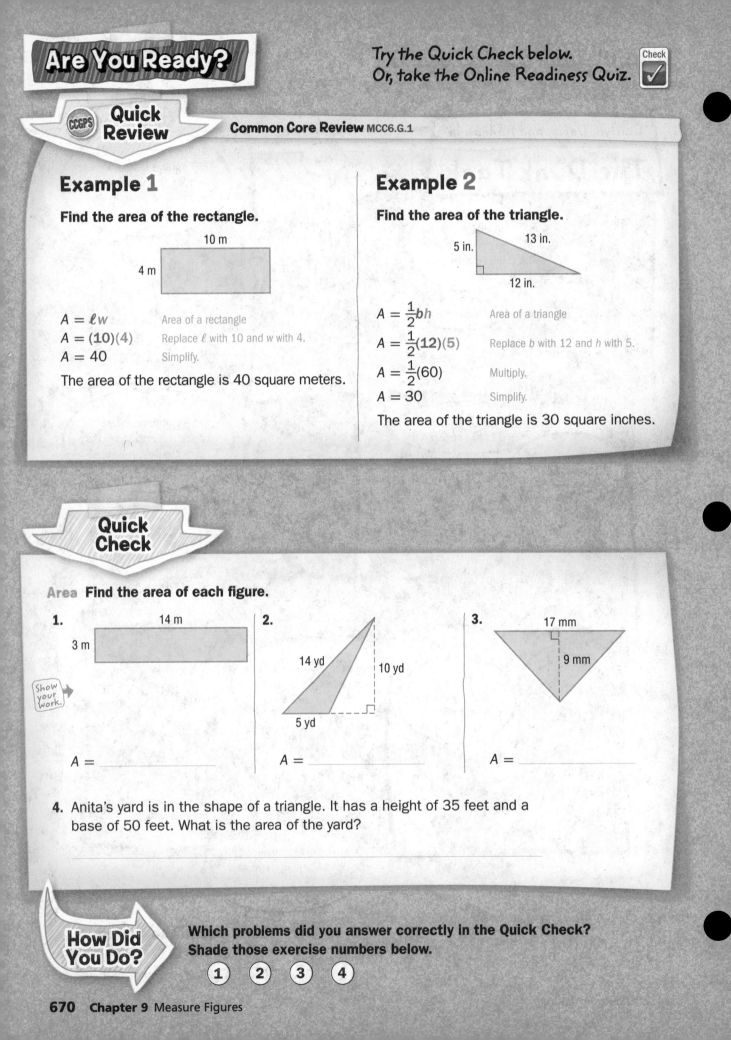

10 m

4 m

$A = \ell w$	Area of a rectangle
$A = (10)(4)$	Replace ℓ with 10 and w with 4.
$A = 40$	Simplify.

The area of the rectangle is 40 square meters.

Example 2

Find the area of the triangle.

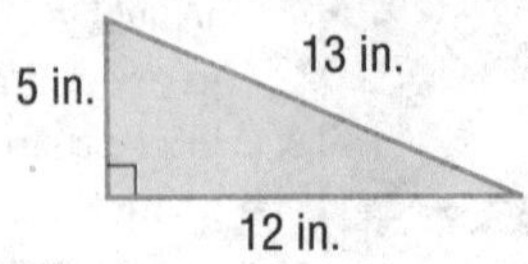

$A = \frac{1}{2}bh$	Area of a triangle
$A = \frac{1}{2}(12)(5)$	Replace b with 12 and h with 5.
$A = \frac{1}{2}(60)$	Multiply.
$A = 30$	Simplify.

The area of the triangle is 30 square inches.

Quick Check

Area **Find the area of each figure.**

1. 14 m, 3 m

$A =$ ______

2.

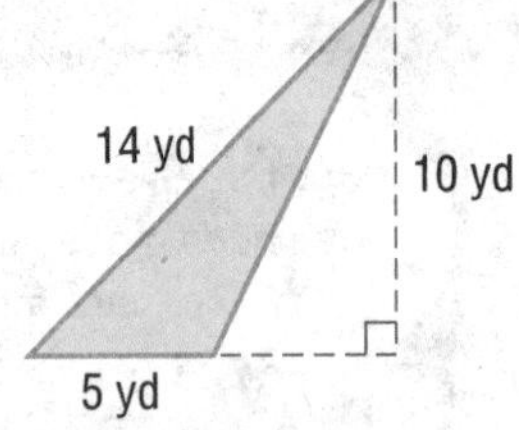

$A =$ ______

3.

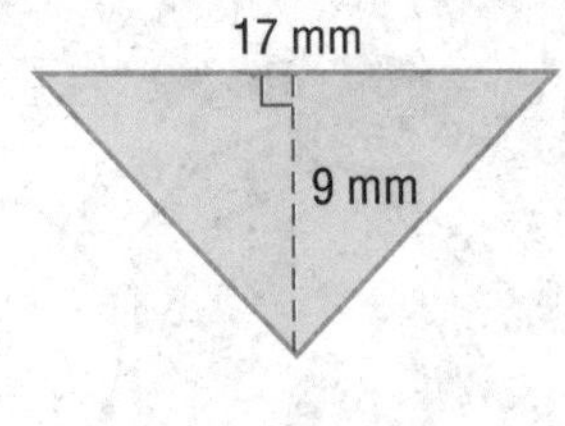

$A =$ ______

4. Anita's yard is in the shape of a triangle. It has a height of 35 feet and a base of 50 feet. What is the area of the yard?

______

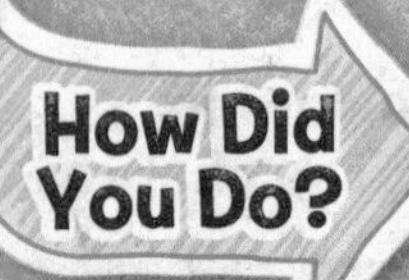

Which problems did you answer correctly in the Quick Check? Shade those exercise numbers below.

1 2 3 4

Inquiry Lab

Circumference

HOW is the circumference of a circle related to its diameter?

Content Standards
MCC7.G.4

Mathematical Practices
1, 3, 6

The distance around a flying disc, or its *circumference*, is 37.7 centimeters. The distance across the disc through its center, or its *diameter*, is 12 centimeters. How is the circumference of a circular object, such as a flying disc, related to its diameter?

What do you know? ______________________________

____

What do you need to find? ______________________________

____

Investigation

Step 1 Cut a piece of string the length of the circumference of a circular object such as a jar lid. Use a centimeter ruler to measure the length of the string to the nearest tenth of a centimeter. Record this measurement in the table below.

Object	Circumference (C)	Diameter (d)	$\frac{C}{d}$
Disc	37.7 cm	12 cm	

Step 2 Measure the diameter of the lid. Record this measurement in the table.

Step 3 Use a calculator to find the ratio of the circumference of the Frisbee to its diameter. Then use a calculator to find the ratio of the circumference to the diameter of the circular object you measured in Steps 1 and 2. Round answers to the nearest hundredth.

Step 4 Repeat Steps 1 through 4 for other circular objects.

Collaborate

Work with a partner to answer the following questions.

1. Refer to the table in the Investigation. Describe the ratio $\frac{C}{d}$ for the values you calculated. ______________________________

Make a Prediction **Measure the diameter of two different circular objects. Predict each circumference. Then check your predictions by measuring. Record your values in the table below.**

	Object	Diameter	Predicted Circumference	Measured Circumference
2.				
3.				

Analyze

Work with a partner to answer the following question.

4. **Reason Inductively** Look for a pattern in the measurements you recorded in both tables. Write a formula that relates the circumference C of a circle to its diameter d. ______________________________

5. **Be Precise** The *radius* of a circle is one half of its diameter. Write a formula that relates the circumference of a circle to its radius r. __________

Reflect

6. **Construct an Argument** In Exercise 4, you wrote a formula to represent the relationship between circumference and diameter. In your own words, what is the definition of a formula? ______________________________

7. **Inquiry** HOW is the circumference of a circle related to its diameter?

____

Circumference

What You'll Learn

Scan the lesson. List two headings you would use to make an outline of the lesson.

- ______________________________
- ______________________________

Essential Question

HOW do measurements help you describe real-world objects?

Vocabulary

circle
center
circumference
diameter
radius
pi π

Common Core GPS

Content Standards
MCC7.G.4

Mathematical Practices
1, 3, 4, 6, 8

Vocabulary Start-Up

A **circle** is the set of all points in a plane that are the same distance from a point, called the **center**. The **circumference** is the distance around a circle. The **diameter** is the distance across a circle through its center. The **radius** is the distance from the center to any point on the circle.

Fill in each box with one of the following terms: *center*, *diameter*, and *radius*.

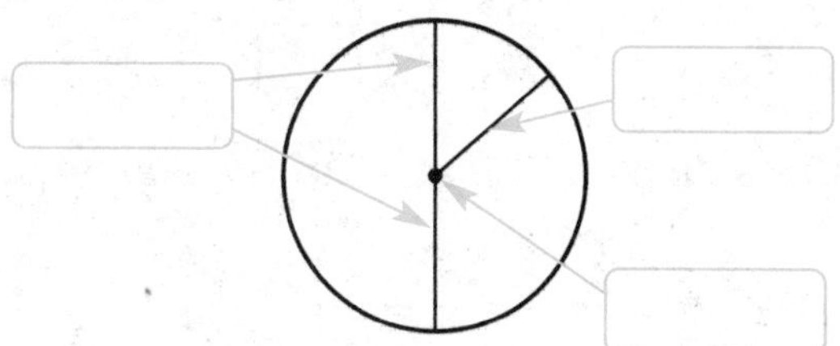

Real-World Link

1. The table shows the approximate measurements of two sizes of hula hoops.

Size	Radius (in.)	Diameter (in.)	Circumference (in.)
child	14	28	88
adult	20	40	126

a. Describe the relationship between the diameter and radius of each hula hoop. ______________________________

b. Describe the relationship between the circumference and diameter of each hula hoop. ______________________________

Key Concept

Radius and Diameter

Words The diameter d of a circle is twice its radius r. The radius r of a circle is half of its diameter d.

Symbols $d = 2r$ $r = \frac{d}{2}$

Work Zone

Examples

1. The diameter of a circle is 14 inches. Find the radius.

$r = \frac{d}{2}$ Radius of circle

$r = \frac{14}{2}$ Replace d with 14.

$r = 7$ Divide.

The radius is 7 inches.

STOP and Reflect

The diameter of a circle is 36 inches. Circle the radius.

72 in. 18 in.

2. The radius of a circle is 8 feet. Find the diameter.

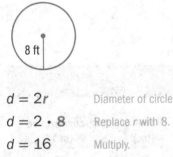

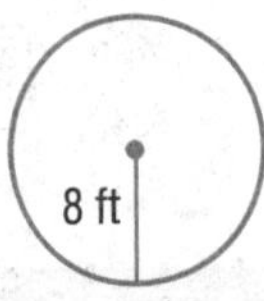

$d = 2r$ Diameter of circle

$d = 2 \cdot 8$ Replace r with 8.

$d = 16$ Multiply.

The diameter is 16 feet.

Got It? Do these problems to find out.

Find the radius or diameter of each circle with the given dimension.

a. $d = 23$ cm **b.** $r = 3$ in.

c. $d = 16$ yd **d.** $r = 5.2$

Show your work.

a. ________

b. ________

c. ________

d. ________

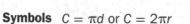

Circumference

Key Concept

Words The circumference of a circle is equal to π times its diameter or π times twice its radius.

Model

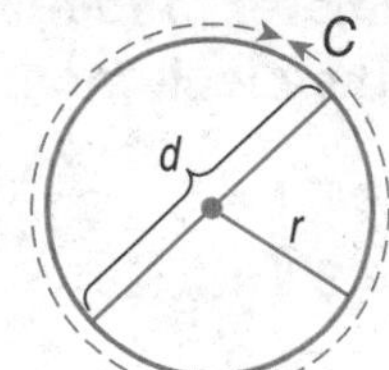

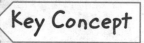

Symbols $C = \pi d$ or $C = 2\pi r$

In the Inquiry Lab, you learned that $\frac{C}{d} \approx 3$. The exact ratio is represented by the Greek letter **π (pi)**. The value of π is 3.1415926... . The decimal never ends, but it is often approximated as 3.14.

Another approximation for π is $\frac{22}{7}$. Use this value when the radius or diameter is a multiple of 7 or has a multiple of 7 in its numerator if the radius is a fraction.

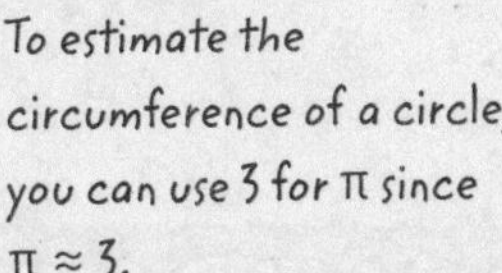

Estimation

To estimate the circumference of a circle, you can use 3 for π since $\pi \approx 3$.

Example

3. Find the circumference of a circle with a radius of 21 inches.

Since 21 is a multiple of 7, use $\frac{22}{7}$ for π.

$C = 2\pi r$	Circumference of a circle
$C \approx 2 \cdot \frac{22}{7} \cdot 21$	Replace π with $\frac{22}{7}$ and r with 21.
$C \approx 2 \cdot \frac{22}{\cancel{7}_1} \cdot \frac{\cancel{21}^3}{1}$	Divide by the GCF, 7.
$C \approx 132$	Simplify.

The circumference of the circle is about 132 inches.

Got It? Do these problems to find out.

Find the circumference of each circle. Use $\frac{22}{7}$ for π.

e.

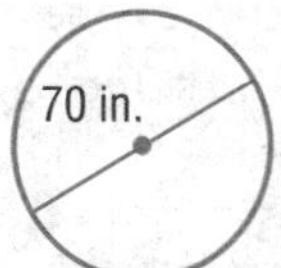

f.

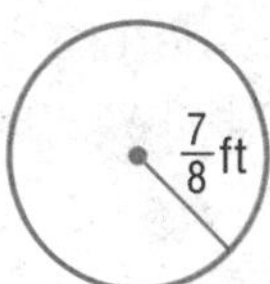

e. ________

f. ________

Example

4. Big Ben is a famous clock tower in London, England. The diameter of the clock face is 23 feet. Find the circumference of the clock face. Round to the nearest tenth.

$C = \pi d$	Circumference of a circle
$C \approx \mathbf{3.14}(23)$	Replace π with 3.14 and d with 23.
$C \approx 72.2$	Multiply.

So, the distance around the clock is about 72.2 feet.

Got It? Do this problem to find out.

Show your work.

g. A circular fence is being placed to surround a tree. The diameter of the fence is 4 feet. How much fencing is used? Use 3.14 for π. Round to the nearest tenth if necessary.

g. ________

Guided Practice

Find the radius or diameter of each circle with the given dimension. (Examples 1 and 2)

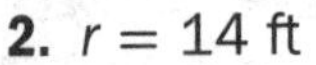

Show your work.

1. $d = 3$ m ______

2. $r = 14$ ft ______

3. $d = 20$ in. ______

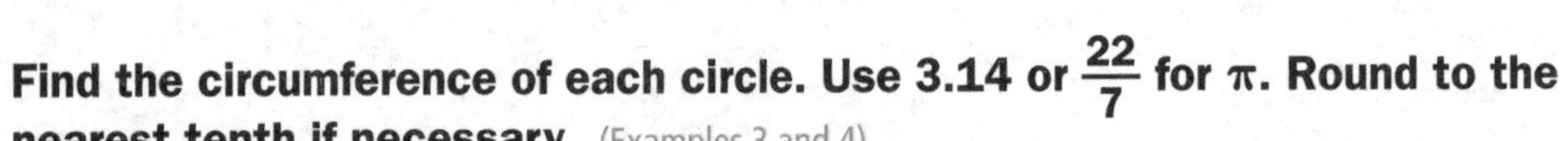

Find the circumference of each circle. Use 3.14 or $\frac{22}{7}$ for π. Round to the nearest tenth if necessary. (Examples 3 and 4)

4. 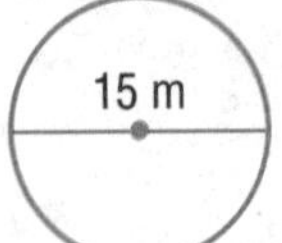

______

5. 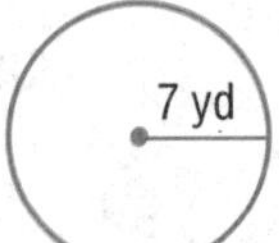

______

6. **Building on the Essential Question** A circle has a circumference of about 16.3 meters and a diameter of about 5.2 meters. What is the relationship between the circumference and diameter of this circle?

Rate Yourself!

How confident are you about finding the circumference? Check the box that applies.

For more help, go online to access a Personal Tutor.

Name ______________________ My Homework ______________________

Independent Practice

Go online for Step-by-Step Solutions

Find the radius or diameter of each circle with the given dimensions. (Examples 1 and 2)

1. $d = 5$ mm ________

2. $d = 24$ ft ________

3. $r = 17$ cm ________

Find the circumference of each circle. Use 3.14 or $\frac{22}{7}$ for π. Round to the nearest tenth if necessary. (Example 3)

4. 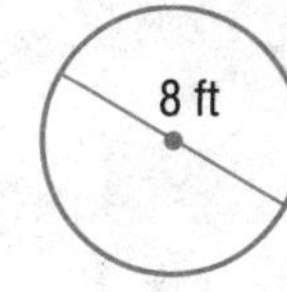

5. 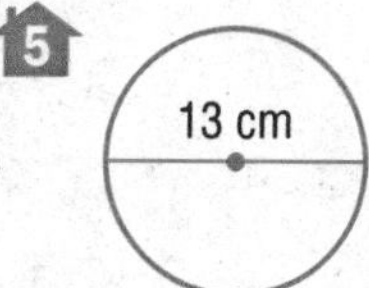

6. 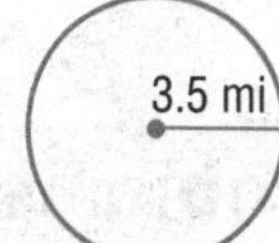

7. The largest tree in the world by volume is in Sequoia National Park. The diameter at the base is 36 feet. If a person with outstretched arms can reach 6 feet, how many people would it take to reach around the base of the tree? (Example 4)

8. The Belknap shield volcano is located in the Cascade Range in Oregon. The volcano is circular and has a diameter of 5 miles. What is the circumference of this volcano. Round your answer to the nearest tenth? (Example 4)

9. CCGPS **Be Precise** Refer to the circle at the right.

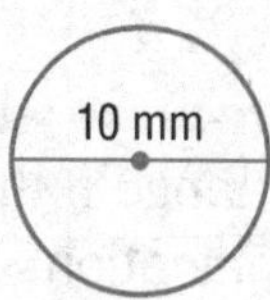

a. Find the circumference of the circle. Use 3 as the estimate of π.

b. Find the circumference of the circle using 3.14 for π.

c. Another estimate of π is 3.14159. Find the circumference using this estimate.

d. What do you notice about the estimate used for π and the circumference of the circle?

Copy and Solve **For Exercises 10-14, show your work on a separate piece of paper.**

Find the diameter given each circumference. Use 3.14 for π.

10. a satellite dish with a circumference of 957.7 meters

11. a basketball hoop with a circumference of 56.52 inches

12. a nickel with a circumference of about 65.94 millimeters

Find the distance around each figure. Use 3.14 for π.

13.

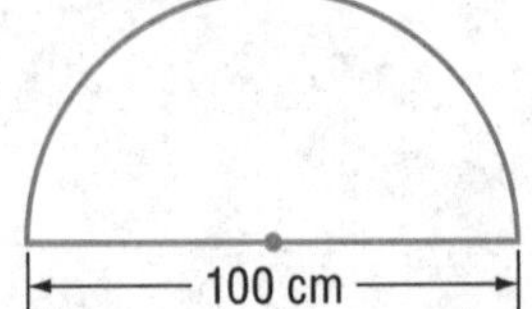

14.

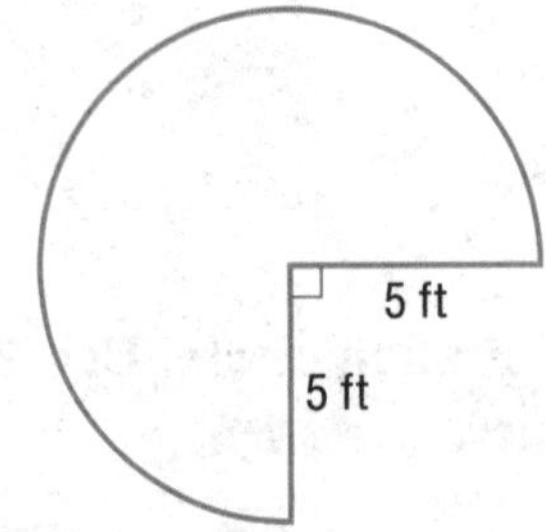

H.O.T. Problems Higher Order Thinking

15. CCGPS **Justify Conclusions** Determine if the circumference of a circle with a radius of 4 feet will be greater or less than 24 feet. Explain.

16. CCGPS **Model with Mathematics** Draw and label a circle that has a diameter more than 5 inches, but less than 10 inches. Estimate its circumference and then find its circumference using a calculator. Compare your results.

17. CCGPS **Persevere with Problems** Analyze how the circumference of a circle would change if the diameter was doubled. Provide an example to support your explanation.

Georgia Test Practice

18. An above-ground circular swimming pool is 18 feet in diameter. How does the pool's diameter d compare to its circumference C?

Ⓐ $d \approx \frac{1}{2}C$ Ⓑ $d \approx 2C$ Ⓒ $d \approx 3C$ Ⓓ $d \approx \frac{1}{3}C$

Name ______ My Homework ______

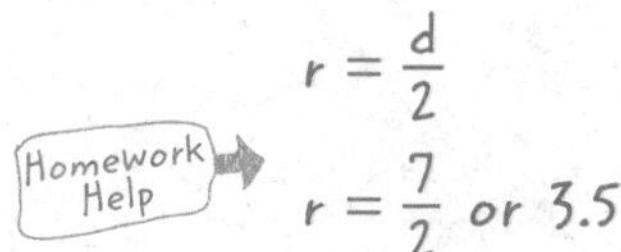

Extra Practice

Find the radius or diameter of each circle with the given dimensions.

19. $d = 7$ in. 3.5 in.

Homework Help

$r = \frac{d}{2}$

$r = \frac{7}{2}$ or 3.5

20. $d = 30$ m ______

21. $r = 36$ ft ______

Find the circumference of each circle. Use 3.14 or $\frac{22}{7}$ for π.

22.

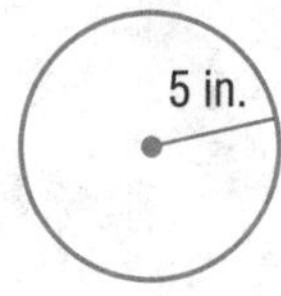

______

23.

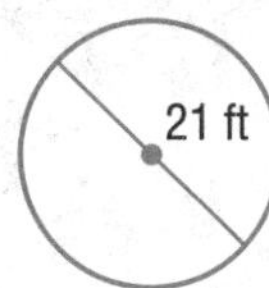

______

24.

______

25. a button with a radius of 21 millimeters

______

26. a dunk tank with a radius of 36 inches

______

27. The diameter of a music CD is 12 centimeters. Find the circumference of a CD to the nearest tenth. ______

28. At a local park, Sara can choose between two circular paths to walk. One path has a diameter of 120 yards, and the other has a radius of 45 yards. How much farther can Sara walk on the longer path than the shorter path if she walks around the path once? ______

29. CCGPS **Identify Repeated Reasoning** The diagram at the right is made up of circles with the same center. The innermost circle has a diameter of 1 unit. Each circle moving outward has a diameter one more unit than the previous. Without calculating, how much longer is the circumference of each circle? ______

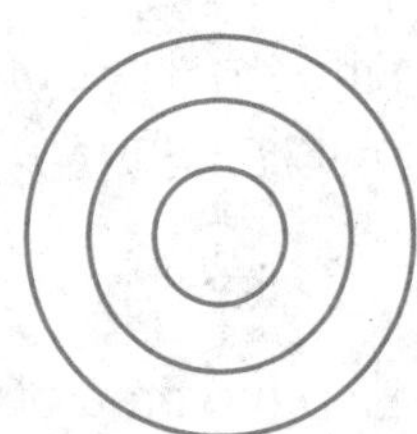

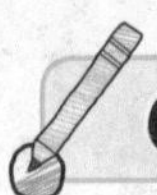

Georgia Test Practice

30. A circle with center at point O is shown below.

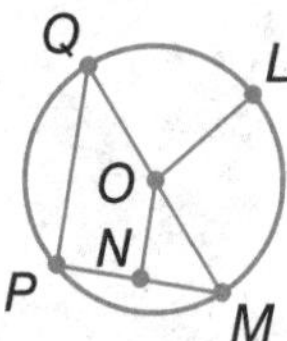

Which line segment is half the length of diameter QM?

Ⓐ Segment ON

Ⓑ Segment PM

Ⓒ Segment QP

Ⓓ Segment OL

31. A bicycle wheel has spokes for support. Each spoke extends from the center of the wheel to the rim. Which method can be used to find the circumference of the bicycle wheel?

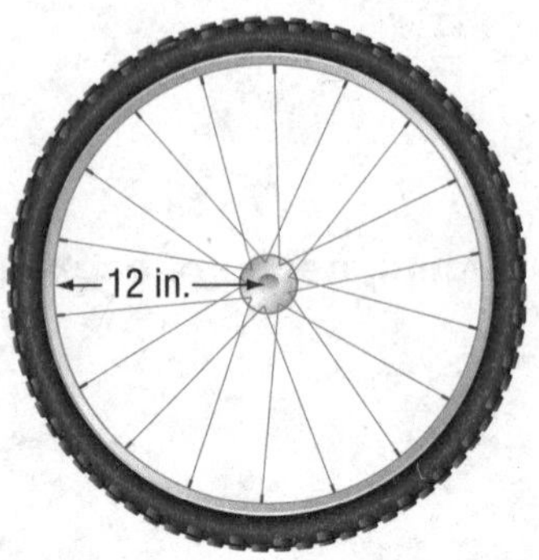

Ⓕ Multiply the diameter by π and by 2.

Ⓖ Divide the diameter by π.

Ⓗ Multiply the radius by π.

Ⓘ Multiply the radius by π and by 2.

32. **Short Response** The circumference of the Ferris wheel at the county fair is 78.5 feet. What is the diameter of the Ferris wheel, in feet?

Use 3.14 for π. ______

Common Core Review

Find the area of each trapezoid. MCC6.G.1

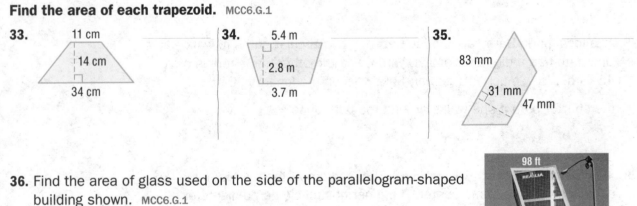

33. ______

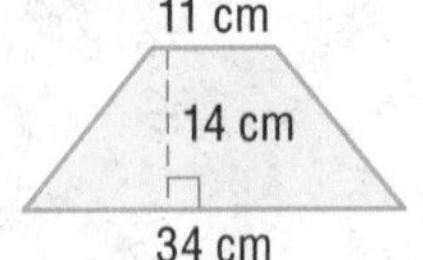

34. ______

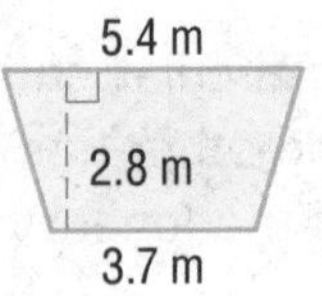

35. ______

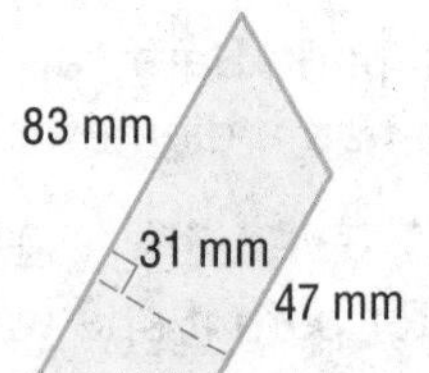

36. Find the area of glass used on the side of the parallelogram-shaped building shown. MCC6.G.1

______

37. Find the area of a triangle with a base of 25 inches and a height of 30 inches. MCC6.G.1

______

Murat Taner/Getty Images

Inquiry Lab
Area of Circles

HOW are the circumference and area of a circle related?

CCGPS Content Standards MCC7.G.4
Mathematical Practices 1, 3, 6

Message Centers Mrs. Allende wants to create a family message center on a wall in her house. There are 4 family members, including Mrs. Allende. She decides to paint 1 circle for each family member using magnetic paint. Each circle will have a 12-inch radius. How do you find the area of a circle?

Dad
Mom
Sis
Jr.
Soccer Practice 4PM

What do you know? ______________________________

What do you need to find? ______________________________

Investigation

Let's develop a formula for finding the area of a circle.

Step 1 Fold a paper plate in half four times to divide it into 16 equal sections.

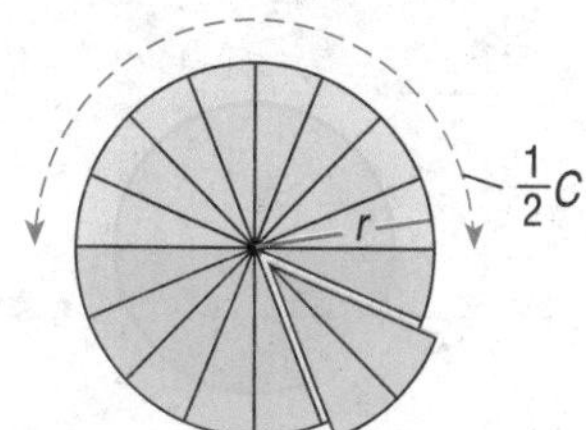

Step 2 Label the radius r as shown. Let C represent the circumference of the circle.

Step 3 Cut out each section. Reassemble the sections to form a parallelogram-shaped figure.

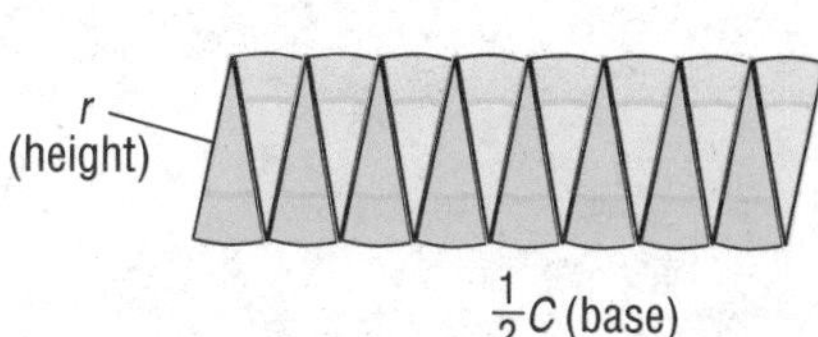

So, r represents the __________ of the parallelogram and $\frac{1}{2}C$ represents its __________.

Collaborate

Refer to the Investigation. Work with a partner to answer the following questions.

1. What expressions represent the measurements of the base and the height?

Show your work. Base: ________ Height: ________

2. CCGPS **Be Precise** Substitute these values into the formula for the area of a parallelogram, $A = b \times h$. Write the new formula. ________

3. Replace C with the expression for the circumference of a circle, $2\pi r$. Simplify the equation and describe what it represents.

____

Analyze

Work with a partner to complete the table for each circle with the given radius. Use 3.14 for π. Round to the nearest hundredth.

	Radius (in.)	Circumference (in.)	Area (in^2)
	1	6.28	3.14
4.	2		
5.	3		
6.	4		

7. CCGPS **Justify Conclusions** Is the circumference to radius relationship linear? Is the area to radius relationship linear? Explain.

____

____

____

Reflect

8. Inquiry HOW are the circumference and area of a circle related?

____

____

Lesson 2

Area of Circles

What You'll Learn

Predict two things you will learn about area.

-
-

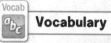

Essential Question

HOW do measurements help you describe real-world objects?

Vocabulary

semicircle

Common Core GPS

Content Standards
MCC7.G.4

Mathematical Practices
1, 3, 4

Real-World Link

Pets Adrianne bought an 8-foot leash for her dog.

1. Adrianne wants to find the distance the dog runs when it runs one circle with the leash fully extended. Should she calculate the circumference or area? Explain.

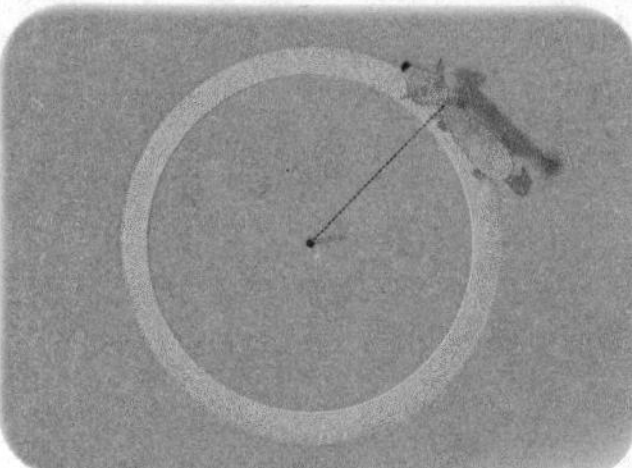

2. Suppose she wants to find the amount of running room the dog has with the leash fully extended. Should she calculate the circumference or area? Explain.

3. Describe a real-world situation that would involve finding the area of a circle.

4. Describe a real-world situation that would involve finding the circumference of a circle.

Key Concept

Find the Area of a Circle

Words The area A of a circle equals the product of π and the square of its radius r.

Model

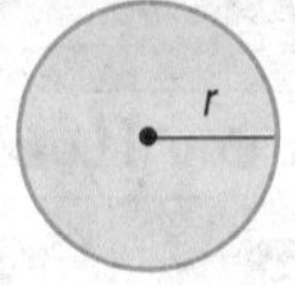

Symbols $A = \pi r^2$

Work Zone

Examples

1. Find the area of the circle. Use 3.14 for π.

2 in.

Estimate $3 \times 2 \times 2 = 12$

$A = \pi r^2$ Area of a circle

$A \approx 3.14 \cdot 2^2$ Replace r with 2.

$A \approx 3.14 \cdot 4$ $2^2 = 2 \cdot 2 = 4$

$A \approx 12.56$ Multiply.

Check for Reasonableness $12.56 \approx 12$ ✓

The area of the circle is approximately 12.56 square inches.

2. Find the area of a circle with a radius of 14 centimeters. Use $\frac{22}{7}$ for π.

Estimate $3 \times 14 \times 14 = 588$

$A = \pi r^2$ Area of a circle

$A \approx \frac{22}{7} \cdot 14^2$ Replace π with $\frac{22}{7}$ and r with 14.

$A \approx \frac{22}{7} \cdot 196$ $14^2 = 14 \cdot 14 = 196$

$A \approx \frac{22}{\cancel{7}_1} \cdot \cancel{196}^{28}$ Divide by the GCF, 7.

$A \approx 616$ Multiply.

Check for Reasonableness $616 \approx 588$ ✓

The area of the circle is approximately 616 square centimeters.

STOP and Reflect

Cross out the formula that is not used for finding the area of a circle.

$A = \pi r^2$ $A = 3.14r^2$

$A = \frac{22}{7}r^2$ $A = \frac{1}{2}bh$

Got It? Do this problem to find out.

Show your work.

a. Find the area of a circle with a radius of 3.2 centimeters. Round to the nearest tenth.

a. ________

Example

3. Find the area of the face of the Virginia quarter with a diameter of 24 millimeters. Use 3.14 for π. Round to the nearest tenth if necessary.

The radius is $\frac{1}{2}(24)$ or 12 millimeters.

$A = \pi r^2$ Area of a circle

$A \approx 3.14 \cdot 12^2$ Replace r with 12.

$A \approx 452.16$ Multiply.

The area is approximately 452.2 square millimeters.

Calculating with π
When evaluating expressions involving π, using the π key on a calculator will result in a different approximation.

Got It? Do this problem to find out.

b. The bottom of a circular swimming pool with a diameter of 30 feet is painted blue. How many square feet are blue?

b. ____________

Area of Semicircles

A **semicircle** is half of a circle. The formula for the area of a semicircle is $A = \frac{1}{2}\pi r^2$.

Example

4. Find the area of the semicircle. Use 3.14 for π. Round to the nearest tenth.

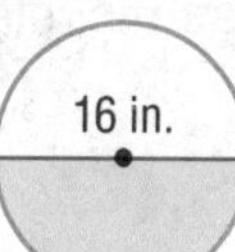

$A = \frac{1}{2}\pi r^2$ Area of a semicircle

$A \approx \frac{1}{2}\pi 8^2$ Replace r with 8.

$A \approx 0.5(3.14)(8^2)$ Multiply. Use 3.14 for π.

$A \approx 100.5$ Simplify.

The area of the semicircle is approximately 100.5 square inches.

Got It? Do this problem to find out.

c. Find the approximate area of a semicircle with a radius of 6 centimeters.

c. ____________

Example

5. On a basketball court, there is a semicircle above the free-throw line that has a radius of 6 feet. Find the area of the semicircle. Use 3.14 for π. Round to the nearest tenth.

$A = \frac{1}{2}\pi r^2$	Area of a semicircle
$A \approx 0.5(3.14)(6^2)$	Replace π with 3.14 and r with 6.
$A \approx 0.5(3.14)(36)$	$6^2 = 6 \cdot 6 = 36$
$A \approx 56.5$	Multiply.

So, the area of the semicircle is approximately 56.5 square feet.

Guided Practice

Find the area of each circle. Round to the nearest tenth. Use 3.14 or $\frac{22}{7}$ for π. (Examples 1–3)

1.

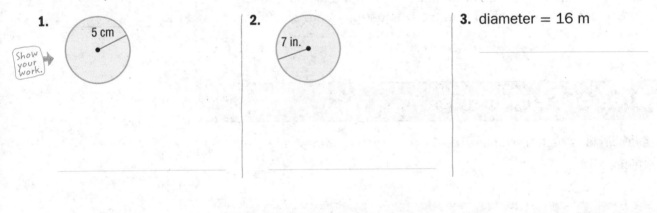

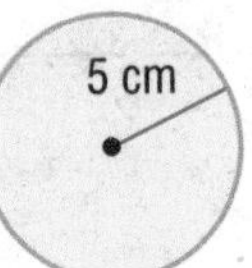

2.

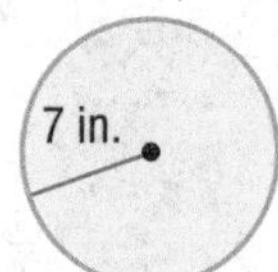

3. diameter = 16 m

4. Rondell draws the semicircle shown at the right. What is the area of the semicircle?

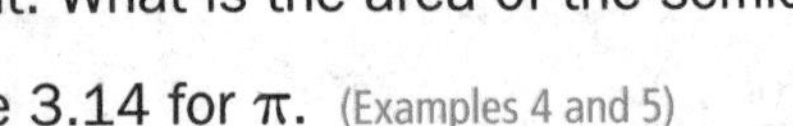

Use 3.14 for π. (Examples 4 and 5)

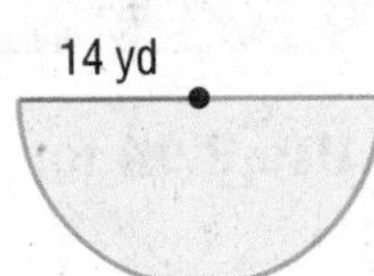

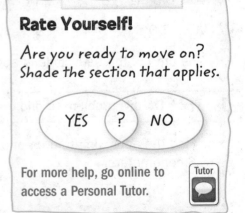

5. **Building on the Essential Question** Name one way the circumference and area of a circle are the same and one way they are different.

Rate Yourself!

Are you ready to move on? Shade the section that applies.

For more help, go online to access a Personal Tutor.

Name ________________ My Homework ________________

Independent Practice

Go online for Step-by-Step Solutions

Find the area of each circle. Round to the nearest tenth. Use 3.14 or $\frac{22}{7}$ for π. (Examples 1–3)

1.
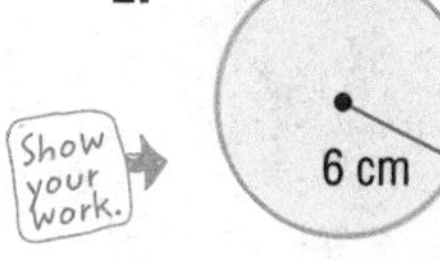

2.
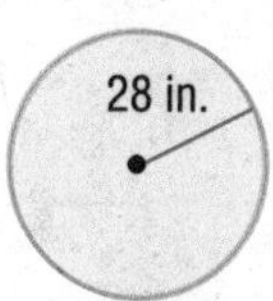

3.
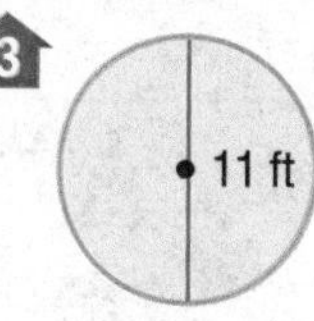

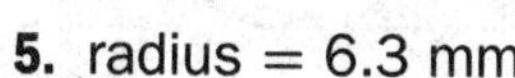

4. diameter = 10.5 in.

5. radius = 6.3 mm

6. radius = $3\frac{1}{4}$ yd

7. Refer to the pets problem at the beginning of this lesson. Find the area, to the nearest tenth, of grass that Adrianne's dog may run in if the leash is 9 feet long. (Example 3) ________________

8. A rotating sprinkler that sprays water at a radius of 11 feet is used to water a lawn. Find the area of the lawn that is watered. Use 3.14 for π. (Example 3) ________________

Find the area of each semicircle. Round to the nearest tenth. Use 3.14 for π. (Example 4)

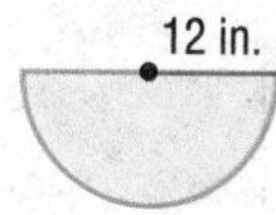

10.
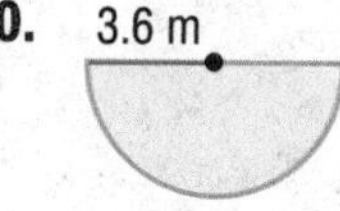

11. 20.4 yd

12. The tunnel opening shown is a semicircle. Find the area, to the nearest tenth, of the opening of the tunnel enclosed by the semicircle. (Example 5)

13. **Justify Conclusions** Harry's Pizzeria is having a sale on medium and large pizzas. Medium pizzas are 10 inches in diameter and cost $7.99. Large pizzas are 14 inches in diameter and cost $14.99. Which size pizza is the better deal? Explain. (*Hint*: Find the cost per square inch of each pizza.)

H.O.T. Problems Higher Order Thinking

14. **Model with Mathematics** Write a real-world problem that involves finding the area of two circles. Then solve your problem.

15. **Reason Inductively** If the length of the radius of a circle is doubled, how does that affect the circumference and area? Explain.

 **Persevere with Problems Find the area of the shaded region in each figure. Round to the nearest tenth.**

16.

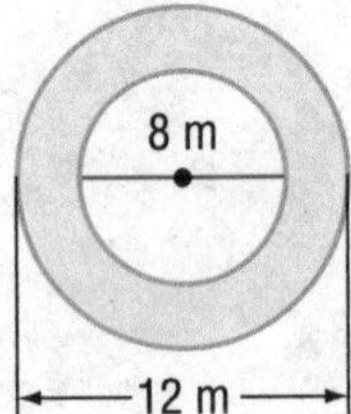

17.

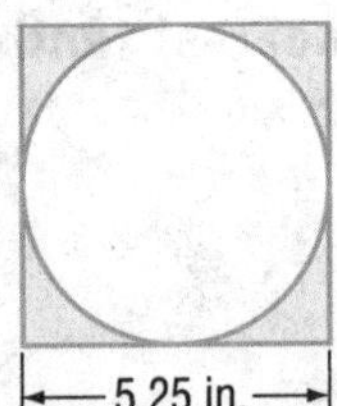

18.

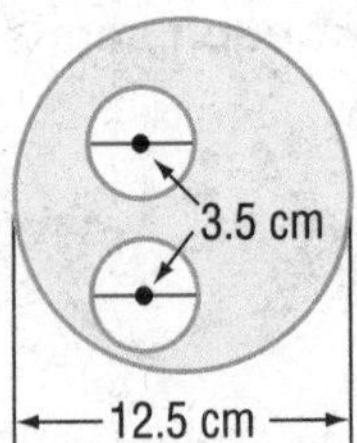

Georgia Test Practice

19. Which equation could be used to find the area in square inches of a circle with a diameter of 12 inches?

Ⓐ $A = 6 \times \pi$

Ⓑ $A = \pi \times 6^2$

Ⓒ $A = 12 \times \pi$

Ⓓ $A = \pi \times 12^2$

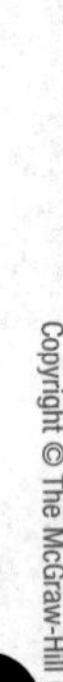

Name ____________ My Homework ____________

Extra Practice

Find the area of each circle. Round to the nearest tenth. Use 3.14 or $\frac{22}{7}$ for π.

20.

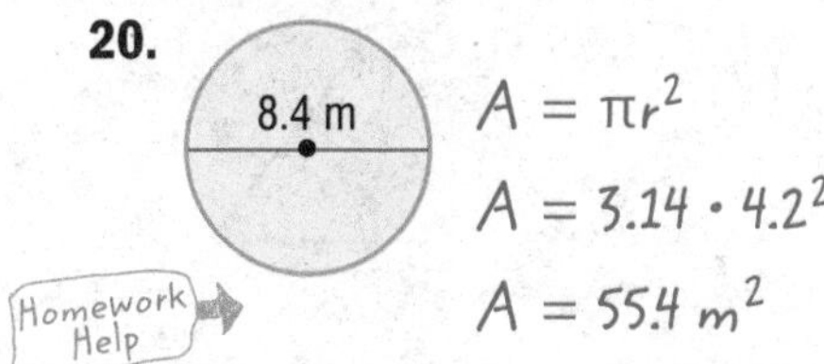

$3.14 \times 4.2 \times 4.2 = 55.4\ m^2$

21.

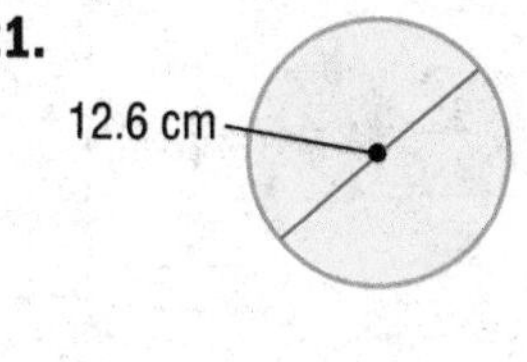

22.

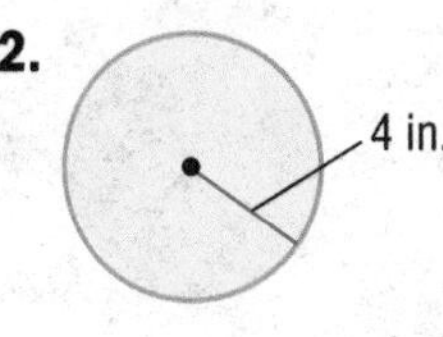

23. diameter = 10.8 yd

24. radius = $3\frac{4}{5}$ ft

25. radius = 9.3 mm

26. Find the area of the Girl Scout patch shown if the diameter is 1.25 inches. Round to the nearest tenth.

Find the area of each semicircle. Round to the nearest tenth. Use 3.14 for π.

27.

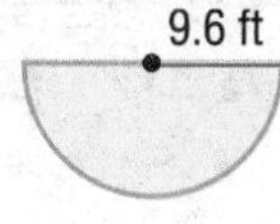

28.

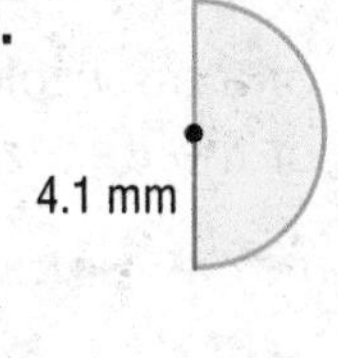

29.

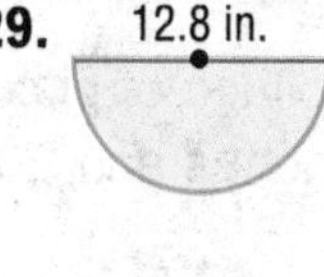

30. A window that is in the shape of a semicircle has a diameter of 28 inches. Find the area of the window. Round to the nearest tenth.

31. CCGPS **Justify Conclusions** Which has a greater area, a triangle with a base of 100 feet and a height of 100 feet or a circle with diameter of 100 feet? Justify your selection.

32. A radio station sends a signal in a circular area with an 80-mile radius. Find the approximate area in square kilometers that receives the signal. (*Hint*: 1 square mile ≈ 2.6 square kilometers)

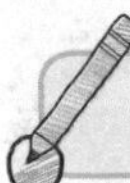

Georgia Test Practice

33. A distance measuring wheel is used to measure long distances by rotating 360 degrees.

Which of the following best describes the distance in one 360-degree rotation?

Ⓐ the area of the wheel

Ⓑ the radius of the wheel

Ⓒ the diameter of the wheel

Ⓓ the circumference of the wheel

34. Which two figures have the same area shaded?

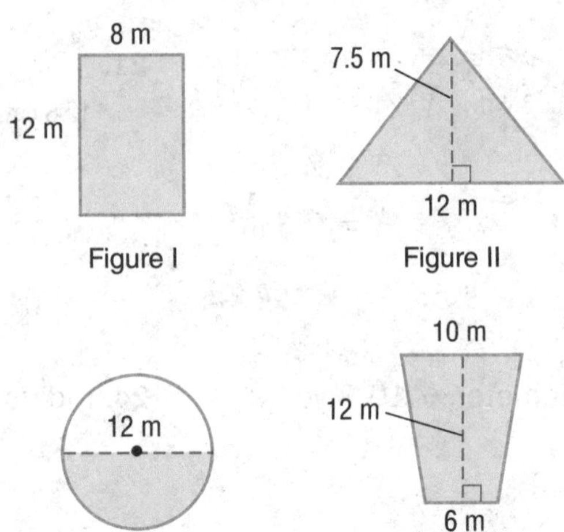

Ⓕ Figure I and Figure IV

Ⓖ Figure I and Figure II

Ⓗ Figure II and Figure IV

Ⓘ Figure II and Figure III

Common Core Review

35. A frame for a collage of pictures is in the shape of a trapezoid. The two bases are 15 inches and 20 inches. The height of the trapezoid is 12 inches. What is the area enclosed by the frame? MCC6.G.1 ________

Find the area of each parallelogram. Round to the nearest tenth if necessary. MCC6.G.1

36.

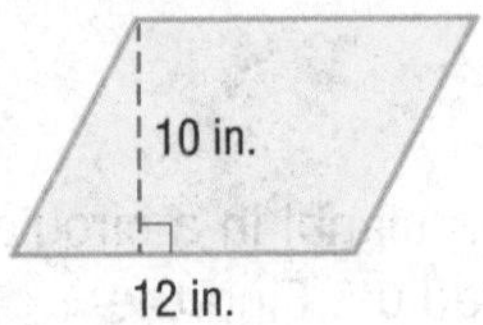

37.

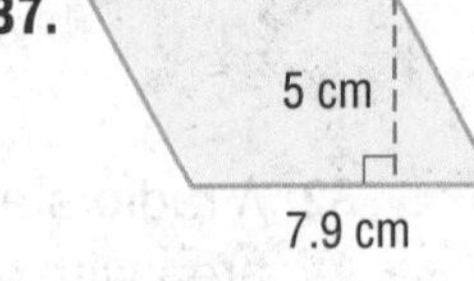

38.

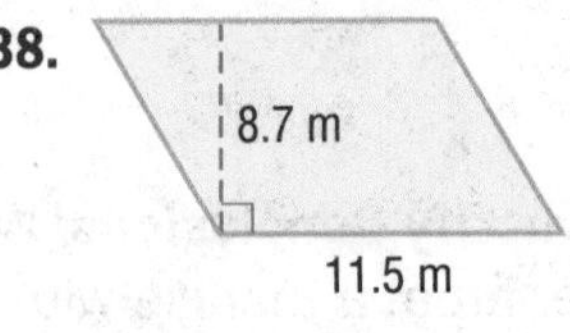

Area of Composite Figures

What You'll Learn

List two real-world scenarios in which you would use the area of a composite figure.

-

-

Essential Question

HOW do measurements help you describe real-world objects?

Vocabulary

composite figure

Common Core GPS

Content Standards
MCC7.G.4, MCC7.G.6

Mathematical Practices
1, 2, 3, 4

Real-World Link

Stained Glass Windows An image of a stained glass window is shown below.

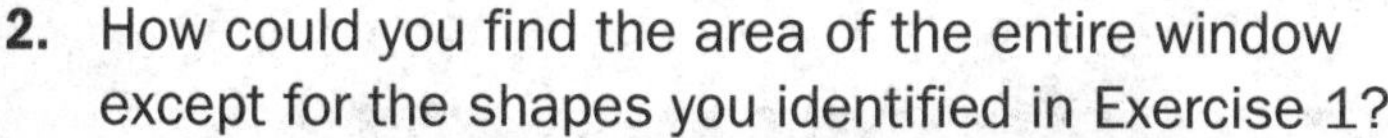

1. Identify two of the shapes that make up the window.

2. How could you find the area of the entire window except for the shapes you identified in Exercise 1?

3. Draw a figure that is made up of a triangle and a rectangle on the grid below. Then find the area of your figure by counting square units.

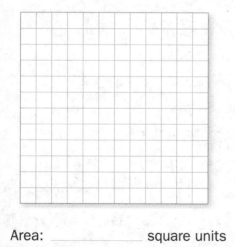

Area: ______ square units

Work Zone

Find the Area of a Composite Figure

A **composite figure** is made up of two or more shapes.

To find the area of a composite figure, decompose the figure into shapes with areas you know. Then find the sum of these areas.

Shape	Words	Formula
Parallelogram	The area A of a parallelogram is the product of any base b and its height h.	$A = bh$
Triangle	The area A of a triangle is half the product of any base b and its height h.	$A = \frac{1}{2}bh$
Trapezoid	The area A of a trapezoid is half the product of the height h and the sum of the bases, b_1 and b_2.	$A = \frac{1}{2}h(b_1 + b_2)$
Circle	The area A of a circle is equal to π times the square of the radius r.	$A = \pi r^2$

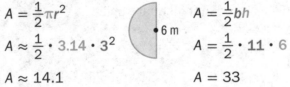

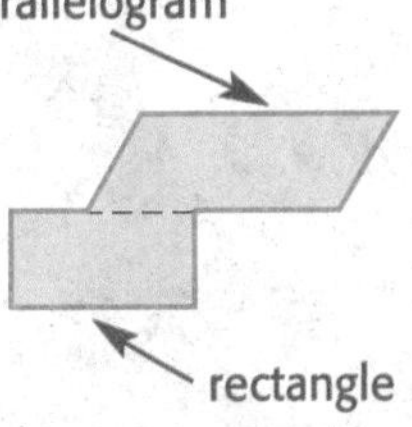

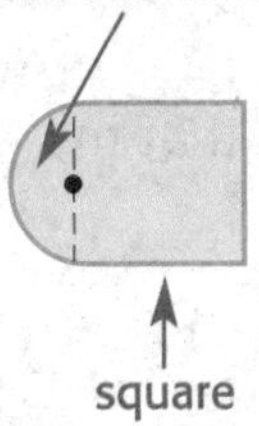

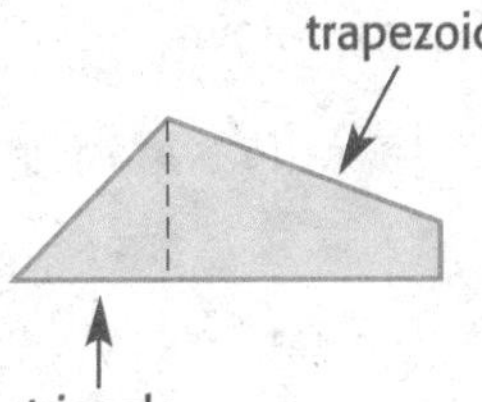

Example

1. Find the area of the composite figure.

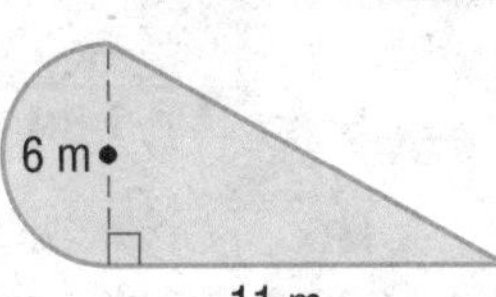

The figure can be separated into a semicircle and a triangle.

Area of semicircle

$A = \frac{1}{2}\pi r^2$

$A \approx \frac{1}{2} \cdot 3.14 \cdot 3^2$

$A \approx 14.1$

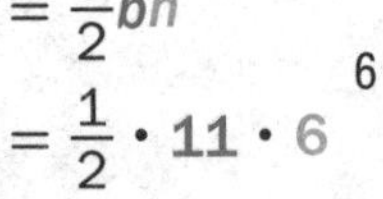

Area of triangle

$A = \frac{1}{2}bh$

$A = \frac{1}{2} \cdot 11 \cdot 6$

$A = 33$

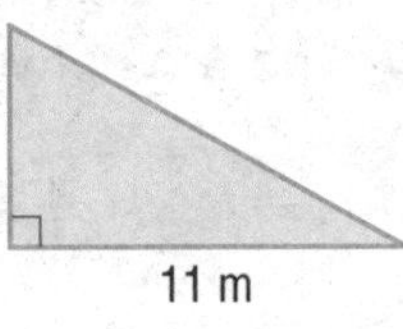

The area of the figure is about 14.1 + 33 or 47.1 square meters.

Got It? Do this problem to find out.

Show your work.

a. Find the area of the figure. Round to the nearest tenth if necessary.

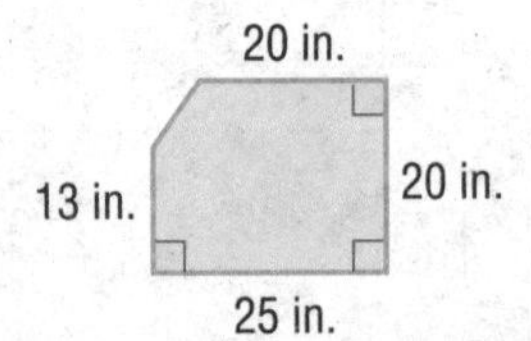

a. ____________

Example

2. A miniature golf hole is composed of a trapezoid and a parallelogram. How many square feet of turf does the hole cover?

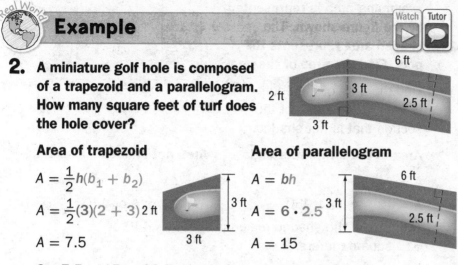

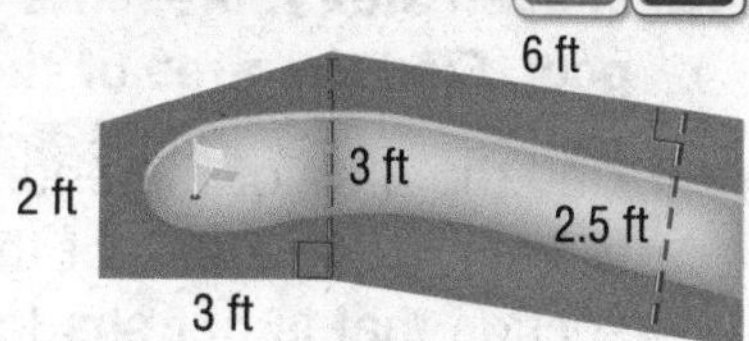

Area of trapezoid	**Area of parallelogram**
$A = \frac{1}{2}h(b_1 + b_2)$	$A = bh$
$A = \frac{1}{2}(3)(2 + 3)$	$A = 6 \cdot 2.5$
$A = 7.5$	$A = 15$

So, 7.5 + 15 or 22.5 square feet of turf will be needed.

Got It? **Do this problem to find out.**

b. Pedro's father is building a shed. How many square feet of wood are needed to build the back of the shed shown at the right?

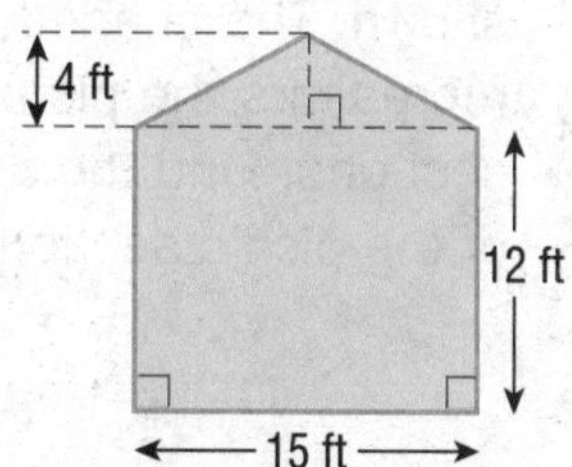

b. ______________

Find the Area of a Shaded Region

Use the areas you know to find the area of a shaded region.

Examples

3. Find the area of the shaded region.

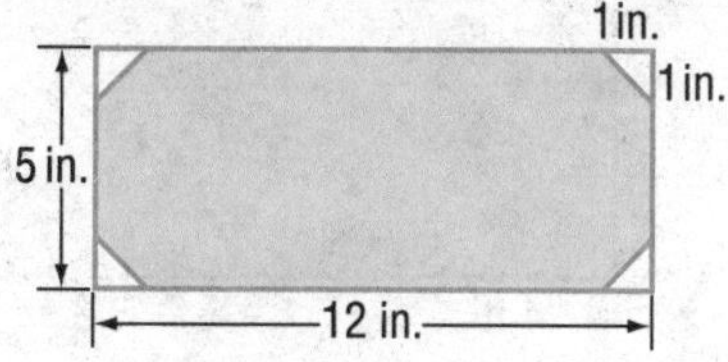

Find the area of the rectangle and subtract the area of the four triangles.

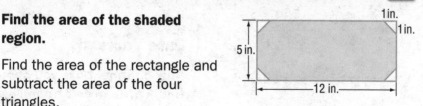

Area of rectangle		**Area of triangles**	
$A = \ell w$		$A = 4 \cdot \left(\frac{1}{2}bh\right)$	
$A = 12 \cdot 5$	$\ell = 12, w = 5$	$A = 4 \cdot \frac{1}{2} \cdot 1 \cdot 1$	$b = 1, h = 1$
$A = 60$	Simplify.	$A = 2$	Simplify.

The area of the shaded region is 60 – 2 or 58 square inches.

Congruent Triangles

Congruent triangles have corresponding sides and angles that are congruent.

4. The blueprint for a hotel swimming area is represented by the figure shown. The shaded area represents the pool. Find the area of the pool.

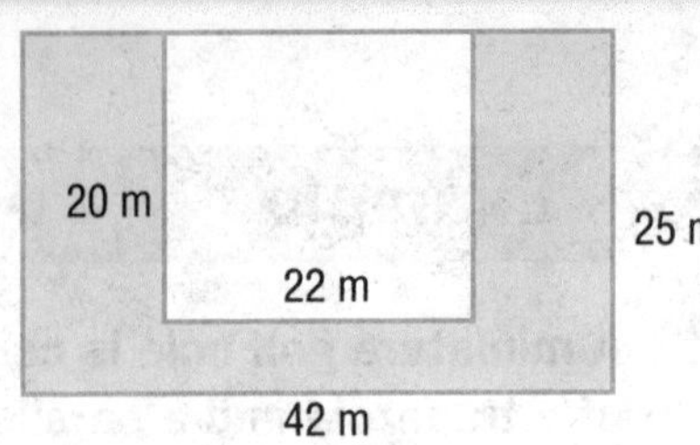

Find the area of the entire rectangle and subtract the section that is not shaded.

Area of the entire rectangle	**Area not shaded**
$A = \ell w$	$A = \ell w$
$A = 42 \cdot 25$ or 1,050	$A = 22 \cdot 20$ or 440

The area of the shaded region is 1,050 − 440 or 610 square meters.

Got It? **Do this problem to find out.**

c. A diagram for a park is shown. The shaded area represents the picnic sections. Find the area of the picnic sections.

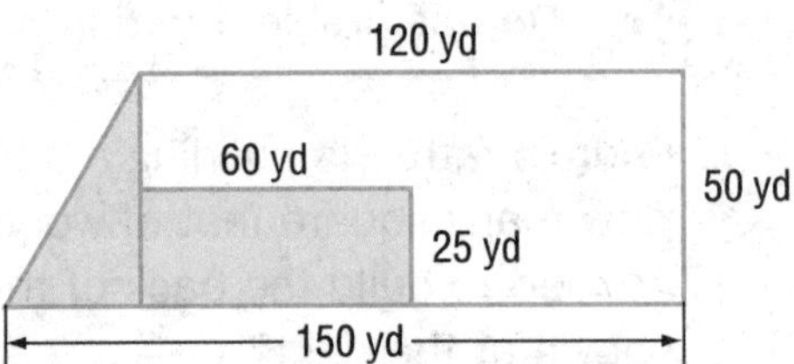

c. ______

Guided Practice

1. Mike installed the window shown. How many square feet is the window? Round to the nearest tenth. Use 3.14 for π.

Show your work. (Examples 1 and 2) ______

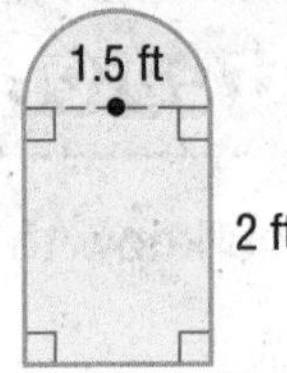

2. A triangle is cut from a rectangle. Find the area of the shaded region.

(Examples 3 and 4) ______

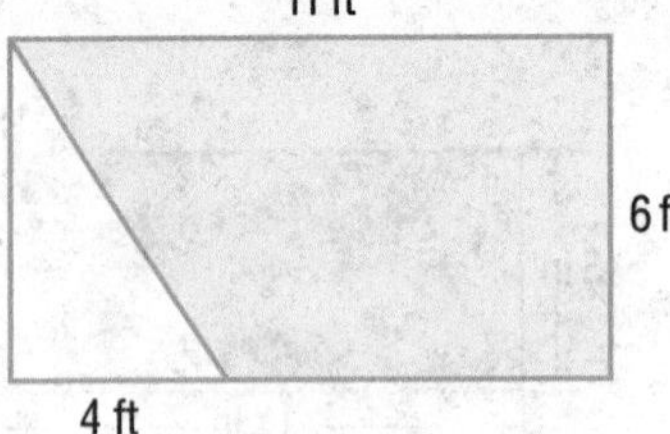

3. **Building on the Essential Question** Is your answer to Exercise 1 an exact or approximate answer? Explain.

______

______

______

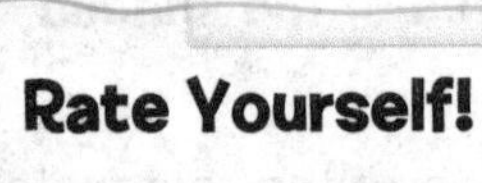

Rate Yourself!

How confident are you about finding the area of composite figures? Check the box that applies.

For more help, go online to access a Personal Tutor.

Name ______________________ My Homework ______________

Independent Practice

Go online for Step-by-Step Solutions

Find the area of each figure. Round to the nearest tenth if necessary. (Example 1)

1. 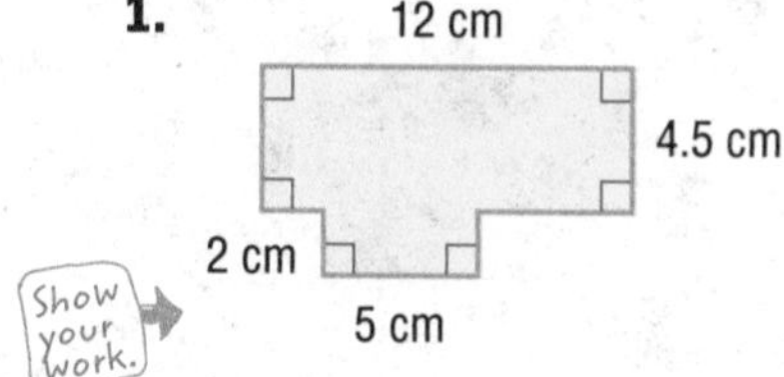

Show your work.

2. 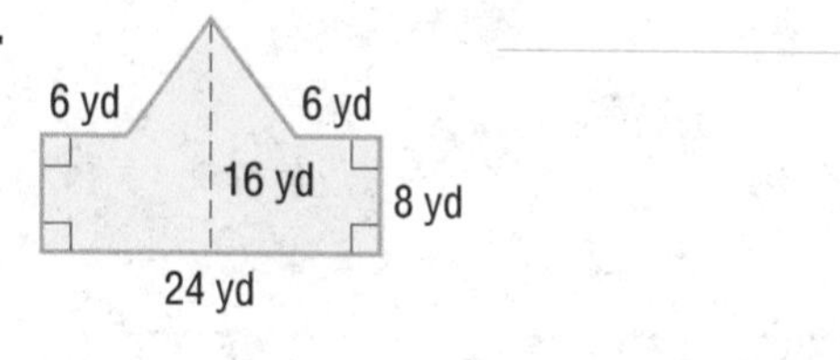

3. 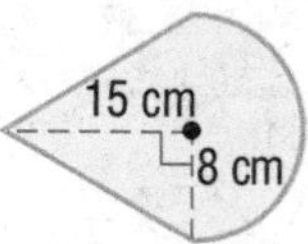

4. 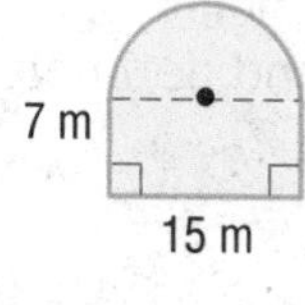

5. 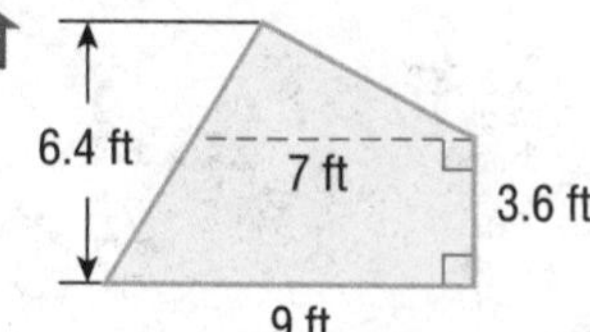

6. 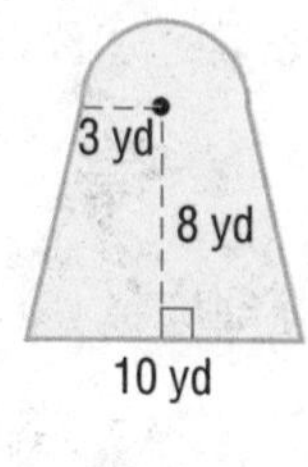

7. Daniel is constructing a deck like the one shown. What is the area of the deck? (Example 2)

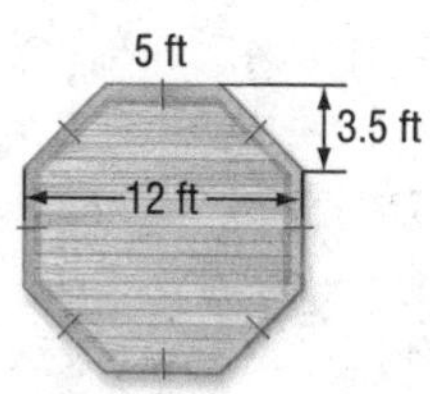

Find the area of the shaded region. Round to the nearest tenth if necessary. (Examples 3 and 4)

8. 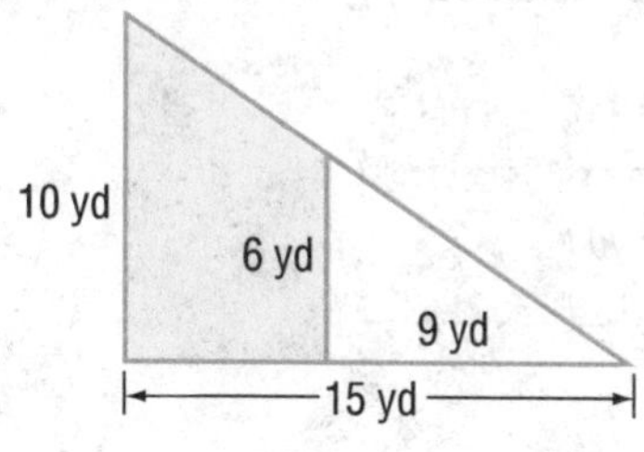

9. 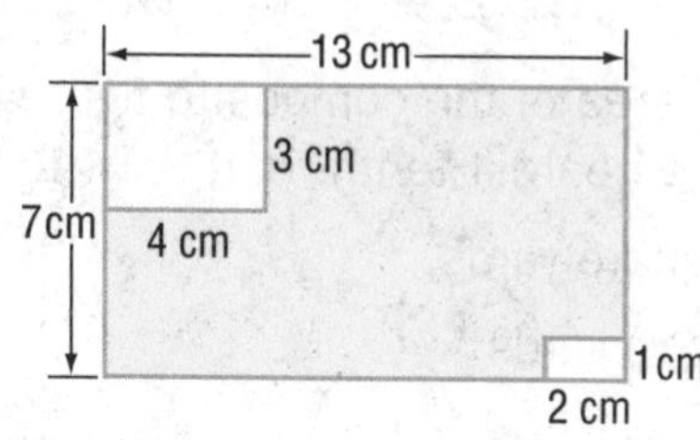

10. CCGPS **Persevere with Problems** Zoe's mom is carpeting her bedroom and needs to know the amount of floor space. How many square feet of carpeting are needed for the room? If she is also installing baseboards on the bottom of all the walls, how many feet of baseboards are needed? ______

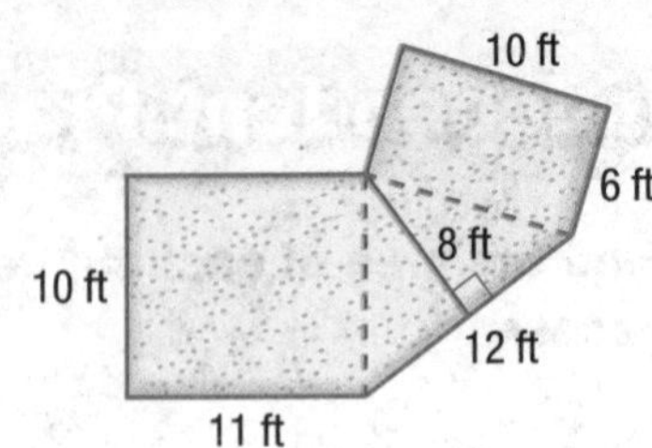

H.O.T. Problems Higher Order Thinking

11. CCGPS **Persevere with Problems** The composite figure shown is made from a rectangle and a triangle. The area of the rectangle is 32 square feet. Find the area and perimeter of the entire figure.

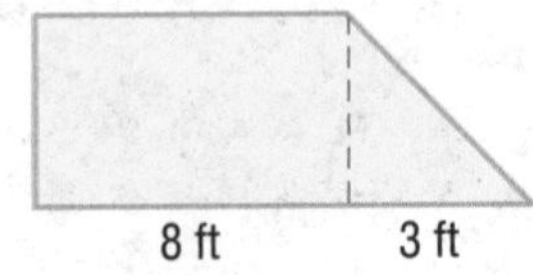

______

12. CCGPS **Reason Abstractly** The side length of the square in the figure at the right is *x* units. Write expressions that represent the perimeter and area of the figure.

______

13. CCGPS **Persevere with Problems** In the diagram shown at the right, a 2-foot-wide flower border surrounds the heart-shaped pond. What is the area of the border?

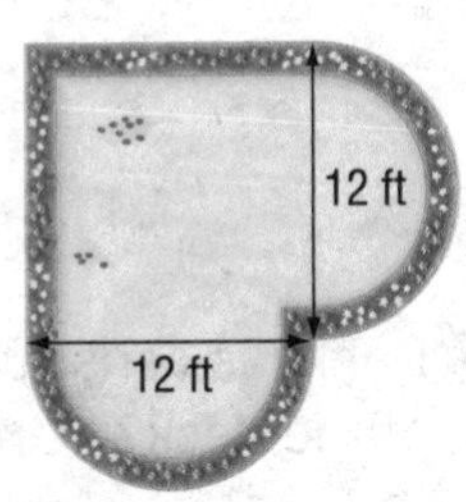

______

Georgia Test Practice

14. What is the area of the composite figure shown at the right. Round to the nearest tenth. Use 3.14 for π.

Ⓐ 73.5 square yards

Ⓑ 60 square yards

Ⓒ 58 square yards

Ⓓ 54.2 square yards

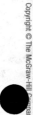

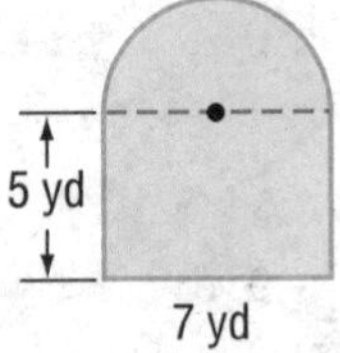

Extra Practice

Find the area of each figure. Round to the nearest tenth if necessary.

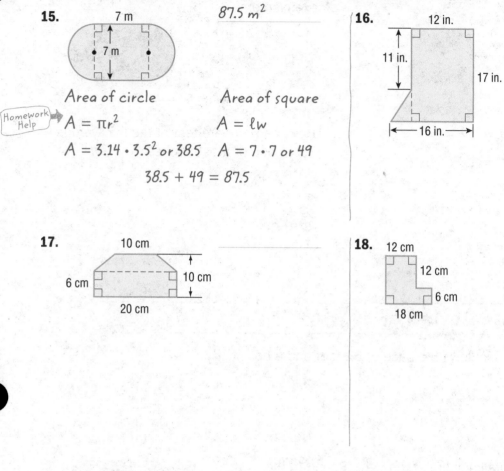

15. 87.5 m^2

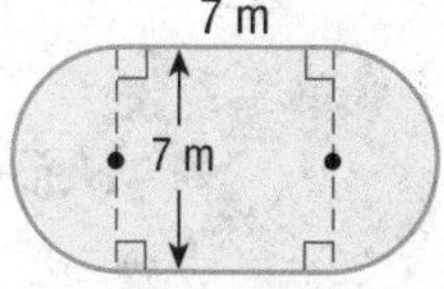

Area of circle

$A = \pi r^2$

$A = 3.14 \cdot 3.5^2$ or 38.5

Area of square

$A = \ell w$

$A = 7 \cdot 7$ or 49

$38.5 + 49 = 87.5$

16. ____

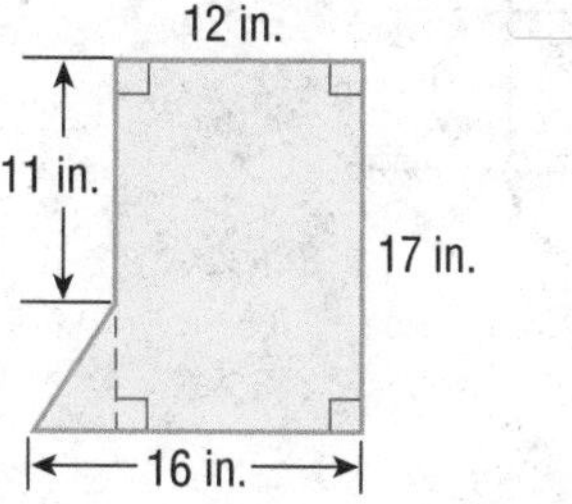

17. ____

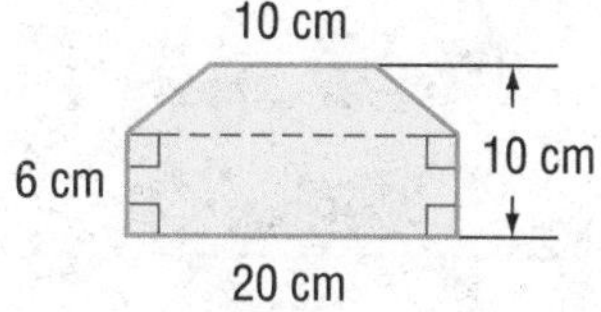

18. ____

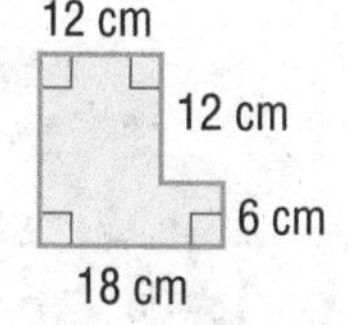

19. A necklace comes with a gold pendant. What is the area of the pendant in square centimeters? ____

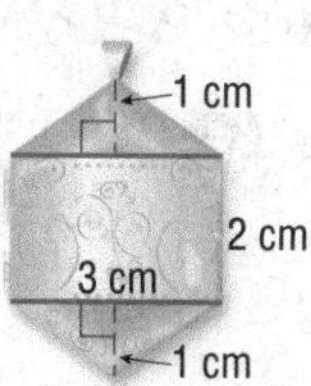

Find the area of the shaded region. Round to the nearest tenth if necessary.

20.

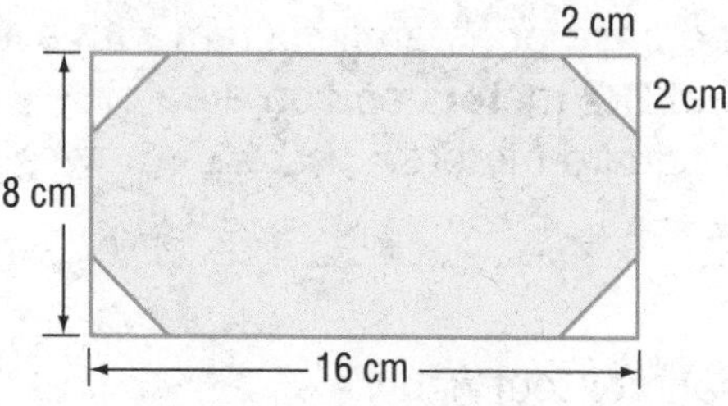

____

21.

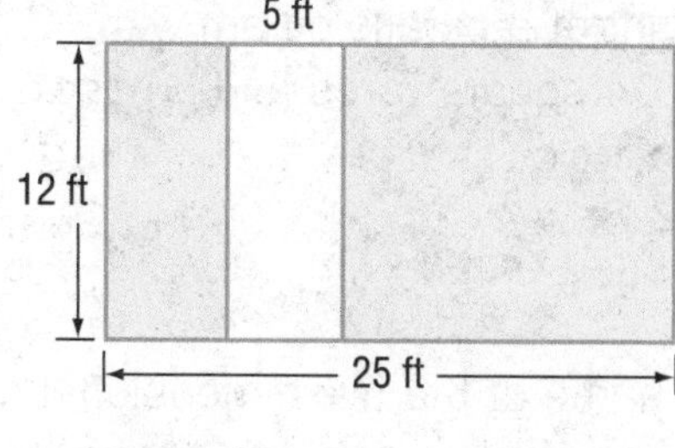

____

Georgia Test Practice

22. What is the total area of the figure shown?

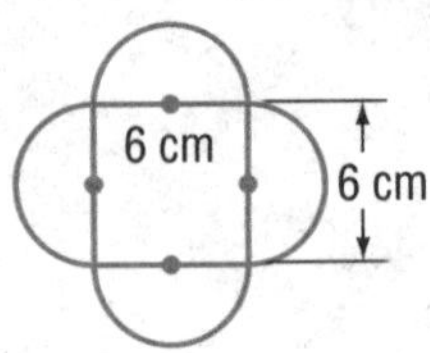

Ⓐ 92.5 cm^2
Ⓑ 64.3 cm^2
Ⓒ 56.5 cm^2
Ⓓ 36.0 cm^2

23. The Patels' backyard has a rectangular vegetable garden and a triangular pet exercise area.

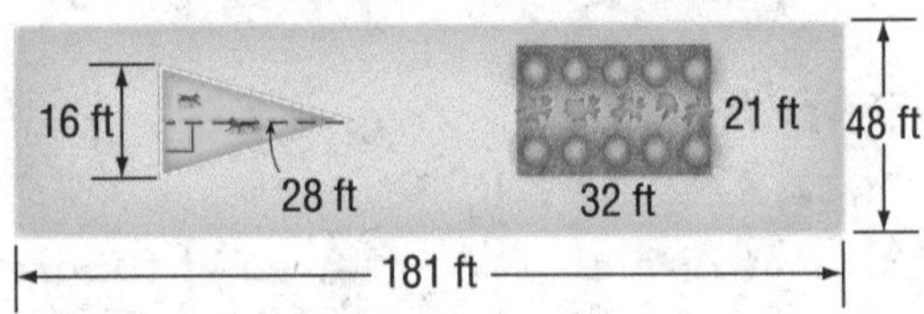

How many square feet of the backyard is *not* in one of these areas?

Ⓕ 8,688 ft^2
Ⓖ 7,792 ft^2
Ⓗ 4,887 ft^2
Ⓘ 896 ft^2

CCGPS Common Core Review

24. What is the area of a triangle with a base of 52 feet and a height of 38 feet? **MCC6.G.1** ______

25. Find the area of the parallelogram at the right. Round to the nearest tenth. **MCC6.G.1** ______

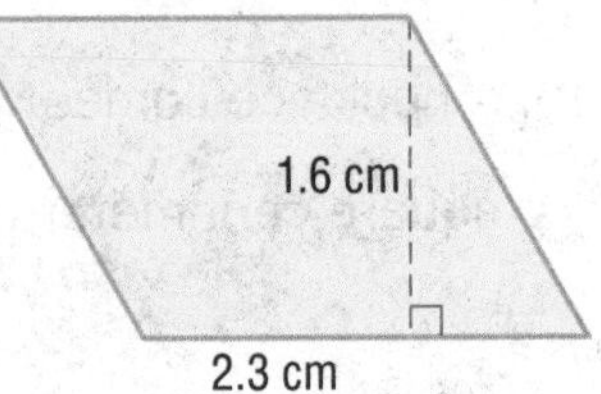

26. Find the height of a parallelogram with an area of 104 square yards and a base of 8 yards. **MCC6.G.1**

______

27. Find the base of a parallelogram with a height of 3.2 meters and an area of 15.04 square meters. **MCC6.G.1**

______

28. What is the name of the two-dimensional figure that is made of four right angles and four congruent sides? **MCC5.G.4**

______

Volume of Prisms

What You'll Learn

List two headings you would use to make an outline of the lesson.

- ______________________________
- ______________________________

Essential Question

HOW do measurements help you describe real-world objects?

Vocabulary

volume

Common Core GPS

Content Standards
MCC7.G.6

Mathematical Practices
1, 2, 3, 4

Vocabulary Start-Up

Recall that a prism is a polyhedron with two parallel, congruent bases. The bases of a *rectangular prism* are rectangles, and the bases of a *triangular prism* are triangles.

Write *rectangular prism* or *triangular prism* on the line below each figure.

1. 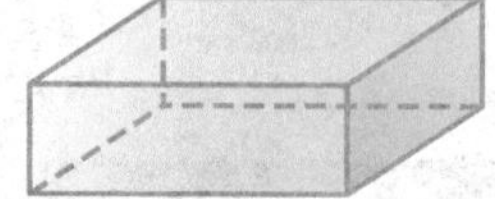

____

2. 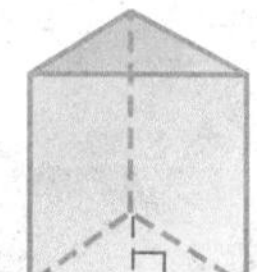

____

Real-World Link

1. Suppose you observed the camping tent shown from directly above. What geometric figure would you see?

____

2. What formula would you use to find the area of this figure?

____

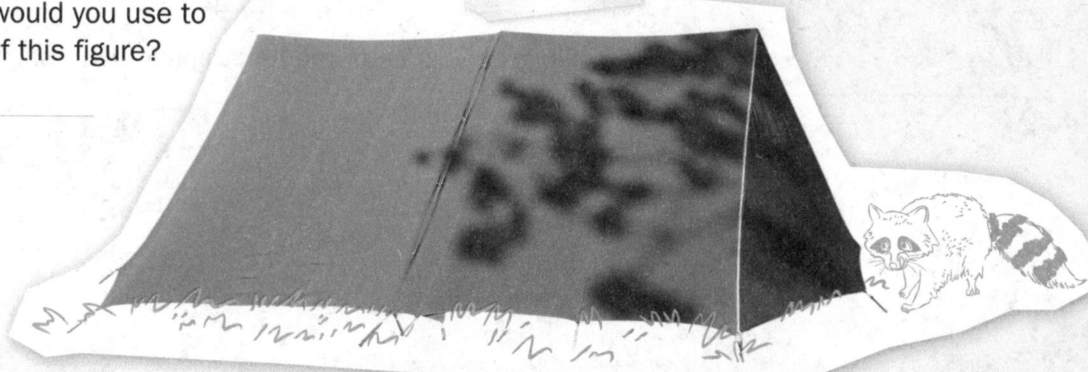

Key Concept Volume of a Rectangular Prism

Words The volume V of a rectangular prism is the product of the length ℓ, the width w, and the height h. It is also the area of the base B times the height h.

Model

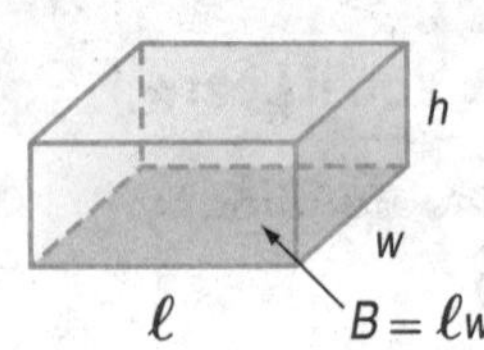

Symbols $V = \ell wh$ or $V = Bh$

Work Zone

The **volume** of a three-dimensional figure is the measure of space it occupies. It is measured in cubic units such as cubic centimeters (cm^3) or cubic inches (in^3).

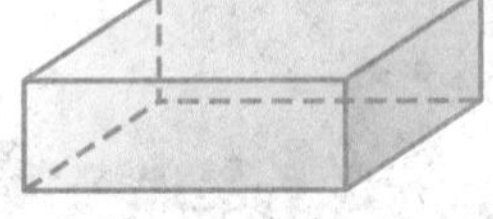

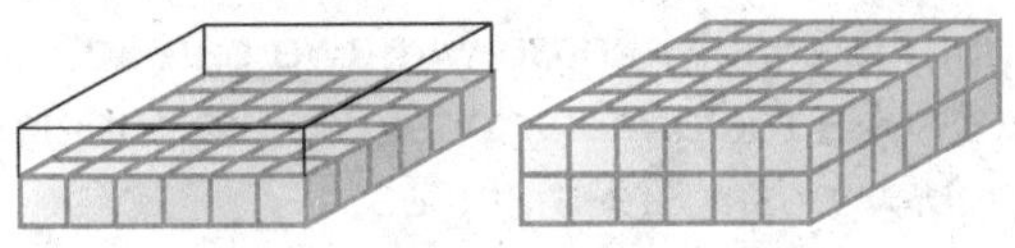

It takes 2 layers of 36 cubes to fill the box. So, the volume of the box is 72 cubic centimeters.

Decomposing Figures

Think of the volume of the prism as consisting of three congruent slices. Each slice contains the base area, 20 square centimeters, and a height of 1 centimeter.

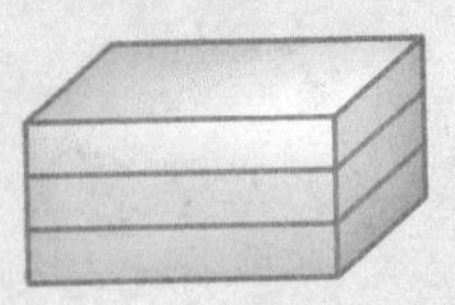

Example

1. Find the volume of the rectangular prism.

3 cm, 4 cm, 5 cm

$V = \ell wh$	Volume of a prism
$V = 5 \cdot 4 \cdot 3$	$\ell = 5$, $w = 4$, and $h = 3$
$V = 60$	Multiply.

The volume is 60 cubic centimeters or 60 cm^3.

Got It? **Do this problem to find out.**

Show your work.

a. Find the volume of the rectangular prism shown below.

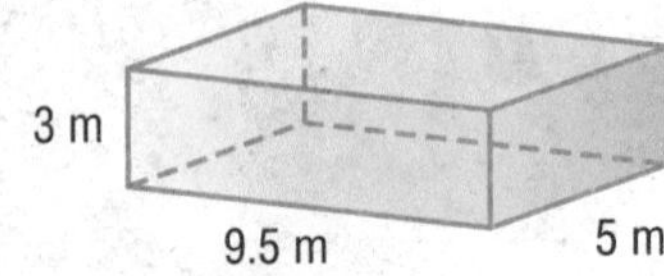

a. ______

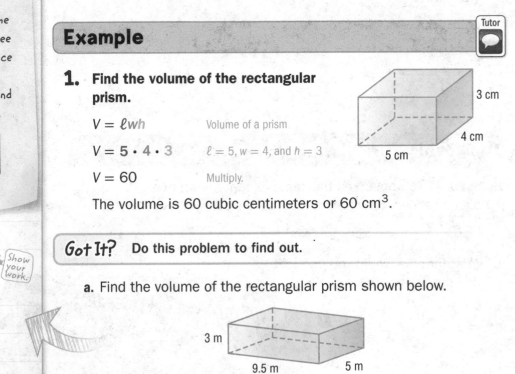

Volume of a Triangular Prism

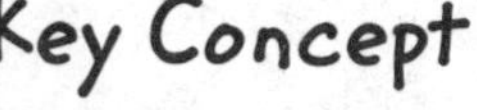

Words The volume V of a triangular prism is the area of the base B times the height h.

Symbols $V = Bh$, where B is the area of the base.

Model

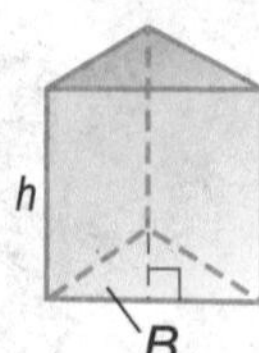

Height
Do not confuse the height of the triangular base with the height of the prism.

The diagram below shows that the volume of a triangular prism is also the product of the area of the base B and the height h of the prism.

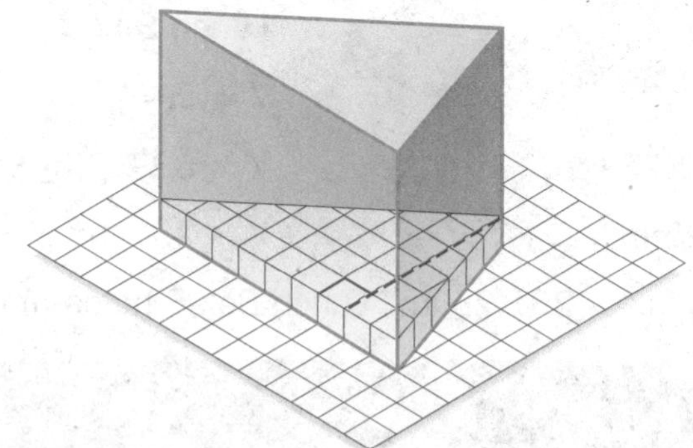

Example

2. Find the volume of the triangular prism shown.

The area of the triangle is $\frac{1}{2} \cdot 6 \cdot 8$, so replace B with $\frac{1}{2} \cdot 6 \cdot 8$.

6 ft
9 ft
8 ft

$V = Bh$	Volume of a prism
$V = \left(\frac{1}{2} \cdot 6 \cdot 8\right)h$	Replace B with $\frac{1}{2} \cdot 6 \cdot 8$.
$V = \left(\frac{1}{2} \cdot 6 \cdot 8\right)9$	The height of the prism is 9.
$V = 216$	Multiply.

The volume is 216 cubic feet or 216 ft^3.

Before finding the volume of a prism, identify the base. In Example 2, the base is a triangle, so you replace B with $\frac{1}{2}bh$.

Got It? **Do this problem to find out.**

b. Find the volume of the triangular prism.

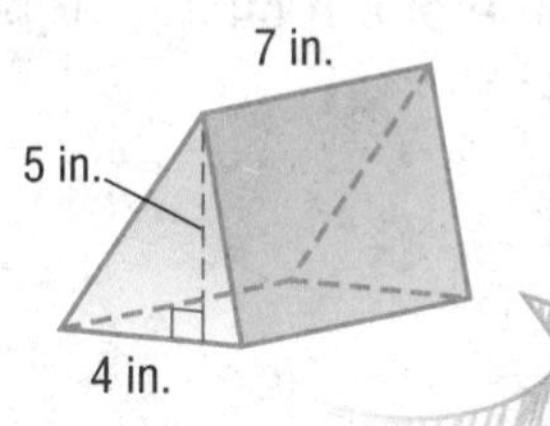

b. ________

Example

3. Which lunch box holds more food?

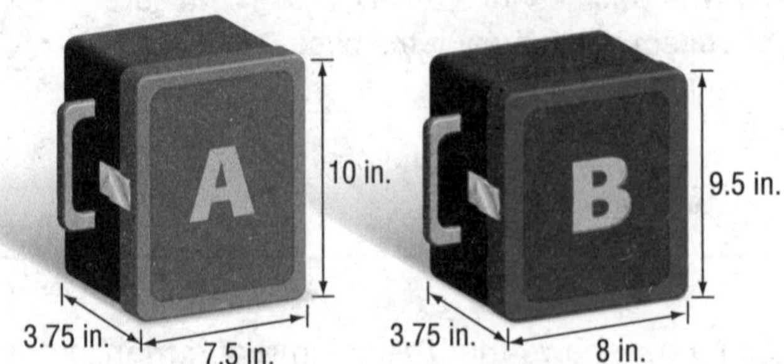

Find the volume of each lunch box. Then compare.

Lunch Box A

$V = \ell wh$

$V = 7.5 \cdot 3.75 \cdot 10$

$V = 281.25 \text{ in}^3$

Lunch Box B

$V = \ell wh$

$V = 8 \cdot 3.75 \cdot 9.5$

$V = 285 \text{ in}^3$

Since $285 \text{ in}^3 > 281.25 \text{ in}^3$, Lunch Box B holds more food.

Guided Practice

Find the volume of each prism. Round to the nearest tenth if necessary. (Examples 1–2)

1.

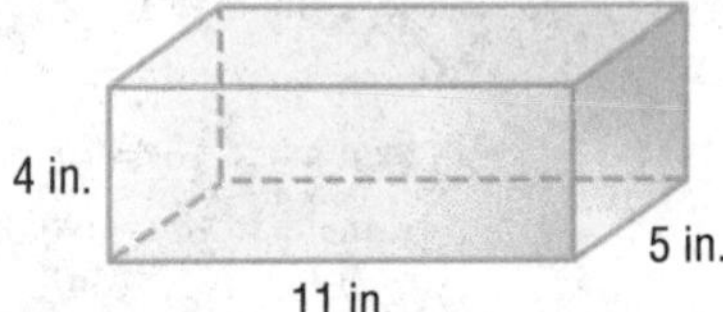

2.

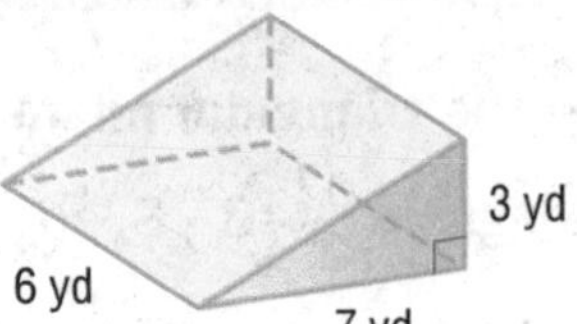

3. One cabinet measures 3 feet by 2.5 feet by 5 feet. A second measures 4 feet by 3.5 feet by 4.5 feet. Which volume is greater? Explain. (Example 3)

4. **Building on the Essential Question** Compare and contrast finding the volume of a rectangular prism and a triangular prism.

Rate Yourself!

How confident are you about finding volume for prisms? Check the box that applies.

For more help, go online to access a Personal Tutor.

FOLDABLES *Time to update your Foldable!*

Name ______________________ My Homework ______________________

Independent Practice

Go online for Step-by-Step Solutions 

Find the volume of each prism. Round to the nearest tenth if necessary.
(Examples 1–2)

1. 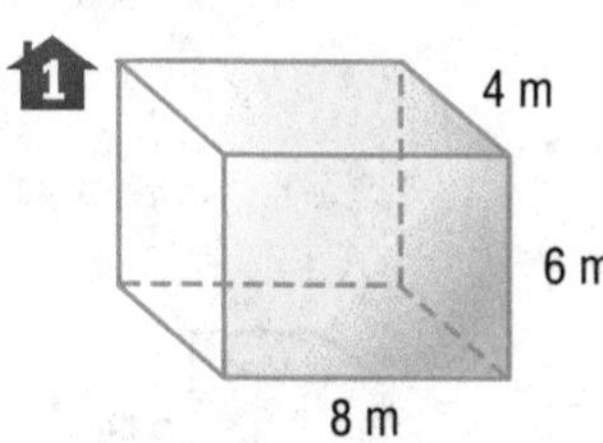

2. 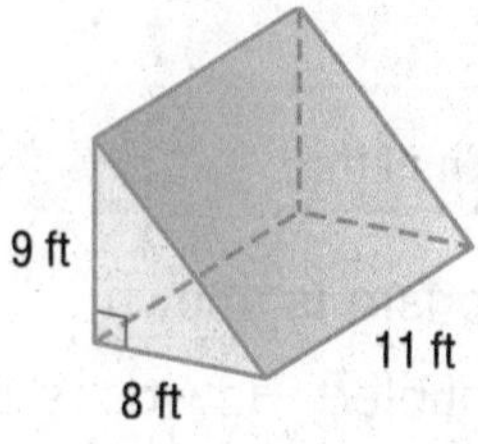

3. 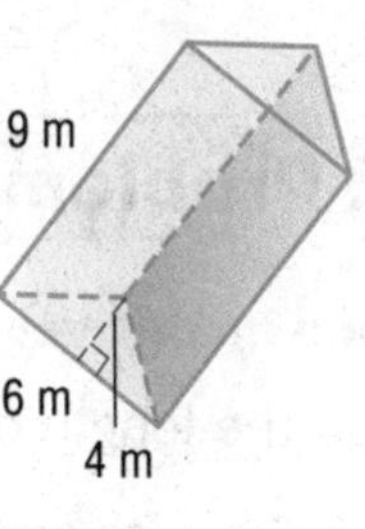

Show your work.

4. Which container holds more detergent? Justify your answer. (Example 3)

Soapy Suds: 13 in., 8 in., 12 in.

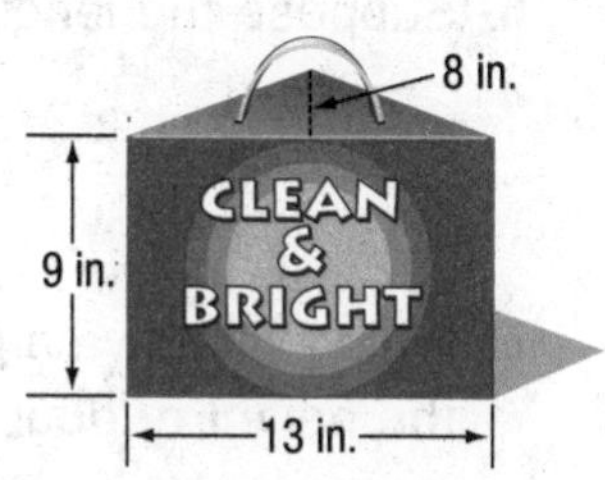

5. **CCGPS Model with Mathematics** Refer to the graphic novel frame below.

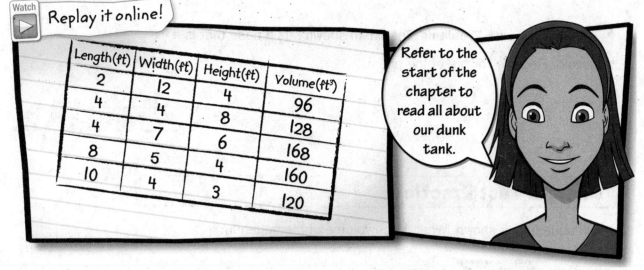

Watch Replay it online!

Length (ft)	Width (ft)	Height (ft)	Volume (ft^3)
2	12	4	96
4	4	8	128
4	7	6	168
8	5	4	160
10	4	3	120

Refer to the start of the chapter to read all about our dunk tank.

a. Are there any other possible dimensions for the dunk tank?

b. Which dimensions are reasonable for a dunk tank? Explain.

6. The diagram shows the dimensions of an office. It costs about \$0.11 per year to air condition one cubic foot of space. On average, how much does it cost to air condition the office for one month? ______

12 ft
25 ft
32 ft

H.O.T. Problems Higher Order Thinking

7. CCGPS **Reason Inductively** A rectangular prism is shown.

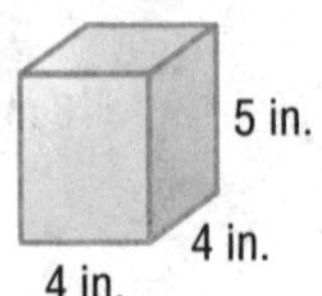

a. Suppose the length of the prism is doubled. How does the volume change? Explain your reasoning. ______

b. Suppose the length, width, and height are each doubled. How does the volume change? ______

c. Which will have a greater effect on the volume of the prism: doubling the height or doubling the width? Explain your reasoning.

______

8. CCGPS **Persevere with Problems** The prism shown has a base that is a trapezoid. Find the volume of the prism. ______

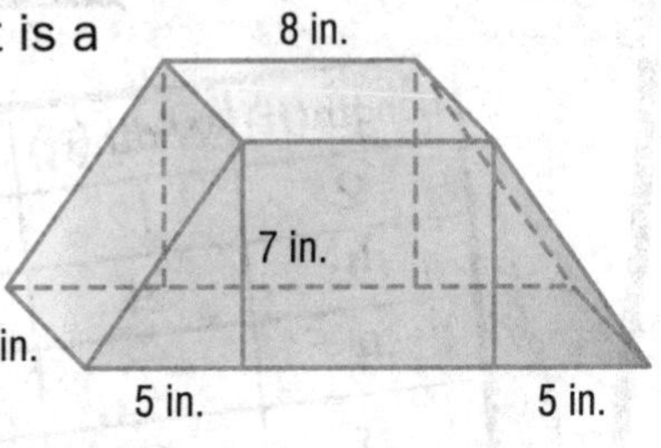

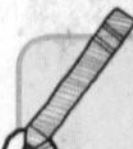

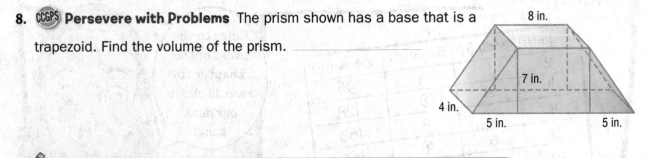

Georgia Test Practice

9. A fish aquarium is shown. What is the volume of the aquarium?

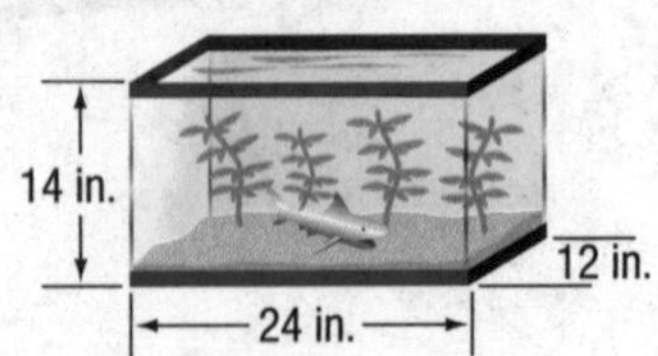

Ⓐ 168 in^3

Ⓑ 342 in^3

Ⓒ 2,016 in^3

Ⓓ 4,032 in^3

Name ________________ My Homework ________________

Extra Practice

Find the volume of each prism. Round to the nearest tenth if necessary.

10. 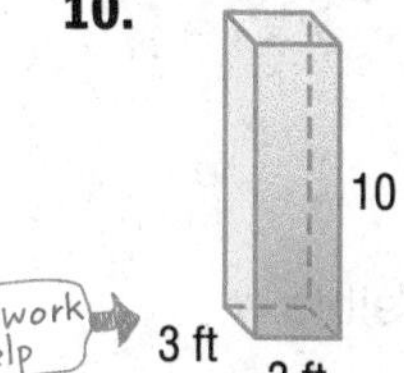

90 ft³

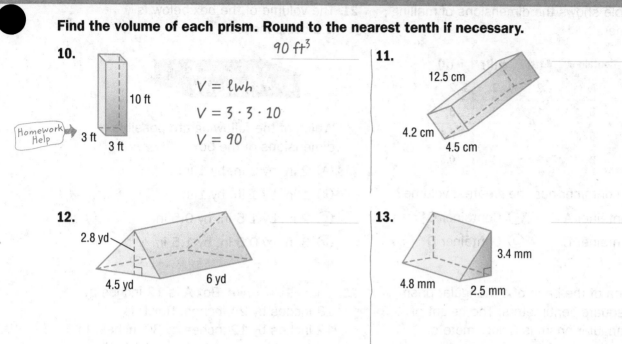

$V = lwh$

$V = 3 \cdot 3 \cdot 10$

$V = 90$

11. 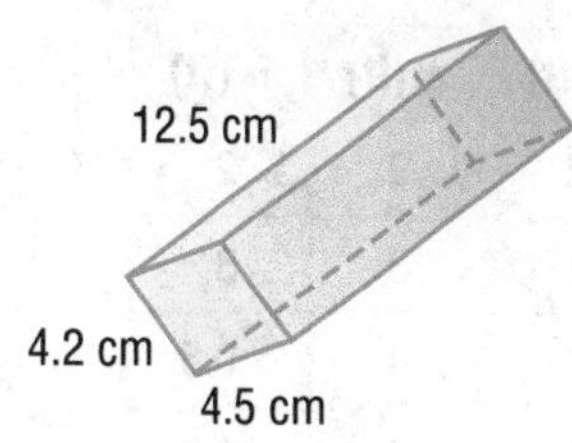

12. 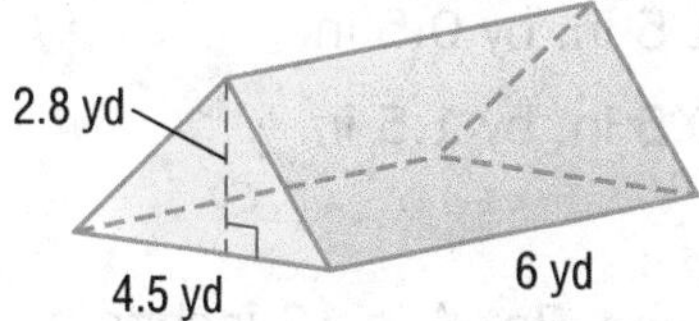

13. 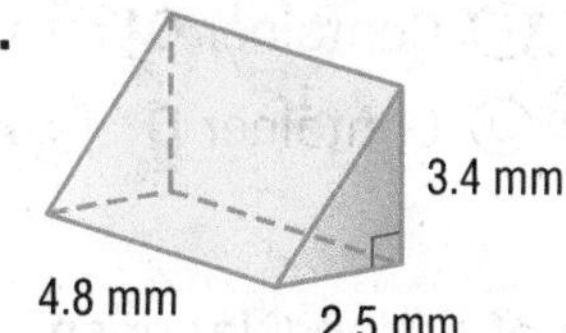

14. A toy company makes rectangular sandboxes that measure 6 feet by 5 feet by 1.2 feet. A customer buys a sandbox and 40 cubic feet of sand. Did the customer buy too much or too little sand? Justify your answer.

15. The base of a rectangular prism has an area of 19.4 square meters and the prism has a volume of 306.52 cubic meters. Write an equation that can be used to find the height *h* of the prism. Then find the height of the prism.

Find the volume of each prism.

16. 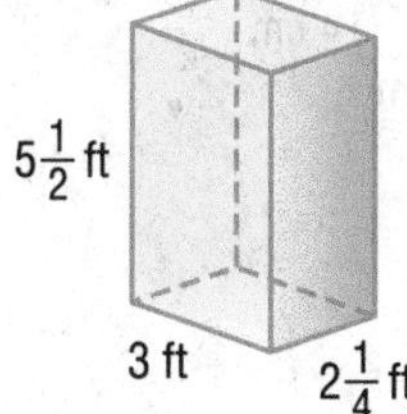

17. 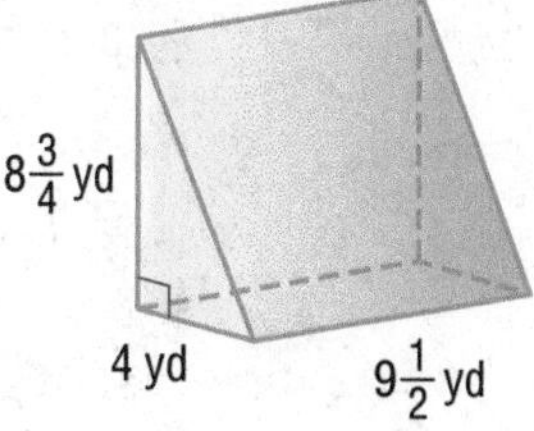

18. CCGPS **Reason Abstractly** Write a formula for finding the volume of a cube. Use an exponent and the variable s to represent the side lengths. Then use the formula to find the volume of a cube with side lengths of 7 inches.

Georgia Test Practice

19. The table shows the dimensions of mailing containers.

Container	ℓ (ft)	w (ft)	h (ft)
A	2	2	2
B	1	3	3
C	3	4	0.5
D	3	2	0.5

Which container has the greatest volume?

Ⓐ Container A Ⓒ Container C

Ⓑ Container B Ⓓ Container D

20. The area of the base of a triangular prism is 50 square centimeters. The height of the triangular prism is 8 centimeters. Which represents the volume of the triangular prism?

Ⓕ 58 cm^2 Ⓗ 400 cm^2

Ⓖ 58 cm^3 Ⓘ 400 cm^3

21. The volume of the box below is 1.5 cubic inches.

Which of the following are possible dimensions of the box?

Ⓐ 2 in. by 2 in. by 1 in.

Ⓑ 1 in. by 1 in. by 1 in.

Ⓒ 2 in. by 1.5 in. by 0.5 in.

Ⓓ 3 in. by 0.5 in. by 1.5 in.

22. **Short Response** Box A is 12 inches by 18 inches by 24 inches. Box B is 12 inches by 12 inches by 30 inches. In cubic inches, how much greater is the volume of Box A?

______

CCGPS Common Core Review

Find the perimeter of each figure. MCC4.MD.3

23. 4.3 m, 4.3 m, 4.3 m, 4.3 m, 4.3 m, 4.3 m

______

24.

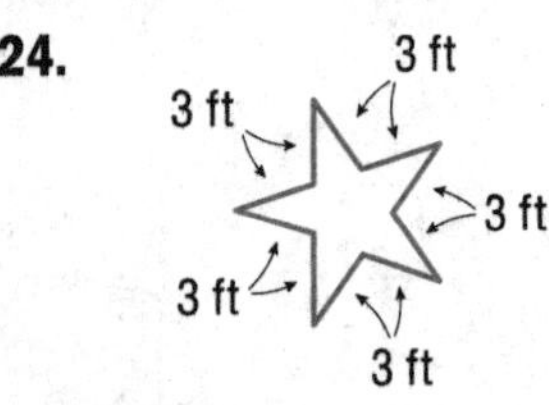

______

25.

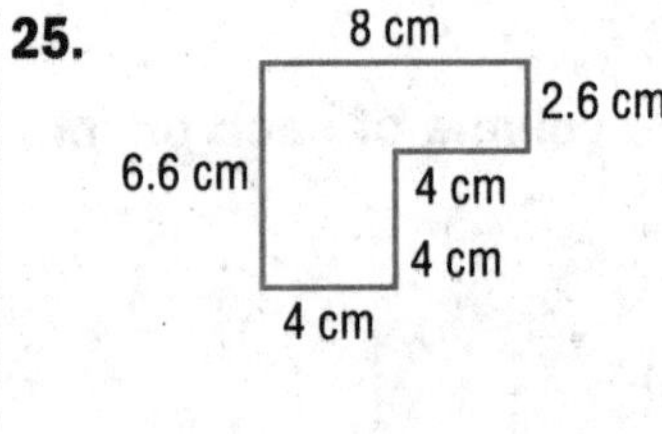

______

26. Write a formula for finding the perimeter of a square. Use your formula to find the perimeter of a square with side length of 0.5 inch. MCC6.G.3

______

Solve a Simpler Problem

Content Standards
MCC7.G.4, MCC7.G.6
Mathematical Practices
1, 3

Case #1 Playgrounds

Liam is helping to mulch the play area at the community center. The diagram shows the dimensions of the play area.

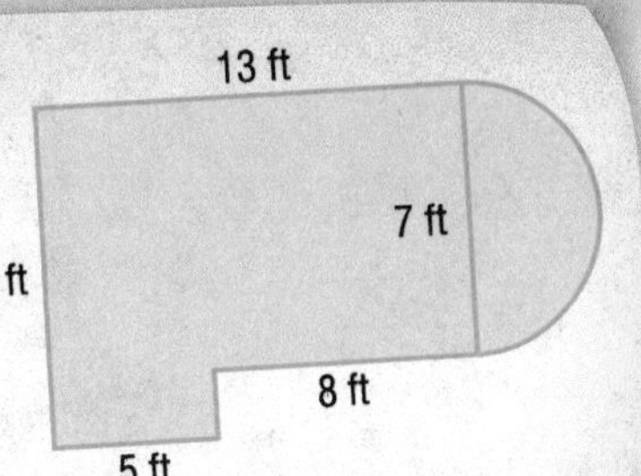

What is the area of the play area to be mulched? Round to the nearest tenth if necessary.

1 Understand *What are the facts?*

You know the shape and dimensions of the play area.

2 Plan *What is your strategy to solve this problem?*

Find the area of the two rectangles and the semi-circle, and then add.

3 Solve *How can you apply the strategy?*

Area of Rectangle 1	Area of Rectangle 2	Area of Semi-Circle
$A = \ell w$	$A = \ell w$	$A = \frac{\pi r^2}{2}$
$A = 5 \cdot 10$	$A = 8 \cdot 7$	$A = \frac{3.14 \cdot (3.5)^2}{2}$
$A =$ ☐	$A =$ ☐	$A =$ ☐

The total area is ☐ + ☐ + ☐ or ☐ square feet.

4 Check *Does the answer make sense?*

The play area is about $13 \cdot 10$ or 130 square feet. So, an answer of ☐ square feet is reasonable.

Analyze the Strategy

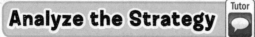

CCGPS **Reason Inductively** Why is breaking this problem into simpler parts a good strategy to solve it?

Case #2 Wallpaper

Dora is painting a wall in her house.

What is the area that will be painted?

1 Understand

Read the problem. What are you being asked to find?

I need to find ________________________.

What information do you know?

The picture shows the wall is ________ long and ________ high.

There is a window that is ________ by ________.

2 Plan

Choose a problem-solving strategy.

I will use the ____________________ strategy.

3 Solve

Use your problem-solving strategy to solve the problem.

Find the area of the wall. Then subtract the area of the window.

The dimensions of the wall are ☐ feet by ☐ feet.

So, the area of the wall is ☐ × ☐ = ☐ ft^2.

The dimensions of the window are ☐ feet by ☐ feet.

So, the area of the window is ☐ × ☐ = ☐ ft^2.

☐ – ☐ = ☐

So, ________________________.

4 Check

Use information from the problem to check your answer.

Use estimation to check the reasonableness of your answer. The area of the wall is approximately 10 × 12 = ☐ ft^2. The answer is reasonable.

Collaborate Work with a small group to solve the following cases. Show your work on a separate piece of paper.

Case #3 Woodworking

Two workers can make two chairs in two days.

How many chairs can 8 workers working at the same rate make in 20 days?

Case #4 Tips

Ebony wants to leave an 18% tip for a $19.82 restaurant bill.

Does she have enough for the tip if she has $4? Explain.

Case #5 Continents

The land area of Earth is 57,505,708 square miles.

Find the approximate land area of each continent.

Continent	Percent of Earth's Land
Asia	30
Africa	20.2
North America	16.5

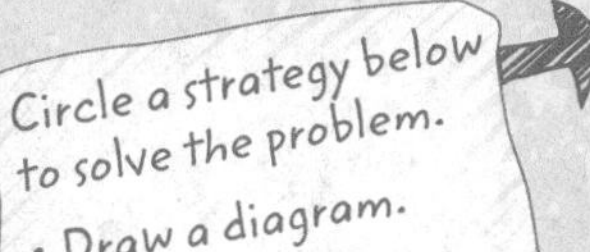

Circle a strategy below to solve the problem.
- Draw a diagram.
- Make a model.
- Determine reasonable answers.

Case #6 Fountains

Mr. Flores has a circular fountain with a radius of 5 feet. He plans on installing a brick path around the fountain.

What will be the area of the path? Round to the nearest tenth.

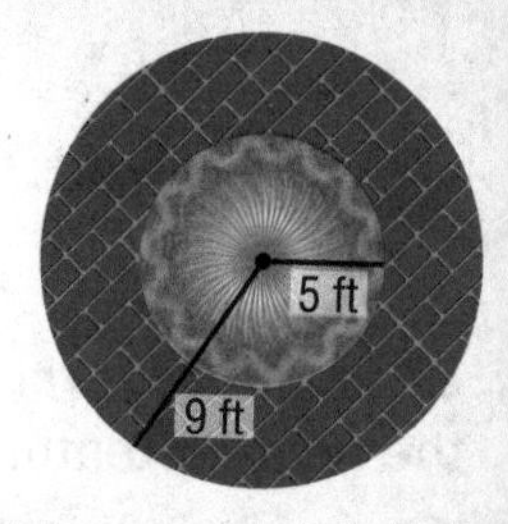

Mid-Chapter Check

Vocabulary Check

1. **Be Precise** Define *circumference*. Explain how to find the circumference of a circle. (Lesson 1)

2. Fill in the blank in the sentence below with the correct term. (Lesson 3)

   A ______________________ is made up of two or more shapes.

Skills Check and Problem Solving

Find the circumference and area of each circle. Use 3.14 for π. Round to the nearest tenth if necessary. (Lessons 1 and 2)

3. circumference = ________

   area = ________

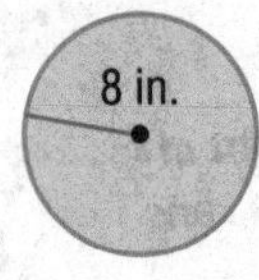

4. circumference = ________

   area = ________

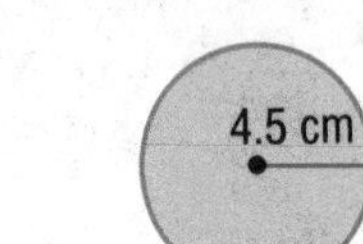

5. circumference = ________

   area = ________

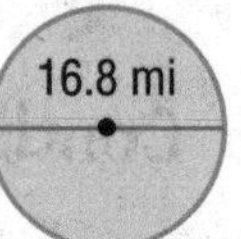

6. The dimensions of a cardboard box are shown in the figure at the right. What is the volume of the box? (Lesson 4)

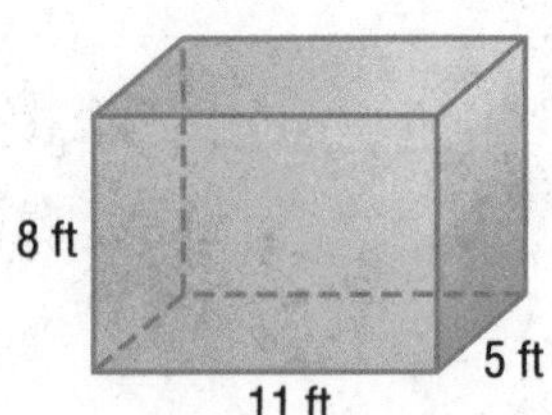

7. **Georgia Test Practice** What is the area of the figure at the right? Round to the nearest tenth. (Lesson 3)

   Ⓐ 30.4 cm^2
   Ⓑ 35.1 cm^2
   Ⓒ 39.8 cm^2
   Ⓓ 49.3 cm^2

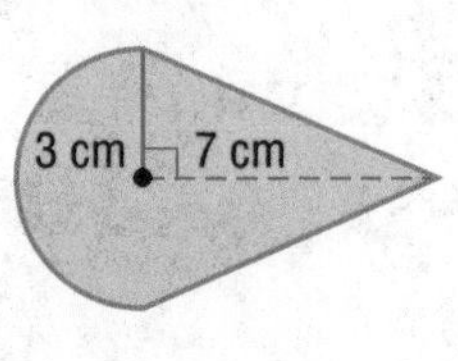

Inquiry Lab

Volume of Pyramids

WHAT is the relationship between the volume of a prism and the volume of a pyramid with the same base area and height?

Content Standards
MCC7.G.6

Mathematical Practices
1, 3, 5

Movie Theaters A movie theater offers two different containers of popcorn: a square prism and a square pyramid. Both containers are 4 inches tall and have a base area of 16 square inches. Determine the container that holds more popcorn.

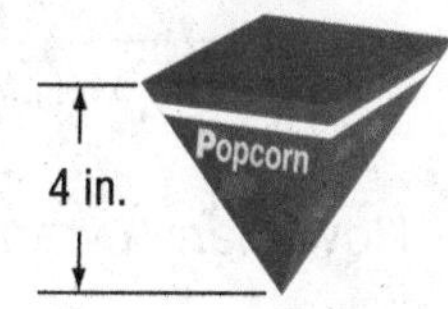

Investigation

Nets are two-dimensional patterns of three-dimensional figures.

Step 1 Draw the nets of the popcorn containers shown below onto card stock. Cut out and tape each net to form its shape. The prism and pyramid will be open. The pyramid is composed of ☐ congruent isosceles triangles with bases of 4 inches and heights of $4\frac{1}{2}$ inches.

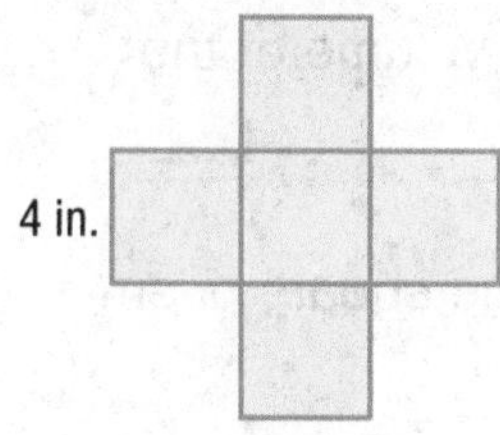

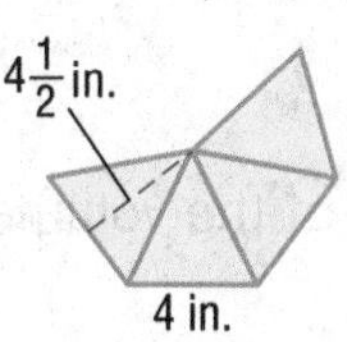

Step 2 Fill the pyramid with rice. Pour the rice from the pyramid into the prism and repeat until the prism is full. Slide a ruler across the top to level the amount.

It took ☐ pyramids of rice to fill the prism.

So, the square ________ container holds more popcorn than the square ________ container.

Collaborate

Use Math Tools **Work with a partner to repeat the Investigation with a rectangular prism and a rectangular pyramid.**

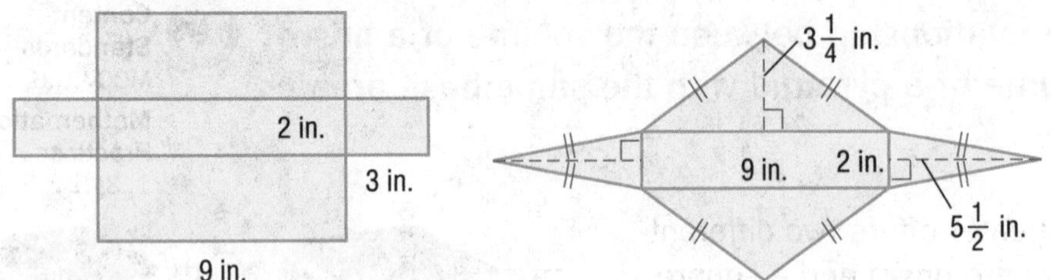

1. How many pyramids of rice did it take to fill the prism?

2. What is true about the bases of your rectangular prism and rectangular pyramid? the heights?

3. Refer to the Investigation. What is true about the bases of the square prism and square pyramid? the heights?

Analyze

4. What fraction of the volume of the rectangular prism is the volume of the rectangular pyramid? ____________

5. Refer to the Investigation. What fraction of the volume of the square prism is the volume of the square pyramid? ____________

6. **Reason Inductively** How can you find volume of a pyramid given a prism with the same base area and height?

Reflect

7.  WHAT is the relationship between the volume of a prism and the volume of a pyramid with the same base area and height?

Lesson 5

Volume of Pyramids

What You'll Learn

Scan the lesson. Write the definitions of lateral face and pyramid.

- lateral face ______________________

____

- pyramid ______________________

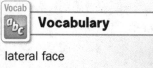

Essential Question

HOW do measurements help you describe real-world objects?

Vocabulary

lateral face

Common Core GPS

Content Standards
MCC7.G.6

Mathematical Practices
1, 3, 4, 6

Real-World Link

Sand Sculpture Dion is helping his mother build a sand sculpture at the beach in the shape of a pyramid. The square pyramid has a base with a length and width of 12 inches each and a height of 14 inches.

1. Label the dimensions of the sand sculpture on the square pyramid below.

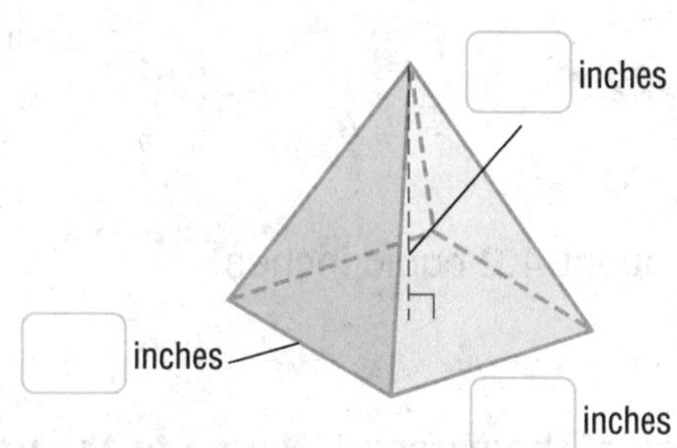

2. What is the area of the base of the pyramid?

____

3. What is the volume of a square prism with the same dimensions as the pyramid?

____

Key Concept Volume of a Pyramid

Words The volume V of a pyramid is one third the area of the base B times the height of the pyramid h.

Symbols $V = \frac{1}{3}Bh$

Model

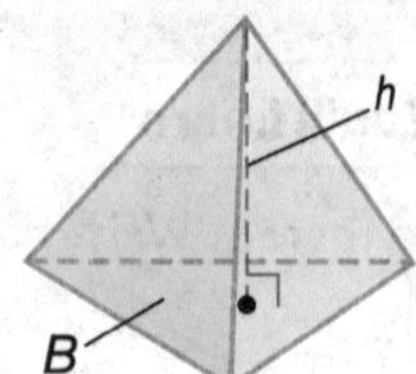

Work Zone

In a polyhedron, any face that is not a base is called a **lateral face**. The lateral faces of a pyramid meet at a common vertex. The height of a pyramid is the distance from the vertex perpendicular to the base.

Examples

1. Find the volume of the pyramid. Round to the nearest tenth.

$V = \frac{1}{3}Bh$ Volume of a pyramid

$V = \frac{1}{3}(3.2 \cdot 1.4)2.8$ $B = 3.2 \cdot 1.4, h = 2.8$

$V \approx 4.2$ Simplify.

The volume is about 4.2 cubic inches.

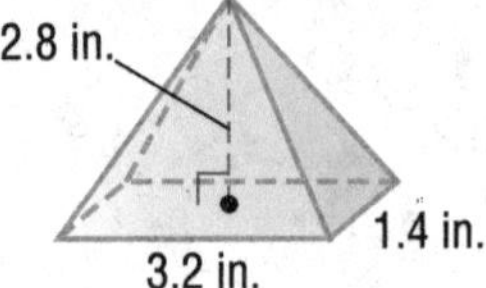

2. Find the volume of the pyramid. Round to the nearest tenth.

$V = \frac{1}{3}Bh$ Volume of a pyramid

$V = \frac{1}{3}\left(\frac{1}{2} \cdot 8.1 \cdot 6.4\right)11$ $B = \frac{1}{2} \cdot 8.1 \cdot 6.4, h = 11$

$V = 95.04$ Simplify.

The volume is about 95.0 cubic meters.

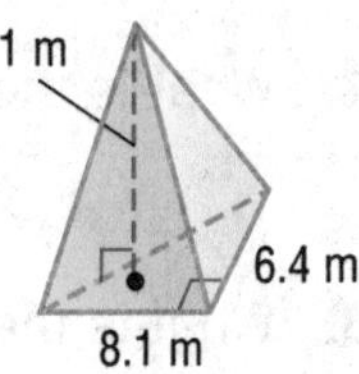

Got It? Do this problem to find out.

a. Find the volume of a pyramid that has a height of 9 centimeters and a rectangular base with a length of 7 centimeters and a width of 3 centimeters.

a. ______________

Find the Height of a Pyramid

You can also use the formula for the volume of a pyramid to find a missing height.

Examples

3. The rectangular pyramid shown has a volume of 90 cubic inches. Find the height of the pyramid.

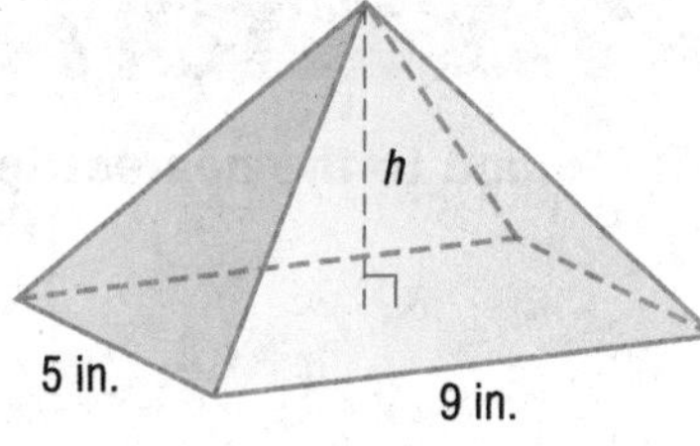

$V = \frac{1}{3}Bh$	Volume of a pyramid
$90 = \frac{1}{3}(9 \cdot 5)h$	$V = 90$, $B = 9 \cdot 5$
$90 = 15h$	Multiply.
$\frac{90}{15} = \frac{15h}{15}$	Divide by 15.
$6 = h$	Simplify.

The height of the pyramid is 6 inches.

4. A triangular pyramid has a volume of 44 cubic meters. It has an 8-meter base and a 3-meter height. Find the height of the pyramid.

$V = \frac{1}{3}Bh$	Volume of a pyramid
$44 = \frac{1}{3}\left(\frac{1}{2} \cdot 8 \cdot 3\right)h$	$V = 44$, $B = \frac{1}{2} \cdot 8 \cdot 3$
$44 = 4h$	Multiply.
$\frac{44}{4} = \frac{4h}{4}$	Divide by 4.
$11 = h$	Simplify.

h
3 m
8 m

The height of the pyramid is 11 meters.

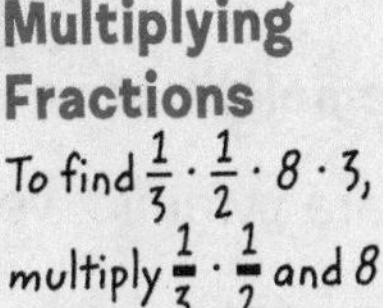

Multiplying Fractions
To find $\frac{1}{3} \cdot \frac{1}{2} \cdot 8 \cdot 3$, multiply $\frac{1}{3} \cdot \frac{1}{2}$ and $8 \cdot 3$ to get $\frac{1}{6}$ and 24, then find $\frac{1}{6}$ of 24.

Got It? Do these problems to find out.

b. A triangular pyramid has a volume of 840 cubic inches. The triangular base has a base length of 20 inches and a height of 21 inches. Find the height of the pyramid.

c. A rectangular pyramid has a volume of 525 cubic feet. It has a base of 25 feet by 18 feet. Find the height of the pyramid.

b. ________

c. ________

Example

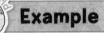

5. Kamilah is making a model of the Food Guide Pyramid for a class project. Find the volume of the square pyramid.

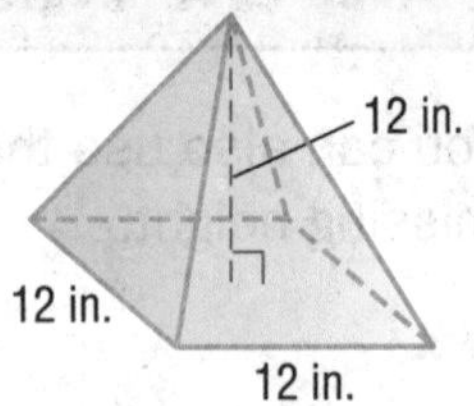

$V = \frac{1}{3}Bh$ Volume of a pyramid

$V = \frac{1}{3}(12 \cdot 12)12$ $B = 12 \cdot 12, h = 12$

$V = 576$ Multiply.

The volume is 576 cubic inches.

Guided Practice

Find the volume of each pyramid. Round to the nearest tenth if necessary. (Examples 1 and 2)

1. 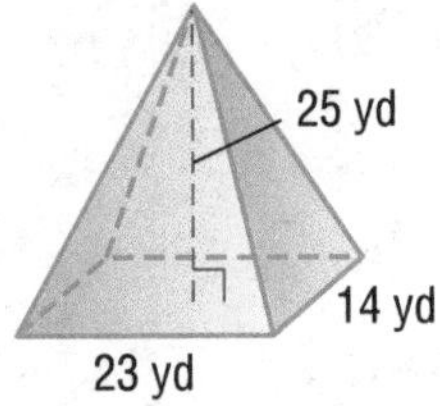

______

2. 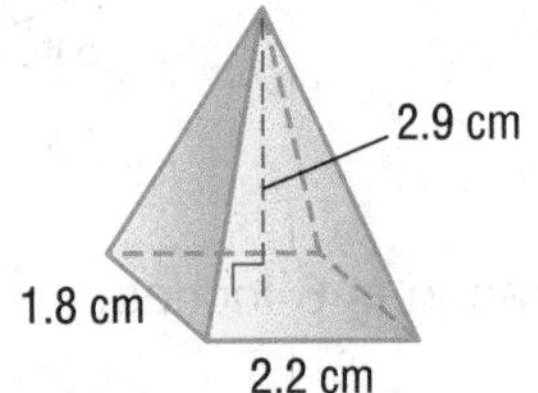

______

Find the height of each pyramid. (Examples 3 and 4)

3. square pyramid: volume 1,024 cm^3; base edge 16 cm ______

4. triangular pyramid: volume 48 in^3; base edge 9 in.; base height 4 in. ______

5. The Transamerica Pyramid is a skyscraper in San Francisco. The rectangular base has a length of 175 feet and a width of 120 feet. The height is 853 feet.

Find the volume of the building. (Example 5) ______

6. **Building on the Essential Question** When you are finding the volume of a pyramid, why is it important to know the shape of the base of the pyramid?

______

______

Rate Yourself!

How well do you understand volume of pyramids? Circle the image that applies.

Clear

Somewhat Clear

Not So Clear

For more help, go online to access a Personal Tutor.

FOLDABLES *Time to update your Foldable!*

Independent Practice

Go online for Step-by-Step Solutions 

Find the volume of each pyramid. Round to the nearest tenth if necessary. (Examples 1 and 2)

1\. 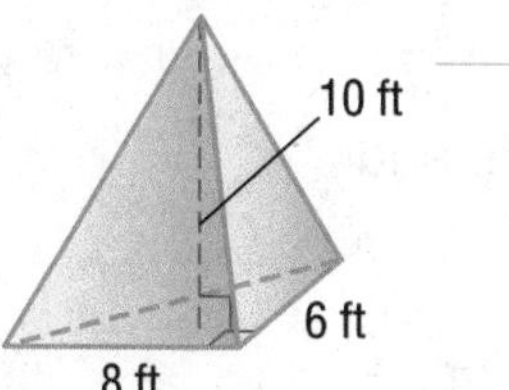

2\. 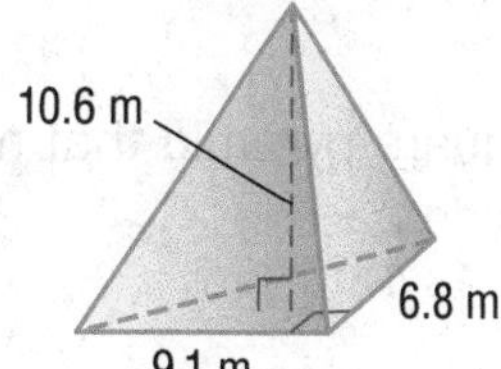

3\. 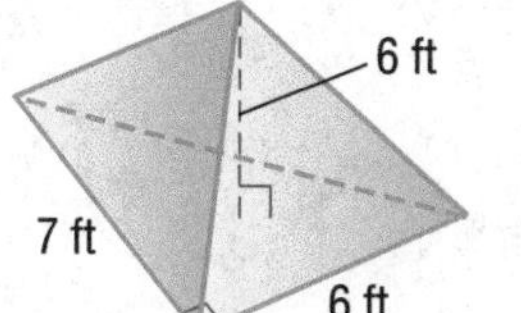

4\. 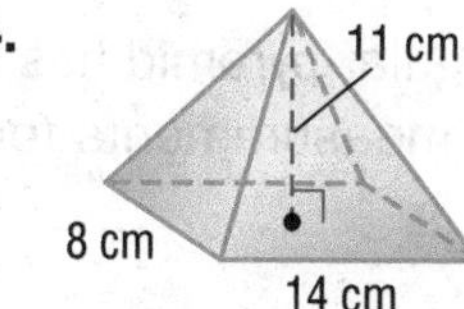

Find the height of each pyramid. (Examples 3 and 4)

5\. rectangular pyramid: volume 448 in^3; base edge 12 in.; base length 8 in.

6\. triangular pyramid: volume 270 cm^3; base edge 15 cm; height of base 4 cm

7\. A glass pyramid has a height of 4 inches. Its rectangular base has a length of 3 inches and a width of 2.5 inches. Find the volume of glass used to create the pyramid. (Example 5)

8\. The Pyramid Arena in Memphis, Tennessee, is a square pyramid that is 321 feet tall. The base has 600-foot sides. Find the volume of the pyramid. (Example 5)

9. **Reason Inductively** A rectangular pyramid has a length of 14 centimeters, a width of 9 centimeters, and a height of 10 centimeters. Explain the effect on the volume if each dimension were doubled.

10. Find the height of a square pyramid that has a volume of $25\frac{3}{5}$ meters and a base with 4 meter sides.

H.O.T. Problems Higher Order Thinking

11. **Be Precise** A rectangular pyramid has a volume of 160 cubic feet. Find two possible sets of measurements for the base area and height of the pyramid.

12. **Persevere with Problems** A square pyramid and a cube have the same bases and volumes. How are their heights related? Explain.

13. **Reason Inductively** The two figures shown have congruent bases. How does the volume of the two square pyramids in Figure B compare to the volume of the square pyramid in Figure A?

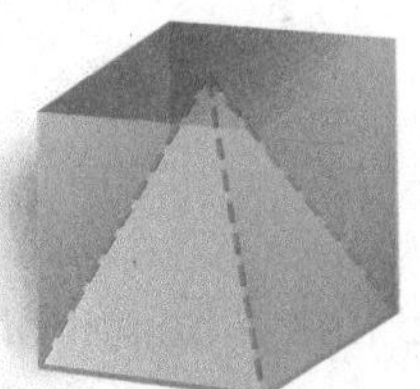
Figure A

Figure B

Georgia Test Practice

14. A rectangular pyramid has a base 18 inches by 30 inches and a height of 36 inches. Which is closest to the volume of the pyramid in cubic inches?

Ⓐ 5,000 in^3 Ⓒ 6,500 in^3

Ⓑ 6,000 in^3 Ⓓ 7,500 in^3

Name ______________________ My Homework ______________________

Extra Practice

Find the volume of each pyramid. Round to the nearest tenth if necessary.

15. 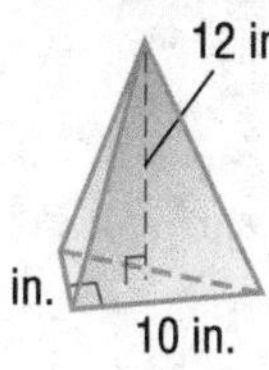

60 in³

Homework Help

$V = \frac{1}{3}Bh$

$V = \frac{1}{3}\left(\frac{1}{2} \cdot 10 \cdot 3\right)12$

$V = 60$

16. 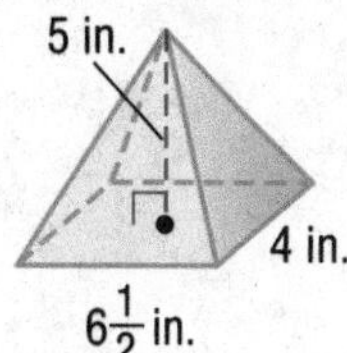

______

17. 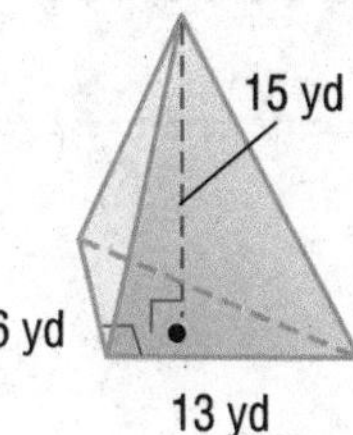

______

18. 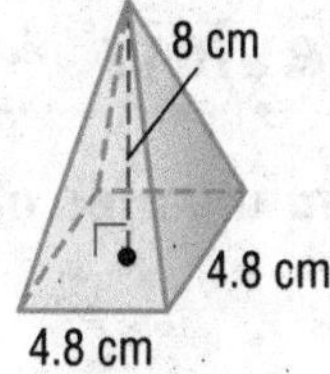

______

Find the height of each pyramid.

19. square pyramid: volume 297 ft^3; area of the base 81 ft^2

______

20. hexagonal pyramid: volume 1,320 ft^3; area of the base 120 ft^2

______

21. square pyramid: volume 550 in^3; area of the base 75 in^2

______

22. rectangular pyramid: volume 3,800 m^3; area of the base 300 m^2

______

23. An ancient stone pyramid has a height of 13.6 meters. The edges of the square base are 16.5 meters. Find the volume of the stone pyramid.

______

Georgia Test Practice

24. The rectangular pyramid has a volume of 1,560 cubic inches. What is the height of the pyramid?

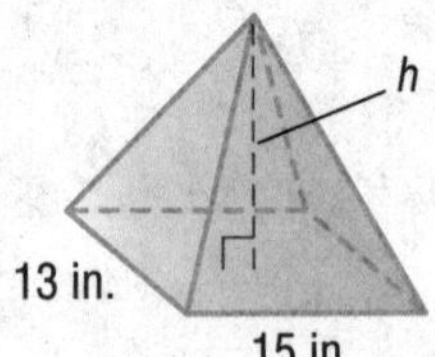

Ⓐ 8 in.
Ⓑ 24 in.
Ⓒ 30 in.
Ⓓ 48 in.

25. Find the volume of the rectangular pyramid. Round to the nearest tenth.

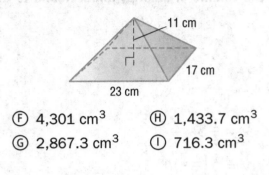

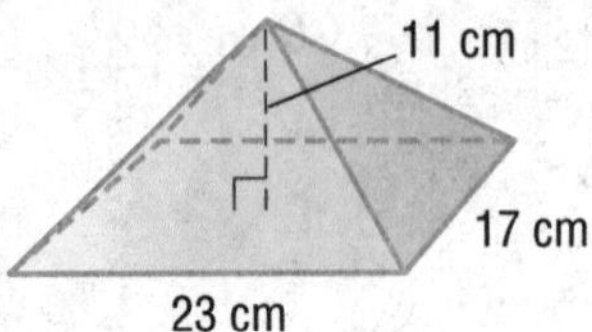

Ⓕ 4,301 cm^3
Ⓖ 2,867.3 cm^3
Ⓗ 1,433.7 cm^3
Ⓘ 716.3 cm^3

Common Core Review

Convert each length to feet. Find the area of each figure in square feet.
MCC5.MD.1

26. ________

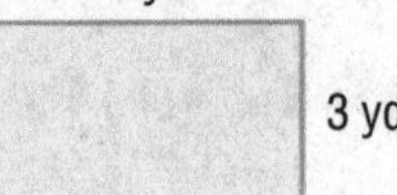

27. ________

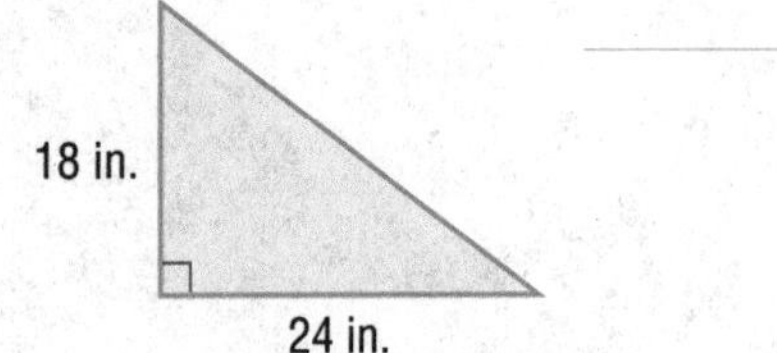

28. ________

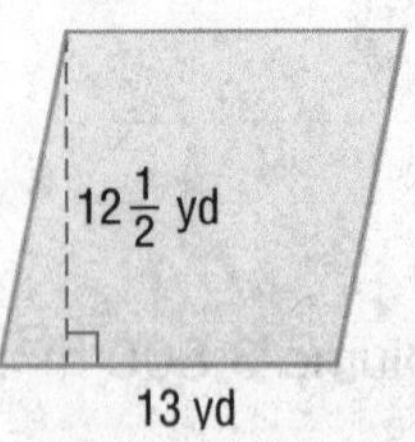

29. ________

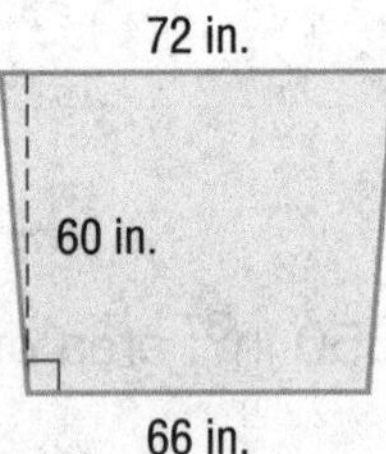

30. If the area of one face of a cube is 32 square inches, what is the total area of all the faces of the cube? MCC6.G.1

____

Nets of Three-Dimensional Figures

HOW can models and nets help you find the surface area of prisms?

Content Standards
MCC7.G.6

Mathematical Practices
1, 3, 6

Nets Nets are used to design and manufacture items such as boxes and labels. Find the shapes that make up the net of a cereal box.

Investigation 1

Make a net from a rectangular prism.

Step 1 Use an empty cereal box. Cut off one of the two top flaps. The remaining top flap is the top face.

Step 2 Label the top and bottom faces using a green marker. Label the front and back faces using a blue marker. Label the left and right faces using a red marker.

Step 3 Carefully cut along the three edges of the top face. Then cut down each vertical edge.

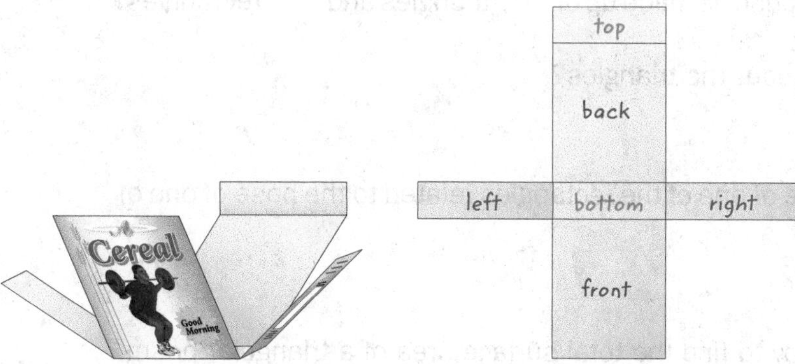

The net of a cereal box is made up of a total of ☐ rectangles.

What do you notice about the top and bottom faces, the left and right faces, and the front and back faces?

____

Investigation 2

Make a triangular prism from a net.

Step 1 Draw a net on a piece of card stock with the dimensions shown below.

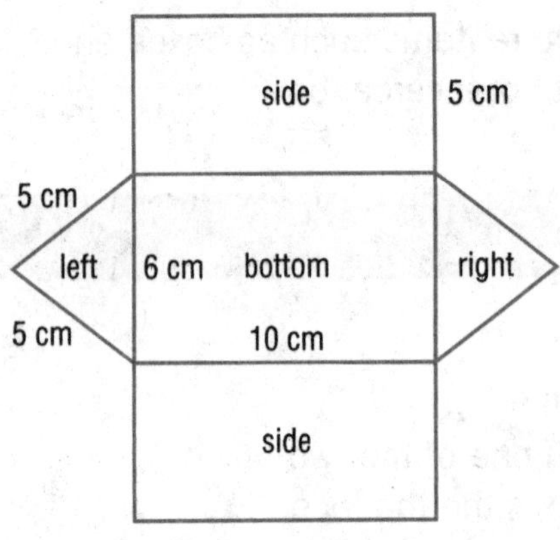

Step 2 Fold the net into a triangular prism. Tape together adjacent edges.

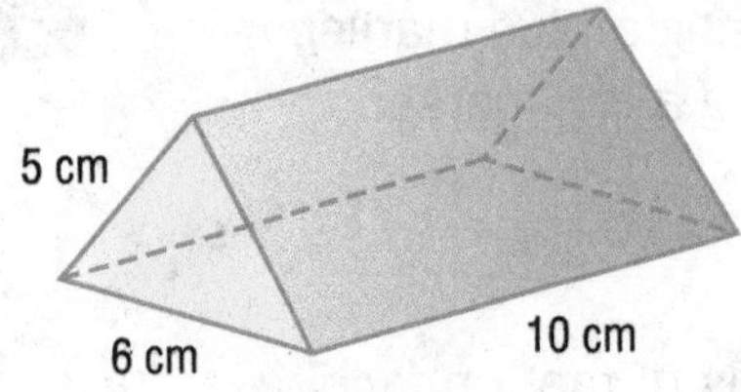

The triangular prism is made up of ☐ triangles and ☐ rectangles.

What is true about the triangles?

____

How is the side of one of the rectangles related to the base of one of the triangles?

____

Explain one way to find the total surface area of a triangular prism.

____

____

____

Work with a partner to solve each problem.

1. A net of a rectangular prism that is 24 inches by 18 inches by 4 inches is shown. The net of the prism is labeled with *top*, *bottom*, *side*, and *end*. Fill in the boxes to find the total area of the rectangular prism.

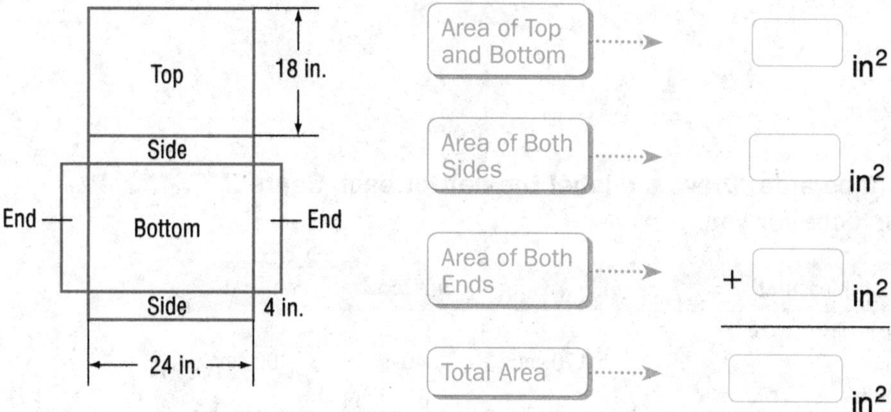

2. A net of a triangular prism is shown. Fill in the boxes to find the total area of the triangular prism.

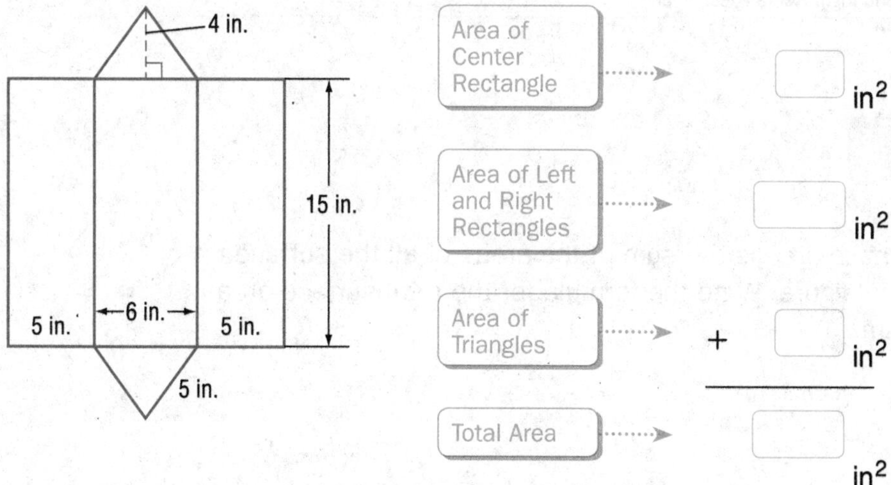

Analyze

Work with a partner.

3. **Reason Inductively** Suppose Ladell wants to wrap a present in a container that is a rectangular prism. How can he determine the amount of wrapping paper that he will need? ______

______

______

Circle each correct surface area. Draw and label the net for each figure if needed. The first one is done for you.

	Prism	Measures	Surface Area		
	Rectangular	Length: 10 cm Width: 8 cm Height: 5 cm	170 cm^2	340 cm^2	400 cm^2
4.	Rectangular	Length: 3 ft Width: 2 ft Height: 5 ft	30 ft^2	31 ft^2	62 ft^2
5.	Rectangular	Length: 2 m Width: 1 m Height: 1.5 m	3 m^2	6.5 m^2	13 m^2
6.	Triangular	Area of Top and bottom Triangles: 3 mm^2 Area of Center Rectangle: 12 mm^2 Area of Left and Right Rectangles: 10 mm^2	25 mm^2	28 mm^2	38 mm^2
7.	Triangular	Area of Top and bottom Triangles: 6 in^2 Area of Center Rectangle: 50.4 in^2 Area of Left and Right Rectangles: 56 in^2	174.4 in^2	118.4 in^2	112.4 in^2

Reflect

8. **Be Precise** *Surface area* is the sum of the areas of all the surfaces of a three-dimensional figure. Write the formula for the total surface area of a rectangular prism.

______

______

9. **Inquiry** HOW can models and nets help you find the surface area of prisms? ______

______

______

Surface Area of Prisms

What You'll Learn

Scan the lesson. List two headings you would use to make an outline of the lesson.

-

-

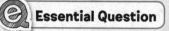

Essential Question

HOW do measurements help you describe real-world objects?

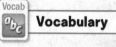

Vocabulary

surface area

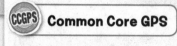

Common Core GPS

Content Standards
MCC7.G.6

Mathematical Practices
1, 3, 4, 6

Real-World Link

Message Board Members of a local recreation center are permitted to post messages on 8.5-inch by 11-inch paper on the board. Assume the signs are posted vertically and do not overlap, as shown below.

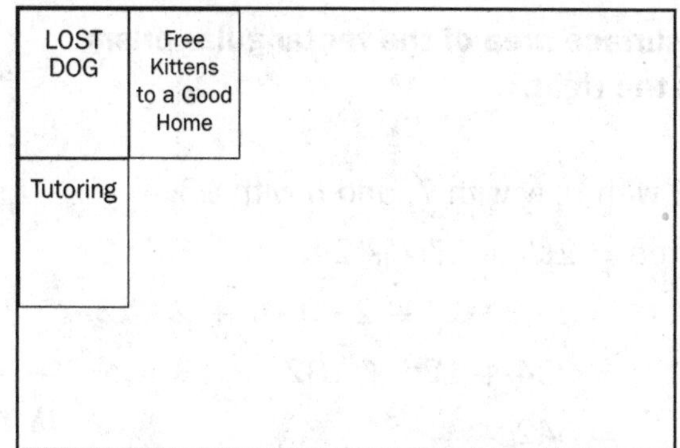

1. Suppose 6 messages fit across the board widthwise.

   What is the width of the board in inches? ☐ inches

2. Suppose 3 messages fit down the board lengthwise.

   What is the length of the board in inches? ☐ inches

3. What is the area in square inches of the message board?

4. Messages can also be posted on the other side of the board. What is the total area of the front and back of the board in square inches?

Work Zone

Key Concept: Surface Area of a Rectangular Prism

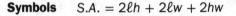

Words The surface area $S.A.$ of a rectangular prism with base ℓ, width w, and height h is the sum of the areas of its faces.

Model

Symbols $S.A. = 2\ell h + 2\ell w + 2hw$

The sum of the areas of all the surfaces, or faces, of a three-dimensional figure is the **surface area**. In the previous Inquiry Lab, you used a net to find the surface area of a rectangular prism. You can also use a formula to find surface area.

When you find the surface area of a three-dimensional figure, the units are square units, not cubic units.

Example

1. Find the surface area of the rectangular prism shown at the right.

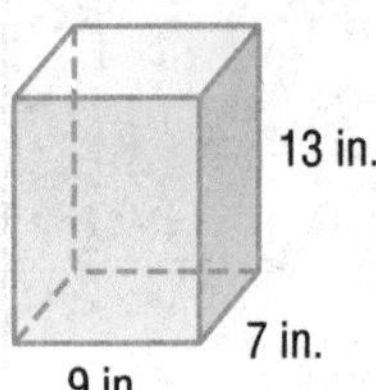

Replace ℓ with 9, w with 7, and h with 13.

$$\begin{aligned} \text{surface area} &= 2\ell h + 2\ell w + 2hw \\ &= 2 \cdot 9 \cdot 13 + 2 \cdot 9 \cdot 7 + 2 \cdot 13 \cdot 7 \\ &= 234 + 126 + 182 \quad \text{Multiply first. Then add.} \\ &= 542 \end{aligned}$$

The surface area of the prism is 542 square inches.

Got It? Do these problems to find out.

Find the surface area of each rectangular prism.

a.

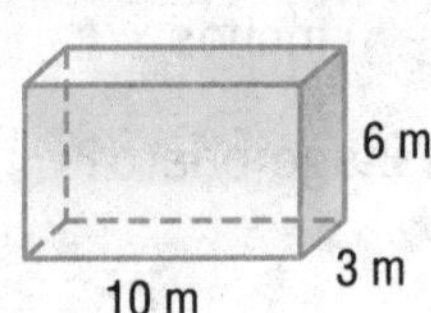

b.

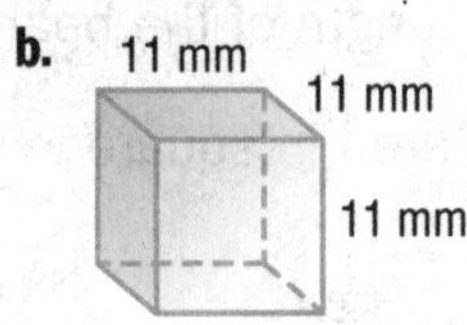

a. ________

b. ________

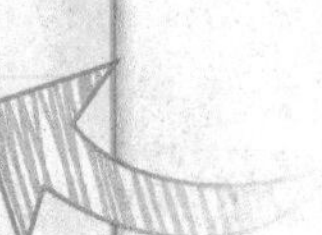

Example

2. Domingo built a toy box 60 inches long, 24 inches wide, and 36 inches high. He has 1 quart of paint that covers about 87 square feet of surface. Does he have enough to paint the outside of the toy box? Justify your answer.

Step 1 Find the surface area of the toy box.

Replace ℓ with 60, w with 24, and h with 36.

$$\begin{aligned}\text{surface area} &= 2\ell h + 2\ell w + 2hw \\ &= 2 \cdot 60 \cdot 36 + 2 \cdot 60 \cdot 24 + 2 \cdot 36 \cdot 24 \\ &= 8{,}928 \text{ in}^2\end{aligned}$$

Step 2 Find the number of square inches the paint will cover.

$1 \text{ ft}^2 = 1 \text{ ft} \times 1 \text{ ft}$ — Replace 1 ft with 12 in.

$= 12 \text{ in.} \times 12 \text{ in.}$ — Multiply.

$= 144 \text{ in}^2$

So, 87 square feet is equal to 87×144 or 12,528 square inches.

Since $12{,}528 > 8{,}928$, Domingo has enough paint.

137.94
76.38
162.14

Consistent Units

Since the surface area of the toy box is expressed in inches, convert 87 ft^2 to square inches so that all measurements are expressed using the same units.

Got It? **Do this problem to find out.**

c. The largest corrugated cardboard box ever constructed measured about 23 feet long, 9 feet high, and 8 feet wide. Would 950 square feet of paper be enough to cover the box? Justify your answer.

c. ______

40
100
125

Surface Area of Triangular Prisms

To find the surface area of a triangular prism, it is more efficient to find the area of each face and calculate the sum of all of the faces rather than using a formula.

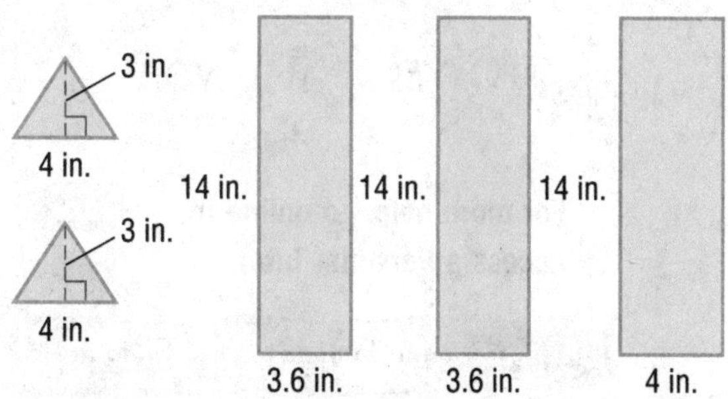

112
80
70

156

Example

3. Marty is mailing his aunt the package shown. How much cardboard is used to create the shipping container?

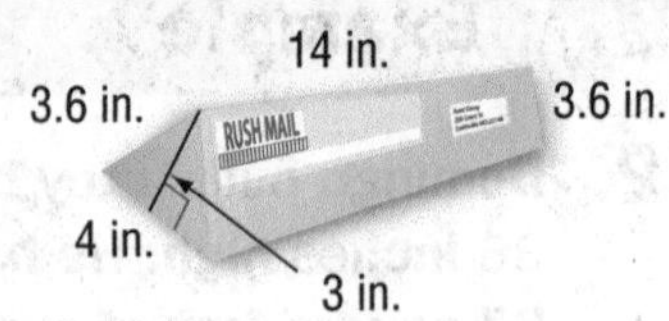

Find the area of each face and add.

The area of each triangle is $\frac{1}{2} \cdot 4 \cdot 3$ or 6.

The area of two of the rectangles is $14 \cdot 3.6$ or 50.4. The area of the third rectangle is $14 \cdot 4$ or 56.

The sum of the areas of the faces is $6 + 6 + 50.4 + 50.4 + 56$ or 168.8 cubic inches.

Got It? **Do this problem to find out.**

d. ________

d. Find the surface area of the triangular prism.

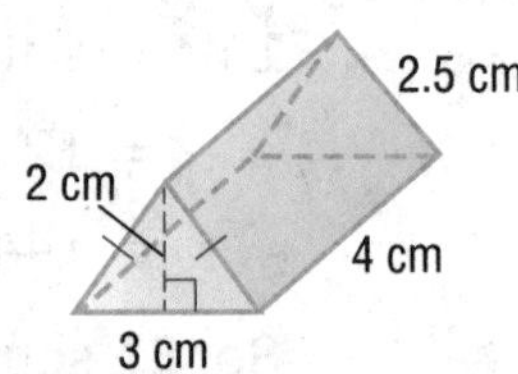

Guided Practice

Find the surface area of each prism. (Examples 1–3)

1.

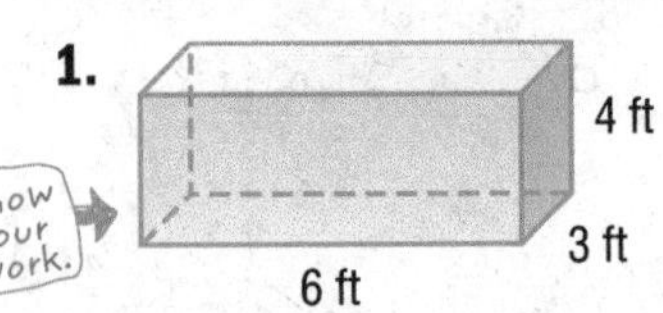

____

2.

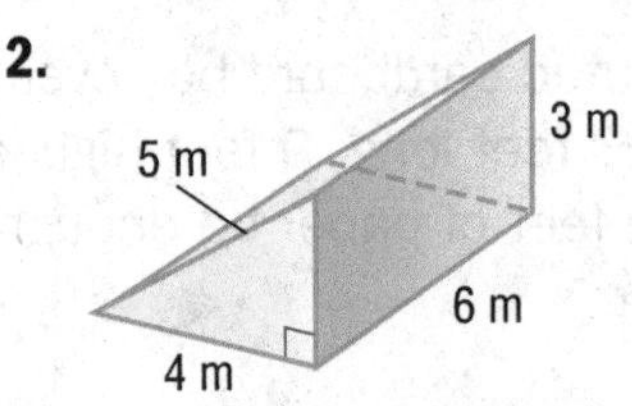

____

3. **Building on the Essential Question** Why is the surface area of a three-dimensional figure measured in square units rather than in cubic units?

Rate Yourself!
Are you ready to move on?
Shade the section that applies.
YES
?
NO
For more help, go online to access a Personal Tutor.
Tutor
FOLDABLES Time to update your Foldable!

Name ______ My Homework ______

Independent Practice

Go online for Step-by-Step Solutions

Find the surface area of each rectangular prism. Round to the nearest tenth if necessary. (Example 1)

1.

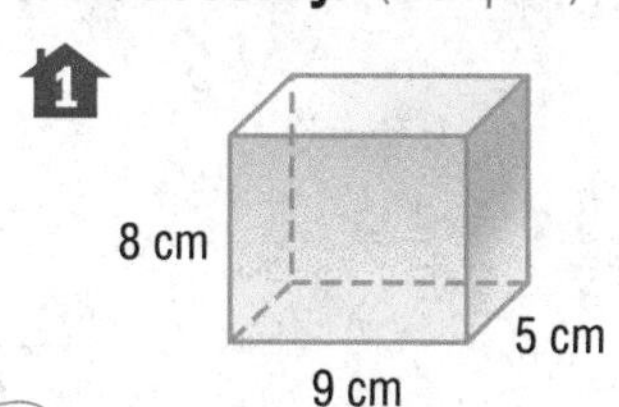

Show your work.

2. ______

12 ft
1.7 ft
6.4 ft

3. When making a book cover, Anwar adds an additional 20 square inches to the surface area to allow for overlap. How many square inches of paper will Anwar use to make a book cover for a book 11 inches long, 8 inches wide, and 1 inch high? (Example 2) ______

Find the surface area of each triangular prism. (Example 3)

4. ______

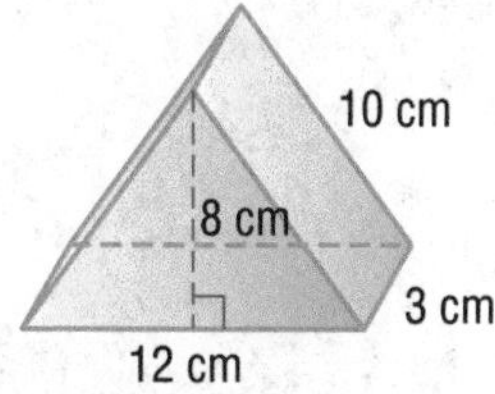

5. ______

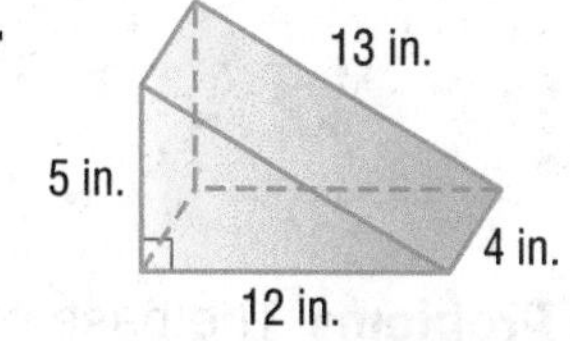

6. CCGPS **Model with Mathematics** Refer to the graphic novel in Lesson 4 and the one below. What whole number dimensions would allow the students to maximize the volume while keeping the surface area at most 160 square feet? Explain. ______

Watch
Replay it online!
We are designing a dunk tank. Remember, we want to maximize the volume and minimize the surface area.
Dunk Tank

7. Write a formula for the surface area *S.A.* of a cube in which each side measures *x* units.

8. A company will make a cereal box with whole number dimensions and a volume of 100 cubic centimeters. If cardboard costs $0.05 per 100 square centimeters, what is the least cost to make 100 boxes?

H.O.T. Problems Higher Order Thinking

9. CCGPS **Reason Inductively** Determine if the following statement is *true* or *false*. Explain your reasoning.

If you double one of the dimensions of a rectangular prism, the surface area will double.

10. CCGPS **Persevere with Problems** The base of the prism shown at the right is a regular hexagon with side lengths of 8 centimeters. The area of one of its bases is about 166 square centimeters. What is the surface area of this hexagonal prism?

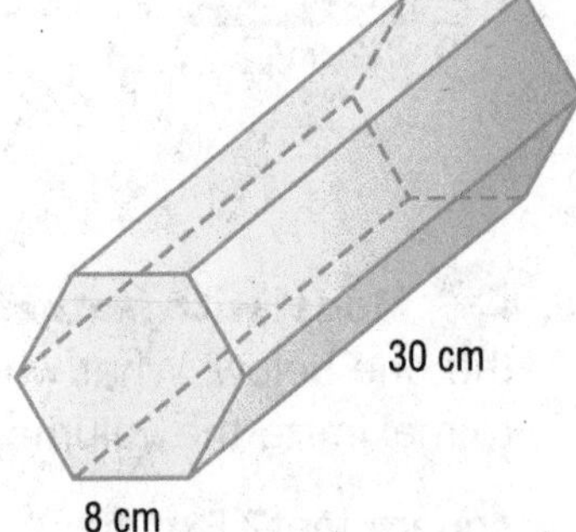

11. CCGPS **Persevere with Problems** The figure at the right is made by placing a cube with 12-centimeter sides on top of another cube with 15-centimeter sides. Find the surface area.

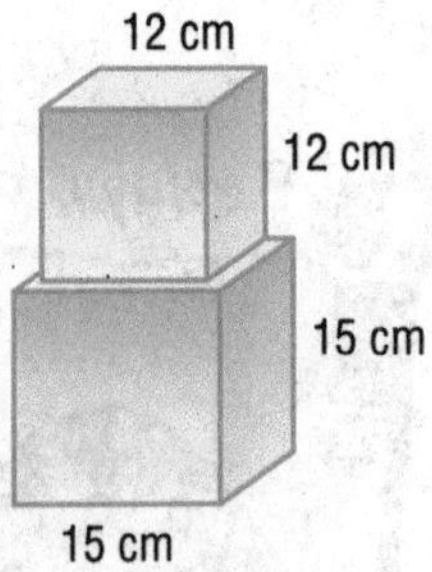

Georgia Test Practice

12. What is the surface area of the rectangular prism shown?

Ⓐ $600\frac{1}{2}$ yd^2 Ⓒ 662.7 yd^2

Ⓑ 659.7 yd^2 Ⓓ 700 yd^2

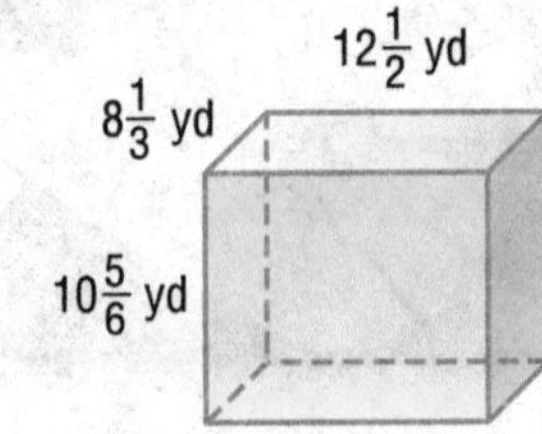

Name ________________________ My Homework ________________

Extra Practice

Find the surface area of each prism. Round to the nearest tenth if necessary.

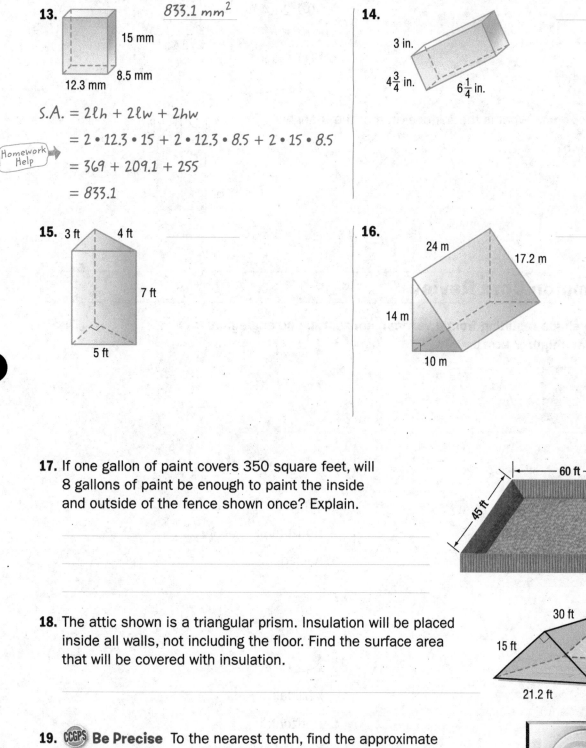

13. $833.1\ mm^2$

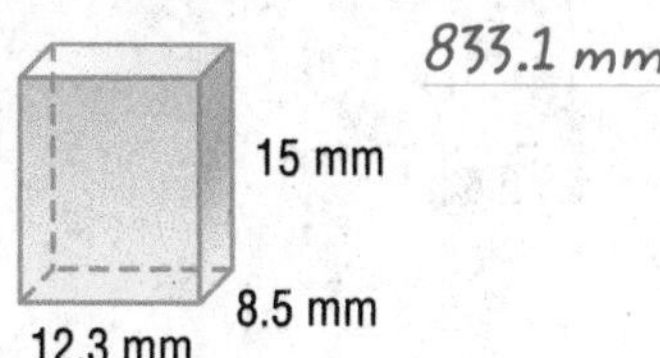

$S.A. = 2\ell h + 2\ell w + 2hw$

Homework Help

$= 2 \cdot 12.3 \cdot 15 + 2 \cdot 12.3 \cdot 8.5 + 2 \cdot 15 \cdot 8.5$

$= 369 + 209.1 + 255$

$= 833.1$

14. ____________

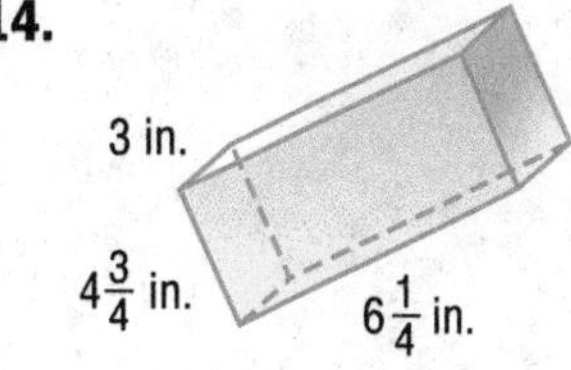

15. ____________

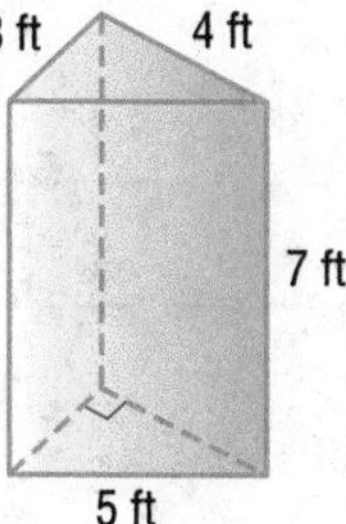

16. ____________

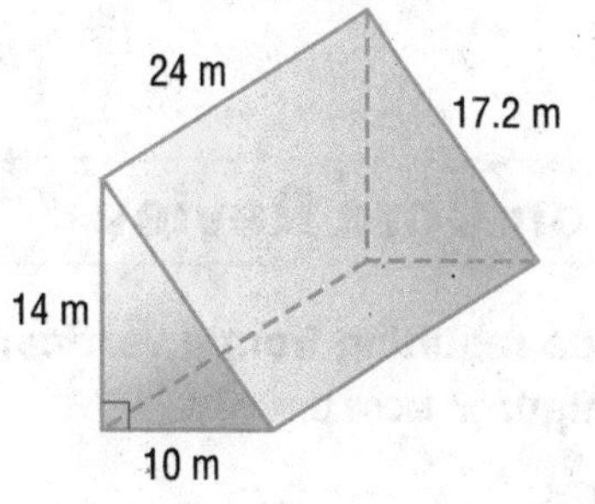

17. If one gallon of paint covers 350 square feet, will 8 gallons of paint be enough to paint the inside and outside of the fence shown once? Explain.

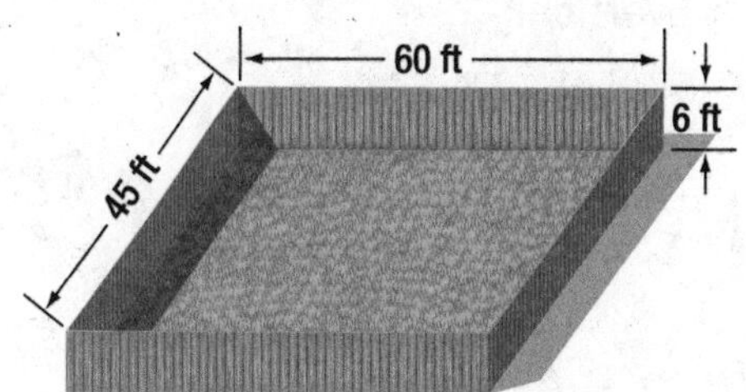

____

____

____

18. The attic shown is a triangular prism. Insulation will be placed inside all walls, not including the floor. Find the surface area that will be covered with insulation.

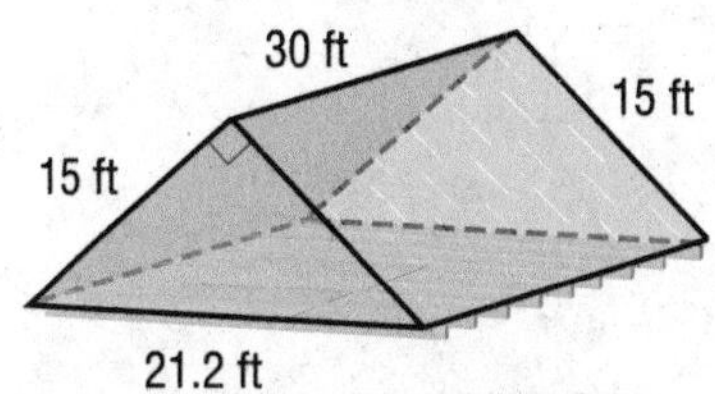

____

19. CCGPS **Be Precise** To the nearest tenth, find the approximate amount of plastic covering the outside of the CD case.

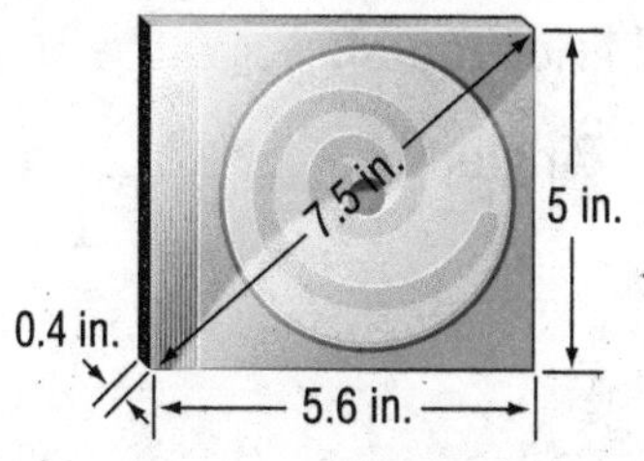

____

Georgia Test Practice

20. Which of the following expressions represents the surface area of a cube with side length w?

Ⓐ w^3

Ⓑ $6w^2$

Ⓒ $6w^3$

Ⓓ $2w + 4w^2$

21. How much cardboard is needed to make the box shown?

Ⓕ 37.5 ft^2

Ⓖ 24.4 ft^2

Ⓗ 8 ft^2

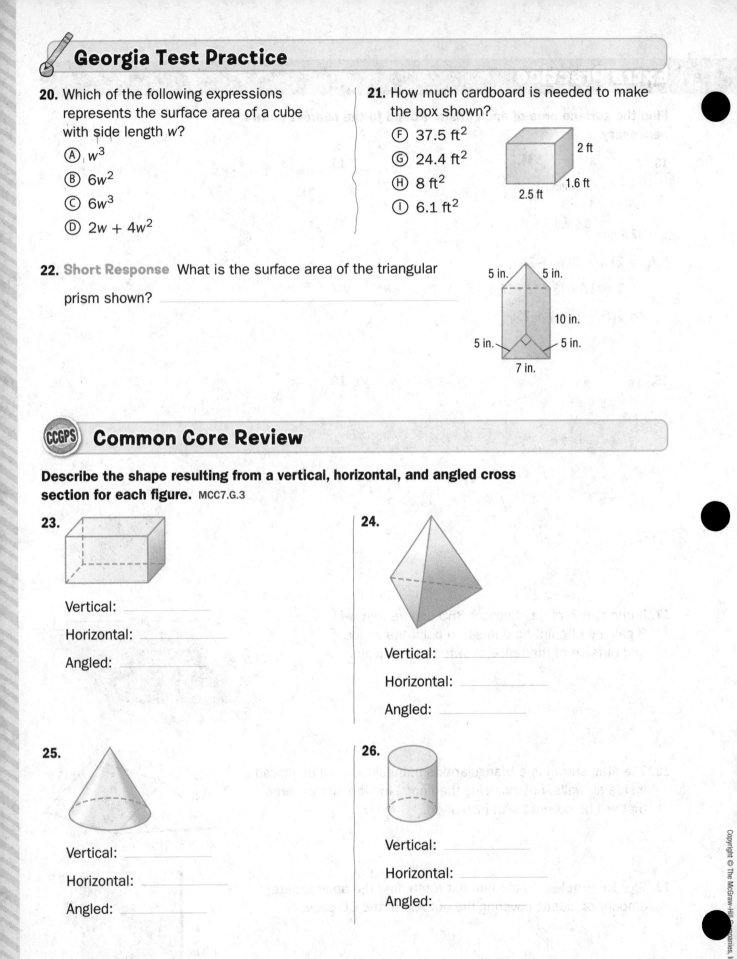

Ⓘ 6.1 ft^2

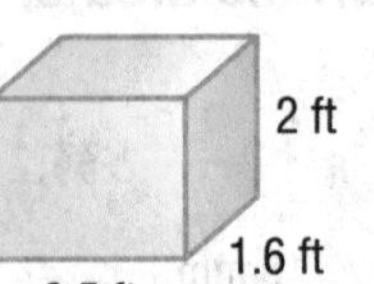

22. **Short Response** What is the surface area of the triangular prism shown? ______________________

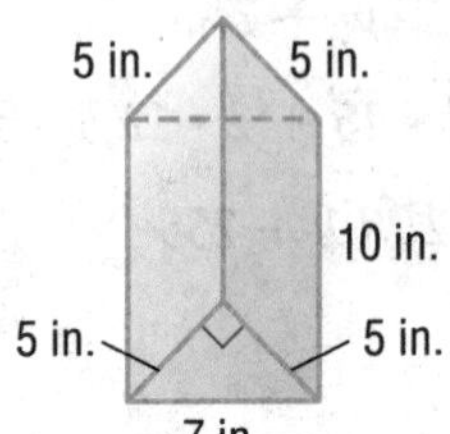

Common Core Review

Describe the shape resulting from a vertical, horizontal, and angled cross section for each figure. MCC7.G.3

23.

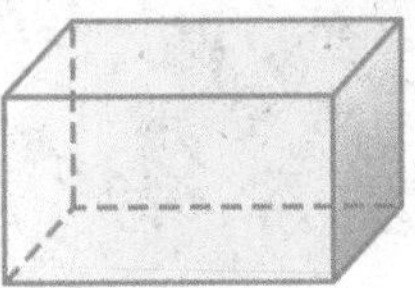

Vertical: ______________

Horizontal: ______________

Angled: ______________

24.

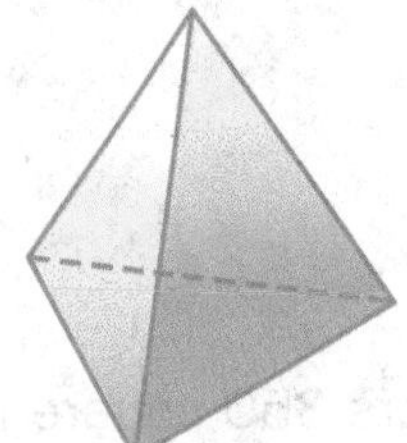

Vertical: ______________

Horizontal: ______________

Angled: ______________

25.

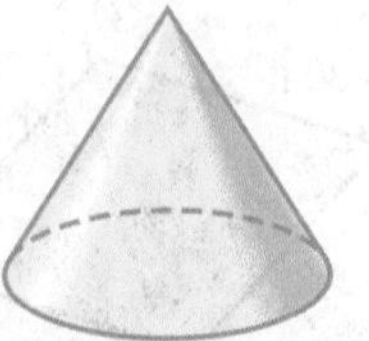

Vertical: ______________

Horizontal: ______________

Angled: ______________

26.

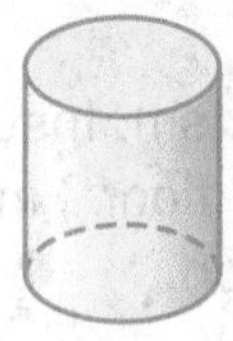

Vertical: ______________

Horizontal: ______________

Angled: ______________

Inquiry Lab

Relate Surface Area and Volume

HOW does the shape of a rectangular prism affect its volume and surface area?

Content Standards
MCC7.G.6

Mathematical Practices
1, 3, 4

Blocks You can arrange blocks in many ways. How can you arrange 8 blocks to create the least possible surface area?

What do you know? ______________________________

____

What do you need to find? ______________________________

____

Investigation 1

Tools

Step 1 Create a rectangular prism using 8 centimeter cubes. Record the dimensions in the table below. Find and record the volume and surface area of the prism.

Rectangular Prism	Length (cm)	Width (cm)	Height (cm)	Volume (cm^3)	Surface Area (cm^2)
1	2	2			
2					
3					

Step 2 Repeat Step 1 for as many different rectangular prisms as you can create with 8 cubes.

Does the volume change when the prism changes? Explain.

____

____

The rectangular prism measuring ☐ × ☐ × ☐ has the least surface area.

Investigation 2

Blocks Suppose you make structures in the shape of the ones shown below. What is the volume of each structure? Which structure has the lesser surface area?

Figure 1

Figure 2

Step 1 Use centimeter cubes to create the rectangular prism shown in Figure 1. Write its dimensions, volume, and surface area in the table below.

Rectangular Prism	Length (cm)	Width (cm)	Height (cm)	Volume (cm^3)	Surface Area (cm^2)
Figure 1	3				
Figure 2					

Step 2 Use centimeter cubes to create the rectangular prism shown in Figure 2. Write its dimensions, volume, and surface area in the table.

Step 3 Compare the volume and surface areas of Figure 1 and Figure 2.

What do you notice about the volume of Figure 1 and Figure 2?

____

The surface area of Figure 1 is ____ square centimeters.

The surface area of Figure 2 is ____ square centimeters.

Compare the surface areas using an inequality.

____ square centimeters $<$ ____ square centimeters

So, Figure ____ has the lesser surface area.

Collaborate

Work with a partner. Compare the two figures that have the same volume. Then determine which figure has a greater surface area.

1.

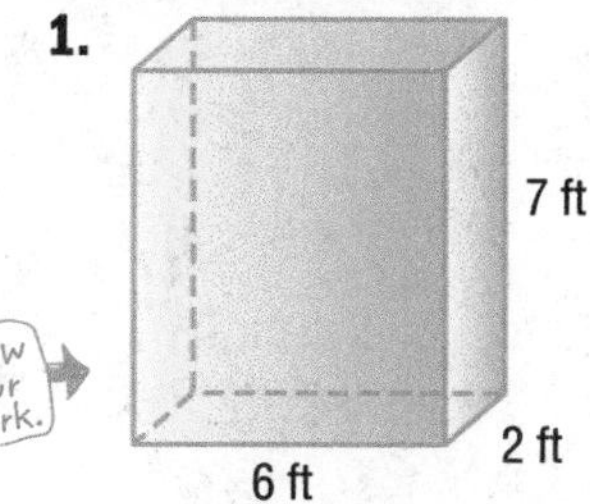

Figure 1

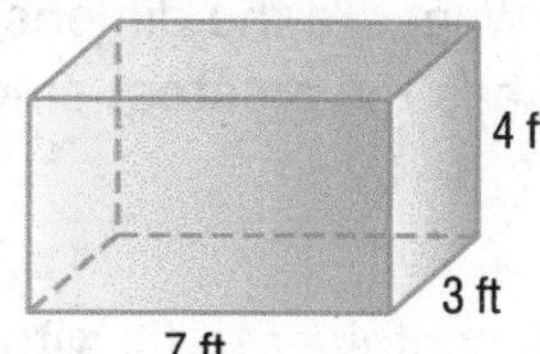

Figure 2

Surface Area: ______ Surface Area: ______

2.

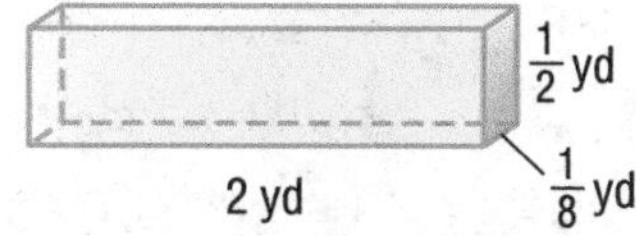

0.5 yd

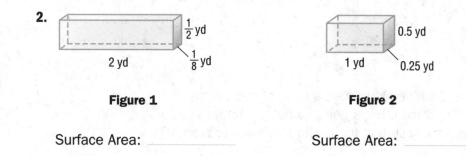

1 yd 0.25 yd

Figure 1

Figure 2

Surface Area: ______ Surface Area: ______

3.

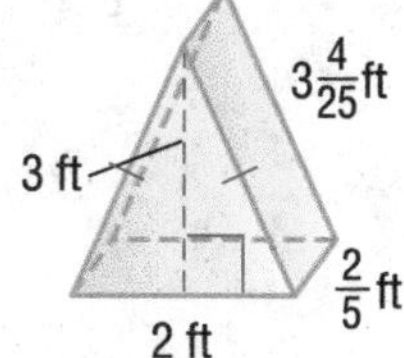

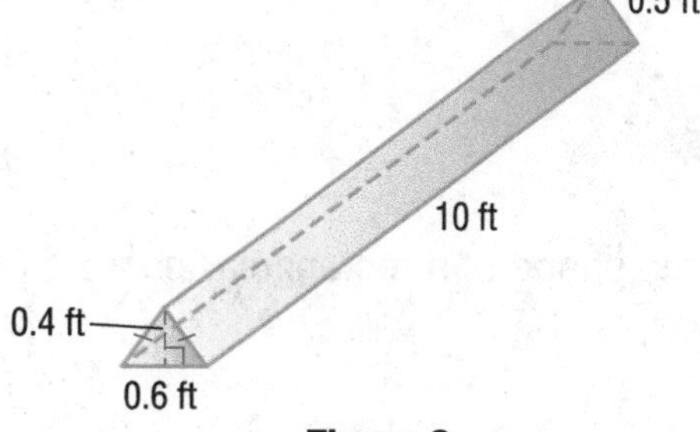

Figure 1

Figure 2

Surface Area: ______ Surface Area: ______

Work with a partner to solve the following problems.

4. Monique sews together pieces of fabric to make rectangular gift boxes. She only uses whole numbers. What are the dimensions of a box with a volume of 50 cubic inches that has the greatest amount of surface area?

5. Thomas is creating a decorative container to fill with colored sand. He uses only whole numbers. The top of the container is open. What are the dimensions of the rectangular prism that holds 100 cubic inches with the least amount of surface area?

6. CCGPS **Model with Mathematics** Draw a sketch of a triangular prism with a volume of 120 cubic units and a surface area of 184 square units.

7. CCGPS **Construct an Argument** Zack needs to melt a stick of butter that measures 5 inches by 1 inch by 1 inch. He is going to put the butter in a pan on top of the stove. Explain why cutting the butter into smaller pieces will help the butter melt faster.

Reflect

8. Inquiry HOW does the shape of a rectangular prism affect its volume and surface area?

Lesson 7

Surface Area of Pyramids

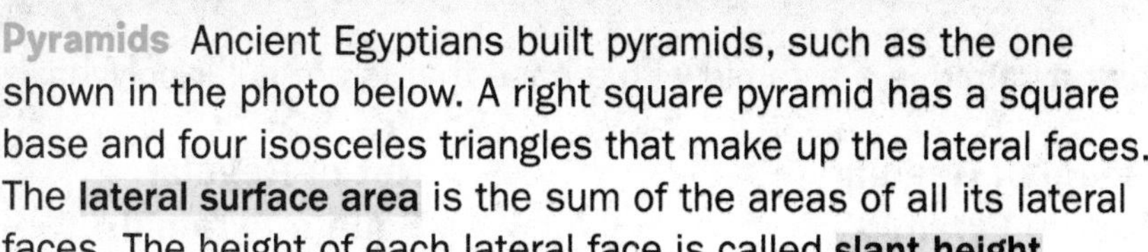

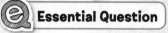

What You'll Learn

Scan the lesson. Write the definitions of slant height and lateral surface area.

- slant height ______________________________
- lateral surface area ______________________________

Essential Question

HOW do measurements help you describe real-world objects?

Vocabulary

lateral surface area
slant height
regular pyramid

Common Core GPS

Content Standards
MCC7.G.6

Mathematical Practices
1, 3, 4, 5

Vocabulary Start-Up

Pyramids Ancient Egyptians built pyramids, such as the one shown in the photo below. A right square pyramid has a square base and four isosceles triangles that make up the lateral faces. The **lateral surface area** is the sum of the areas of all its lateral faces. The height of each lateral face is called **slant height**.

1. Fill in the blanks on the diagram below with the terms *slant height* and *lateral face*.

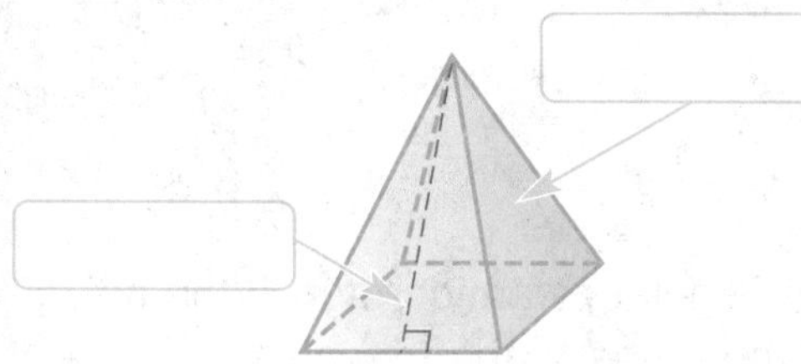

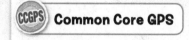

2. Draw a net of a square pyramid.

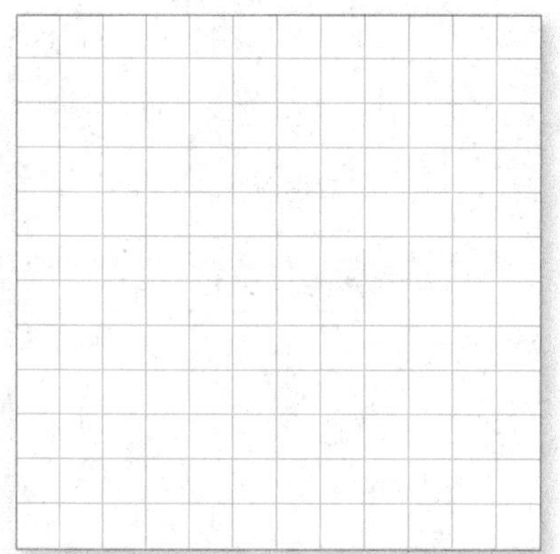

Key Concept: Surface Area of a Pyramid

Work Zone

Lateral Area

Words The lateral surface area *L.A.* of a regular pyramid is half the perimeter *P* of the base times the slant height ℓ.

Model

slant height ℓ
area of base *B*
perimeter of base *P*

Symbols $L.A. = \frac{1}{2}P\ell$

Total Surface Area

Words The total surface area *S.A.* of a regular pyramid is the lateral area *L.A.* plus the area of the base *B*.

Symbols $S.A. = B + L.A.$ or $S.A. = B + \frac{1}{2}P\ell$

A **regular pyramid** is a pyramid with a base that is a regular polygon.

Model of Regular Square Pyramid

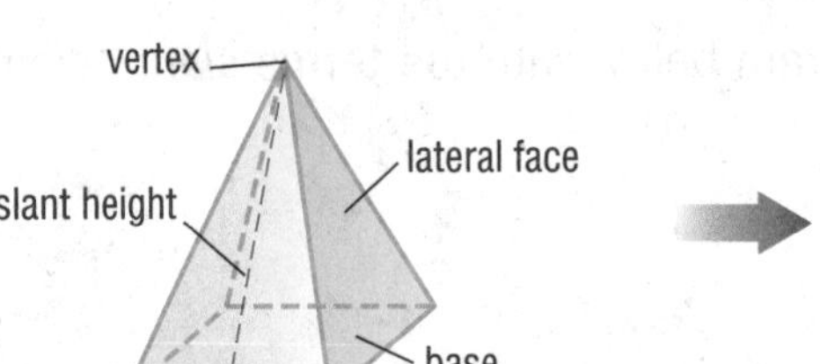

Net of Regular Square Pyramid

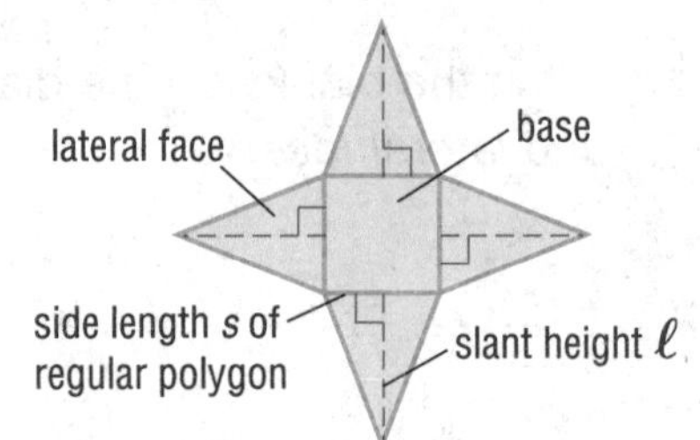

To find the lateral area *L.A.* of a regular pyramid, refer to the net. The lateral area is the sum of the areas of the triangles.

$L.A. = 4\left(\frac{1}{2}s\ell\right)$ Area of the lateral faces

$L.A. = \frac{1}{2}(4s)\ell$ Commutative Property of Multiplication

$L.A. = \frac{1}{2}P\ell$ The perimeter of the base *P* is 4s.

The total surface area of a regular pyramid is the lateral surface area *L.A.* plus the area of the base *B*.

$$S.A. = B + \frac{1}{2}P\ell$$

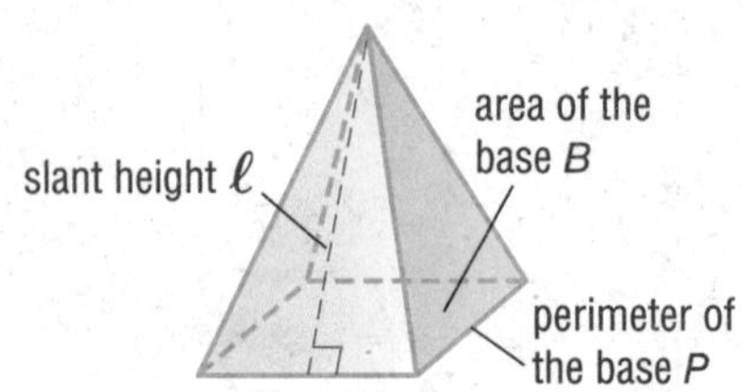

Examples

1. Find the total surface area of the pyramid. Round to the nearest tenth.

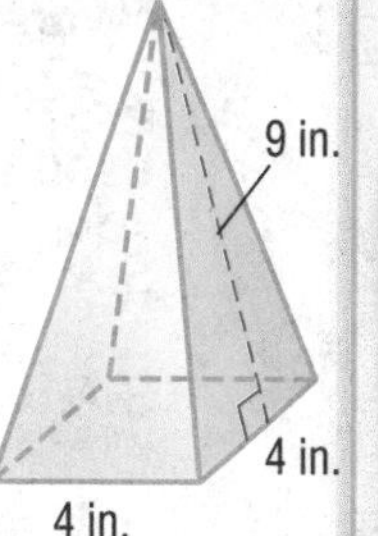

$S.A. = B + \frac{1}{2}P\ell$	Surface area of a pyramid
$S.A. = 16 + \frac{1}{2}(16 \cdot 9)$	$B = 4 \cdot 4$, $P = 4 \cdot 4$ or 16, $\ell = 9$
$S.A. = 88$	Simplify.

The surface area is 88 square inches.

Perimeter of a Square
The formula for the perimeter of a square is $P = 4s$.

2. Find the total surface area of the pyramid with a base area of 111 square meters.

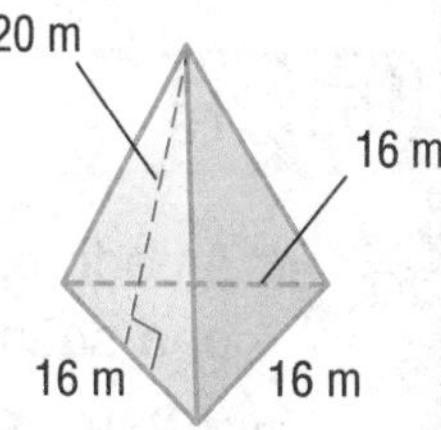

$S.A. = B + \frac{1}{2}P\ell$	Surface area of a pyramid
$S.A. = 111 + \frac{1}{2}(48 \cdot 20)$	$B = 111$, $P = 16 + 16 + 16$ or 48, $\ell = 20$
$S.A. = 591$	Simplify.

The surface area of the pyramid is 591 square meters.

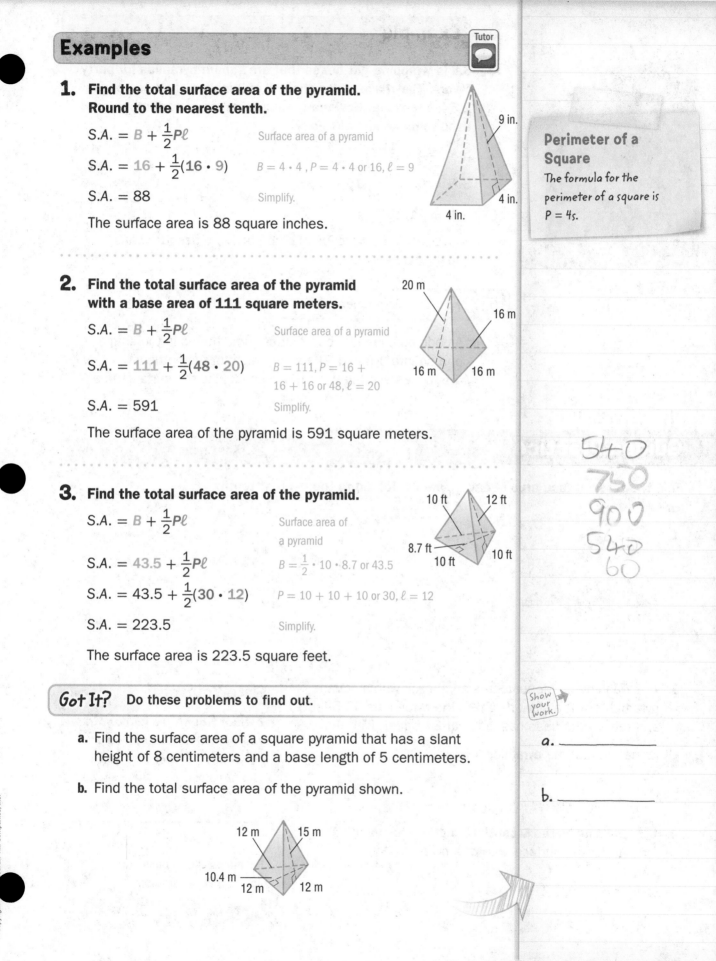

3. Find the total surface area of the pyramid.

10 ft, 12 ft, 8.7 ft, 10 ft, 10 ft

$S.A. = B + \frac{1}{2}P\ell$	Surface area of a pyramid
$S.A. = 43.5 + \frac{1}{2}P\ell$	$B = \frac{1}{2} \cdot 10 \cdot 8.7$ or 43.5
$S.A. = 43.5 + \frac{1}{2}(30 \cdot 12)$	$P = 10 + 10 + 10$ or 30, $\ell = 12$
$S.A. = 223.5$	Simplify.

The surface area is 223.5 square feet.

Got It? Do these problems to find out.

a. Find the surface area of a square pyramid that has a slant height of 8 centimeters and a base length of 5 centimeters.

a. ________

b. Find the total surface area of the pyramid shown.

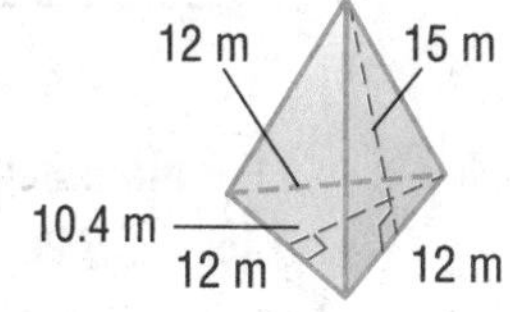

b. ________

Example

4. Sal is wrapping gift boxes that are square pyramids for party favors. They have a slant height of 3 inches and base edges 2.5 inches long. How many square inches of card stock are used to make one gift box?

$S.A. = B + \frac{1}{2}P\ell$ Surface area of a pyramid

$S.A. = 6.25 + \frac{1}{2}(10 \cdot 3)$ $B = 2.5^2$ or 6.25, $P = 4(2.5)$ or 10, $\ell = 3$

$S.A. = 21.25$ Simplify.

So, 21.25 square inches of card stock are used to make one gift box.

Got It? **Do this problem to find out.**

c. Amado purchased a bottle of perfume that is in the shape of a square pyramid. The slant height of the bottle is 4.5 inches and the base is 2 inches. Find the surface area.

c. ______

Guided Practice

Find the total surface area of each pyramid. Round to the nearest tenth. (Examples 1–3)

1. ______

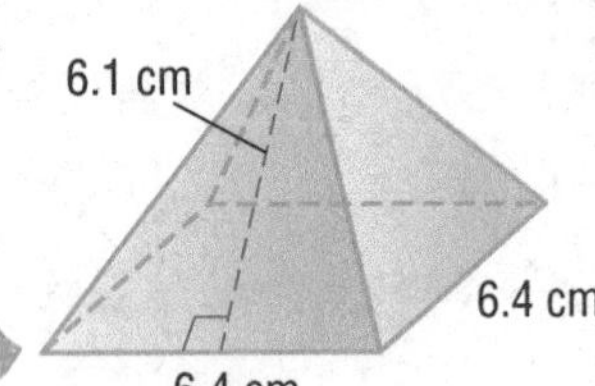

2. ______

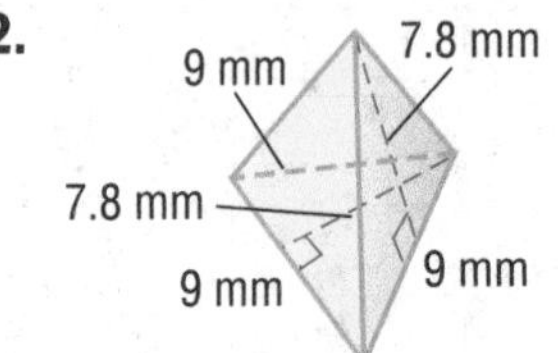

3. The Washington Monument is an obelisk with a square pyramid top. The slant height of the pyramid is 55.5 feet, and the square base has sides of 34.5 feet. Find the lateral area of the pyramid. (Example 4) ______

4. **Building on the Essential Question** Justify the formula for the surface area of a pyramid.

______

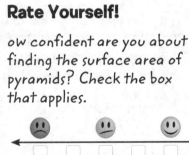

Rate Yourself!

ow confident are you about finding the surface area of pyramids? Check the box that applies.

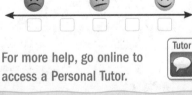

For more help, go online to access a Personal Tutor.

FOLDABLES Time to update your Foldable!

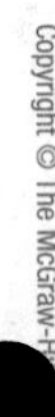

Name ______________________ My Homework ______________________

Independent Practice

Go online for Step-by-Step Solutions

eHelp 

Find the total surface area of each pyramid. Round to the nearest tenth. (Examples 1–3)

1. 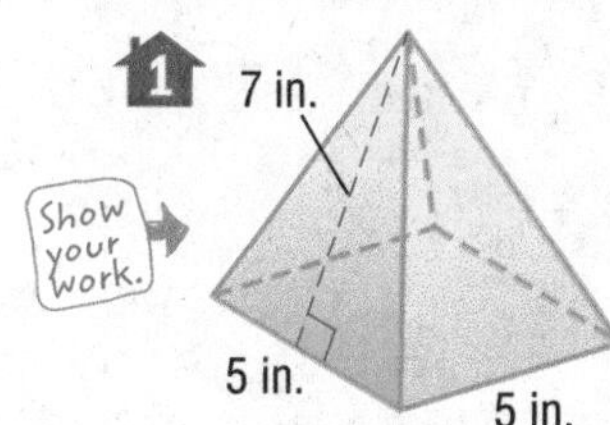

____

2. 15 mm
17 mm
17 mm
17 mm
$A \approx 125$ mm^2

____

3. 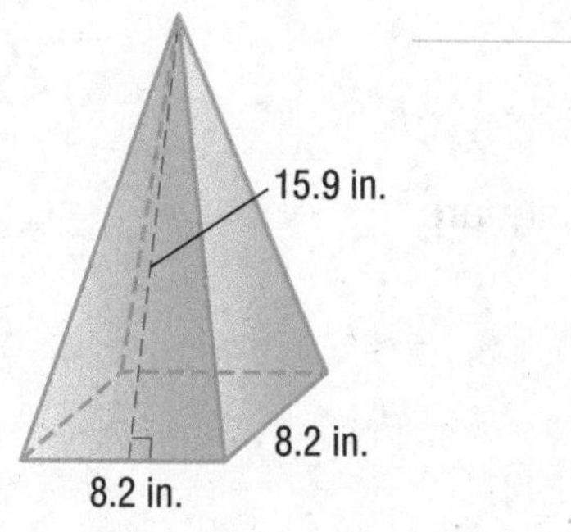

____

4. 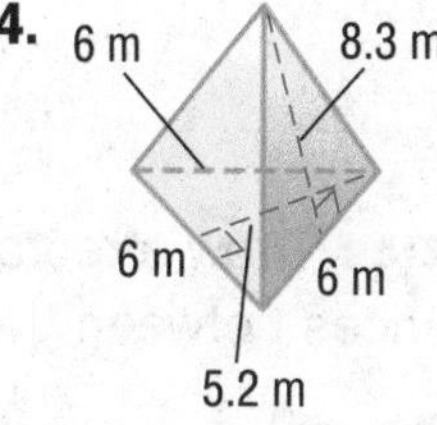

____

5. A triangular pyramid has a slant height of 0.75 foot. The equilateral triangular base has a perimeter of 1.2 feet and an area of about 0.07 square foot. Find the approximate surface area. (Example 4)

____

6. The gemstone shown is a square pyramid that has a base with sides 3.4 inches long. The slant height of the pyramid is 3.8 inches. Find the surface area of the gemstone. (Example 4)

____

7. Isaac is building a birdhouse for a class project. The birdhouse is a regular hexagonal pyramid. The base has side lengths of 3 inches and an area of about 24 square inches. The slant height is 6 inches. Find the approximate surface area of the birdhouse. (Example 4)

____

8.  **Persevere with Problems** A square pyramid has a surface area of 175 square inches. The square base has side lengths of 5 inches. Find the slant height of the pyramid.

9. A square pyramid has a lateral area of 107.25 square centimeters and a slant height of 8.25 centimeters. Find the length of each side of its base.

H.O.T. Problems Higher Order Thinking

10. **Justify Conclusions** Suppose you could climb to the top of the Great Pyramid of Giza in Egypt. Which path would be shorter, climbing a lateral edge or the slant height? Justify your response.

11. **Model with Mathematics** Draw a rectangular pyramid and a square pyramid. Explain the differences between the two.

Rectangular Pyramid **Square Pyramid**

Georgia Test Practice

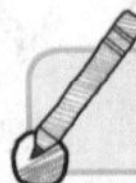

12. Which is the best estimate for the surface area of the pyramid?

Ⓐ 107 ft^2 Ⓒ 429 ft^2

Ⓑ 180 ft^2 Ⓓ 608 ft^2

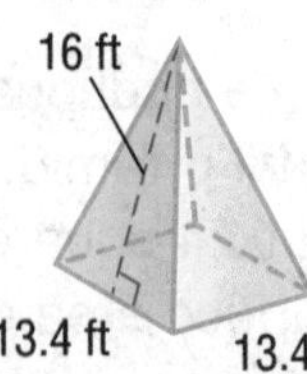

Extra Practice

Find the total surface area of each pyramid. Round to the nearest tenth.

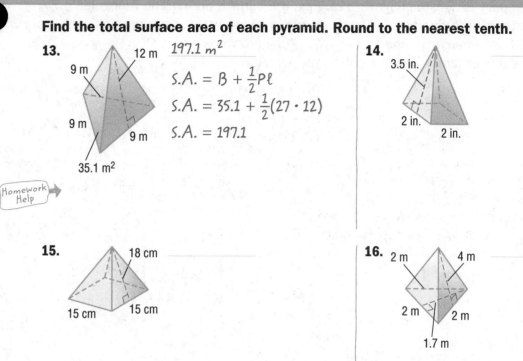

13. 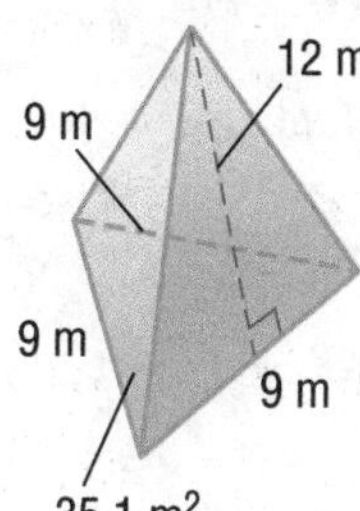

197.1 m^2

$S.A. = B + \frac{1}{2}P\ell$

$S.A. = 35.1 + \frac{1}{2}(27 \cdot 12)$

$S.A. = 197.1$

Homework Help

14. 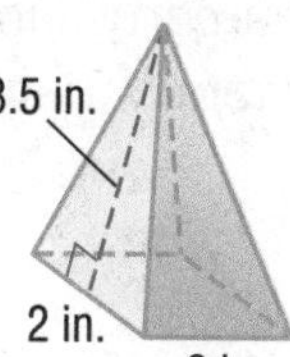

______

15. 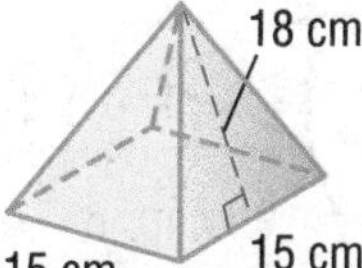

______

16. 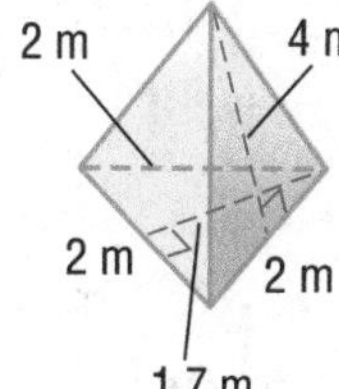

______

17. A square pyramid has a slant height of $4\frac{2}{3}$ feet. The base has side lengths of $2\frac{1}{4}$ feet. Find the surface area. ______

18. A building in San Francisco is shaped like a square pyramid. It has a slant height of 856.1 feet and each side of its base is 145 feet long. Find the lateral area of the building. ______

19. CCGPS **Use Math Tools** Complete the organizer below to help you remember what each part of the formula for the surface area of a pyramid represents.

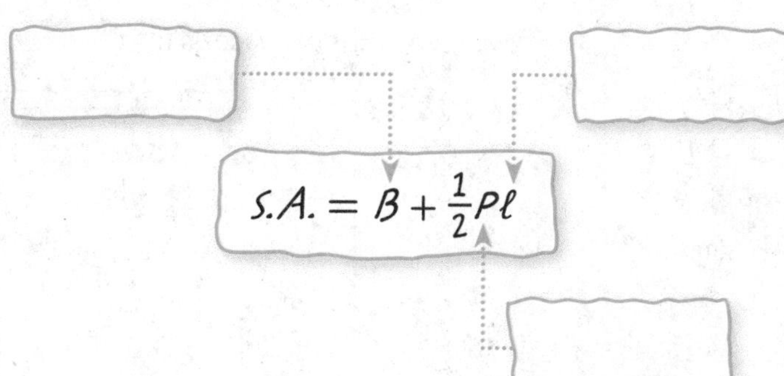

Georgia Test Practice

20. An entertainment company is constructing a tent in the shape of a square pyramid, without a floor, to be used at a party. Find the number of square feet of fabric that will be required.

Ⓐ 1,500 ft^2

Ⓑ 1,700 ft^2

Ⓒ 2,250 ft^2

Ⓓ 2,550 ft^2

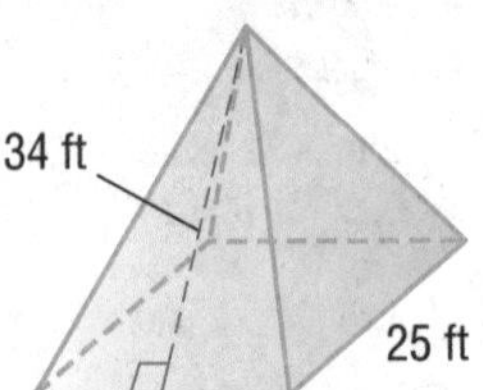

21. Find the surface area of the triangular pyramid shown with a base area of 27.7 square yards.

Ⓕ 39.3 yd^2

Ⓖ 117.9 yd^2

Ⓗ 171.7 yd^2

Ⓘ 213.5 yd^2

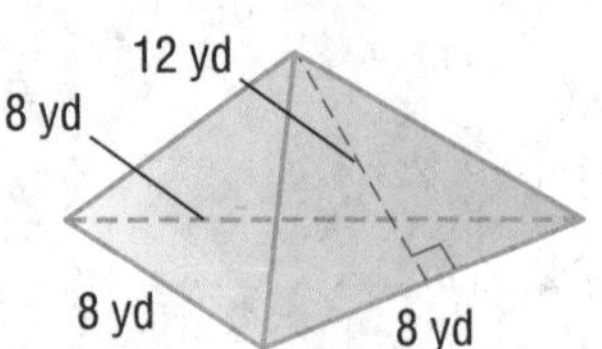

22. **Short Response** The net of a paperweight is shown to the right. What is the lateral surface area of the paperweight?

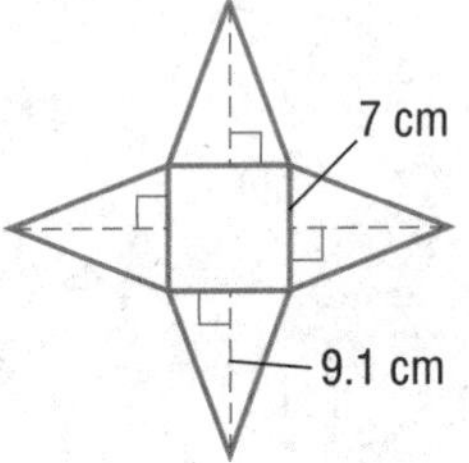

Common Core Review

Find the surface area of each prism. MCC7.G.6

23.

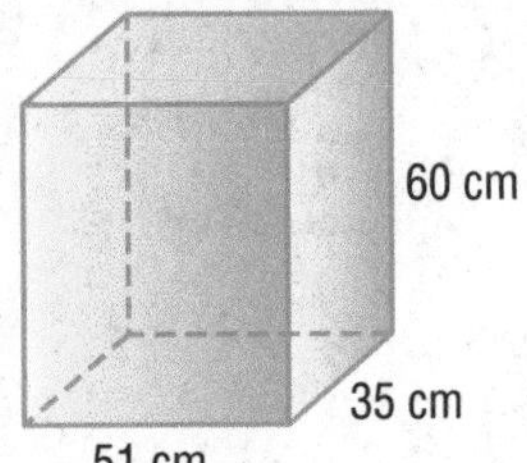

24.

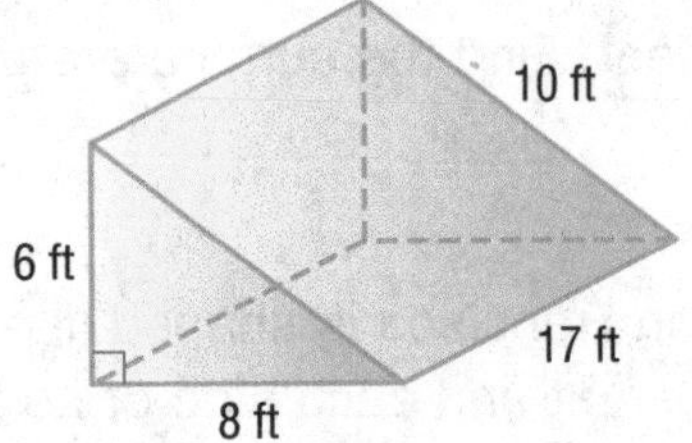

25. The volume of the prism shown below is 140 cubic meters. Find the height of the prism. MCC7.G.6

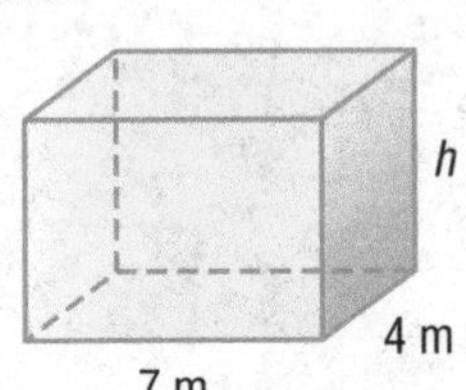

26. The volume of the prism shown below is 10,360 cubic feet. Find the width of the prism. MCC7.G.6

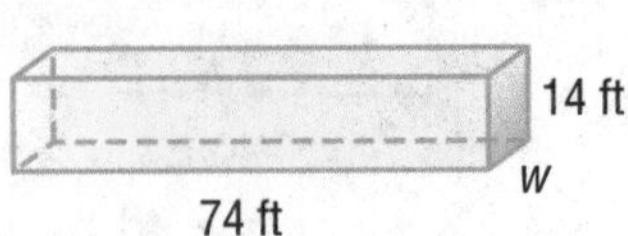

Composite Figures

HOW can you find the volume and surface area of a composite figure?

Content Standards
MCC7.G.6

Mathematical Practices
1, 3, 4

Architecture A company made a model of a new office building. The building is composed of rectangular prisms. You can use centimeter cubes to find the volume and surface area of the building model.

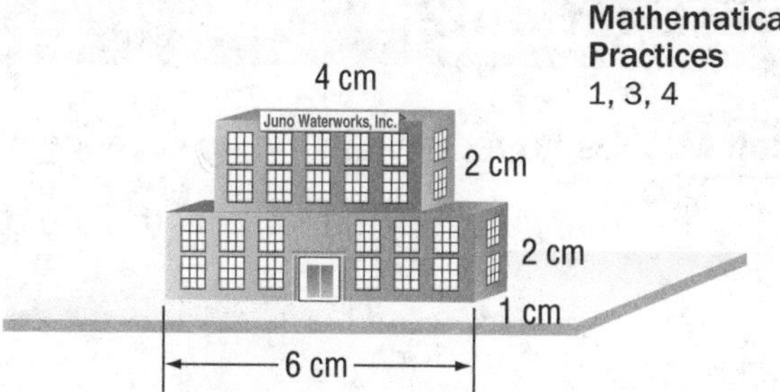

Investigation 1

Tools

The model is a *composite figure* made of two rectangular prisms.

Step 1 Model the top and bottom rectangular prisms using cubes.

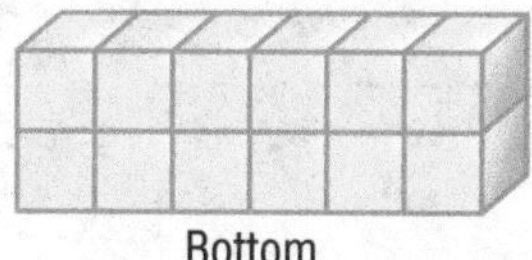

Bottom

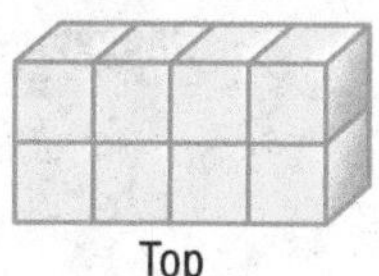

Top

Step 2 Count the cubes to find the dimensions. Write the dimensions in the table below. Then use the cube models to find the volume of and surface area of both prisms. Write these measures in the table below step 3.

Step 3 Use the table to find the volume and surface area of the entire building model. Write these measures in the composite row of the table.

Model	Length (cm)	Width (cm)	Height (cm)	Volume (cm^3)	Surface Area (cm^3)
Bottom	6	1			
Top					
Composite					

School Mr. Wendell's class made a model of a house. The model was composed of a rectangular prism and a triangular prism. Determine the volume and surface area of the model house.

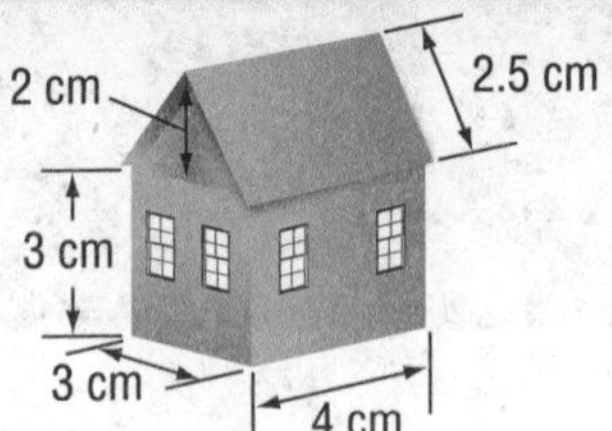

Investigation 2

Step 1 Use a rectangular prism to model the bottom of the house. Use a triangular prism to model the top of the house.

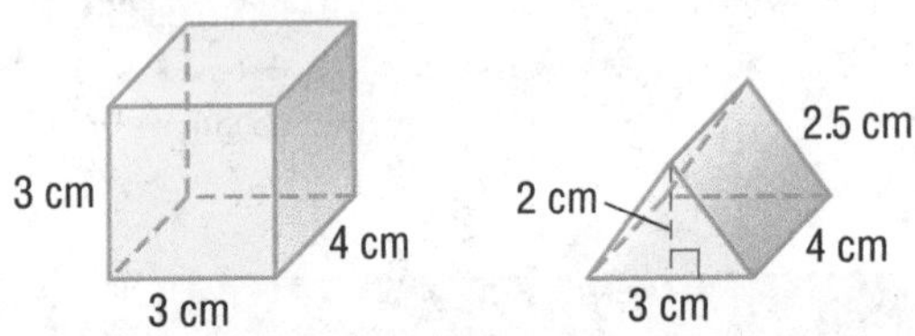

Step 2 Complete the tables below using the models from Step 1.

Prism	Length (cm)	Width (cm)	Height (cm)
Rectangular	4	3	

Prism	Length (cm)	Base (cm)	Height (cm)
Triangular	4	3	

Step 3 Use the information from the tables and the models to find the total volume of the model house.

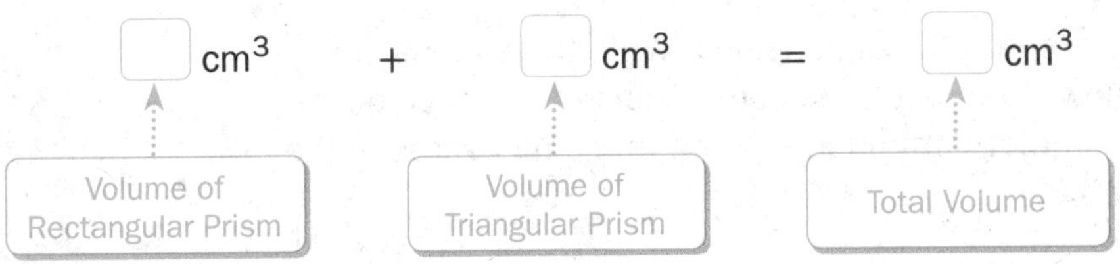

Step 4 Use the information from the tables and the models to find the total surface area of the model house.

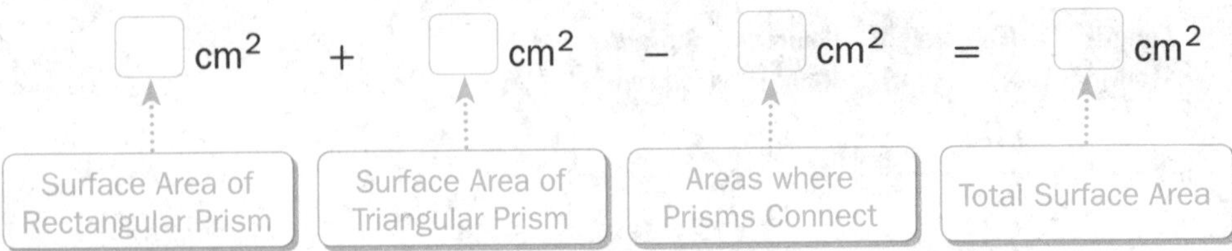

The total volume of the model house is ☐ cubic centimeters.

The total surface area is ☐ square centimeters.

Work with a partner.

1. **Model with Mathematics** Use the top, side, and front views to build a figure using centimeter cubes.

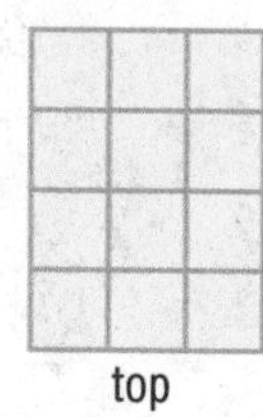
top

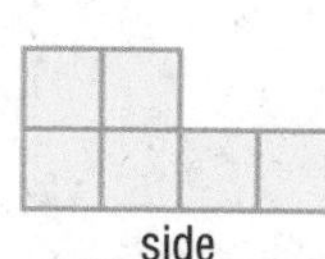
side

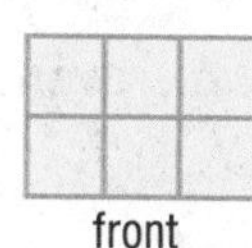
front

a. Make a sketch of the figure you built.

b. Find the volume and surface area of the figure.

Volume: ________ Surface Area: ________

Refer to the figure at the right for Exercises 2–4.

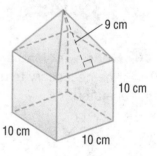

2. The figure is comprised of a ________ and a square ________.

3. Complete the following to find the volume of the figure.

a. The volume of the cube is ☐ cubic centimeters.

b. The volume of the square pyramid is 250 cubic centimeters.

c. So, the volume of the composite figure is ☐ cubic centimeters.

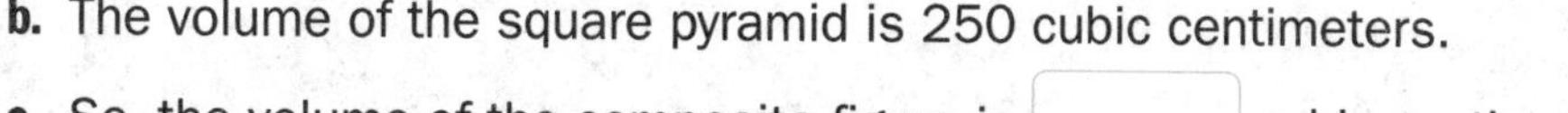

4. Complete the following to find the surface area of the figure.

a. The surface area of the cube is ☐ square centimeters.

b. The surface area of the square pyramid is ☐ square centimeters.

c. The area where the figures overlap is ☐ square centimeters.

d. The surface area of the composite figure is ☐ square centimeters.

Analyze

CCGPS Reason Inductively Work with a partner. Write each of the following statements in the correct location. One statement is done for you.

5. *measured in square units*
6. *measured in cubic units*
7. *involves adding measures of each figure*
8. *involves subtracting where figures overlap*

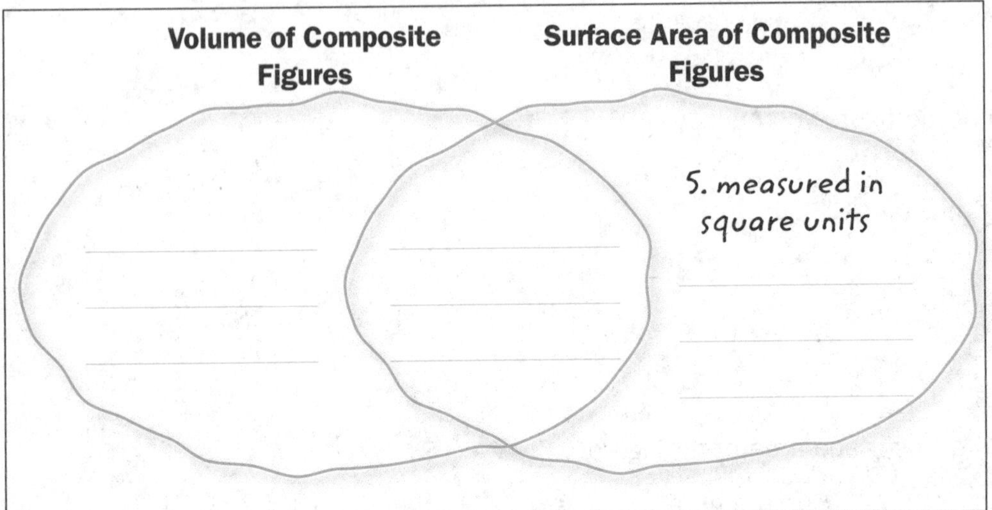

Reflect

9. CCGPS **Model with Mathematics** Describe a real-world situation where it might be necessary to use a model or a drawing to find the volume or surface area.

10. Inquiry HOW can you find the volume and surface area of a composite figure?

Lesson 8

Volume and Surface Area of Composite Figures

What You'll Learn

Scan the lesson. List two headings you would use to make an outline of the lesson.

-

-

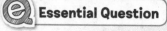

Essential Question

HOW do measurements help you describe real-world objects?

Common Core GPS

Content Standards
MCC7.G.6

Mathematical Practices
1, 3, 4

Real-World Link

Kaylee and Miles are making a bat house for their backyard like the one shown. They need to determine the surface area to find how much wood they will need.

1. What three-dimensional figures make up the bat house?

2. What method could you use to find the surface area of the bat house?

3. Suppose you wanted to find the volume of the bat house. What method could you use?

Work Zone

Volume of a Composite Figure

The volume of a composite figure can be found by separating the figure into solids whose volumes you know how to find.

Examples

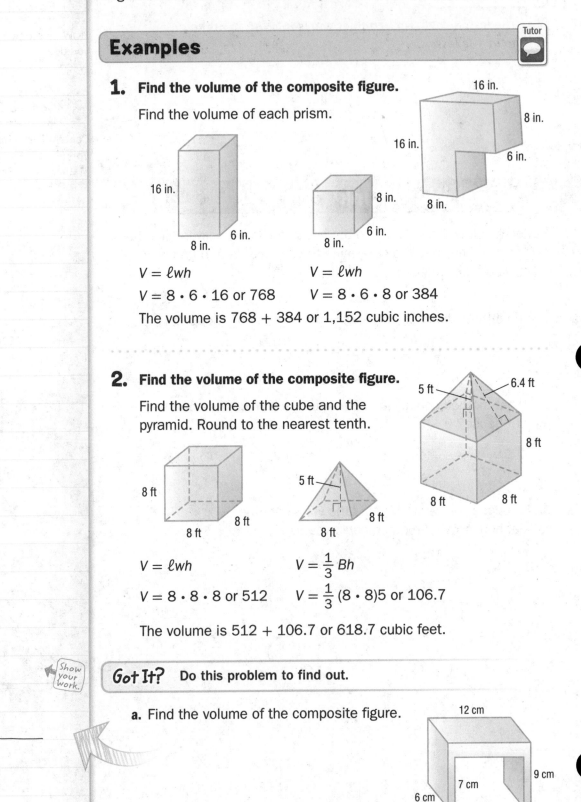

1. Find the volume of the composite figure.

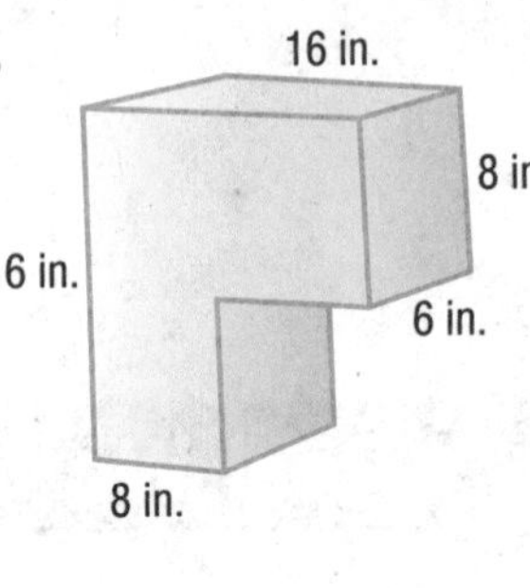

Find the volume of each prism.

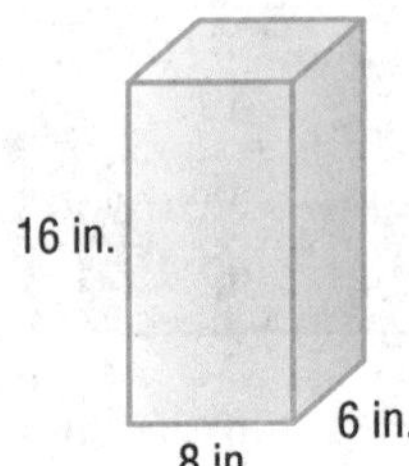

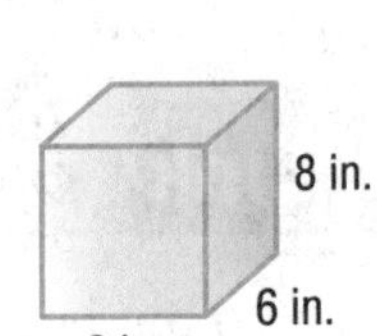

$V = \ell wh$ $\quad$ $V = \ell wh$

$V = 8 \cdot 6 \cdot 16$ or 768 $\quad$ $V = 8 \cdot 6 \cdot 8$ or 384

The volume is $768 + 384$ or 1,152 cubic inches.

2. Find the volume of the composite figure.

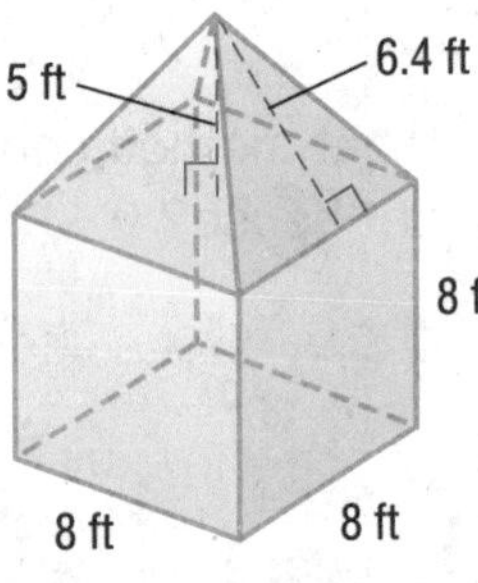

Find the volume of the cube and the pyramid. Round to the nearest tenth.

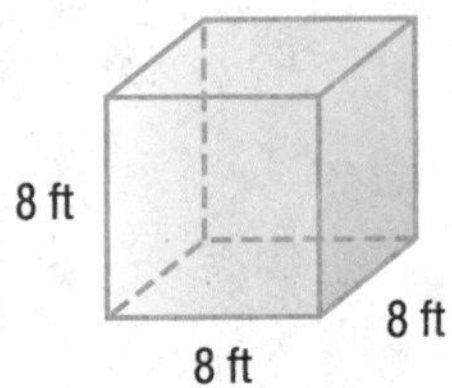

$V = \ell wh$ $\quad$ $V = \frac{1}{3}Bh$

$V = 8 \cdot 8 \cdot 8$ or 512 $\quad$ $V = \frac{1}{3}(8 \cdot 8)5$ or 106.7

The volume is $512 + 106.7$ or 618.7 cubic feet.

Got It? **Do this problem to find out.**

a. Find the volume of the composite figure.

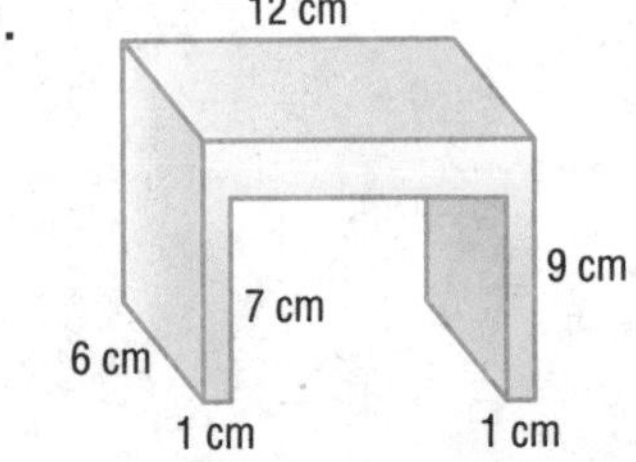

a. ________

Surface Area of a Composite Figure

You can also find the surface area of composite figures by finding the areas of the faces that make up the composite figure.

Examples

3. Find the surface area of the figure in Example 1.

The surface is made up of three different polygons.

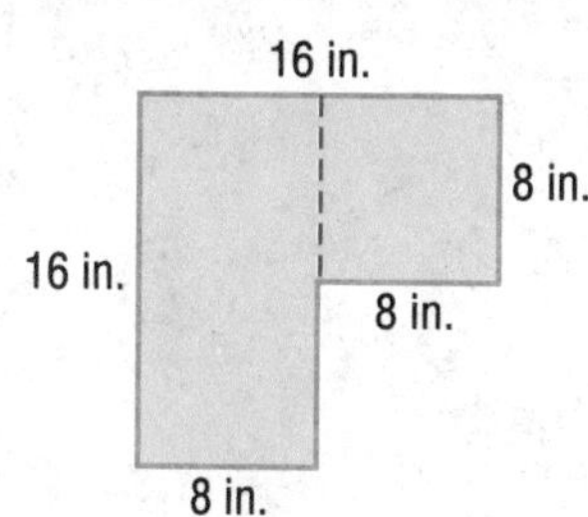

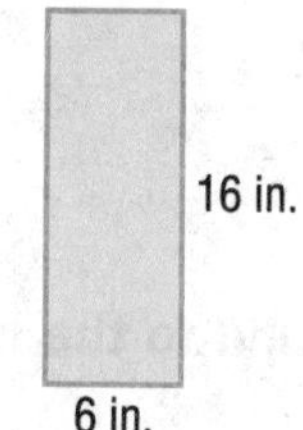

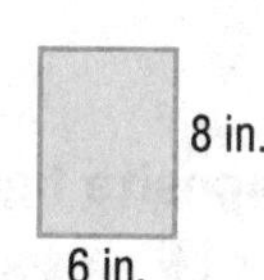

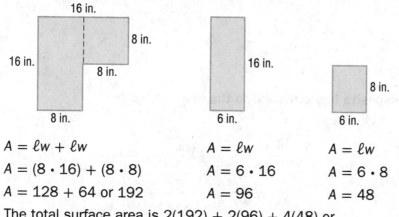

$A = \ell w + \ell w$	$A = \ell w$	$A = \ell w$
$A = (8 \cdot 16) + (8 \cdot 8)$	$A = 6 \cdot 16$	$A = 6 \cdot 8$
$A = 128 + 64$ or 192	$A = 96$	$A = 48$

The total surface area is $2(192) + 2(96) + 4(48)$ or 768 square inches.

4. Find the surface area of the composite figure in Example 2.

The figure is made up of two different polygons.

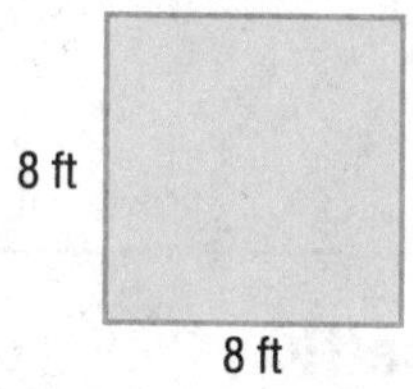

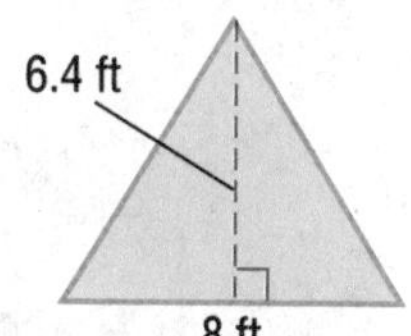

$A = \ell w$	$A = \frac{1}{2}bh$
$A = 8 \cdot 8$ or 64	$A = \frac{1}{2} \cdot 8 \cdot 6.4$ or 25.6

The total surface area is $5(64) + 4(25.6)$ or 422.4 square centimeters.

Surface Area
To make it easier to see each face, sketch the faces and label the dimensions of each.

Got It? Do this problem to find out.

b. Find the surface area of the steps that are represented by the composite figure shown.

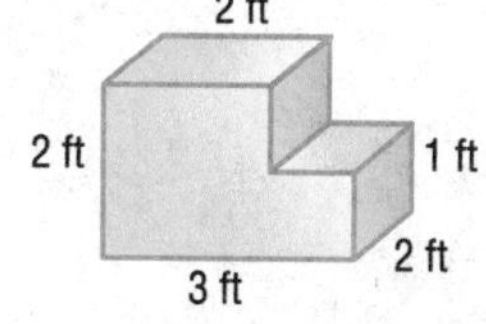

b. ______________

Guided Practice

Find the volume of each composite figure. Round to the nearest tenth if necessary. (Examples 1 and 2)

1.

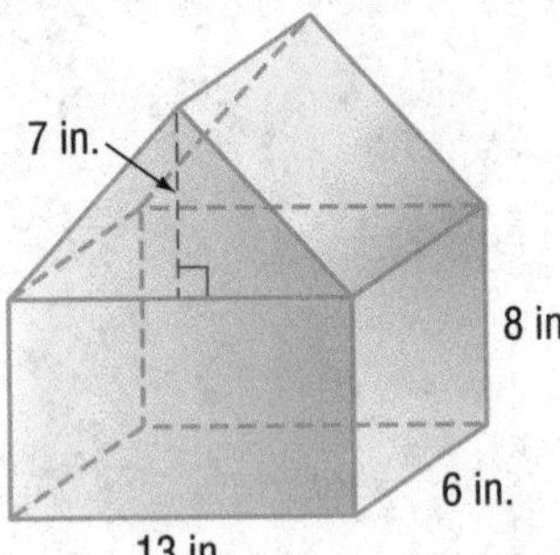

Show your work.

2.

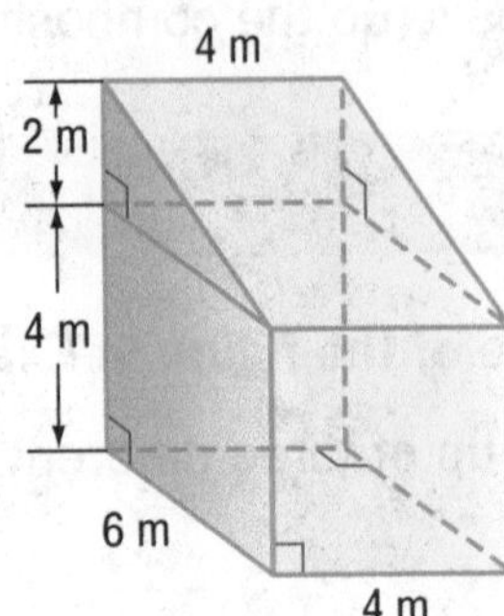

Find the surface area of each composite figure. Round to the nearest tenth if necessary. (Examples 3 and 4)

3.

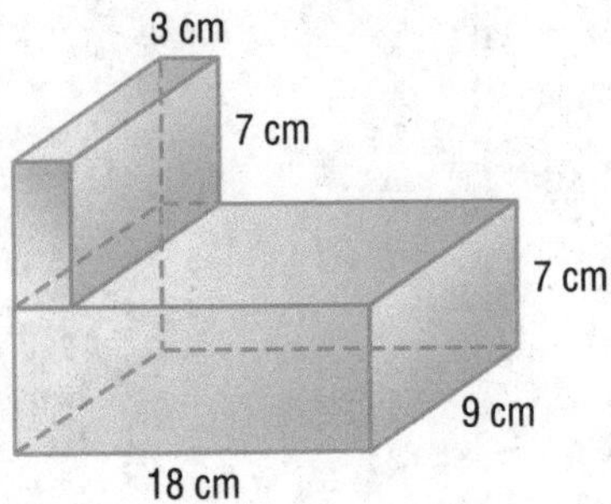

4.

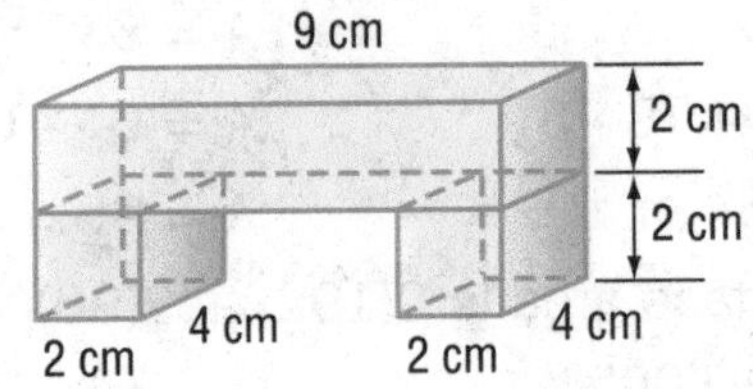

5. **Building on the Essential Question** How do the previous lessons in this chapter help you find the surface area and volume of a composite figure?

Rate Yourself!

Are you ready to move on? Shade the section that applies.

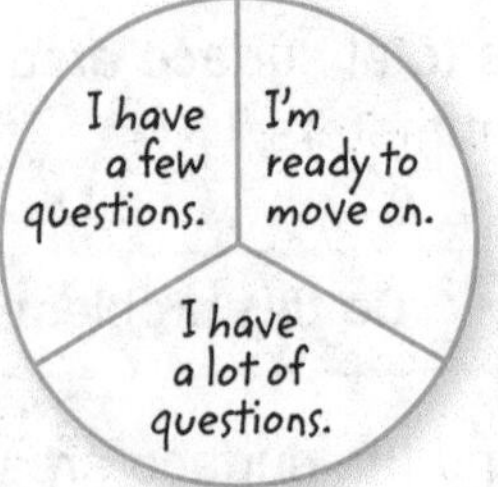

For more help, go online to access a Personal Tutor.

Name ______________________ My Homework ______________________

Independent Practice

eHelp Go online for Step-by-Step Solutions 

Find the volume of each composite figure. Round to the nearest tenth if necessary. (Examples 1 and 2)

1. 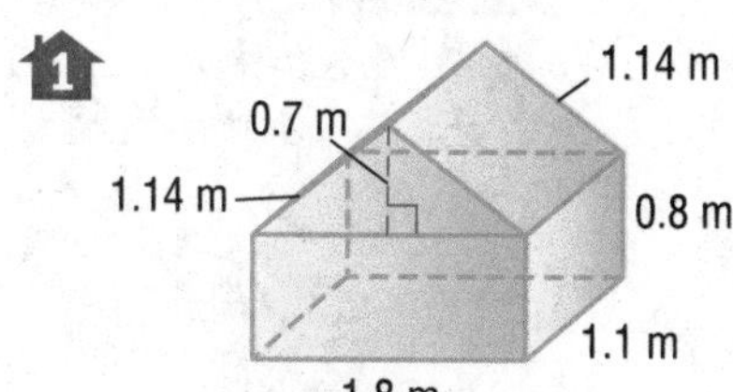

2.

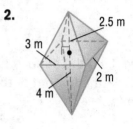

Find the surface area of each composite figure. Round to the nearest tenth if necessary. (Examples 3 and 4)

3. 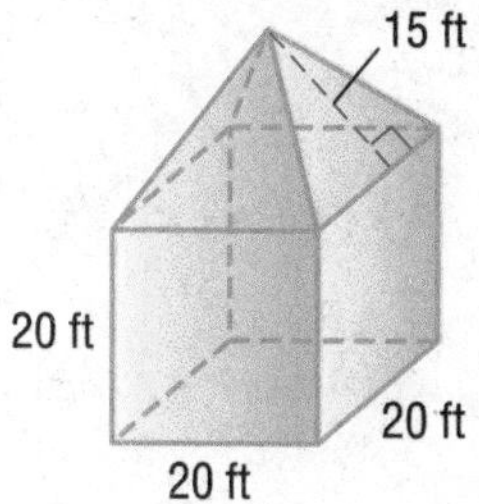

4. 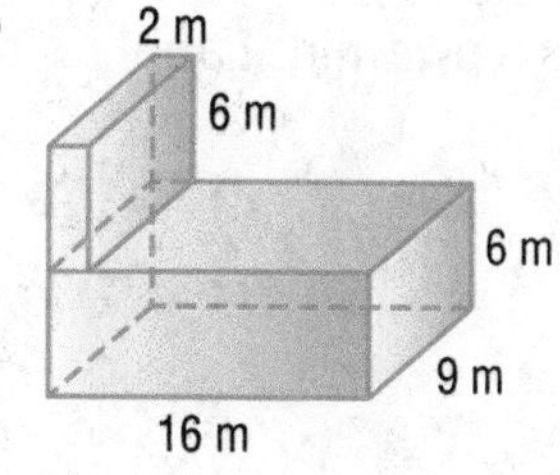

5. Find the volume of the figure at the right in cubic feet. Round to the nearest tenth. (Examples 1 and 2)

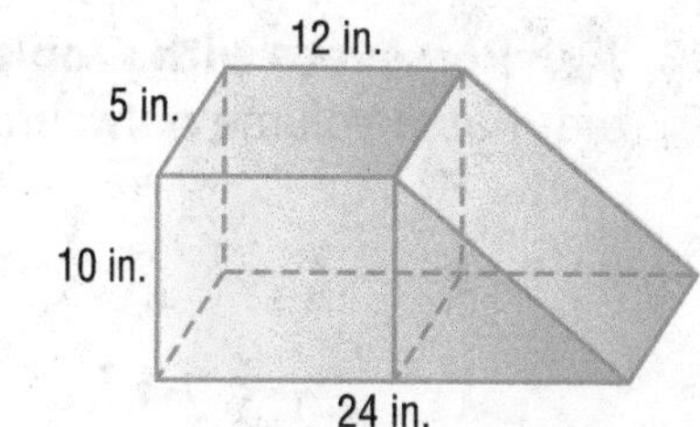

6. **Reason Inductively** The swimming pool at the right is being filled with water. Find the number of cubic feet that it will take to fill the swimming pool. (*Hint:* The area of a trapezoid is $A = \frac{1}{2}h(b_1 + b_2)$.) (Examples 1 and 2)

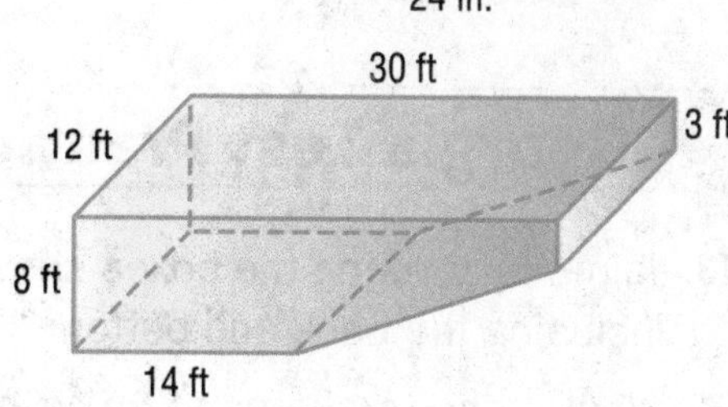

Copy and Solve For Exercises 7–8, show your work on a separate piece of paper. Round to the nearest tenth. (Examples 1- 4)

7. Find the surface area of the figure in Exercise 1.

8. Find the volume of the figure in Exercise 4.

9. A carryout container is shown. The bottom base is a 4-inch square and the top base is a 4-inch by 6-inch rectangle. The height of the container is 5 inches. Find the volume of food that it holds.

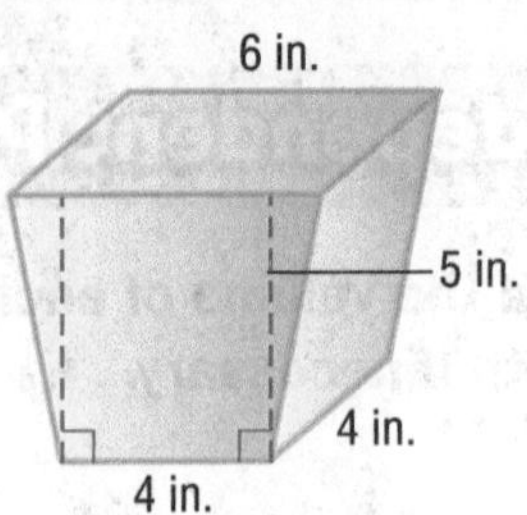

10. Refer to the house shown. Find the surface area and volume of the house. Do not include the bottom of the house when calculating the surface area.

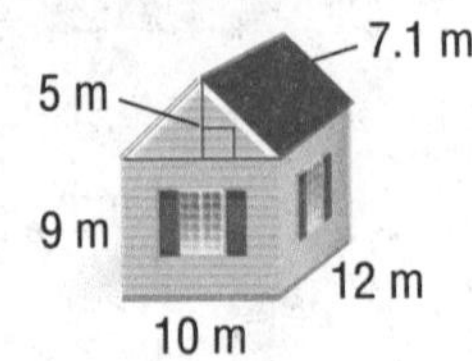

H.O.T. Problems Higher Order Thinking

11. CCGPS **Model with Mathematics** Draw a composite figure that is made up of a cube and a square pyramid. Label its dimensions and find the volume of the figure.

12. CCGPS **Persevere with Problems** Draw an example of a composite figure that has a volume between 250 and 300 cubic units.

Georgia Test Practice

13. Jaime is covering the boxes shown in felt, including the back and bottom.

What is the total area to be covered with felt?

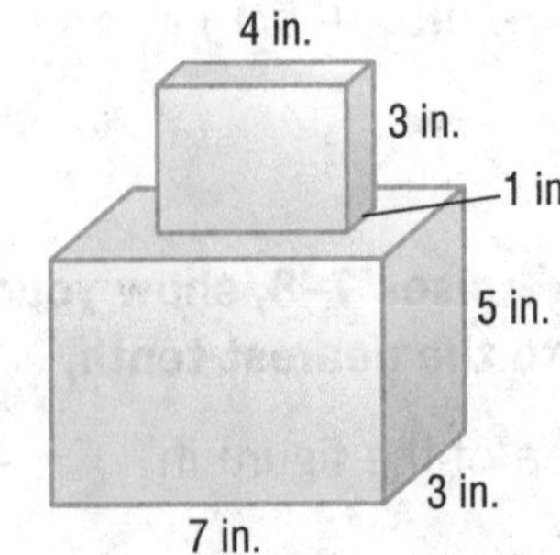

Ⓐ 23 in^2

Ⓑ 117 in^2

Ⓒ 172 in^2

Ⓓ 1,260 in^2

Extra Practice

Find the volume of each composite figure. Round to the nearest tenth if necessary.

14. 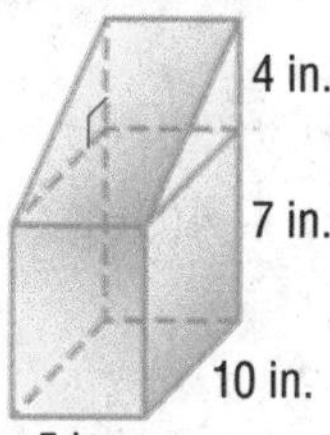

450 in³

Homework Help

Rectangular Prism

$V = \ell wh$

$V = 5 \cdot 10 \cdot 7$

$V = 350$

Triangular Prism

$V = Bh$

$V = \frac{1}{2} \cdot 10 \cdot 4 \cdot 5$

$V = 100$

Total Volume = 350 + 100 or 450 in^3

15. 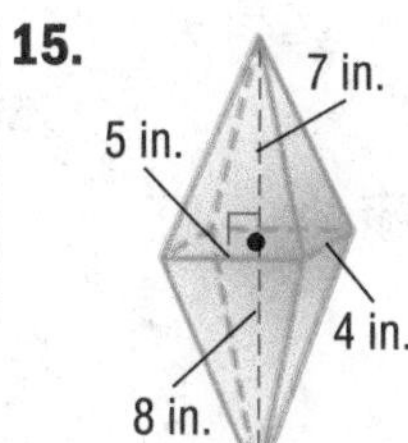

______

Find the surface area of each composite figure. Round to the nearest tenth if necessary.

16. 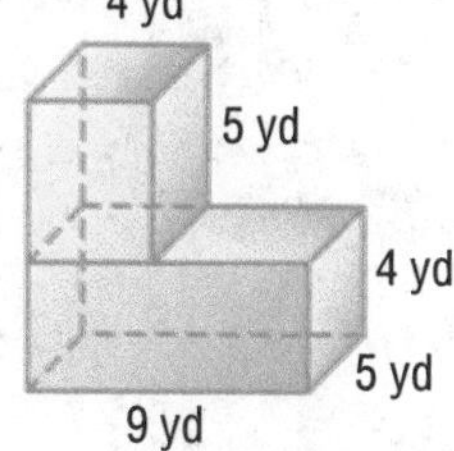

______

17. 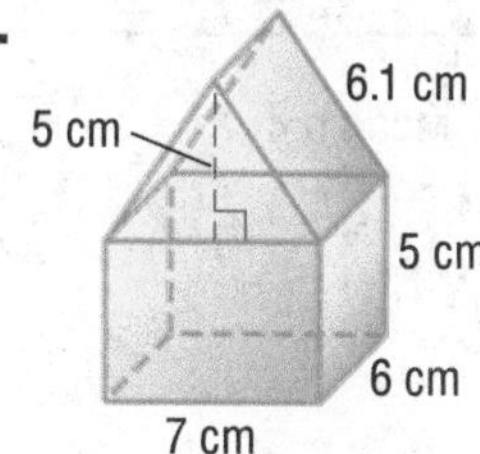

______

18. CCGPS **Find the Error** Seth is finding the surface area of the composite figure shown. Find his mistake and correct it.

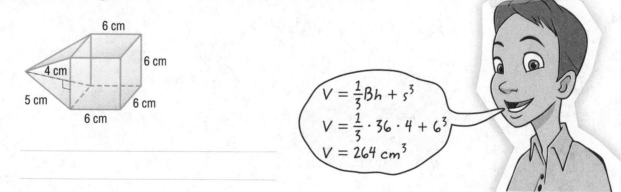

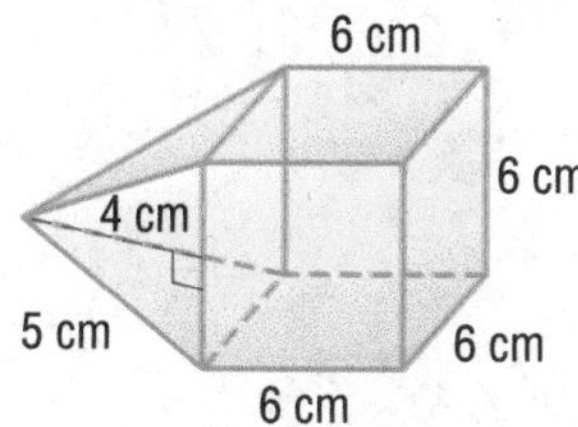

______

______

______

$V = \frac{1}{3}Bh + s^3$
$V = \frac{1}{3} \cdot 36 \cdot 4 + 6^3$
$V = 264 \text{ cm}^3$

Georgia Test Practice

19. What is the volume of the figure below? Round to the nearest tenth.

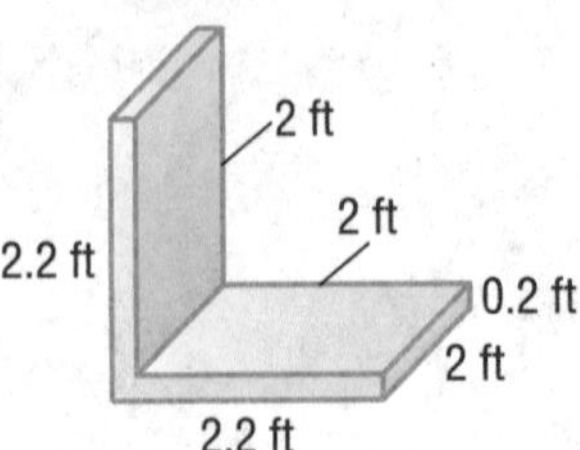

Ⓐ 0.7 ft^3

Ⓑ 1.7 ft^3

Ⓒ 17 ft^3

Ⓓ 27 ft^3

20. Which expression represents the surface area of the figure in Exercise 19?

Ⓕ $4(2.2 \cdot 2 \cdot 0.2)$

Ⓖ $4(2.2) + 4(2) + 4(0.2)$

Ⓗ $2(4) + 2(4.4) + 2(0.44) + 4(0.4)$

Ⓘ $4(4) + 2(4.4) + 2(0.44) + 4(0.4)$

21. **Short Response** Explain how you would find the volume of the composite figure. Then find the volume.

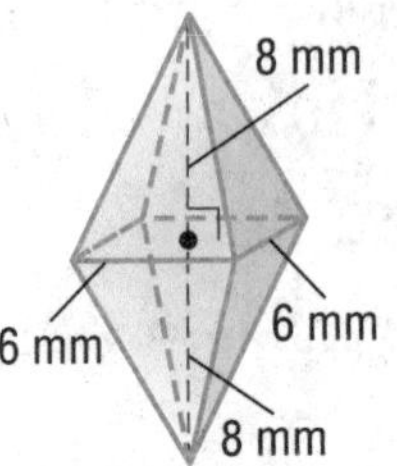

____

____

CCGPS Common Core Review

Draw a net for each figure. MCC6.G.4

22.

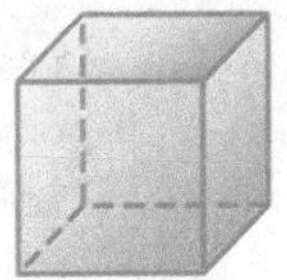

Show your work.

23.

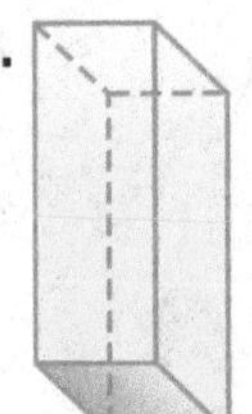

24.

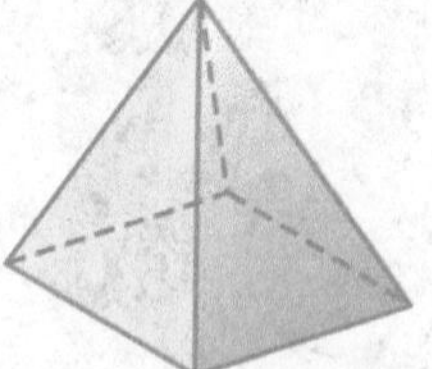

25.

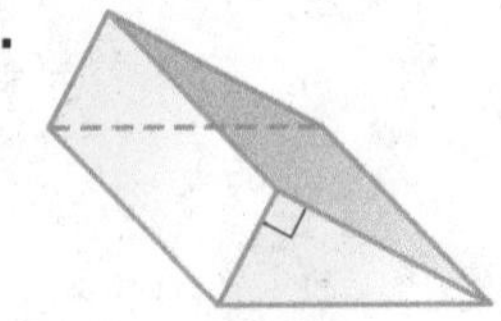

21ST CENTURY CAREER in Landscape Architecture

Landscape Architect

Do you have an artistic side, and do you enjoy being outdoors? If so, a career in landscape design might be a perfect fit for you. Landscape architects design outside areas such as yards, parks, playgrounds, campuses, shopping centers, and golf courses. Their designed areas are not only meant to be beautiful, but also functional and compatible with the natural environment. A landscape architect must be proficient in mathematics, science, and the use of computer-aided design.

Explore college and careers at ccr.mcgraw-hill.com

Is This the Career for You?

Are you interested in a career as a landscape architect? Take some of the following courses in high school.

- Algebra
- Botany
- Drafting/Illustrative Design Technology
- Geometry
- Architectural Design

Find out how math relates to a career in Landscape Architecture.

Planting in Circles

For each problem, use the information in the designs.

1. In Design 2, what is the radius of the larger grassy area? ______
2. The small circular fountain in Design 1 is surrounded by a stone wall. Find the circumference of the wall. Use $\frac{22}{7}$ for π. ______
3. Find the circumference of the smaller grassy area in Design 2. Use 3.14 for π. ______
4. In Design 2, how much greater is the lawn area in the larger circle than in the smaller circle? Use 3.14 for π. ______
5. In Design 2, the smaller circle is surrounded by a path 1 meter wide. What is the circumference of the path? Use the π key on a calculator and round to the nearest tenth. ______
6. In Design 1, the area of the large circular patio is about 201.1 square feet. What is the radius of the patio? Round to the nearest foot. ______

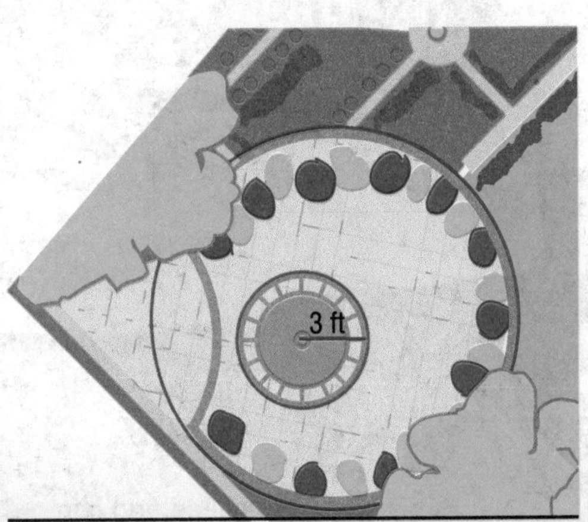

Design 1

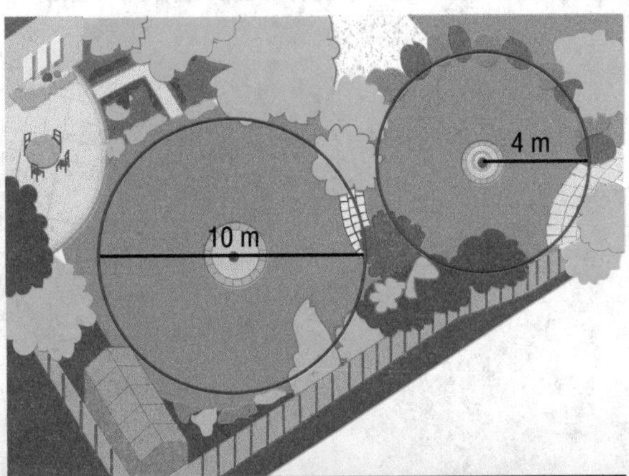

Design 2

Career Project

It's time to update your career portfolio! Download free landscaping software from the Internet and use it to create your own landscape design. Include a list of all the plants, materials, and hard elements used in your design. Also, provide an estimate of the total cost of the landscaping project.

What is something you really want to do in the next ten years?

-
-
-
-
-

Chapter Review

Vocabulary Check

Complete each sentence using the vocabulary list at the beginning of the chapter. Then circle the word that completes the sentence in the word search.

1. The distance across a circle through its center is called the ______________.

2. The ______________ is the distance from the center to any point on the circle.

3. A ______________ is the set of all points in a plane that are the same distance from a point.

4. The point in a circle from which all other points are equidistant is called the ______________.

5. The distance around a circle is the ______________.

6. The ratio of circumference to diameter is called ______________.

7. A ______________ is half of a circle.

8. A ______________ figure is made up of two or more shapes.

9. The ______________ of a three-dimensional figure is the measure of the space it occupies.

10. The sum of the areas of all the faces of a three-dimensional figure is the ______________ area.

11. The triangular faces of a pyramid that are not bases are ______________ faces.

12. The height of each lateral face of a pyramid is called the ______________ height.

Key Concept Check

Use Your FOLDABLES

Use your Foldable to help review the chapter.

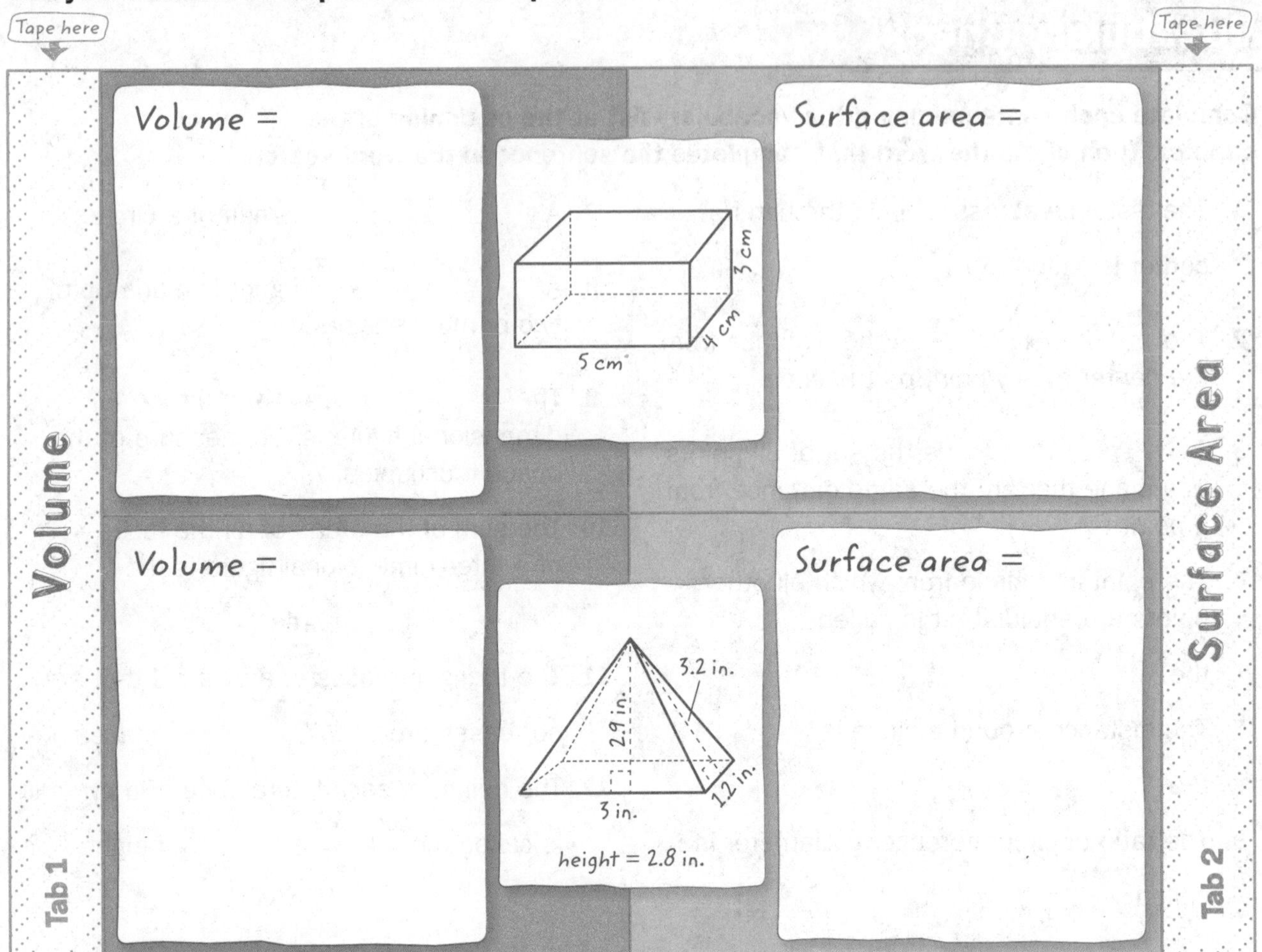

Got it?

Circle the correct term or number to complete each sentence.

1. The diameter of a circle is (twice, three times) its radius.
2. The area of a circle equals the product of pi and the square of its (radius, diameter).
3. The volume of a rectangular prism can be found by multiplying the area of the base times the (length, height).
4. To find the surface area of a triangular prism, find the area of each face and calculate the (sum, product) of all the faces.

Problem Solving

For Exercises 1–3, use 3.14 for π. Round to the nearest tenth.

1. The radius of the center circle of a basketball court is 6 feet. What is the circumference of the center circle? (Lesson 1)

2. A coin has a diameter of about 30 millimeters. What is the area of the coin? (Lesson 2)

3. CCGPS **Justify Conclusions** Tanya and Paco are making a game for the school carnival. They cut out and remove three congruent circles from the rectangular board shown at the right. What is the area of the board after the circles are removed? Explain. (Lesson 3)

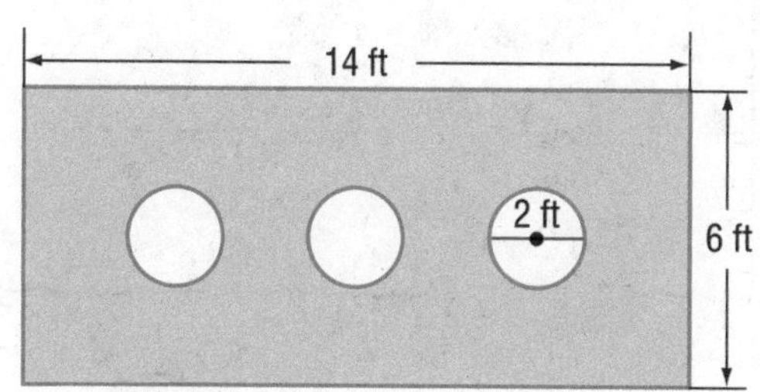

4. The dimensions of the bed of a dump truck are: length 20 feet, width 7 feet, and height $9\frac{1}{2}$ feet. What is the volume of the bed of the dump truck? (Lesson 4)

5. Mrs. Delgado stores cookies in a pyramid-shaped jar that is 12 inches high and has a square base with side lengths of 14 inches. Find the volume of the jar. Round to the nearest tenth. (Lesson 5)

6. Jess bought a pyramid-shaped crystal. The rectangular base of the crystal measures 9 centimeters by 8 centimeters and has a slant height of 12 centimeters. What is the surface area of the crystal? (Lesson 7)

Reflect

Answering the Essential Question

Use what you learned about measuring figures to complete the graphic organizer.

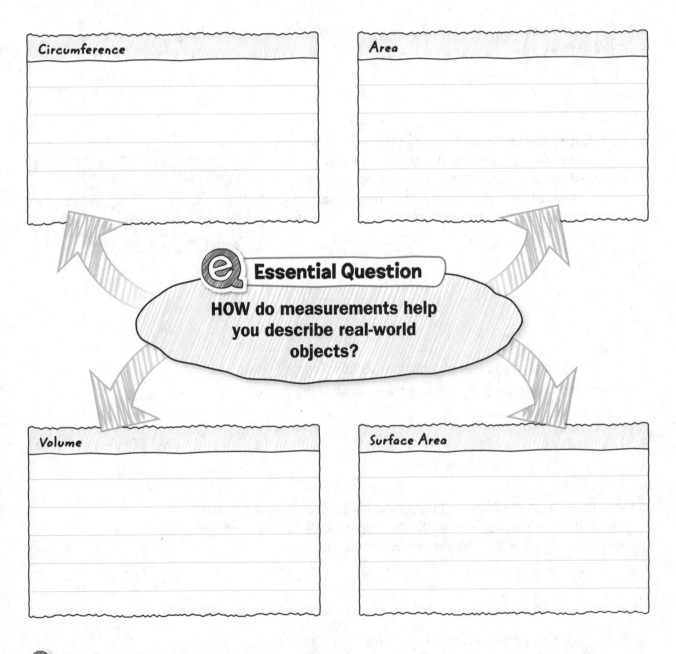

Circumference

Area

Essential Question

HOW do measurements help you describe real-world objects?

Volume

Surface Area

Answer the Essential Question. HOW do measurements help you describe real-world objects?

UNIT 6

Probability

Essential Question

WHY is learning mathematics important?

Chapter 10
Probability

Probability describes the likelihood of an event occurring. In this chapter, you will develop probability models and find probabilities of simple and compound events.

Chapter 10

Probability

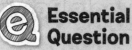

Essential Question

HOW can you predict the outcome of future events?

Common Core GPS

Content Standards
MCC7.SP.5, MCC7.SP.6, MCC7.SP.7, MCC7.SP.7a, MCC7.SP.7b, MCC7.SP.8, MCC7.SP.8a, MCC7.SP.8b, MCC7.SP.8c

Mathematical Practices
1, 3, 4, 5

Math in the Real World

Probability is the likelihood or chance of an event occurring.

At the beginning of a football game, a coin is tossed to determine which team receives the ball first. Fill in the table below to indicate the number of times a team would expect to win the coin toss based on the number of games played.

HOME | 50 | AWAY

Number of Games	Number of Coin Toss Wins
4	
10	
22	
50	

FOLDABLES® Study Organizer

Cut out the correct Foldable from the FL pages in the back of this book.

Place your Foldable on the Key Concept page toward the end of this chapter.

Use the Foldable throughout this chapter to help you learn about probability.

What Tools Do You Need?

Vocabulary

complementary events
compound event
dependent events
experimental probability
fair
Fundamental Counting Principle
independent events
outcome
permutation
probability
random
relative frequency
sample space
simple event
simulation
theoretical probability
tree diagram
uniform probability model
unfair

Review Vocabulary

Fractions, Decimals, and Percents Equivalent rational numbers are numbers that have the same value. For example, three-fourths is equivalent to 0.75 or 75%.

A probability can be expressed as a fraction, decimal, or percent. For each rational number, write the missing equivalent values. Write fractions in simplest form.

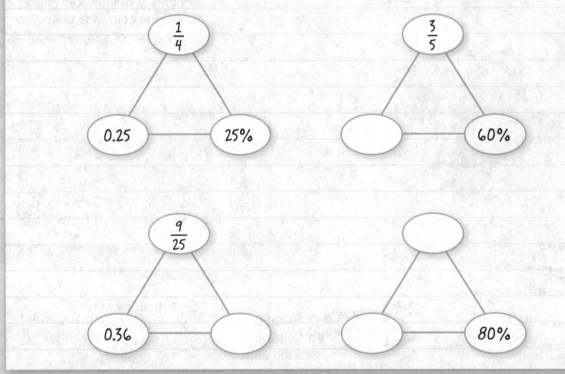

When Will You Use This?

Your Turn! **You will solve this problem in the chapter.**

Are You Ready?

Try the Quick Check below.
Or, take the Online Readiness Quiz.

Quick Review

Common Core Review MCC5.NBT.5, MCC6.NS.4

Example 1

Write $\frac{21}{28}$ in simplest form.

$$\frac{21}{28} = \frac{3}{4} \quad (\div 7)$$

Divide the numerator and denominator by the GCF, 7.

Example 2

Find 7 • 6 • 5 • 4.

$$7 \cdot 6 \cdot 5 \cdot 4 = 42 \cdot 5 \cdot 4$$
$$= 210 \cdot 4$$
$$= 840$$

Multiply from left to right.

Quick Check

Fractions **Write each fraction in simplest form.**

1. $\frac{5}{15} =$ ______
2. $\frac{3}{18} =$ ______
3. $\frac{8}{12} =$ ______
4. $\frac{12}{20} =$ ______

Show your work.

Products **Find each product.**

5. $6 \cdot 5 =$ ______
6. $10 \cdot 9 \cdot 8 =$ ______
7. $4 \cdot 3 \cdot 2 \cdot 1 =$ ______

8. Suppose you listen to 9 songs each hour for 5 hours every day this week. How many songs will you have listened to this week?

______

How Did You Do?

Which problems did you answer correctly in the Quick Check? Shade those exercise numbers below.

① ② ③ ④ ⑤ ⑥ ⑦ ⑧

Lesson 1

Probability of Simple Events

What You'll Learn

Scan the lesson. Predict two things you will learn about probability.

-
-

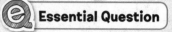

Essential Question

HOW can you predict the outcome of future events?

Vocabulary

probability
outcome
simple event
random
complementary events

Common Core GPS

Content Standards
MCC7.SP.5, MCC7.SP.7, MCC7.SP.7a

Mathematical Practices
1, 3, 4

Vocabulary Start-Up

Probability is the chance that some event will occur. A **simple event** is one outcome or a collection of outcomes. What is an **outcome**?

Math Definition		Real-World Definition
A possible result in a probability experiment.	Outcome	

Real-World Link

For a sledding trip, you randomly select one of the four hats shown. Complete the table to show the possible outcomes.

Hat Selection Outcomes			
Outcome 1	green hat	**Outcome 3**	
Outcome 2		**Outcome 4**	

1. Write a ratio that compares the number of blue hats to the total number of hats. ______

2. Describe a hat display in which you would have a better chance of selecting a red hat.

______

Key Concept **Probability**

Work Zone

Words The probability of an event is a ratio that compares the number of favorable outcomes to the number of possible outcomes.

Symbols $P(event) = \frac{\text{number of favorable outcomes}}{\text{number of possible outcomes}}$

STOP and Reflect

In the space below, describe an example of a simple event that is certain to occur.

The probability of a chance event is a number between 0 and 1 that expresses the likelihood of the event occurring. Greater numbers indicate greater likelihood. A probability near 0 indicates an unlikely event, a probability around $\frac{1}{2}$ indicates an event that is neither unlikely nor likely, and a probability near 1 indicates a likely event.

Probability can be written as a fraction, decimal, or percent.

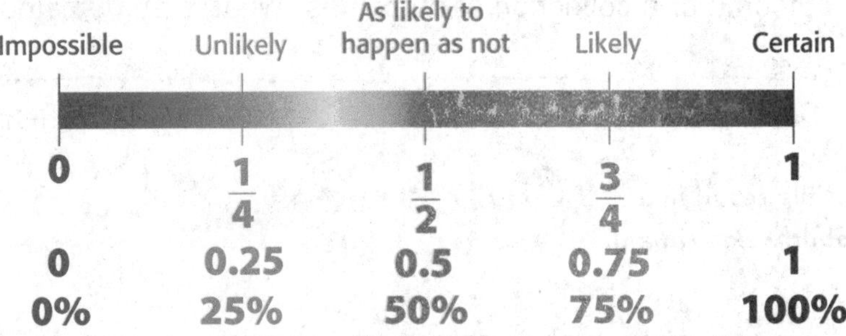

Outcomes occur at **random** if each outcome is equally likely to occur.

Example

There are six equally likely outcomes if a number cube with sides labeled 1 through 6 is rolled.

1. Find *P*(6) or the probability of rolling a 6.

There is only one 6 on the number cube.

$$P(6) = \frac{\text{number of favorable outcomes}}{\text{number of possible outcomes}}$$

$$= \frac{1}{6}$$

The probability of rolling a 6 is $\frac{1}{6}$, or about 17%, or about 0.17.

Got It? **Do this problem to find out.**

a. A coin is tossed. Find the probability of the coin landing on heads. Write your answer as a fraction, percent, and decimal.

a. ______

Example

2. Find the probability of rolling a 2, 3, or 4 on the number cube.

The word *or* indicates that the number of favorable outcomes needs to include the numbers 2, 3, and 4.

$$P(2, 3, \text{or } 4) = \frac{\text{number of favorable outcomes}}{\text{number of possible outcomes}}$$

$$= \frac{3}{6} \text{ or } \frac{1}{2} \quad \text{Simplify.}$$

The probability of rolling a 2, 3, or 4 is $\frac{1}{2}$, 50%, or 0.5.

Got It? Do these problems to find out.

The spinner at the right is spun once. Find the probability of each event. Write each answer as a fraction, percent, and decimal.

b. $P(\text{F})$ **c.** $P(\text{D or G})$ **d.** $P(\text{vowel})$

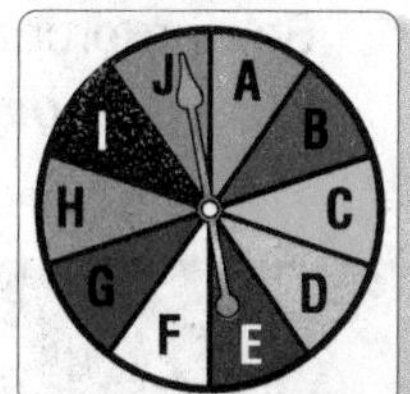

b. ____________

c. ____________

d. ____________

Find Probability of the Complement

Complementary events are two events in which either one or the other must happen, but they cannot happen at the same time. For example, a coin can either land on heads or *not* land on heads. The sum of the probability of an event and its complement is 1 or 100%.

Complement
In everyday language complement means the quantity required to make something complete. This is similar to the math meaning.

Example

3. Find the probability of *not* rolling a 6 in Example 1.

The probability of *not* rolling a 6 and the probability of rolling a 6 are complementary. So, the sum of the probabilities is 1.

$P(6) + P(\text{not } 6) = 1$ $P(6)$ and $P(\text{not } 6)$ are complements.

$\frac{1}{6} + P(\text{not } 6) = 1$ Replace $P(6)$ with $\frac{1}{6}$.

$\frac{1}{6} + \frac{5}{6} = 1$ THINK $\frac{1}{6}$ plus what number equals 1?

The probability of *not* rolling a 6 is $\frac{5}{6}$, or about 83% or 0.83.

Got It? Do this problem to find out.

e. A bag contains 5 blue, 8 red, and 7 green marbles. A marble is selected at random. Find the probability the marble is *not* red.

e. ____________

Example

4. Mr. Harada surveyed his class and discovered that 30% of his students have blue eyes. Identify the complement of this event. Then find its probability.

The complement of having blue eyes is *not* having blue eyes. The sum of the probabilities is 100%.

$P(\text{blue eyes}) + P(\textit{not}\text{ blue eyes}) = 100\%$	P(blue eyes) and P(*not* blue eyes) are complements.
$30\% + P(\textit{not}\text{ blue eyes}) = 100\%$	Replace P(blue eyes) with 30%.
$30\% + 70\% = 100\%$	**THINK** 30% plus what number equals 100%?

So, the probability that a student does *not* have blue eyes is 70%, 0.7, or $\frac{7}{10}$.

Guided Practice

A letter tile is chosen randomly. Find the probability of each event. Write each answer as a fraction, percent, and decimal. (Examples 1–3)

1. P(D) ______

2. P(S, V, or L) ______

3. P(*not* D) ______

4. The probability of choosing a "Go Back 1 Space" card in a board game is 25%. Describe the complement of this event and find its probability. (Example 4) ______

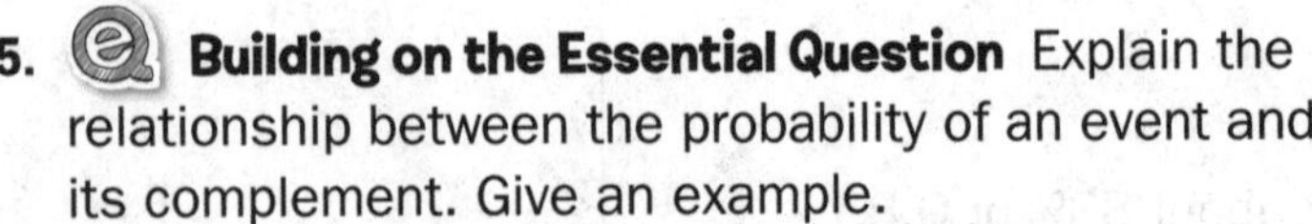

5. **Building on the Essential Question** Explain the relationship between the probability of an event and its complement. Give an example.

Rate Yourself!

How confident are you about finding the probability of simple events? Shade the ring on the target.

For more help, go online to access a Personal Tutor.

FOLDABLES Time to update your Foldable!

Independent Practice

Go online for Step-by-Step Solutions

The spinner shown is spun once. Find the probability of each event. Write each answer as a fraction, percent, and decimal. (Examples 1–3)

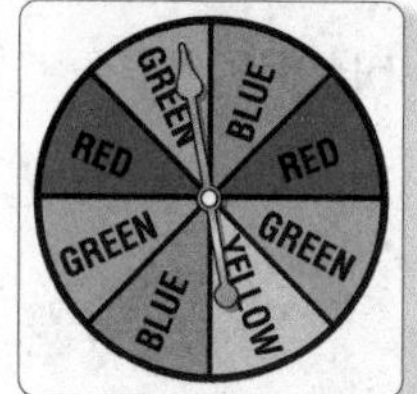

1. P(blue)

2. P(red or yellow)

3. P(*not* brown)

4. P(*not* green)

5. Refer to the table on air travel at selected airports. Suppose a flight that arrived at El Centro is selected at random. What is the probability that the flight did *not* arrive on time? Write the answer as a fraction, decimal, and percent. Explain your reasoning. (Example 4)

Air Travel	
Airport	Arrivals (Percent on-time)
El Centro (CA)	80
Baltimore (MD)	82

6. **Model with Mathematics** Refer to the graphic novel frame below. Jamar and Theresa decide to create a music mix and include an equal number of songs from each genre. What is the probability that any given song would be from the hip-hop genre? ____________

One jelly bean is picked, without looking, from the dish. Write a sentence that explains how likely it is for each event to happen.

7. black

8. purple, red, or yellow

H.O.T. Problems Higher Order Thinking

9. CCGPS **Persevere with Problems** The probability of landing in a certain section on a spinner can be found by considering the size of the angle formed by that section. On spinner shown, the angle formed by the yellow section is one-fourth of the angle formed by the entire circle. So, P(yellow) $= \frac{1}{4}$, 0.25, or 25%.

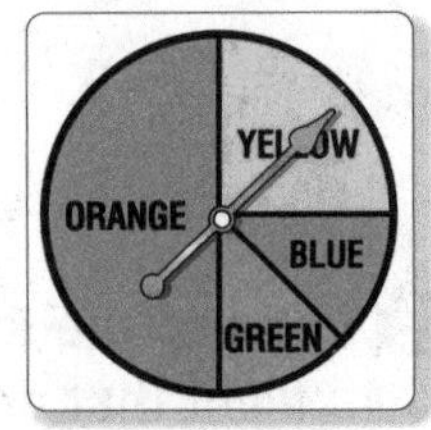

a. Determine *P*(green) and *P*(orange) for the spinner. Write the probabilities as fractions, decimals, and percents.

b. Determine *P*(*not* yellow).

10. CCGPS **Persevere with Problems** A bag contains 6 red, 4 blue, and 8 green marbles. How many marbles of each color should be added so that the total number of marbles is 27, but the probability of randomly selecting one marble of each color remains unchanged?

Georgia Test Practice

11. A miniature golf course has a bucket with 7 yellow, 6 green, 3 blue, and 8 red golf balls. If Tamika draws a ball at random from the bucket, what is the probability that she will *not* draw a green golf ball?

Ⓐ $\frac{1}{4}$ Ⓑ $\frac{1}{3}$ Ⓒ $\frac{2}{3}$ Ⓓ $\frac{3}{4}$

Name ____________ My Homework ____________

Extra Practice

Ten cards numbered 1 through 10 are mixed together and then one card is drawn. Find the probability of each event. Write each answer as a fraction, percent, and decimal.

12. *P*(8)

$\frac{1}{10}$, 10%, or 0.1

Only 1 card has an 8. So, P(8) is $\frac{1}{10}$, 10%, or 0.1.

Homework Help

13. *P*(7 or 9)

$\frac{1}{5}$, 20%, or 0.2

There is 1 card with a 7 and 1 card with a 9. So, P(7 or 9) is $\frac{2}{10}$ or $\frac{1}{5}$, or 20%, or 0.2.

14. *P*(less than 5)

15. *P*(greater than 3)

16. *P*(odd)

17. *P*(even)

18. *P*(*not* a multiple of 4)

19. *P*(*not* 5, 6, 7, or 8)

20. *P*(divisible by 3)

21. Of the students at Grant Middle School, 63% are girls. The school newspaper is randomly selecting a student to be interviewed. Describe the complement of selecting a girl and find the probability of the complement. Write the answer as a fraction, decimal, and percent.

22. The table shows the number of dogs and cats at a groomer. If a pet is selected at random to be groomed, find the probability that Patches the cat will be selected. Then find the probability that a cat will be selected.

Pets at the Groomer	
Cats	**Dogs**
12	16

23. CCGPS **Persevere with Problems** For a certain game, the probability of choosing a card with the number 13 is $\frac{8}{1,000}$. Find the probability of *not* choosing a card with the number 13. Then describe the likelihood of the event occurring.

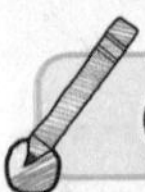

Georgia Test Practice

24. Joel has a bowl containing the mints shown in the table.

Color	Number
Red	5
Orange	3
Yellow	1
Green	6

If he randomly chooses one mint from the bowl, what is the probability that the mint is orange?

Ⓐ $\frac{1}{5}$ Ⓒ $\frac{11}{15}$

Ⓑ $\frac{2}{3}$ Ⓓ $\frac{4}{5}$

25. **Short Response** Max has 50 songs on his MP3 player. If he plays a song at random, what is the probability that it is a rock song? ______________

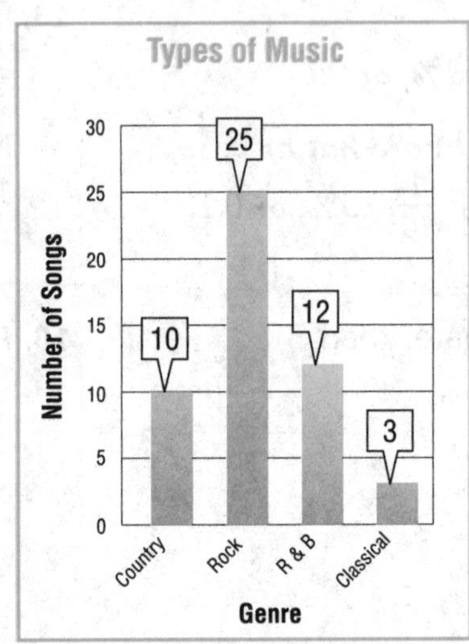

26. What is the probability of the spinner landing on an A, C, or D?

Ⓕ $\frac{1}{4}$ Ⓗ $\frac{1}{2}$

Ⓖ $\frac{3}{8}$ Ⓘ $\frac{3}{4}$

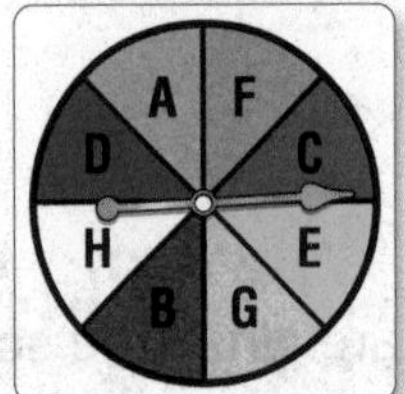

CCGPS Common Core Review

Compare each decimal using <, >, or =. MCC5.NBT.3b

27. 0.2 ◯ 0.3

28. 0.75 ◯ 0.7

29. 5.89 ◯ 5.899

30. Dwayne misses 12% of his foul shots and Bryan misses 0.2 of his foul shots. Write 12% and 0.2 as fractions in simplest form. Then compare the fractions to determine who misses more foul shots. MCC6.NS.7b

____

Inquiry Lab
Relative Frequency

Inquiry HOW is probability related to relative frequency?

CCGPS Content Standards MCC7.SP.6, MCC7.SP.7, MCC7.SP.7a

Mathematical Practices 1, 3

In a board game, you get an extra turn if you roll doubles or two of the same number.

You can conduct an experiment to find the relative frequency of rolling doubles using two number cubes. **Relative frequency** is the ratio of the number of experimental successes to the number of experimental attempts.

Investigation

Tools 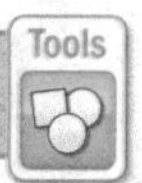

Step 1 The table shows all of the possible outcomes for rolling two number cubes. Shade all of the possible outcomes that are doubles.

The probability of rolling doubles is ________.

(1, 1)	(2, 1)	(3, 1)	(4, 1)	(5, 1)	(6, 1)
(1, 2)	(2, 2)	(3, 2)	(4, 2)	(5, 2)	(6, 2)
(1, 3)	(2, 3)	(3, 3)	(4, 3)	(5, 3)	(6, 3)
(1, 4)	(2, 4)	(3, 4)	(4, 4)	(5, 4)	(6, 4)
(1, 5)	(2, 5)	(3, 5)	(4, 5)	(5, 5)	(6, 5)
(1, 6)	(2, 6)	(3, 6)	(4, 6)	(5, 6)	(6, 6)

Step 2 Roll two number cubes and record the number of doubles in the table. Repeat the experiment 50 times.

Number of Rolls	Number of Doubles
50	

Step 3 Find the relative frequency of rolling doubles. Use the ratio $\frac{\text{number of times doubles were rolled}}{\text{number of rolls}}$. ________

Are the ratios in Steps 1 and 3 of the Investigation the same? Explain why or why not.

____

Suppose the number cubes are rolled 100 times. Would you expect the results to be the same? Explain why or why not.

____

Collaborate

Work with a partner.

1. Place a paperclip around the tip of a pencil. Then place the tip on the center of the spinner. Spin the paperclip 40 times. Record the results in the table below.

Section	A	B	C	D
Frequency				
Relative Frequency				

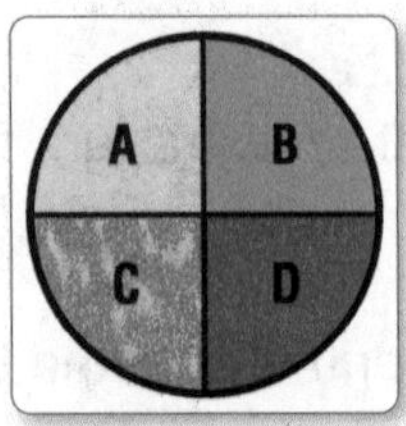

The spinner above is spun once. Find the probability of each event.

2. $P(\text{A})$ ______

3. $P(\text{B})$ ______

4. $P(\text{C})$ ______

5. $P(\text{D})$ ______

Analyze

6. Based on your results from the spinner experiment, are the outcomes of A, B, C, or D equally likely? ______

7. CCGPS **Reason Inductively** What would you expect to happen to the long-run relative frequency of spinning an A as you increase the number of spins from 40 to 1,000? ______

Reflect

8. CCGPS **Justify Conclusions** If you rolled a number cube 600 times, approximate the relative frequency of rolling a 3 or 6. Explain your reasoning to a classmate. ______

9. Inquiry HOW is probability related to relative frequency?

Theoretical and Experimental Probability

Scan the lesson. Write the definitions of theoretical probability and experimental probability.

- theoretical probability: ______

- experimental probability: ______

Essential Question

HOW can you predict the outcome of future events?

Vocabulary

uniform probability model
theoretical probability
experimental probability

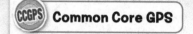

Common Core GPS

Content Standards
MCC7.SP.7, MCC7.SP.7a, MCC7.SP.7b

Mathematical Practices
1, 3, 4

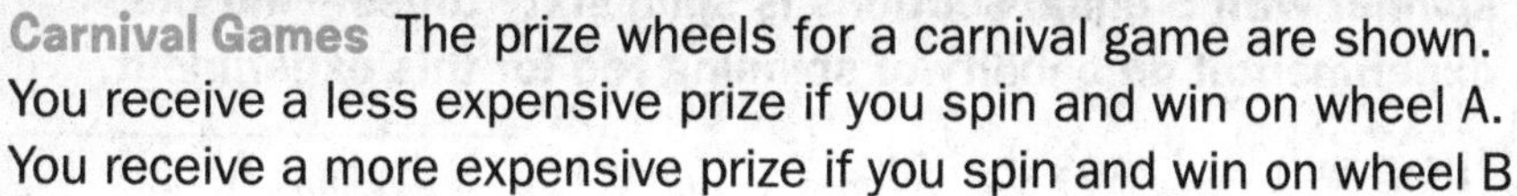

Carnival Games The prize wheels for a carnival game are shown. You receive a less expensive prize if you spin and win on wheel A. You receive a more expensive prize if you spin and win on wheel B.

Wheel A

Wheel B

In a **uniform probability model**, each outcome has an equal probability of happening.

1. Which wheel has uniform probability? ______

2. Use a paperclip and the tip of your pencil to spin each wheel 4 times. Record your results.

Spin	Wheel A	Wheel B
1		
2		
3		
4		

3. Why do you think winners on wheel A receive a less expensive prize than winners on wheel B?

______

______

Work Zone

Experimental and Theoretical Probability

Theoretical probability is based on uniform probability — what *should* happen when conducting a probability experiment. **Experimental probability** is based on relative frequency — what *actually* occurrs during such an experiment.

The theoretical probability and the experimental probability of an event may or may not be the same. As the number attempts increases, the theoretical probability and the experimental probability should become closer in value.

Trials
A trial is one experiment in a series of successive experiments.

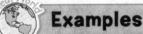

Examples

1. The graph shows the results of an experiment in which a spinner with 3 equal sections is spun sixty times. Find the experimental probability of spinning red for this experiment.

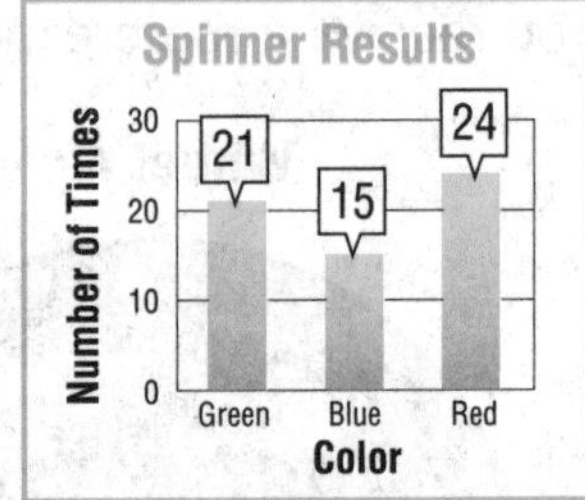

The graph indicates that the spinner landed on red 24 times, blue 15 times, and green 21 times.

$$P(\text{red}) = \frac{\text{number of times red occurs}}{\text{total number of spins}}$$

$$= \frac{24}{60} \text{ or } \frac{2}{5}$$

The experimental probability of spinning red is $\frac{2}{5}$.

2. Compare the experimental probability you found in Example 1 to its theoretical probability.

The spinner has three equal sections: red, blue, and green. So, the theoretical probability of spinning red is $\frac{1}{3}$. Since $\frac{2}{5} \approx \frac{1}{3}$, the experimental probability is close to the theoretical probability.

Show your work.

Got It? Do these problems to find out.

a. Refer to Example 1. If the spinner was spun 3 more times and landed on green each time, find the experimental probability of spinning green for this experiment.

b. Compare the experimental probability you found in Exercise a to its theoretical probability.

a. ________

b. ________

Examples

3. Two number cubes are rolled together 20 times. A sum of 9 is rolled 8 times. What is the experimental probability of rolling a sum of 9?

$$P(9) = \frac{\text{number of times a sum of 9 occurs}}{\text{total number of rolls}}$$

$$= \frac{8}{20} \text{ or } \frac{2}{5}$$

The experimental probability of rolling a sum of 9 is $\frac{2}{5}$.

4. Compare the experimental probability you found in Example 3 to its theoretical probability. If the probabilities are not close, explain a possible reason for the discrepancy.

When rolling two number cubes, there are 36 possible outcomes. The theoretical probability of rolling a sum of 9 is $\frac{4}{36}$ or $\frac{1}{9}$.

Rolls with Sum of 9	
First Cube	**Second Cube**
3	6
4	5
5	4
6	3

Since $\frac{1}{9}$ is not close to $\frac{2}{5}$, the experimental probability is *not* close to the theoretical probability. One possible explanation is that there were not enough trials.

Got It? Do these problems to find out.

c. In Example 3, what is the experimental probability of rolling a sum that is *not* 9?

d. Two coins are tossed 10 times. Both coins land on heads 6 times. Compare the experimental probability to the theoretical probability. If the probabilities are not close, explain a possible reason for the discrepancy.

e. Suppose three coins are tossed 10 times. All three coins land on heads 1 time. Compare the experimental probability to the theoretical probability. If the probabilities are not close, explain a possible reason for the discrepancy.

c. ____________

d. ____________

e. ____________

Predict Future Events

Theoretical and experimental probability can be used to make predictions about future events.

Example

Solving Proportions

The cross products of any proportion are equal.

$\frac{29}{100} = \frac{x}{5,000}$

5. Last year, a DVD store sold 670 action DVDs, 580 comedy DVDs, 450 drama DVDs, and 300 horror DVDs. If a media buyer expects to sell 5,000 DVDs this year. Based on these results, how many comedy DVDs should she buy? Explain.

2,000 DVDs were sold and 580 were comedy. So, the probability is $\frac{580}{2,000}$ or $\frac{29}{100}$.

$\frac{29}{100} = \frac{x}{5,000}$ Write a proportion.

$29 \cdot 5,000 = 100 \cdot x$ Find the cross products.

$145,000 = 100x$ Multiply.

$1,450 = x$ Divide each side by 100.

She should buy about 1,450 comedy DVDs.

Guided Practice

1. A coin is tossed 50 times, and it lands on heads 28 times. Find the experimental probability and the theoretical probability of the coin landing on heads. Then, compare the experimental and theoretical probabilities. (Examples 1–4)

2. Yesterday, 50 bakery customers bought muffins and 11 of those customers bought banana muffins. If 100 customers buy muffins tomorrow, how many would you expect to buy a banana muffin? (Example 5)

3. **Building on the Essential Question** How are experimental probability and theoretical probability alike?

Rate Yourself!

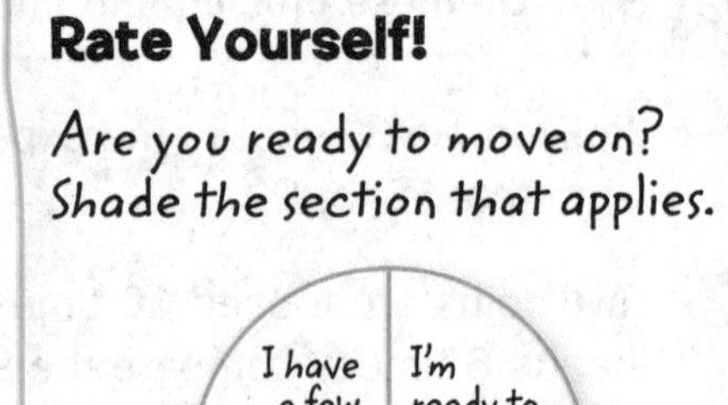
Are you ready to move on?
Shade the section that applies.

I have a few questions.
I'm ready to move on.
I have a lot of questions.

For more help, go online to access a Personal Tutor.

FOLDABLES Time to update your Foldable!

Name ______________________ My Homework ______________________

Independent Practice

Go online for Step-by-Step Solutions 

1. A number cube is rolled 20 times and lands on 1 two times and on 5 four times. Find each experimental probability. Then compare the experimental probability to the theoretical probability. (Examples 1–4)
   a. landing on 5

   b. *not* landing on 1

2. The spinner at the right is spun 12 times. It lands on blue 1 time. (Examples 1–4)

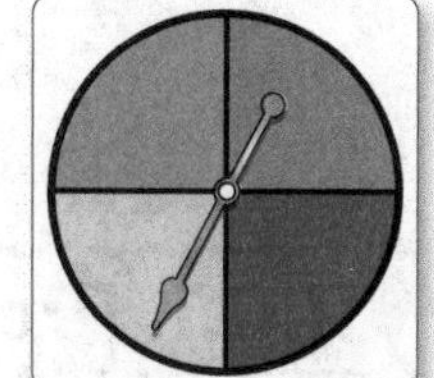

   a. What is the experimental probability of the spinner landing on blue?

   b. Compare the experimental and theoretical probabilities of the spinner landing on blue. If the probabilities are not close, explain a possible reason for the discrepancy.

3. Use the graph of a survey of 70 zoo visitors who were asked to name their favorite animal exhibit. (Example 5)
   a. Suppose 540 people visit the zoo. Predict how many people will choose the monkey exhibit as their favorite. ______
   b. Suppose 720 people visit the zoo. Predict how many people will choose the penguin exhibit as their favorite. ______

What is your Favorite Animal Exhibit?

Exhibit	Tally	Frequency
Bears	𝍸 I	6
Elephants	𝍸 𝍸 𝍸 II	17
Monkeys	𝍸 𝍸 𝍸 𝍸 I	21
Penguins	𝍸 𝍸 III	13
Snakes	𝍸 𝍸 III	13

4. CCGPS **Make a Conjecture** Cross out the part of the concept circle that does *not* belong. Then describe the relationship among the remaining parts.

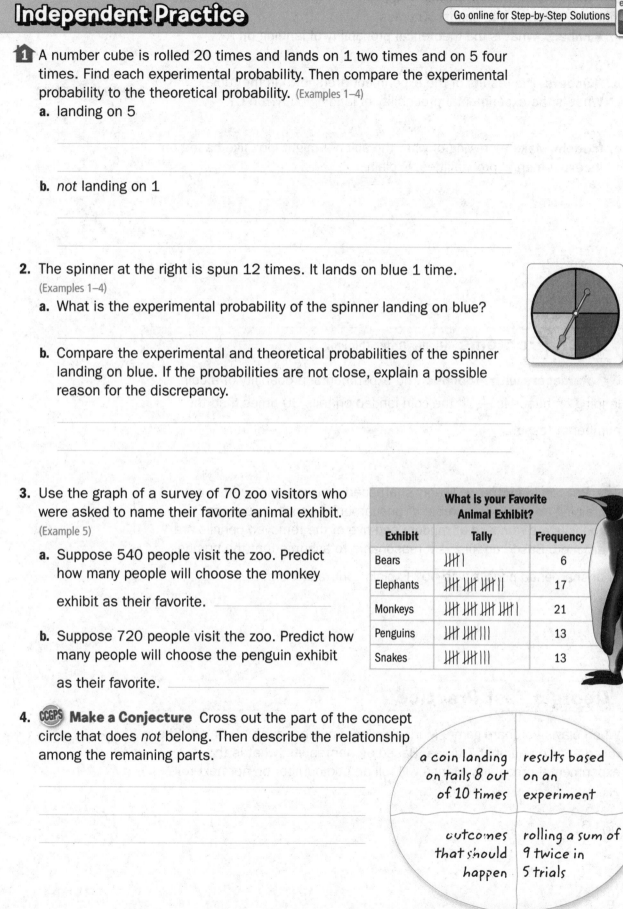

a coin landing on tails 8 out of 10 times	results based on an experiment
outcomes that should happen	rolling a sum of 9 twice in 5 trials

5 **CCGPS Multiple Representations** A spinner with three equal-sized sections marked A, B, and C is spun 100 times.

a. **Numbers** What is the theoretical probability of landing on A?

b. **Numbers** The results of the experiment are shown in the table. What is the experimental probability of landing on A? on C?

Section	Frequency
A	24
B	50
C	26

c. **Models** Make a drawing of what the spinner might look like based on its experimental probabilities. Explain.

H.O.T. Problems Higher Order Thinking

6. **CCGPS Persevere with Problems** The experimental probability of a coin landing on heads is $\frac{7}{12}$. If the coin landed on tails 30 times, find the number of tosses.

7. **CCGPS Reason Inductively** Twenty sharpened pencils are placed in a box containing an unknown number of unsharpened pencils. Suppose 15 pencils are removed at random and five of the removed pencils are sharpened. Based on this, is it reasonable to assume that the number of unsharpened pencils was 40? Explain your reasoning.

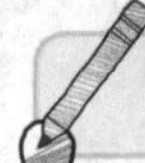

Georgia Test Practice

8. When playing a board game, Marisol rolled a number cube 10 times. She rolled an even number 7 times. Based on her results, what is the experimental probability Marisa will roll an odd number on her next roll?

Ⓐ $\frac{1}{6}$

Ⓑ $\frac{3}{10}$

Ⓒ $\frac{7}{10}$

Ⓓ $\frac{5}{6}$

Extra Practice

For Exercises 9 and 10, find each experimental probability. Then compare the experimental probability to its theoretical probability. If the probabilities are not close, explain a possible reason for the discrepancy.

9. A coin is tossed 20 times. It lands on heads 9 times.

$P(\text{heads}) = \frac{\text{number of times heads occurs}}{\text{total number of coin tosses}} = \frac{9}{20}$

Homework Help

The experimental probability of $\frac{9}{20}$ is close to the theoretical probability of $\frac{1}{2}$.

10. A heart is randomly chosen 7 out of 12 times from the cards shown.

____

____

____

____

Solve.

11. Last month, customers at a gift shop bought 40 birthday cards, 19 congratulations cards, 20 holiday cards, and 21 thank you cards. Suppose 125 customers buy greeting cards next month. How many would you expect to buy a birthday card?

____

12. Use the graph at the right.

a. What is the probability that a mother received a gift of flowers or plants? Write the probability as a fraction in simplest form.

____

b. Suppose 400 mothers will receive a gift. Predict how many will receive flowers or plants.

____

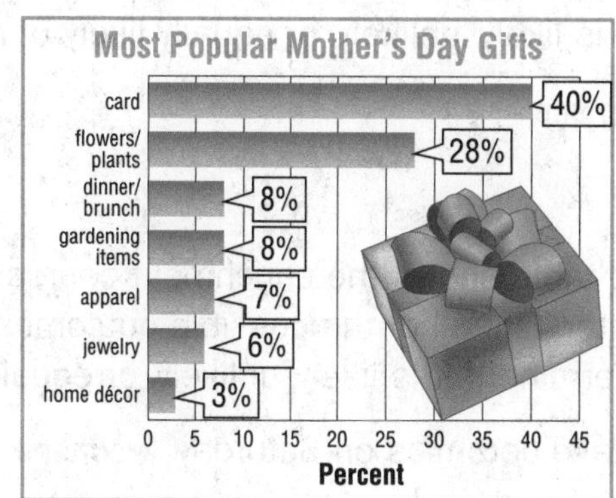

Georgia Test Practice

13. The table shows Mitch's record for the last thirty par-3 holes he has played.

Mitch's Golf Results	
Score	**Number of Holes**
2	4
3	14
4	9
5	3

Based on this record, what is the probability that Mitch will score a 2 or 3 on the next par-3 hole?

Ⓐ $\frac{7}{9}$

Ⓑ $\frac{3}{5}$

Ⓒ $\frac{3}{10}$

Ⓓ $\frac{9}{50}$

14. J.R. tossed a coin 100 times.

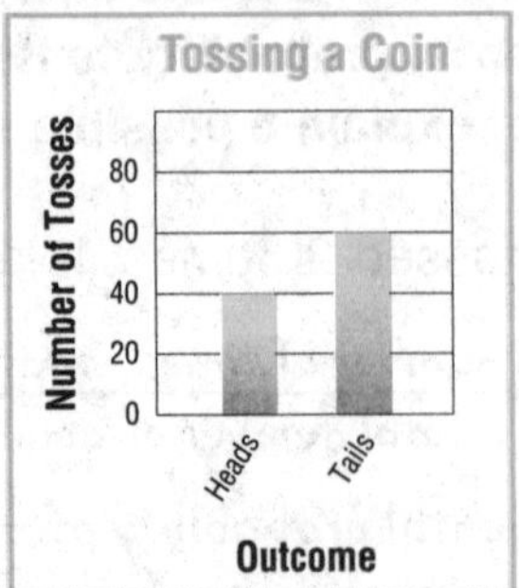

Based on his results, what is the experimental probability of J.R. tossing tails on the next toss?

Ⓕ $\frac{1}{5}$

Ⓖ $\frac{2}{3}$

Ⓗ $\frac{3}{5}$

Ⓘ $\frac{4}{5}$

Common Core Review

For Exercises 15 and 16, circle the greater probability. MCC7.SP.5

15. The spinner at the right is spun.

P(red) P(not red)

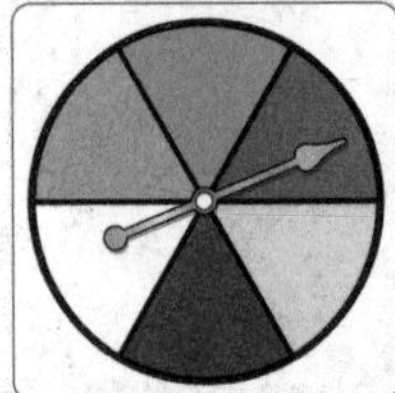

16. A number cube is rolled.

P(multiple of 3) P(prime number)

17. A restaurant offers three flavors of ice cream on its dessert menu: vanilla, chocolate, and strawberry. Dessert options are sundaes or ice cream cones. List all of the possible desserts. Then determine if it is likely, unlikely, or equally likely of randomly choosing a sundae.

MCC7.SP.5 ______________________________

____

18. The table shows the enrichment courses offered at a community arts center. List all of the possible outcomes of the classes. Then determine if it is likely, unlikely, or equally likely of randomly choosing to take ceramics on Saturday. MCC7.SP.5 ______________________________

Course Offering	Days of Class
ceramics painting photography	Friday Saturday

____

____

Inquiry Lab

Fair and Unfair Games

HOW can you determine if a game is fair?

Content Standards
MCC7.SP.7, MCC7.SP.7a, MCC7.SP.7b

Mathematical Practices
1, 3

In a counter-toss game, players toss three two-color counters. The winner of each game is determined by how many counters land with either the red or yellow side facing up. Find out if this game is fair or unfair.

Mathematically speaking, a two-player game is **fair** if each player has an equal chance of winning. A game is **unfair** if there is not such a chance.

Work in pairs to play the game described above.

Step 1 Player 1 tosses the counters. If 2 or 3 counters land red-side up, Player 1 wins. If 2 or 3 counters land yellow-side up, Player 2 wins. Record the results in the table below. Place a check in the winner's column for each game.

Game	Player 1	Player 2	Game	Player 1	Player 2
1			6		
2			7		
3			8		
4			9		
5			10		

Step 2 Player 2 then tosses the counters and the results are recorded.

Step 3 Continue alternating turns until the counters have been tossed 10 times.

Based on your results, do you think the game is fair or unfair? Circle your response below.

Fair Unfair

Collaborate

Work with a partner.

1. Complete the organized list of all the possible outcomes resulting from one toss of the three counters described in Investigation 1.

Counter 1	Counter 2	Counter 3	Outcome
red	red	red	red, red, red

2. In the outcome column of the table above, draw a circle around the outcomes that are a win for Player 1. Draw a box around the outcomes that are a win for Player 2.

3. Calculate the theoretical probability of each player winning. Write each probability as a fraction and as a percent. Then determine if the game is fair or unfair.

4. Use your results from Investigation 1 to calculate the experimental probability of each player winning.

Reflect

5. CCGPS **Justify Conclusions** Compare the probabilities you found in Exercises 3 and 4. Explain any discrepancies.

6. CCGPS **Reason Inductively** Predict the number of times Player 1 would win if the game were played 100 times. Explain your reasoning.

David and Lyn made up a game using a plastic cup. A cup is tossed. If it lands right-side up or open-end down, David wins. If it lands on its side, Lyn wins. Is this game fair?

Investigation 2

Work in pairs to play the game and determine if David and Lyn created a fair game.

Step 1 Player 1 tosses the cup. If it lands right-side up or open-end down, Player 1 gets a point. If the cup lands on its side, Player 2 gets a point. Record your results in the table below.

Toss	Player 1	Player 2	Toss	Player 1	Player 2
1			6		
2			7		
3			8		
4			9		
5			10		

Step 2 Player 2 then tosses the cup and the results are recorded.

Step 3 Continue alternating turns until there is a total of 10 tosses.

Based on your results, do you think the game David and Lyn created is fair or unfair? Circle your response below.

Fair Unfair

There are three possible outcomes when tossing the cup and David wins if two of those outcomes happen. It may appear that David has a better chance of winning, however this is not necessarily true.

Explain why Lyn actually has a better chance at winning the game.

____

____

____

What was the experimental probability for the cup landing right-side up or open-end down?

____

Collaborate

Work with a partner.

7. A game involves rolling two number cubes. Player 1 wins the game if the total of the numbers rolled is 5 or if a 5 is shown on one or both number cubes. Otherwise, Player 2 wins. Fill in the table for all of the possible outcomes of rolling two number cubes.

	1	2	3	4	5	6
1	1 + 1 = 2	1 + 2 = 3	1 + 3 = 4	1 + 4 = 5	1 + 5 = 6	1 + 6 = 7
2	2 + 1 = 3					
3						
4						
5						
6						

8. Shade in the cells of the table in which Player 1 is a winner.

Analyze

9. For the number cube game, calculate the theoretical probability of each player winning. Write each probability as a fraction and as a percent.

____

____

10. CCGPS **Justify Conclusions** Is the number cube game fair? Explain.

____

____

11. If the number cube game is fair, explain how you could change the game so that it is unfair. If the game is unfair, explain how you could change the game to make it fair. ______________________________

____

Reflect

12. Inquiry HOW can you determine if a game is fair? ______________________________

____

Lesson 3

Probability of Compound Events

What You'll Learn

Scan the lesson. List two headings you would use to make an outline of the lesson.

- ______________________________
- ______________________________

Essential Question

HOW can you predict the outcome of future events?

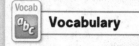

Vocabulary

sample space
tree diagram
compound event

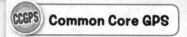

Common Core GPS

Content Standards
MCC7.SP.8, MCC7.SP.8a, MCC7.SP.8b

Mathematical Practices
1, 3, 4, 5

Real-World Link

Travel Aimee wants to pack enough items to create 6 different outfits. She packs 1 jacket, 3 shirts, and 2 pairs of jeans. Can Aimee create 6 different outfits from her clothing items?

1. Complete the table below.

Outfit	Clothing Items
1	jacket, shirt 1, jeans 1
2	jacket, shirt 1, jeans 2
3	jacket, shirt 2, jeans 1
4	jacket, shirt 2,
5	jacket, shirt 3,
6	jacket,

2. The table is an example of an organized list. What is another way to show the different outfits that Aimee can create?

3. Describe another situation for which you might want to list all of the possible outcomes.

Work Zone

Find a Sample Space

The set of all of the possible outcomes in a probability experiment is called the **sample space**. Organized lists, tables, and **tree diagrams** can be used to represent the sample space.

Examples

1. The three students chosen to represent Mr. Balderick's class in a school assembly are shown. All three of them need to sit in a row on the stage. Use a list to find the sample space for the different ways they can sit in a row.

Students
Adrienne
Carlos
Greg

Use A for Adrienne, C for Carlos, and G for Greg. Use each letter exactly once.

ACG AGC CAG CGA GAC GCA

So, the sample space consists of 6 outcomes.

2. A car can be purchased in blue, silver, red, or purple. It also comes as a convertible or hardtop. Use a table or a tree diagram to find the sample space for the different styles in which the car can be purchased.

Color	Top
blue	convertible
blue	hardtop
silver	convertible
silver	hardtop
red	convertible
red	hardtop
purple	convertible
purple	hardtop

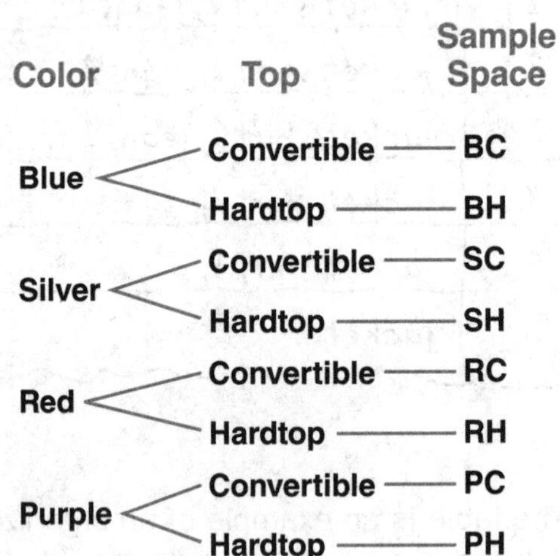

Using either method, the sample space consists of 8 outcomes.

Show your work.

Got It? Do this problem to find out.

a. The table shows the sandwich choices for a picnic. Find the sample space using a list, table, or tree diagram for a sandwich consisting of one type of meat and one type of bread.

Meat	Bread
ham turkey	rye sourdough white

a. ______

Find Probability

A **compound event** consists of two or more simple events. The probability of a compound event, just as with simple events, is the fraction of outcomes in the sample space for which the compound event occurs.

Example

3. Suppose you toss a quarter, a dime, and a nickel. Find the sample space. What is the probability of getting three tails?

Make a tree diagram to show the sample space.

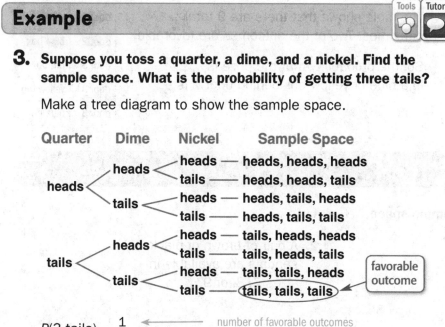

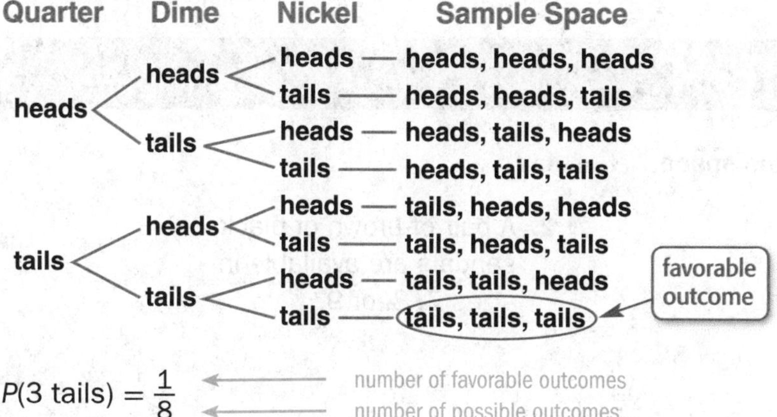

$P(3 \text{ tails}) = \frac{1}{8}$ ← number of favorable outcomes ← number of possible outcomes

So, the probability of getting three tails is $\frac{1}{8}$.

Got It? **Do this problem to find out.**

b. The animal shelter has both male and female Labrador Retrievers in yellow, brown, or black. There is an equal number of each kind. What is the probability of choosing a female yellow Labrador Retriever? Show your work in the space below.

Random
When choosing an outcome, assume that each outcome is chosen randomly.

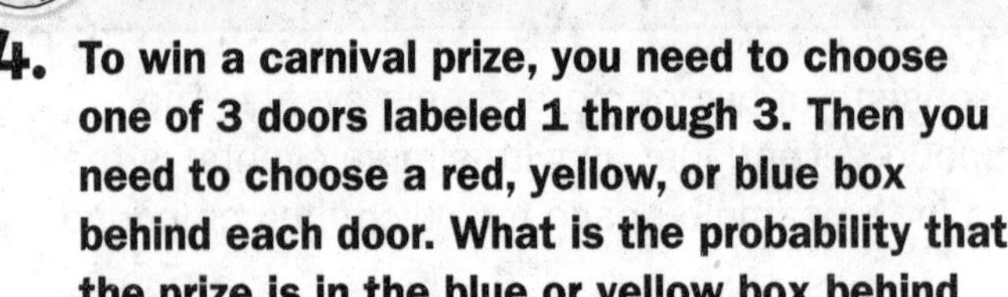

Example

4. To win a carnival prize, you need to choose one of 3 doors labeled 1 through 3. Then you need to choose a red, yellow, or blue box behind each door. What is the probability that the prize is in the blue or yellow box behind door 2?

Outcomes	
door 1	red box
door 1	yellow box
door 1	blue box
door 2	red box
door 2	yellow box
door 2	blue box
door 3	red box
door 3	yellow box
door 3	blue box

The table shows that there are 9 total outcomes. Two of the outcomes are favorable.

So, the probability that the prize is in a blue or yellow box behind door 2 is $\frac{2}{9}$.

Guided Practice

For each situation, find the sample space. (Examples 1–2)

1. A coin is tossed twice.

2. A pair of brown or black sandals are available in sizes 7, 8, or 9.

3. Gerardo spins a spinner with four equal sections, labeled A, B, C, and D, twice. If letter A is spun at least once, Gerardo wins. Otherwise, Odell wins. Use a list to find the sample space. Then find the probability that Odell wins. (Examples 3–4)

4. **Bulding on the Essential Question** How do tree diagrams, tables, and lists help you find the probability of a compound event?

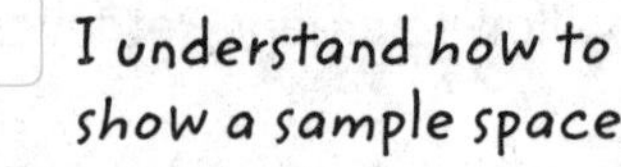

Rate Yourself!

☐ I understand how to show a sample space.

Great! You're ready to move on!

☐ I still have questions about showing a sample space.

No Problem! Go online to access a Personal Tutor.

Name ______________________ My Homework ______________________

Independent Practice

Go online for Step-by-Step Solutions 

For each situation, find the sample space. (Examples 1–2)

1. tossing a coin and spinning the spinner at the right

2. picking a number from 1 to 5 and choosing the color red, white, or blue

3. choosing a purple, green, black, or silver bike having 10, 18, 21, or 24 speeds

4. choosing a letter from the word SPACE and choosing a consonant from the word MATH

For each game, find the sample space. Then find the indicated probability. (Examples 3–4)

5. Alana tosses 2 number cubes. She wins if she rolls double sixes.

   Find P(Alana wins). ______________________

6. Ming rolls a number cube, tosses a coin, and chooses a card from two cards marked A and B. If an even number and heads appears, Ming wins, no matter which card is chosen. Otherwise Lashonda wins.

   Find P(Ming wins). ______________________

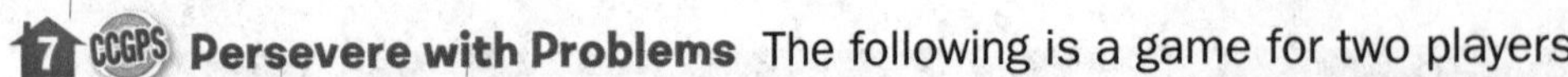

7. **Persevere with Problems** The following is a game for two players.

- Three counters are labeled according to the table at the right.
- Toss the three counters.
- If exactly 2 counters match, Player 1 scores a point. Otherwise, Player 2 scores a point.

Counters	Side 1	Side 2
Counter 1	red	blue
Counter 2	red	yellow
Counter 3	blue	yellow

Find the probability that each player scores a point.

H.O.T. Problems Higher Order Thinking

8. **Persevere with Problems** Refer to Exercise 7. Do the two players both have an equal chance of winning? Explain.

9. **Find the Error** Caitlyn wants to determine the probability of guessing correctly on two true-false questions on her history test. She draws the tree diagram below using C for correct and I for incorrect. Find her mistake and correct it.

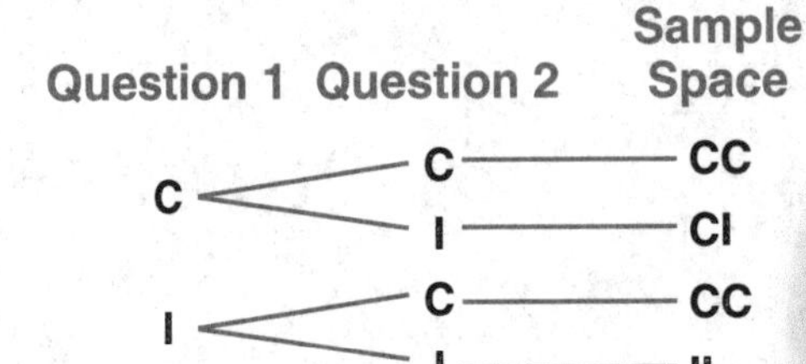

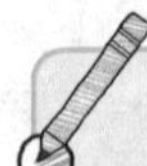

Georgia Test Practice

10. A coffee shop offers 2 types of coffee: regular and decaffeinated; 3 types of flavoring: vanilla, hazelnut, and caramel; and 2 choices of topping: with or without whipped cream. How many possible choices are there?

Ⓐ 12 choices

Ⓑ 14 choices

Ⓒ 16 choices

Ⓓ 18 choices

Name ______________________ My Homework ______________________

Extra Practice

11. Three-course dinners can be made from the menu shown. Find the sample space for a dinner consisting of an appetizer, entrée, and dessert.

Appetizers	Entrees	Desserts
Soup	Steak	Carrot cake
Salad	Chicken	Apple pie

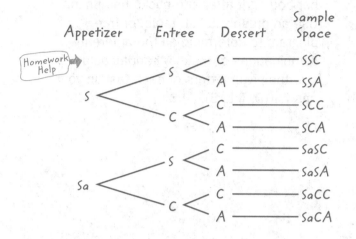

Homework Help

Appetizer	Entree	Dessert	Sample Space
S	S	C	SSC
		A	SSA
	C	C	SCC
		A	SCA
Sa	S	C	SaSC
		A	SaSA
	C	C	SaCC
		A	SaCA

12. Mr. and Mrs. Romero are expecting triplets. Suppose the chance of each child being a boy is 50% and of being a girl is 50%. Find the probability of each event.

a. *P*(all three children will be boys) ______

b. *P*(at least one boy and one girl) ______

c. *P*(two boys and one girl) ______

d. *P*(at least two girls) ______

Copy and Solve For Exercises 13 and 14, show your work on a separate piece of paper.

13. The University of Oregon's football team has many different uniforms. The coach can choose from four colors of jerseys and pants: green, yellow, white, and black. There are three helmet options: green, white, and yellow. Also, there are the same four colors of socks and two colors of shoes, black and yellow.

a. How many jersey/pant combinations are there?

b. If the coach picks a jersey/pant combination at random, what is the probability he will pick a yellow jersey with green pants?

c. Use a tree diagram to find all of the possible shoe and sock combinations.

14. CCGPS **Use Math Tools** Use the Internet or another source to find the top five best-selling animated movies. Then create a list of the possibilities for choosing a movie and choosing a wide-screen or full-screen version.

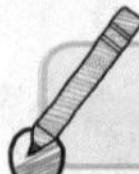

Georgia Test Practice

15. Mr. Zajac will choose one student from each of the two groups below to present their history report to the class.

Group 1
Ava
Antoine
Greg

Group 2
Mario
Brooke

Which set shows all the possible choices?

Ⓐ {(Ava, Mario), (Antoine, Mario), (Greg, Mario)}

Ⓑ {(Ava, Antoine), (Antoine, Greg), (Brooke, Mario)}

Ⓒ {(Ava, Mario), (Antoine, Mario), (Greg, Mario), (Ava, Brooke), (Antoine, Brooke), (Greg, Brooke)}

Ⓓ {(Brooke, Antoine), (Mario, Greg), (Ava, Brooke), (Mario, Antoine)}

16. Short Response Miranda needs to get dressed (D), brush her teeth (T), pack her lunch (L), and make her bed (B) before she leaves for school. She always makes her bed right after she packs her lunch. Use an organized list, table, or tree diagram to determine all the different combinations of tasks Miranda could do. Use the given letters of each task in your answer (D, T, L, B).

Common Core Review

Eight cards numbered 1–8 are shuffled together. A card is drawn at random. Find the probability of each event. MCC7.SP.5

17. P(8) ______

18. P(greater than 5) ______

19. P(even) ______

20. P(3 or 7) ______

21. What is the probability of rolling a number greater than 4 on a number cube? Explain. MCC7.SP.5

Simulations

What You'll Learn

Scan the lesson. Predict two things you will learn about simulations.

-
-

Essential Question

HOW can you predict the outcome of future events?

Vocabulary

simulation

Common Core GPS

Content Standards
MCC7.SP.8, MCC7.SP.8c

Mathematical Practices
1, 3, 4

Real-World Link

Music Downloads A new electronics store is opening at the mall. One out of six new customers will receive a free music download. The winners are chosen at random. On Monday, the store had 50 customers. You can act out or *simulate* 50 random customers by using the random number generator on a graphing calculator.

Type in the following keystrokes to set 1 as the lower bound and 6 as the upper bound for 50 trials.

Keystrokes: MATH ◀ 5 1 , 6 , 50) ENTER

The screen should look similar to the screen shown to the below.

A set of 50 numbers ranging from 1 to 6 appears. Use the right arrow key to see the next number in the set.

1. Let the number 3 represent a customer who wins a free download. Write the experimental probability of winning a download.

2. Compare the experimental probabilities found in Exercise 1 to the theoretical probability of winning a download.

Work Zone

Model Equally Likely Outcomes

A **simulation** is an experiment that is designed to model the action in a given situation. For example, you used a random number generator to simulate rolling a number cube. Simulations often use models to act out an event that would be impractical to perform.

Example

1. A cereal company is placing one of eight different trading cards in its boxes of cereal. If each card is equally likely to appear in a box of cereal, describe a model that could be used to simulate the cards you would find in 15 boxes of cereal.

Choose a method that has 8 possible outcomes, such as tossing 3 coins. Let each outcome represent a different card.

For example, the outcome of all three coins landing heads up could simulate finding card 1.

Toss 3 coins to simulate the cards that might be in 15 boxes of cereal. Repeat 15 times.

Coin Toss Simulation			
Outcome	**Card**	**Outcome**	**Card**
HHH	1	TTT	5
HHT	2	TTH	6
HTH	3	THT	7
HTT	4	THH	8

Got It? Do this problem to find out.

a. A restaurant is giving away 1 of 5 different toys with its children's meals. If the toys are given out randomly, describe a model that could be used to simulate which toys would be given with 6 children's meals.

a. 

Example

2. Every student who volunteers at the concession stand during basketball games will receive a free school T-shirt. The T-shirts come in 3 different designs.

Design a simulation that could be used to model this situation. Use your simulation to find how many times a student must volunteer in order to get all 3 T-shirts.

Use a spinner divided into 3 equal sections. Assign each section one of the T-shirts. Spin the spinner until you land on each section.

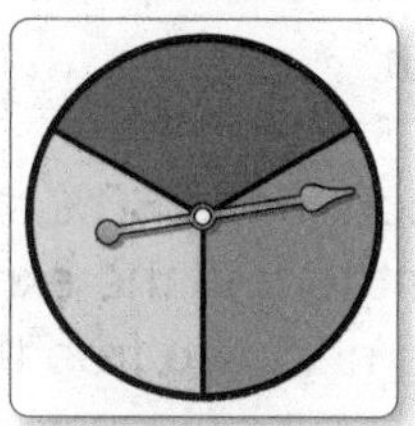

first spin

second spin

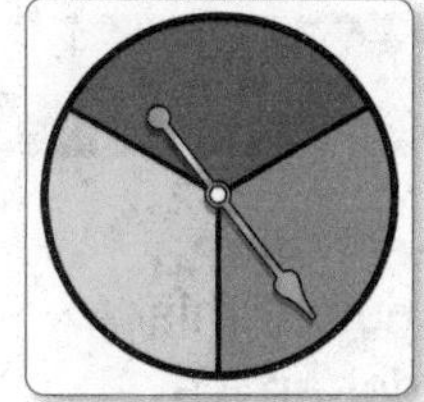

third spin

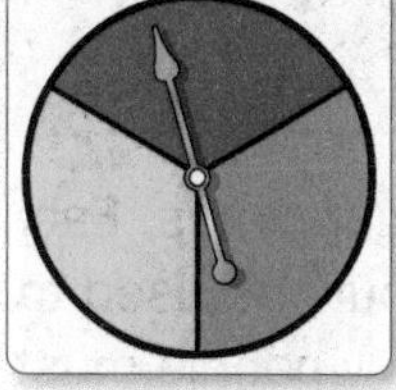

fourth spin

Based on this simulation, a student should volunteer 4 times in order to get all 3 T-shirts.

Got It? Do this problem to find out.

b. Mr. Chen must wear a dress shirt and a tie to work. Each day he picks one of his 6 ties at random. Design a simulation that could be used to model this situation. Use your simulation to find how many days Mr. Chen must work in order to wear all of his ties.

b. ______________

Model Unequally Likely Outcomes

Simulations can also be used to model events in which the outcomes are not equally likely.

STOP and Reflect

How could you simulate a 20% chance? Write your answer below.

Example

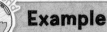

3. There is a 60% chance of rain for each of the next two days. Describe a method you could use to find the experimental probability of having rain on both of the next two days.

Place 3 red and 2 blue marbles in a bag. Let 60% or $\frac{3}{5}$ of them represent rain. Let 40% or $\frac{2}{5}$ of them represent no rain.

Randomly pick one marble to simulate the first day. Replace the marble and pick again to simulate the second day. Find the probability of rain on both days.

Show your work.

Got It? **Do this problem to find out.**

c. During the regular season, Jason made 80% of his free throws. Describe an experiment to find the experimental probability of Jason making his next two free throws.

c. ____________

Guided Practice

Check

1. An ice cream store offers waffle cones or sugar cones. Each is equally likely to be chosen. Describe a model that could be used to simulate this situation. Based on your simulation, how many people must order an ice cream cone in order to sell all possible combinations? (Examples 1 and 2)

2. An electronics store has determined that 45% of its customers buy a wide-screen television. Describe a model that you could use to find the experimental probability that the next three television-buying customers will buy a wide-screen television. (Example 3)

3. **Building on the Essential Question** Explain how using a simulation is related to experimental probability.

Rate Yourself!

How well do you understand simulations? Circle the image that applies.

Clear | Somewhat Clear | Not So Clear

For more help, go online to access a Personal Tutor.

Name ______________________ My Homework ______________________

Independent Practice

Go online for Step-by-Step Solutions

eHelp

1. The questions on a multiple-choice test each have 4 answer choices. Describe a model that you could use to simulate the outcome of guessing the correct answers to a 50-question test. (Example 1)

2. A game requires drawing balls numbered 0 through 9 for each of four digits to determine the winning number. Describe a model that could be used to simulate the selection of the number. (Example 1)

CCGPS **Model with Mathematics Describe a model you could use to simulate each event.**

3. A jar of cookies contains 18 different types of cookies. Each type is equally likely to be chosen. Based on your simulation, how many times must a cookie be chosen in order to get each type? (Example 2)

4. A cooler contains 5 bottles of lemonade, 4 bottles of water, and 3 bottles of juice. Each type is equally likely to be chosen. Based on your simulation, how many times must a drink be chosen in order to get each type? (Example 3)

5. Players at a carnival game win about 30% of the time. Based on your simulation, what is the experimental probability that the next four players will win. (Example 3)

6. **Model with Mathematics** Suppose a mouse is placed in the maze at the right. If each decision about direction is made at random, create a simulation to determine the probability that the mouse will find its way out before coming to a dead end or going out the In opening.

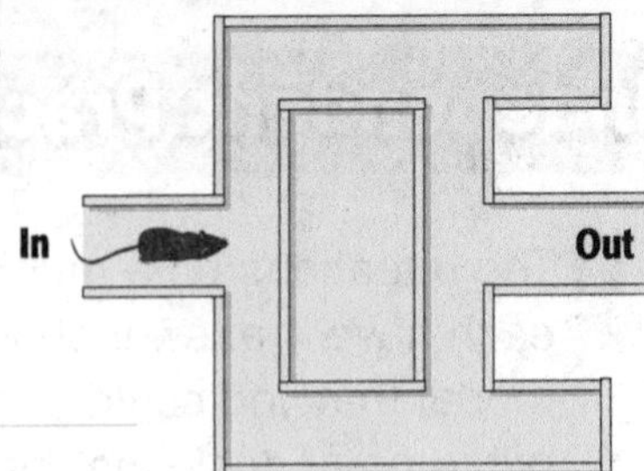

H.O.T. Problems Higher Order Thinking

7. **Model with Mathematics** Describe a situation that could be represented by a simulation. What objects could be used in your simulation?

8. **Persevere with Problems** A simulation uses cards numbered 0 through 9 to generate five 2-digit numbers. A card is selected for the tens digit and not replaced. Then a card for the ones digit is drawn and not replaced. The process is repeated until all the cards are used. If the simulation is performed 10 times, about how many times could you expect a 2-digit number to begin with a 5? Explain.

9. **Justify Conclusions** Determine whether the following statement is *sometimes*, *always*, or *never* true. Justify your answer.

A spinner can be used to model equally likely outcomes.

Georgia Test Practice

10. Donté has homework in language arts and science. He randomly picks up one of the 2 homework folders. Which simulation could be used to model the selection of one of the folders?

Ⓐ rolling a number cube
Ⓑ tossing a coin
Ⓒ spinning a spinner with 3 equal sections
Ⓓ spinning a spinner with 4 equal sections

Name ____________________ My Homework ____________________

Extra Practice

11. A store employee randomly gives scratch-off discount cards to the first 50 customers. The cards offer discounts of 10%, 20%, 25%, 30%, or 40%. There is an equal chance of receiving any of the 5 cards. Describe a model that could be used to simulate the discount received by 4 customers.

Homework Help

Use a spinner with 5 equal sections to represent the 5 different discounts. Spin 4 times to simulate 4 customers receiving cards.

12. On average, 75% of the days in Henderson county are sunny, with little or no cloud cover. Describe a model that you could use to find the experimental probability of sunny days each day for a week in Henderson county.

CCGPS **Model with Mathematics** **Describe a model you could use to simulate each event.**

13. Every student who participated in field day activities received a water bottle. The water bottles came in 2 different colors. Based on your simulation, how many students had to receive a water bottle in order to distribute water bottles in both colors?

14. A field hockey team wins 80% of its games. Based on your simulation, what is the experimental probability of the team winning its next 3 games?

15. There are 4 different magazines on Hannah's nightstand. Each evening, she randomly selects one magazine to read. Based on your simulation, how many days must she select a magazine in order to read all 4 magazines?

Georgia Test Practice

16. Marcus placed 8 blue tiles and 12 red tiles in a container. He plans to draw a tile, record its color, and replace it in the container before drawing another. Suppose Marcus does this 50 times. How many times should he expect to draw a red tile?

Ⓐ 8
Ⓑ 12
Ⓒ 20
Ⓓ 30

17. Claire tosses a coin and rolls a number cube 100 times. How many times should she expect to have the coin show heads and roll a 1 or a 2?

Ⓕ 17
Ⓖ 33
Ⓗ 50
Ⓘ 66

Common Core Review

Solve. MCC7.SP.5, MCC7.SP.7

18. A local video store has advertised that one out of every four customers will receive a free box of popcorn with their video rental. So far, 15 out of 75 customers have received popcorn. Compare the experimental and theoretical probabilities of receiving popcorn.

____

____

19. Dana received $25 for her birthday. She spent a total of $24.50 on a DVD. In how many different ways can she receive her change if she did not receive any pennies nor 50-cent pieces? Use an organized table to show the sample space. ______________

20. Describe the complement of rolling 3 on a number cube. Then find its probability. ______________

HOW do simulations help you understand the probability of events happening?

Content Standards
MCC7.SP.8, MCC7.SP.8c
Mathematical Practices
1, 3

Coupons A local shop randomly gives coupons to 3 out of every 8 customers. Use a spinner to determine the probability that a customer will receive a coupon two days in a row.

Investigation 1

Step 1 A spinner with eight equal sections can be used to simulate the situation. Label three of the sections with the letter C to represent the people that receive a coupon. Label five of the sections with the letter D to represent the people that do not receive a coupon.

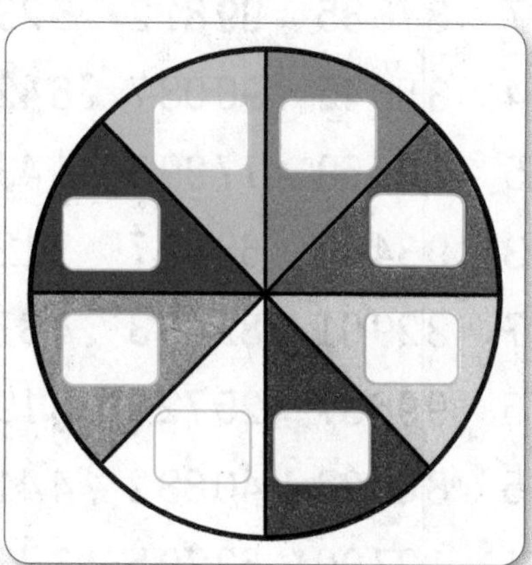

Step 2 Every two spins of the spinner represents one trial. Use a paperclip and the tip of your pencil to spin the spinner twice and record the results in the table. Perform a total of 15 trials.

Trial	Spin 1	Spin 2	Trial	Spin 1	Spin 2	Trial	Spin 1	Spin 2
1			6			11		
2			7			12		
3			8			13		
4			9			14		
5			10			15		

Based on your results, what is the experimental probability that a customer will receive a coupon two days in a row?

You can also use a random number table to simulate a compound event.

There is a 10% chance of rain for a city on Sunday and a 20% chance of rain on Monday. Use a random number table to find the probability that it will rain on both days.

Investigation 2

Step 1 A random number table has random digits in rows that can be grouped in different combinations as needed. These digits are arranged in groups of 5, but the grouping often does not matter. Since the situation we want to represent involves two days, continue drawing lines to separate the numbers into two-digit numbers.

48587	49460	89640	30270
19507	87835	99812	52353
11364	35645	90087	64254
87045	39769	77995	14316
69913	93449	68497	31270
81827	32901	82033	43714
33386	99637	25725	31900
41575	86692	40882	44123
77351	12790	62795	77307

Step 2 Using the digits 0 through 9, assign one digit in the tens place for rain on Sunday and assign two different digits in the ones place for rain on Monday. For example, the digit 1 in the tens place can represent rain occurring on Sunday and the digits 1 and 2 in the ones place can represent rain occurring on Monday.

Step 3 Find the numbers in the table that have a 1 in the tens place and either a 1 or 2 in the ones place. Those numbers are 11 and 12. Circle those numbers in the table.

Step 4 Find the probability using the numbers found in Step 3.

There were ☐ instances of the random numbers 11 and 12 occurring out of 90 random numbers.

So, the probability that it will rain on both days is $\frac{\square}{90}$ or $3\frac{1}{3}$%.

Collaborate

Work with a partner.

1. Luke plays goalie on his soccer team. He usually stops 2 out of every 6 penalty kicks. Label the sections of the spinner at the right. Then use the spinner to determine the experimental probability that Luke stops 2 penalty kicks in a row.

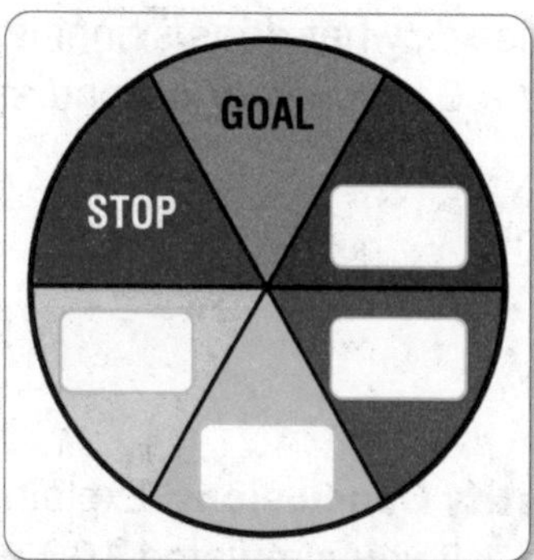

Trial	Spin 1	Spin 2	Trial	Spin 1	Spin 2	Trial	Spin 1	Spin 2
1			6			11		
2			7			12		
3			8			13		
4			9			14		
5			10			15		

The experimental probability is ______________.

2. Suppose 40% of customers who enter a pet store own a cat. What is the probability that it will take at least 4 customers before a cat owner enters the store? Use a random number table to simulate this compound event.

In the table below, separate the numbers into groups of 4. Then use the digits 0, 1, 2, and 3 to represent people who own cats. You are looking for groups of 4 numbers that do *not* contain a 0, 1, 2, or 3. Circle those groups.

1877 1	473 74	36 541	8 3454
9790 7	409 78	34 947	7 8482
2607 1	126 44	94 567	3 5467
0245 9	784 67	06 161	8 5897
(4448) 0	717 16	13 166	4 4096
7276 9	189 74	24 186	5 0866
3584 2	784 78	45 468	1 5441
5843 8	374 87	16 187	8 9892
8371 1	546 31	19 846	0 8483

In this case, the probability is $\frac{\square}{45}$ or 15.6%.

So, the experimental probability that it takes at least 4 customers before a cat owner enters the store is 15.6%.

Analyze

3. In Exercise 1, what does spinning a Stop on your first spin, and spinning a Goal on your second spin represent in this situation?

4. CCGPS **Justify Conclusions** Explain how your results might change for Exercise 1 if you simulated 100 penalty kicks.

5. In Exercise 2, why were the numbers from the random number table separated into groups of four?

6. In Exercise 2, you could have used any 4 numbers to represent cat owners. Complete the simulation four more times using the numbers in the table to represent the cat owners.

Numbers that Represent Cat Owners	Experimental Probability
4, 5, 6, 7	$\frac{\square}{45}$
0, 1, 8, 9	$\frac{\square}{45}$
3, 4, 5, 6	$\frac{\square}{45}$

Reflect

7. Inquiry HOW do simulations help you understand the probability of events happening?

Content Standards
MCC7.SP.8, MCC7.SP.8c
Mathematical Practices
1, 4

Case #1 Winning Serves

Edie has been practicing her volleyball serve every day after school. She hits a good serve an average of 3 out of 4 times.

What is the probability that Edie will hit two good serves in a row?

Understand ***What are the facts?***

You know that Edie hits a good serve an average of 3 out of 4 times. Act it out with a spinner.

Plan ***What is your strategy?***

Spin a spinner, numbered 1 to 4, two times. If the spinner lands on 1, 2, or 3, she hits a good serve. If the spinner lands on 4, she doesn't. Repeat the experiment 10 times.

Solve ***How can you apply the strategy?***

Here are some possible results. Circle the columns that show two good serves. The first two are done for you.

Trials	1	2	3	4	5	6	7	8	9	10
First Spin	4	1	4	3	1	2	2	1	3	2
Second Spin	2	3	3	2	1	4	1	4	3	3

The circled columns show that six out of 10 trials resulted in two good serves in a row. So, the probability is ______%.

Check ***Does the answer make sense?***

Repeat the experiment several times to see whether the results agree.

Analyze the Strategy

Reason Inductively Describe an advantage of using the *act it out* strategy?

Tools

Case #2 Tests

James uses a spinner with four equal sections to answer a five-question multiple-choice quiz. Each question has choices A, B, C, and D.

Is this a good way to answer the quiz questions?

1 Understand

- **Read the problem. What are you being asked to find?**

I need to find ____

____.

- **What information do you know?**

The spinner has 4 equal parts. There are 5 multiple-choice questions.

The answer choices are A, B, C, and D.

2 Plan

- **Choose a problem-solving strategy.**

I will use the ______________________________ strategy.

3 Solve

Use your problem-solving strategy to solve the problem.
Spin a spinner with four equal parts labeled A, B, C, and D five times. Repeat the experiment two times. Make a table of the results.

Question	1	2	3	4	5
Trial 1					
Trial 2					

With each spin there is an equal chance of landing on any section. Since the probability of an answer being A, B, C, or D is ____________ likely, any answer choice is possible.

Is using a spinner to answer a multiple-choice question a good idea? ________

4 Check

Use information from the problem to check your answer.
Repeat the experiment several times to see if the results agree.

Collaborate Work with a small group to solve the following cases. Show your work on a separate piece of paper.

Case #3 Chess

A chess tournament will be held and 32 students will participate. If a player loses one match, he or she will be eliminated.

How many total games will be played in the tournament?

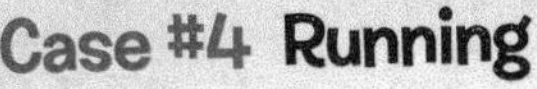

Case #4 Running

Six runners are entered in a race. Assume there are no ties.

In how many ways can first and second places be awarded?

Case #5 School

Suppose rolling an even number on a number cube corresponds to an answer of true and rolling an odd number corresponds to an answer of false.

Determine whether rolling the number cube is a good way to answer a five-question true-false quiz. Justify your answer.

Circle a strategy below to solve the problem.
- Make a table.
- Solve a simpler problem.
- Look for a pattern.

Case #6 Algebra

The figure shown at the right is known as Pascal's Triangle.

Make a conjecture for the numbers in the 6th row.

Mid-Chapter Check

Vocabulary Check

1. Define *probability*. Give an example of the probability of a simple event. (Lesson 1)

2. Fill in the blank in the sentence below with the correct term. (Lesson 4)

   A(n) ______________ is an experiment that is designed to act out a given situation.

Skills Check and Problem Solving

The table shows the number of science fiction, action, and comedy movies Jason has in his collection. Suppose one movie is selected at random. Find each probability. Write as a fraction in simplest form. (Lesson 1)

Type of Movie	
Science Fiction	10
Action	7
Comedy	3

3. P(science fiction) ________

4. P(*not* action) ________

5. A coin is tossed 20 times. It lands heads 4 times. Compare the experimental probability to its theoretical probability. If the probabilities are not close, explain a possible reason for the discrepancy. (Lesson 2)

6. A weather forecaster predicts a 30% chance of rain for each of the next three days. Describe a way to simulate the chance that it will rain the next three days. (Lesson 4)

7. **Georgia Test Practice** For breakfast, a customer can choose two different items from the following list: eggs, pancakes, waffles, oatmeal, bacon, or a muffin. How many different breakfast meals are possible? (Lesson 3)

   Ⓐ 8 Ⓑ 15 Ⓒ 20 Ⓓ 30

Fundamental Counting Principle

What You'll Learn

Scan the lesson. List two headings you would use to make an outline of the lesson.

- ______________________________
- ______________________________

Essential Question

HOW can you predict the outcome of future events?

Vocabulary

Fundamental Counting Principle

Common Core GPS

Content Standards
MCC7.SP.5, MCC7.SP.8, MCC7.SP.8a, MCC7.SP.8b

Mathematical Practices
1, 3, 4

Real-World Link

Classes Tyler wants to take a class at the community center. The table shows the class options he is considering. All of the classes are offered only on Monday and Tuesday.

Class	Day
Drawing Martial Arts Dance	Monday Tuesday

1. According to the table, how many classes is he considering? ________

2. How many days are the classes offered?

   ____

3. Complete the tree diagram to find the number of different class and day outcomes.

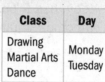

Class	Day	Sample Space
Drawing	Monday	Drawing, Monday
	Tuesday	Drawing, Tuesday
Martial Arts	________	Martial Arts, Monday
	________	________
________	________	________
	________	________

4. Find the product of the two numbers you found in Exercises 1 and 2. How does the number of outcomes compare to the product?

   ____

Key Concept Fundamental Counting Principle

If event M has m possible outcomes and event N has n possible outcomes, then event M followed by event N has $m \times n$ possible outcomes.

Work Zone

You can use multiplication instead of making a tree diagram to find the number of possible outcomes in a sample space. This is called the **Fundamental Counting Principle**.

Example

1. Find the total number of outcomes when a coin is tossed and a number cube is rolled.

A coin has 2 possible outcomes. A number cube has 6 possible outcomes. Multiply the possible outcomes of each event.

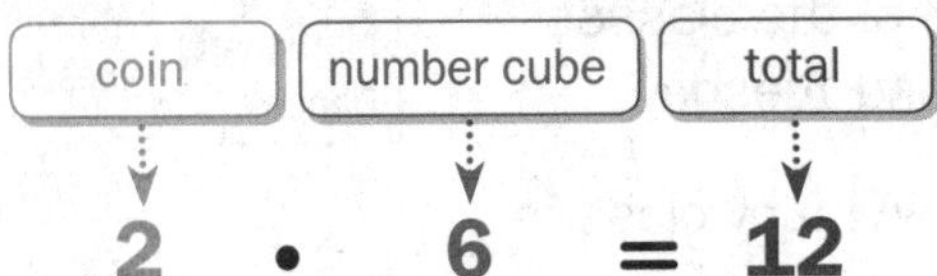

Fundamental Counting Principle

There are 12 different outcomes.

Check Draw a tree diagram to show the sample space.

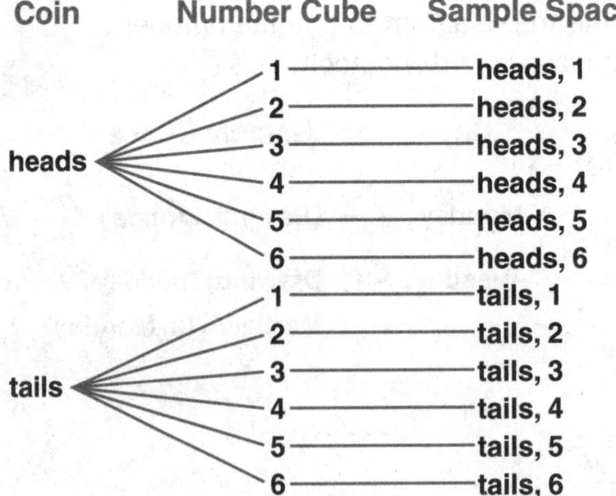

The tree diagram also shows that there are 12 outcomes. ✓

Got It? **Do this problem to find out.**

a. Find the total number of outcomes when choosing from bike helmets that come in three colors and two styles.

a. ________

Find Probability

You can use the Fundamental Counting Principle to help find the probability of events.

Examples

2. Find the total number of outcomes from rolling a number cube with sides labeled 1–6 and choosing a letter from the word NUMBERS. Then find the probability of rolling a 6 and choosing an M.

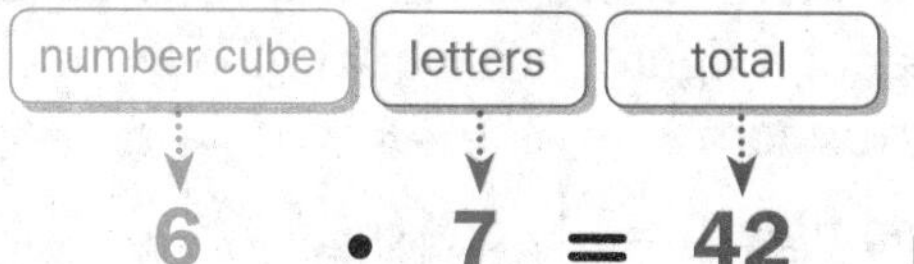

$6 \cdot 7 = 42$ Fundamental Counting Principle

There are 42 different outcomes.

There is only one favorable outcome. So, the probability of rolling a 6 and choosing an M is $\frac{1}{42}$ or about 2%.

3. Find the number of different jeans available at The Jeans Shop. Then find the probability of randomly selecting a size 32 × 34 slim fit. Is it likely or unlikely that the jeans would be chosen?

The Jeans Shop

Waist Size	Length (in.)	Style
30	30	slim fit
32	32	bootcut
34	34	loose fit
36		
38		

Jean Size
In men's jeans, the size is labeled waist x length. So, a 32 x 34 is a 32-inch waist with a 34-inch length.

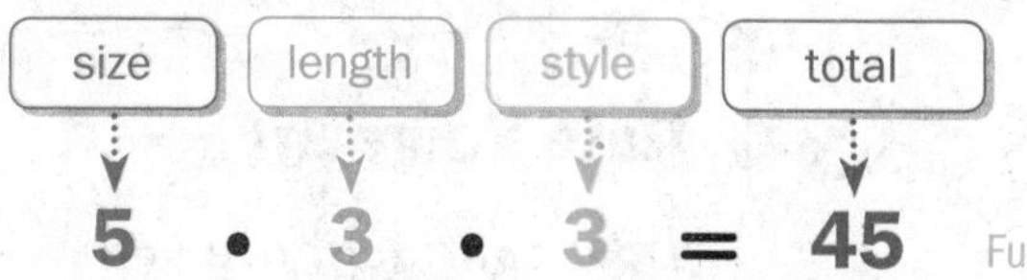

$5 \cdot 3 \cdot 3 = 45$ Fundamental Counting Principle

There are 45 different types of jeans to choose. Out of the 45 possible outcomes, only one is favorable. So, the probability of randomly selecting a 32 × 34 slim fit is $\frac{1}{45}$ or about 2%.

It is very unlikely that the size would be chosen at random.

Got It? **Do this problem to find out.**

b. Two number cubes are rolled. What is the probability that the sum of the numbers on the cubes is 12? How likely is it that the sum would be 12?

b. ____________

Example

4. A box of toy cars contains blue, orange, yellow, red, and black cars. A separate box contains a male and a female action figure. What is the probability of randomly choosing an orange car and a female action figure? Is it likely or unlikely that this combination is chosen?

First, find the number of possible outcomes.

There are 5 choices for the car and 2 choices for the action figure.

$5 \cdot 2 = 10$ Fundamental Counting Principal

There are 10 possible outcomes. There is one way to choose an orange car and a female action figure. It is very unlikely that this combination is chosen at random.

$P(\text{orange car, female action figure}) = \frac{1}{10}$ or 10%.

Guided Practice

1. Use the Fundamental Counting Principle to find the number of outcomes from tossing a quarter, a dime, and a nickel. (Example 1)

2. How many outcomes are possible when rolling a number cube and picking a cube from 4 different colored cubes? (Example 1)

3. Find the number of different outfits that can be made from 3 sweaters, 4 blouses, and 6 skirts. Then find the probability of randomly selecting a particular sweater-blouse-skirt outfit. Is the probability of this event likely or unlikely? (Examples 2–4)

4. **Building on the Essential Question** Compare and contrast tree diagrams and the Fundamental Counting Principle.

Rate Yourself!

How confident are you about using the Fundamental Counting Principle? Shade the ring on the target.

For more help, go online to access a Personal Tutor.

Name ______________________ My Homework ______________________

Independent Practice

Go online for Step-by-Step Solutions

Use the Fundamental Counting Principle to find the total number of outcomes for each situation. (Example 1)

1. choosing a bagel with one type of cream cheese from the list shown in the table

______

Bagels	Cream Cheese
Plain Blueberry Cinnamon raisin Garlic	Plain Chive Sun-dried tomato

2. choosing a sandwich and a side from the list shown in the table

______

Sandwiches	Sides
Ham Turkey Roast Beef Tuna Salad Vegetarian	Pasta Salad Fruit Cup Potato Chips Side Salad

3. picking a month of the year and a day of the week ______

4. choosing from a comedy, horror, or action movie each shown in four different theaters

______

5. Find the number of possible routes from Eastland to Johnstown that pass through Harping. Then find the probability that State and Fairview will be used if a route is selected at random. State the probability as a fraction and percent. (Examples 2–3)

______

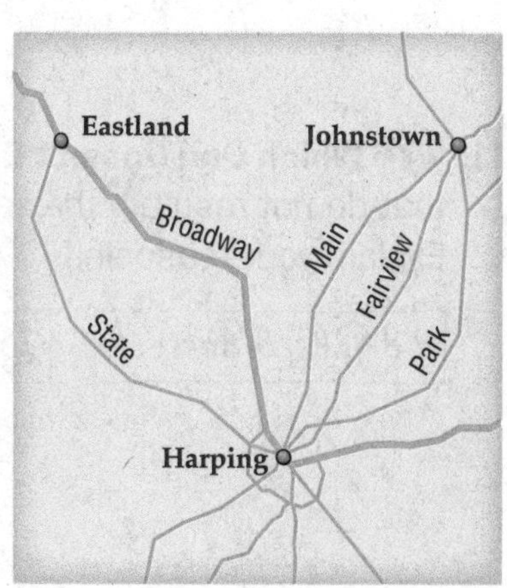

6. Find the number of possible choices for a 2-digit password that is greater than 19. Then find the number of possible choices for a 4-digit Personal Identification Number (PIN) if the digits cannot be repeated. (Example 1)

______

7. An electronics company makes educational apps for 5 subjects, including math. The app has 10 versions, with a different avatar in each version. One version has an avatar that looks similar to a lion. The company is randomly giving free apps to its customers. Find the probability of randomly receiving a math app with a lion avatar. How likely is the probability of receiving this app at random? (Examples 2–4)

______

8. A sandwich shop offers 4 different meats and 2 different cheeses. Suppose the sandwich shop offers 24 different meat-cheese sandwiches. How many different breads does the sandwich shop use?

9. CCGPS **Justify Conclusions** A store offers 32 different T-shirt designs and 11 choices of color. Is the store's advertisement true? Explain.

H.O.T. Problems Higher Order Thinking

10. CCGPS **Persevere with Problems** Determine the number of possible outcomes when tossing one coin, two coins, and three coins. Then determine the number of possible outcomes for tossing *n* coins. Describe the strategy you used.

11. CCGPS **Which One Doesn't Belong?** Identify the choices for events *M* and *N* that do not result in the same number of outcomes as the other two. Explain your reasoning.

9 drinks, 8 desserts	18 shirts, 4 pants	10 groups, 8 activities

Georgia Test Practice

12. A bakery offers white, chocolate, or yellow cakes with white or chocolate icing. There are also 24 designs that can be applied to a cake. If all orders are equally likely, what is the probability that a customer will order a white cake with white icing in a specific design?

Ⓐ $\frac{1}{30}$

Ⓑ $\frac{1}{64}$

Ⓒ $\frac{1}{120}$

Ⓓ $\frac{1}{144}$

Name ________________________ My Homework ________________

Extra Practice

Use the Fundamental Counting Principle to find the total number of outcomes for each situation.

13. rolling a number cube and spinning a spinner with eight equal sections 48

$6 \cdot 8 = 48$

14. tossing a coin and selecting one letter from the word MATH ______

15. selecting one sweatshirt from a choice of five sweatshirts and one pair of pants from a choice of four pairs of pants ______

16. selecting one entrée from a choice of nine entrées and one dessert from a choice of three desserts ______

17. rolling a number cube and tossing two coins ______

18. choosing tea in regular, raspberry, lemon, or peach; sweetened or unsweetened; and in a glass or bottle ______

19. A cafeteria offers oranges, apples, or bananas as its fruit option. It offers peas, green beans, or carrots as the vegetable option. Find the number of fruit and vegetable options. If the fruit and the vegetable are chosen at random, what is the probability of getting an orange and carrots? Is it likely or unlikely that a customer would get an orange and carrots?

____

20. CCGPS **Justify Conclusions** The table shows cell phone options offered by a wireless phone company. If a phone with one payment plan and one accessory is given away at random, predict the probability that it will be Brand B and have a headset. Explain your reasoning.

Phone Brands	Payment Plans	Accessories
Brand A	Individual	Leather case
Brand B	Family	Car mount
Brand C	Business	Headset
	Government	Travel charger

____

____

____

____

Georgia Test Practice

21. A number cube is rolled and a marble is drawn from a bag containing 3 red and 3 yellow marbles. What is the probability of the number cube landing on 1 and the marble being yellow?

Ⓐ $\frac{1}{8}$

Ⓑ $\frac{1}{10}$

Ⓒ $\frac{1}{12}$

Ⓓ $\frac{1}{18}$

22. A movie theater offers a combo special with 3 different drink sizes and 3 different popcorn sizes. From how many different combos can a customer choose?

Ⓕ 6

Ⓖ 9

Ⓗ 15

Ⓘ 27

23. Short Response Hat Shack sells 9 different styles of hats in several different colors for 2 different sports teams. If the company makes 108 kinds of hats, how many different colors do they make? ________

Hat Shack		
Styles	**Colors**	**Teams**
9	?	2

Common Core Review

Find each probability. MCC7.SP.8

24. A coin is tossed and a spinner with 4 equal sections labeled W–Z is spun. Find *P*(heads and Z).

____

25. A pizza shop offers a single item pizza with choice of pepperoni, green peppers, pineapple, sausage, or mushroom toppings. The pizza can be thick crust or thin crust. Find *P*(thick crust).

____

Describe a model that could be used to simulate each situation. MCC7.SP.8c

26. There is a fifty percent chance of rain on Monday.

____

27. A restaurant randomly gives away 1 of 6 toys. Determine the number of times a child needs to visit the restaurant to receive all 6 toys.

____

____

Lesson 6

Permutations

What You'll Learn

Scan the lesson. List two real-world scenarios that would involve using permutations.

- ______________________________
- ______________________________

 **Essential Question**

HOW can you predict the outcome of future events?

Vocabulary

permutation

Common Core GPS

Content Standards
MCC7.SP.8, MCC7.SP.8a

Mathematical Practices
1, 3, 4

Real-World Link

Scheduling Colt is planning his Saturday. He wants to mow the grass, go swimming, and do his homework. How many different ways are there to arrange what he wants to do?

Fill in the blanks of the organized list below to find all of the possible arrangements of the activities.

1: Mowing	2: Swimming	3: Homework
1: Mowing	2: Homework	3: ______
1: Swimming	2: Mowing	3: Homework
1: Swimming	2: Homework	3: ______
1: Homework	2: ______	3: ______
1: ______	2: ______	3: ______

1. How many choices does Colt have for his first activity?

____

2. Once the first activity is selected, how many choices does Colt have for the second activity?

____

3. Once the first and second activities are selected, how many choices does Colt have for the third activity?

____

Work Zone

Find a Permutation

A **permutation** is an arrangement, or listing, of objects in which order is important.

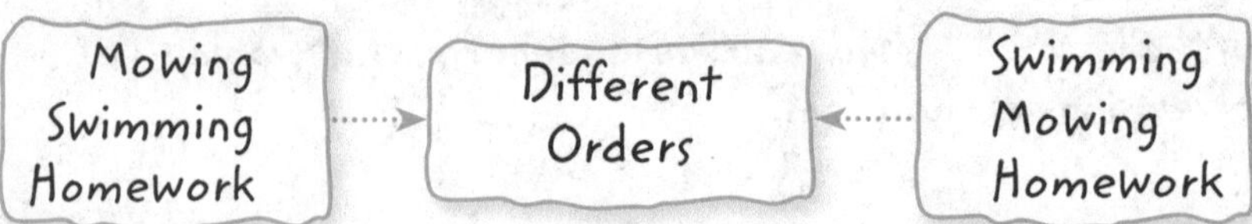

You can use the Fundamental Counting Principle to find the number of permutations.

Examples

1. Julia is scheduling her first three classes. Her choices are math, science, and language arts. Use the Fundamental Counting Principle to find the number of different ways Julia can schedule her first three classes.

There are **3** choices for the first class.

There are **2** choices that remain for the second class.

There is **1** choice that remains for the third class.

$$3 \cdot 2 \cdot 1 = 6$$ ← the number of permutations of 3 classes

There are 6 possible arrangements, or permutations, of the 3 classes.

2. An ice cream shop has 31 flavors. Carlos wants to buy a three-scoop cone with three different flavors. How many cones could he buy if the order of the flavors is important?

There are 31 choices for the first scoop, 30 choices for the second scoop, and 29 choices for the third scoop.

Use the Fundamental Counting Principle.

$31 \cdot 30 \cdot 29 = 26{,}970$

Carlos could buy 26,970 different cones.

Show your work.

Got It? Do these problems to find out.

a. In how many ways can the starting six players of a volleyball team stand in a row for a picture?

b. In a race with 7 runners, in how many ways can the runners end up in first, second, and third place?

a. ________

b. ________

The symbol $P(31, 3)$ represents the number of permutations of 31 things taken 3 at a time.

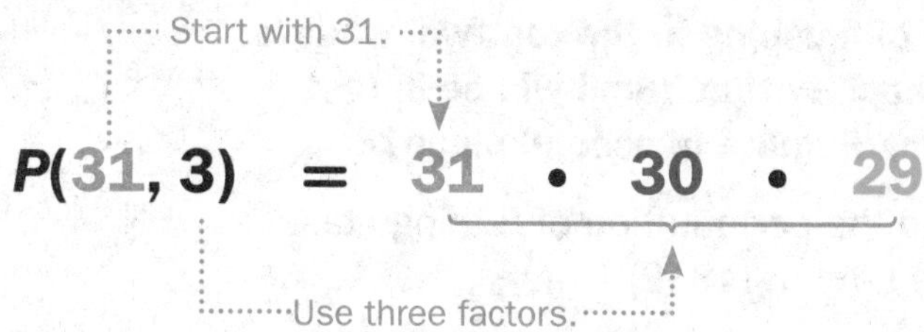

Example

3. Find $P(8, 3)$.

$P(8, 3) = 8 \cdot 7 \cdot 6$ or 336 8 things taken 3 at a time

Got It? Do these problems to find out.

c. $P(12, 2)$ **d.** $P(4, 4)$ **e.** $P(10, 5)$

c. ________

d. ________

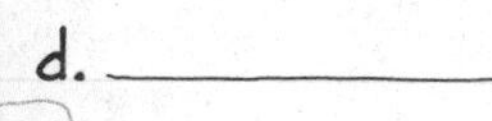

e. ________

Find Probabililty

Permutations can be used when finding probabilities of real-world situations.

Examples

4. Ashley's MP3 player has a setting that allows the songs to play in a random order. She has a playlist that contains 10 songs. What is the probability that the MP3 player will randomly play the first three songs in order?

First find the permutation of ten things taken three at a time or $P(10, 3)$.

10 songs — Choose 3

$$P(10, 3) = 10 \cdot 9 \cdot 8$$
$$= 720$$

10 choices for the 1st song
9 choices for the 2nd song
8 choices for the 3rd song

So, there are 720 different ways to play the first 3 songs. Since you want the first three songs in order, there is only 1 out of the 720 ways to do this.

So, the probability that the first 3 songs will play in order is $\frac{1}{720}$.

Notation

In Example 4, the notation P(10, 3) indicates a permutation while the notation P(playing the first three songs in order) indicates probability.

5. **A swimming event features 8 swimmers. If each swimmer has an equally likely chance of finishing in the top two, what is the probability that Yumii will be in first place and Paquita in second place?**

Swimmers	
Octavia	Eden
Natasha	Paquita
Calista	Samantha
Yumii	Lorena

First find the permutation of 8 things taken two at a time or $P(8, 2)$.

$$P(8, 2) = 8 \cdot 7$$
$$= 56$$

There are 56 possible arrangements, or permutations, of the two places. Since there is only one way of having Yumii come in first and Paquita second, the probability of this event is $\frac{1}{56}$.

Reasonable Answers

A possible probability of $\frac{1}{56}$ indicates that it is very unlikely that Yumii will finish first and Paquita will finish second.

Got It? **Do this problem to find out.**

f. Two different letters are randomly selected from the letters in the word *math*. What is the probability that the first letter selected is *m* and the second letter is *h*?

f. ___________

Guided Practice

1. In how many ways can a president, vice president, and secretary be randomly selected from a class of 25 students? (Examples 1 and 2) ___________

2. Find the value of $P(5, 3)$. (Example 3) ___________

3. Adrianne, Julián, and two of their friends will sit in a row at a baseball game. If each friend is equally likely to sit in any seat, what is the probability that Adrianne will sit in the first seat and Julián will sit in the second seat? (Examples 4 and 5) ___________

4. **Building on the Essential Question** HOW can you find the number of permutations of a set of objects?

Rate Yourself!

☐ I understand how to find permutations.

Great! You're ready to move on!

☐ I still have questions about finding permutations.

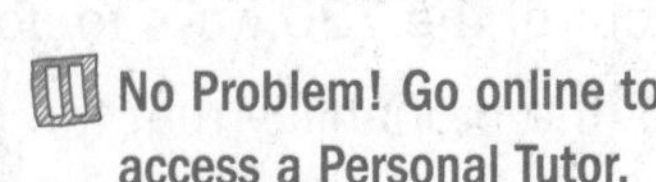

Name ______ My Homework ______

Independent Practice

Go online for Step-by-Step Solutions 

1. In the Battle of the Bands contest, in how many ways can the four participating bands perform? (Examples 1 and 2)

2. A garage door code has 5 digits. If no digit is repeated, how many codes are possible?

Find each value. Use a calculator if needed. (Example 3)

3. $P(7, 4)$ ______

4. $P(12, 5)$ ______

5. $P(8, 8)$ ______

6. You have five seasons of your favorite TV show on DVD. If you randomly select two of them from a shelf, what is the probability that you will select season one first and season two second? (Examples 4 and 5)

7. CCGPS **Model with Mathematics** The graphic novel frame below explains how the survey has students rank their favorite kinds of music. In how many ways can the survey be answered? ______

Watch
Replay it online!
Our survey asked teens to place a 1, 2, 3, 4, or 5 next to each type of music.
That's going to give us a bunch of answer arrangements.
Our survey lists country, classical, hip-hop, oldies, and alternative as music options.

8. A certain number of friends are waiting in line to board a new roller coaster. They can board the ride in 5,040 different ways. How many friends are in line?

9 The Coughlin family discovered they can stand in a row for their family portrait in 720 different ways. How many members are in the Coughlin family?

10. Howland Middle School assigns a four-digit identification number to each student. The number is made from the digits 1, 2, 3, and 4, and no digit is repeated. If assigned randomly, what is the probability that an ID number will end with a 3?

H.O.T. Problems Higher Order Thinking

11. CCGPS **Model with Mathematics** Describe a real-world situation that has 6 permutations.

12. CCGPS **Persevere with Problems** There are 1,320 ways for three students to win first, second, and third place during a debate match. How many students are there on the debate team? Explain your reasoning.

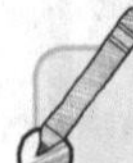

Georgia Test Practice

13. A baseball coach is deciding on the batting order for his nine starting players with the pitcher batting last. How many batting orders are possible?

Ⓐ 8 Ⓒ 40,320

Ⓑ 72 Ⓓ 362,880

Name ______ My Homework ______

Extra Practice

14. How many permutations are possible of the letters in the word FRIEND? 720

$6 \cdot 5 \cdot 4 \cdot 3 \cdot 2 \cdot 1 = 720$

15. How many different 3-digit numbers can be formed using the digits 9, 3, 4, 7, and 6? Assume no number can be used more than once. ______

Find each value. Use a calculator if needed.

16. $P(9, 2)$ ______

17. $P(5, 5)$ ______

18. $P(7, 7)$ ______

19. The members of the Evergreen Junior High Quiz Bowl team are listed in the table. If a captain and an assistant captain are chosen at random, what is the probability that Walter is selected as captain and Mi-Ling as co-captain? ______

Evergreen Junior High Quiz Bowl Team	
Jamil	Luanda
Savannah	Mi-Ling
Tucker	Booker
Ferdinand	Nina
Walter	Meghan

20. Alex, Aiden, Dexter, and Dion are playing a video game. If they each have an equally likely chance of getting the highest score, what is the probability that Dion will get the highest score and Alex the second highest? ______

21. A child has wooden blocks with the letters shown below. Find the probability that the child randomly arranges the letters in the order TIGER. ______

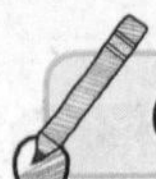

Georgia Test Practice

22. **Short Response** The five finalists in a random drawing are shown. Find the probability that Sean is awarded first prize and Teresa is awarded second prize.

Finalists
Cesar
Teresa
Sean
Nikita
Alfonso

23. The schools listed below are finalists in a science competition. In how many ways can they finish in first, second, and third place?

Finalists
Chester Middle School
Glenwood Middle School
Lincoln Middle School
River Valley Middle School
South Middle School

Ⓐ 15
Ⓑ 20
Ⓒ 60
Ⓓ 120

Common Core Review

A card is pulled from a stack of 30 cards labeled 1–30. Find each probability. Write as a fraction in simplest form. MCC7.SP.5

24. *P*(greater than 5) _____

25. *P*(*not* 1) _____

26. *P*(an even number) _____

27. A cross country athlete has a white, a red, and a gray sweatshirt. She has black and gray running pants. Use a tree diagram to show the possible combinations of training outfits. MCC7.SP.8b

Inquiry Lab

Independent and Dependent Events

HOW can one event impact a second event in a probability experiment?

Content Standards
MCC7.SP.8, MCC7.SP.8b, MCC7.SP.8c

Mathematical Practices
1, 3

Fun Jeanie wants to go to the movies and Kate wants to go skating. They decide by doing a simulation. They place two red counters in a bag to represent going to the movies and two white counters to represent going skating. If they draw or remove two red counters, they will go to the movies. If they draw two white counters they will go skating. If they draw a red and a white counter, they will stay home.

You can simulate this activity using counters.

Investigation

Step 1 Place two red counters and two white counters in a paper bag.

Step 2 Without looking, draw a counter from the bag and record its color in the table below. Place the counter back in the bag.

Step 3 Without looking, draw a second counter and record its color in the table. The two colors are one trial. Place the counter back in the bag.

Step 4 Repeat until you have 18 trials.

Trial	1st Color	2nd Color	Trial	1st Color	2nd Color	Trial	1st Color	2nd Color
1			7			13		
2			8			14		
3			9			15		
4			10			16		
5			11			17		
6			12			18		

What is the experimental probability that the girls will go to the movies?

___

Collaborate

Work with a partner.

1. Complete the same experiment from the Investigation. Except do not replace the counter after the first draw for each trial. Record your results.

Trial	1st Color	2nd Color	Trial	1st Color	2nd Color	Trial	1st Color	2nd Color
1			7			13		
2			8			14		
3			9			15		
4			10			16		
5			11			17		
6			12			18		

What is the experimental probability that the girls will go to the movies?

Analyze

The tree diagrams below represent the possible outcomes for the Investigation and for Exercise 1. Use the diagrams to answer Exercises 2-3.

Investigation

1st Draw	2nd Draw	Outcome
R	R	RR
	R	RR
	W	RW
	W	RW
W	R	WR
	R	WR
	W	WW
	W	WW

Exercise 1

1st Draw	2nd Draw	Outcome
R	R	RR
	W	RW
	W	RW
W	R	WR
	R	WR
	W	WW

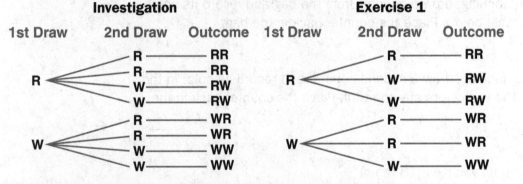

2. What is the theoretical probability of drawing two reds in the Investigation? In Exercise 1? ____________

3. **CCGPS Reason Inductively** Is there a better chance that the girls will go to the movies if the counters are replaced after the first draw? Explain.

Reflect

4. **Inquiry** HOW can one event impact a second event in a probability experiment? ____________

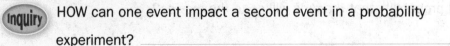

Independent and Dependent Events

What You'll Learn

Scan the lesson. Write the definitions of dependent events and independent events.

- independent events: ______________________________

- dependent events: ______________________________

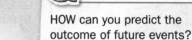

Essential Question

HOW can you predict the outcome of future events?

Vocabulary

independent events
dependent events

Common Core GPS

Content Standards
MCC7.SP.8, MCC7.SP.8a, MCC7.SP.8b

Mathematical Practices
1, 3, 4

Vocabulary Start-Up

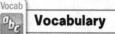

When one event does not affect the outcome of the other event, the events are **independent events**. For example, if you toss a coin twice, the first toss has no affect on the second toss. Complete the graphic organizer below.

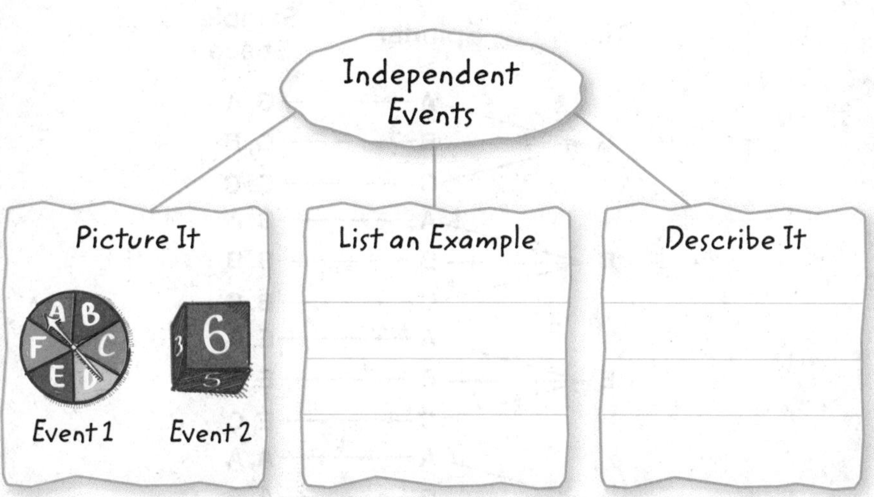

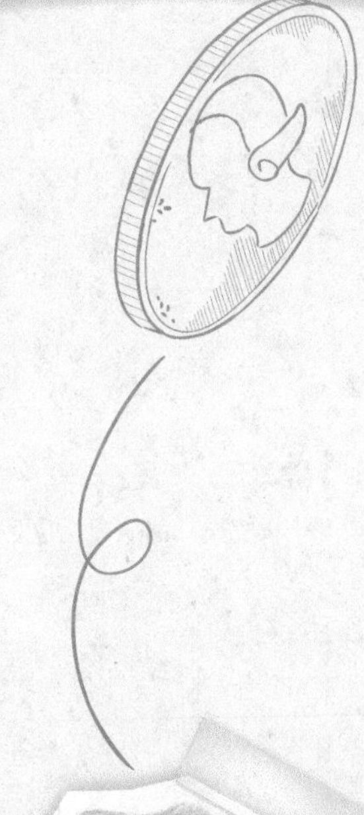

Real-World Link

Independent is a common word in the English language. Use a dictionary to look up its definition. Explain how the dictionary definition can help you remember the mathematical definition of *independent*. ______________________________

Work Zone

Key Concept Probability of Independent Events

Words The probability of two independent events can be found by multiplying the probability of the first event by the probability of the second event.

Symbols $P(A \text{ and } B) = P(A) \cdot P(B)$

You can use organized lists, tables, tree diagrams, or multiplication to find the probability of compound events.

Examples

1. One letter tile is selected and the spinner is spun. What is the probability that both will be a vowel?

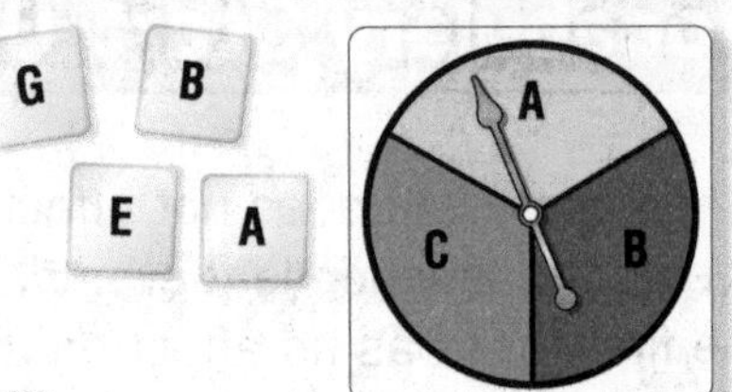

Method 1 **Make a Tree Diagram**

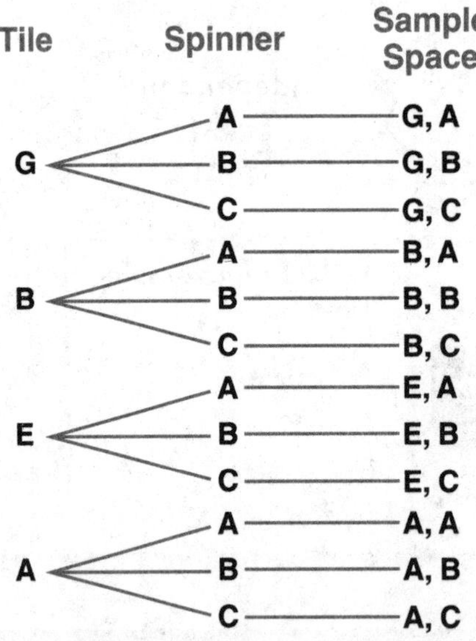

There are 12 outcomes. Two outcomes contain only vowels. The probability that both will be a vowel is $\frac{2}{12}$ or $\frac{1}{6}$.

Method 2 **Use Multiplication**

$P(\text{selecting a vowel}) = \frac{2}{4}$ or $\frac{1}{2}$. $P(\text{spinning a vowel}) = \frac{1}{3}$.

$P(\text{both vowels}) = \frac{1}{2} \cdot \frac{1}{3}$ or $\frac{1}{6}$. Multiply the probabilities.

So, using either method the probability is $\frac{1}{6}$.

2. The spinner and number cube shown are used in a game. What is the probability of a player *not* spinning blue and then rolling a 3 or 4?

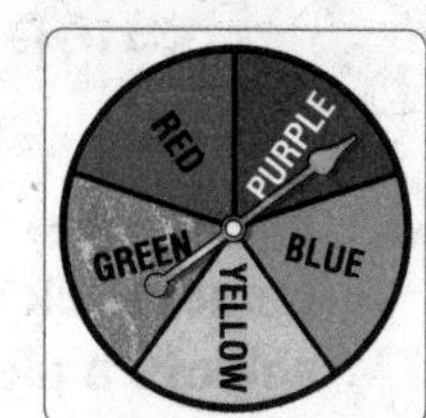

You are asked to find the probability of the spinner *not* landing on blue and rolling a 3 or 4 on a number cube. The events are independent because spinning the spinner does not affect the outcome of rolling a number cube.

First, find the probability of each event.

$P(\textit{not}\text{ blue}) = \frac{4}{5}$ ← number of ways not to spin blue / number of possible outcomes

$P(3 \text{ or } 4) = \frac{2}{6} \text{ or } \frac{1}{3}$ ← number of ways to roll 3 or 4 / number of possible outcomes

Then, find the probability of both events occurring.

$P(\textit{not}\text{ blue and 3 or 4}) = \frac{4}{5} \cdot \frac{1}{3}$ — $P(A \text{ and } B) = P(A) \cdot P(B)$

$= \frac{4}{15}$ — Multiply.

The probability is $\frac{4}{15}$.

Check Make an organized list, table, or a tree diagram to show the sample space.

Got It? **Do this problem to find out.**

a. A game requires players to roll two number cubes to move the game pieces. The faces of the cubes are labeled 1 through 6. What is the probability of rolling a 2 or 4 on the first number cube and then rolling a 5 on the second?

a. ______

Probability of Dependent Events

Key Concept

Words If two events *A* and *B* are dependent, then the probability of both events occurring is the product of the probability of *A* and the probability of *B* after *A* occurs.

Symbols $P(A \text{ and } B) = P(A) \cdot P(B \text{ following } A)$

If the outcome of one event affects the outcome of another event, the events are called **dependent events**. For example, you have a bag with blue and green marbles. You pick one marble, do not replace it, and pick another one.

Example

3. There are 4 oranges, 7 bananas, and 5 apples in a fruit basket. Ignacio selects a piece of fruit at random and then Terrance selects a piece of fruit at random. Find the probability that two apples are chosen.

Since the first piece of fruit is not replaced, the first event affects the second event. These are dependent events.

$P(\text{first piece is an apple}) = \frac{5}{16}$ ← number of apples / total pieces of fruit

$P(\text{second piece is an apple}) = \frac{4}{15}$ ← number of apples left / total pieces of fruit left

$P(\text{two apples}) = \frac{\overset{1}{\cancel{5}}}{\underset{4}{\cancel{16}}} \cdot \frac{\overset{1}{\cancel{4}}}{\underset{3}{\cancel{15}}} \text{ or } \frac{1}{12}.$

The probability that two apples are chosen is $\frac{1}{12}$.

Show your work.

b. ______

c. ______

Got It? Do these problems to find out.

Refer to the situation above. Find each probability.

b. P(two bananas)

c. P(orange then apple)

Guided Practice

Check

A penny is tossed and a number cube is rolled. Find each probability. (Examples 1-2)

1. P(tails and 3) ______

2. P(heads and odd) ______

3. Cards labeled 5, 6, 7, 8, and 9 are in a stack. A card is drawn and not replaced. Then, a second card is drawn at random. Find the probability of drawing two even numbers.

(Example 3) ______

4. **Building on the Essential Question** Explain the difference between independent events and dependent events.

______

Rate Yourself!

Are you ready to move on? Shade the section that applies.

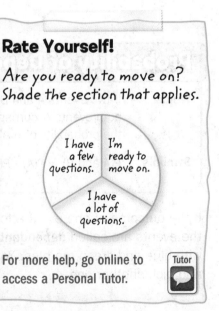

I have a few questions.
I'm ready to move on.
I have a lot of questions.

For more help, go online to access a Personal Tutor.

Tutor

Name ______________________ My Homework ______________________

Independent Practice

Go online for Step-by-Step Solutions

A number cube is rolled and a marble is selected at random from the bag at the right. Find each probability. Show your work. (Example 1)

Show your work.

1. P(1 and red) ______

2. P(3 and purple) ______

3. P(even and yellow) ______

4. P(odd and *not* green) ______

5. A carnival game wheel has 12 equal sections. One of the sections contains a star. To win a prize, players must land on the section with the star on two consecutive spins. What is the probability of a player winning? (Example 2) ______

6. A standard set of dominoes contains 28 tiles, with each tile having two sides of dots from 0 to 6. Of these tiles, 7 have the same number of dots on each side. If four players each randomly choose a tile, without replacement, what is the probability that each chooses a tile with the same number of dots on each side? (Example 3) ______

Mrs. Ameldo's class has 5 students with blue eyes, 7 with brown eyes, 4 with hazel eyes, and 4 with green eyes. Two students are selected at random. Find each probability. (Example 3)

7. P(green then brown) ______

8. P(two blue) ______

9. P(hazel then blue) ______

10. P(brown then blue) ______

11. **Reason Inductively** You and a friend plan to see 2 movies over the weekend. You can choose from 6 comedy, 2 drama, 4 romance, 1 science fiction, or 3 action movies. You write the movie titles on pieces of paper, place them in a bag, and each randomly select a movie. What is the probability that neither of you selects a comedy? Is this a dependent or independent event? Explain.

H.O.T. Problems Higher Order Thinking

12. **Model with Mathematics** There are 9 marbles representing 3 different colors. Write a problem where 2 marbles are selected at random without replacement and the probability is $\frac{1}{6}$.

13. **Find the Error** A spinner with equal sections numbered from 1 to 5 is spun twice. Raul is finding the probability that both spins will result in an even number. Find his mistake and correct it.

14. **Justify Conclusions** Determine whether the following statement is *true* or *false*. If false, provide a counterexample.
If two events are independent, then the probability of both events is less than 1.

Georgia Test Practice

15. A jar contains 6 aqua beads and 4 black beads. If two beads are selected at random, with replacement, what is the probability that both beads will be aqua?

Ⓐ $\frac{1}{3}$

Ⓑ $\frac{9}{25}$

Ⓒ $\frac{3}{5}$

Ⓓ $\frac{9}{10}$

Extra Practice

A number cube is rolled and a letter is selected from the word AMERICA. Find each probability. Show your work.

16. *P*(less than 4 and vowel) $\frac{1}{7}$

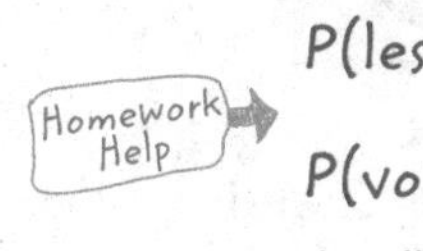

$P(\text{less than } 4) = \frac{1}{2}$

$P(\text{vowel}) = \frac{4}{7}$

$\frac{1}{2} \cdot \frac{4}{7} = \frac{4}{14} \text{ or } \frac{1}{7}$

17. *P*(greater than 1 and a consonant) ________

18. A number cube is rolled and a coin is tossed. What is the probability of the cube landing on 5 or 6 and the coin landing on heads?

____

19. A laundry basket contains 18 blue socks and 24 black socks. What is the probability of randomly picking, without replacement, 2 black socks from the basket?

____

20. 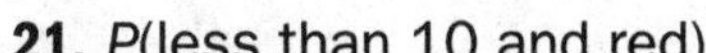 **Persevere with Problems** Corbin is playing a board game that requires rolling two number cubes to move a game piece. He needs to roll a sum of 6 on his first turn and then a sum of 10 on his second turn to land on the next two bonus spaces. What is the probability that Corbin will roll a sum of 6 and then a sum of 10 on his next two turns? ________

Copy and Solve Solve Exercises 21–24 on a separate sheet of paper. A card is pulled from a stack of 15 cards labeled 1–15 and the spinner shown is spun. Find each probability.

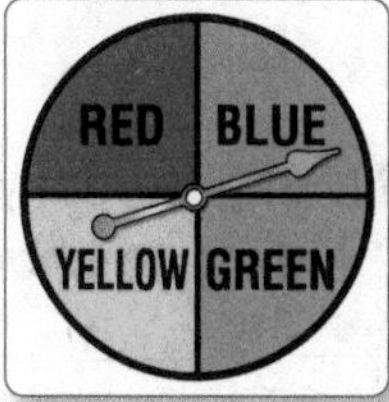

21. *P*(less than 10 and red)

22. *P*(odd and red or blue)

23. *P*(even and blue)

24. *P*(prime number and blue)

Maddie is packing for a trip. In her closet, there are 3 red, 4 black, 2 green, and 2 yellow blouses. She randomly selects 2 blouses. Find each probability.

25. *P*(red and red)

26. *P*(black and yellow)

27. *P*(red and black)

28. *P*(green and green)

Georgia Test Practice

29. Juan is holding four straws of different lengths. Four of his friends each randomly pick a straw. Milo picks first, and keeps the shortest straw. What is the probability that Frank will get the longest straw if he picks second?

Ⓐ $\frac{1}{4}$

Ⓑ $\frac{1}{2}$

Ⓒ $\frac{1}{3}$

Ⓓ $\frac{1}{5}$

30. The spinners are each spun once.

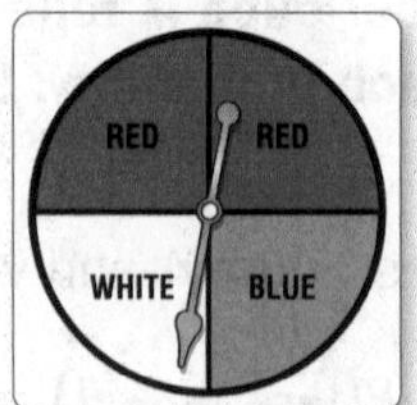

What is the probability of spinning 2 and white?

Ⓕ $\frac{1}{16}$

Ⓖ $\frac{1}{4}$

Ⓗ $\frac{2}{5}$

Ⓘ $\frac{3}{5}$

Common Core Review

31. A magazine rack contains 5 sports magazines, 7 news magazines, and 10 fashion magazines. After a magazine is chosen, it is *not* replaced. Find the probability of randomly choosing two fashion magazines. MCC7.SP.8a

32. Each week, Ryan's mother has him randomly choose a chore that he must complete from the list shown. The first week, he chose washing the dishes. What is the probability that Ryan will choose washing the dishes two more weeks in a row? MCC7.SP.5

Weekly Chores
Collecting the trash
Folding the laundry
Cleaning the house
Washing the dishes
Cutting the grass

33. In how many different orders can a person watch 3 different videos? Use a list to show the sample space. MCC7.SP.8b

21ST CENTURY CAREER in Medicine

Pediatricians

Do you have compassion, a sense of humor, and the ability to analyze data? You might want to consider a career in medicine. Pediatricians care for the health of infants, children, and teenagers. They diagnose illnesses, interpret diagnostic tests, and prescribe and administer treatment.

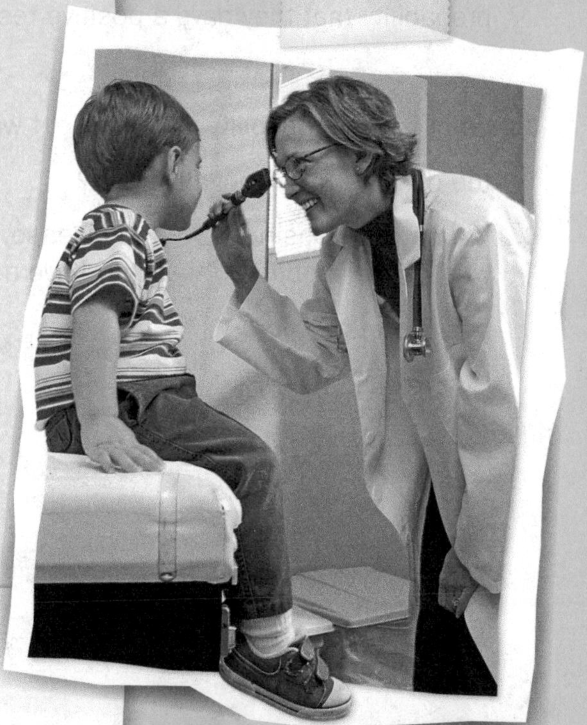

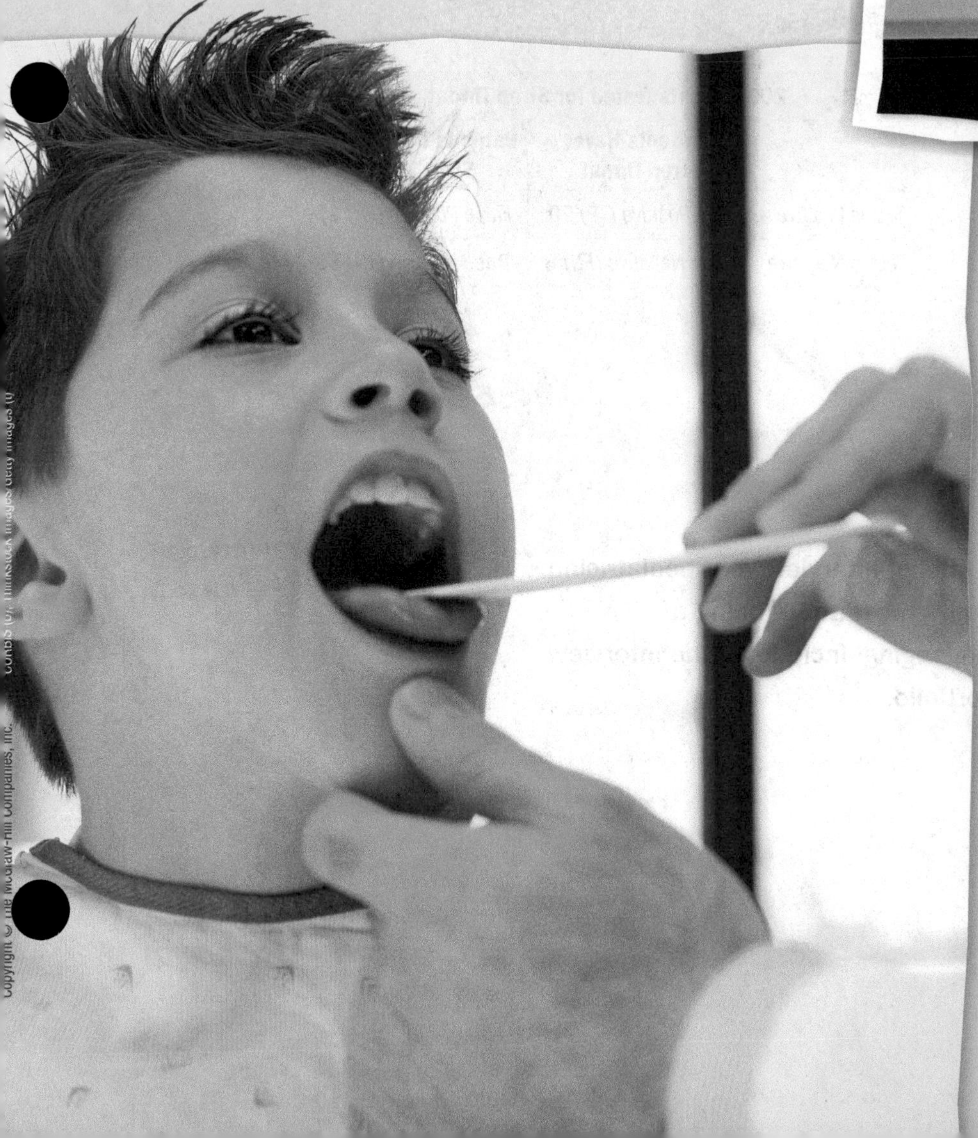

College & Career READINESS

Explore college and careers at ccr.mcgraw-hill.com

Is This the Career for You?

Are you interested in a career as a pediatrician? Take some of the following courses in high school.

- Algebra
- Biology
- Calculus
- Chemistry
- Psychology

Find out how math relates to a career in Medicine.

On Call for Kids

Use the information in the table below to solve each problem. Round to the nearest tenth, if necessary. Write each answer as a percent rounded to the nearest whole number.

1. What is the probability that one of the patients tested has strep throat? ________
2. If a patient has strep throat, what is the probability that they have a positive test? ________
3. What is the probability that a patient with the disease has a negative test? ________
4. If a patient does not have the disease, what is the probability that they have a positive test? ________
5. What is the probability that a patient that does *not* have strep throat tested negative for the disease? ________
6. The *positive predictive value,* or *PPV,* is the probability that a patient with a positive test result will have the disease. What is the PPV? ________
7. The *negative predictive value,* or *NPV,* is the probability that a patient with a negative test result will not have the disease. What is the NPV? ________

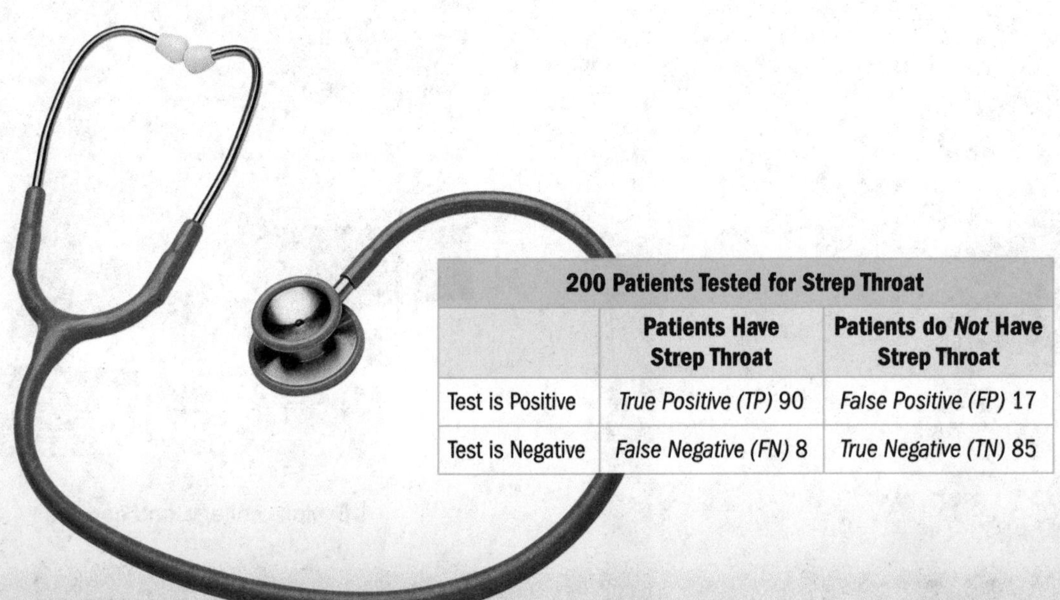

200 Patients Tested for Strep Throat

	Patients Have Strep Throat	Patients do *Not* Have Strep Throat
Test is Positive	*True Positive (TP)* 90	*False Positive (FP)* 17
Test is Negative	*False Negative (FN)* 8	*True Negative (TN)* 85

Career Project

It's time to update your career portfolio! Interview your pediatrician. Be sure to ask what he or she enjoys most about being a pediatrician and what is most challenging. Include all the interview questions and answers in your portfolio.

What are some short term goals you need to achieve to become a pediatrician?

-
-
-
-
-

Photodisc Collection/Getty Images

Chapter Review

Vocabulary Check

Unscramble each of the clue words. After unscrambling all of the terms, use the numbered letters to find a sentence assoicated with probability.

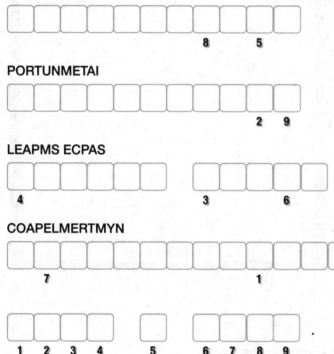

HELATCORTEI

☐☐☐☐☐☐☐☐☐☐☐ (box 8 = 8, box 10 = 5)

PORTUNMETAI

☐☐☐☐☐☐☐☐☐☐☐ (box 10 = 2, box 11 = 9)

LEAPMS ECPAS

☐☐☐☐☐☐ ☐☐☐☐☐ (box 1 = 4; second word box 1 = 3, box 4 = 6)

COAPELMERTMYN

☐☐☐☐☐☐☐☐☐☐☐☐☐ (box 2 = 7, box 10 = 1)

☐☐☐☐ ☐ ☐☐☐☐ .

1 2 3 4 5 6 7 8 9

Complete each sentence using one of the unscrambled words above.

1. The ______________ is the set of all of the possible outcomes of a probability experiment.

2. A ______________ is an arrangement, or listing, of objects in which order is important.

3. The ______________ probability is based on what should happen when conducting a probability experiment.

4. Two events in which one or the other must happen, but they cannot happen at the same time are ______________.

Key Concept Check

Use Your FOLDABLES

Use your Foldable to help review the chapter.

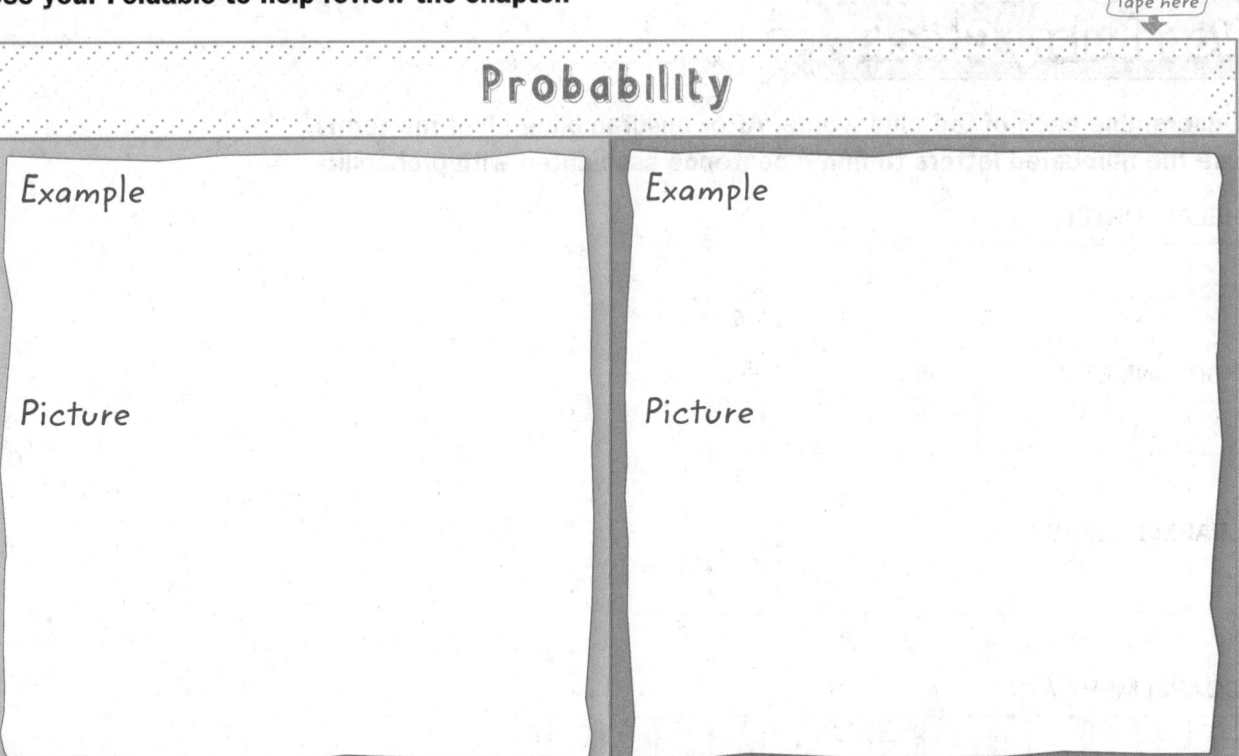

Got it?

Match each term or phrase on the left with the words on the right.

1. Based on what actually occurred in a probability experiment
2. The outcome of one event affects the outcome of a separate event
3. Consists of two or more simple events
4. Can be used to find the sample space

a. compound event

b. experimental probability

c. Fundamental Counting Principle

d. dependent event

e. tree diagrams

f. organized lists

Problem Solving

For Exercises 1 and 2, a number cube is rolled. The table shows the results. (Lesson 2)

Number	Times Rolled
1	7
2	9
3	10
4	12
5	6
6	6

1. What is the experimental probability that the next roll will be four?

2. How does the experimental probability of rolling 4 compare to the theoretical probability? Provide a reason for any discrepancy.

3. Ginger and Micah are playing a game in which a coin is tossed twice. If heads comes up exactly once, Ginger wins. Otherwise, Micah wins. Find the sample space using a tree diagram. Then find the probability that Ginger wins. (Lesson 3)

4. In how many ways can the picture frames shown be arranged in a line on the wall? (Lesson 6) ____________

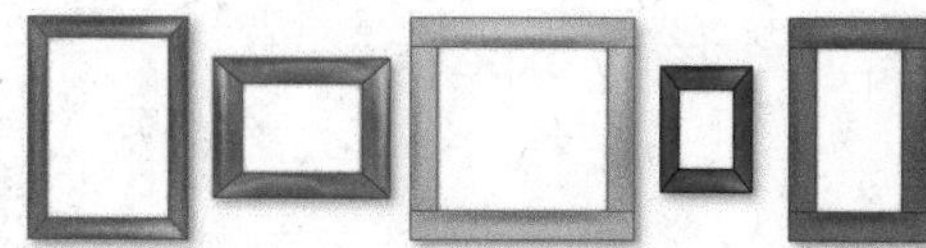

5. A bag of animal crackers contains 6 monkeys, 5 giraffes, 6 elephants, and 3 tigers. Maria selects a cracker at random. Then Bryan selects a cracker at random. What is the probability that two tigers are chosen? (Lesson 7)

Reflect

Answering the Essential Question

Use what you learned about probability to complete the graphic organizer.

Theoretical Probability

Experimental Probability

Essential Question

HOW can you predict the outcome of future events?

Sample Space

Simulation

Answer the Essential Question. HOW can you predict the outcome of future events?

COLLABORATIVE PROJECT

Become a Travel Expert Without proper planning, a family vacation could end up costing a fortune! In this project you will:

- **Collaborate** with your classmates as you research the cost of a family vacation.
- **Share** the results of your research in a creative way.
- **Reflect** on how you use mathematics to describe change and model real-world situations.

By the end of this project, you will be ready to plan a family vacation without breaking the bank.

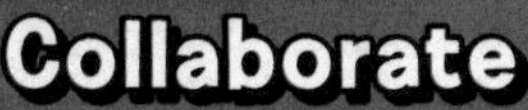

Collaborate

Go Online Work with your group to research and complete each activity. You will use your results in the Share section on the following page.

1. Research the cost for a family of four to fly round trip to a destination of your choosing. Record the cost of a flight that is nonstop and one that has at least one extra stop. Make sure to include the cost of the tax.

2. Research two different rental cars that would be available at a local company. Compare the miles per gallon (mpg) that each car averages on the highway. How much gas would you use for each car if you were going to be traveling 450 miles on your trip?

3. If you are traveling out of the country you will need to know the current exchange rates. Record the exchange rate for three different countries. How much is $100 worth in those countries?

4. Choose a vacation spot that is a city in the United States. Find a popular restaurant for tourists in your city and look up their menu online. Calculate the cost for a dinner that feeds four people. Don't forget the tip.

5. Different states have different sales tax rates. Choose three different states. Research the sales tax rate for each of those states. Then, determine the total cost of buying jeans that cost $50 plus the sales tax.

With your group, decide on a way to share what you have learned about the cost of a family vacation. Some suggestions are listed below, but you can also think of other creative ways to present your information. Remember to show how you used mathematics in your project!

- Use your creative writing skills to write journal entries or blogs. Your writing should describe how you were able to save money while traveling on your vacations.
- Act as a travel agent to put together one domestic and one international travel package for a family of four. Create a digital brochure to explain each package.

Check out the note on the right to connect this project with other subjects.

Financial Literacy *Imagine that you are the director of tourism for your state. Write a script for a commercial that is trying to encourage tourists to visit. Your script should include:*

- *unique activities found in your state*
- *ways of traveling in your state*

6. **Answer the Essential Question** How can you use mathematics to describe change and model real-world situations?

   a. How did you use what you learned about ratios and proportional reasoning to describe change and model the real-world situations in this project?

   b. How did you use what you learned about percents to describe change and model the real-world situations in this project?

COLLABORATIVE PROJECT

Explore the Ocean Depths For this project, imagine that your dream job is to become an oceanographer. In this project you will:

- **Collaborate** with your classmates as you research information about the ocean.
- **Share** the results of your research in a creative way.
- **Reflect** on how mathematical ideas can be represented.

Collaborate

Go Online **Work with your group to research and complete each activity. You will use your results in the Share section on the following page.**

1. About $\frac{2}{3}$ of Earth is covered by ocean. Research the five oceans of the world and create a table that shows about what fraction each ocean is of that $\frac{2}{3}$.

2. What is the greatest ocean depth? Find out and then display it on a vertical number line along with other facts about what you can find at different ocean depths.

3. Coral reefs are the home of many ocean creatures. Look up some facts about the state of coral reefs in the world today and display them in a creative way.

4. Choose three different types of whales that live in the ocean. Compare things like their size, the amount of food they eat, or the climate in which they live. Organize the information in a table or graph.

5. Research one of the larger icebergs in the Arctic Ocean. Sketch an image of the iceberg next to a vertical number line that shows the approximate top and bottom of the iceberg. Remember, about $\frac{7}{8}$ of an iceberg is under water.

Share

With your group, decide on a way to share what you have learned about ocean depths. Some suggestions are listed below, but you could also think of other creative ways to present your information. Remember to show how you used mathematics in your project!

- Use presentation software to organize what you have learned in this project. Share your presentation with the class.
- Imagine you need to apply for funds to go on a deep sea exploration. Write a persuasive letter or speech that highlights the importance of studying ocean depths.

Check out the note on the right to connect this project with other subjects.

Environmental Literacy Research an animal that lives in the ocean that is on the endangered species list. Give a presentation to your class that answers the following questions:

- What are some of the causes for the animals being on the endangered species list?
- What efforts are currently being made to protect the animal you chose?

Reflect

6. **Answer the Essential Question** How can mathematical ideas be represented?

   a. How were mathematical ideas involving integers represented in the information you discovered about oceans?

   b. How were mathematical ideas involving rational numbers represented in the information you discovered about oceans?

COLLABORATIVE PROJECT

Watch

Stand Up and Be Counted The U.S. Census is used to determine the number of U.S. House of Representative members that each state is assigned. In this project you will:

- **Collaborate** with your classmates as you research Census data and the U.S. House of Representatives.
- **Share** the results of your research in a creative way.
- **Reflect** on how you can communicate mathematical ideas effectively.

Collaborate

Go Online Work with your group to research and complete each activity. You will use your results in the Share section on the following page.

1. Explore the official U.S. Census web site to find the 2010 state populations. There will be interactive maps that display this information. Write down a few facts you find interesting.

2. Create a table that displays the population and the number of U.S. Representatives for your state and three other states. Then create a line plot for the number of U.S. Representatives.

3. Write an equation that uses any state's population x and its number of U.S. Representative members y to describes the number of people per U.S. Representative z.

4. Use your equation from Exercise 3 to determine the approximate number of people per U.S. Representative for the four states you chose. Interpret the results.

5. Look at the 2000 and 2010 census. How did the population of your state and states in your region change? Did the population change affect the number of U.S. Representatives assigned?

6. States can be categorized by population size and density. Write at least two inequalities that compare the states using these categories.

Share

With your group, decide on a way to share what you have learned about the U.S. House of Representatives and state populations. Some suggestions are listed below, but you can also think of other creative ways to present your information. Remember to show how you used mathematics to complete each of the activities in this project!

- Act as a Census representative and create a presentation to encourage people to participate in the census and explain why it is important.
- Write a letter or email to your Representative about what you learned in this project and how it can be used to improve your community.

Check out the note on the right to connect this project with other subjects.

with Social Studies

Civic Literacy *Research the Electoral College. Some questions to consider are:*

- *Why was it established?*
- *What is the relationship between the United States House of Representatives and the Electoral College?*

Reflect

7. **Answer the Essential Question** How can you communicate mathematical ideas effectively?

   a. How did you use what you learned about expressions to help you communicate mathematical ideas effectively in this project?

   b. How did you use what you learned about equations and inequalities to help you communicate mathematical ideas effectively in this project?

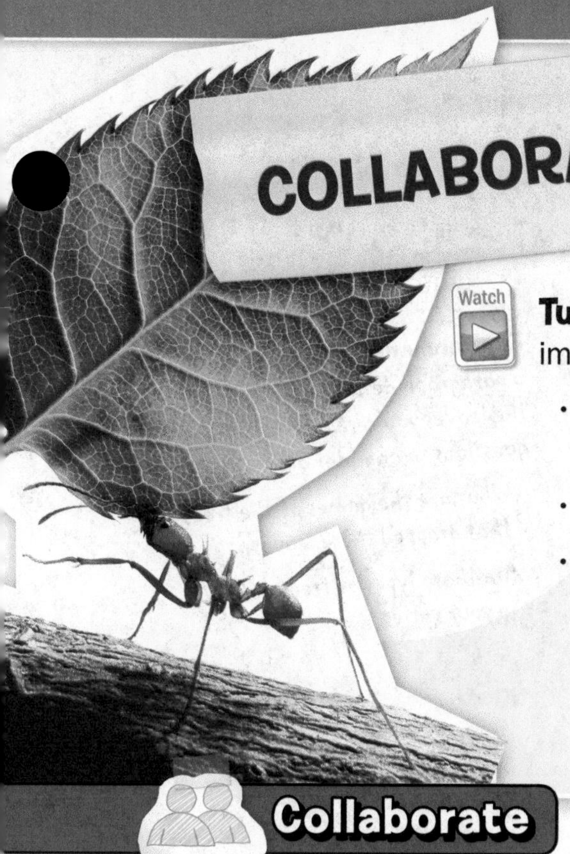

COLLABORATIVE PROJECT

Watch

Turn Over a New Leaf The flatness of leaves serves an important purpose. In this project you will:

- **Collaborate** with your classmates as you research the primary function of leaves.
- **Share** the results of your research in a creative way.
- **Reflect** on how you use different measurements to solve real-life problems.

Collaborate

Go Online Work with your group to research and complete each activity. You will use your results in the Share section on the following page.

1. Suppose you have a cube that is 10 centimeters on each side. Find the volume, surface area, and surface area to volume ratio.

2. Start with the cube from Activity 1 and imagine slicing it horizontally into ten equal sections. Arrange the sections in a 5-by-2-by-1 prism. Find the volume, surface area, and surface area to volume ratio.

3. Compare and contrast the volume, surface area, and surface area to volume ratio from Exercises 1 and 2.

4. Trace the outline of a leaf onto centimeter grid paper. Estimate the volume of the leaf. (Assume the height of your leaf is 0.1 centimeter.) Estimate the surface area. (You can ignore the edge of the leaf.) Find the surface area to volume ratio.

5. Do research to find the primary function of a leaf. Explain how the surface area to volume ratio of a leaf aids in its function.

6. Find examples from nature or man-made objects that have a small surface area to volume ratio. Explain the benefits.

With your group, decide on a way to share what you have learned about the surface area to volume ratio of leaves. Some suggestions are listed below, but you could also think of other creative ways to present your information. Remember to show how you used mathematics to complete each of the activities in this project!

- Create a digital presentation that compares two types of leaves. Use what you learned about surface area to volume ratios in your presentation.
- Imagine you discovered a new type of leaf. Create an annotated diagram of your leaf. The annotations should include the type of information you learned in this project.

Check out the note on the right to connect this project with other subjects.

Environmental Literacy Write a paragraph detailing facts about the leaves you researched. Some questions to consider are:

- What are the names of the trees that dropped these leaves?
- Are these types of trees common in your state?

6. **Answer the Essential Question** How can you use different measurements to solve real-life problems?

   a. How did what you learned about geometric figures help you use different measurements to solve real-life problems in this project?

   b. How did what you learned about measuring figures to help you use different measurements to solve real-life problems in this project?

COLLABORATIVE PROJECT

Math Genes A Punnett Square is a graphical way to predict the genetic traits of offspring. In this project you will:

- **Collaborate** with your classmates as you research genetics and the Punnet Square.
- **Share** the results of your research in a creative way.
- **Reflect** on why learning mathematics is important.

Complete the activities below and discover the fun you can have with genetics.

Collaborate

Go Online **Work with your group to research and complete each activity. You will use your results in the Share section on the following page.**

1. Use the Internet to research Punnett Squares and their role in genetics. Write a paragraph describing your findings.

2. Create sample genes for pet traits. Then create a Punnett Square using those traits. Describe what each outcome represents. Include a graph with your explanation.

3. Refer to Exercise 2. How many different genetic outcomes are possible according to your Punnett Square? What is the probability of each outcome occurring?

4. Create three word problems that involve using probability and the Punnett Squares to help answer the questions.

5. Collect two or more genetic-related information samples about students in your class. For example, you can collect data on attached/unattached earlobes. Analyze the data and make a prediction about the genetics of the entire school. Draw an appropriate graph of your results.

Share

With your group, decide on a way to share what you have learned about genetics and Punnett Squares. Some suggestions are listed below, but you can also think of other creative ways to your present your information. Remember to show how you used mathematics to complete each of the activities in this project.

- Create a digital presentation of the facts you learned about genetics.
- Act as a genetic scientist. Write a journal entry that explains your current research on predicting traits passed down from generations.

Check out the note on the right to connect this project with other subjects.

with Health

Health Literacy *Select a health condition or disease and research how genetics may play a part in the disease. Write 1–2 paragraphs explaining how genetics may influence someone's risk of getting the disease and steps that can be taken to reduce the risk factors.*

Reflect

6.  **Answer the Essential Question** Why is learning mathematics important?

   a. How did what you learned about probability help you to understand why learning mathematics is important?

   b. How did what you learned about statistics help you to understand why learning mathematics is important?

Glossary/Glosario

Go online for the eGlossary. 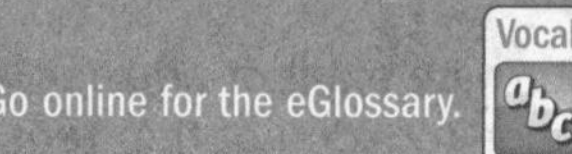

The eGlossary contains words and definitions in the following 13 languages:

Arabic	Cantonese	Hmong	Spanish	Urdu
Bengali	English	Korean	Tagalog	Vietnamese
Brazilian Portuguese	Haitian Creole	Russian		

English

Aa

absolute value The distance the number is from zero on a number line.

acute angle An angle with a measure greater than 0° and less than 90°.

acute triangle A triangle having three acute angles.

Addition Property of Equality If you add the same number to each side of an equation, the two sides remain equal.

Addition Property of Inequality If you add the same number to each side of an inequality, the inequality remains true.

Additive Identity Property The sum of any number and zero is the number.

additive inverse Two integers that are opposites. The sum of an integer and its additive inverse is zero.

adjacent angles Angles that have the same vertex, share a common side, and do not overlap.

algebra A branch of mathematics that involves expressions with variables.

algebraic expression A combination of variables, numbers, and at least one operation.

Español

valor absoluto Distancia a la que se encuentra un número de cero en la recta numérica.

ángulo agudo Ángulo que mide más de 0° y menos de 90°.

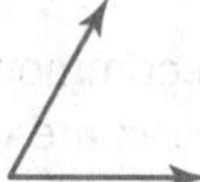

triángulo acutángulo Triángulo con tres ángulos agudos.

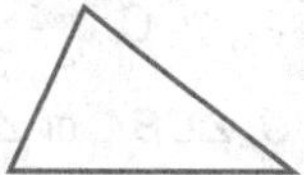

propiedad de adición de la igualdad Si sumas el mismo número a ambos lados de una ecuación, los dos lados permanecen iguales.

propiedad de desigualdad en la suma Si se suma el mismo número a cada lado de una desigualdad, la desigualdad sigue siendo verdadera.

propiedad de identidad de la suma La suma de cualquier número y cero es el mismo número.

inverso aditivo Dos enteros opuestos.

ángulos adyacentes Ángulos que comparten el mismo vértice y un común lado, pero no se sobreponen.

álgebra Rama de las matemáticas que trata de las expresiones con variables.

expresión algebraica Combinación de variables, números y por lo menos una operación.

alternate exterior angles Angles that are on opposite sides of the transversal and outside the parallel lines.

ángulos alternos externos Ángulos en lados opuestos de la trasversal y afuera de las rectas paralelas.

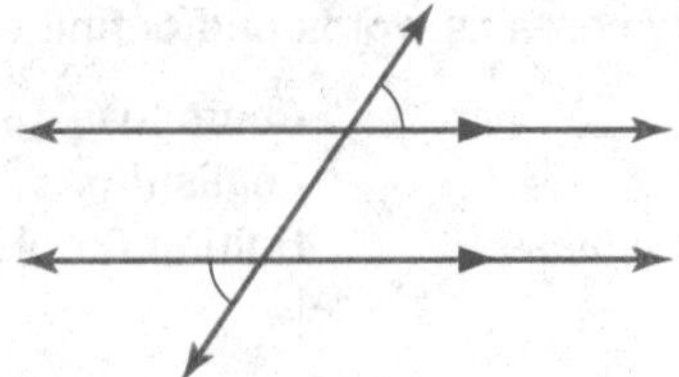

alternate interior angles Angles that are on opposite sides of the transversal and inside the parallel lines.

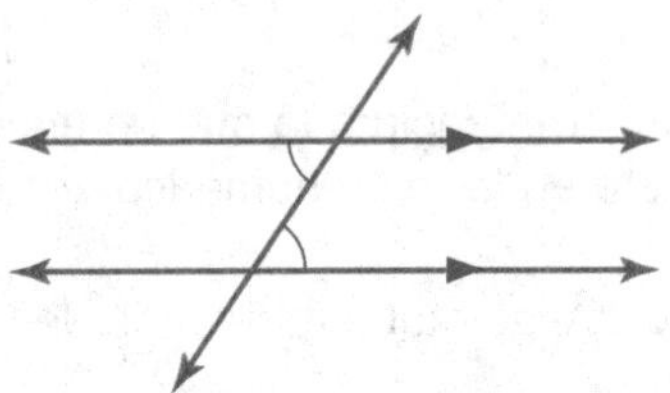

ángulos alternos internos Ángulos en lados opuestos de la trasversal y dentro de las rectas paralelas.

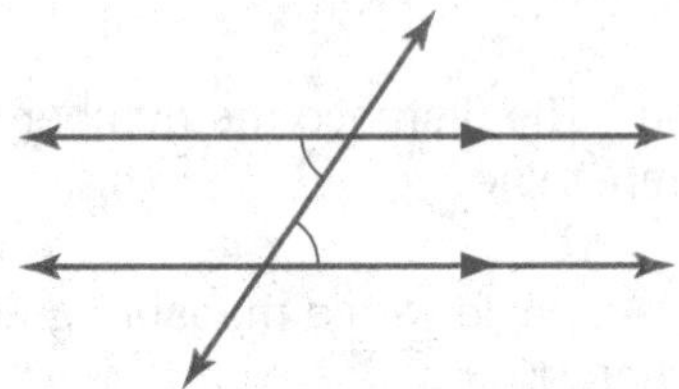

angle Two rays with a common endpoint form an angle. The rays and vertex are used to name the angle.

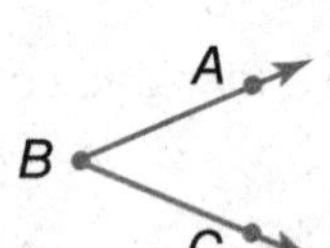

$\angle ABC$, $\angle CBA$, or $\angle B$

ángulo Dos rayos con un extremo común forman un ángulo. Los rayos y el vértice se usan para nombrar el ángulo.

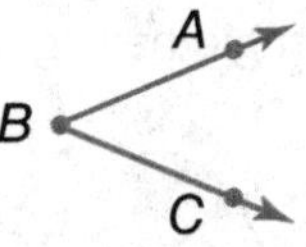

$\angle ABC$, $\angle CBA$ o $\angle B$

arithmetic sequence A sequence in which the difference between any two consecutive terms is the same.

sucesión aritmética Sucesión en la cual la diferencia entre dos términos consecutivos es constante.

Associative Property The way in which numbers are grouped does not change their sum or product.

propiedad asociativa La forma en que se agrupan números al sumarlos o multiplicarlos no altera su suma o producto.

Bb

bar notation In repeating decimals, the line or bar placed over the digits that repeat. For example, $2.\overline{63}$ indicates that the digits 63 repeat.

notación de barra Línea o barra que se coloca sobre los dígitos que se repiten en decimales periódicos. Por ejemplo, $2.\overline{63}$ indica que los dígitos 63 se repiten.

base In a power, the number used as a factor. In 10^3, the base is 10. That is, $10^3 = 10 \times 10 \times 10$.

base En una potencia, el número usado como factor. En 10^3, la base es 10. Es decir, $10^3 = 10 \times 10 \times 10$.

base One of the two parallel congruent faces of a prism.

base Una de las dos caras paralelas congruentes de un prisma.

biased sample A sample drawn in such a way that one or more parts of the population are favored over others.

muestra sesgada Muestra en que se favorece una o más partes de una población.

box plot A method of visually displaying a distribution of data values by using the median, quartiles, and extremes of the data set. A box shows the middle 50% of the data.

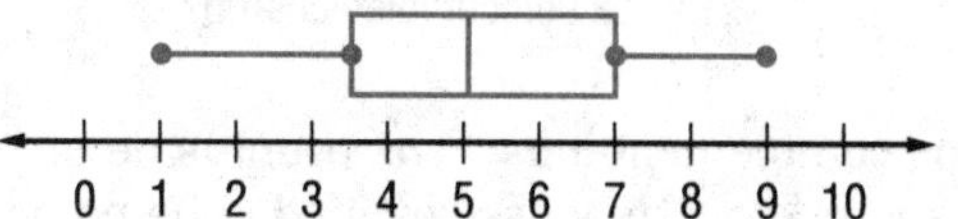

diagrama de caja Un método de mostrar visualmente una distribución de valores usando la mediana, cuartiles y extremos del conjunto de datos. Una caja muestra el 50% del medio de los datos.

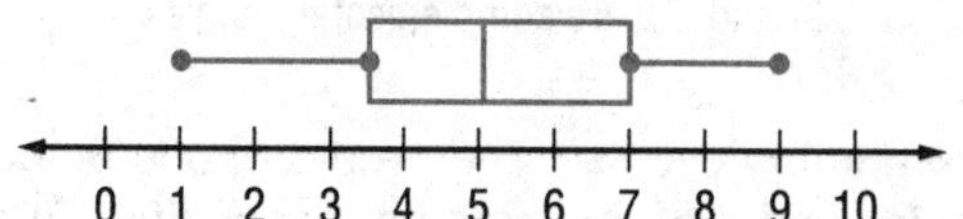

Cc

center The point from which all points on circle are the same distance.

centro El punto desde el cual todos los puntos en una circunferencia están a la misma distancia.

circle The set of all points in a plane that are the same distance from a given point called the center.

círculo Conjunto de todos los puntos de un plano que están a la misma distancia de un punto dado denominado "centro".

circle graph A graph that shows data as parts of a whole. In a circle graph, the percents add up to 100.

Area of Oceans

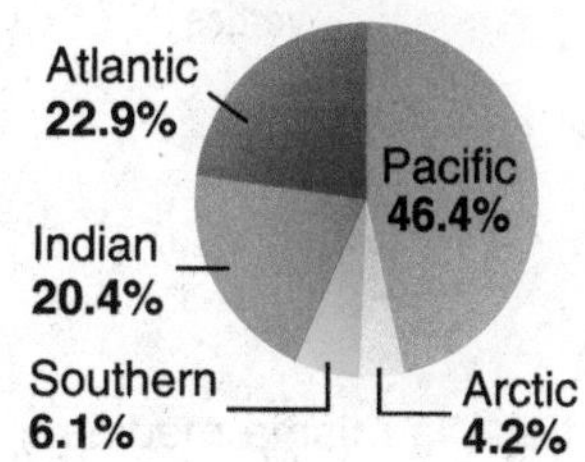

gráfica circular Gráfica que muestra los datos como partes de un todo. En una gráfica circular los porcentajes suman 100.

Área de superficie de los océanos

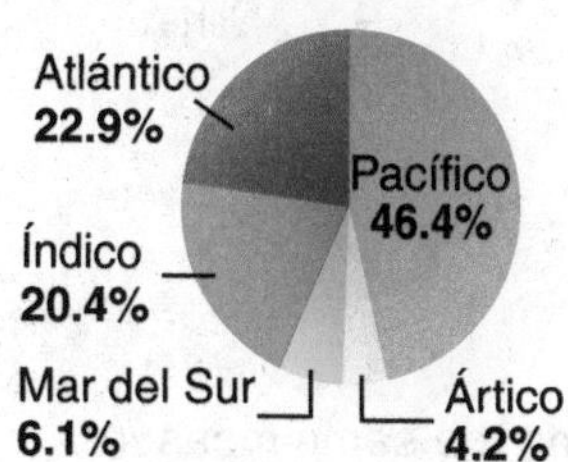

circumference The distance around a circle.

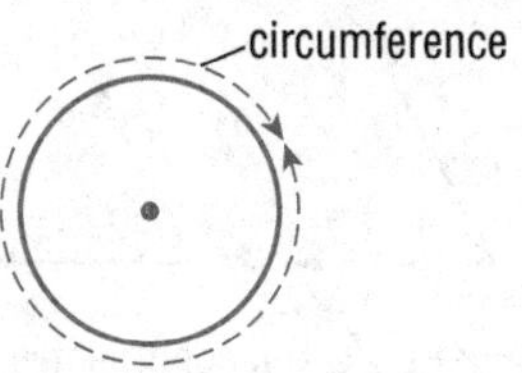

circunferencia Distancia en torno a un círculo.

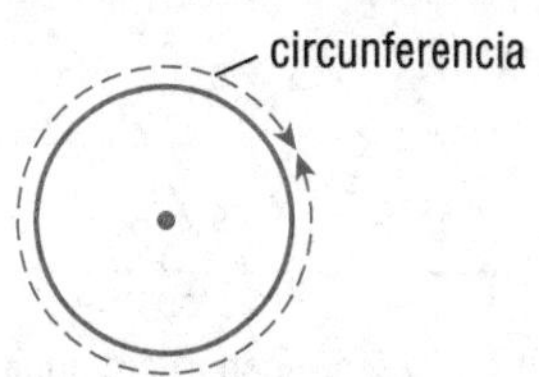

coefficient The numerical factor of a term that contains a variable.

coeficiente El factor numérico de un término que contiene una variable.

common denominator A common multiple of the denominators of two or more fractions. 24 is a common denominator for $\frac{1}{3}$, $\frac{5}{8}$, and $\frac{3}{4}$ because 24 is the LCM of 3, 8, and 4.

común denominador El múltiplo común de los denominadores de dos o más fracciones. 24 es un denominador común para $\frac{1}{3}$, $\frac{5}{8}$ y $\frac{3}{4}$ porque 24 es el mcm de 3, 8 y 4.

Commutative Property The order in which two numbers are added or multiplied does not change their sum or product.

propiedad conmutativa El orden en que se suman o multiplican dos números no altera el resultado.

complementary angles Two angles are complementary if the sum of their measures is 90°.

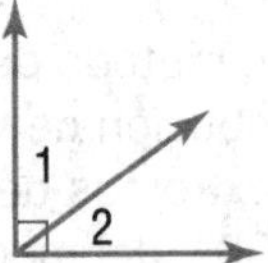

∠1 and ∠2 are complementary angles.

ángulos complementarios Dos ángulos son complementarios si la suma de sus medidas es 90°.

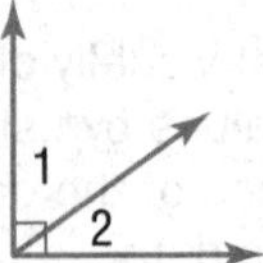

∠1 y ∠2 son complementarios.

complementary events The events of one outcome happening and that outcome not happening. The sum of the probabilities of an event and its complement is 1 or 100%. In symbols, $P(A) + P(not\ A) = 1$.

eventos complementarios Los eventos de un resultado que ocurre y ese resultado que no ocurre. La suma de las probabilidades de un evento y su complemento es 1 ó 100. En símbolos $P(A) + P(no\ A) = 1$.

complex fraction A fraction $\frac{A}{B}$ where A or B are fractions and B does not equal zero.

fracción compleja Una fracción $\frac{A}{B}$ en la cual A o B son fracciones y B no es igual a cero.

composite figure A figure that is made up of two or more three-dimensional figures.

figura compuesta Figura formada por dos o más figuras tridimensionales.

compound event An event consisting of two or more simple events.

evento compuesto Un evento que consiste en dos o más eventos simples.

cone A three-dimensional figure with one circular base connected by a curved surface to a single vertex.

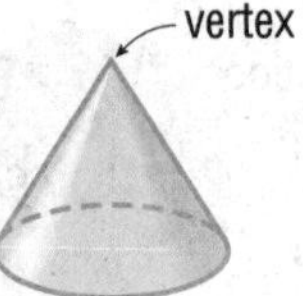

cono Una figura tridimensional con una base circular conectada por una superficie curva para un solo vértice.

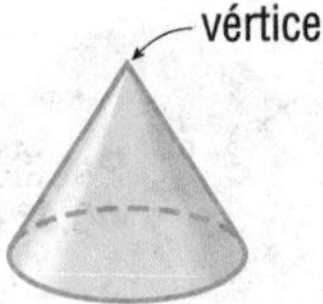

congruent Having the same measure.

congruente Que tiene la misma medida.

congruent angles Angles that have the same measure.

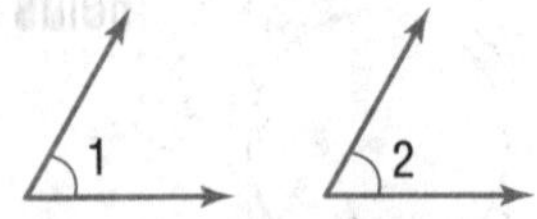

∠1 and ∠2 are congruent angles.

ángulos congruentes Ángulos que tienen la misma medida.

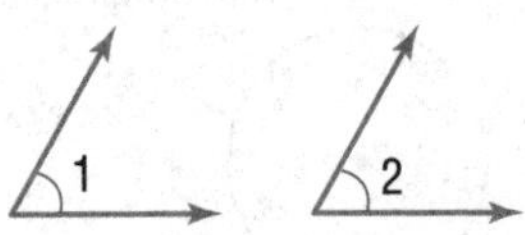

∠1 y ∠2 son congruentes.

congruent figures Figures that have the same size and same shape and corresponding sides and angles with equal measure.

figuras congruentes Figuras que tienen el mismo tamaño y la misma forma y los lados y los ángulos correspondientes tienen igual medida.

congruent segments Sides with the same length.

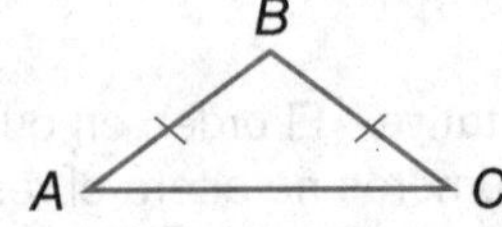

Side $\overline{AB}$ is congruent to side $\overline{BC}$.

segmentos congruentes Lados con la misma longitud.

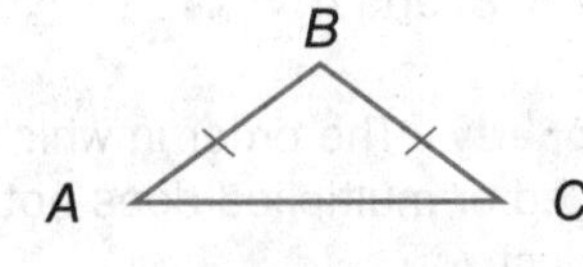

$\overline{AB}$ es congruente a $\overline{BC}$.

constant A term that does not contain a variable.

constante Término que no contiene ninguna variable.

constant of proportionality A constant ratio or unit rate of two variable quantities. It is also called the constant of variation.

constante de proporcionalidad Una razón constante o tasa por unidad de dos cantidades variables. También se llama constante de variación.

constant of variation The constant ratio in a direct variation. It is also called the constant of proportionality.

constante de variación Una razón constante o tasa por unidad de dos cantidades variables. También se llama constante de proporcionalidad.

constant rate of change The rate of change in a linear relationship.

razón constante de cambio Tasa de cambio en una relación lineal.

continuous data Data that take on any real number value. It can be determined by considering what numbers are reasonable as part of the domain.

datos continuos Datos que asumen cualquier valor numérico real. Se pueden determinar al considerar qué números son razonables como parte del dominio.

convenience sample A sample which consists of members of a population that are easily accessed.

muestra de conveniencia Muestra que incluye miembros de una población fácilmente accesibles.

coordinate plane A plane in which a horizontal number line and a vertical number line intersect at their zero points. Also called a coordinate grid.

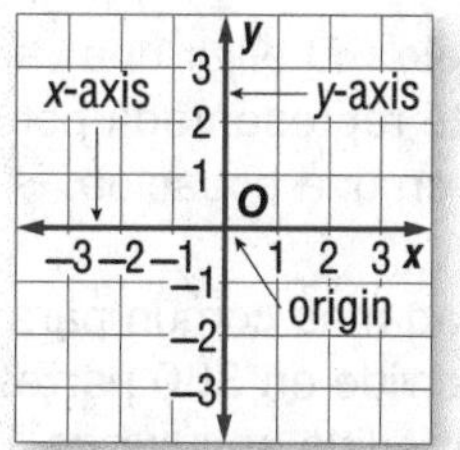

plano de coordenadas Plano en el cual se han trazado dos rectas numéricas, una horizontal y una vertical, que se intersecan en sus puntos cero. También conocido como sistema de coordenadas.

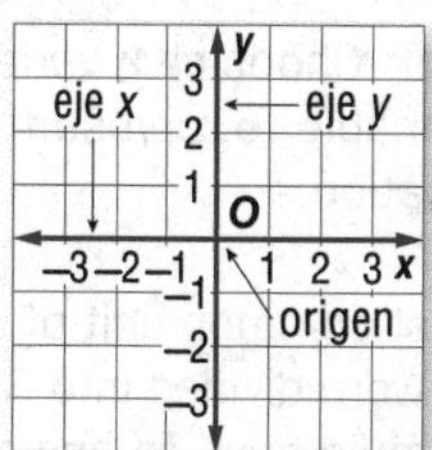

coplanar Lines or points that lie in the same plane.

coplanar Líneas o puntos situados en el mismo plano.

corresponding angles Angles in the same position on parallel lines in relation to a transversal.

ángulos correspondientes Ángulos que están en la misma posición sobre rectas paralelas en relación con la transversal.

corresponding sides The sides of similar figures that are in the same relative postion.

lados correspondientes Lados de figuras semejantes que estan en la misma posición.

counterexample A specific case which proves a statement false.

contraejemplo Caso específico que demuestra la falsedad de un enunciado.

cross product The product of the numerator of one ratio and the denominator of the other ratio. The cross products of any proportion are equal.

producto cruzado Producto del numerador de una razón por el denominador de la otra razón. Los productos cruzados de cualquier proporción son iguales.

cross section The cross section of a solid and a plane.

sección transversal Intersección de un sólido con un plano.

cube root One of three equal factors of a number. If $a^3 = b$, then a is the cube root of b. The cube root of 125 is 5 since $5^3 = 125$.

raíz cúbica Uno de tres factores iguales de un número. Si $a^3 = b$, entonces a es la raíz cúbica de b. La raíz cúbica de 125 es 5, dado que $5^3 = 125$.

cubed The product in which a number is a factor three times. Two cubed is 8 because $2 \times 2 \times 2 = 8$.

al cubo El producto de un número por sí mismo, tres veces. Dos al cubo es 8 porque $2 \times 2 \times 2 = 8$.

cylinder A three-dimensional figure with two parallel congruent circular bases connected by a curved surface.

cilindro Una figura tridimensional con dos paralelas congruentes circulares bases conectados por una superficie curva.

Dd

decagon A polygon having ten sides.

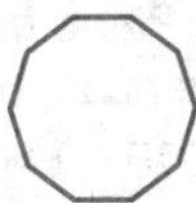

decágono Un polígono con diez lados.

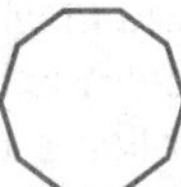

defining a variable Choosing a variable and a quantity for the variable to represent in an expression or equation.

definir una variable El eligir una variable y una cantidad que esté representada por la variable en una expresión o en una ecuacion.

degrees The most common unit of measure for angles. If a circle were divided into 360 equal-sized parts, each part would have an angle measure of 1 degree.

grados La unidad más común para medir ángulos. Si un círculo se divide en 360 partes iguales, cada parte tiene una medida angular de 1 grado.

dependent events Two or more events in which the outcome of one event affects the outcome of the other event(s).

eventos dependientes Dos o más eventos en que el resultado de un evento afecta el resultado de otro u otros eventos.

dependent variable The variable in a relation with a value that depends on the value of the independent variable.

variable dependiente La variable en una relación cuyo valor depende del valor de la variable independiente.

derived unit A unit that is derived from a measurement system base unit, such as length, mass, or time.

unidad derivada Unidad que se deriva de una unidad básica de un sistema de medidas, como la longitud, la masa o el tiempo.

diagonal A line segment that connects two nonconsecutive vertices.

diagonal Segmento de recta que une dos vértices no consecutivos de un polígono.

diameter The distance across a circle through its center.

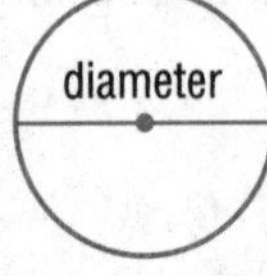

diámetro Segmento que pasa por el centro de un círculo y lo divide en dos partes iguales.

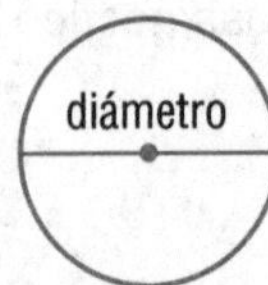

dimensional analysis The process of including units of measurement when you compute.

análisis dimensional Proceso que incluye las unidades de medida al hacer cálculos.

direct variation The relationship between two variable quantities that have a constant ratio.

variación directa Relación entre las cantidades de dos variables que tienen una tasa constante.

discount The amount by which the regular price of an item is reduced.

descuento Cantidad que se le rebaja al precio regular de un artículo.

discrete data When solutions of a function are only integer values. It can be determined by considering what numbers are reasonable as part of the domain.

datos discretos Cuando las soluciones de una función son solo valores enteros. Se pueden determinar considerando qué números son razonables como parte del dominio.

disjoint events Events that cannot happen at the same time.

eventos disjuntos Eventos que no pueden ocurrir al mismo tiempo.

Distributive Property To multiply a sum by a number, multiply each addend of the sum by the number outside the parentheses. For any numbers a, b, and c, $a(b + c) = ab + ac$ and $a(b - c) = ab - ac$.

Example: $2(5 + 3) = (2 \times 5) + (2 \times 3)$ and $2(5 - 3) = (2 \times 5) - (2 \times 3)$

propiedad distributiva Para multiplicar una suma por un número, multiplíquese cada sumando de la suma por el número que está fuera del paréntesis. Sean cuales fuere los números a, b, y c, $a(b + c) = ab + ac$ y $a(b - c) = ab - ac$.

Ejemplo: $2(5 + 3) = (2 \cdot 5) + (2 \cdot 3)$ y $2(5 - 3) = (2 \cdot 5) - (2 \cdot 3)$

Division Property of Equality If you divide each side of an equation by the same nonzero number, the two sides remain equal.

propiedad de igualdad de la división Si divides ambos lados de una ecuación entre el mismo número no nulo, los lados permanecen iguales.

Division Property of Inequality When you divide each side of an inequality by a negative number, the inequality symbol must be reversed for the inequality to remain true.

propiedad de desigualdad en la división Cuando se divide cada lado de una desigualdad entre un número negativo, el símbolo de desigualdad debe invertirse para que la desigualdad siga siendo verdadera.

domain The set of input values for a function.

dominio El conjunto de valores de entrada de una función.

double box plot Two box plots graphed on the same number line.

doble diagrama de caja Dos diagramas de caja sobre la misma recta numérica.

double dot plot A method of visually displaying a distribution of two sets of data values where each value is shown as a dot above a number line.

doble diagrama de puntos Un método de mostrar visualmente una distribución de dos conjuntos de valores donde cada valor se muestra como un punto arriba de una recta numérica.

Ee

edge The line segment where two faces of a polyhedron intersect.

borde El segmento de línea donde se cruzan dos caras de un poliedro.

enlargement An image larger than the original.

ampliación Imagen más grande que la original.

equation A mathematical sentence that contains an equals sign, =, stating that two quantities are equal.

ecuación Enunciado matemático que contiene el signo de igualdad = indicando que dos cantidades son iguales.

equiangular In a polygon, all of the angles are congruent.

equiangular En un polígono, todos los ángulos son congruentes.

equilateral In a polygon, all of the sides are congruent.

equilátero En un polígono, todos los lados son congruentes.

equilateral triangle A triangle having three congruent sides.

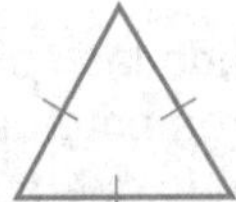

triángulo equilátero Triángulo con tres lados congruentes.

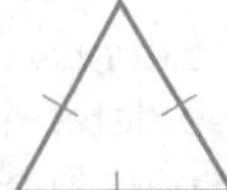

equivalent equations Two or more equations with the same solution.

ecuaciones equivalentes Dos o más ecuaciones con la misma solución.

equivalent expressions Expressions that have the same value.

expresiones equivalentes Expresiones que tienen el mismo valor.

equivalent ratios Two ratios that have the same value.

razones equivalentes Dos razones que tienen el mismo valor.

evaluate To find the value of an expression.

evaluar Calcular el valor de una expresión.

experimental probability An estimated probability based on the relative frequency of positive outcomes occurring during an experiment. It is based on what *actually* occurred during such an experiment.

probabilidad experimental Probabilidad estimada que se basa en la frecuencia relativa de los resultados positivos que ocurren durante un experimento. Se basa en lo que *en realidad* ocurre durante dicho experimento.

exponent In a power, the number that tells how many times the base is used as a factor. In 5^3, the exponent is 3. That is, $5^3 = 5 \times 5 \times 5$.

exponente En una potencia, el número que indica las veces que la base se usa como factor. En 5^3, el exponente es 3. Es decir, $5^3 = 5 \times 5 \times 5$.

exponential form Numbers written with exponents.

forma exponencial Números escritos usando exponentes.

Ff

face A flat surface of a polyhedron.

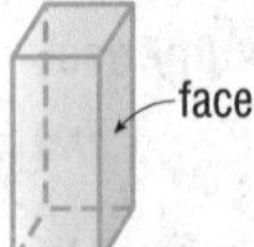

cara Una superficie plana de un poliedro.

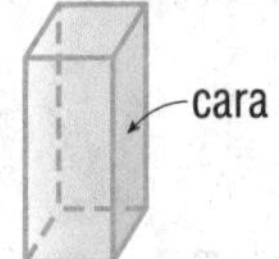

factor To write a number as a product of its factors.

factorizar Escribir un número como el producto de sus factores.

factored form An expression expressed as the product of its factors.

forma factorizada Una expresión expresada como el producto de sus factores.

factors Two or more numbers that are multiplied together to form a product.

factores Dos o más números que se multiplican entre sí para formar un producto.

fair game A game where each player has an equally likely chance of winning.

juego justo Juego donde cada jugador tiene igual posibilidad de ganar.

first quartile For a data set with median *M*, the first quartile is the median of the data values less than *M*.

primer cuartil Para un conjunto de datos con la mediana *M*, el primer cuartil es la mediana de los valores menores que *M*.

formula An equation that shows the relationship among certain quantities.

fórmula Ecuación que muestra la relación entre ciertas cantidades.

function A relationship which assigns exactly one output value for each input value.

función Relación que asigna exactamente un valor de salida a cada valor de entrada.

function rule The operation performed on the input of a function.

regla de función Operación que se efectúa en el valor de entrada.

function table A table used to organize the input numbers, output numbers, and the function rule.

tabla de funciones Tabla que organiza las entradas, la regla y las salidas de una función.

Fundamental Counting Principle Uses multiplication of the number of ways each event in an experiment can occur to find the number of possible outcomes in a sample space.

Principio Fundamental de Contar Este principio usa la multiplicación del número de veces que puede ocurrir cada evento en un experimento para calcular el número de posibles resultados en un espacio muestral.

Gg

gram A unit of mass in the metric system equivalent to 0.001 kilogram. The amount of matter an object can hold.

gramo Unidad de masa en el sistema métrico que equivale a 0.001 de kilogramo. La cantidad de materia que puede contener un objeto.

graph The process of placing a point on a number line or on a coordinate plane at its proper location.

graficar Proceso de dibujar o trazar un punto en una recta numérica o en un plano de coordenadas en su ubicación correcta.

gratuity Also known as a tip. It is a small amount of money in return for a service.

gratificación También conocida como propina. Es una cantidad pequeña de dinero en retribución por un servicio.

Hh

heptagon A polygon having seven sides.

heptágono Polígono con siete lados.

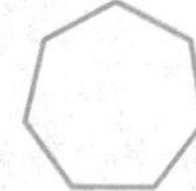

hexagon A polygon having six sides.

hexágono Polígono con seis lados.

histogram A type of bar graph used to display numerical data that have been organized into equal intervals.

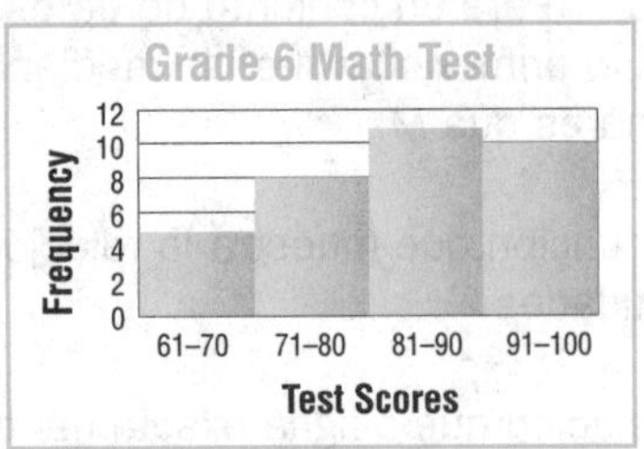

histograma Tipo de gráfica de barras que se usa para exhibir datos que se han organizado en intervalos iguales.

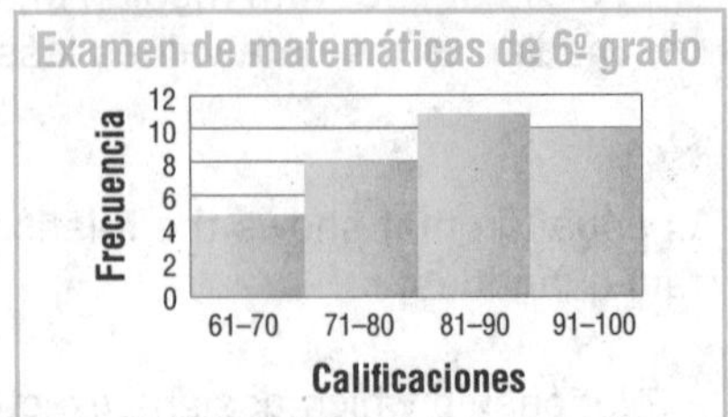

Ii

Identity Property of Zero The sum of an addend and zero is the addend. Example: $5 + 0 = 5$

propiedad de identidad del cero La suma de un sumando y cero es igual al sumando. Ejemplo: $5 + 0 = 5$

independent events Two or more events in which the outcome of one event does not affect the outcome of the other event(s).

eventos independientes Dos o más eventos en los cuales el resultado de uno de ellos no afecta el resultado de los otros eventos.

independent variable The variable in a function with a value that is subject to choice.

variable independiente Variable en una función cuyo valor está sujeto a elección.

indirect measurement Finding a measurement using similar figures to find the length, width, or height of objects that are too difficult to measure directly.

medición indirecta Hallar una medición usando figuras semejantes para calcular el largo, ancho o altura de objetos que son difíciles de medir directamente.

inequality An open sentence that uses $<, >, \neq, \leq$, or $\geq$ to compare two quantities.

desigualdad Enunciado abierto que usa $<, >, \neq, \leq$ o $\geq$ para comparar dos cantidades.

integer Any number from the set $\{\ldots, -4, -3, -2, -1, 0, 1, 2, 3, 4, \ldots\}$, where ... means continues without end.

entero Cualquier número del conjunto $\{\ldots, -4, -3, -2, -1, 0, 1, 2, 3, 4, \ldots\}$, donde ... significa que continúa sin fin.

interquartile range A measure of variation in a set of numerical data. It is the distance between first and third quartiles of the data set.

rango intercuartil Una medida de la variación en un conjunto de datos numéricos. Es la distancia entre el primer y el tercer cuartiles del conjunto de datos.

inverse variation A relationship where the product of x and y is a constant k. As x increases in value, y decreases in value, or as y decreases in value, x increases in value.

variación inversa Relación en la cual el producto de x y y es una constante k. A medida que aumenta el valor de x, disminuye el valor de y o a medida que disminuye el valor de y, aumenta el valor de x.

irrational number A number that cannot be expressed as the ratio of two integers.

número irracional Número que no se puede expresar como el razón de dos enteros.

isosceles triangle A triangle having at least two congruent sides.

triángulo isósceles Triángulo que tiene por lo menos dos lados congruentes.

Kk

kilogram The base unit of mass in the metric system. One kilogram equals 1,000 grams.

kilogramo Unidad básica de masa del sistema métrico. Un kilogramo equivale a 1,000 gramos.

Ll

lateral face In a polyhedron, a face that is not a base.

cara lateral En un poliedro, las caras que no forman las bases.

lateral surface area The sum of the areas of all of the lateral faces of a solid.

área de superficie lateral Suma de las áreas de todas las caras de un sólido.

least common denominator (LCD) The least common multiple of the denominators of two or more fractions. You can use the LCD to compare fractions.

mínimo común denominador (mcd) El menor de los múltiplos de los denominadores de dos o más fracciones. Puedes usar el mínimo común denominador para comparar fracciones.

like fractions Fractions that have the same denominators.

fracciones semejantes Fracciones que tienen los mismos denominadores.

like terms Terms that contain the same variables raised to the same power. Example: 5*x* and 6*x* are like terms.

términos semejante Términos que contienen las mismas variables elevadas a la misma potencia. Ejemplo: 5*x* y 6*x* son *términos semejante*.

line graph A type of statistical graph using lines to show how values change over a period of time.

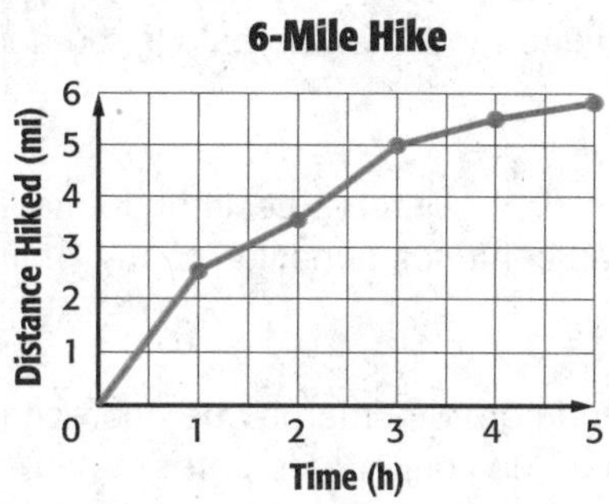

gráfica lineal Tipo de gráfica estadística que usa segmentos de recta para mostrar cómo cambian los valores durante un período de tiempo.

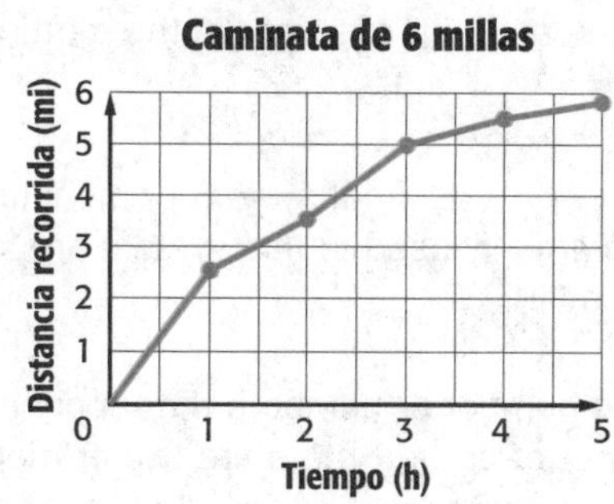

linear expression An algebraic expression in which the variable is raised to the first power.

expresión lineal Expresión algebraica en la cual la variable se eleva a la primera potencia.

linear function A function for which the graph is a straight line.

función lineal Función cuya gráfica es una recta.

linear relationship A relationship for which the graph is a straight line.

relación lineal Una relación para la cual la gráfica es una línea recta.

liter The base unit of capacity in the metric system. The amount of dry or liquid material an object can hold.

litro Unidad básica de capacidad del sistema métrico. La cantidad de materia líquida o sólida que puede contener un objeto.

Mm

markdown An amount by which the regular price of an item is reduced.

rebaja Una cantidad por la cual el precio regular de un artículo se reduce.

markup The amount the price of an item is increased above the price the store paid for the item.

margen de utilidad Cantidad de aumento en el precio de un artículo por encima del precio que paga la tienda por dicho artículo.

mean The sum of the data divided by the number of items in the data set.

media La suma de los datos dividida entre el número total de artículos en el conjunto de datos.

mean absolute deviation A measure of variation in a set of numerical data, computed by adding the distances between each data value and the mean, then dividing by the number of data values.

desviación media absoluta Una medida de variación en un conjunto de datos numéricos que se calcula sumando las distancias entre el valor de cada dato y la media, y luego dividiendo entre el número de valores.

measures of center Numbers that are used to describe the center of a set of data. These measures include the mean, median, and mode.

medidas del centro Números que se usan para describir el centro de un conjunto de datos. Estas medidas incluyen la media, la mediana y la moda.

measures of variation A measure used to describe the distribution of data.

medidas de variación Medida usada para describir la distribución de los datos.

median A measure of center in a set of numerical data. The median of a list of values is the value appearing at the center of a sorted version of the list—or the mean of the two central values, if the list contains an even number of values.

mediana Una medida del centro en un conjunto de dados númericos. La mediana de una lista de valores es el valor que aparace en el centro de una versíon ordenada de la lista, o la media de dos valores centrales si la lista contiene un número par de valores.

meter The base unit of length in the metric system.

metro Unidad fundamental de longitud del sistema métrico.

metric system A decimal system of measures. The prefixes commonly used in this system are kilo-, centi-, and milli-.

sistema métrico Sistema decimal de medidas. Los prefijos más comunes son kilo-, centi- y mili-.

mode The number or numbers that appear most often in a set of data. If there are two or more numbers that occur most often, all of them are modes.

moda El número o números que aparece con más frecuencia en un conjunto de datos. Si hay dos o más números que ocurren con más frecuencia, todosellos son modas.

monomial A number, variable, or product of a number and one or more variables.

monomio Número, variable o producto de un número y una o más variables.

Multiplication Property of Equality If you multiply each side of an equation by the same nonzero number, the two sides remain equal.

propiedad de multiplicación de la igualdad Si multiplicas ambos lados de una ecuación por el mismo número no nulo, lo lados permanecen iguales.

Multiplication Property of Inequality When you multiply each side of an inequality by a negative number, the inequality symbol must be reversed for the inequality to remain true.

propiedad de desigualdad en la multiplicación Cuando se multiplica cada lado de una desigualdad por un número negativo, el símbolo de desigualdad debe invertirse para que la desigualdad siga siendo verdadera.

Multiplicative Identity Property The product of any number and one is the number.

propiedad de identidad de la multiplicación El producto de cualquier número y uno es el mismo número.

Multiplicative Property of Zero The product of any number and zero is zero.

propiedad del cero en la multiplicación El producto de cualquier número y cero es cero.

multiplicative inverse Two numbers with a product of 1. For example, the multiplicative inverse of $\frac{2}{3}$ is $\frac{3}{2}$.

inverso multiplicativo Dos números cuyo producto es 1. Por ejemplo, el inverso multiplicativo de $\frac{2}{3}$ es $\frac{3}{2}$.

Nn

negative exponent Any nonzero number to the negative *n* power. It is the multiplicative inverse of its *n*th power.

exponente negativo Cualquier número que no sea cero a la potencia negative de *n*. Es el inverso multiplicativo de su *en*ésimo potencia.

negative integer An integer that is less than zero. Negative integers are written with a − sign.

entero negativo Número menor que cero. Se escriben con el signo −.

net A two-dimensional figure that can be used to build a three-dimensional figure.

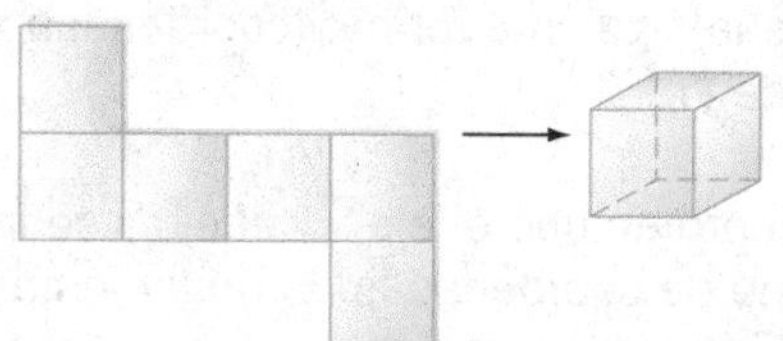

red Figura bidimensional que sirve para hacer una figura tridimensional.

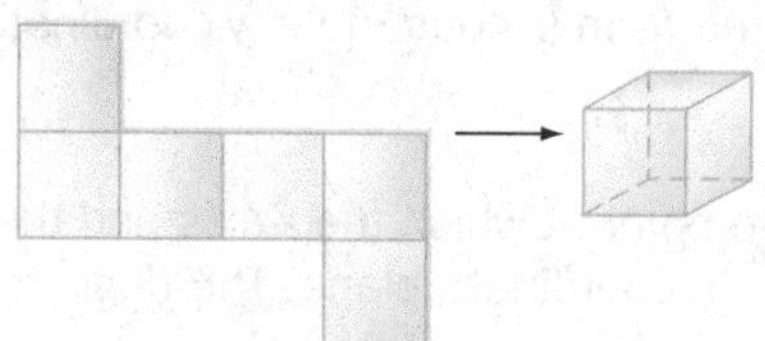

nonagon A polygon having nine sides.

enágono Polígono que tiene nueve lados.

nonlinear function A function for which the graph is *not* a straight line.

nonlinear function Función cuya gráfica *no* es una línea recta.

nonproportional The relationship between two ratios with a rate or ratio that is not constant.

no proporcional Relación entre dos razones cuya tasa o razón no es constante.

numerical expression A combination of numbers and operations.

expresión numérica Combinación de números y operaciones.

Oo

obtuse angle Any angle that measures greater than 90° but less than 180°.

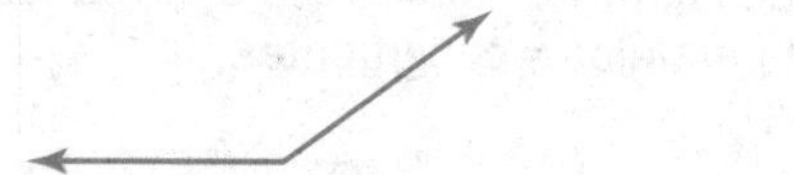

ángulo obtuso Cualquier ángulo que mide más de 90° pero menos de 180°.

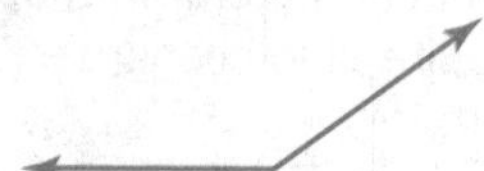

obtuse triangle A triangle having one obtuse angle.

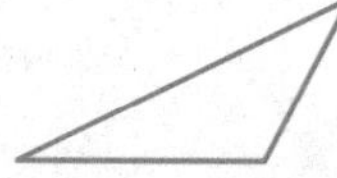

triángulo obtusángulo Triángulo que tiene un ángulo obtuso.

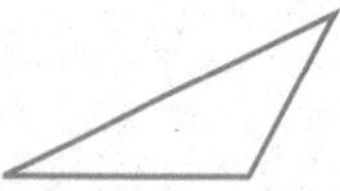

octagon A polygon having eight sides.

octágono Polígono que tiene ocho lados.

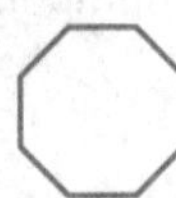

opposites Two integers are opposites if they are represented on the number line by points that are the same distance from zero, but on opposite sides of zero. The sum of two opposites is zero.

opuestos Dos enteros son opuestos si, en la recta numérica, están representados por puntos que equidistan de cero, pero en direcciones opuestas. La suma de dos opuestos es cero.

order of operations The rules to follow when more than one operation is used in a numerical expression.

1. Evaluate the expressions inside grouping symbols.
2. Evaluate all powers.
3. Multiply and divide in order from left to right.
4. Add and subtract in order from left to right.

orden de las operaciones Reglas a seguir cuando se usa más de una operación en una expresión numérica.

1. Primero, evalúa las expresiones dentro de los símbolos de agrupación.
2. Evalúa todas las potencias.
3. Multiplica y divide en orden de izquierda a derecha.
4. Suma y resta en orden de izquierda a derecha.

ordered pair A pair of numbers used to locate a point in the coordinate plane. An ordered pair is written in the form (x-coordinate, y-coordinate).

par ordenado Par de números que se utiliza para ubicar un punto en un plano de coordenadas. Se escribe de la siguiente forma: (coordenada x, coordenada y).

origin The point at which the x-axis and the y-axis intersect in a coordinate plane. The origin is at (0, 0).

origen Punto en que el eje x y el eje y se intersecan en un plano de coordenadas. El origen está ubicado en (0, 0).

outcome Any one of the possible results of an action. For example, 4 is an outcome when a number cube is rolled.

resultado Cualquiera de los resultados posibles de una acción. Por ejemplo, 4 puede ser un resultado al lanzar un cubo numerado.

outlier A data value that is either much *greater* or much *less* than the median.

valor atípico Valor de los datos que es mucho *mayor* o mucho *menor* que la mediana.

Pp

parallel lines Lines in a plane that never intersect.

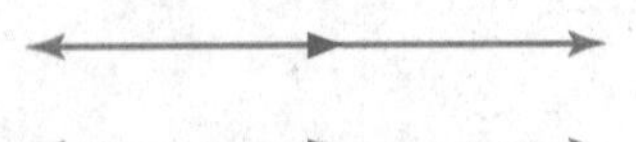

rectas paralelas Rectas en un plano que nunca se intersecan.

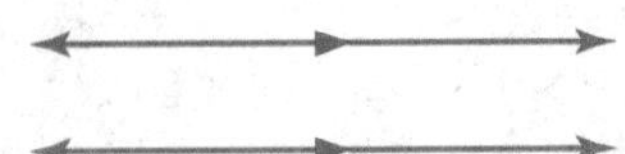

parallelogram A quadrilateral with opposite sides parallel and opposite sides congruent.

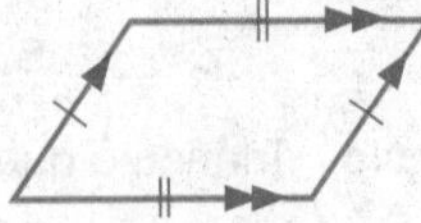

paralelogramo Cuadrilátero cuyos lados opuestos son paralelos y congruentes.

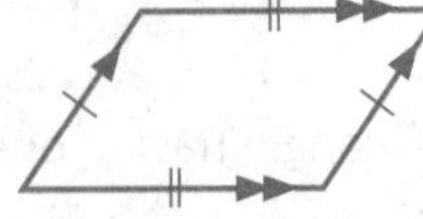

pentagon A polygon having five sides.

percent equation An equation that describes the relationship between the part, whole, and percent.

$$\text{part} = \text{percent} \cdot \text{whole}$$

percent error A ratio that compares the inaccuracy of an estimate (amount of error) to the actual amount.

percent of change A ratio that compares the change in a quantity to the original amount.

$$\text{percent of change} = \frac{\text{amount of change}}{\text{original amount}}$$

percent of decrease A negative percent of change.

percent of increase A positive percent of change.

percent proportion One ratio or fraction that compares part of a quantity to the whole quantity. The other ratio is the equivalent percent written as a fraction with a denominator of 100.

$$\frac{\text{part}}{\text{whole}} = \frac{\text{percent}}{100}$$

perfect squares Numbers with square roots that are whole numbers. 25 is a perfect square because the square root of 25 is 5.

permutation An arrangement, or listing, of objects in which order is important.

perpendicular lines Lines that meet or cross each other to form right angles.

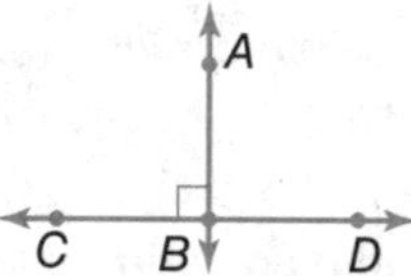

pi The ratio of the circumference of a circle to its diameter. The Greek letter π represents this number. The value of pi is 3.1415926. . . . Approximations for pi are 3.14 and $\frac{22}{7}$.

plane A two-dimensional flat surface that extends in all directions.

pentágono Polígono que tiene cinco lados.

ecuación porcentual Ecuación que describe la relación entre la parte, el todo y el por ciento.

$$\text{parte} = \text{por ciento} \cdot \text{todo}$$

porcentaje de error Una razón que compara la inexactitud de una estimación (cantidad del error) con la cantidad real.

porcentaje de cambio Razón que compara el cambio en una cantidad a la cantidad original.

$$\text{porcentaje de cambio} = \frac{\text{cantidad del cambio}}{\text{cantidad original}}$$

porcentaje de disminución Porcentaje de cambio negativo.

porcentaje de aumento Porcentaje de cambio positivo.

proporción porcentual Razón o fracción que compara parte de una cantidad a toda la cantidad. La otra razón es el porcentaje equivalente escrito como fracción con 100 de denominador.

$$\frac{\text{parte}}{\text{todo}} = \frac{\text{porcentaje}}{100}$$

cuadrados perfectos Números cuya raíz cuadrada es un número entero. 25 es un cuadrado perfecto porque la raíz cuadrada de 25 es 5.

permutación Arreglo o lista de objetos en la cual el orden es importante.

rectas perpendiculares Rectas que al encontrarse o cruzarse forman ángulos rectos.

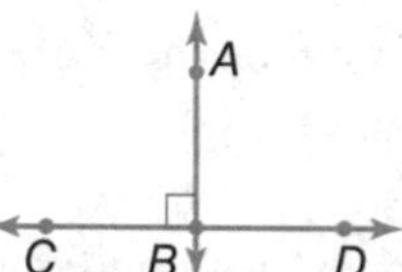

pi Relación entre la circunferencia de un círculo y su diámetro. La letra griega π representa este número. El valor de pi es 3.1415926. . . . Las aproximaciones de pi son 3.14 y $\frac{22}{7}$.

plano Superficie bidimensional que se extiende en todas direcciones.

polygon A simple closed figure formed by three or more straight line segments.

polígono Figura cerrada simple formada por tres o más segmentos de recta.

polyhedron A three-dimensional figure with faces that are polygons.

poliedro Una figura tridimensional con caras que son polígonos.

population The entire group of items or individuals from which the samples under consideration are taken.

población El grupo total de individuos o de artículos del cual se toman las muestras bajo estudio.

positive integer An integer that is greater than zero. They are written with or without a + sign.

entero positivo Entero que es mayor que cero; se escribe con o sin el signo +.

powers Numbers expressed using exponents. The power 3^2 is read *three to the second power,* or *three squared.*

potencias Números que se expresan usando exponentes. La potencia 3^2 se lee *tres a la segunda potencia o tres al cuadrado.*

precision The ability of a measurement to be consistently reproduced.

precisión Capacidad que tiene una medición de poder reproducirse consistentemente.

principal The amount of money deposited or borrowed.

capital Cantidad de dinero que se deposita o se toma prestada.

prism A polyhedron with two parallel congruent faces called bases.

prisma Un poliedro con dos caras congruentes paralelas llamadas bases.

probability The chance that some event will happen. It is the ratio of the number of favorable outcomes to the number of possible outcomes.

probabilidad La posibilidad de que suceda un evento. Es la razón del número de resultados favorables al número de resultados posibles.

probability model A model used to assign probabilities to outcomes of a chance process by examining the nature of the process.

modelo de probabilidad Un modelo usado para asignar probabilidades a resultados de un proceso aleatorio examinando la naturaleza del proceso.

properties Statements that are true for any number or variable.

propiedades Enunciados que son verdaderos para cualquier número o variable.

proportion An equation stating that two ratios or rates are equivalent.

proporción Ecuación que indica que dos razones o tasas son equivalentes.

proportional The relationship between two ratios with a constant rate or ratio.

proporcional Relación entre dos razones con una tasa o razón constante.

pyramid A polyhedron with one base that is a polygon and three or more triangular faces that meet at a common vertex.

pirámide Un poliedro con una base que es un polígono y tres o más caras triangulares que se encuentran en un vértice común.

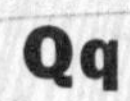

quadrant One of the four regions into which the two perpendicular number lines of the coordinate plane separate the plane.

y-axis
Quadrant II Quadrant I
O x-axis
Quadrant III Quadrant IV

quadrilateral A closed figure having four sides and four angles.

quartile A value that divides the data set into four equal parts.

cuadrante Una de las cuatro regiones en que dos rectas numéricas perpendiculares dividen el plano de coordenadas.

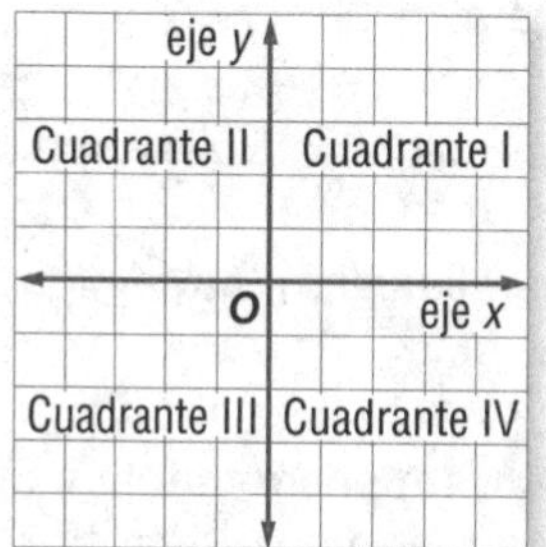

cuadrilátero Figura cerrada que tiene cuatro lados y cuatro ángulos.

cuartil Valor que divide el conjunto de datos en cuatro partes iguales.

radical sign The symbol used to indicate a nonnegative square root, $\sqrt{\ }$.

radius The distance from the center of a circle to any point on the circle.

random Outcomes occur at random if each outcome occurs by chance. For example, rolling a number on a number cube occurs at random.

range The set of output values for a function.

range The difference between the greatest and least data value.

rate A ratio that compares two quantities with different kinds of units.

rate of change A rate that describes how one quantity changes in relation to another. A rate of change is usually expressed as a unit rate.

signo radical Símbolo que se usa para indicar una raíz cuadrada no negativa, $\sqrt{\ }$.

radio Distancia desde el centro de un círculo hasta cualquiera de sus puntos.

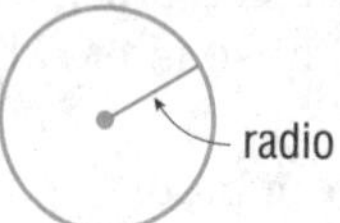

azar Los resultados ocurren aleatoriamente si cada resultado ocurre por casualidad. Por ejemplo, sacar un número en un cubo numerado ocurre al azar.

rango Conjunto de valores de salida para una función.

rango La diferencia entre el número mayor y el menor en un conjunto de datos.

tasa Razón que compara dos cantidades que tienen distintas unidades de medida.

tasa de cambio Tasa que describe cómo cambia una cantidad con respecto a otra. Por lo general, se expresa como tasa unitaria.

rational numbers The set of numbers that can be written in the form $\frac{a}{b}$, where a and b are integers and $b \neq 0$.
Examples: $1 = \frac{1}{1}, \frac{2}{9}, -2.3 = -2\frac{3}{10}$

real numbers A set made up of rational and irrational numbers.

reciprocal The multiplicative inverse of a number.

rectangle A parallelogram having four right angles.

rectangular prism A prism that has two parallel congruent bases that are rectangles.

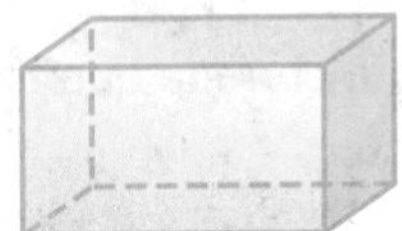

reduction An image smaller than the original.

regular polygon A polygon that has all sides congruent and all angles congruent.

regular pyramid A pyramid whose base is a regular polygon and in which the segment from the vertex to the center of the base is the altitude.

relation Any set of ordered pairs.

relative frequency A ratio that compares the frequency of each category to the total.

repeating decimal The decimal form of a rational number.

rhombus A parallelogram having four congruent sides.

right angle An angle that measures exactly 90°.

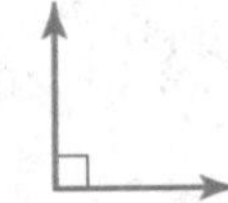

números racionales Conjunto de números que puede escribirse en la forma $\frac{a}{b}$ donde a y b son números enteros y $b \neq 0$.
Ejemplos: $1 = \frac{1}{1}, \frac{2}{9}, -2.3 = -2\frac{3}{10}$

números reales Conjunto de números racionales e irracionales.

recíproco El inverso multiplicativo de un número.

rectángulo Paralelogramo con cuatro ángulos rectos.

prisma rectangular Un prisma con dos bases paralelas congruentes que son rectángulos.

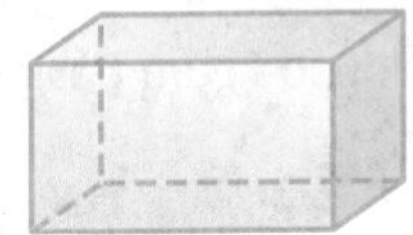

reducción Imagen más pequeña que la original.

polígono regular Polígono con todos los lados y todos los ángulos congruentes.

pirámide regular Pirámide cuya base es un polígono regular y en la cual el segmento desde el vértice hasta el centro de la base es la altura.

relación Cualquier conjunto de pares ordenados.

frecuencia relativa Razón que compara la frecuencia de cada categoría al total.

decimal periódico La forma decimal de un número racional.

rombo Paralelogramo que tiene cuatro lados congruentes.

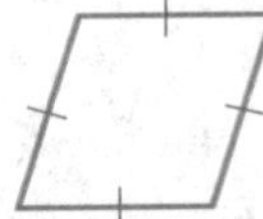

ángulo recto Ángulo que mide exactamente 90°.

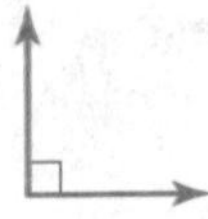

right triangle A triangle having one right angle.

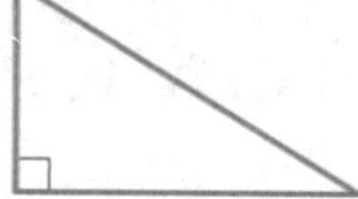

triángulo rectángulo Triángulo que tiene un ángulo recto.

Ss

sales tax An additional amount of money charged on items that people buy.

impuesto sobre las ventas Cantidad de dinero adicional que se cobra por los artículos que se compran.

sample A randomly selected group chosen for the purpose of collecting data.

muestra Grupo escogido al azar o aleatoriamente que se usa con el propósito de recoger datos.

sample space The set of all possible outcomes of a probability experiment.

espacio muestral Conjunto de todos los resultados posibles de un experimento probabilístico.

scale The scale that gives the ratio that compares the measurements of a drawing or model to the measurements of the real object.

escala Razón que compara las medidas de un dibujo o modelo a las medidas del objeto real.

scale drawing A drawing that is used to represent objects that are too large or too small to be drawn at actual size.

dibujo a escala Dibujo que se usa para representar objetos que son demasiado grandes o demasiado pequeños como para dibujarlos de tamaño natural.

scale factor A scale written as a ratio without units in simplest form.

factor de escala Escala escrita como una razón sin unidades en forma simplificada.

scale model A model used to represent objects that are too large or too small to be built at actual size.

modelo a escala Réplica de un objeto real, el cual es demasiado grande o demasiado pequeño como para construirlo de tamaño natural.

scalene triangle A triangle having no congruent sides.

triángulo escaleno Triángulo sin lados congruentes.

scatter plot In a scatter plot, two sets of related data are plotted as ordered pairs on the same graph.

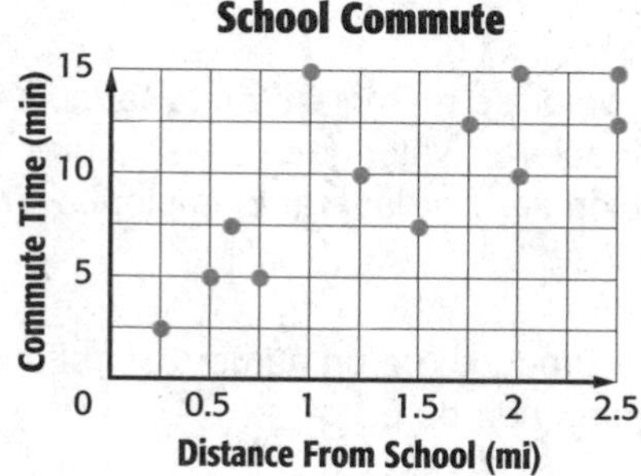

diagrama de dispersión Diagrama en que dos conjuntos de datos relacionados aparecen graficados como pares ordenados en la misma gráfica.

selling price The amount the customer pays for an item.

precio de venta Cantidad de dinero que paga un consumidor por un artículo.

semicircle Half of a circle. The formula for the area of a semicircle is $A = \frac{1}{2}\pi r^2$.

semicírculo Medio círculo La fórmula para el área de un semicírculo es $A = \frac{1}{2}\pi r^2$.

sequence An ordered list of numbers, such as 0, 1, 2, 3 or 2, 4, 6, 8.

sucesión Lista ordenada de números, como 0, 1, 2, 3 ó 2, 4, 6, 8.

similar figures Figures that have the same shape but not necessarily the same size.

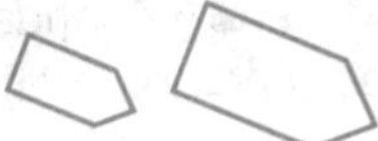

figuras semejantes Figuras que tienen la misma forma, pero no necesariamente el mismo tamaño.

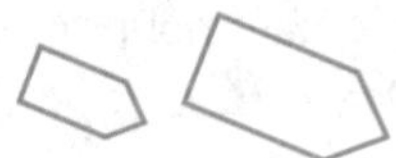

similar solids Solids with the same shape. Their corresponding linear measures are proportional.

sólidos semejantes Sólidos con la misma forma. Sus medidas lineales correspondientes son proporcionales.

simple event One outcome or a collection of outcomes.

eventos simples Un resultado o una colección de resultados.

simple interest The amount paid or earned for the use of money. The formula for simple interest is $I = prt$.

interés simple Cantidad que se paga o que se gana por el uso del dinero. La fórmula para calcular el interés simple es $I = prt$.

simple random sample An unbiased sample where each item or person in the population is as likely to be chosen as any other.

muestra aleatoria simple Muestra de una población que tiene la misma probabilidad de escogerse que cualquier otra.

simplest form An expression is in simplest form when it is replaced by an equivalent expression having no like terms or parentheses.

expresión mínima Expresión en su forma más simple cuando es reemplazada por una expresión equivalente que no tiene términos similares ni paréntesis.

simplify Write an expression in simplest form.

simplificar Escribir una expresión en su forma más simple.

simulation An experiment that is designed to model the action in a given situation.

simulación Un experimento diseñado para modelar la acción en una situación dada.

slant height The height of each lateral face.

altura oblicua Altura de cada cara lateral.

slope The rate of change between any two points on a line. It is the ratio of vertical change to horizontal change. The slope tells how steep the line is.

pendiente Razón de cambio entre cualquier par de puntos en una recta. Es la razón del cambio vertical al cambio horizontal. La pendiente indica el grado de inclinación de la recta.

solution A replacement value for the variable in an open sentence. A value for the variable that makes an equation true. Example: The *solution* of $12 = x + 7$ is 5.

solución Valor de reemplazo de la variable en un enunciado abierto. Valor de la variable que hace que una ecuación sea verdadera. Ejemplo: La *solución* de $12 = x + 7$ es 5.

square The product of a number and itself. 36 is the square of 6.

cuadrado Producto de un número por sí mismo. 36 es el cuadrado de 6.

square A parallelogram having four right angles and four congruent sides.

square root The factors multiplied to form perfect squares.

squared The product of a number and itself. 36 is the square of 6.

standard form Numbers written without exponents.

statistics The study of collecting, organizing, and interpreting data.

straight angle An angle that measures exactly 180°.

Subtraction Property of Equality If you subtract the same number from each side of an equation, the two sides remain equal.

Subtraction Property of Inequality If you subtract the same number from each side of an inequality, the inequality remains true.

supplementary angles Two angles are supplementary if the sum of their measures is 180°.

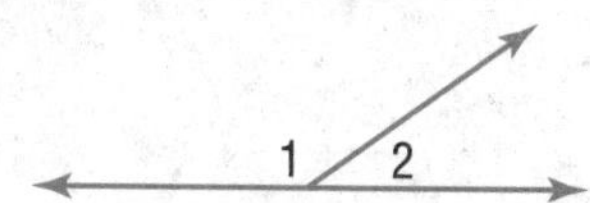

∠1 and ∠2 are supplementary angles.

surface area The sum of the areas of all the surfaces (faces) of a three-dimensional figure.

survey A question or set of questions designed to collect data about a specific group of people, or population.

systematic random sample A sample where the items or people are selected according to a specific time or item interval.

cuadrado Paralelogramo con cuatro ángulos rectos y cuatro lados congruentes.

al cuadrado Factores multiplicados para formar cuadrados perfectos.

raíz cuadrada El producto de un número por sí mismo. 36 es el cuadrado de 6.

forma estándar Números escritos sin exponentes.

estadística Estudio que consiste en recopilar, organizar e interpretar datos.

ángulo llano Ángulo que mide exactamente 180°.

propiedad de sustracción de la igualdad Si restas el mismo número de ambos lados de una ecuación, los dos lados permanecen iguales.

propiedad de desigualdad en la resta Si se resta el mismo número a cada lado de una desigualdad, la desigualdad sigue siendo verdadera.

ángulos suplementarios Dos ángulos son suplementarios si la suma de sus medidas es 180°.

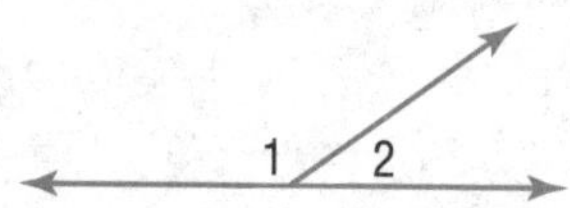

∠1 y ∠2 son suplementarios.

área de superficie La suma de las áreas de todas las superficies (caras) de una figura tridimensional.

encuesta Pregunta o conjunto de preguntas diseñadas para recoger datos sobre un grupo específico de personas o población.

muestra aleatoria sistemática Muestra en que los elementos o personas se eligen según un intervalo de tiempo o elemento específico.

Tt

term Each number in a sequence.

term A number, a variable, or a product or quotient of numbers and variables.

terminating decimal A repeating decimal which has a repeating digit of 0.

término Cada número en una sucesión.

término Número, variable, producto o cociente de números y de variables.

decimal finito Un decimal periódico que tiene un dígito que se repite que es 0.

theoretical probability The ratio of the number of ways an event can occur to the number of possible outcomes. It is based on what *should* happen when conducting a probability experiment.

probabilidad teórica Razón del número de maneras en que puede ocurrir un evento al número de resultados posibles. Se basa en lo que *debería* pasar cuando se conduce un experimento probabilístico.

three-dimensional figure A figure with length, width, and height.

figura tridimensional Figura que tiene largo, ancho y alto.

third quartile For a data set with median M, the third quartile is the median of the data values greater than M.

tercer cuartil Para un conjunto de datos con la mediana M, el tercer cuartil es la mediana de los valores mayores que M.

tip Also known as a gratuity, it is a small amount of money in return for a service.

propina También conocida como gratificación; es una cantidad pequeña de dinero en recompensa por un servicio.

transversal The third line formed when two parallel lines are intersected.

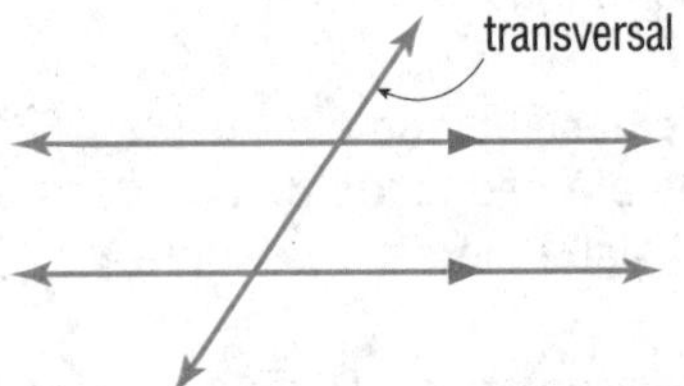

transversal Tercera recta que se forma cuando se intersecan dos rectas paralelas.

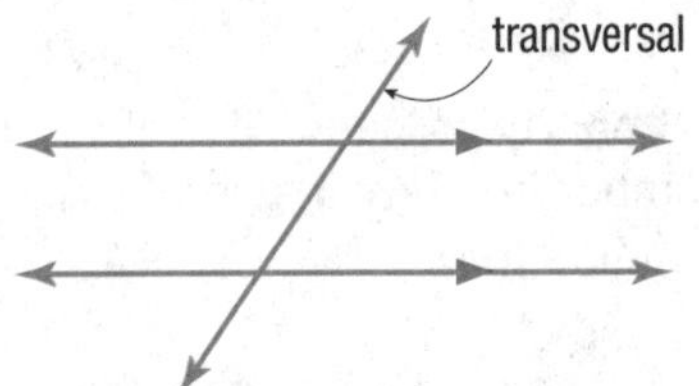

trapezoid A quadrilateral with one pair of parallel sides.

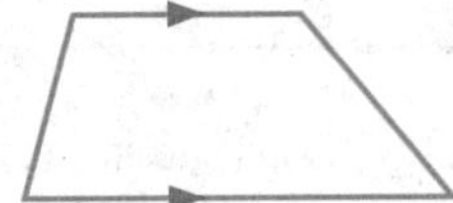

trapecio Cuadrilátero con un único par de lados paralelos.

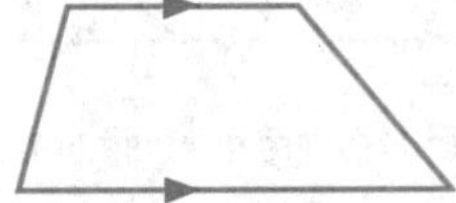

tree diagram A diagram used to show the sample space.

diagrama de árbol Diagrama que se usa para mostrar el espacio muestral.

triangle A figure with three sides and three angles.

triángulo Figura con tres lados y tres ángulos.

triangular prism A prism that has two parallel congruent bases that are triangles.

prisma triangular Un prisma que tiene dos bases congruentes paralelas que triángulos.

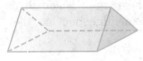

two-step equation An equation having two different operations.

ecuación de dos pasos Ecuación que contiene dos operaciones distintas.

two-step inequality An inequality than contains two operations.

desigualdad de dos pasos Desigualdad que contiene dos operaciones.

Uu

unbiased sample A sample representative of the entire population.

muestra no sesgada Muestra que se selecciona de modo que se representativa de la población entera.

unfair game A game where there is not a chance of each player being equally likely to win.

juego injusto Juego donde cada jugador no tiene la misma posibilidad de ganar.

uniform probability model A probability model which assigns equal probability to all outcomes.

modelo de probabilidad uniforme Un modelo de probabilidad que asigna igual probabilidad a todos los resultados.

unit rate A rate that is simplified so that it has a denominator of 1 unit.

tasa unitaria Tasa simplificada para que tenga un denominador igual a 1.

unit ratio A unit rate where the denominator is one unit.

razón unitaria Tasa unitaria en que el denominador es la unidad.

unlike fractions Fractions with different denominators.

fracciones con distinto denominador Fracciones cuyos denominadores son diferentes.

Vv

variable A symbol, usually a letter, used to represent a number in mathematical expressions or sentences.

variable Símbolo, por lo general una letra, que se usa para representar un número en expresiones o enunciados matemáticos.

vertex A vertex of an angle is the common endpoint of the rays forming the angle.

vertex

vértice El vértice de un ángulo es el extremo común de los rayos que lo forman.

vértice

vertex The point where three or more faces of a polyhedron intersect.

vértice El punto donde tres o más caras de un poliedro se cruzan.

vertex The point at the tip of a cone.

vértice El punto en la punta de un cono.

vertical angles Opposite angles formed by the intersection of two lines. Vertical angles are congruent.

1 2

$\angle 1$ and $\angle 2$ are vertical angles.

ángulos opuestos por el vértice Ángulos opuestos formados por la intersección de dos rectas. Los ángulos opuestos por el vértice son congruentes.

1 2

$\angle 1$ y $\angle 2$ son ángulos opuestos por el vértice.

visual overlap A visual demonstration that compares the centers of two distributions with their variation, or spread.

superposición visual Una demostración visual que compara los centros de dos distribuciones con su variación, o magnitud.

volume The number of cubic units needed to fill the space occupied by a solid.

volumen Número de unidades cúbicas que se requieren para llenar el espacio que ocupa un sólido.

voluntary response sample A sample which involves only those who want to participate in the sampling.

muestra de respuesta voluntaria Muestra que involucra sólo aquellos que quieren participar en el muestreo.

x-axis The horizontal number line in a coordinatWe plane.

eje x La recta numérica horizontal en el plano de coordenadas.

x-coordinate The first number of an ordered pair. It corresponds to a number on the x-axis.

coordenada x El primer número de un par ordenado. Corresponde a un número en el eje x.

y-axis The vertical number line in a coordinate plane.

eje y La recta numérica vertical en el plano de coordenadas.

y-coordinate The second number of an ordered pair. It corresponds to a number on the y-axis.

coordenada y El segundo número de un par ordenado. Corresponde a un número en el eje y.

zero pair The result when one positive counter is paired with one negative counter. The value of a zero pair is 0.

par nulo Resultado de hacer coordinar una ficha positiva con una negativa. El valor de un par nulo es 0.

Chapter 1 Integers

Chapter 1 Are You Ready?

1. 6 **3.** 24

4–9.

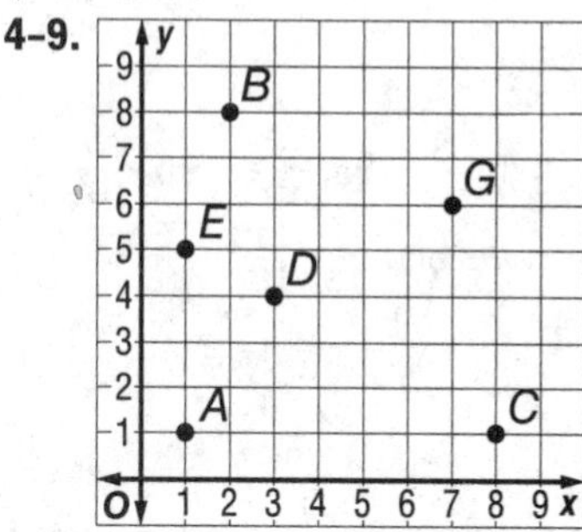

Lesson 1-1 Independent Practice

1. 9 **3.** −53

5

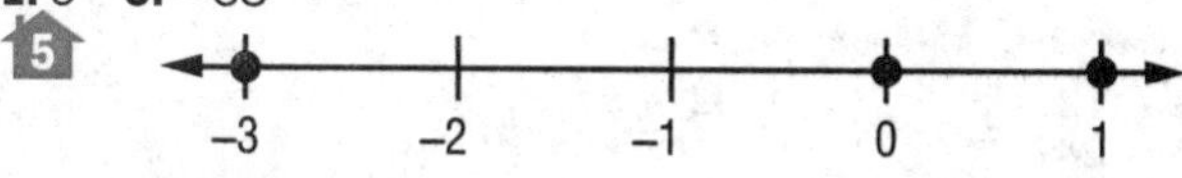

7. 10 **9** 8 **11.** −7 **13.** $299.97; |−200| + |−40| + |−60| = 200 + 40 + 60 = 300 **15.** always; It is true if *A* and *B* are both positive or if *A* or *B* is negative, and if both *A* and *B* are negative. **17.** A

Lesson 1-1 Extra Practice

19. 12

21.

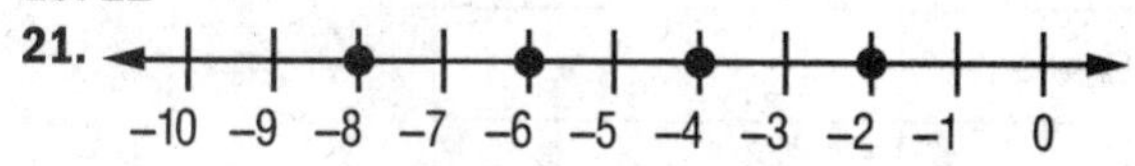

23. 11 **25.** 25 **27.** 5 **29.** C **31.** Wednesday **33.** (0, −2); *y*-axis **35.** (1, 1); I

36–39.

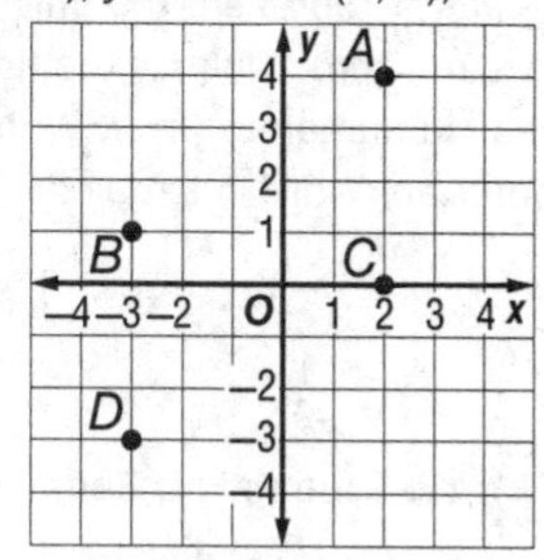

Lesson 1-2 Independent Practice

1. −38 **3.** 16 **5** 0 **7.** 9 **9.** −4 **11** green; profit of $1; white; profit of $3; black; profit of $3 **13.** Sample answer: In science, atoms may contain 2 positive charges and 2 negative charges. In business, a stock's value may fall 0.75 one day and rise 0.75 the next day. **15.** *a* **17.** *m* + (−15)

Lesson 1-2 Extra Practice

19. 13 **21.** −6 **23.** 15 **25.** 22 **27.** −19 **29.** −5 + (−15) + 12; The team has lost a total of 8 yards. **31.** D **33.** −8 + (−3) = −11 **35.** −8 **37.** 4 **39.** 5

Lesson 1-3 Independent Practice

1. −10 **3** −12 **5.** −30 **7.** 23 **9.** 104 **11.** 0 **13** **a.** 2,415 ft **b.** 3,124 ft **c.** 627 ft **d.** 8 ft **15.** 16 **17.** Sample answer: −5 − 11 = −5 + (−11) = −16; Add 5 and 11 and keep the negative sign. **19.** He did not find the additive inverse of −18. −15 − (−18) = −15 + 18 or 3. The correct answer is 3. **21.** D

Lesson 1-3 Extra Practice

23. 35 **25.** −14 **27.** 6 **29.** 15 **31.** 11 **33.** 1 **35.** A **37.** 10 − 12 **39.** 195 **41.** 12 **43.** 2

Problem-Solving Investigation Look for a Pattern

Case 3. Add the previous 2 terms; 89, 144
Case 5. 13 toothpicks

Lesson 1-4 Independent Practice

1. −96 **3.** 36 **5** −64 **7** 5(−650); −3,250; Ethan burns 3,250 Calories each week. **9.** 5 black T-shirts

11.

×	+	−
+	+	−
−	−	+

Sample answer: When you multiply a negative and a positive integer, the product is negative. When you multiply two negative integers the product is positive. **13.** Sample answer: Evaluate −7 + 7 first. Since −7 + 7 = 0, and any number times 0 is 0, the value of the expression is 0. **15.** D

Lesson 1-4 Extra Practice

17. 160 **19.** −64 **21.** −45 **23.** 12(−4); −48; Lily's gift card has $48 less than its starting amount. **25.** 16 **27.** −12 **29.** 648 **31.** −243 **33.** Sample answer: The answer should be −24. A negative multiplied by a negative will be positive. Then, if it is multiplied by a negative it will be negative. **35.** 8(−15); −120 **37.** A **39.** < **41.** >

43.

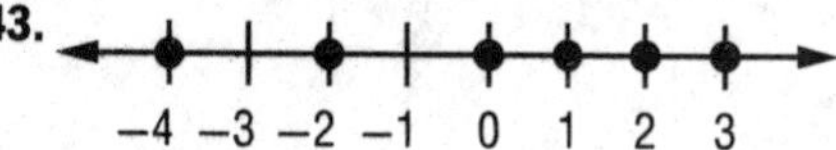

Lesson 1-5 Independent Practice

1. −10 **3** 5 **5.** −11 **7.** −2 **9.** −3 **11.** −6 **13** −$60 miles per hour **15.** 4 **17.** 16 **19.** No; Sample answer: 9 ÷ 3 ≠ 3 ÷ 9 **21.** −2 **23.** B

Lesson 1-5 Extra Practice

25. 9 **27.** 4 **29.** 9 **31.** −12 **33.** 2 **35.** −10°F; The boiling point decreases 10°F at an altitude of 5,000 ft. **37.** B **39.** 4; Sample answer: Christopher answered 6 questions incorrectly. If each question is worth the same, each incorrect answer is worth −24 ÷ 6 or −4 points. So, Nythia answered −16 ÷ (−4) or 4 questions incorrectly. **41.** −9 **43.** 5 **45.** III

Chapter Review Vocabulary Check

1. additive **3.** integers **5.** opposites

Chapter Review Key Concept Check

1. not correct; $|-5| + |2| = 5 + 2$ or 7 **3.** not correct; $-24 \div |-2| = -24 \div 2 = -12$

Chapter Review Problem Solving

1.

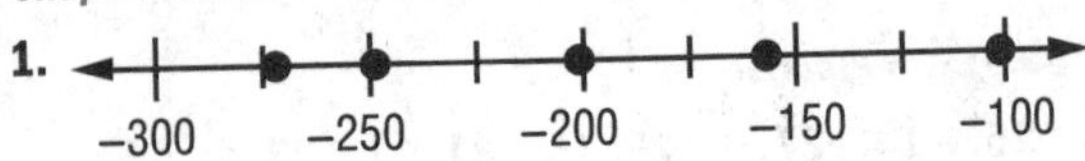

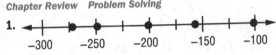

3. 100°C **5.** 4(−2); $33

Chapter 2 Rational Numbers

Chapter 2 Are You Ready?

1. $\frac{2}{3}$ **3.** $\frac{8}{11}$

4–7.

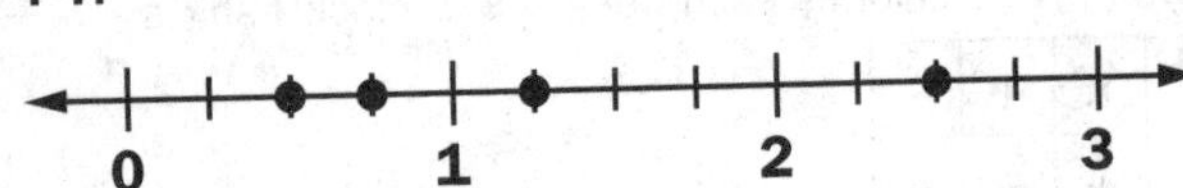

Lesson 2-1 Independent Practice

1. 0.5 **3** 0.125 **5.** −0.66 **7.** 5.875 **9.** $-0.\overline{8}$ **11.** $-0.\overline{72}$ **13.** $-\frac{1}{5}$ **15.** $5\frac{24}{25}$ **17** $10\frac{1}{2}$ **19.** Sample answer: $\frac{3}{5}$ **21.** Sample answer: $3\frac{1}{7} \approx 3.14286$ and $3\frac{10}{71} \approx 3.14085$; Since 3.1415926... is between $3\frac{1}{7}$ and $3\frac{10}{71}$, Archimedes was correct.

Lesson 2-1 Extra Practice

23. 0.8 **25.** $-0.\overline{4}$ **27.** 0.75 **29.** $\frac{17}{50}$ **31.** $-\frac{13}{1}$ **33.** $-\frac{16}{5}$ **35.** D **37.** B **39.** 0.1

41–43.

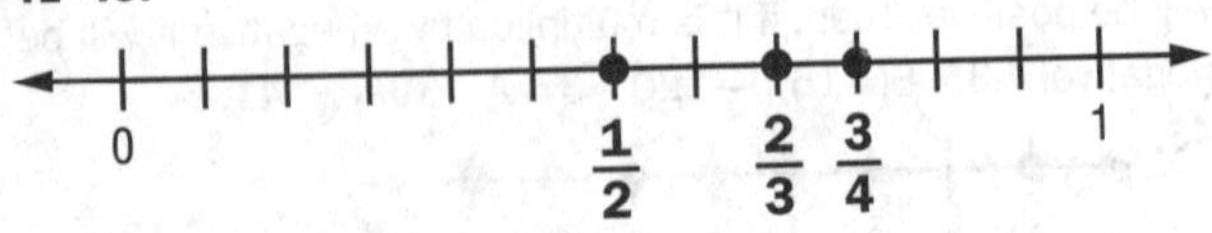

Lesson 2-2 Independent Practice

1. >

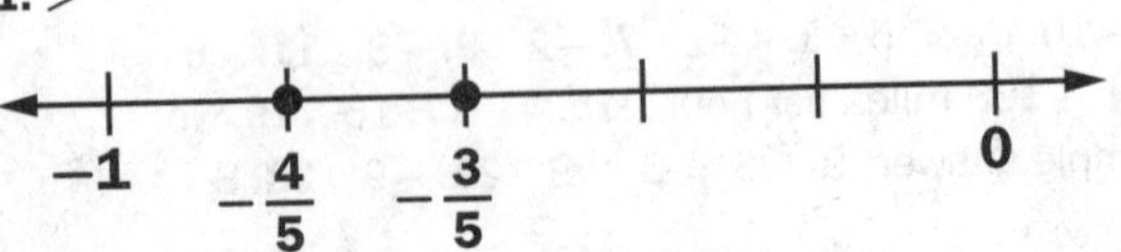

3. > **5** first quiz **7.** $-\frac{5}{8}$, −0.62, −0.615 **9** < **11.** Yes; $69\frac{1}{8} < 69\frac{6}{8}$. **13.** Sample answer: $\frac{63}{32}$ is closest to 2 because the difference of $\frac{63}{32}$ and 2 is the least.

Lesson 2-2 Extra Practice

15. < **17.** < **19.** Jim; $\frac{10}{16} > \frac{4}{15}$ **21.** −1.4, −1.25, $-1\frac{1}{25}$ **23.** C **25.** D **27.** > **29.** > **31.** >

Lesson 2-3 Independent Practice

1. $1\frac{4}{7}$ **3.** $-\frac{2}{3}$ **5** $-1\frac{1}{2}$ **7** $\frac{3}{14}$ **9a.** $\frac{33}{100}$ **9b.** $\frac{67}{100}$ **9c.** $\frac{41}{100}$ **11.** Sample answer: $\frac{11}{18}$ and $\frac{5}{18}$; $\frac{11}{18} - \frac{5}{18} = \frac{6}{18}$, which simplifies to $\frac{1}{3}$. **13.** C

Lesson 2-3 Extra Practice

15. $-1\frac{2}{3}$ **17.** $\frac{1}{4}$ **19.** $\frac{1}{9}$ **21.** $1\frac{47}{100}$ **23.** $\frac{1}{2}$c **25.** D **27.** 4 **29.** < **31.** < **33.** 28 **35.** 60

Lesson 2-4 Independent Practice

1 $\frac{13}{24}$ **3.** $1\frac{2}{5}$ **5.** $\frac{4}{9}$ **7.** $-\frac{26}{45}$ **9.** $1\frac{11}{18}$

11 Subtraction; Sample answer: To find how much time remained, subtract $\left(\frac{1}{6} + \frac{1}{4}\right)$ from $\frac{2}{3}$; $\frac{1}{4}$ h

13.

Homework	Fraction of Time	
	Pepita	Francisco
Math	$\frac{1}{6}$	$\frac{1}{2}$
English	$\frac{2}{3}$	$\frac{1}{8}$
Science	$\frac{1}{6}$	$\frac{3}{8}$

15. Sample answer: Let $\frac{1}{a}$ and $\frac{1}{b}$ represent the unit fractions, where *a* and *b* are not zero. Multiply the first numerator by *b* and the second numerator by *a*. Write the product over the denominator *ab*. Write in simplest form. **17.** C

Lesson 2-4 Extra Practice

19. $\frac{19}{30}$ **21.** $\frac{11}{20}$ **23.** $-\frac{13}{24}$ **25.** Subtraction; Sample answer: To find how much more turkey Makalaya bought, subtract $\frac{1}{4}$ from $\frac{5}{8}$; $\frac{3}{8}$ lb **27.** Theresa did not rename the fractions using the LCD. $\frac{5}{20} + \frac{12}{20} = \frac{17}{20}$ **29.** I **31.** $1\frac{2}{5}$ **33.** $1\frac{1}{100}$ **35.** $7\frac{7}{10}$ **37.** 26 **39.** 27

Lesson 2-5 Independent Practice

1. $9\frac{5}{9}$ **3.** $8\frac{3}{5}$ **5** $7\frac{5}{12}$ **7.** $4\frac{14}{15}$ **9.** $4\frac{1}{3}$

11 Subtraction; the width is shorter than the length; $1\frac{3}{4}$ ft

13. −5 **15.** $13\frac{5}{9}$ **17.** Sample answer: A board with a length of $3\frac{7}{8}$ ft needs to be cut from a $5\frac{1}{2}$–foot existing board. How much wood will be left after the cut is made?; $1\frac{5}{8}$ ft **19.** B

Lesson 2-5 Extra Practice

21. $18\frac{17}{24}$ **23.** $7\frac{5}{7}$ **25.** $5\frac{7}{8}$ **27.** Subtraction twice; the amount of flour is less than the original amount; $2\frac{2}{3}$ c **29.** $7\frac{1}{8}$ yd **31.** D **33.** 5; 8; 40 **35.** 5; 11; 55 **37.** 14 mi; Sample answer: $6\frac{4}{5} \approx 7$ and $1\frac{3}{4} \approx 2$; $7 \times 2 = 14$

Problem-Solving Investigation Draw a Diagram

Case 3. $\frac{3}{8}$ **Case 5.** $\frac{1}{4}$ mi

Lesson 2-6 Independent Practice

1. $\frac{3}{32}$ **3.** $-4\frac{1}{2}$ **5.** $\frac{1}{6}$ **7** $\frac{3}{8}$ **9.** −1 **11** $\frac{1}{16}$ **13.** $\frac{1}{3} \times \left(\frac{11}{16}\right) = \frac{11}{48}$ **15.** Sample answer: Three fourths of the students at Walnut Middle School were on the honor roll. Of that group, only $\frac{1}{8}$ of them received all As. What fraction of the students received all As? **17.** A

Lesson 2-6 Extra Practice

19. $\frac{1}{9}$ **21.** $\frac{1}{4}$ **23.** $2\frac{1}{6}$ **25.** $\frac{3}{16}$ **27.** $-\frac{8}{27}$ **29.** broccoli: $1\frac{7}{8}$ c, pasta: $5\frac{5}{8}$ c, salad dressing: 1 c, cheese: 2 c; Multiply each amount by $1\frac{1}{2}$. **31.** B **33.** $<$ **35.** $\frac{1}{18} \div \frac{1}{3} = \frac{1}{6}$; $\frac{1}{18} \div \frac{1}{6} = \frac{1}{3}$ **37.** $6\frac{3}{4} \div 1\frac{1}{5} = 5\frac{5}{8}$; $6\frac{3}{4} \div 5\frac{5}{8} = 1\frac{1}{5}$ **39.** $5\frac{1}{4}$ pints

Lesson 2-7 Independent Practice

1. 12.7 **3** 128.17 **5.** 0.04 **7.** 15.75 **9.** 1.5 **11.** 887.21 mL **13** 1.5 lb **15.** 1,000 mL or 1 L **17.** 0.031 m, 0.1 ft, 0.6 in., 1.2 cm **19.** 0.7 gal, 950 mL, 0.4 L, $1\frac{1}{4}$ c **21.** C

Lesson 2-7 Extra Practice

23. 158.76 **25.** 121.28 **27.** 41.89 **29.** 2 L **31.** 3 gal **33.** 4 mi **35.** B **37.** 5.7 **39.** 15,840 **41.** 1 **43.** 5 **45.** 1

Lesson 2-8 Independent Practice

1. $\frac{7}{16}$ **3** $\frac{1}{15}$ **5.** $\frac{2}{9}$ **7** 84 movies **9.** $1\frac{1}{4}$

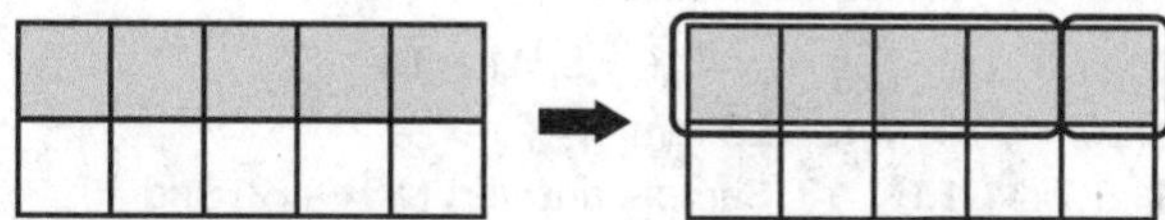

Sample answer: The model on the left shows that one half of a rectangle with ten sections is five sections. Two fifths of ten sections is four sections. The model on the right shows the five sections divided into $1\frac{1}{4}$ groups of four sections. **11.** $\frac{1}{6}$ of a dozen; 2 folders **13.** $\frac{10}{3}$

Lesson 2-8 Extra Practice

15. $\frac{2}{3}$ **17.** $-7\frac{4}{5}$ **19.** 11 servings **21.** $\frac{1}{2}$ **23.** C **25.** $\frac{9}{20}$ **27.** $\frac{46}{63}$ **29.** $\frac{3}{4}$ ft **31a.** $\frac{5}{8}$ mi **31b.** $\frac{13}{16}$ mi

Chapter Review Vocabulary Check

1. bar notation **3.** common denominator **5.** terminating

Chapter Review Key Concept Check

1. $\frac{3}{5}$ **3.** denominator **5.** multiply

Chapter Review Problem Solving

1. $5.1\overline{3}$ min **3.** $1\frac{5}{8}$ c **5.** $\frac{7}{30}$; Sample answer: The product of $\frac{7}{20}$ and $\frac{2}{3}$ is $\frac{14}{60}$ or $\frac{7}{30}$. **7.** 140 oz

Chapter 3 Expressions

Chapter 3 Are You Ready?

1. 16 **3.** 16 **5.** −50 **7.** 25

Lesson 3-1 Independent Practice

1. 34 **3** 3 **5.** 3 **7.** 2 **9.** −1 **11** 50 + 0.17*m*; \$75.50 **13.** 9.1 **15.** 37.85 **17.** Sample answer: The fee to rent a bicycle is \$10 plus \$5 for each hour. The expression $5x + 10$ represents the total cost for renting a bicycle for *x* hours. **19.** B

Lesson 3-1 Extra Practice

21. 4 **23.** −12 **25.** 5 **27.** \$8.75 **29.** G **31.** Let $h =$ the height; $h - 8$ **33.** Let $j =$ the number of Jacob's goals; $2j$ **35.** 4(8) + 3(5); \$47

Lesson 3-2 Independent Practice

1. 7 is added to the previous term; 28, 35, 42 **3** 8 is added to the previous term; 58, 66, 74 **5.** 0.8 is added to the previous term; 5.6, 6.4, 7.2 **7** 3*n*; 36 in.

9a.

x	1	2	3	4	5
y	3	6	9	12	15

9b. 3*n*

9c.

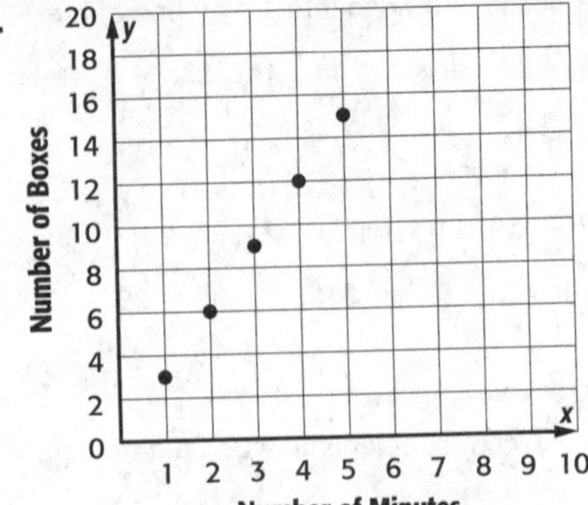

Sample answer: The number of boxes increases by 3 each minute. The points appear to fall in a straight line passing through the origin. **9d.** 135 boxes **11.** + 1, + 2, + 3, + 4, ...; 16, 22, 29 **13.** B

Lesson 3-2 Extra Practice

15. 10 is added to the previous term; 46, 56, 66 **17.** 1.5 is added to the previous term; 10.5, 12.0, 13.5 **19.** 4 is added to the previous term; 20.6, 24.6, 28.6 **21.** 25 is added to the previous term; 120, 145, 170 **23a.** Each figure is 8 less than the previous figure. **23b.** 40, 32 **25.** 33, 30, 27 **27.** D **29.** $2n + 3$ **31.** 27 **33.** 10,000 **35.** 16,807

Lesson 3-3 Independent Practice

1. Commutative (+) **3** Associative (+) **5.** false; Sample answer: $(24 \div 4) \div 2 \neq 24 \div (4 \div 2)$

7. $= (15 + 12) + 8a$ Associative (+)
$= 27 + 8a$ Simplify.

9 $= 3x \cdot (x \cdot 7)$ Commutative (×)
$= (3x \cdot x) \cdot 7$ Associative (×)
$= 3x^2 \cdot 7$ Simplify.
$= 3 \cdot 7 \cdot x^2$ Commutative (×)
$= (3 \cdot 7) \cdot x^2$ Associative (×)
$= 21x^2$ Simplify.

11. $[7 + (47 + 3)][5 \cdot (2 \cdot 3)]$, Associative (+); $(7 + 50)[5 \cdot (2 \cdot 3)]$, Simplify; $57[5 \cdot (2 \cdot 3)]$, Simplify; $57[(5 \cdot 2) \cdot 3]$, Associative (×); $57 \cdot 10 \cdot 3$, Simplify; $(57 \cdot 10) \cdot 3$, Associative (×); $570 \cdot 3$, Simplify; 1,710 **13.** Blake incorrectly multiplied both the 5 and m by 4. He should have used the Associative Property to group the 5 and 4 together, simplify, and then multiply by m. $4 \cdot (5 \cdot m) = 20m$ **15.** C

Lesson 3-3 Extra Practice

17. Commutative (×) **19.** Associative (+) **21.** 48 s; Sample answer: 12.4 + 12.6 = 25 and 11.8 + 11.2 = 23, 25 + 23 = 48

23. $= (18 + 5) + 6m$ Associative (+)
$= 23 + 6m$ Simplify.

25. $= 10 \cdot 7 \cdot y$ Commutative (×)
$= (10 \cdot 7) \cdot y$ Associative (×)
$= 70y$ Simplify.

27. C **29.** 2.29 + 2.50 + 2.21 **31.** 76 **33.** 88 **35.** 1.5

Lesson 3-4 Independent Practice

1. 33 **3** −30 **5.** 4 **7.** $-12x + 24$ **9.** $30 - 6q$ **11.** $-15 + 3b$ **13** \$27.40; 4(\$7.00 − \$0.15) = $4 \cdot 7 - 4 \cdot 0.15$

15. 315;
$9(30 + 5) = 9(30) + 9(5)$
$= 270 + 45$

17. 672;
$(100 + 12)6 = 100(6) + 12(6)$
$= 600 + 72$

19. 488;
$4(120 + 2) = 4(120) + 4(2)$
$= 480 + 8$

21. Sample answer: $6(2a + 3b - c)$ **23.** $2a + ay + 2b + by$

Lesson 3-4 Extra Practice

25. −72 **27.** −40 **29.** $10b + 40$ **31.** \$31.96; 4(\$8.00 − \$0.01) = $4 \cdot 8 - 4 \cdot 0.01$ **33.** $0.5xy - 0.5xz$ **35.** $-12mn + 24mp$ **37.** $-6a + 4b$ **39.** $8(x + 4)$; $8x + 32$ **41.** H **43.** \$448.50; 30(\$15.00 − \$0.05) = $30 \cdot 15 - 30 \cdot 0.05$ **45.** 756 **47.** 4; x

Problem-Solving Investigation Make a Table

Case 3. 55 containers **Case 5.** 18 toothpicks

Lesson 3-5 Independent Practice

1. terms: 2, $3a$, $9a$; like terms: $3a$, $9a$; coefficients: 3, 9; constant: 2 **3.** terms: 9, $-z$, 3, $-2z$; like terms: 9 and 3, $-z$ and $-2z$; coefficients: −1, −2; constants: 9, 3 **5.** $11c$ **7.** $1.03t$; \$74.16 **9** $2x + 30$ **11** **a.** $7 + 5x + 4y + 2z$ **b.** \$43 **13.** $16a + 8b + 4$ **15.** Sample answer: $3x + x - 7$; coefficients: 3, 1; constant: −7 **17.** $8x^2 + 10x - 3$; $8x^2 + 10x - 3 = 8(2)^2 + 10(2) - 3 = 49$ and $8x^2 - 2x + 12x - 3 = 8(2)^2 - 2(2) + 12(2) - 3 = 49$

Lesson 3-5 Extra Practice

19. terms: 4, $5y$, $-6y$, y; like terms: $5y$, $-6y$, y; coefficients: 5, −6, 1; constant: 4 **21.** terms: $-3d$, 8, $-d$, −2; like terms: $-3d$ and $-d$, 8 and −2; coefficients: −3, −1; constants: 8, −2 **23.** $2 + 4d$ **25.** $2m - 2$ **27.** $7m - 20$ **29.** $20x + 9$ **31.** $38g + 36h - 38$ **33.** $3x - 10y$ **35.** 7(5)(4); \$140 **37.** b = cost of a book; $4b$ **39.** 7

Lesson 3-6 Independent Practice

1. $11x + 11$ **3** $4x - 16$ **5.** $4x + 14$ **7.** $(10x + 18)$ mm; 118 mm **9** $-x + 2$ **11.** $8.7x - 1.6$ **13.** Sample answer: $(10x + 2)$ and $(-15x + 2)$ **15.** $2x + 1$; The expression $2x + 1$ will always be odd when x is an integer because when an integer is doubled, the result is always even. Adding one to the result will give an odd number.

Lesson 3-6 Extra Practice

17. $-4x + 16$ **19.** $-2x - 2$ **21.** $-6x + 5$ **23.** $(24x + 9)$ yd; 177 yd **25.** D **27.** $(4x - 36)$ m **29.** 56 **31.** 66 **33.** 23 students; Sample answer: $6 + 4 = 10$, $5 + 8 = 13$, $10 + 13 = 23$

Lesson 3-7 Independent Practice

1 $5x + 2$ **3.** $2x + 2$ **5.** $8x - 12$ **7.** $5x - 2$; 248 customers **9** $x + 0.51$

11. Sample answer: The additive inverse of $(2x + 1)$ is $(-2x - 1)$.

$$\begin{aligned}(5x + 3) - (2x + 1) &= (5x + 3) + (-2x - 1)\\ &= 5x + 3 + (-2x) + (-1)\\ &= 5x + (-2x) + 3 + (-1)\\ &= 3x + 2\end{aligned}$$

13. $-x + 5$

Lesson 3-7 Extra Practice

15. $-10x - 11$ **17.** $3x + 13$ **19.** $7x + 5$ **21.** $2x - 11$; 5 questions **23.** $-1\frac{1}{2}x + 1\frac{1}{2}$ **25.** $4x - 15$ **27.** $5x + 3$ **29.** $(12x - 4)$ ft; 32 ft **31.** $-\frac{1}{4}$ **33.** $\frac{1}{8}$ **35.** $\frac{2}{3}$

Lesson 3-8 Independent Practice

1. 24 **3** $36k$ **5.** cannot be factored **7** 4 units by $(x - 2)$ units **9.** $(x + 2)$ dollars **11.** $5(x + 4)$ units^2 **13.** $4(5x + 19)$ units^2 **15.** Sample answer: $20m$ and $12mn$ **17.** B

Lesson 3-8 Extra Practice

19. $6rs$ **21.** $20x$ **23.** $25xy$ **25.** $6(3x + 1)$ **27.** $5(2x - 7)$ **29.** $10(3x - 4)$ **31.** $(2x + 5)$ in. **33.** $\frac{2}{3}(x + 9)$ **35.** $\frac{5}{6}(x - 36)$ **37.** $\frac{3}{8}(x + 48)$ **39.** D **41.** $4x + 4$ **43.** $14b + 35$

45.

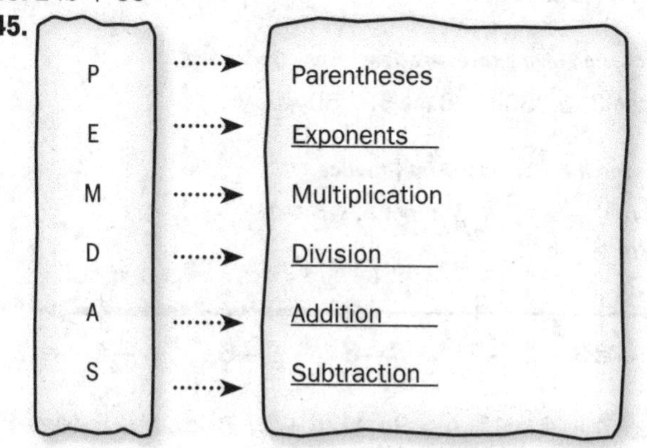

Chapter Review Vocabulary Check

Across

3. simplest form **7.** sequence **11.** counter example **13.** define

Down

1. equivalent **5.** variable **9.** term

Chapter Review Key Concept Check

1. $1 + 3$ **3.** $2x - 4$ **5.** $3(x + 7)$

Chapter Review Problem Solving

1. $5.75h + 8.95s$; \$62 **3.** 49 points; Sample answer: $8 + 12 = 20$, $13 + 7 = 20$, $20 + 20 + 9 = 49$ **5.** $5(x - 5)°$

Chapter 4 Equations and Inequalities

Chapter 4 Are You Ready?

1. $p + 3$ **3.** $g + 10$ **5.** 17 **7.** 1 **9.** 35

Lesson 4-1 Independent Practice

1. 7 **3** 17 **5.** -1

7

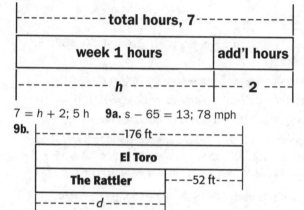

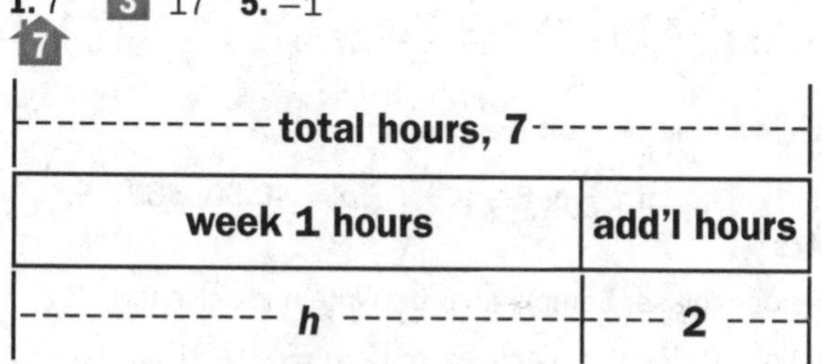

$7 = h + 2$; 5 h **9a.** $s - 65 = 13$; 78 mph

9b.

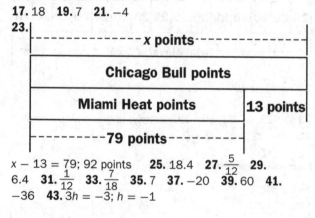

176 ft
El Toro
The Rattler
52 ft
d

$d + 52 = 176$; 124 ft **9c.** The solution of each equation is 170; Colossos is 170 feet tall. **11.** $115 + 115 + 65 + x = 360$; 65 **13.** She should have subtracted 5 from each side; -13 **15.** C

Lesson 4-1 Extra Practice

17. 18 **19.** 7 **21.** -4

23.

x points
Chicago Bull points
Miami Heat points
13 points
79 points

$x - 13 = 79$; 92 points **25.** 18.4 **27.** $\frac{5}{12}$ **29.** 6.4 **31.** $\frac{1}{12}$ **33.** $\frac{7}{18}$ **35.** 7 **37.** -20 **39.** 60 **41.** -36 **43.** $3h = -3$; $h = -1$

Lesson 4-2 Independent Practice

1. 7 **3.** 8 **5.** 80 **7** -5 **9.** -90 **11** $205 = \frac{d}{3}$; 615 mi

13a.

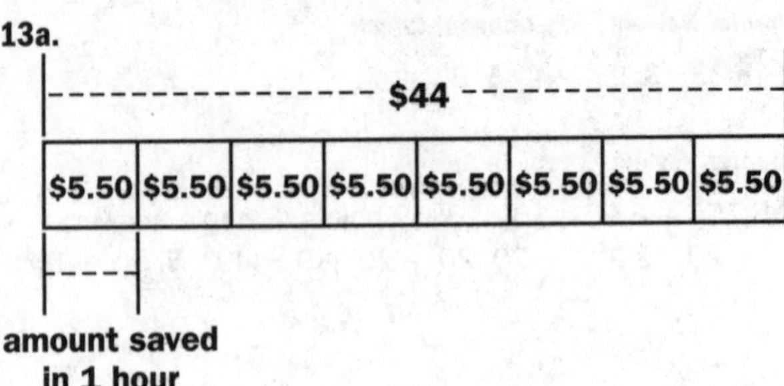

13b. $5.5x = 44$ **13c.** Sample answer: Divide each side by 5.5. Then simplify. $x = 8$ **15.** True; Sample answer: Multiply each side of the equation by $\frac{1}{5}$ instead of dividing each side by 5. **17.** D

Lesson 4-2 Extra Practice

19. 4 **21.** 70 **23.** −120 **25.** $50 = 25t$; 2 s **27.** C **29.** G **31.** $5\frac{5}{7}$ **33.** $\frac{16}{7}$ **35.** $\frac{95}{9}$ **37.** 9 **39.** $\frac{14}{45}$ **41.** $\frac{1}{6}$

Lesson 4-3 Independent Practice

1. 5 **3** 3 **5.** $\frac{20}{3}$ or $6\frac{2}{3}$ **7** $\frac{3}{4}p = 46.50$; \$62 **9.** Emily's homeroom class; Sample answer: Write and solve the equations $0.75e = 15$ and $\frac{2}{3}s = 12$; $e = 20$ and $s = 18$; Since $20 > 18$, Emily's homeroom class has more students. **11.** 20; Sample answer: Solve to $8 = \frac{m}{4}$, find that $m = 32$. So, replace m with 32 to find $32 - 12 = 20$. **13.** Sample answer: Multiply each side by 2. Then divide each side by $(b_1 + b_2)$. So, $\frac{2A}{b_1 + b_2} = h$.

Lesson 4-3 Extra Practice

15. 7 **17.** −3.8 **19.** $-\frac{125}{12}$ or $-10\frac{5}{12}$

21.

$\frac{7}{15}$ of elevation, 140 ft

20	20	20	20	20	20	20	20	20	20	20	20	20	20	20

total elevation, x ft

$140 = \frac{7}{15}x$; 300 ft

23. D **25.** G **27.** 50 **29.** multiply; divide; add; subtract **31.** $30 - (2 \times 8 + 2 \times 2 + 4)$; \$6

Lesson 4-4 Independent Practice

1. 3 **3** 7 **5.** −3

7.

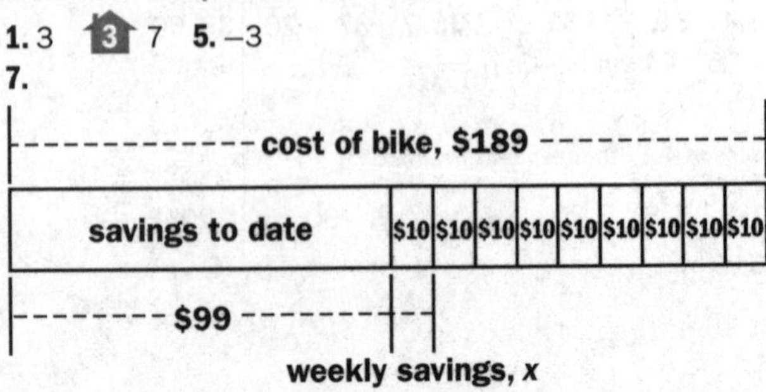

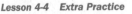

$189 = 10x + 99$; 9 weeks

9. 2.25 **11** **a.** −9°C **b.** 92.2°F **13.** No, none of the Fahrenheit temperatures convert to the same temperature in Celsius. Only −40°F = −40°C. **15.** B

Lesson 4-4 Extra Practice

17. −4 **19.** 4 **21.** 36

23a.

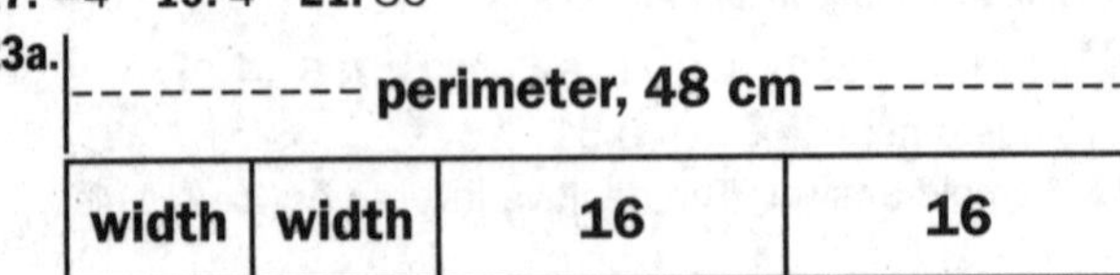

23b. $48 = 32 + 2w$; 8 cm **23c.** Sample answer: Using either method, you would subtract first and then divide **25.** 7 days **27.** $6 \cdot 10 + 6 \cdot n$ or $60 + 6n$ **29.** $5(x + 7)$ **31.** $10(t + 3)$ **33.** $2(m + 6)$

Lesson 4-5 Independent Practice

1. 6 **3** −14 **5.** −3.2 **7** $3(\ell + 5) = 60$; 15 in. **9a.** $12(m - 2.57) = 0.36$ **9b.** Sample answer: I first divided each side by 12 and then added 2.57 to each side; \$2.60. **11.** Sample answer: Marisol should have divided by six before subtracting three; $6(x + 3) = 21$, $x + 3 = 3.5$, $x = 3.5 - 3$, $x = 0.5$ **13.** A

Lesson 4-5 Extra Practice

15. 16 **17.** −2 **19.** 78 **21.** $5\frac{3}{4}$ or 5.75 **23.** $1.20\left(n + 2\frac{1}{2}\right) = 4.50$; 1.25 or $1\frac{1}{4}$ pounds **25.** $\frac{1}{b}$ **27.** 2; See answer 31 for graph. **29.** 3; See answer 31 for graph **31.** −2

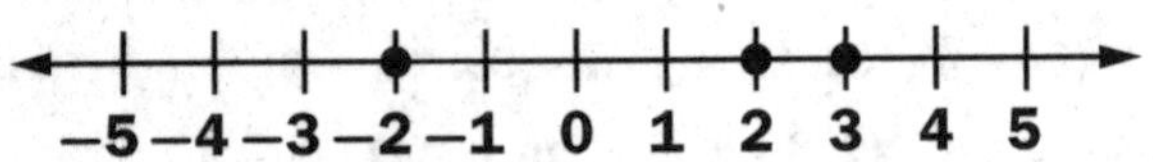

33. 3 **35.** 1, 2, 3

Problem-Solving Investigation Work Backward

Case 3. 1,250 ft **Case 5.** 7:50 A.M.

Lesson 4-6 Independent Practice

1. $h \leq -8$ **3** $5 < n$ **5.** $x > -1$
7. $m \geq -6$;

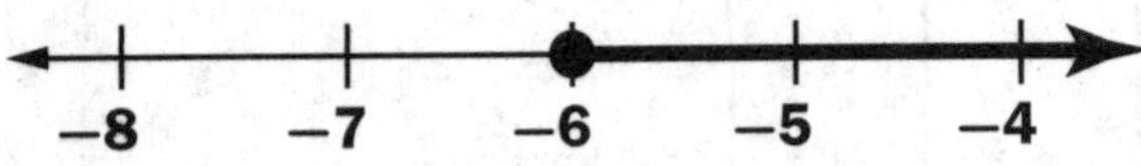

9 $n + 4 > 13$; $n > 9$ **11.** $p + 17 \leq 26$; $p \leq 9$; Nine additional players or fewer can make the team. **13a.** $42 + x \geq 74$; $x \geq 32$ **13b.** $74 + y \geq 110$; $y \geq 36$ **15.** Sample answer: $x + 3 < 25$ **17.** A

Lesson 4-6 Extra Practice

19. $m \leq 4.3$
21. $-5 < a$

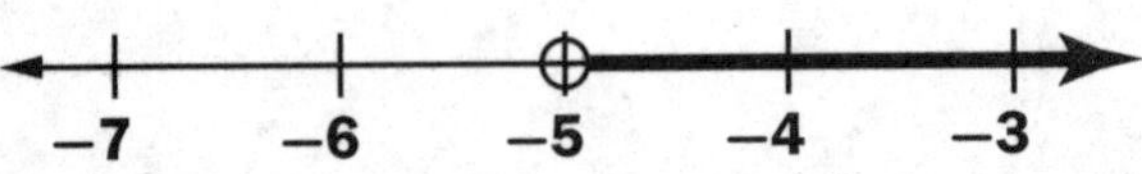

23. $n - 8 < 10$; $n < 18$ **25.** $68 + c \leq 125$; $c \leq 57$; The salesman has 57 cars or less left to sell.

27. $2\frac{2}{3} > x$ or $x < 2\frac{2}{3}$

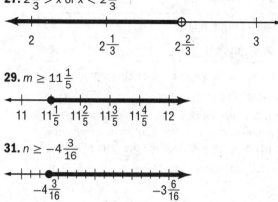

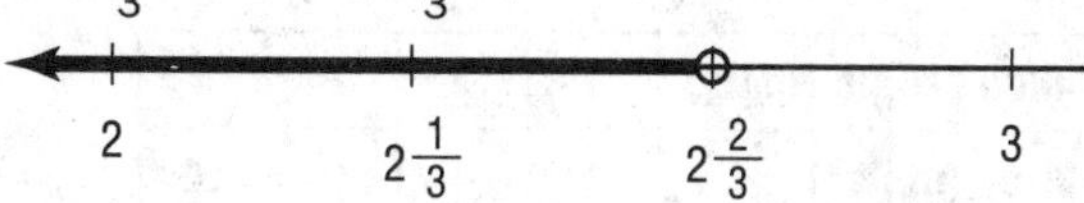

29. $m \geq 11\frac{1}{5}$

11 $11\frac{1}{5}$ $11\frac{2}{5}$ $11\frac{3}{5}$ $11\frac{4}{5}$ 12

31. $n \geq -4\frac{3}{16}$

$-4\frac{3}{16}$ $-3\frac{6}{16}$

33. I **35.** $50 + x \geq 268$; \$218 **37.** -4; See answer 41 for graph. **39.** -2; See answer 41 for graph.

41. -6;

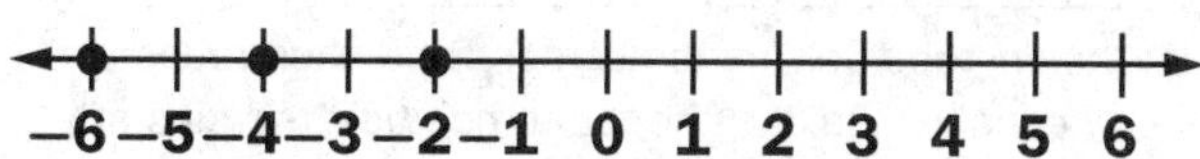

43. $\{-3, -2, -1, 0, 1, 2, 3\}$

Lesson 4-7 Independent Practice

1. $y < 3$ **3.** $180 \leq m$ **5.** $m \geq 56$ **7.** $n \leq 4.5$

9. $w \leq -45$

11. $4 < t$

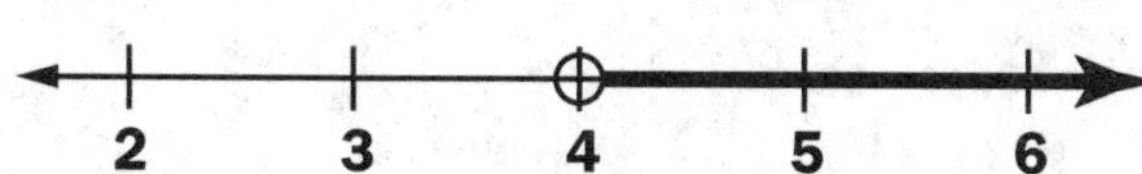

13. $x \leq -32$

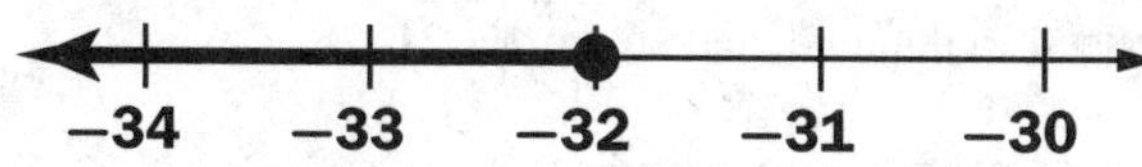

15. Sample answer: The inequalities $-2x > 12$, $\frac{x}{2} < -3$, and $-7 > x - 1$ are equal to $x < -6$. The inequality $-2 < x + 4$ is equal to $x > -6$. **17.** $4 + 5n \leq 34$; $n \leq 6$

19. at least a 15

Lesson 4-7 Extra Practice

21. $n < 2$ **23.** $5 < r$ or $r > 5$ **25.** $t < -70$

27. $w > 13$

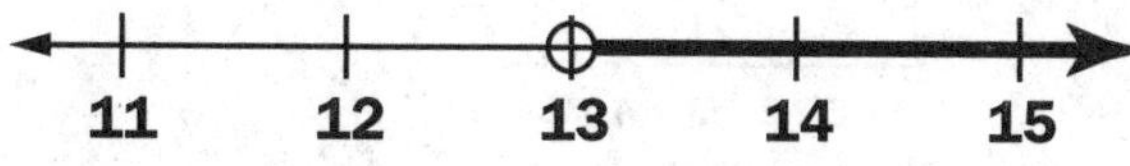

29. $-20 \geq t$ or $t \leq -20$

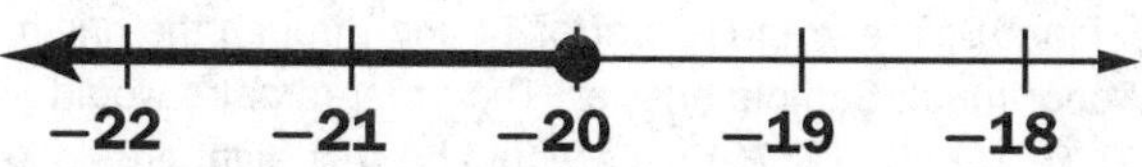

31. $0.5x > 15$; $x > 30$; A person should play more than 30 games. **33.** $5n < -45$; $n < -9$ **35.** F **37.** -3

39. 3 **41.** $3\frac{6}{7}$

Lesson 4-8 Independent Practice

1. $x \geq 1$;

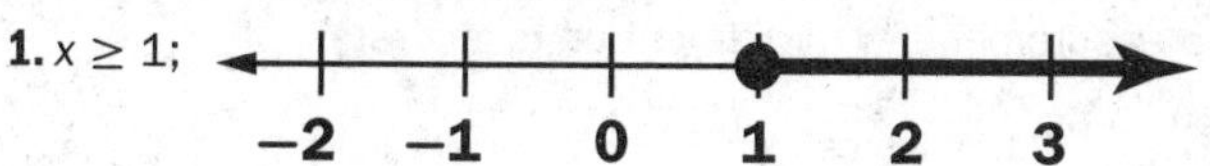

3. $x > 12$

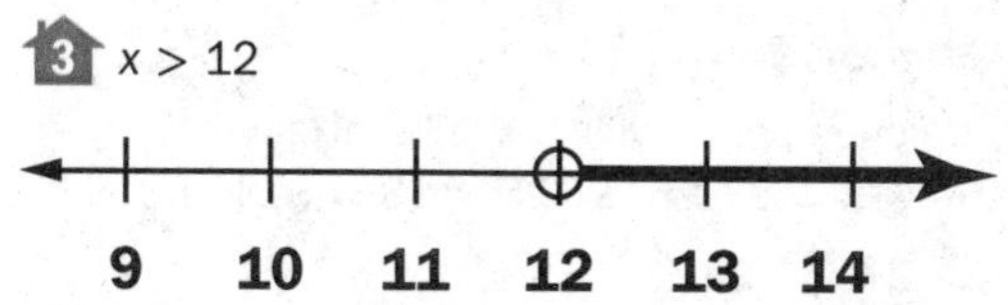

5. $30 + 7x \geq 205$; $x \geq 25$ hours; He will have to work at least 25 hours. **7.** $\frac{x}{-5} + 1 \leq 7$; $x \geq -30$

9. $-2x - 6 > -18$; $x < 6$ **11.** Sample answer: $-2x + 5 > -7$ **13.** Sample answer: $\frac{x}{2} + 5 \geq 30$ **15.** at least 17 points **17.** B

Lesson 4-8 Extra Practice

19. $x \leq -8$

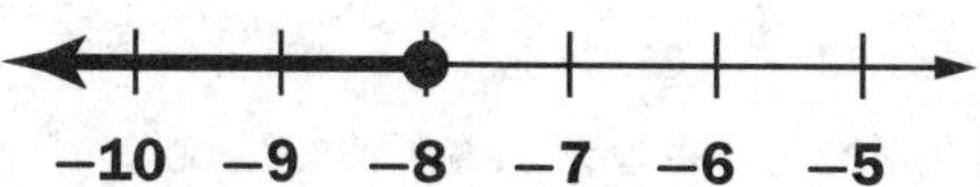

21. $x \geq 42$

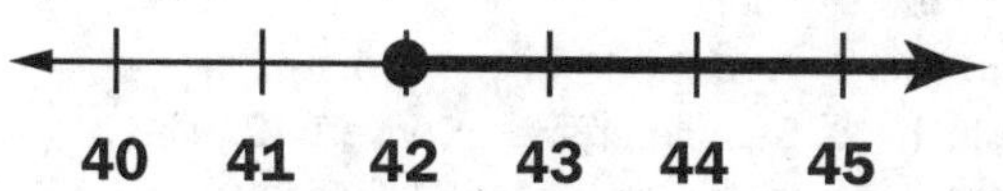

23. $75 + 5s \geq 125$; $s \geq 10$; Audrey needs to make at least 10 sales for her pay to be \$125. **25.** A **27.** I

29. $y < -6$

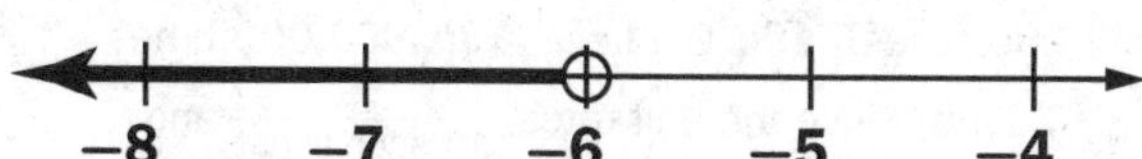

31. 8 **33.** $\frac{1}{2}$

Chapter Review Key Concept Check

1. f **3.** a

Chapter Review Problem Solving

1. 2 m **3.** $300 = 7.5r$; 40 mph **5.** $x + 120 \leq 180$; Ben can lift up to 60 pounds more. **7.** $50c + 600 \geq 1{,}250$; Mr. Walker must sell at least 13 computers.

Chapter 5 Ratios and Proportional Reasoning

Chapter 5 Are You Ready?

1. $\frac{2}{15}$ **3.** $\frac{1}{51}$ **5.** No; $\frac{12}{20} = \frac{3}{5}$, $\frac{15}{30} = \frac{1}{2}$

Lesson 5-1 Independent Practice

1. 60 mi/h **3.** 3.5 m/s **5.** Sample answer: about \$0.50 per pair **7.** 510 words **9a.** 20.04 mi/h

b. about 1.5 h **13.** Sometimes; a ratio that compares two measurements with different units is a rate, such as $\frac{\text{2 miles}}{\text{10 minutes}}$. **15.** C

Lesson 5-1 Extra Practice

17. 203.75 Calories per serving **19.** 32 mi/gal
21. $108.75 ÷ 15 = $7.25, $7.25 × 18 = $130.50
23. C **25.** G **27.** $\frac{2}{7}$ **29.** $\frac{2}{3}$

Lesson 5-2 Independent Practice

1. $1\frac{1}{2}$ **3.** $\frac{4}{27}$ **5.** $\frac{2}{25}$ **7.** $6 per yard **9.** $\frac{5}{6}$ page
11. $\frac{39}{250}$ **13.** $\frac{11}{200}$ **15.** Sample answer: If one of the numbers in the ratio is a fraction, then the ratio can be a complex fraction. **17.** $\frac{1}{2}$

Lesson 5-2 Extra Practice

19. 4 **21.** $\frac{1}{10}$ **23.** $\frac{1}{10}$ **25.** 8 costumes **27.** $\frac{3}{125}$
29. $\frac{1}{12}$ **31.** D **33.** C **35.** 24 **37.** 32 **39.** 1,000

Lesson 5-3 Independent Practice

1. 115 mi/h **3.** 322,000 m/h **5.** 6.1 mi/h
7. 7,200 Mb/h **9.** Sample answer: Convert 42 miles per hour to miles per minute. **11.** 461.5 yd/h

Lesson 5-3 Extra Practice

13. 1,760 **15.** 66 **17.** 35.2 **19a.** 6.45 ft/s
19b. 2,280 times **19c.** 0.11 mi **19d.** 900,000 times
21. H **23.** no; Since the unit rates, $\frac{\$9}{\text{1 baseball hat}}$ and $\frac{\$8}{\text{1 baseball hat}}$ are not the same, the rates are not equivalent.

25.

Payment	$22	÷ 2 × 5	$55
Hours	2	÷ 2 × 5	5

Lesson 5-4 Independent Practice

1.

Time (days)	1	2	3	4
Water (L)	225	450	675	900

Yes; the time to water ratios are all equal to $\frac{1}{225}$.
3. The table for Desmond's Time shows a proportional relationship. The ratio between the time and the number of laps is always 73.
5. a. yes; Sample answer:

Side Length (units)	1	2	3	4
Perimeter (units)	4	8	12	16

The side length to perimeter ratio for side lengths of 1, 2, 3, and 4 units is $\frac{1}{4}$, $\frac{2}{8}$ or $\frac{1}{4}$, $\frac{3}{12}$ or $\frac{1}{4}$, $\frac{4}{16}$ or $\frac{1}{4}$. Since these ratios are all equal to $\frac{1}{4}$, the measure of the side length of a square is proportional to the square's perimeter.
b. no; Sample answer:

Side Length (units)	1	2	3	4
Area (units^2)	1	4	9	16

The side length to area ratio for side lengths of 1, 2, 3, and 4 units is $\frac{1}{1}$ or 1, $\frac{2}{4}$ or $\frac{1}{2}$, $\frac{3}{9}$ or $\frac{1}{3}$, $\frac{4}{16}$ or $\frac{1}{4}$. Since these ratios are not equal, the measure of the side length of a square is not proportional to the square's area.
7. It is not proportional because the ratio of laps to time is not consistent; $\frac{4}{1} \neq \frac{6}{2} \neq \frac{8}{3} \neq \frac{10}{4}$. **9.** B

Lesson 5-4 Extra Practice

11.

Degrees Celsius	0	10	20	30
Degrees Fahrenheit	32	50	68	86

No; the degrees Celsius to degrees Fahrenheit ratios are not all equal. **13a.** No; the fee to ride tickets ratios are not equal. **13b.** no; Sample answer: The fee increase is inconsistent. The table shows an increase of $4.50 from 5 to 10 tickets, an increase of $4 from 10 to 15 tickets, and an increase of $2.50 from 15 to 20 tickets.

15.

n	30	60	120	173
p	90	180	360	519

17. 20 **19.** 12 **21.** 3

Problem-Solving Investigation The Four-Step Plan

Case 3. $360 **Case 5.** Add 2 to the first term, 3 to the second, 4 to the third, and so on; 15, 21, 28.

Lesson 5-5 Independent Practice

1.

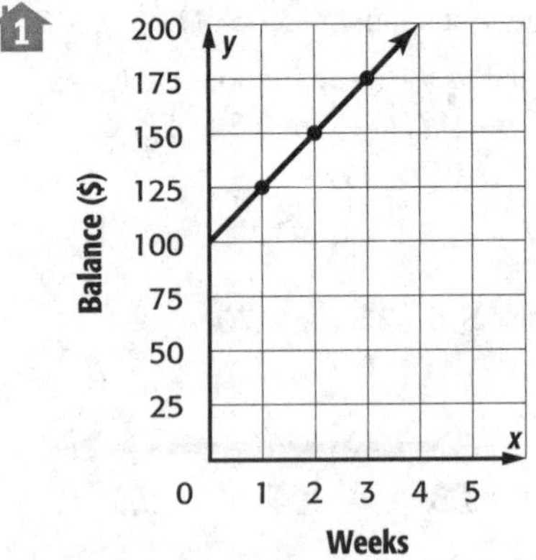

Not proportional; The graph does not pass through the origin.
3. Plant B; The graph is a straight line through the origin.
5. Proportional; Sample answer: The ordered pairs would be (0, 0), (1, 35), (2, 70). This would be a straight line through the origin.

7. 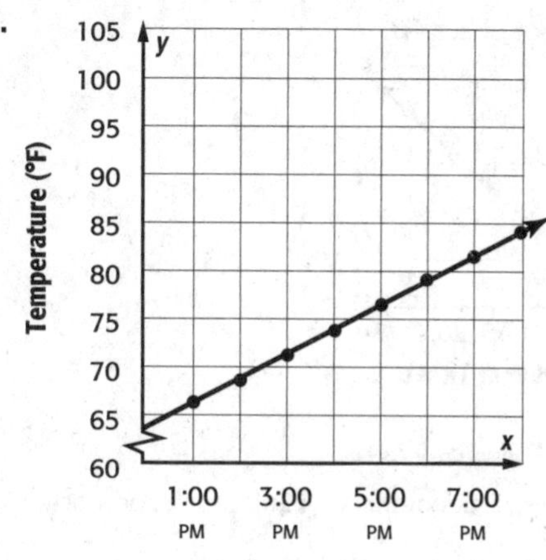

Not proportional; The graph does not pass through the origin.

Lesson 5-5 Extra Practice

9. Not proportional; The graph does not pass through the origin. **11.** Not proportional; The graph does not pass through the origin. **13.** The number of heartbeats is proportional to the number of seconds because the graph is a straight line through the origin. **15.** Samora's; The graph is a straight line through the origin. **17.** $\frac{5}{1}$ **19.** $\frac{1}{5}$

Lesson 5-6 Independent Practice

1 40 **3.** 3.5 **5.** $\frac{2}{5} = \frac{x}{20}$; 8 ounces **7** $c = 0.50p$; $4.00 **9.** $\frac{360}{3} = \frac{n}{7}$; 840 visitors **11.** 256 *c*; Sample answer: The ratio of cups of mix to cups of water is 1:8, which means that the proportion $\frac{1}{8} = \frac{32}{x}$ is true and can be solved. **13.** 18 **15.** B

Lesson 5-6 Extra Practice

17. 7.2 **19.** $\frac{6}{7} = \frac{c}{40}$; about 34 patients **21.** $s = 45w$; $360 **23.** B **25.** No, the ratios for each age and height are not equal. **27.** Yes; the unit rate is $\frac{15}{1}$ or $15 per hour. **29.** 500 kB/min

Lesson 5-7 Independent Practice

1 6 m per s **3** $9 per shirt; Sample answer: The point (0, 0) represents 0 T-shirts purchased and 0 dollars spent. The point (1, 9) represents 9 dollars spent for 1 T-shirt. **5.** 10 inches per hour

7. Sample answer:

Feet	Inches
3	18
6	36
9	54
12	72

9. C

Lesson 5-7 Extra Practice

11. $0.03 per minute **13.** Josh; sample answer: The unit rate for Ramona is $9 per hour. The unit rate for Josh is $10 per hour. **15.** A

17.

Input	Add 4	Output
1	1 + 4	5
2	2 + 4	6
3	3 + 4	7
4	4 + 4	8

19.

Input	Multiply by 2	Output
1	1 × 2	2
2	2 × 2	4
3	3 × 2	6
4	4 × 2	8

21.

Input	Add 6	Output
4	?	10
5	?	11
6	?	12
7	?	13

Lesson 5-8 Independent Practice

1 $\frac{50}{1}$ or 50; Adriano read 50 pages every hour.

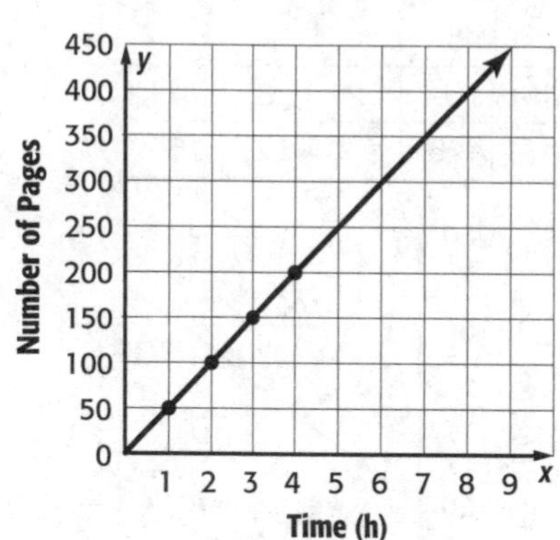

3 **a.** It shows that car A travels 120 miles in 2 hours. **b.** It shows that car B travels 67.5 miles in 1.5 hours. **c.** the speed of each car at that point **d.** the average speed of the car **e.** Car A; the slope is steeper.

5. Marisol found $\frac{\text{run}}{\text{rise}}$. Her answer should be $\frac{3}{2}$. **7.** D

Lesson 5-8 Extra Practice

9a. It costs $20 to rent a paddle boat from Water Wheels for 1 hour. **9b.** It costs $50 to rent a paddle boat from Fun in the Sun for 2 hours.

Selected Answers

11.

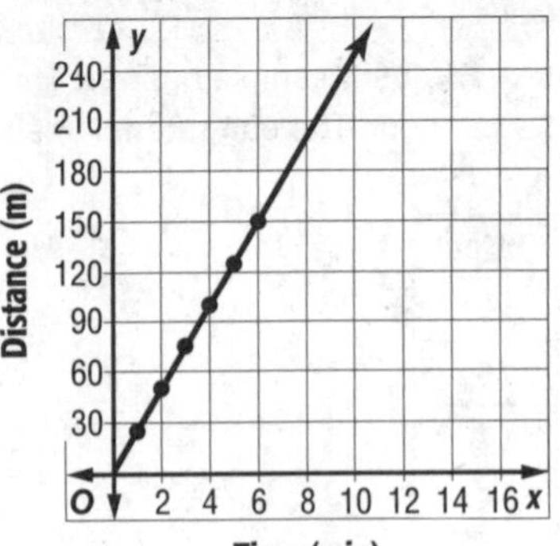

13.

Homework Problems

d

80 70 60 50 40 30 20 10 0

1 2 3 4 5 6 x

Time (h)

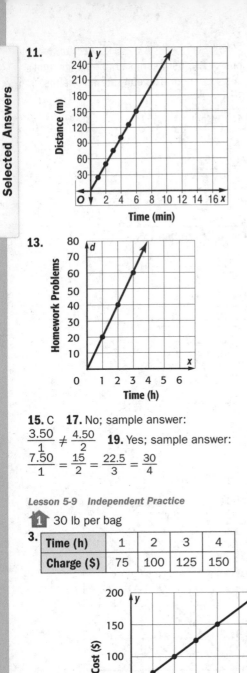

15. C **17.** No; sample answer: $\frac{3.50}{1} \neq \frac{4.50}{2}$ **19.** Yes; sample answer: $\frac{7.50}{1} = \frac{15}{2} = \frac{22.5}{3} = \frac{30}{4}$

Lesson 5-9 Independent Practice

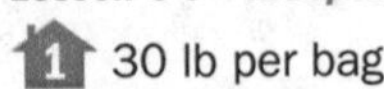

1 30 lb per bag

3.

Time (h)	1	2	3	4
Charge ($)	75	100	125	150

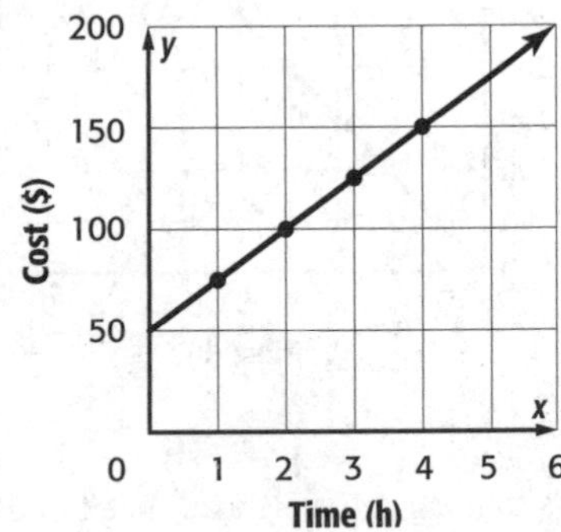

No; sample answer: $\frac{75}{1} \neq \frac{100}{2}$; Because there is no constant ratio and the line does not go through the origin, there is no direct variation. **5** no **7.** no **9.** $y = \frac{7}{4}x$; 21 **11.** $y = \frac{1}{4}x$; −28 **13.** Sample answer: 9; $5\frac{1}{2}$; 36; 22 **15.** C

Lesson 5-9 Extra Practice

17. 7 c **19.** yes; 0.2 **21.** C **23.** yes; 36

25. $\frac{8}{1}$; Each ticket costs $8.

Cost ($)

250 200 150 100 50 0

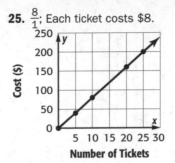

y

x

5 10 15 20 25 30

Number of Tickets

Chapter Review Vocabulary Check

1. rate **3.** ordered **5.** complex **7.** slope **9.** proportion **11.** Dimensional

Chapter Review Key Concept Check

1. denominator **3.** vertical change to horizontal change

Chapter Review Problem Solving

1. the 16-ounce bottle **3.** No; Sample answer: The cost for 1 month of service is $60, while the cost for 2 months is $90; $\frac{60}{1} \neq \frac{90}{2}$ **5.** 721.8 lb

Chapter 6 Percents

Chapter 6 Are You Ready?

1. 48 **3.** $70 **5.** 72.5% **7.** 92%

Lesson 6-1 Independent Practice

1. 120.9 **3.** $147.20 **5** 17.5 **7.** 1.3 **9.** 30.1 **11.** $7.19 at Pirate Bay, $4.46 at Funtopia, $9.62 at Zoomland **13.** 4 **15** 0.61 **17.** 520 **19.** 158 **21.** 0.14 **23.** Sample answer: It is easiest to use a fraction when the denominator of the fraction is a multiple of the number. If this is not the case, a decimal may be easier to use.

Lesson 6-1 Extra Practice

25. 45.9 **27.** 14.7 **29.** $54 **31.** 0.3 **33.** 2.25 **35.** $19.95 **35.** D **37.** 91.8 **39.** 133.92 **41.** 160

Lesson 6-2 Independent Practice

1. 35

$\frac{1}{2} \cdot 70 = 35$

$0.1 \cdot 70 = 7$ and

$5 \cdot 7 = 35$

3 18

$\frac{1}{5} \cdot 90 = 18$

$0.1 \cdot 90 = 9$ and

$2 \cdot 9 = 18$

5. 168

$\frac{7}{10} \cdot 240 = 168$

$0.1 \cdot 240 = 24$ and

$7 \cdot 24 = 168$

7. 720

$(2 \cdot 320) + \left(\frac{1}{4} \cdot 320\right) = 720$

9. 2

$0.01 \cdot 500 = 5$ and

$\frac{2}{5} \cdot 5 = 2$

11 about 96 mi; $0.01 \cdot 12{,}000 = 120$ and $\frac{4}{5} \cdot 120 = 96$

13. 6

$\frac{2}{3} \cdot 9 = 6$

15. 24

$\frac{1}{10} \cdot 240 = 24$

17a. Sample answer: about 260 canned foods; $200 + 0.3 \cdot 200$ **17b.** Sample answer: about 780 canned foods; $600 + 0.3 \cdot 600$ **19.** sometimes; Sample answer: one estimate for 37% of 60 is $\frac{2}{5} \cdot 60 = 24$.

Lesson 6-2 Extra Practice

21. 135

23. 90

$\frac{9}{10} \cdot 100 = 90$

$0.1 \cdot 100 = 10$ and

$9 \cdot 10 = 90$

25. 0.7

$0.01 \cdot 70 = 0.7$

27. about 12 muscles; $\frac{3}{10} \cdot 40 = 12$ **29a.** Sample answer: 420; $\frac{7}{10} \cdot 600 = 420$ **29b.** Greater; both the number of passes and the percent were rounded up. **29c.** Tony Romo; sample answer: 64% of 520 must be greater than 64% of 325. **31.** G **33.** 300 **35.** $\frac{1}{4}$

Lesson 6-3 Independent Practice

1. 25% **3** 75 **5.** 36 **7.** $68 **9.** 80 **11** 0.2% **13a.** about 3.41% **13b.** about 24,795.62 km **13c.** about 6,378.16 km **15.** 20% of 500, 20% of 100, 5% of 100; If the percent is the same but the base is greater, then the part is greater. If the base is the same but the percent is greater, then the part is greater.

Lesson 6-3 Extra Practice

17. 45 **19.** 20 **21.** 20% **23.** 8 pencils; $0.25 \times 8 = 2$ **25.** 120% **27.** A **29.** 60% **31.** $\frac{3}{20}$ **33.** $\frac{8}{15}$ **35.** $\frac{7}{25}$

Lesson 6-4 Independent Practice

1 50%; $75 = n \cdot 150$ **3.** 63.7; $p = 0.65 \cdot 98$ **5.** 6; $p = 0.24 \cdot 25$ **7.** 50 books **9** **a.** 37% **b.** 31% **11.** 0.3; $p = 0.004 \cdot 82.1$ **13.** 115%; $230 = n \cdot 200$ **15.** Sample answer: If the percent is less than 100%, then the part is less than the whole; if the percent equals 100%, then the part equals the whole; if the percent is greater than 100%, then the part is greater than the whole.

Lesson 6-4 Extra Practice

17. 20% **19.** 25%; $98 = n \cdot 392$ **21.** 4.4; $1.45 = 0.33 \cdot w$ **23.** 42.5; $17 = 0.4 \cdot w$ **25.** $17 = n \cdot 27$; 63% **27.** $6.15; $0.25 \cdot 6 = 0.15$ and $6 + 0.15 = 6.15$ **29.** F **31.** $<$ **33.** $<$ **35.** 140; There are 140 students that participate in fall sports.

Problem-Solving Investigation Determine Reasonable Answers

Case 3. 70 families **Case 5.** 240 students; Sample answer: $0.6 \times 400 = 240$

Lesson 6-5 Independent Practice

1. 20%; increase **3** 25%; decrease **5.** 41%; decrease **7** 28% **9.** 38%; decrease **11a.** 100% **11b.** 300% **13.** about 4.2% **15.** He did not write a ratio comparing the change to the original amount. It should have had a denominator of $52 and the percent of change would be about 140%.

Lesson 6-5 Extra Practice

17. 50%; decrease **19.** 33%; increase **21a.** about 3.8%; increase **21b.** about 2.9%; decrease **23.** 25% **25.** 6,500 comments **27.** 200% **29.** 45.93 **31.** 49,695.72 mi

Lesson 6-6 Independent Practice

1. $69.60 **3** $1,605 **5** $35.79 **7.** $334.80 **9.** $10.29 **11.** 7% **13.** $54, $64.80; The percent of gratuity is 20%. All of the other pairs have a gratuity of 15%.

Lesson 6-6 Extra Practice

15. $103.95 **17.** $7.99 **19.** $96.26 **21.** Yes; $84 was earned. 5% × $70 = $3.50; $70 + $3.50 = $73.50; 15% × $70 = $10.50; $73.50 + $10.50 = $84 **23.** B **25.** Store B; The total cost of the boots at store A is $58.19. The total cost of the boots at store B is $56.98. **27.** 57.85 **29.** $50

Lesson 6-7 Independent Practice

1. $51.20 **3** $6.35 **5** $4.50 **7a.** $28.76, $25.29, $28.87 **7b.** Funtopia **9.** $9.00 **11.** Sample answers are given.

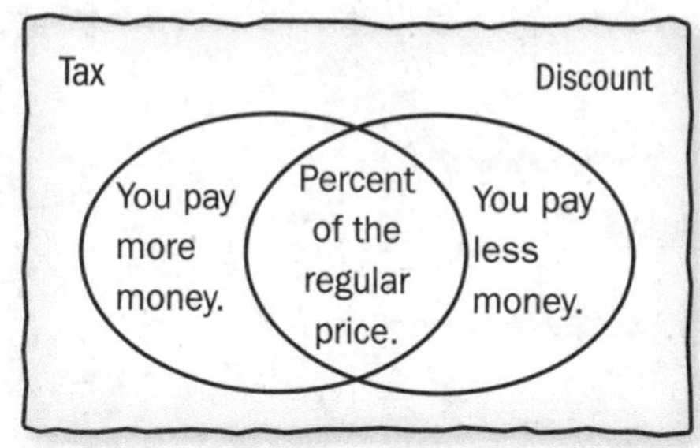

Selected Answers

13. $25

Lesson 6-7 Extra Practice

15. \$102.29 **17.** \$169.15 **19.** Mr. Chang; \$22.50 < \$23.99 **21.** A **23.** 29%; increase **25.** 35%; decrease **27.** Carlos, 18 months; Karen, 16 months; Beng, 14 months

Lesson 6-8 Independent Practice

1. \$38.40 **3.** \$5.80 **5** \$1,417.50 **7.** \$75.78 **9** **a.** 5% **b.** Yes; he would have \$5,208. **11.** Sample answer: If the rate is increased by 1%, then the interest earned is \$60 more. If the time is increased by 1 year, then the interest earned is \$36 more. **13.** C

Lesson 6-8 Extra Practice

15. \$6.25 **17.** \$123.75 **19.** \$45.31 **21.** \$14.06 **23.** C

25–28.

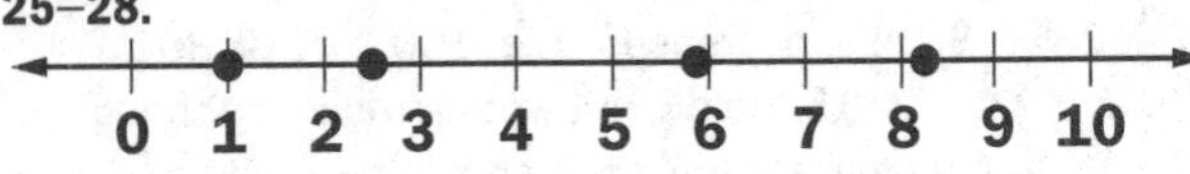

29. Belinda; Sample answer: Since 6 > 4, 5.6 > 5.4. So, Belinda walks a longer distance to school.

Lesson 6-9 Independent Practice

1 102.6 mi **3** 12 cm; $\frac{1}{300}$ **5.** 108 ft^2 **7.** 3x; about $6\frac{1}{3}$ ft or 6 feet 4 in.

Lesson 6-9 Extra Practice

9. 50 km **11.** 102.5 km **13.** $109\frac{3}{8}$ ft **15.** 3,420 ft^2 **17.** H **19.** 5 feet **21.** 21

Chapter Review Vocabulary Check

Down

1. increase **3.** markdown **5.** selling **7.** discount **9.** sales tax

Across

11. interest

Chapter Review Key Concept Check

1. 300 **3.** 18 **5.** 12

Chapter Review Problem Solving

1. 21 students; 12% = 0.12, 0.12(175) = 21 **3.** 5% **5.** \$18

Chapter 7 Statistics

Chapter 7 Are You Ready?

1. Rihanna **3.** 75

Lesson 7-1 Independent Practice

1. $\frac{3}{10}$, 0.3, or 30% **3** $\frac{2}{25}$, 0.08, or 8% **5** 9 students **7.** About 143 students prefer humor books, and the number of students that prefer nonfiction is 88. So, there are about 55 more students who prefer humor books to nonfiction books. **9.** about 100 times **11.** D

Lesson 7-1 Extra Practice

13. 36 games **15.** about 6 free throws **17.** $n = 27 \cdot 2.38$ **19.** D **21.** 35 **23.** 14.4 **25.** 2

Lesson 7-2 Independent Practice

1 The conclusion is valid. This is an unbiased systematic random sample. **3** This is a simple random sample. So, the sample is valid; about 205 people. **5.** Sample answer: Questions should be asked in a neutral manner. For example, the question "You really don't like Brand X, do you?" might not get the same answer as the question "Do you prefer Brand X or Brand Y?" **7.** Sometimes; Sample answer: The sample needs to represent the entire population to be valid. **9.** Sample answer: The sample will be biased because it is a convenience sample. Marisol will be asking only basketball fans.

Lesson 7-2 Extra Practice

11. This is an unbiased, simple random sample because randomly selected Californians were surveyed. So, the conclusion is valid. **13.** This is an unbiased, systematic random sample. So, the conclusion is valid; 304 students. **15.** The survey results in a convenience sample; Sample answer: The school district should survey every tenth family living within the school district's boundaries. **17.** F **19.** median; Sample answer: She scored better than the mean on four of the tests. She scored lower than the mode on four of the tests.

Lesson 7-3 Independent Practice

1 Graph B; Sample answer: The ratio of the area of the gas pumps in the graph on the right are not proportional to the cost of gas. **3** The median or the mode because they are much closer in value to most of the data.

5.

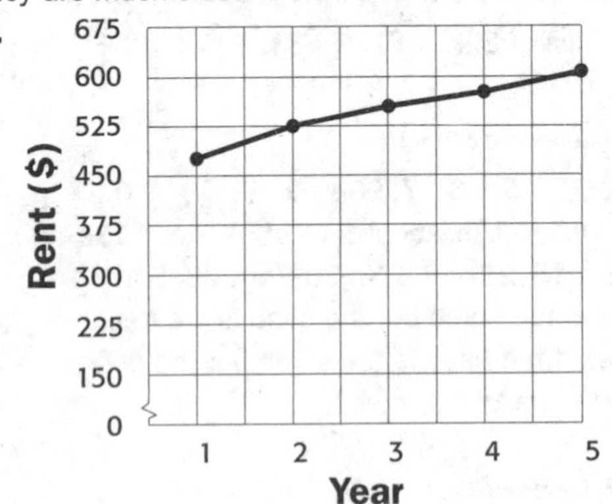

7. Sample answer: Since the graph makes it seem as if rent has been stable, a person may choose to become a tenant. **9.** C

Lesson 7-3 Extra Practice

11. Sample answer: The scale of the graph is not divided into equal intervals, so differences in heights appear less than they actually are. **13.** Sample answer: The mode is 100, but she only received 100 two times out of 6 tests. **15.** 225 min; Sample answer: The ratios of the area of the cell phones are not proportional to the number of minutes.

Problem-Solving Investigation *Use a Graph*

Case 3. Sample answer: 2017

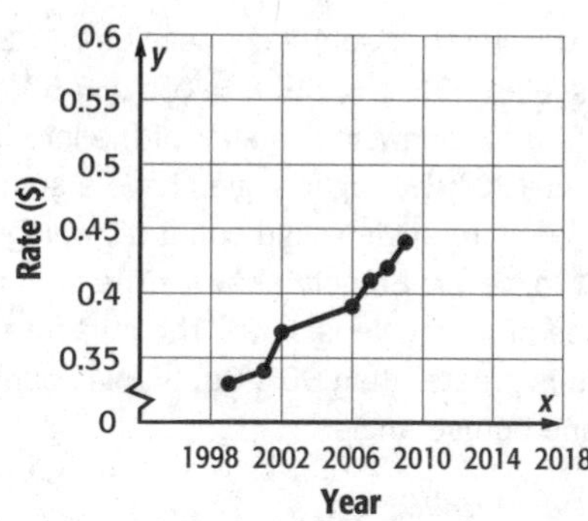

Case 5. Sample answer: about $34

Lesson 7-4 *Independent Practice*

1 Sample answer: The times at Lucy's Steakhouse have a median of 20 minutes with an interquartile range of 20 minutes. The times at Gary's Grill have a median of 15 minutes with an interquartile range of 10 minutes. In general, a customer will wait longer at Lucy's Steakhouse. **3a.** Plant A: 2.75, 0.75; Plant B: 3.1; 0.7

3b.

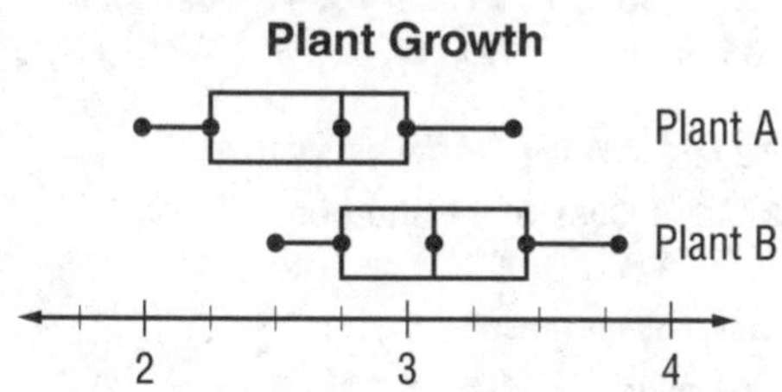

3c. Sample answer: Both populations have similar interquartile ranges. The median for Plant A is higher. So, Plant B generally showed more growth. **5.** The data shown in the histograms are only shown in intervals. Specific values are not shown. **7.** A

Lesson 7-4 *Extra Practice*

9. this season; Sample answer: Both seasons' scores have a median of 20 points, but last season's scores have an interquartile range of 15 points while this season's interquartile range is 10 points. So, the football team's performance was more consistent this season. **11.** Sample answer: 2, 4, 4, 5, 8, 9, 10 **13.** 12.5 mph **15.** Sample answer: There is a peak at 3 and a gap between 5 and 7.

Lesson 7-5 *Independent Practice*

1 box plot; shows the median

3.

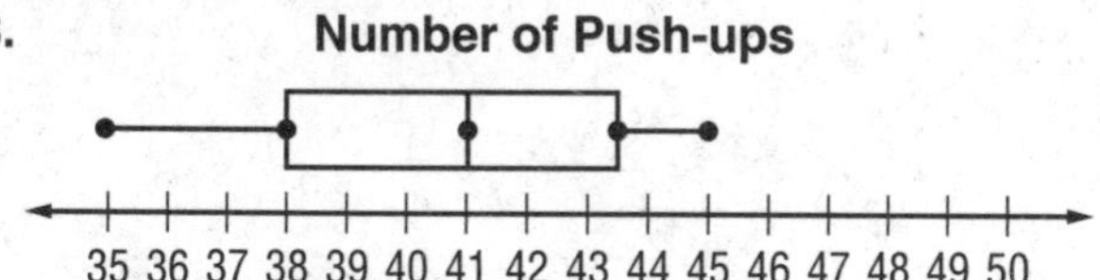

A box plot is an appropriate graph because there is a large set of data and it will show the measures of variation of the data set. This graph has a median of 41. **5a.** Situation B; Sample answer: A bar graph can show the number of customers who made a purchase by each individual age. **5b.** Yes; Sample answer: line plot; A line plot shows the frequency of data on a number line. **7.** always; Sample answer: The sections of the circle graph can be taken from the bars of the graph and the percents can be found by dividing each bar's value by the total number of data values. **9.** C

Lesson 7-5 *Extra Practice*

11. circle graph; compares parts to a whole

13a.

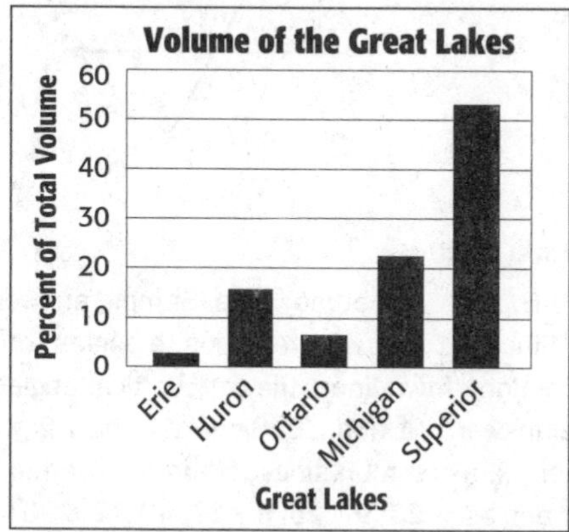

13b. Sample answer: The circle graph is most appropriate because it shows how each lake compares to the whole.

15.

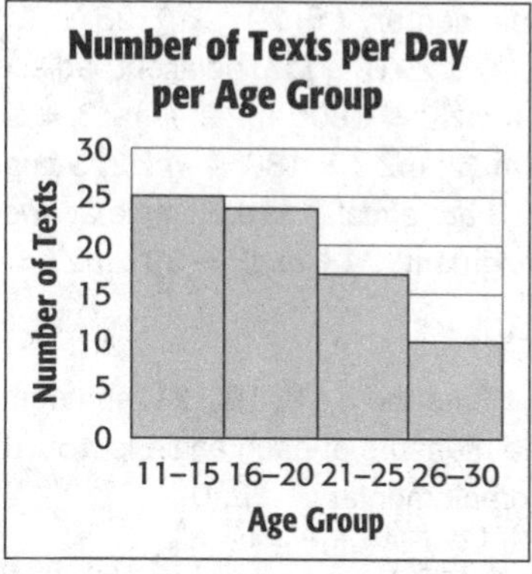

A histogram is an appropriate graph because the data is given in intervals. The graph shows people ages 26–30 text the least amount. **17.** I **19.** 65 men; 65 women

Chapter Review *Vocabulary Check*

Across

5. population **9.** sample

Down

1. systematic **3.** simple **7.** unbiased

Chapter Review *Key Concept Check*

1. survey **3.** biased sample

Chapter Review *Problem Solving*

1. $\frac{3}{10}$ or 0.3 or 30% **3.** This is a systematic random sample. **5.** Sample answer: The median score for Class A is about 6 points lower than the median score for Class B. **7.** no; Sample answer: A circle graph compares parts of the data to the whole.

Chapter 8 Geometric Figures

Chapter 8 Are You Ready?

1. 40° **3.** 90° **5.** 6.72 yd^2

Lesson 8-1 Independent Practice

1. ∠ABC, ∠CBA, ∠B, ∠4; acute **3** ∠MNP, ∠PNM, ∠N, ∠1; obtuse **5** neither **7.** adjacent **9.** vertical **11.** 11 **15.** True; Sample answer:

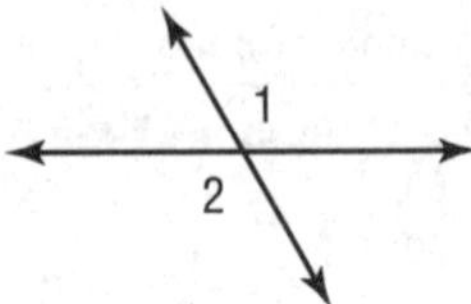

17. A

Lesson 8-1 Extra Practice

19. ∠HKI, ∠IKH, ∠K, ∠8; obtuse **21a.** Sample answer: ∠1 and ∠3; Since ∠1 and ∠3 are opposite angles formed by the intersection of two lines, they are vertical angles. **21b.** Sample answer: ∠1 and ∠2; Since ∠1 and ∠2 share a common vertex, a common side, and do not overlap, they are adjacent angles. **23.** 9 **25.** B **27.** 40 **29.** 90° **31.** $\overline{AB}$, $\overline{BA}$

Lesson 8-2 Independent Practice

1. neither **3** supplementary **5.** 20 **7** 23 **9.** Sample answer: ∠CGK, ∠KGJ **11a.** adjacent; adjacent; vertical **11b.** $m\angle 1 + m\angle 2 = 180°$; $m\angle 2 + m\angle 3 = 180°$ **11c.** $m\angle 1 = 180° - m\angle 2$; $m\angle 3 = 180° - m\angle 2$; Sample answer: $m\angle 1$ and $m\angle 3$ are equal. **11d.** Sample answer: Vertical angles are congruent. **13.** $m\angle E = 39°$, $m\angle F = 51°$

Lesson 8-2 Extra Practice

15. supplementary **17.** neither **19.** 16 **21.** sometimes; Sample answer: If the measure of each angle is 45°, then the two angles are complementary. **23.** D

25. square

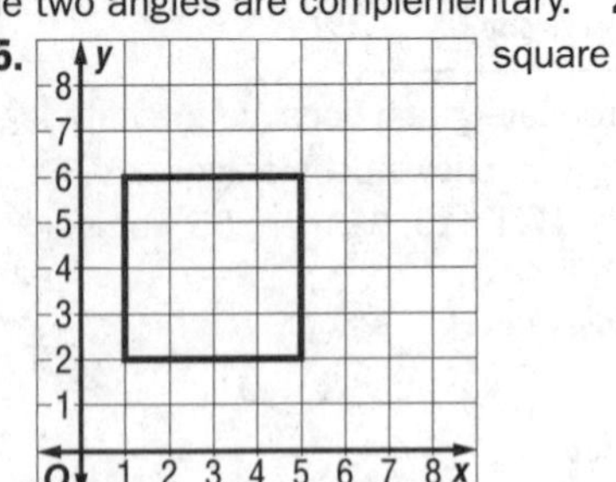

27. parallelogram

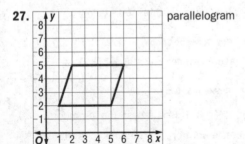

Lesson 8-3 Independent Practice

1 Sample answer: acute equilateral

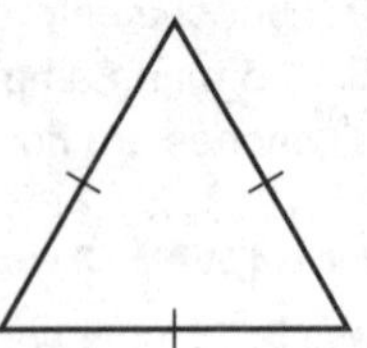

3 acute equilateral **5.** obtuse isosceles **7.** 118 **9.** acute isosceles **11.** $a = 55$; $b = 65$; $c = 60$; $d = 30$ **13a.** never; Sample answer: The sum of the interior angles of a triangle is 180°. Two right angles have a sum of 180°. This means the third angle would equal 0°, which is not possible. **13b.** never; Sample answer: The sum of the interior angles of a triangle is 180°. The measure of an obtuse angle is greater than 90°. So, triangle cannot have more than one obtuse angle.

Lesson 8-3 Extra Practice

15. acute isosceles **17.** right scalene **19.** obtuse isosceles; Sample answer:

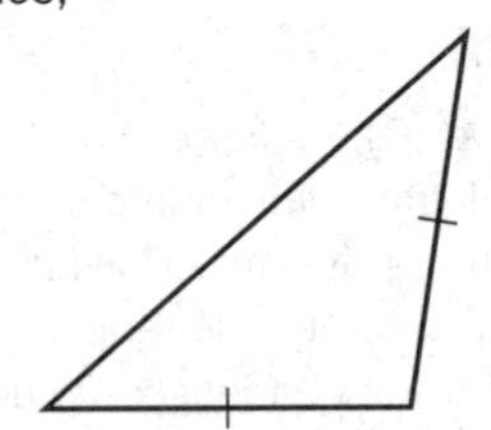

21. 90 **23.** 53° **25.** 30 **27.** B **29.** 47 **31.** 32 ft^2 **33.** 25 m^2 **35.** 36 in^2

Problem-Solving Investigation Make a Model

Case 3. 15 tables **Case 5.** 41 squares

Lesson 8-4 Independent Practice

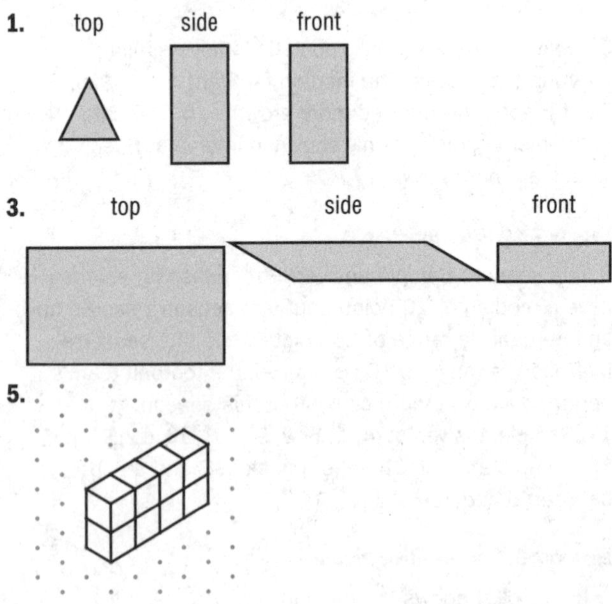

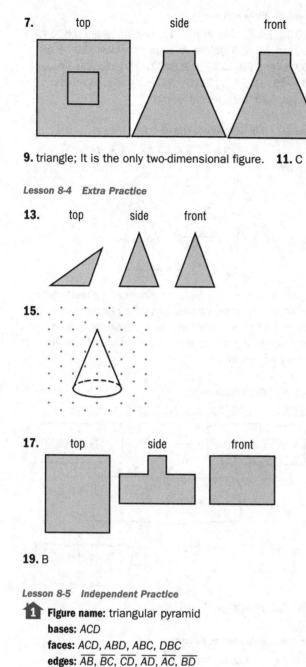

7.

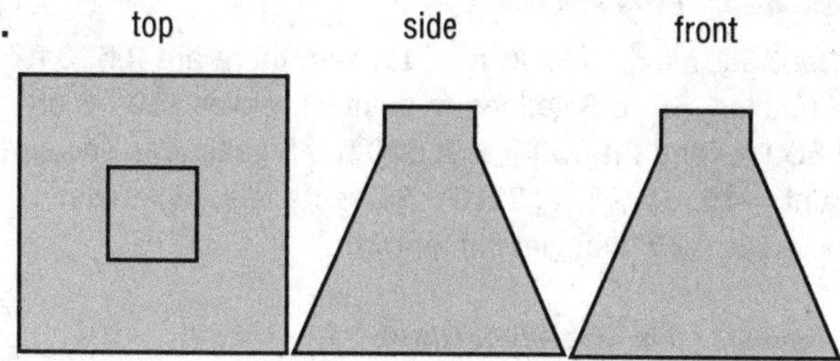

9. triangle; It is the only two-dimensional figure. **11.** C

Lesson 8-4 Extra Practice

13.

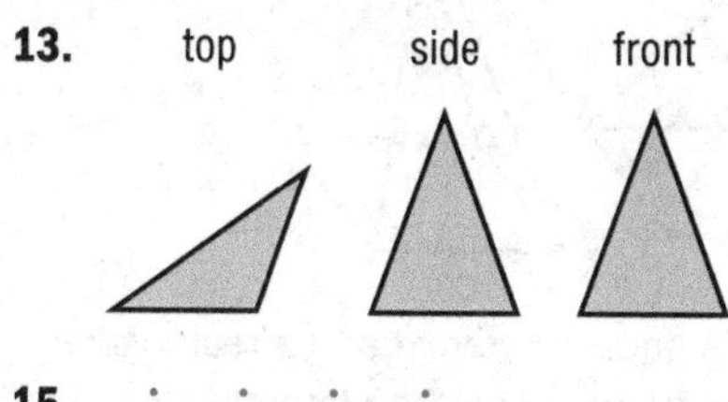

15.

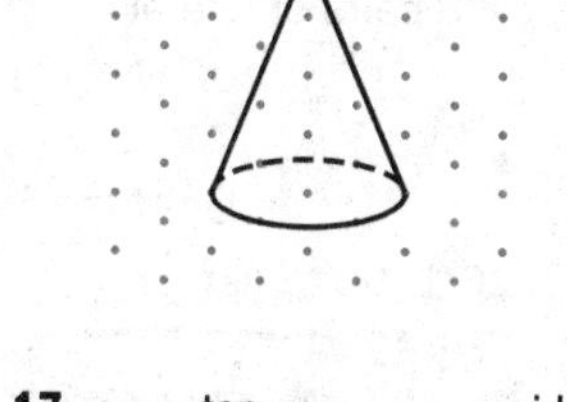

17.

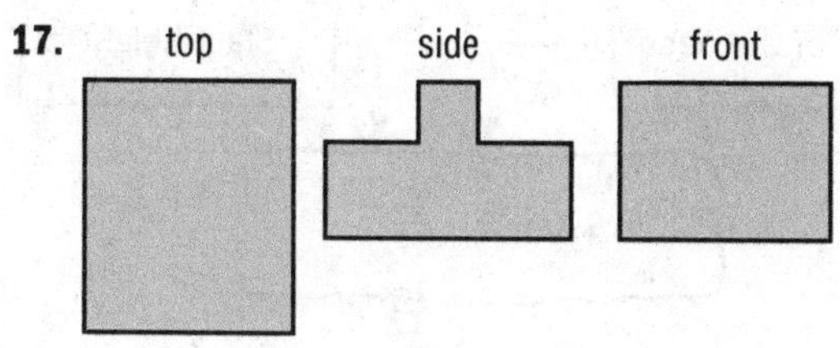

19. B

Lesson 8-5 Independent Practice

1 **Figure name:** triangular pyramid
bases: *ACD*
faces: *ACD*, *ABD*, *ABC*, *DBC*
edges: $\overline{AB}$, $\overline{BC}$, $\overline{CD}$, $\overline{AD}$, $\overline{AC}$, $\overline{BD}$
vertices: *A*, *B*, *C*, *D*

3 rectangle **5.** triangle **7.** False; two planes intersect at a line, which is an infinite number of points.
9. Sometimes; a rectangular prism has 2 bases and 4 faces, but a triangular prism has 2 bases and 3 faces.
11. C

Lesson 8-5 Extra Practice

13. Figure name: rectangular prism
bases: *ABCD*, *EFGH*, *ABFE*, *DCGH*, *ADHE*, *BCGF*
faces: *ABCD*, *EFGH*, *ABFE*, *DCGH*, *ADHE*, *BCGF*
edges: $\overline{AB}$, $\overline{BC}$, $\overline{CD}$, $\overline{AD}$, $\overline{EF}$, $\overline{FG}$, $\overline{GH}$, $\overline{EH}$, $\overline{AE}$, $\overline{BF}$, $\overline{CG}$, $\overline{DH}$
vertices: *A*, *B*, *C*, *D*, *E*, *F*, *G*, *H*

15. curve **17.** Because there are two parallel, congruent triangular bases, it is a triangular prism. **19.** F
21. trapezoid **23.** parallelogram

Chapter Review Vocabulary Check

Across
11. equilateral **15.** complementary
Down
1. adjacent **3.** supplementary **5.** triangle **7.** vertical
9. acute **13.** right

Chapter Review Key Concept Check

1. vertex **3.** 90°

Chapter Review Problem Solving

1. Sample answer: vertical: ∠1 and ∠3; adjacent: ∠1 and ∠2 **3.** 40
5.

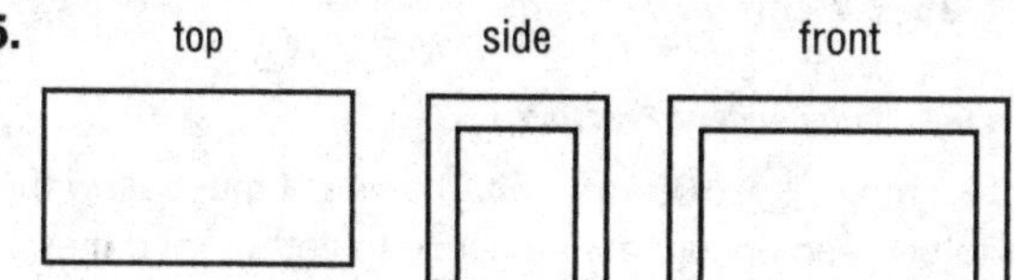

Chapter 9 Measure Figures

Chapter 9 Are You Ready?

1. 42 sq m **3.** 76.5 sq mm

Lesson 9-1 Independent Practice

1. 2.5 mm **3.** 34 cm **5** 3.14 × 13 = 40.8 cm **7** 19 people **9a.** 30 mm **9b.** 31.4 mm
9c. 31.4159 mm **9d.** Sample answer: The more decimal places of the estimate of π, the more precise the circumference. **11.** 18 in. **13.** 257 cm **15.** Greater than; Sample answer: Since the radius is 4 feet, the diameter is 8 feet. Since π is a little more than 3, the circumference will be a little more than 3 times 8, or 24 feet. **17.** The circumference would double. For example, with a diameter of 4 feet, the circumference is about 12.6 feet. With a diameter of 8 feet, the circumference is about 25.1 feet.

Lesson 9-1 Extra Practice

19. 3.5 in. **21.** 72 ft **23.** $\frac{22}{7} \times 21 = 66$ ft **25.** $\frac{22}{7} \times 42 = 132$ mm **27.** 37.7 cm **29.** Each is π, or about 3.14, units longer than the previous circle. **31.** I
33. 315 cm^2 **35.** 2,015 mm^2 **37.** 375 in^2

Lesson 9-2 Independent Practice

1. $3.14 \times 6 \times 6 = 113.0$ cm^2 **3** $3.14 \times 5.5 \times 5.5 = 95.0$ ft^2 **5.** $3.14 \times 6.3 \times 6.3 = 124.6$ mm^2
7. 254.3 ft^2 **9.** 226.1 in^2 **11.** 163.3 yd^2 **13.** The large pizza; the medium pizza's area is 78.5 square inches and costs $0.102 per square inch. The large pizza's area is 153.86 square inches and costs $0.097 per square inch.
15. When the radius of a circle is doubled, the circumference doubles and the area is 4 times as large. In the formula for area of a circle, the radius is squared, so when the radius of a circle is doubled, the area is 2^2 or 4 times as large. **17.** 5.9 in^2 **19.** D

Lesson 9-2 Extra Practice

21. $3.14 \times 6.3 \times 6.3 = 124.6$ cm² **23.** $3.14 \times 5.4 \times 5.4 = 91.6$ yd² **25.** $3.14 \times 9.3 \times 9.3 = 271.6$ mm² **27.** 144.7 ft² **29.** 64.3 in² **31.** circle; $\frac{1}{2} \cdot 100 \cdot 100 < 3 \cdot 50 \cdot 50$ **33.** D **35.** 210 in² **37.** 39.5 cm²

Lesson 9-3 Independent Practice

1. 64 cm² **3.** 220.5 cm² **5.** 38.6 ft² **7.** 119.5 ft² **9.** 77 cm² **11.** 38 ft²; 28 ft **13.** 110.8 ft²

Lesson 9-3 Extra Practice

15. 87.5 m² **17.** 180 cm² **19.** 9 cm² **21.** 240 ft² **23.** G **25.** 3.7 cm² **27.** 4.7 m

Lesson 9-4 Independent Practice

1. 192 m³ **3.** 108 m³ **5b.** The height must allow the water to be deep enough for someone to get wet and the length and width must allow a person to fit. So the first and last sets of dimensions would not work. **7a.** Sample answer: There is a direct relationship between the volume and the length. Since the length is doubled, the volume is also doubled. **7b.** The volume is eight times greater. **7c.** Neither; Sample answer: doubling the height will result in a volume of $4 \cdot 4 \cdot 10$ or 160 in³; doubling the width will result in a volume of $4 \cdot 8 \cdot 5$ or 160 in³. **9.** D

Lesson 9-4 Extra Practice

11. 236.3 cm³ **13.** 20.4 mm³ **15.** $306.52 = 19.4h$; 15.8 m **17.** $166\frac{1}{4}$ yd³ **19.** B **21.** C **23.** 25.8 m **25.** 29.2 cm

Problem-Solving Investigation Solve a Simpler Problem

Case 3. 80 chairs **Case 5.** Sample answer: Asia, 17,251,712.4 mi²; Africa, 11,616,153.02 mi²; N. America, 9,488,441.82 mi²

Lesson 9-5 Independent Practice

1. 80 ft³ **3.** 42 ft³ **5.** 14 in. **7.** 10 in³ **9.** The volume is eight times greater; Sample answer: Since each dimension is two times greater, the volume is $2 \times 2 \times 2$ or eight times greater. **11.** Sample answer: first set: area of the base, 40 ft²; height of the pyramid, 12 ft; second set: area of the base, 30 ft²; height of the pyramid, 16 ft **13.** The volumes are the same.

Lesson 9-5 Extra Practice

15. 60 in³ **17.** 195 yd³ **19.** 11 ft **21.** 22 in. **23.** 1,234.2 m³ **25.** H **27.** 1.5 ft² **29.** 28.75 ft²

Lesson 9-6 Independent Practice

1. 314 cm² **3.** 207 in² **5.** 180 in² **7.** $S.A. = 6x^2$ **9.** False; Sample answer: A $9 \times 7 \times 13$ rectangular prism has a surface area of $2(9 \times 13) + 2(9 \times 7) + 2(13 \times 7)$ or 542 square units. Doubling the length, the surface area is $2(18 \times 13) + 2(18 \times 7) + 2(13 \times 7)$ or 902 square units. $2 \times 542 \neq 902$ **11.** 1,926 cm²

Lesson 9-6 Extra Practice

13. 833.1 mm² **15.** 96 ft² **17.** Yes; there are 2,520 ft² of fencing. Since 8 gallons of paint will cover $350 \cdot 8$ or 2,800 ft² and 2,800 ft² > 2,520 ft², 8 gallons is enough paint. **19.** 64.5 in² **21.** G **23.** rectangle; rectangle; rectangle **25.** triangle; circle; oval

Lesson 9-7 Independent Practice

1. 95 in² **3.** 328 in² **5.** 0.52 ft² **7.** 78 in² **9.** 6.5 cm

11.

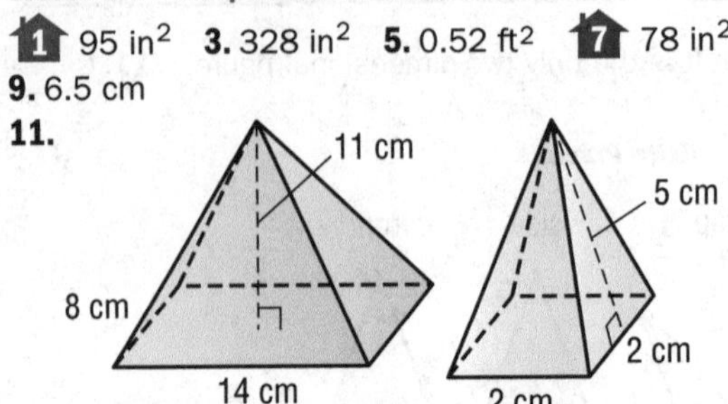

Sample answer: Both a square pyramid and a rectangular pyramid have isosceles triangles as their lateral faces. All the lateral faces are congruent on a square pyramid but, on a rectangular pyramid, the opposite pairs of lateral faces are congruent.

Lesson 9-7 Extra Practice

13. 197.1 m² **15.** 765 cm² **17.** 26.1 ft²

19.

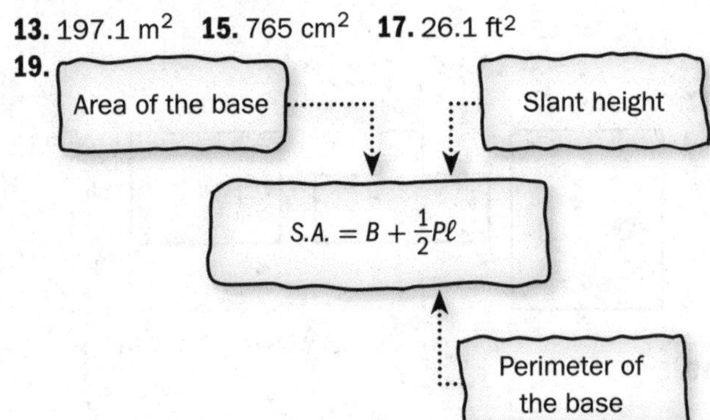

21. H **23.** 13,890 cm² **25.** 5 m

Lesson 9-8 Independent Practice

1. 2.3 m³ **3.** 2,600 ft² **5.** 0.5 ft³ **7.** 10.4 m² **9.** 100 in³ **13.** C

Lesson 9-8 Extra Practice

15. 100 in³ **17.** 280.2 cm² **19.** B **21.** Sample answer: Find the volume of 2 pyramids.; 192 mm³

23.

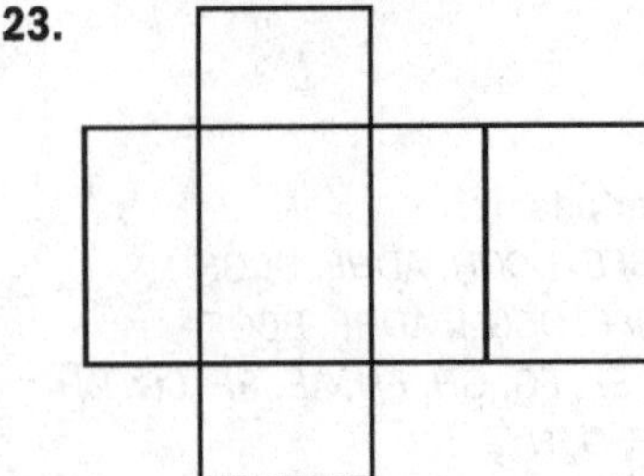

25.

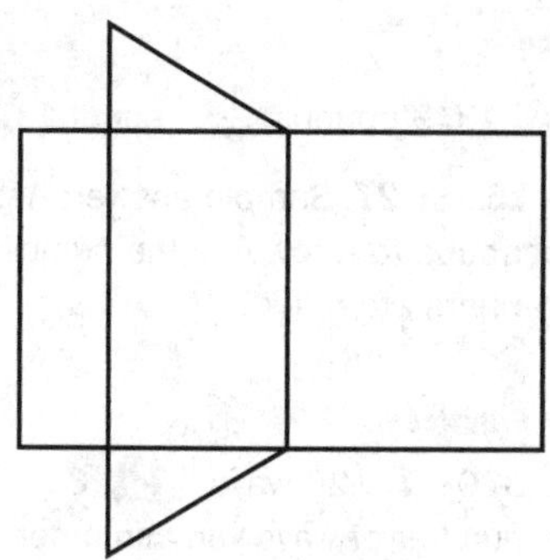

Chapter Review *Vocabulary Check*

1. diameter **3.** circle **5.** circumference **7.** semicircle **9.** volume **11.** lateral

Chapter Review *Key Concept Check*

1. twice **3.** height

Chapter Review *Problem Solving*

1. 37.7 ft **3.** 74.6 ft^2; Sample answer: Find the area of the board. Then subtract the area of the circles. **5.** 784 in^3

Chapter 10 Probability

Chapter 10 *Are You Ready?*

1. $\frac{1}{3}$ **3.** $\frac{2}{3}$ **5.** 30 **7.** 24

Lesson 10-1 *Independent Practice*

1. $\frac{1}{4}$, 25%, or 0.25 **3** $\frac{1}{1}$, 100%, or 1 **5** $\frac{1}{5}$, 0.2, or 20%; Sample answer: Since 80% arrive on time, that means that 20% do not arrive on time. **7.** Picking a black jelly bean is impossible since the probability of picking a black jelly bean is 0%. **9a.** $\frac{1}{8}$, 0.125, 12.5%; $\frac{1}{2}$, 0.5, 50% **9b.** $\frac{1}{8}$, 0.125, 12.5% **11.** D

Lesson 10-1 *Extra Practice*

13. $\frac{1}{5}$, 20%, 0.2 **15.** $\frac{7}{10}$, 70%, or 0.7 **17.** $\frac{1}{2}$, 50%, or 0.5 **19.** $\frac{3}{5}$, 60%, or 0.6 **21.** The complement of selecting a girl is selecting a boy. The probability of the complement is $\frac{37}{100}$, 0.37, or 37%. **23.** $\frac{124}{125}$, 99.2%, or 0.992; It is very likely that card 13 will *not* be chosen. **25.** $\frac{1}{2}$, 0.5, or 50% **27.** < **29.** <

Lesson 10-2 *Independent Practice*

1 **a.** $\frac{1}{5}$; The experimental probability is close to the theoretical probability of $\frac{1}{6}$. **b.** $\frac{9}{10}$; The experimental probability is close to the theoretical probability of $\frac{5}{6}$. **3a.** 162 people **3b.** about 134 people **5** **a.** $\frac{1}{3}$ tosses **b.** $\frac{6}{25}$, $\frac{13}{50}$

c.

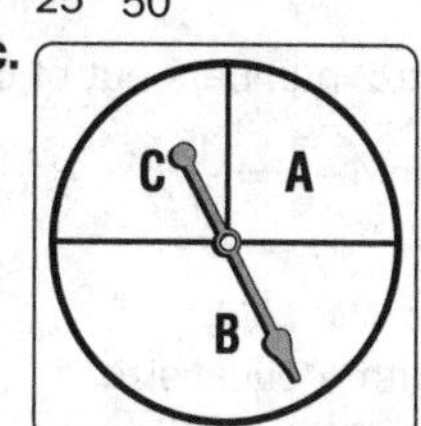

Sample answer: Section B should be one half of the spinner and sections A and C should each be one fourth of the spinner. **7.** Yes; Sample answer: $\frac{5 \text{ sharpened}}{10 \text{ unsharpened}} = \frac{20 \text{ sharpened}}{x \text{ unsharpened}}$. So, $x = 40$.

Lesson 10-2 *Extra Practice*

9. $P(\text{heads}) = \frac{\text{number of times heads occurs}}{\text{total number of coin tosses}} = \frac{9}{20}$; The experimental probability of $\frac{9}{20}$ is close to the theoretical probability of $\frac{1}{2}$. **11.** 50 customers **13.** B **15.** *P*(not red) **17.** vanilla sundae, vanilla cone, chocolate sundae, chocolate cone, strawberry sundae, strawberry cone; equally likely

Lesson 10-3 *Independent Practice*

1. H1, H2, H3, H4, H5, T1, T2, T3, T4, T5

3 purple 10, purple 18, purple 21, purple 24, green 10, green 18, green 21, green 24, black 10, black 18, black 21, black 24, silver 10, silver 18, silver 21, silver 24

5. $\frac{1}{36}$;

1, 1	1, 2	1, 3	1, 4	1, 5	1, 6
2, 1	2, 2	2, 3	2, 4	2, 5	2, 6
3, 1	3, 2	3, 3	3, 4	3, 5	3, 6
4, 1	4, 2	4, 3	4, 4	4, 5	4, 6
5, 1	5, 2	5, 3	5, 4	5, 5	5, 6
6, 1	6, 2	6, 3	6, 4	6, 5	6, 6

7 *P*(Player 1) = $\frac{6}{8}$ or $\frac{3}{4}$; *P*(Player 2) = $\frac{2}{8}$ or $\frac{1}{4}$; RRB, RYB, RRY, RYY, BRB, BYB, BYY, BRY **9.** The first outcome in the I bracket should be IC.

Lesson 10-3 *Extra Practice*

11.

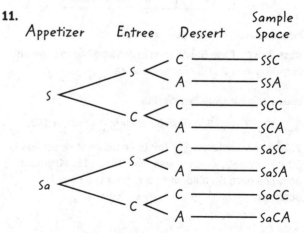

Appetizer	Entree	Dessert	Sample Space
S	S	C	SSC
		A	SSA
	C	C	SCC
		A	SCA
Sa	S	C	SaSC
		A	SaSA
	C	C	SaCC
		A	SaCA

13a. 16 combinations **13b.** $\frac{1}{16}$ **13c.** 8 combinations **15.** C **17.** $\frac{1}{8}$ **19.** $\frac{1}{2}$ **21.** $\frac{1}{3}$; There are 2 numbers out of 6 on a number cube that are greater than 4. $\frac{2}{6} = \frac{1}{3}$

Lesson 10-4 Independent Practice

1 Sample answer: Spin a spinner with 4 equal-size sections 50 times. **3.** Sample answer: Spin a spinner divided into 3 equal sections and roll a number cube. Repeat the simulation until all types of cookies are obtained. **5.** Sample answer: Use 3 red marbles to represent winning and 7 blue marbles to represent losing. Draw 1 marble 4 times, replacing the marble each time. **7.** Sample answer: a survey of 100 people voting on whether or not to enact a tax increase, where each person is equally likely to vote yes or no. Toss a coin 100 times. **9.** Sample answer: sometimes; The spinner must have equal-sized sections.

Lesson 10-4 Extra Practice

11. Sample answer: Use a spinner with 5 equal sections to represent the 5 discounts. Spin 4 times to represent 4 customers receiving cards. **13.** Sample answer: Toss a coin. Heads represents one color and tails represents the other. Repeat until both are selected. **15.** Sample answer: Spin a spinner with 4 equal sections. Each section represents one of the magazines. Repeat the simulation until all possible magazines are selected. **17.** F

19. 10 ways;

Number of Quarters	Number of Dimes	Number of Nickels
2	0	0
1	2	1
1	1	3
1	0	5
0	5	0
0	4	2
0	3	4
0	2	6
0	1	8
0	0	10

Problem-Solving Investigation Act It Out

Case 3. 31 **Case 5.** no; Sample answer: The experiment only produces 2 or 3 correct answers.

Lesson 10-5 Independent Practice

1 12 **3.** 84 **5.** 6 possible routes; $\frac{1}{6}$ or about 17%

7. $\frac{1}{50}$; very unlikely **9** No; the number of selections is $32 \cdot 11$ or 352, which is less than 365. **11.** 10 groups, 8 activities have 80 outcomes; the other two have 72 outcomes.

Lesson 10-5 Extra Practice

13. 48 **15.** 20 **17.** 24 **19.** 9 options; $\frac{1}{9}$ or about 11.1%; unlikely **21.** C **23.** 6 **25.** $\frac{1}{2}$ **27.** Sample answer: Assign each number of a number cube to a toy. Roll the number cube. Repeat until all numbers are rolled.

Lesson 10-6 Independent Practice

1 24 **3.** 840 **5.** 40,320 **7.** 120 ways **9** 6 **11.** Sample answer: The number of ways you can order 3 books on a shelf is $3 \cdot 2 \cdot 1$ or 6. **13.** C

Lesson 10-6 Extra Practice

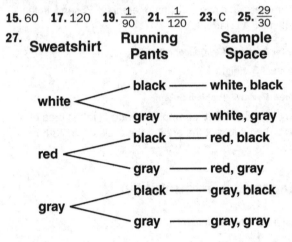

15. 60 **17.** 120 **19.** $\frac{1}{90}$ **21.** $\frac{1}{120}$ **23.** C **25.** $\frac{29}{30}$

27.

Sweatshirt	Running Pants	Sample Space
white	black	white, black
	gray	white, gray
red	black	red, black
	gray	red, gray
gray	black	gray, black
	gray	gray, gray

Lesson 10-7 Independent Practice

1. $\frac{1}{24}$ **3** $\frac{1}{8}$ **5.** $\frac{1}{144}$ **7** $\frac{7}{95}$ **9.** $\frac{1}{19}$ **11.** $\frac{3}{8}$; dependent event; after the first piece of paper is chosen, there is one less from which to choose. **13.** Sample answer: Spinning the spinner twice represents two independent events. The probability of getting an even number is $\frac{2}{5}$ each time; $\frac{2}{5} \cdot \frac{2}{5}$ or $\frac{4}{25}$. **15** B

Lesson 10-7 Extra Practice

17. $\frac{5}{14}$ **19.** $\frac{92}{287}$ **21.** $\frac{3}{20}$ **23.** $\frac{7}{60}$ **25.** $\frac{3}{55}$ **27.** $\frac{6}{55}$ **29.** C **31.** $\frac{15}{77}$ **33.** 6ways; Video 1, Video 2, Video 3; Video 1, Video 3, Video 2; Video 2, Video 1, Video 3; Video 2, Video 3, Video 1; Video 3, Video 1, Video 2; Video 3, Video 2, Video 1

Chapter Review Vocabulary Check

1. sample space **3.** theoretical

Chapter Review Key Concept Check

1. experimental probability **3.** compound event

Chapter Review Problem Solving

1. $\frac{6}{25}$ or 0.24 or 24%

3. $\frac{2}{4}$ or $\frac{1}{2}$;

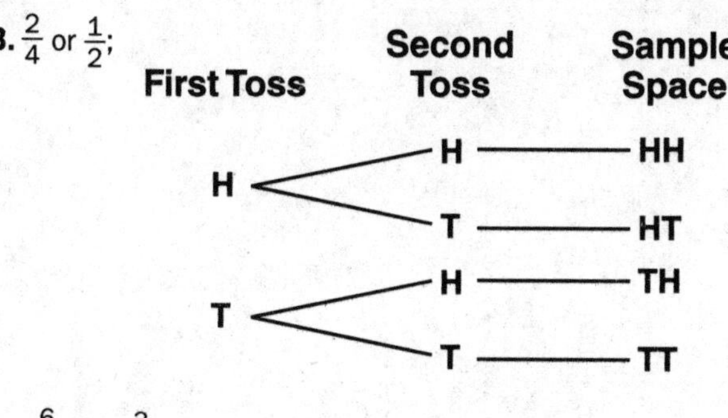

5. $\frac{6}{380}$ or $\frac{3}{190}$

Selected Answers

Index

Ff

Gg

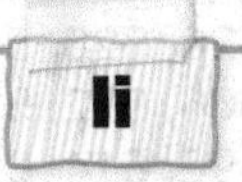

Mm

Nn

Qq

Rr

Ss

Tt

Uu

Vv

Ww

Xx

Yy

Zz

Name ______________________________

=

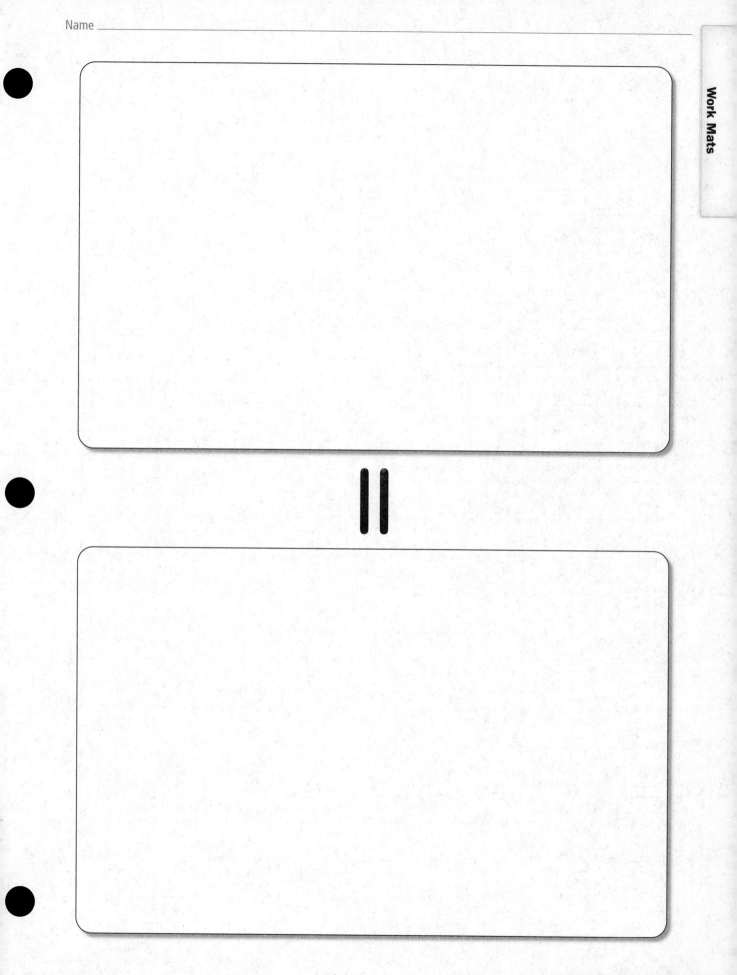

Name ____________________

Name ____________________

Work Mats

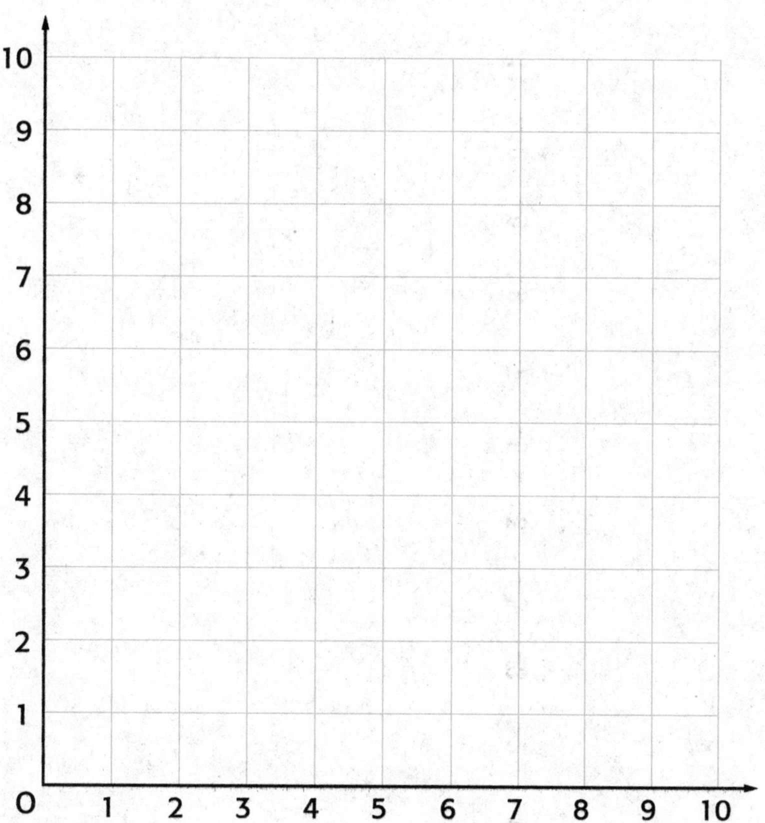

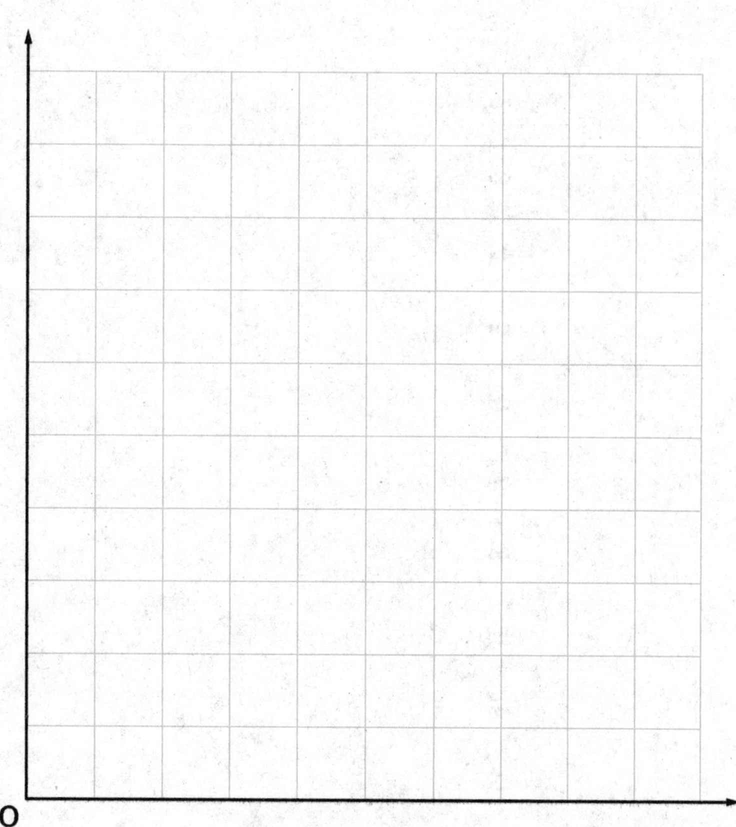

Name ______________________________

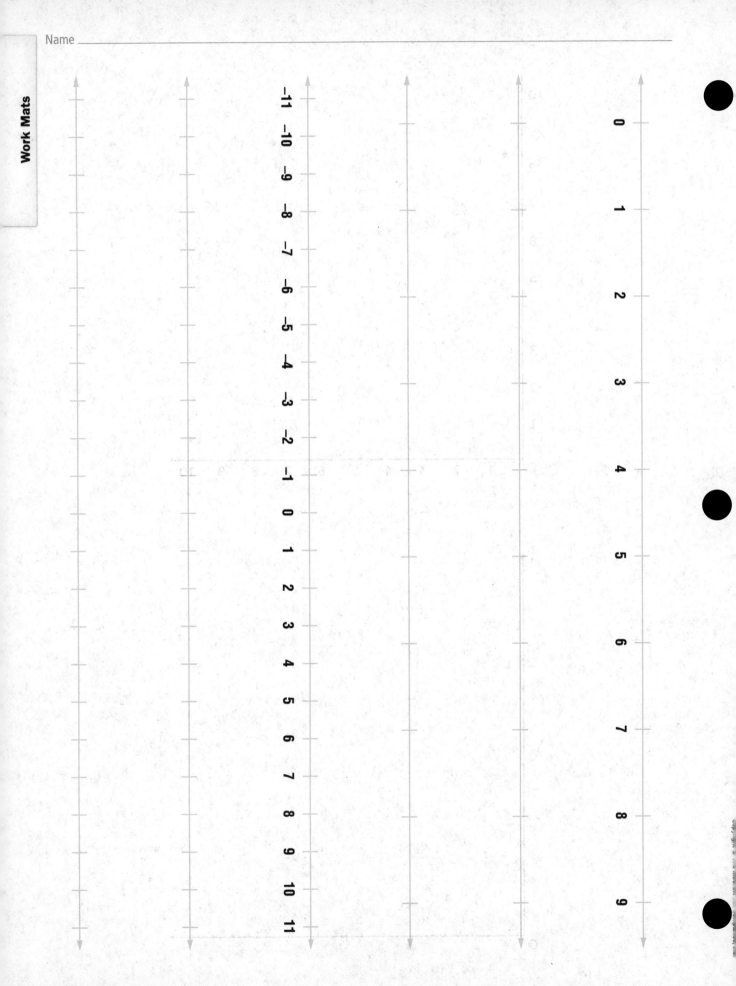

0 1 2 3 4 5 6 7 8 9

–11 –10 –9 –8 –7 –6 –5 –4 –3 –2 –1 0 1 2 3 4 5 6 7 8 9 10 11

Name ______________________________

=

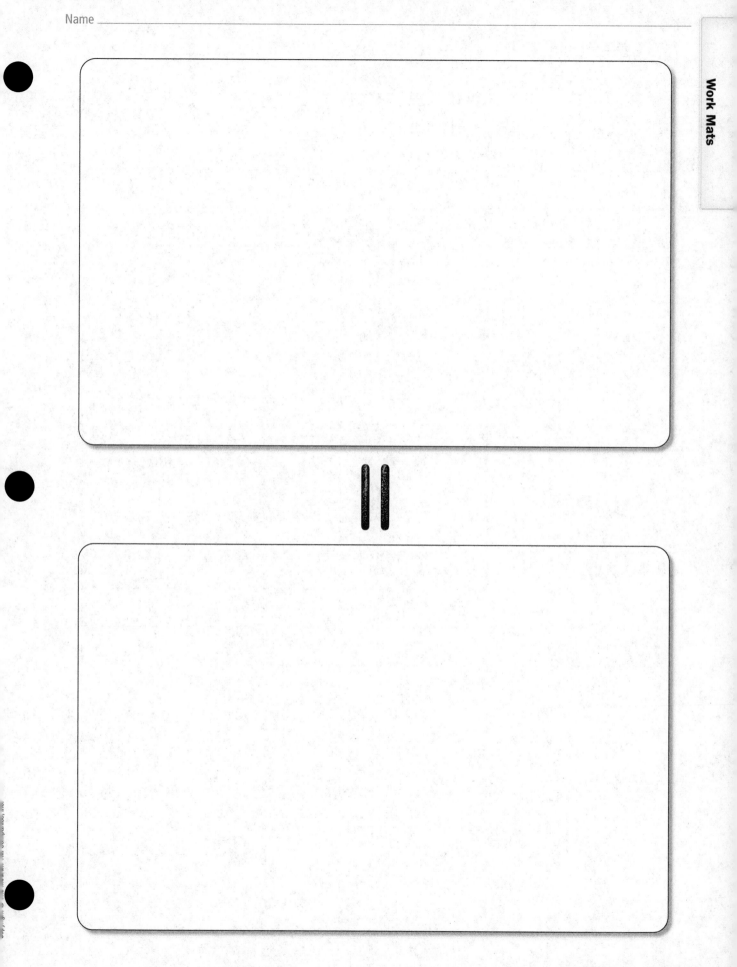

Work Mats

Name ______________________________

Name ______________________________

Name ____________________

Work Mats

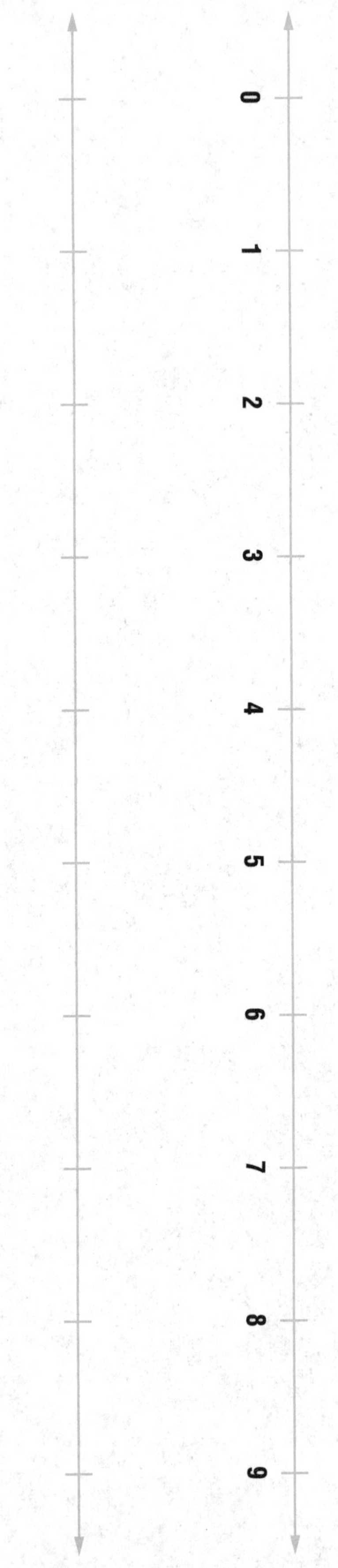

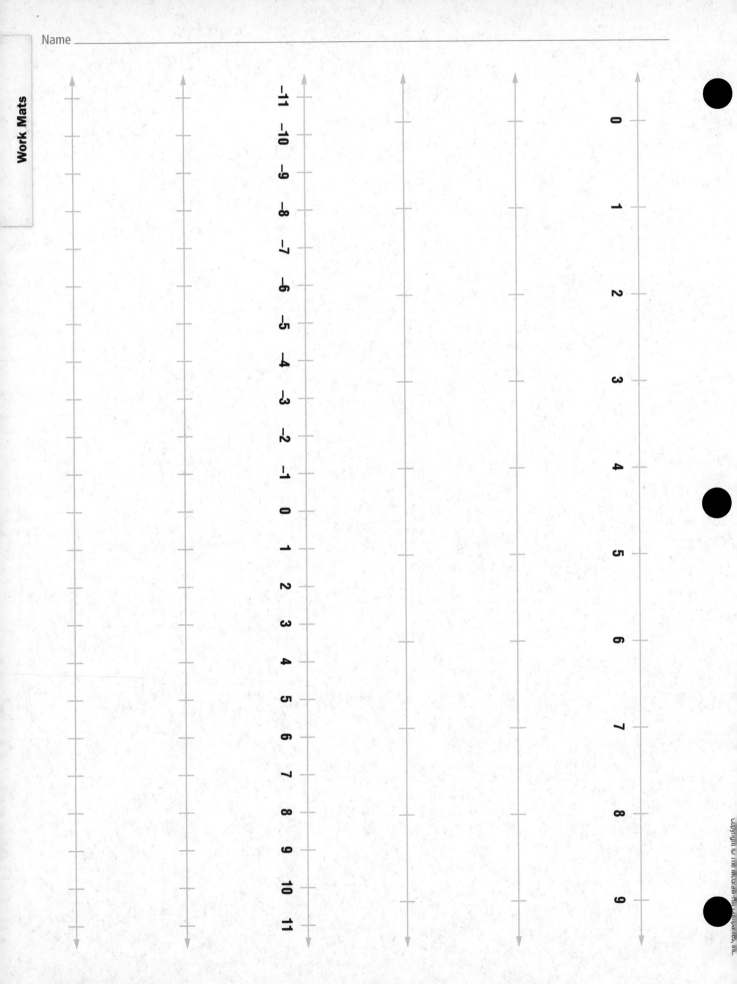

–11 –10 –9 –8 –7 –6 –5 –4 –3 –2 –1 0 1 2 3 4 5 6 7 8 9 10 11

What Are Foldables and How Do I Create Them?

Foldables are three-dimensional graphic organizers that help you create study guides for each chapter in your book.

Step 1 Go to the back of your book to find the Foldable for the chapter you are currently studying. Follow the cutting and assembly instructions at the top of the page.

Step 2 Go to the Key Concept Check at the end of the chapter you are currently studying. Match up the tabs and attach your Foldable to this page. Dotted tabs show where to place your Foldable. Striped tabs indicate where to tape the Foldable.

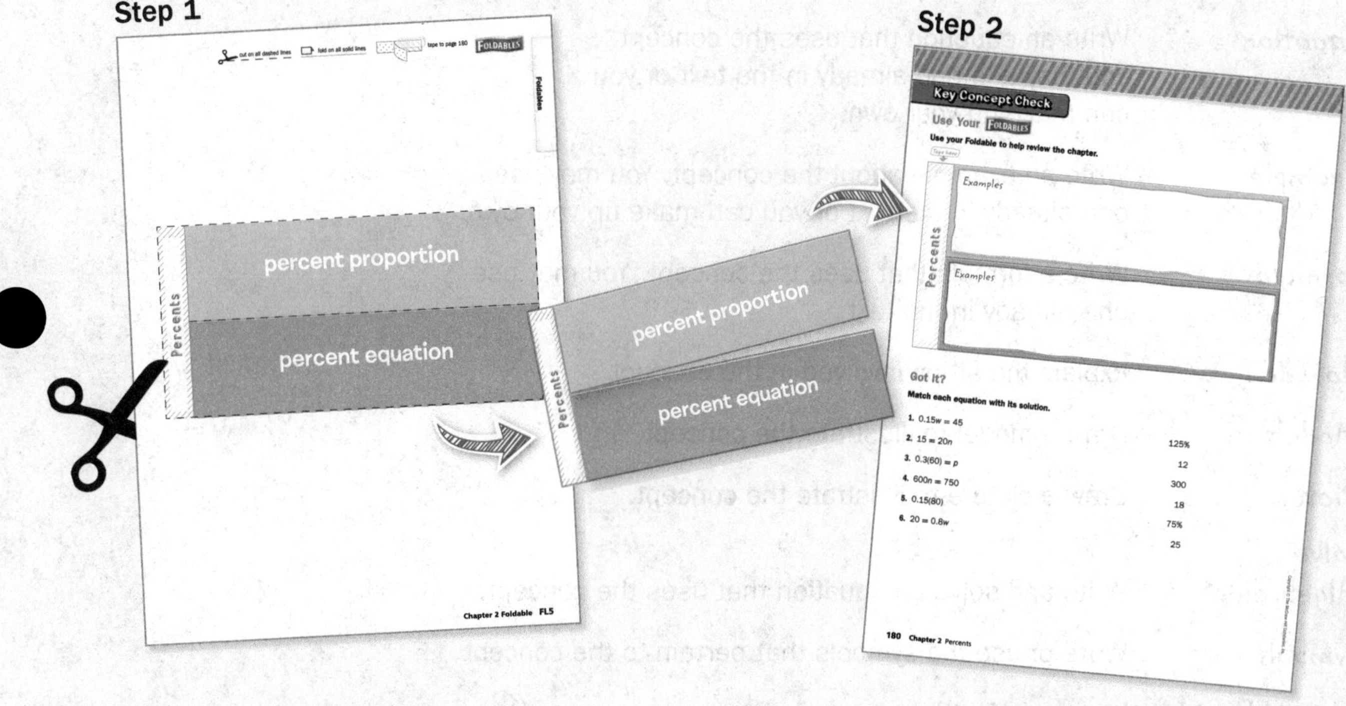

How Will I Know When to Use My Foldable?

When it's time to work on your Foldable, you will see a Foldables logo at the bottom of the **Rate Yourself!** box on the Guided Practice pages. This lets you know that it is time to update it with concepts from that lesson. Once you've completed your Foldable, use it to study for the chapter test.

Rate Yourself!
How well do you understand percent and proportions? Circle the image that applies.
Clear
Somewhat Clear
No So Clear
For more help, go online to access a Personal Tutor.
Tutor
FOLDABLES Time to update your Foldable!

How Do I Complete My Foldable?

No two Foldables in your book will look alike. However, some will ask you to fill in similar information. Below are some of the instructions you'll see as you complete your Foldable. **HAVE FUN** learning math using Foldables!

Instructions and what they mean

Instruction	What it means
Best Used to...	Complete the sentence explaining when the concept should be used.
Definition	Write a definition in your own words.
Description	Describe the concept using words.
Equation	Write an equation that uses the concept. You may use one already in the text or you can make up your own.
Example	Write an example about the concept. You may use one already in the text or you can make up your own.
Formulas	Write a formula that uses the concept. You may use one already in the text.
How do I ...?	Explain the steps involved in the concept.
Models	Draw a model to illustrate the concept.
Picture	Draw a picture to illustrate the concept.
Solve Algebraically	Write and solve an equation that uses the concept.
Symbols	Write or use the symbols that pertain to the concept.
Write About It	Write a definition or description in your own words.
Words	Write the words that pertain to the concept.

Meet Foldables Author Dinah Zike

Dinah Zike is known for designing hands-on manipulatives that are used nationally and internationally by teachers and parents. Dinah is an explosion of energy and ideas. Her excitement and joy for learning inspires everyone she touches.

cut on all dashed lines

fold on all solid lines

tape to page 70

FOLDABLES

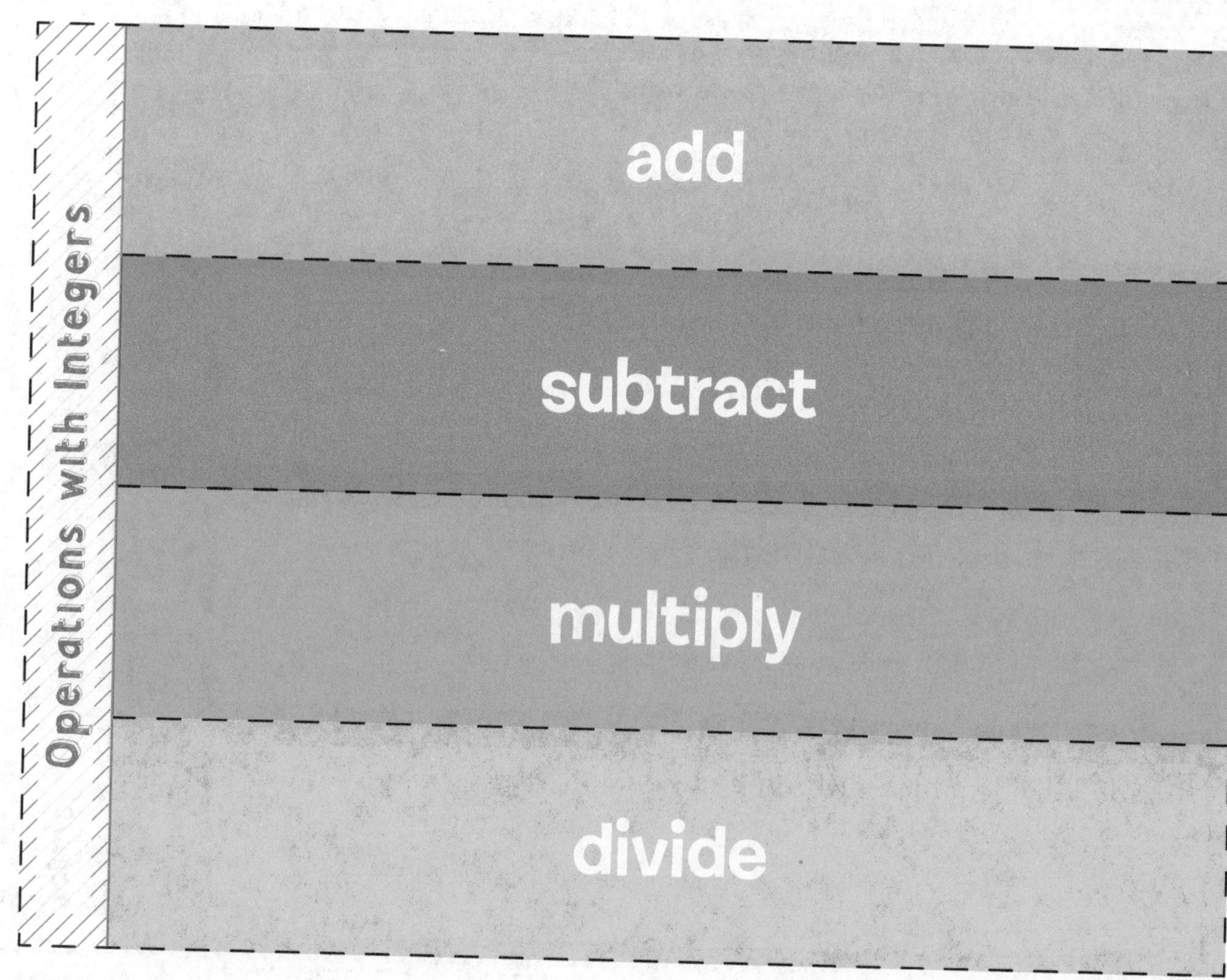

cut on all dashed lines   fold on all solid lines   tape to page 70   FOLDABLES

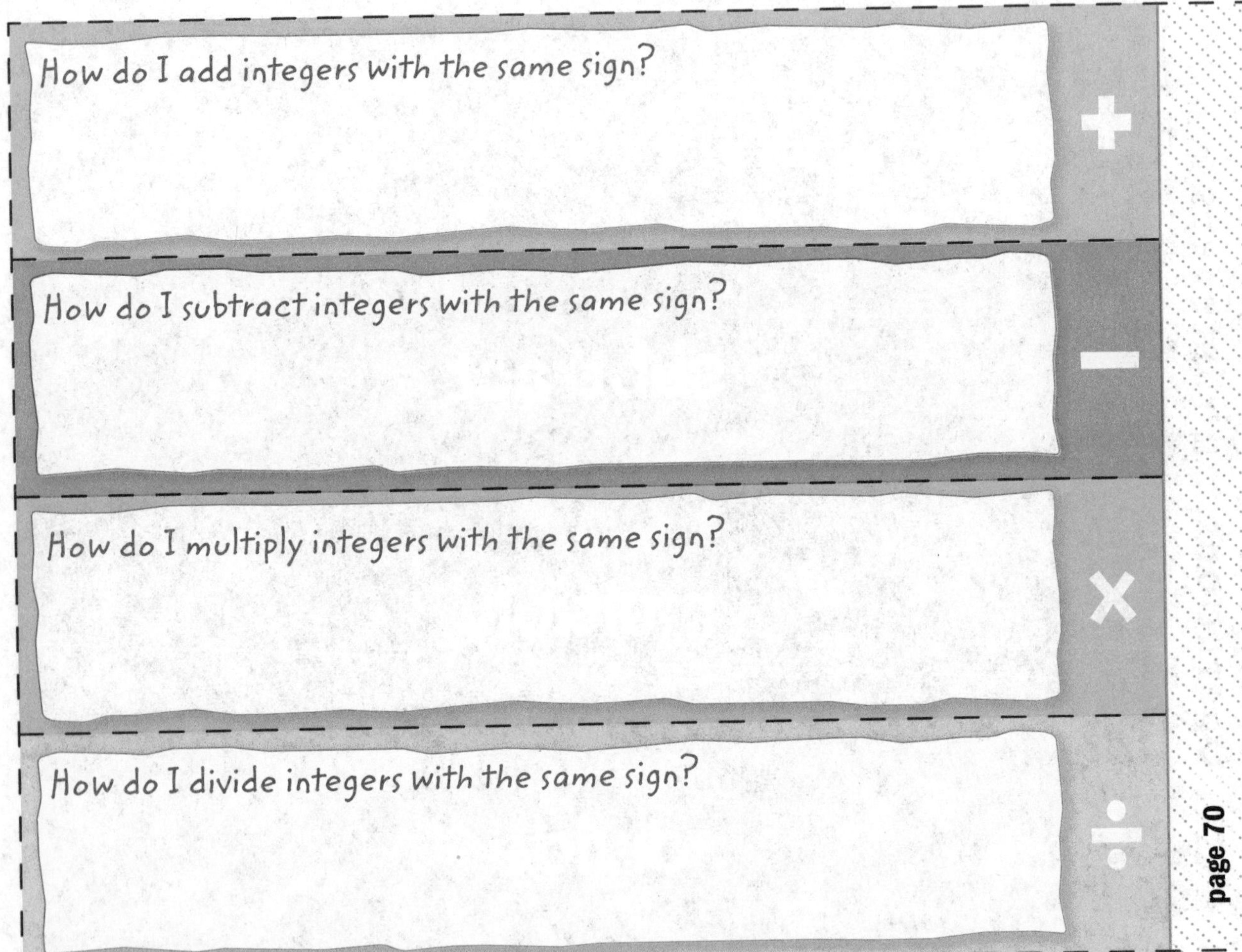
How do I add integers with the same sign?
+
How do I subtract integers with the same sign?
−
How do I multiply integers with the same sign?
×
How do I divide integers with the same sign?
÷
page 70

cut on all dashed lines fold on all solid lines tape to page 154 FOLDABLES

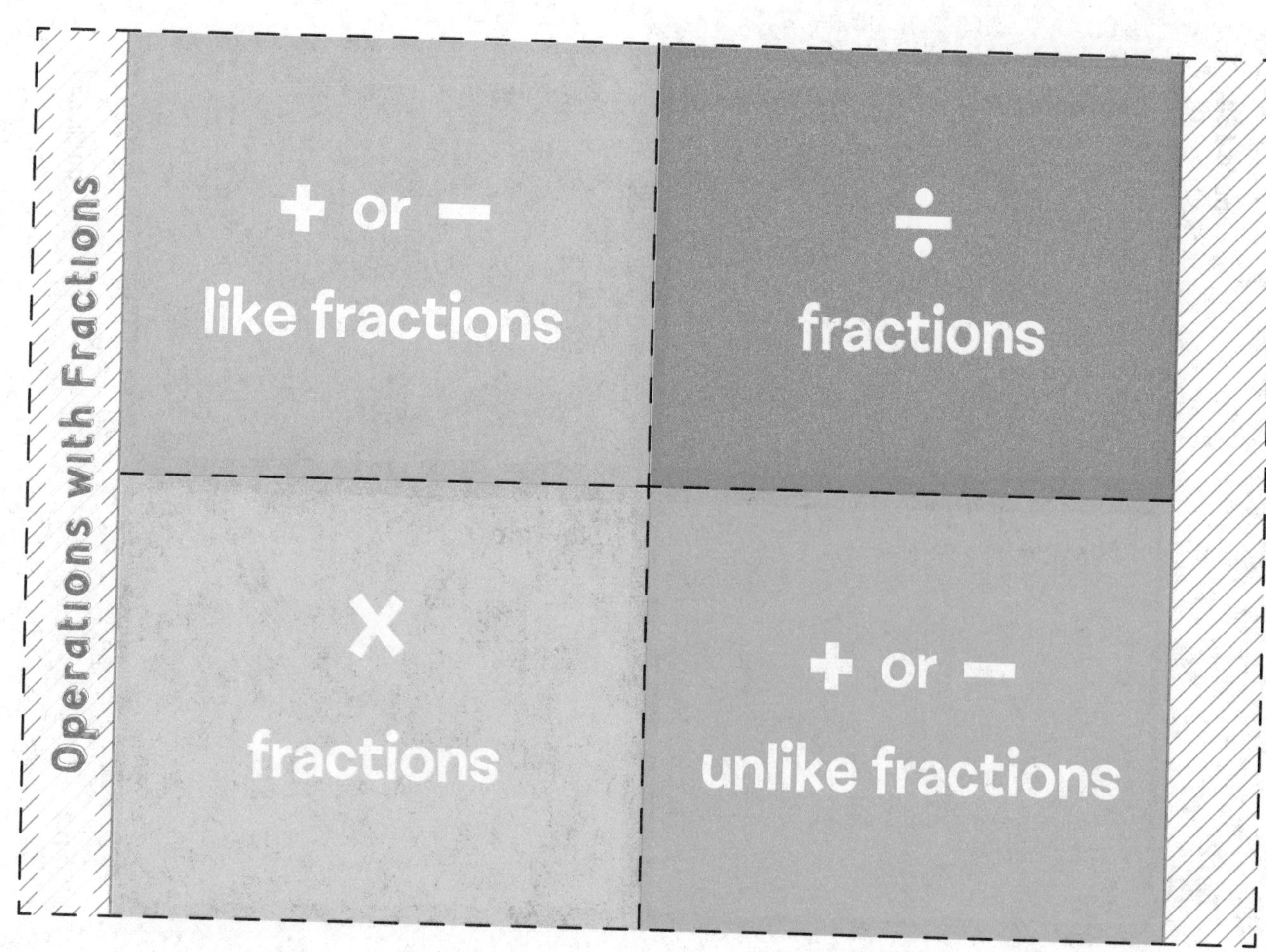

Foldables

cut on all dashed lines   fold on all solid lines   tape to page 154   FOLDABLES

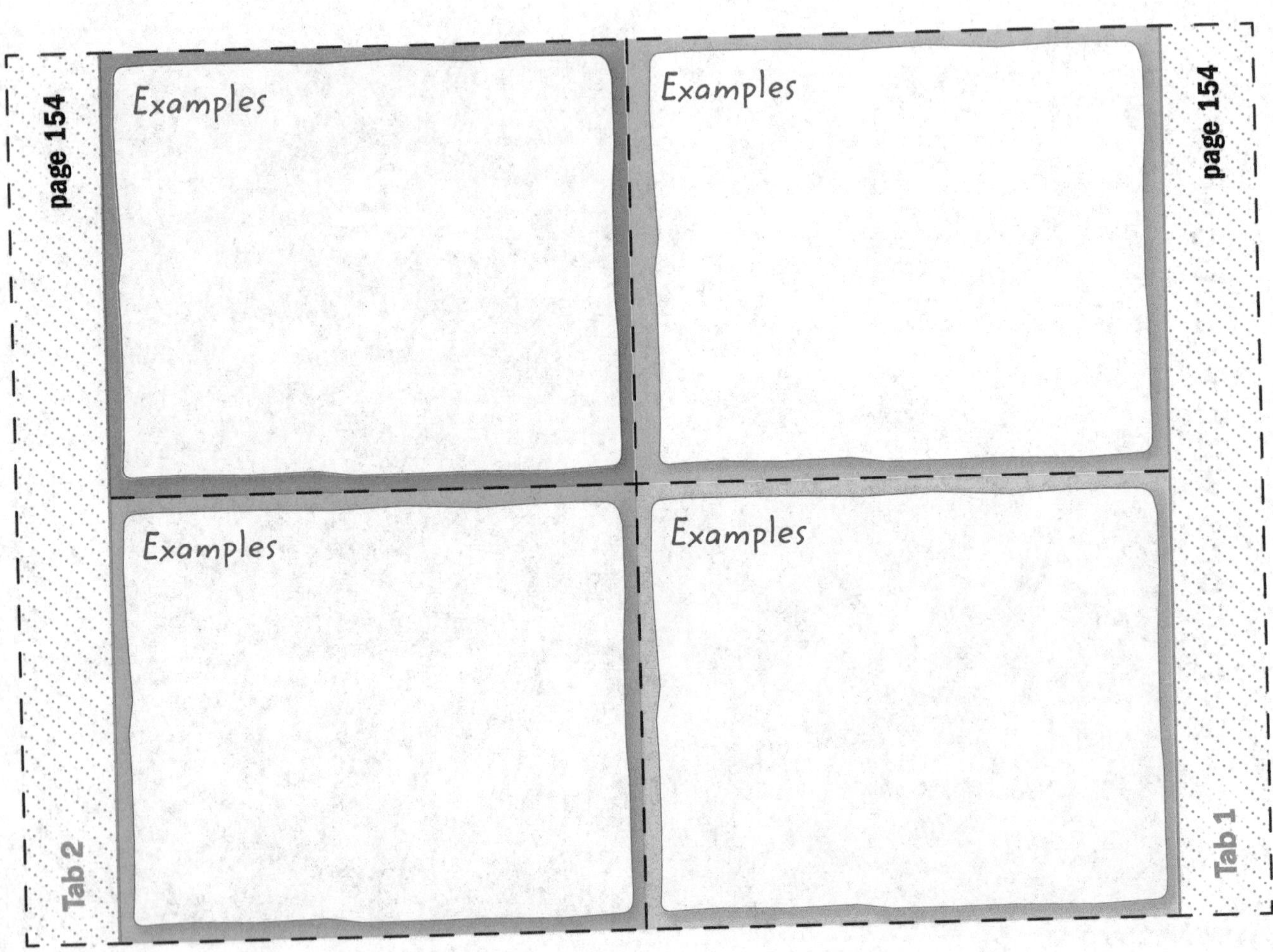

cut on all dashed lines fold on all solid lines tape to page 240 FOLDABLES

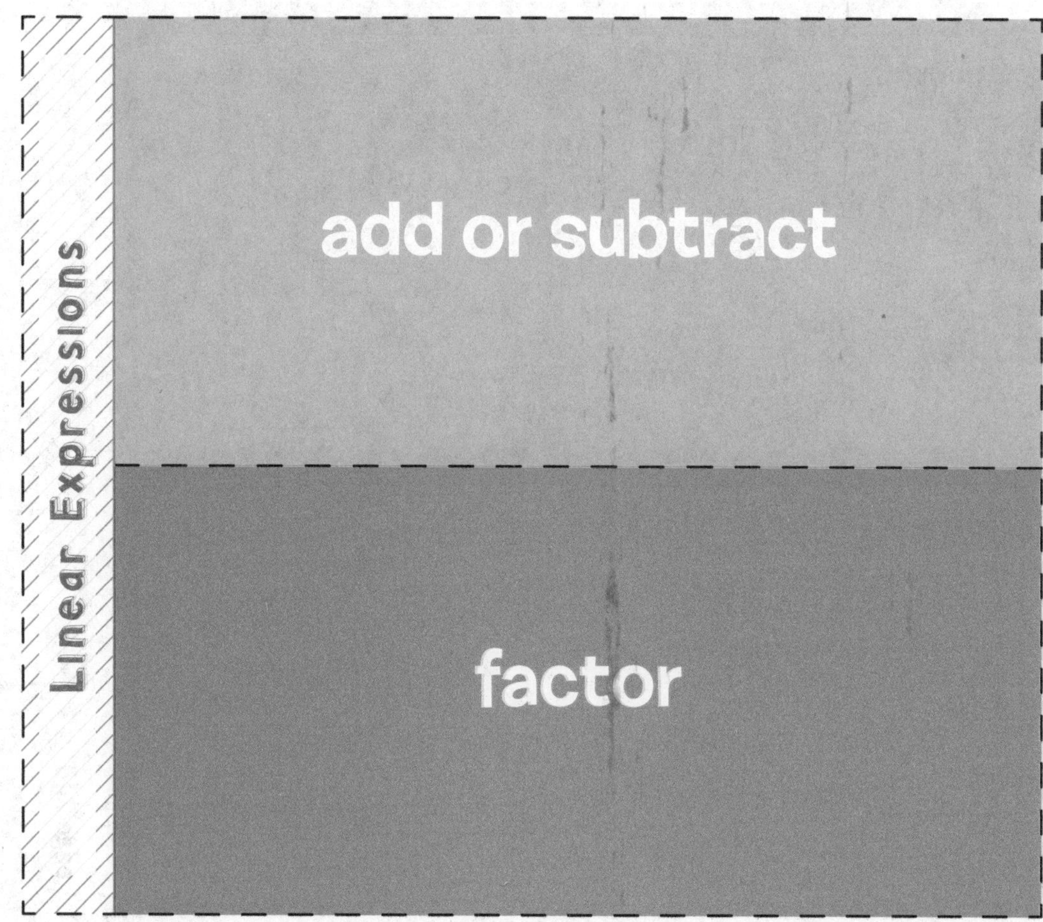

cut on all dashed lines   fold on all solid lines   tape to page 240   FOLDABLES®

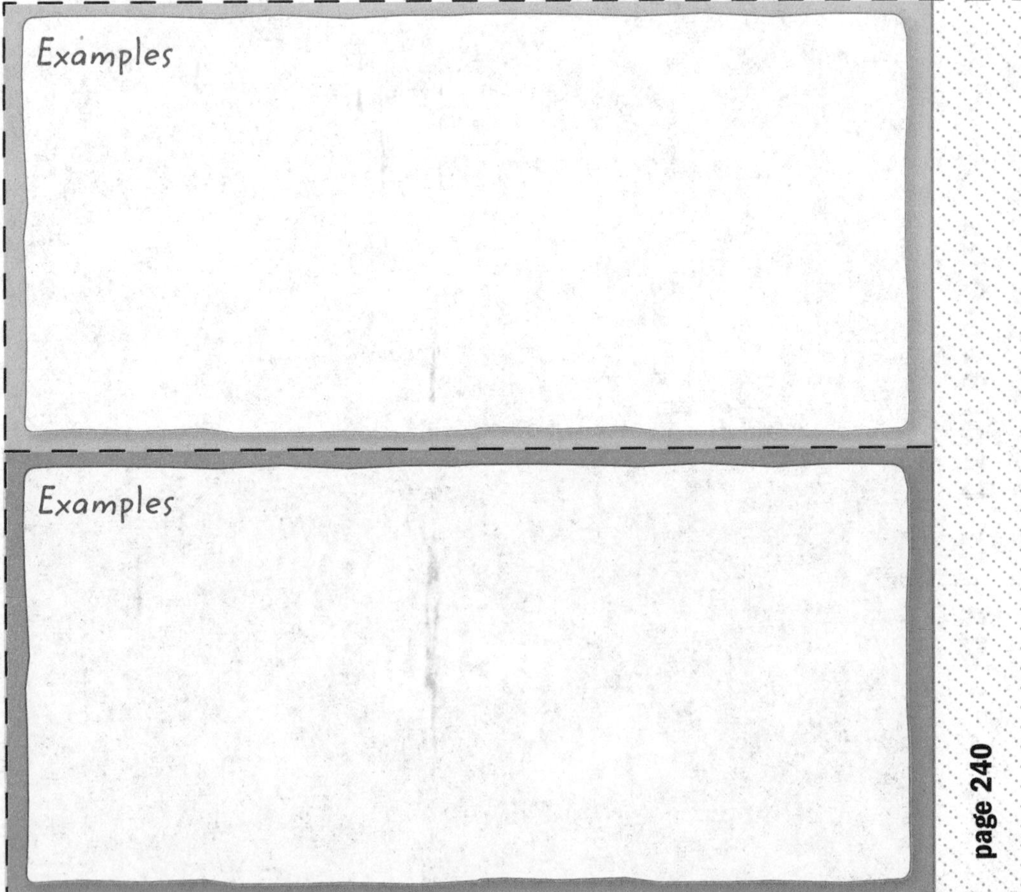

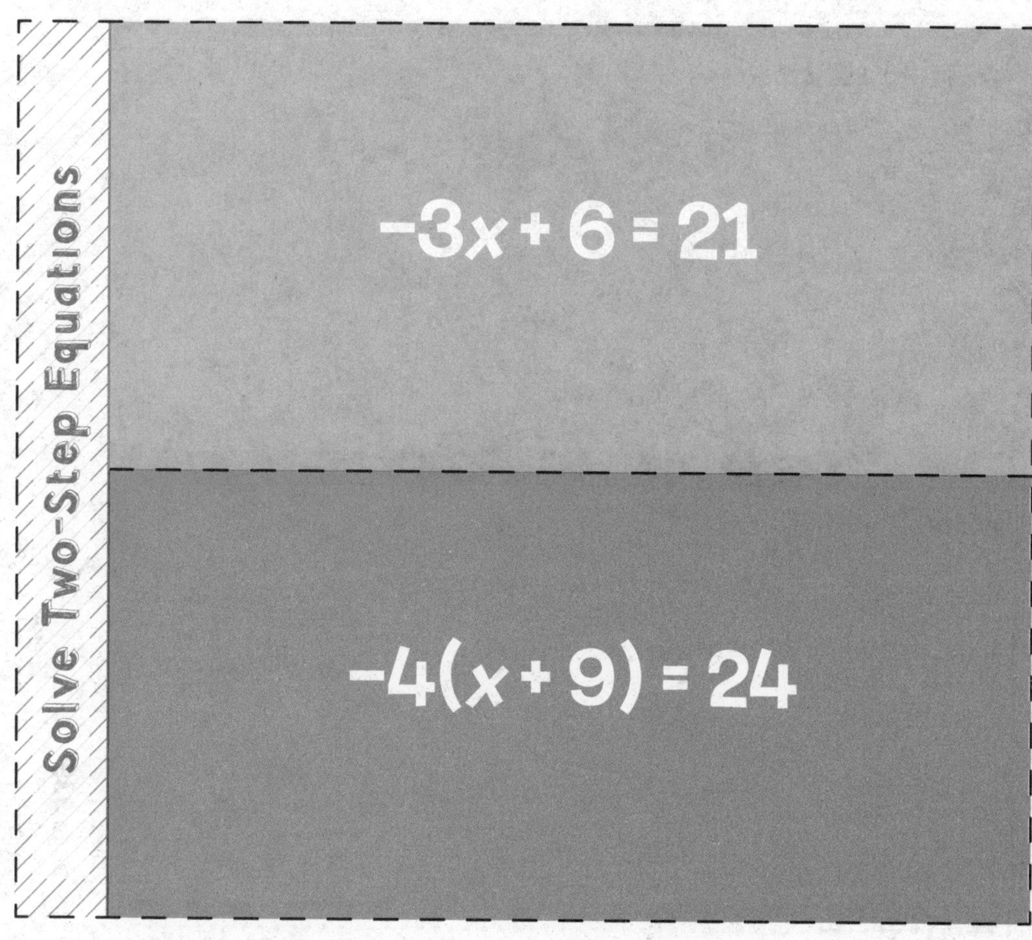
Solve Two-Step Equations
$-3x + 6 = 21$
$-4(x + 9) = 24$

cut on all dashed lines

fold on all solid lines

tape to page 338

FOLDABLES®

Write About It

Write About It

page 338

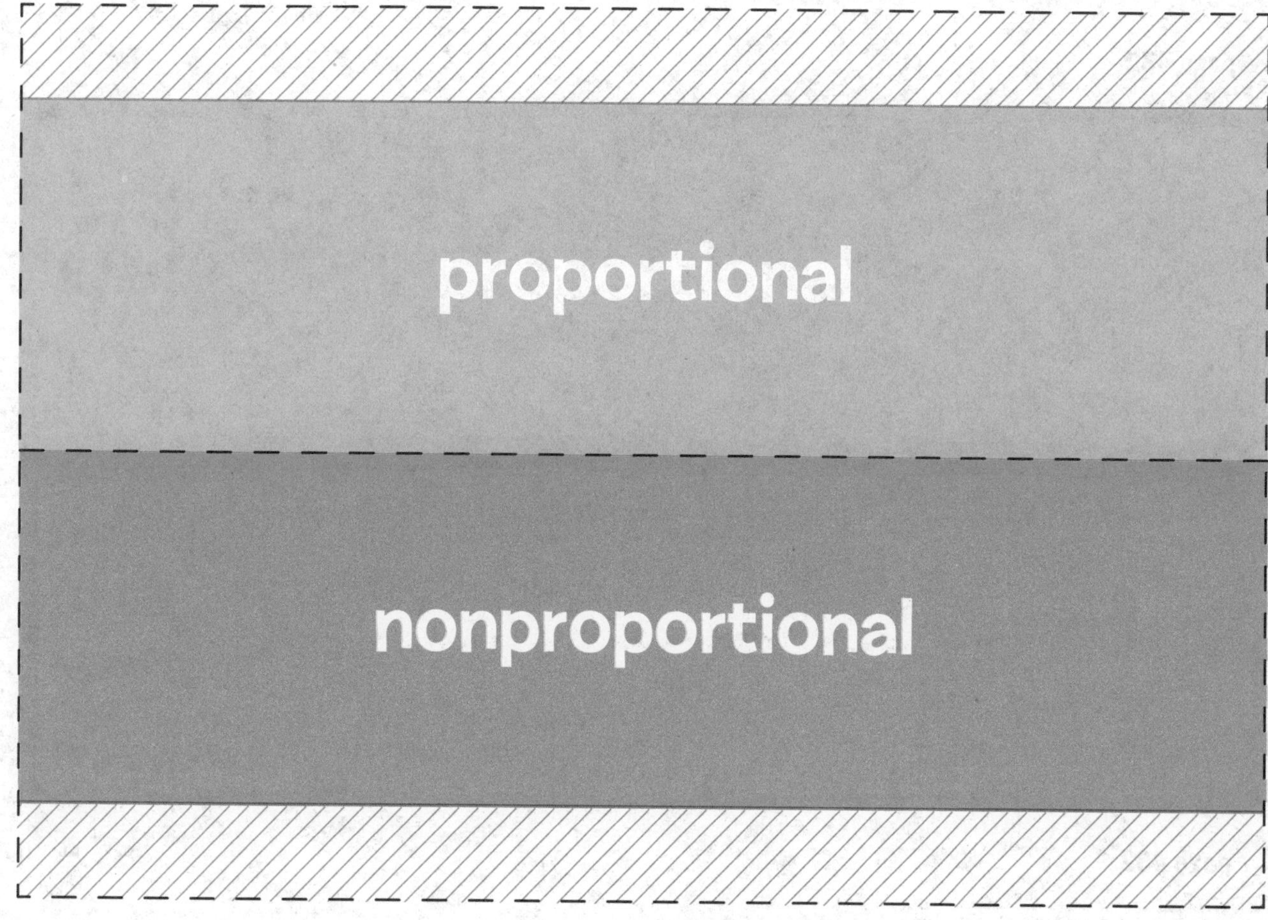
proportional
nonproportional

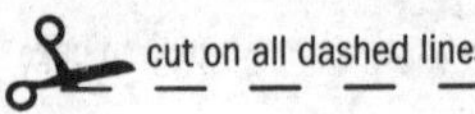

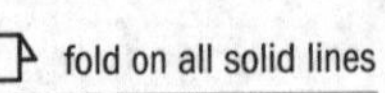

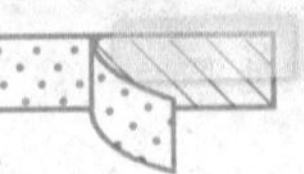

tape to page 432

FOLDABLES®

Foldables

page 432

Tab 1

Write About It

Write About It

page 432

Tab 2

cut on all dashed lines fold on all solid lines tape to page 534 FOLDABLES

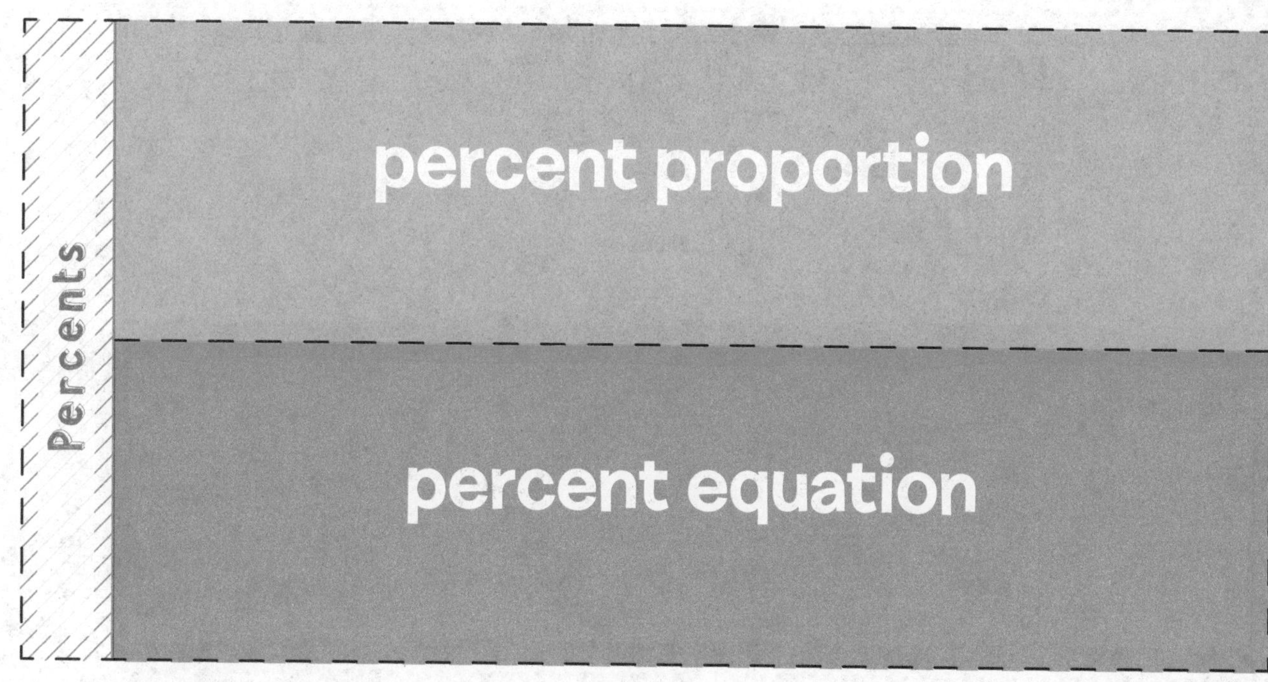

cut on all dashed lines fold on all solid lines tape to page 534

FOLDABLES®

Foldables

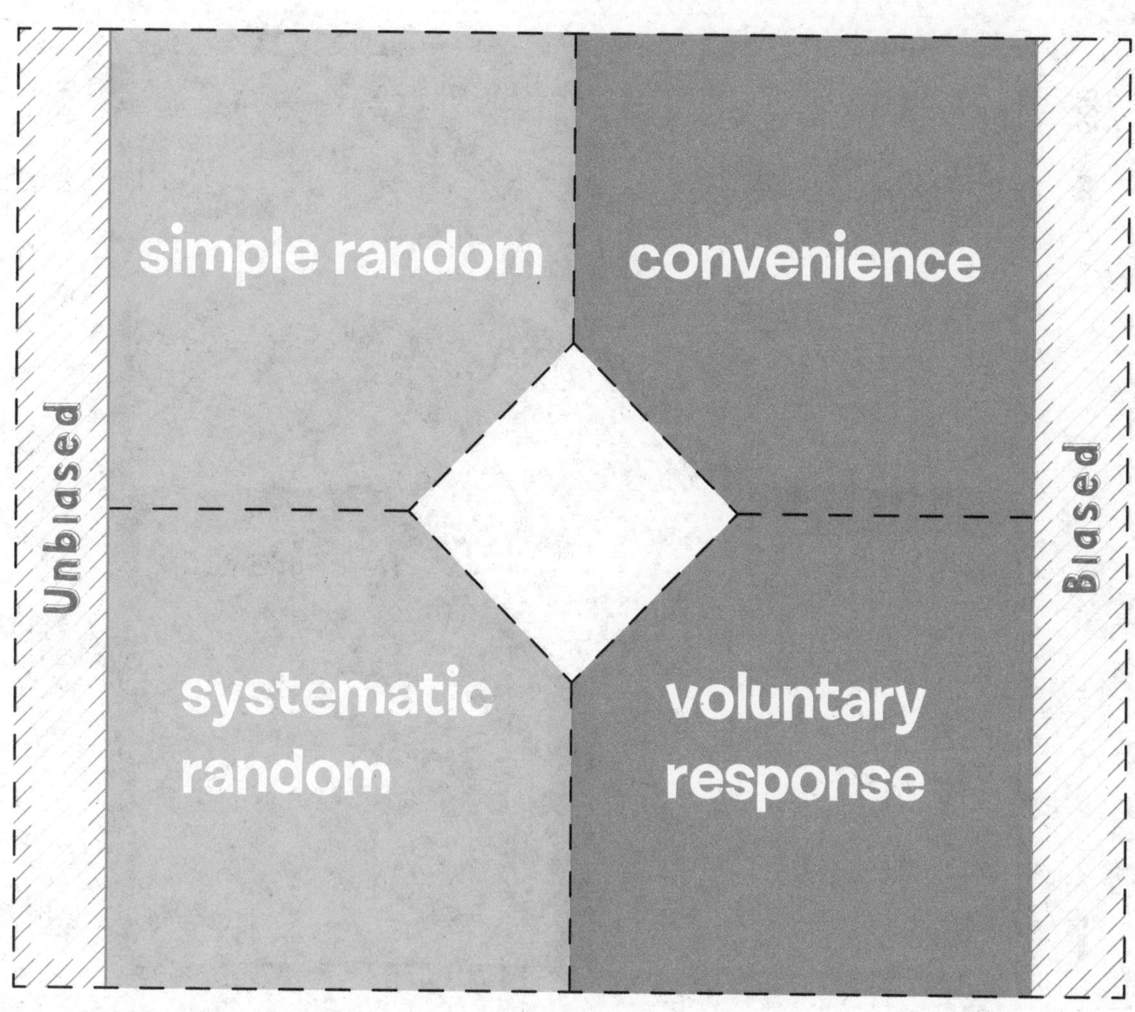
simple random
convenience
Unbiased
Biased
systematic random
voluntary response

cut on all dashed lines
fold on all solid lines
tape to page 600
FOLDABLES®

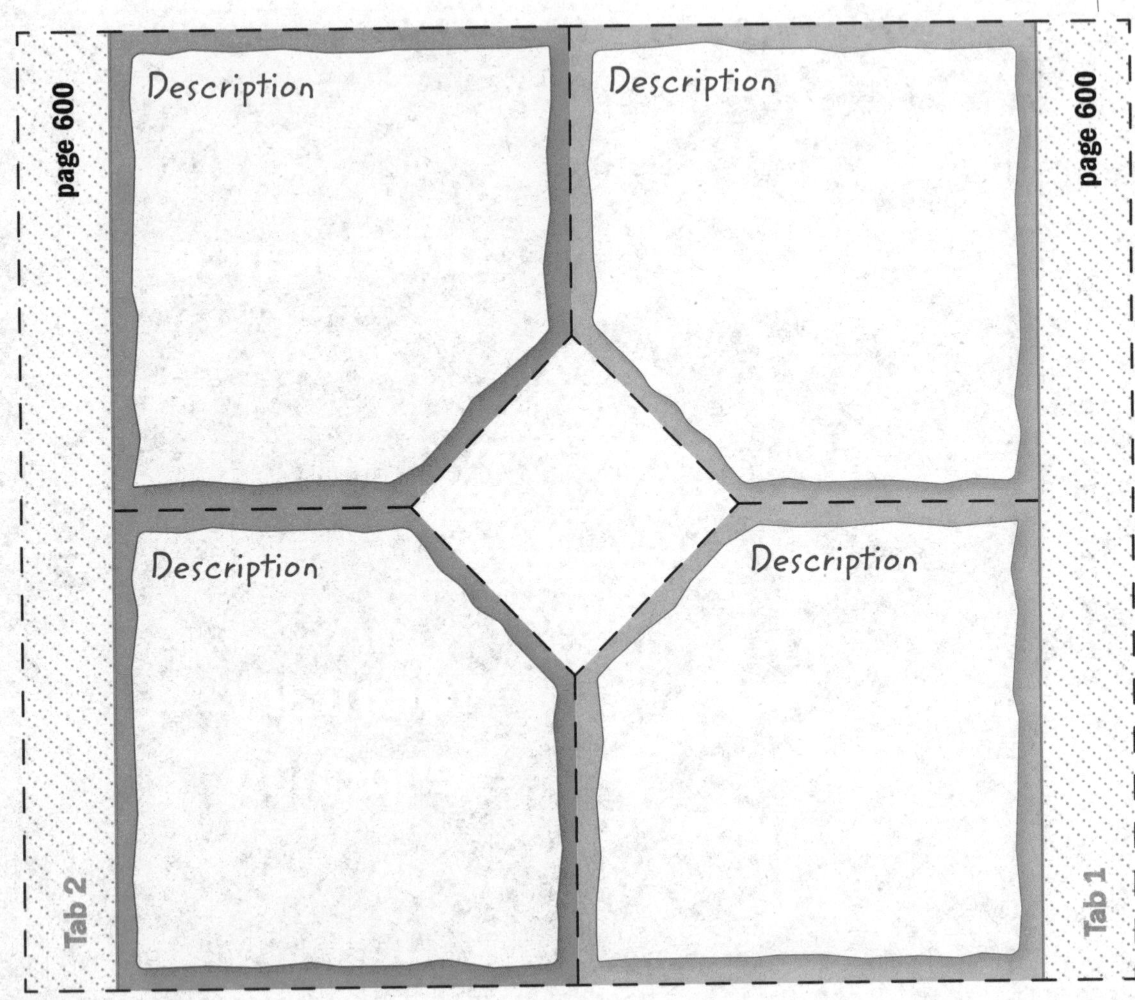

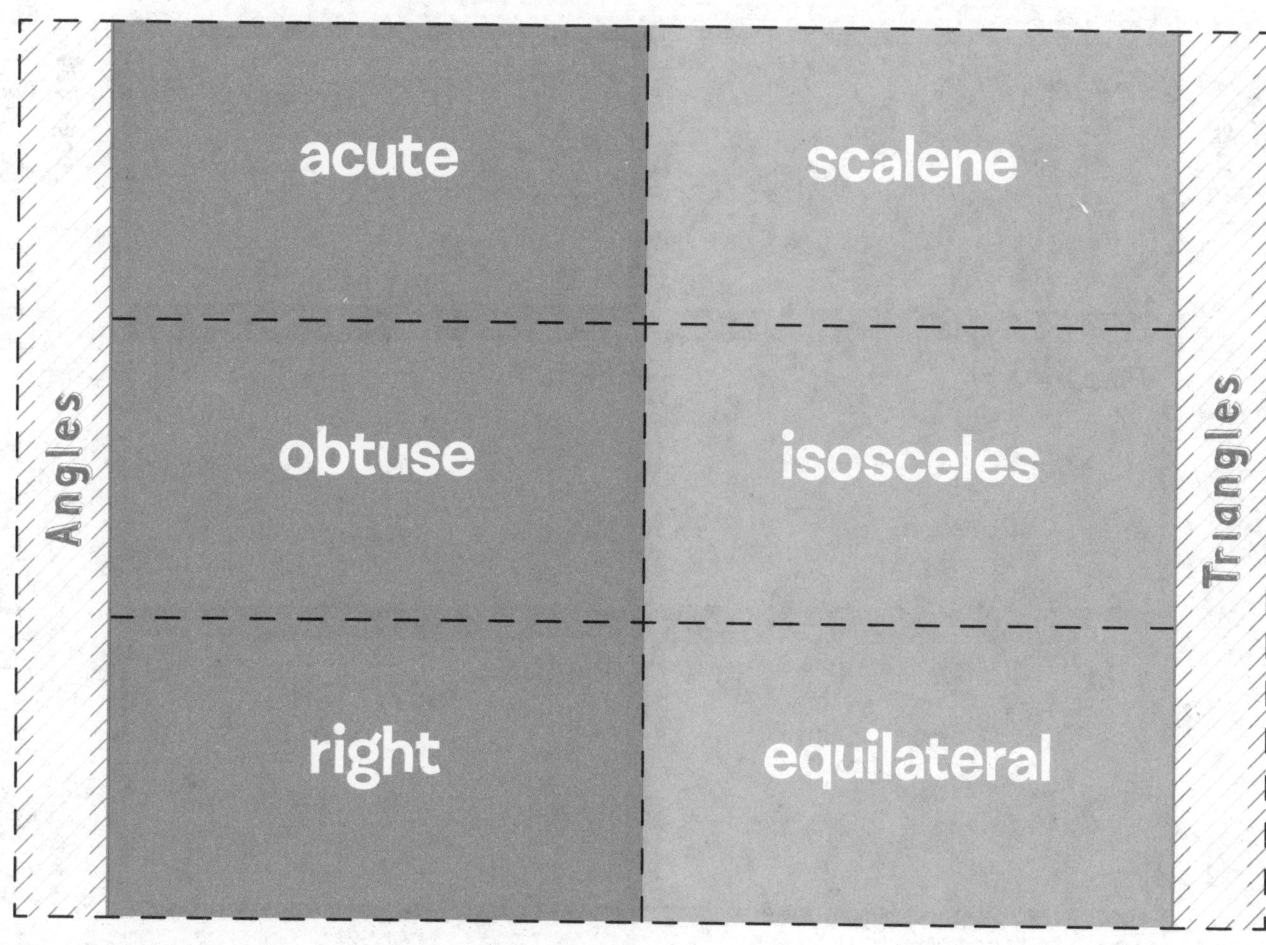
acute
obtuse
right
scalene
isosceles
equilateral
Angles
Triangles

cut on all dashed lines
fold on all solid lines
tape to page 664
FOLDABLES®

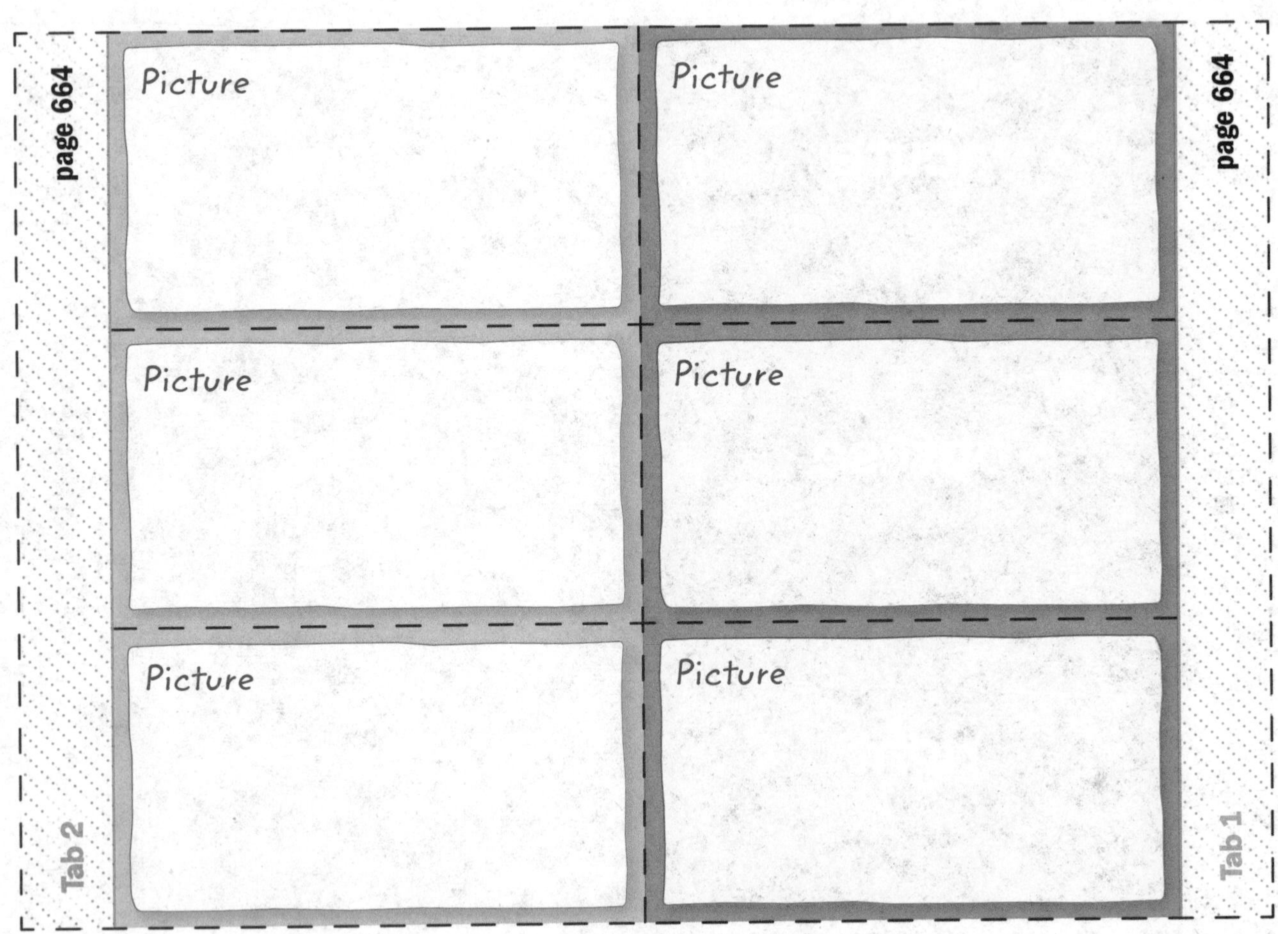

cut on all dashed lines fold on all solid lines tape to page 760 FOLDABLES®

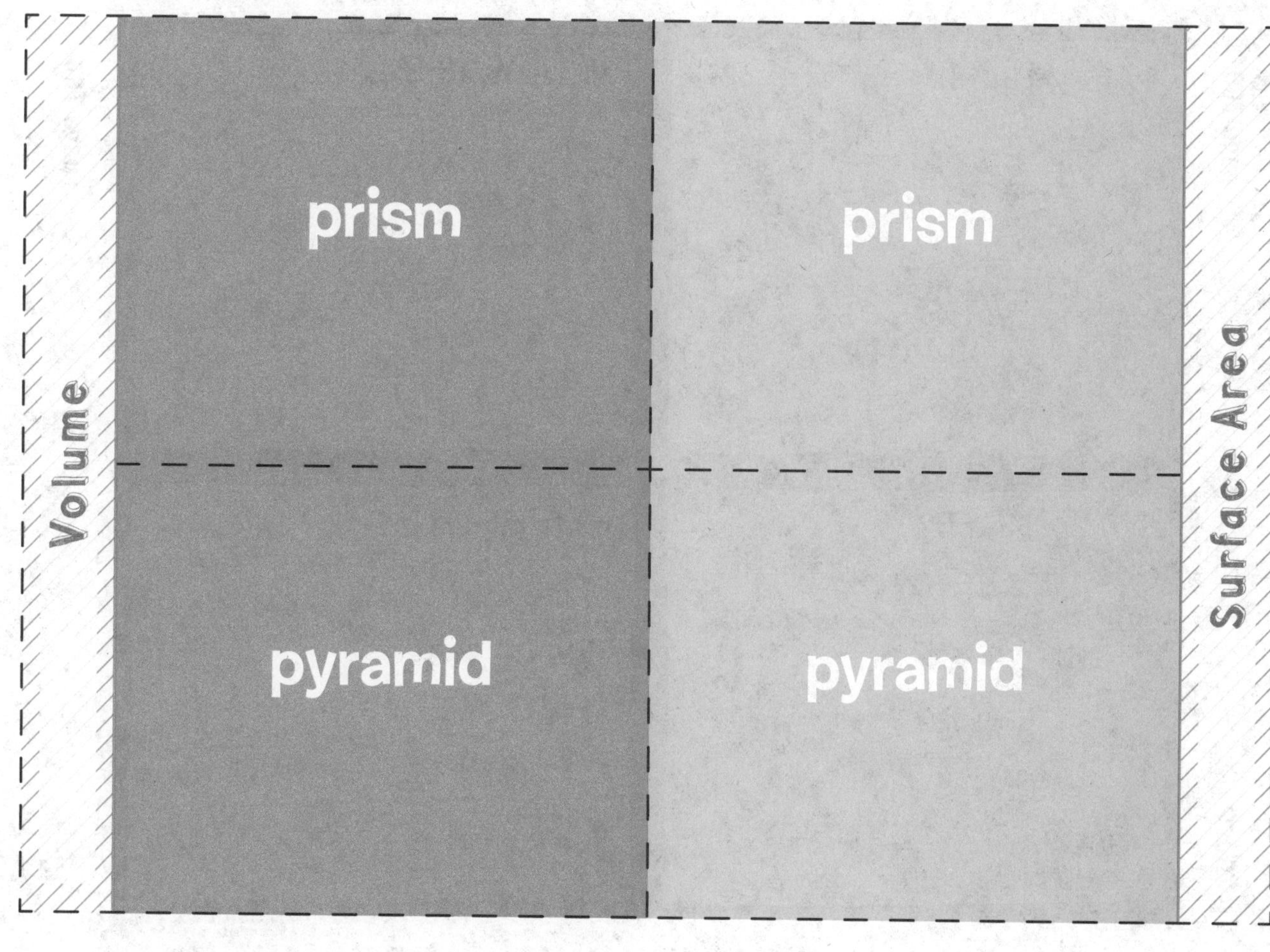

cut on all dashed lines | fold on all solid lines | tape to page 760

FOLDABLES®

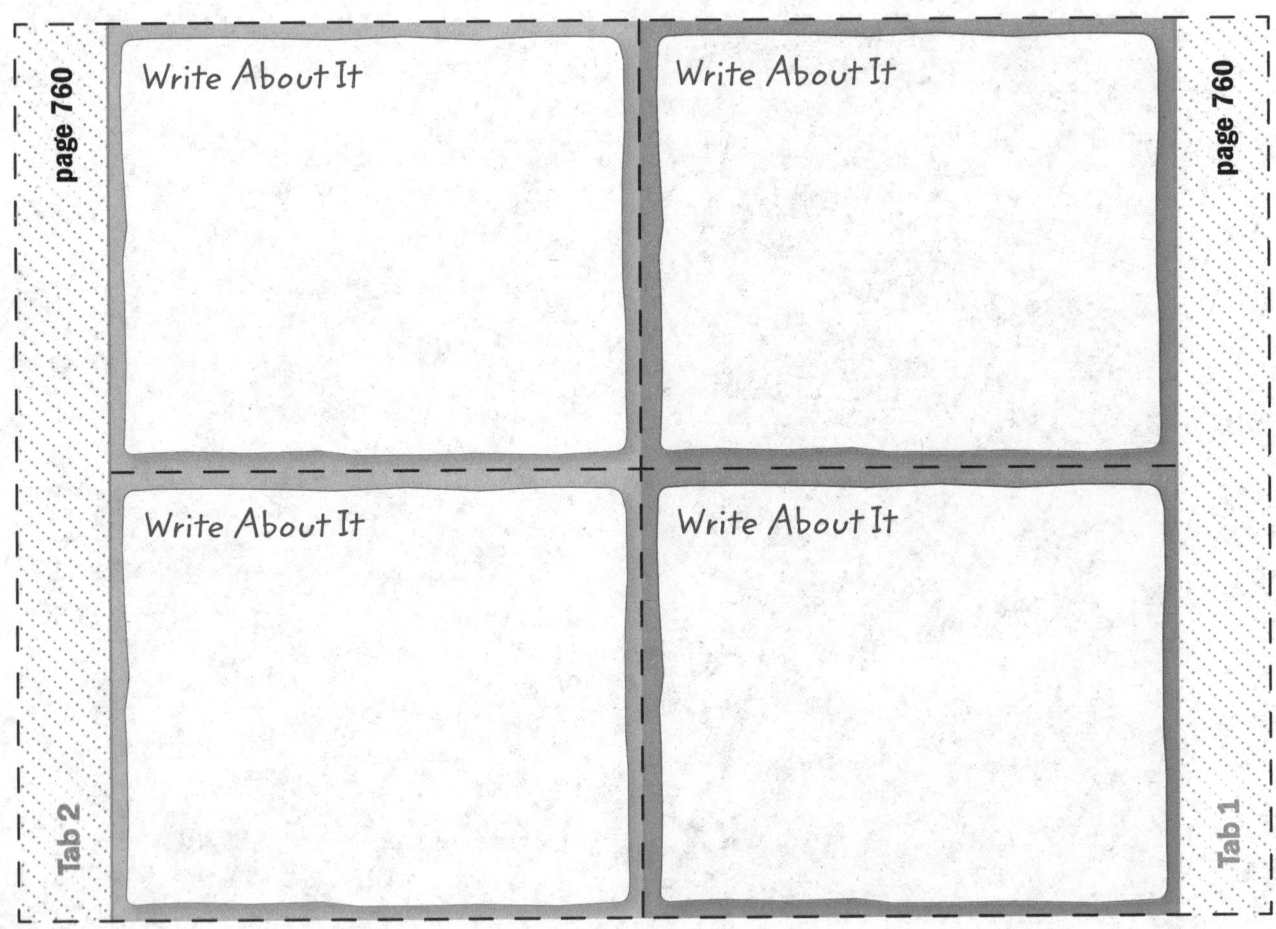

cut on all dashed lines fold on all solid lines tape to page 844 FOLDABLES

Foldables

Probability

simple event

compound event

cut on all dashed lines

fold on all solid lines

tape to page 844

FOLDABLES®

page 844

Definition

Definition

$12x - 18 + 2x$

$\frac{2}{3} \times \frac{-8'}{1} = \frac{-2}{1}$

$-8m - 8 + 15m - 10$

$7m - 18$

$\frac{5}{4} \times \frac{1}{3} = \frac{5}{12}$

$-3(3 - 5 \cdot 2)$

$-3(3 - 10)$

$-4(-3x + 5y)$

$12x - 20y$

$3x + 2 - 9 + x - 8x$

$-4x - 7$

$(7m - 1)(-2)$

$-14m + 2$

$-x(2 - 9)$

$-2x + 9x$

$11x - 8 + 7x - 7$

$18x - 15$

$(11x - 8) + 7(x - 1)$

$11x - 8 + 7x - 7$

$18x - 15$

$8x - 1 - 8x + 1$

x

$-6(5g - 7h + 9 - 10g)$

$-30g + 42h - 54 + 60g$

$30g + 42h - 54$

$7(x - 1) - 2(x - 1$

$7x - 7 - 2x + 2$

$5x - 5$

2pm	3pm
11am	11am
7:30pm	7:30pm
5:45pm	8:30am
1:50pm	1:15pm
8:22am	4:10pm